FATE
AND
FORTUNE

By Brian Innes, Francis King & Neil Powell

CRESCENT BOOKS

New York

Contents

PART 1

Horoscopes

Brian Innes

Contents

1 THE MEANING OF THE HOROSCOPE

Astrology is one of the oldest sciences: kings and generals once kept their personal astrologers, and consulted them whenever they needed advice, for the men who studied the movements of the stars and planets were among the wisest in the ancient world. They kept count of the seasons and predicted the harvest; they could tell when the moon would be bright enough to move an army by night, or dark enough to hide them; and they knew the days of eclipses. With these talents, it was hardly surprising that they claimed also that they could forecast other events from their observations of the heavens – and perhaps they could.

Over the centuries, there have been many people who claimed that they could 'read the stars' and foretell future events. In medieval times, when it was thought that Man, being made in God's image, was a little model of the universe, it seemed logical that the movement of the planets among the stars should be mirrored in human affairs. More recently, as our ideas about the structure of the universe have changed, practitioners of astrology have suggested that they are the inheritors of an ancient wisdom that has been handed down, over the ages, from the oldest astrologers of all.

Whatever secret knowledge the astrologers once had, it is now almost certainly lost. Although the study of the relationship between man and the stars was formerly the most respectable of occupations, the development of the telescope and the formulation of Newton's theories on gravitation soon brought it into disrepute; the gulf between the occult mysteries of astrology and the new science of astronomy began to widen rapidly. 'How can you expect us to believe' exclaimed the reasonable men of the eighteenth century 'that those distant pieces of rock could exert an influence on human beings, affecting their every action and even determining their future?' The short answer is that, of course, they don't.

Look at it this way. Suppose that I have received a letter from my aunt, asking me to meet her; she will be leaving her country home at about 1030, and taking the train. A quick glance at the timetable tells me that the only possible train will arrive at the terminus at 1410. An enquiry at the station will reveal that this train is expected to pull into platform 9. If I could obtain access to the detailed schedules kept by the railway authorities, I would discover the name of the driver, the colour of the engine, its head-code, and a host of other facts.

I take a friend with me to the terminus, and we stand at the end of platform 9. Pointing to the station clock, I tell him that when the two hands are together – the astrological term is 'in conjunction' – a number of things will happen: a blue engine, with the head-code 06 and driven by a man called Tom Cobbett, will draw a train into the platform, and an elderly lady with grey hair will descend from it. I may be wrong – the driver may be a last-minute replacement, the train may be late or directed to another platform – but one thing is certain: these events were not caused by the conjunction of the hands of the clock.

The astrologer works with something very like my railway timetable. Called an *ephemeris*, it tells him where the various planets will be in the heavens at any particular time. Astronomers use tables just like this, and so do all sea and air navigators. Including the sun and moon, which astrologers rather loosely refer to as 'planets' – from the original meaning of the word, 'wanderers' – there are ten bodies which seem to move round Earth against the broad backcloth of the stars. These can be thought of as the ten hands of a giant and very accurate clock, telling us the epoch, the century, the lustrum, the year, the month, the week, the day, the hour, the minute and the second.

But is this all? you may well ask. It most certainly is not. Just as I needed the detailed railway schedule to make some of my predictions, a schedule that was prepared as a fruit of the long experience that the railway planners have, so an astrologer needs to draw on the collected wisdom of generations in the interpretation of a horoscope. This may tell him, for instance, that people born in the early evening toward the end of June, with the moon high in the sky, tend to be gentle, rather dreamy, and emotionally unstable. Or that those born at the beginning of November, soon after sunrise, turn out to be brusque, self-confident and practical, and yet at the same time sympathetic – the sort of person who generally makes a good doctor, in fact.

Fortune, in the guise of an angel in this fifteenth-century German woodcut, turns her wheel to exert the influence of the individual planets. From Mars in the meridian, the planets symbolised here are (in clockwise order) Jupiter, Saturn, Moon, Mercury, Venus and Sun

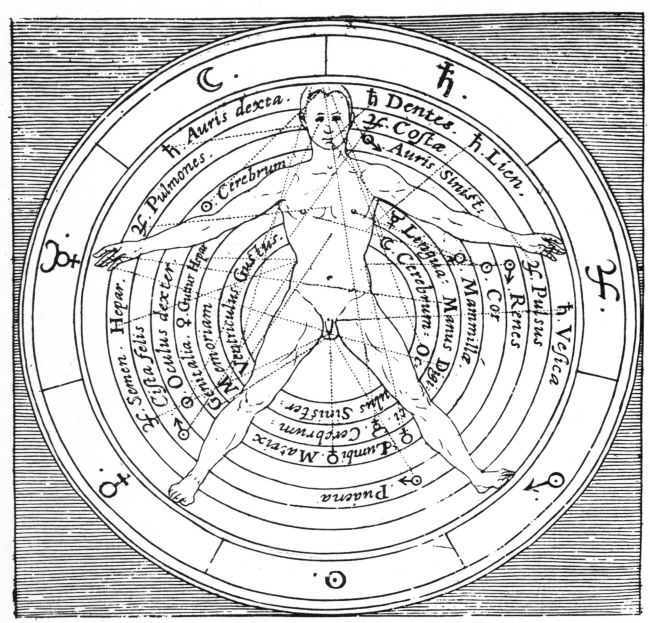

Medieval philosophers believed that, since Man was made in God's image, the human body and mind were like a miniature model of the cosmos. They expressed this in the succinct phrase 'As above, so below', and proposed that by devoting all his energies to a profound study of himself a man could eventually attain complete understanding of the universe. And so, by analogy, changes in one were reflected by changes in the other

But these, of course, are mere generalisations; not everyone born in the morning in early November becomes a doctor, nor are all doctors born at that time. An infinite number of factors can influence any life or any event, and it becomes necessary to distinguish between them. You will find, as you continue your studies and begin to gain experience in the 'reading' of horoscopes, that often you are presented with two or more alternatives, and that quite deliberately you choose one of them. There appears to be no good *reason* for favouring one alternative against another, except that it *seems right*. You are experiencing the first stirrings of a mystic power within yourself.

And, when all is said and done, there is still the possibility that the planets themselves do directly influence our lives on Earth. The sun and the moon most certainly do, as the tides of the sea rise and fall every day. When sun and moon are in conjunction or in opposition, the tides are particularly high; when they are 'square' to one another, the rise and fall of the tide is much less. All the planets exert a gravitational pull, but it is small in comparison with that from the sun or moon, and so we do not generally recognise it. Some of the scientists who are studying the phenomena of sunspots believe that these are the result of solar 'tides' caused by the gravitational pull of other planets. For many years it has been known that an increase in sunspot activity is accompanied by an increase in the 'cosmic rays' that continually bombard Earth; and we also

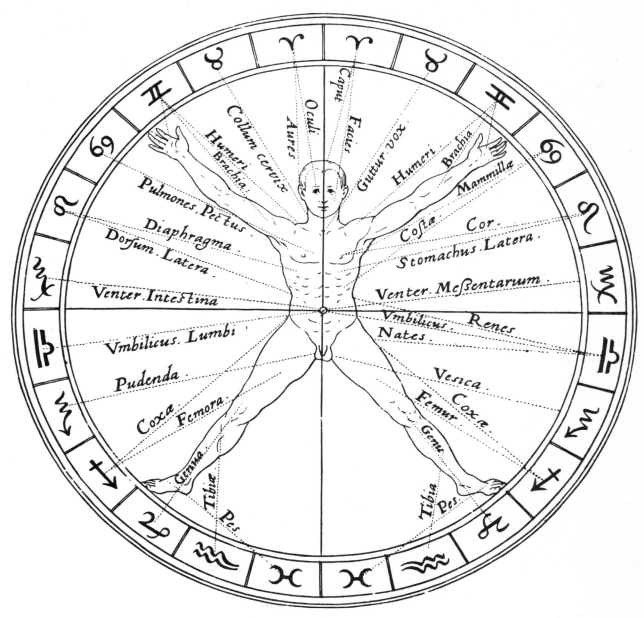

know that these rays have an immeasurable effect on the life of our planet, causing genetic mutations and numerous other phenomena. It would not be too surprising, were a scientist to announce that his experiments had shown a direct correlation between the cosmic ray level at the time of birth and the subsequent development of the individual. Perhaps the astrologer's ephemeris is nothing less than a cosmic tide-table!

The Horoscope
The horoscope is simply a map of part of the heavens; with the observer at the centre, it shows the position of the different planets in relation to him and to one another.

Earth and all the planets travel round the sun in regular orbits, all moving at different speeds according to their size and their distance from the sun. But all these orbits lie in almost the same plane.

Until less than five hundred years ago, man believed that Earth was the centre of the universe. It certainly looked like it: the moon obviously went round Earth, and there was no reason for thinking that the sun did any different. The planets, too, could be seen to go round Earth: they did strange things now and again, like going back on their tracks for several weeks, or even several months, at a time, but since they were under the control of capricious gods and goddesses that was hardly surprising.

Lying far outside our galaxy, the stars seem to form into groups, or constellations,

From the idea of man as a reflection of the cosmos it was a short step to the idea that every part of the human body was under the influence of a particular planet; and from that it was logical to suppose that the signs of the zodiac also represented different parts of the body or their functions. The illustrations on these pages are taken from an encyclopedic work by the great seventeenth century magus Robert Fludd, entitled 'A History of Both Worlds'

which make pictures in the sky, and from the earliest times men have given these groups names. Appearing to lie like a belt round the solar system are twelve of these constellations, which were given names very like their present names thousands of years ago:

♈ Aries, the Ram
♉ Taurus, the Bull
♊ Gemini, the Twins
♋ Cancer, the Crab
♌ Leo, the Lion
♍ Virgo, the Virgin
♎ Libra, the Balance

♏ Scorpio, the Scorpion
♐ Sagittarius, the Centaur
♑ Capricorn, the Goat
♒ Aquarius, the Water-carrier
♓ Pisces, the Fish

As we look out into the night sky from Earth, we can see several of the planets, Mercury or Venus, Mars, Saturn or Jupiter, and these planets seem to be 'in' some of the constellations. This is because we are looking one way or another across the solar system, and can see these planets 'in front of' the constellations far away. If we could see the stars during the day when the sun is shining, we would see the sun also appear to be in one of the constellations. For the whole of one month the sun would appear in one

Bull' or that they are a 'Taurean'. And to an astrologer a statement of this kind means almost nothing at all; it is, after all, exactly the same as saying 'I was born in May', and means little more. Before an astrologer can begin to draw up the simplest horoscope, he needs to know the time to which it refers; and that time must be accurate to, at the very least, two hours – and preferably to within four minutes.

Of course one can make certain generalisations, like the statements above about those born at certain times in June or November. There is a possibility that those born shortly after dawn in the first and second week in May will suffer from respiratory complaints, and there is little doubt that they would be ill-advised to marry someone born at about the same time. But the sun is not one of the most accurate of the hands of our cosmic clock; the moon, and Mercury and Venus and Mars, are just as important, and so is Earth itself, as it turns on its axis. The astrologer needs to know that the Sun was in Taurus, but much more important to him is the sign of the zodiac just rising above the eastern horizon at the moment for which he draws up his horoscope. The position of every other planet can then be calculated very easily, as we shall see.

(Far right) Even the position of moles on the human countenance was believed to be related to the influence of the signs of the zodiac. (Right) Venus 'rules' in Libra by day and Taurus by night. The easy-going, pleasure-loving qualities of Venus, combined with the earthy appetites represented by Taurus, may result in gluttony and self-indulgence

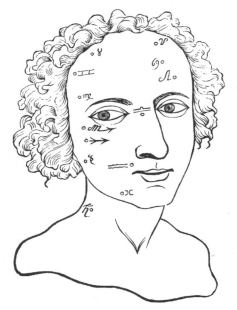

constellation and it would seem to move in a great circle round Earth, taking about a month to pass through each of the twelve constellations in turn.

These twelve constellations are called the Zodiac, from the Greek for 'circle of animals'. The horoscope for any given time is a sketch map showing the positions of the planets in the Zodiac at that moment.

This is what is meant when someone tells you they were born 'under the sign of the

Some simple theory

When astronomers – astrologers, as they then were – began to put forward their theories about the structure of the universe, the idea that Earth was at the centre proved so practical in use that it has remained with us to the present day, and forms the basis of all navigational calculations.

Imagine Earth stationary at the centre of the universe. The planets (a term that includes sun and moon) are moving round

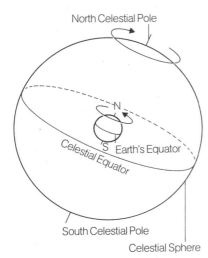

North Celestial Pole

N

Celestial Equator

Earth's Equator

S

South Celestial Pole

Celestial Sphere

(Left) The spatial relationship between the terrestrial sphere, and its equator, and the celestial sphere and equator

equator on the starry sphere. We call this sphere the celestial sphere and the equator the celestial equator. This is shown in the diagram on the left.

But Earth's axis of rotation is not at right angles to the plane of its orbit. Earth, going round the sun, 'leans' (as it were) as it spins, at an angle of 23° 27'. When the northern pole is leaning toward the sun it is summer in the northern hemisphere, and winter in the southern hemisphere; and when it leans the other way, at the opposite point in its orbit, the converse applies. So, as summer approaches, the noon sun appears higher in the sky every day, until it reaches its highest point; this is called the summer solstice, because the sun appears to stand still before starting on its journey back down the sky again. A further result of all this is that the sun shines for more than half the day during the summer months; above the Arctic circle in midsummer the sun never sets. There are only two days every year on which the 24 hours are equally divided between night and day; these are the spring and autumn equinoxes, which are usually on March 20 or 21 and September 22 or 23.

Some four thousand years ago, when the science of astrology was first formulated, the sun 'entered' the constellation of Aries at

Earth in their various orbits, and the whole lot is enclosed in a big sphere on which all the stars are fixed. This sphere is also turning, and the axis of its rotation is in fact the same as the axis of Earth, since the apparent movement of the stars is really due to the fact that Earth is moving. Therefore, since Earth has an equator, which is the circumference of Earth along the direction in which it is turning, we can imagine a similar

(Left) Provided with a model of the celestial sphere, reference books and dividers, the medieval astrologer draws up a horoscope. Another engraving from Fludd's 'History of Two Worlds'

(Below) An eighteenth-century celestial sphere — or rather a representation of the hemisphere of the heavens that can be seen from the northern half of Earth. The moveable horizon can be adjusted to represent the horizon of any observer, whether at the equator or the north pole, but it always cuts the ecliptic at 0°Aries and 0°Libra

the spring equinox. This point on the circle of the zodiac was therefore designated 0°Aries, with the 360° of the circle extending round the heavens from here, 30° to each of the twelve signs of the zodiac.

But Earth is not just 'leaning' as it pursues its orbit; the axis of rotation is also very slowly wobbling, like that of a spinning top. As the centuries pass, the direction in which it leans changes. This was discovered about 120 BC by the great Greek astronomer Hipparchus, and it is called the 'precession of the equinoxes', because the result of this wobbling was that the spring equinox appeared to move gradually through the constellation of Aries and on into Pisces. As we near the end of the twentieth century the spring equinox is moving out of Pisces and into Aquarius. This is the meaning of

the saying that the Age of Aquarius is dawning. Each 'age' lasts about two thousand years, and in another twenty thousand the spring equinox will once more be at 0° Aries. But for navigational and astronomical, as well as for astrological, purposes the spring equinox is still designated 0° Aries, and the circle of the horoscope is divided into the traditional twelve signs of the zodiac from this point.

The Ecliptic

If we made a model of the celestial sphere, putting a light at the centre of Earth, the sun, moon and planets circling in their orbits would cast shadows on to the sphere. The sun's shadow would pass through the constellations of the zodiac, marking a circular track on the celestial sphere, but

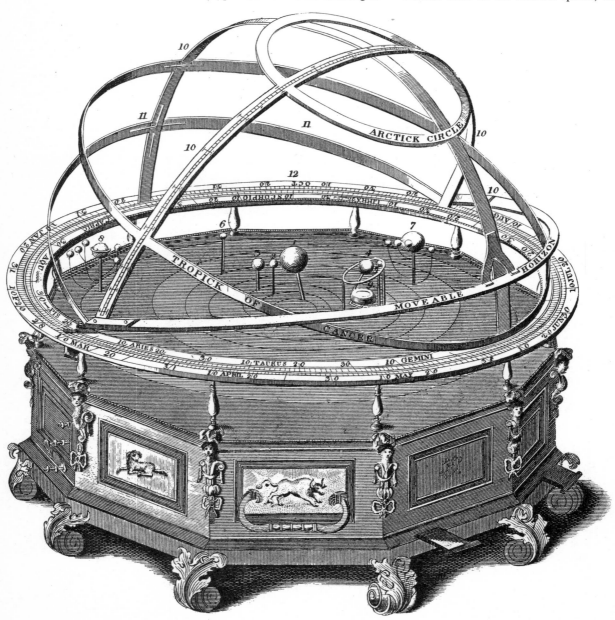

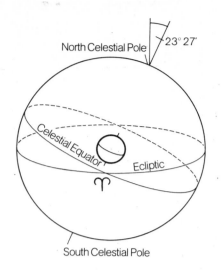

because of the inclination of Earth's axis this circle would be at an angle to the circle of the celestial equator.

The sun's track through the zodiac is called the ecliptic and, as can be seen in the diagram, it cuts the celestial equator at two points. These are the spring and autumn equinoxes, designated as 0° Aries and 0° Libra.

A simple horoscope

We are now in a position to begin drawing a horoscope for any given time. It will not be entirely accurate, because we have not yet dealt with the fact that Earth does not take exactly one year to go round the sun (the reason why Leap Year is necessary every four years), and also because we will ignore the fact that the ecliptic is at an angle to the celestial equator. All the necessary corrections can be dealt with later.

It is necessary to have a book which tells us the positions of the planets at different times throughout the year. Books of ephemeris tables can be bought from specialist booksellers: *Raphael's Ephemeris* is published yearly, and there are other books which provide abbreviated tables for every month over a period of about 150 years. All these publications require a little more knowledge than we yet have at this stage. Later, full details will be provided on how to make use of these tables, and on pages 76–88 there is a condensed ephemeris that will enable you to draw horoscopes for any day between 1880 and 1980.

For the moment, however, to show that there is no mystery about this part of astrology, and nothing whatsoever to which a scientist could take objection, all the calculations will be made with the help of an ordinary nautical almanac. This is exactly the same as that used by navigators

Remember that a horoscope is a sketch map showing the positions of all the planets inside the celestial sphere, and that you are standing on Earth at the centre of this sphere.

For the moment we will make the calculations for an observer in the northern hemisphere; the modifications to be made for the southern hemisphere are very simple. You are facing south and looking up and out at the planets and the stars beyond them. Because Earth is below you, you can of course see only one half of the celestial sphere; the ecliptic rises above the eastern horizon at your left hand and follows a circular track, reaching its highest point in the south, and disappearing below the right hand, western, horizon.

The other half of the circle can be visualised as passing below you. We can represent this as a circle on paper, with south as the highest point of the circle, and east and west at opposite ends of the horizon. And for the twelve constellations we can divide this circle into twelve equal segments of 30° each.

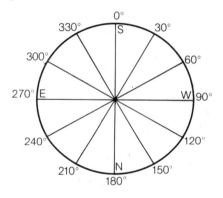

To make the calculations as simple as possible, we have to make just one assumption: that you are standing on the Greenwich meridian, 0° longitude. The sun will be due south and at the highest point in its daily course, at mid-day Greenwich Mean Time.

All the tables in the nautical almanac are based on GMT, and they give the positions of planets in terms of the number of degrees of a circle away (in a clockwise direction) from the Greenwich meridian. This is called the Greenwich Hour Angle (GHA).

Let us draw up a horoscope for 0600 hours on Monday 29 April 1974. For this date and time the almanac lists the following figures:
Sun: GHA = 270° 38.7′
0° Aries: GHA = 306° 49.0′
For practical purposes, we can take these to be respectively 271° and 307°.

We can mark these on to our horoscope circle, in degrees clockwise from the southern meridian, as indicated in the diagram on the following page.

The twelve numbered segments are called 'houses' by astrologers; their importance will be discussed in much greater detail

(Left) The ecliptic, the apparent path of the Sun through the zodiac, is at an angle of 23° 27′ to the celestial equator, and crosses this equator only at 0° Aries and 0° Libra. (Below) Dividing the circle of the zodiac into twelve equal parts

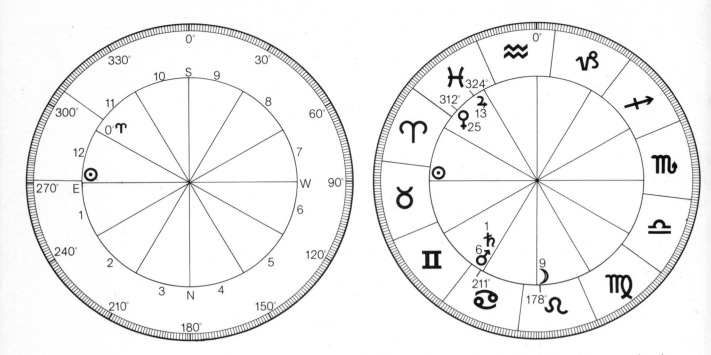

(Above) Plotting a horoscope from figures given in any Nautical Almanac. Once the position of 0°Aries has been established relative to the meridian, the divisions of the zodiac can be plotted, and the positions of the other planets inserted

(Above, opposite) This Egyptian zodiac, from a temple at Dendera, was for long believed to be evidence that the signs of the zodiac were adopted from the Babylonians by the ancient Egyptians. The design, however, has been proved to date from the reign of Augustus in the first century of the Christian era. (Below) An Assyrian stone dated 122BC shows Sun, Moon and Venus, and the signs of Aries and Capricorn, easily recognised

later. For the purposes of this simple explanation the horoscope has been divided equally into twelve houses, and the boundaries between them occur at 0°, 30°, 60°, 90°, 120°, 150°, 180°, 210°, 240°, 270°, 300°, and 330°. The sun has just risen, and, at 271°, is 1° above the eastern horizon.

0° Aries, at 307°, lies 7° inside the eleventh house, and the boundary between the eleventh and twelfth houses is therefore at 7° Aries; and the eastern horizon is at 7° Taurus. The sun is thus in 6° Taurus.

We can now go back to the nautical almanac for the positions of some of the other planets.

☽ Moon: GHA at 0600 hours = 177° 46.4′
♀ Venus: GHA at midnight = 222° 5.9′
   variation 14° 59.9′ per hour
   giving GHA at 0600 hours = 312° 5.3′
   (222° 5.9′ + 6 × 14° 59.9′ = 312° 5.3′)
♃ Jupiter: GHA at midnight = 233° 48.5′
   variation 15° 2.0′ per hour
   giving GHA at 0600 hours = 324° 0.5′
♂ Mars: GHA at midnight = 120° 52.6′
   variation 15° 0.8′ per hour
   giving GHA at 0600 hours = 210° 57.2′
♄ Saturn: GHA at midnight = 125° 35.5′
   variation 15° 2.2′ per hour
   giving GHA at 0600 hours = 215° 48.7′

Now we can enter these angles of approximately 178°, 211°, 216°, 312° and 324° on our chart.

The figures beside the sign for each planet show the number of degrees through which the planet has 'entered' a particular sign of the zodiac. Remember that while the degrees of the Greenwich time circle run clockwise, the degrees of the zodiac run counter-clockwise. This is because Earth turns counterclockwise, so that stars and planets appear

to rise in the east and traverse the sky westward, while Earth carries the 'framework' of the Greenwich time circle with it as it turns.

You will notice that four planets are missing from the chart. Three of them – Uranus, Neptune and Pluto – move so slowly that they are of little use to navigators. And these three planets were not known at all to ancient astrologers: Uranus was not discovered until 1781, Neptune in 1845, and Pluto in 1930. So we can carry out a great deal of our astrological interpretation without bothering about these planets at all.

The fourth is Mercury, which is always very close to the sun; the almanac informs us that it is visible as a morning planet until 27 April, when it comes too close to the sun for observation. This tells us that Mercury rises in the east before the sun, and therefore it is two or three degrees less advanced in Taurus than the sun. In fact, it will be found at about 2° Taurus.

This is as much as a nautical almanac can tell us, and clearly it is not quite enough; like the ancient astrologers, we might manage without Uranus, Neptune and Pluto, but Mercury is a very important planet. Our next stage must be to study the use of a more detailed ephemeris. In some ways it will be simpler, since the positions of the planets will be given directly in degrees of each sign of the zodiac, but it is a little more difficult to work out the eastern horizon and the southern meridian.

We will return to this subject later. For the moment, let us look at the significance of planetary positions. What does it mean, for instance, that the moon is in Leo, or that Mars is in the second house?

According to Aristotle, the seven planets revolved in spheres at mathematically determined distances from Earth. The sphere of earth was covered with water, and beyond this came the spheres of air and fire before the Moon's sphere. Then came the spheres of Mercury, Venus, Sun, Mars, Jupiter and Saturn, all enclosed within the celestial sphere

PTOLEMAICVM,
Machina
EX HYPOTHESI
ICA IN PLA
SPOSITA.

2
THE
PLANETS
AND THE
SIGNS

The Planets and the Signs

So far, we have looked at a horoscope as a simple map of the positions of the planets (a word which includes the Sun and Moon) in the heavens surrounding Earth. We have seen that any one sign of the zodiac represents not that part of the ecliptic occupied by the constellation with the same name, but a symbolic twelfth of the complete circle. It is very like a clock, one sign of the zodiac representing the space (say) from one to two o'clock – an important point to remember being that each zodiac sign occupies a part of the circle representing two hours rather than one.

In fact, in terms of the real zodiac, the Sun appears in each constellation approximately between the following dates:

21 March–18 April	Pisces
18 April–10 May	Aries
10 May–18 June	Taurus
18 June–21 July	Gemini
21 July–10 August	Cancer
10 August–17 September	Leo
17 September–3 November	Virgo
3 November–16 November	Libra
16 November–13 December	Scorpio
13 December–21 January	Sagittarius
21 January–14 February	Capricorn
14 February–21 March	Aquarius

As you can see, even if we were to make allowance for the movement of the equinox and step back these dates by about one month, the division of the horoscope would be very different from the traditional one. Virgo, for instance, a constellation that sprawls across the sky, holds the Sun for about seven weeks, while the Sun is in Libra for less than two. There are some more recent systems that have tried to apply this sort of zodiac division, but for simplicity we shall pursue the traditional path.

Nobody now knows whether the constellations were given their names because they really did look to astrologers like a bull or a crab, or whether because people born with the Sun in that part of the sky tended to have characters that resembled these animals. If we continue to think in terms of a giant cosmic clock, we know that the month after the spring equinox would still be the same time of year, whatever distant stars were visible in the sky. And we continue to call this twelfth of the zodiac Aries, and to observe that people born at this time tend to have some of the wilful, headstrong character of a young ram.

For most people, this is the extent of their knowledge of astrology: 'the sign I was born under'. Millions every day read their 'horoscopes' in newspapers and magazines, and millions every day dismiss astrology with the perfectly legitimate criticism that the same events could not happen tomorrow for everybody born in the same month. The Sun sign is important: it gives us the first inkling of the nature and disposition of the person whose horoscope we are considering. But it is of no greater importance than the ascendant sign, the section of the zodiac rising above the eastern horizon at the moment of birth, or the part of the zodiac in which the Moon was to be found at that time. And the positions of the other planets are of almost equal importance.

The Sun

The Sun, according to the position that it occupies in the sky (the time of day) and in the zodiac (the time of year) affects the real self, the fundamental ego, 'that part of the Universal Spirit imprisoned, for purposes of tuition in constructive Love and Wisdom, in the body of flesh', as A. E. Waite put it.

It is, clearly, one of the most powerful factors to be read in the horoscope. By tradition, the Sun 'rules' in Leo, and he shows much the same characteristics: he represents the father principle. Proud and dignified, strong and dominant, generous and faithful – these are the traits we associate with the Sun.

The Ascendant

The sign rising on the eastern horizon denotes the outward appearance of the subject, the impression that he or she will make upon an objective observer. This covers not only the purely physical characteristics but the mental outlook and behaviour, and all kinds of relations with other people.

Because these traits are the outward-looking ones they are also to a considerable extent under the control of the subject: the *way* in which they are controlled, the direction in which the subject consciously modifies his or her personal appearance, or the personality which is publicly displayed, will also show the influence of the ascendant.

The Moon

The Moon, on the other hand, represents the soul, the desire-nature, the sub-conscious psychological characteristics. It also represents the involuntary part of the human physical body – which includes such functions as the circulation of the blood, the digestion, and numerous nervous reflexes – and the wide range of conditioned responses that we develop from our first moments.

The Moon, which rules the night-time house of Cancer, typifies the feminine principle: protective and sensitive, but changeable and inward-turning. But above all the Moon represents that faculty which is the opposite of everything scientific, and without which there would be no magic – intuition.

Mercury

Many of the planets have given their names to familiar epithets, and from Mercury comes the word 'mercurial' to describe a temperament which is capable of moving rapidly

The signs used for the different planets are derived from little stylised 'glyphs' representing the respective gods and goddesses. Those for Sun and Moon are strictly representational; Mercury is represented by his caduceus (a rod with two snakes twined round it); that for Venus is an archetypal female symbol; Mars has a shield and spear; Jupiter is symbolised by his throne, and Saturn by his scythe (changed into a crutch in the woodcut on the right)

Saturne.	Jupiter.	mars	Sol.	Venus	mercure.	luna.
Saturday.	Thursday.	Tuesday.	Sunday.	Friday.	Wensday.	Munday.

from one subject to another, artful and intelligent, perceptive and versatile, but uncommitted.

In the horoscope, Mercury denotes memory, intelligence and brainwork; it is the planet of communication – a term that covers not only speech and writing, but the literary world and the press, radio and TV.

Venus

The planet Venus was named after the goddess of love and beauty, and in the horoscope Venus represents the aesthetic instincts, the affections, the love of peace and harmony.

As in the case of the naming of the constellations, it would be wrong to take it for granted that the planet was first named after the goddess and that these characteristics were subsequently attributed to it. It is as legitimate to assume that early astrologers, noting the position of this planet in the horoscope, found that the reading of this hand of the cosmic clock was connected with certain aspects of the personality, identified with those of the idealised goddess.

Mars

The epithet 'martial' clearly defines the temperament that Mars denotes. It is the expression of the primal urge, of the forward movement of energy; aggressive, daring, and impulsive. Where Mercury may be taken to typify the young child, and Venus the adolescent, Mars represents the young adult in full possession of his or her powers, like a young stallion.

But the character of Mars must not be thought of as insensitively aggressive. Courage and cheerfulness are equally among the qualities that this planet denotes.

Jupiter

In Latin, Jupiter was alternatively known as Jove, and from the latter name we get the epithet 'jovial', which so aptly typifies the expansive characteristics denoted in the horoscope by this planet.

Jupiter represents physical well-being, material success, an optimistic outlook: the fifth age of man which Shakespeare so well described:

In fair round belly with good capon lined
With eyes severe and beard of formal cut
Full of wise saws and modern instances . . .

Saturn

The most negative aspects of the personality are represented by Saturn; the epithet 'saturnine' describes the element of restraint and emotional coldness that this planet denotes in the horoscope.

Caution and control, pedantic practicality and thrift are the characteristics of Saturn; redeemed in some measure by the qualities of justice and patience. Saturn is in many ways the opposite of Jupiter: for Jupiter's optimism Saturn substitutes pessimism, for expansiveness, restriction.

These were the seven heavenly bodies of antiquity, the only members of the solar system that men could see with the naked eye. Between them, they denoted all the principal qualities of human beings, as well as significant aspects of their fate. Then came the telescope, and Sir Isaac Newton's mathematics. In 1781 Herschel discovered a new planet, which was at first named after him, but subsequently was called Uranus. In 1845 John Couch Adams and Leverrier – independently of one another – calculated

The attribution of one planet to each of the days of the week is a very old concept, first put forward by the Babylonian mathematicians. It survives in many European languages to the present day. In English, Saturnday, Sunday and Moonday are obvious, but the names of the other days of the week are derived from the names of the equivalent Scandinavian gods and goddess, Tyr (Mars), Odin (Mercury), Thor (like Jupiter, a god of thunder) and Frigg (Venus). In French and Italian, the Latin names have survived in Lundi/Lunedi, Mardi/Martedi, Mercredi/Mercoledi, Jeudi/Giovedi and Vendredi/Venedi

the existence of Neptune, which was observed by Galle the following year. And finally, in 1930, Tombaugh discovered Pluto, whose existence had been calculated by Lowell. There is even a possibility that a further planet exists beyond the orbit of Pluto.

Apart from these major planets, there are the moons of Mars, Jupiter, Saturn, Uranus and Neptune, as well as the asteroids; and Leverrier even believed there to be another planet, Vulcan, within the orbit of Mercury – its existence now seems unlikely, although it is possible to buy astrological tables for its movements.

Obviously, all these discoveries came as a blow to traditional astrologers. They felt it a matter of honour to include the new planets, as they were discovered, in their systems. But these new hands on our cosmic clock are relatively slow-moving. They tell us, as we would expect, that people born in one decade differ somewhat from those born in the next, but it would be unwise to be too specific. The experience of three thousand years is incorporated in traditional astrology; two hundred years is insufficient time in which to determine the significance of Uranus and, in the fifty years since it was discovered, even astronomers have learnt little about Pluto.

Nevertheless astrologers, with the invaluable assistance of hindsight, have proposed certain attributes of the newer planets. All the major political revolutions have taken place since the time of the discovery of Uranus – the American War of Independence, the French Revolution, the independence of the Spanish American states, the Russian Revolution, and many more – and so Uranus has been given the attribute of change and disruption.

Neptune, on the other hand, was discovered because of the influence it exerted on the orbit of Uranus: something vaguely subversive seemed to be at work. Spiritualism, which had been in total eclipse for some 1300 years, made its first modern emergence in 1848, and rapidly grew in significance from that date; this has led some astrologers to postulate that Neptune denotes the psychic faculty, and even to suggest that the planet represents an influence that only becomes apparent after death.

As for Pluto, its discovery came at the same time as the rise of the Nazis, and the planet has a prominent place in the horoscope of Hitler. It seems to represent the dark side of mankind – perhaps also the dark side of astrology itself!

It is not possible to relate Pluto to the individual signs of the zodiac. What this planet represents can only be determined by consideration of the horoscope as a whole.

'Good' and 'Bad' Planets
Traditionally, Venus and Jupiter are thought of as good or 'benefic' planets; the extent to which their influence is effective depends upon the position they occupy in the horoscope. Mars and Saturn are bad, or malefic, planets. The way in which these qualities should be taken into account will become apparent later, when we look at the interpretation of the planetary aspects.

The Triplicities
From the very earliest times, mankind has divided all physical matter into the four elements: fire, earth, air and water. The signs of the zodiac can be divided in the same way according to the nature of the temperament that they represent. Each group of three is called a triplicity.

Aries, Leo and Sagittarius are the fire signs, and, like fire, they are wonderful and warming in the right place, and dangerously destructive in places where they should not be. Fire signs denote headstrong natures and noble aims; energy and enthusiasm, ambition, emotion, and love of exaggeration.

Taurus, Virgo and Capricorn are the earth signs: they denote practicality, solidity, shrewdness and diplomacy; an inclination to caution, and a tendency to be suspicious of more lively thinkers.

Gemini, Libra and Aquarius are the air signs. They represent the intellectual qualities: reason, communication, humanity and refinement. Fire cannot burn without air, air moves more freely in the presence of fire.

Cancer, Scorpio and Pisces are the water signs. Water moves, dissolves, reflects; its peaceful exterior can hide deep and treacherous currents. The water signs denote natures that are emotional, hyper-sensitive, easily impressed; at the same time they are artistic, psychic, and naturally extremely sociable.

Rulerships
Each of the seven 'old' planets was given houses of the zodiac in which they ruled. The Sun and Moon, being the king and queen of heaven, each had only one house: the Sun rules in Leo by day, and the Moon in Cancer by night. The other five planets were each given two houses, one for day and one for night. Mercury rules in Virgo by day and Gemini by night; Venus in Libra and Taurus respectively; Mars in Scorpio and Aries; Jupiter in Sagittarius and Pisces; and Saturn in Capricorn and Aquarius. In these houses their influence is greatly strengthened.

The Planets and the Signs
We can now begin to interpret the horoscope. With the knowledge that we have of the characteristics denoted by each of the planets, and of the signs in which they rule, we can look at each twelfth of the zodiac – each 'sign' – and discover what it signifies to have the Sun, the ascendant, the Moon or any of the other heavenly bodies in that section of the heavens.

The science of astronomy is only a recent separation from the ancient science of astrology, which was born more than three thousand years ago in Mesopotamia. Until the invention of the telescope, which revolutionised the observation of the heavens and revealed the existence of three 'new' planets, men had to rely upon the naked eye and primitive instruments such as the astrolabes being used by the astrologers in this illustration from *The Travels of Sir John Mandeville*

Aries

Acting is one of the careers indicated for those with Sun in Aries, like Sir Charles Chaplin. They prefer to supervise their own careers: Chaplin was one of the first film actors to secure financial control of his own films

♈ ARIES: *the night house of Mars*

The spring equinox is the beginning of the zodiacal year, and Aries represents a new beginning. The young ram, with all the year before him, is full of fresh ambitions, and he is not to be diverted from his purpose; he is impulsive, self-centred and concerned only with his personal advancement. Aries is the pioneer in thought and in action, self-reliant and full of energy, but impulsive and headstrong, idealistic rather than down-to-earth.

Aries likes to be appreciated for his positive qualities; but at work, for instance, if he is driven beyond what he feels is a reasonable demand upon his abilities, he may well give in his notice in exasperation, or even revenge himself by some deceitful act. Explain to him what is needed, however, and give him due approval, and he will offer total loyalty.

Aries natives – those with the Sun in this sign – are likely to be full of schemes and new ideas and, if only they can visualise the outcome, they are perfectly capable of carrying their plans through to completion; but it is the picture of the completed work only a short time ahead that carries them forward on a wave of enthusiasm. If the scheme requires patience and dedication, they are unlikely to finish it; they are better fitted to direct and organise than to carry out the work for themselves.

As in all signs, there is a bad side to Aries. Those with the Sun in this sign are generally imaginative and brilliantly persuasive in their talk; when this characteristic is found in excess, they are often given to exaggera-tion and lying. Unhappily, they are too often found out: many unsuccessful confidence tricksters are of this type. The combination of Sun in Aries and Moon in Scorpio is a particularly dangerous one: self-interest, aggressiveness, inconstancy and presumptuousness characterise those whose horoscope contains these indications. Overweening self-pride is found in those who have the Moon in another fire sign.

Aries natives are so full of new ideas and ambitions that they seldom stay long in one job. Suitable careers included those of actor or designer, traveller, architect, free-lance writer – all those, in fact, who prefer to control their own careers and live in what some people regard as an unconventional manner.

Ascendant in Aries: Aries indicates an average stature, a lean and strong body with large bones; a broad head with a narrower chin, altogether rather long in the face; either a ruddy complexion with light or reddish hair and a pinched nose, or dark complexion with dark hair and bushy eyebrows; and quick eyes, generally bluish-grey. Although their general health is sound, Aries natives tend to be somewhat highly-strung, with an inclination to headaches, toothaches, neuralgia, etc. It has been suggested that these nervous disorders stem from trouble with the kidneys.

☽ *Moon in Aries:* This is an unstable indica-tion; those with the Moon in this sign have volatile and impulsive natures, and are given to sudden outbreaks of furious emotion. They fall in love quickly and violently, and

are selfishly possessive of the loved one, tending to dominate all the emotions expressed between them.

On the good side, they show great independence, and seldom lose their tempers for very long.

☿ *Mercury in Aries:* The fiery influence of Aries on the characteristics represented by Mercury results in people of lively temperament, fond of constructive argument and remarkably quick-thinking. They may, however, be carried away by the attractiveness of their arguments, or by thoughts of the personal advantages to be gained from their proposals. In such a situation, they cannot stand interference or delay, and may force a decision by their persuasiveness, or go ahead on their own without due consideration.

♀ *Venus in Aries:* Venus rules in Libra, the sign opposite to Aries, and therefore it is said to be 'in detriment' in the present house. This means that the less attractive characteristics tend to be emphasised: those with Venus in Aries tend to be self-centred and demanding of affection. At the same time they are very extrovert, unlikely to be discouraged from continuing the pursuit of an attractive man or woman if the slightest encouragement is given. Passionately romantic, often genuinely aggressive in their lovemaking, they frequently go too far, revealing an inherent coarseness in their behaviour.

♂ *Mars in Aries:* An almost uncontrollable combination, the overflowing energy and impulsive aggression of Mars added to the personal ambition and self-reliance of Aries. Unfortunately, nothing quite comes up to expectation for the person with Mars in Aries; he constantly feels the need to reassure himself that he is 'the greatest', indulging in ever more daring and impressive deeds. He is the type to make the star sportsman, the racing driver, the boxing champion.

There is leadership, because such a person can inspire enthusiasm in others; but too often he lacks cool organisational ability and tenaciousness, and may well lead such followers as he has blindly into disaster.

♃ *Jupiter in Aries:* The presence of Jupiter in Aries, however, is an excellent indication for leadership. Jupiter tempers the bold creativity of Aries with wisdom and judgment: any new endeavours begun under such an influence will more probably be in the fields of social or educational reform, or in religion, than in some revolutionary enterprise. Nevertheless, the combination of Arician self-interest with the self-importance of Jupiter can sometimes produce unfortunate results: 'at times there is a desire to go on holy crusades that may not be holy in the eyes of others' say Frances Sakoian and Louis Acker. There may be over-confidence, leading to carelessness, particularly in the spending of money. But, all in all, Jupiter in Aries is an indication for good, for energy

properly applied and inspiration to others.

♄ *Saturn in Aries:* Saturn takes some 29 years to pass through all twelve signs of the zodiac and so, in its positive characteristics, it represents the recurrence of similar traits in succeeding generations: where Aries symbolises the first impulse that sets something in motion, Saturn represents the law of cause and effect that brings about the final outcome of the original action, ready for the cycle to be repeated.

Saturn modifies the impulsiveness of Aries, forcing the native to exercise patience and to develop strength of character to survive by his own resources. The self-discipline that this engenders is of the greatest value, but those with this indication find it hard to understand and co-operate with others.

♅ *Uranus in Aries:* Uranus spends about seven years in each sign of the zodiac, and so represents the way in which all people of a similar age display similar characteristics. The human body renews itself completely once every seven years, and this cycle may be seen in operation in everybody's life.

All those born in the years 1928–1934 have Uranus in Aries; they show the impulsiveness and creativity of Aries in their desire for new experiences – their 'seven-

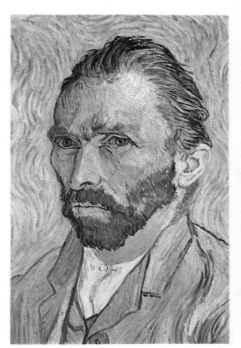

year itch' – and the revolutionary indications of Uranus are shown in the new life-styles that have been developed. But Uranus in Aries can also indicate political fanaticism and violent rejection of the past.

♆ *Neptune in Aries:* Neptune was in Aries between the years 1861 and 1875. Its influence may be seen in the development of new spiritual movements during this period.

New ideas and ambitions characterise Aries natives. Van Gogh (left) was a major innovator in painting; and Thomas Jefferson (above) was the most important influence on the growth of the USA from a group of tiny colonies

Taurus

♉ TAURUS *night house of Venus*

Above all else, Taurus represents strength; not necessarily of body, for the strength may be of character, or of purpose. This is one of the earth signs, denoting solidity and practicality, and Taureans exhibit more determination than any others. 'Extremely strong-willed' says A. E. Waite 'they can be led but never driven'.

The native of Taurus is the builder to the architect of Aries: where Aries may be satisfied with the mere *idea*, it is Taurus who sees that it comes to fruition. Security is an important part of the Taurean way of life, and leads to an emphasis upon physical possessions; it also means that the Taurean is inclined to be conservative and opposed to change. He or she is slow to anger but, when roused, may become violent and lose all control; this is particularly marked if the Moon is in a fire sign.

All those born with the Sun in Taurus are lovers of good food and drink, and they make excellent cooks. When the Moon is in a fire sign – Aries, Leo or Sagittarius – this can lead to less likeable characteristics: gluttony, sensuality and drunkenness.

Taureans may be faithful and generous friends or, where their self-respect is injured, determined enemies: their friendship can then only be regained by an appeal to their better natures. In family life they may sometimes provoke trouble solely for the rather perverse pleasure of 'making friends' again, and for this reason they must be particularly careful in their choice of a partner.

Sun in Taurus indicates a career in the handling of money, in medicine or in chemical manufacture; many Taureans also make good foremen or managers in industry, farmers or chefs. The association of Taurus with the throat is also a recognition of the fact that many Taureans are good singers, making a career either in opera or in more popular fields.

Ascendant in Taurus: Taurus indicates average to short stature, with a heavy, thick-set body, strong and inclining to corpulence; a broad forehead and mouth, often with heavy lips and jaw; big eyes; dark or sandy hair, often curly and rather coarse. The nose may be aquiline, particularly in association with sandy hair, but generally it is thick and rather broad.

The constitution is usually remarkably strong, but the neck and throat may give trouble, and there is a tendency to suffer from respiratory ailments. Taurus's faith in himself is accompanied by a certain lack of faith in the optimism of others, and when he falls seriously ill he is likely to make a quick recovery, whatever the prognosis of the doctors. Nevertheless, 'laziness is fatal to their health, work the best medicine', and they thrive on this prescription.

☽ *Moon in Taurus:* Emotional steadiness and placidity are the indications of the Moon in Taurus, but physical security is necessary in order to achieve this. Fortunately, all domestic and monetary affairs are likely to be dealt with sensibly, and wealth and the good things of life will result. The encouragement

of others may be needed before new schemes can be got under way, but after this persistence will see them through to completion; there is seldom any tendency to abandon one project halfway in favour of another and more attractive one. Moon in Taurus also indicates the kind of person who seems to have an innate understanding of growing things, and who is particularly successful in the garden.

☿ *Mercury in Taurus:* When the importance of Mercury in Taurus is particularly strong – when it is 'well-aspected' – it means marked ability in mathematics and physical sciences; but the conservatism of Taurus in general is inclined to modify the quickness of mind that Mercury represents, leading in some cases to obstinacy of opinion, and even bigotry. Nevertheless, the influence of Mercury on the Taurean is a good one; it represents a leavening of thought, a general liberation of the senses and the development of marked powers of concentration.

♀ *Venus in Taurus:* This is the combination for constancy, emotional stability, and lasting love. It also indicates sensuality: those who have Venus in this sign love physical contact, fine clothes and jewellery, and luxuriously furnished homes; they will always try to make themselves look as young and attractive as possible. Yet, perhaps surprisingly, their sensuality is of a passive kind: they prefer to be the attrac*tive* rather than the attrac*ted*.

Taureans have a natural ability as singers; those with Venus as well as the Sun in this sign may well succeed professionally.

♂ *Mars in Taurus:* The day house of Mars is Scorpio, the sign of the Zodiac diametrically opposite Taurus, and Mars is therefore 'in detriment' in Taurus. The down-to-earth quality represented by Taurus is in conflict with the over-riding energy of Mars – it is as if a fast car is being driven in a muddy country lane. But if a lower gear can be engaged, the power can be properly exploited to practical ends. So Mars in Taurus can be an excellent indication for craftsmen and skilled workers, such as carpenters, engravers and modelmakers; when Venus is well-aspected, sculptors and jewellers may be expected.

When Mars is in a bad position with relation to another planet, there may be obsession with sex and excessive preoccupation with material possessions; this may well show itself in violence in lovemaking and sexual jealousy.

♃ *Jupiter in Taurus:* Jupiter is always the symbol of maturity and sound judgment, and in combination with the commonsense qualities represented by Taurus it signifies reliability, steadiness and spiritual equilibrium. This combination is usually accompanied by the accumulation of wealth, or at the very least by material comfort, and it

becomes essential that those with Jupiter in Taurus should learn not only generosity, but discrimination in the disposition of their money.

When the aspects are bad, the situation can lead to extravagance and dissipation, to ostentation and over-spending.

♄ *Saturn in Taurus:* The time taken by Saturn to complete one cycle of the zodiac is just about the length of the average business

career: most people reach their first position of real responsibility around their twenty-ninth or thirtieth year, and few successful businessmen find it necessary to continue the struggle in the market-place much after the age of sixty. Since Taurus indicates a career in the handling of money, Saturn in Taurus implies success in banking or investments, insurance or some aspect of business management. The cold and restrictive nature of Saturn suggests frugality, and in financial matters this is a virtue. When it is taken to extremes, of course, it leads either to miserliness or to an obsession with material possessions.

♅ *Uranus in Taurus:* In this sign the planet represents obstinacy, determination and resourcefulness; the generation born in the years 1935–41 reached maturity in the late 60s, and this was a period characterised by the introduction of new techniques in accountancy and management. The Taurean concern with material well-being can, however, prove a limiting influence on ambitious schemes of this kind.

♆ *Neptune in Taurus:* Neptune was in Taurus from 1875 to 1888. It was a period that saw the invention of a wide range of devices that have become part of twentieth century life: the telephone, the phonograph, the microphone, and the first practical airship; the building of the first skyscraper, and the establishment of motor car factories. In this way we may see the effect of the combination of the materialism of Taurus with the spiritual influence of Neptune.

Sun in Taurus. The love of music is characterised by the composer Brahms (left); strength of character and purpose were the outstanding attributes of Catherine the Great of Russia (above) and the English Lord Protector, Oliver Cromwell (below)

Gemini

Versatility is frequently the downfall of the Gemini native. Judy Garland (below) was literally destroyed by the demands placed upon her as a young and brilliant film actress; and Marilyn Monroe, exhausted, killed herself (opposite)

♊ GEMINI *night house of Mercury*

Gemini is an Air sign; duality is the fundamental quality of the twins – add the mercurial disposition to this combination and it explains the elusive, contradictory nature of those born with the Sun in this sign. Geminians are naturally two-faced; they may try very hard to be honest and straightforward, but inevitably self-interest leads them into unscrupulousness.

Happy, charming, imaginative, intellectual and restless, they are also likely to lapse suddenly into stolidity, materialism, even sullen pessimism. This is because they can reflect every change in their surroundings; they constantly need variety, and they are very adaptable and versatile. As a result, they have one outstanding virtue: they seldom lose control of themselves or of a situation, and they can make use of their inherent cleverness to come up with a solution for any emergency.

Gemini children need handling with great care. They love intellectual activities, but although they may concentrate hard on studies for a short time they prefer to pick the brains of others, or find some way round the labour of learning. They can be so charming and ingenious about it that parents and teachers may find it difficult to be severe with them – and very soon bad habits can set in that are impossible to eradicate later.

When the Moon is in a fire sign – Aries, Leo or Sagittarius – the typical character of Gemini may be found developed to extremes, placing strain on the nervous disposition.

When they are concerned only for themselves, Gemini natives can be cunning, evasive, unscrupulous and capable of talking their way out of anything; but at their best they make ideal companions, entertaining, witty and excellent storytellers.

It is the versatility of the type that brings about its downfall: Geminians find it difficult to remain too long devoted to any one thing – whether it is a job, or a loved one. It is not that they are intentionally fickle but that, with one side of their nature, they are deeply involved emotionally while, with the other, they immediately begin an intellectual analysis of their intentions.

Among the careers most suitable for people of this type are those of broker or dealer, journalist, barrister or diplomat – in short, any work which combines quick-wittedness with the possibility of fairly regular change of surroundings.

Ascendant in Gemini: The Gemini type is tall, with thin upright body, a long face and colourful features. If the complexion is dark the eyes are usually hazel, large and piercing. Movements are quick and active, and the hands are particularly expressive.

The constitution is not likely to be over strong: the health rapidly breaks down under strain, and catarrh, bronchitis and other diseases should be guarded against.

☽ *Moon in Gemini:* Unless there are particularly good aspects, or other factors which are clearly going to contribute significantly on a practical, down-to-earth, level, the indications of the Moon in Gemini are not good ones, either for the subject or for his or her friends. In this sign, the Moon portends a nervous, restless temperament; this may show itself in almost ceaseless chatter and fidgeting, and few people will be able to endure behaviour of this kind.

Nevertheless, in favourable circumstances, the Moon in Gemini can denote resourcefulness and a quick imagination – the type of temperament that can make a good romantic novelist or a competent actor.

☿ *Mercury in Gemini:* For inventiveness and originality of thought this is an almost unbeatable combination of influences. Mercury rules Gemini: the mutability of the Twins is controlled by the analytical intelligence that Mercury denotes, and the result is that peculiarly logical, questioning approach known as the 'scientific mind'.

There are drawbacks, of course. Although people with this indication are excellent communicators and eloquent speakers, they are so aware of everything that is going on around them that they can easily become distracted and confused. Also, because they can see and assess both sides of an argument, they may find it difficult to come to a decision. In terms of a career, their great versatility, combined with their lack of direction, may make them 'Jack of all trades, master of none'.

♀ *Venus in Gemini:* In the eyes of others, the person with Venus in Gemini may appear to be insincere or superficial, particularly in affairs of the heart. He, or she, likes change and shies away from permanent relationships; but this is not the temperament of a Casanova, because it lacks the sensual drive. It is simply that Venus in Gemini denotes a desire to be friends with everyone, to mix with intellectual equals, and to exchange lighthearted conversation in pleasant surroundings. Frequently this combination is a good indication for literary abilities, and particularly for the writing of poetry.

♂ *Mars in Gemini:* The restlessness of Gemini, combined with the force of Mars, can give a brusqueness to the speech that is not always acceptable. Although those with Mars in this sign have well-developed critical abilities, they may be thought rude in the way in which they express their opinions. They revel in argument and debate, but may become contentious and irritable. Skill in mechanical engineering is also indicated.

♃ *Jupiter in Gemini:* Jupiter brings maturity to the volatile enquiring nature of Gemini; in this sign the planet symbolises a love of such subjects as history, philosophy or the genesis of ideas. In Gemini, Jupiter is 'in detriment', that is in the sign directly opposite Sagittarius, which he rules: the love of learning may turn into a taste for knowledge for its own sake, unsupported by true understanding or even practical experience.

When the indications are good, however,

there are excellent possibilities of extending one's intellectual horizons in all sorts of ways, and of establishing effective partnerships and working friendships. It is important to fight against a tendency to explore too many new subjects, gaining only a superficial acquaintance of each: Jupiter in Gemini represents characteristics that can

make excellent social critics or historians, and it is tempting to gain a reputation by slick plausibility.

♄ *Saturn in Gemini:* The coldly calculating nature symbolised by Saturn combines well with the Geminian character, imposing discipline and logic on the lively intellect. In unfavourable circumstances the effect may be inhibitory, giving rise to excessive scepticism and a tendency to introversion. Nevertheless, the resourcefulness of Gemini can lead to a practical, adaptable nature.

At its best, this combination indicates good opportunities for those who are concerned in solving problems and performing experiments: engineers, research physicists and mathematicians generally gain considerable success, as well as those concerned with drawing-up contracts or keeping books.

♅ *Uranus in Gemini:* Unusual restlessness is the characteristic of the generation born with Uranus in Gemini: they travel frequently, carrying new ideas about the world and making new contacts everywhere. The free exchange of different modes of thinking helps to break down conventional barriers, not only in social relationships but in intellectual matters.

♆ *Neptune in Gemini:* In literature, painting and music, the years 1888–1902 – when Neptune was in Gemini – saw a sudden break away from what had gone before, and the development of a recognisably twentieth-century style. The characteristics of this style have survived to the present day, showing that its influence was strong.

Cunning and unscrupulousness are the essential characteristics of the politician: Gemini natives can talk their way out of anything. But at their best, like John Kennedy, they make entertaining companions and compelling conversationalists

Cancer

Sun in Cancer. Natives of this sign have good memories and sharp ears; they are excellent mimics and, like Gina Lollobrigida, can shine as performers in languages not their own

♋ CANCER *the house of the Moon*

Cancer is a water sign and, like the sea, it responds to the changing influence of its ruler, the Moon. This conflicts oddly with the other side of the nature represented by Cancer, which is characterised by obstinate tenaciousness. The resultant of these two opposing tendencies is seen in the Cancerian's love of theatricality: it is not the stage itself that appeals so much as the excitement of the spectacle, the ebb and flow of passion and action. As a spectator rather than a protagonist, the Cancerian gives his loyalty to one side or the other; deeply moved by the changing fortunes of the hero he supports, he is nevertheless existing in a dream world. This is the type of the devoted football fan who, every Saturday, throws off his inhibitions for a couple of hours but who, if he were ever offered the chance to appear on the field as a player, would almost certainly refuse.

Not that the Cancerian is entirely without the desire to participate. In politics, for example, he or she may be found very active; but it is more likely to be as the anonymous party supporter (shouting 'Sieg Heil!' at a Nuremberg rally, for example) than as the political leader on the platform. When the Moon is in Sagittarius or Virgo, however, the native of Cancer may show great ability as a public speaker.

Although Cancerians are fundamentally conservative and homeloving, they are thus easily carried away by excitement, and they may try to shape their lives in imitation of some romantic ideal. More often than not they are successful, because they are inventive and original and excellent business organisers with a good sense of value. Their homes are likely to be rather dark and mysterious, filled with antiques and curios but essentially comfortable.

Good memory and a sharp ear also characterise those born with the Sun in this sign. They are very good mimics, often almost unconsciously; and they can recall events in remarkable detail years after they have occurred. The ease with which a Cancerian can identify himself with a situation, and the inherent tendency to copy others, means that he should exercise great care in his choice of friends; he will show great sensitivity concerning those whom he loves. Affectionate and sociable by nature, Cancerians nevertheless tend to be shy, and somewhat possessive.

The love of comfort and good living among Cancerians makes them excellent cooks and housekeepers. Secondhand dealers, particularly those selling antiques, and estate agents are also found with the Sun in Cancer; so are many sailors and some very good gardeners.

Ascendant in Cancer: The Cancer type is of average to short stature, with a rather fleshy body and short legs in proportion to the rest of the build. There is a round face, with prominent forehead, pale complexion and small blue or grey eyes; the nose is short, perhaps up-turned, and the hair is brown. There may be a noticeably ungainly walk.

In health matters, the tendency to give way to excitement often leads to gastric and other stomach troubles; pleurisy and dropsy are also associated with Cancer.

☽ *Moon in Cancer:* The influence symbolised by the Moon in the house of its rulership is deeply emotional: the inherent love of home life may manifest itself as an over-dependence on the mother – which the Moon also represents. Certainly domestic security and a happy marriage will figure prominently

in the dreams of the Cancerian, and this ideal will be transferred in time to the children, who may find themselves overwhelmed by parental love and interference.

In fact, those with the Moon in Cancer show an awareness of the feelings and motives of others that is telepathic; on the other hand, they are also so sensitive of their own feelings that they may easily imagine without cause that they have been neglected or insulted.

☿ *Mercury in Cancer:* The emotional bias that Cancer signifies has an unfortunate effect upon the questioning intellect represented by Mercury: whoever has this combination in the horoscope will tend to be subjective and prejudiced in looking at facts, and may even tell lies without consciously appreciating how the truth has been distorted.

On the good side, Mercury in Cancer signifies a retentive memory, one that absorbs information almost unconsciously. At their most sensitive, those with this combination may be telepathic; at a lower level, they may find themselves excessively swayed by appeals to their emotions.

♀ *Venus in Cancer:* This is not a good sign for lovers: their feelings are all too easily hurt, even though they may conceal them behind a calm facade. They may be quite unpredictable in their moods, but one thing is sure: whether their childhood was happy or unhappy they will remember it in detail, and try to build a domestic life of their own which either reconstructs their childhood or makes it what it should have been.

Women with Venus in Cancer are likely to be particularly feminine, and very domestic in their outlook. If there are bad aspects, there may be a tendency to act in a 'spoilt' and sulky way, or to be over-sentimental.

♂ *Mars in Cancer:* When Mars is in Capricorn he is 'exalted'; in Cancer, therefore, diametrically opposite Capricorn, he is in his fall. The significance of this position shows itself in outbursts of irrational anger and periods of frustrated moodiness. If the anger is repressed, it may show itself in other ways, particularly in stomach upsets of a psychosomatic nature.

In the home, irritability can be a problem. However, the forceful energy of Mars can be channelled into creativity, and many of those who show great aptitude for 'do-it-yourself' about the home will be found to have Mars in Cancer.

♃ *Jupiter in Cancer:* Of all the planets, perhaps Jupiter in Cancer represents the happiest inclinations. The maturity of Jupiter controls the emotions of Cancer: the combination exemplifies the best parental attitude, warm and loving yet firm and protective. Generosity, high moral principles, kindness and hospitality are among the virtues shown by those who have Jupiter in this sign, and it is only when the influence is overstrong that these can degenerate into sentimentality, possessive parental love, and self-pampering.

♄ *Saturn in Cancer:* Saturn rules Capricorn, which is the opposite sign, and so his presence in Cancer symbolises repression and isolation. For Cancerians, who love home life so much, this can mean a cold and even unhappy childhood; as compensation, they may take their parental responsibilities with great seriousness. At the same time, they tend to cut themselves off from the true expression of their love in what they may insist is preservation of self-respect but is more likely to be an attempt to safeguard their dignity.

Attempts to establish a secure and stable home-life, with all its necessary comforts, may result in overspending, and resultant financial difficulties.

♅ *Uranus in Cancer:* This combination symbolises the break with home, the departure of the fledglings from the nest; in the adult, it generally indicates an unusual or even eccentric home, individually designed and strikingly decorated. Since Uranus also is connected with occult matters, it is quite possible that the home will show this influence: one room, perhaps, will be given over to meditation or to occasional seances.

♆ *Neptune in Cancer:* With this combination, the telepathic sensitivity represented by Cancer is at its strongest: quite a number of clairvoyants have been born with Neptune in this sign. When the aspects are bad, however, great care should be taken in the exercise of any psychic gifts.

Natives of Cancer are spectators rather than protagonists, ideal qualities for observers of human behaviour like the painter Rembrandt (above, left) or Ernest Hemingway (above)

Leo

♌ LEO *house of the Sun*
Whatever zoologists may tell us now about his lifestyle, the lion remains for all of us a symbol of splendour and pride. And those born with the Sun in Leo seem to have a natural grandeur about them: they are proud, ambitious, masterful, yet sincere and generous. They are born leaders, behaving always as if whatever comes to them is theirs by right, and they love everything big in life.

Trusting and good-hearted as they are, they may suffer intense disillusionment when someone in whom they have had faith does not come up to their expectations; but generally they bring out the best in others, and they themselves seem to thrive in adversity. Leo natives are usually practical and hard-headed; they can go straight to the heart of a problem, are capable of long-lasting effort, and can carry out ambitious schemes to their conclusion. They have strong will-power and a marked degree of self-control; they are at their most effective when they are placed in command of others, and setbacks seem merely to spur them on to greater effort.

In the Leo character there are, of course, tendencies which must be controlled. Overweening pride is the most obvious: haughtiness, boasting, snobbish superiority and disdainfulness are all characteristics to be watched for. There is a tendency, too, to be very obstinate in upholding traditional beliefs, subscribing with complete sincerity to what others may regard as absurd or out-of-date doctrines.

Leo natives are excellent organisers, and make very good managers or foremen; although hardworking, they do not really like manual labour, and tend naturally to take charge of others. Women with the Sun in Leo can find a worthwhile career as social workers. Other typical careers are as orchestral conductors, organists, serious actors or mural painters – anything truly grand in scale or conception.

Ascendant in Leo: Leo indicates a stature usually above average, with a big-boned and well-built body, lean in youth but tending to plumpness in middle life; yellow or blonde hair and a complexion tending to be florid. The head is big and round, with blue or grey eyes; the sight is quick; and the carriage is upright and at times almost stately. In ill health, their good sight may be affected, and they are also liable to suffer from heart diseases, pains in the back and lungs.

☽ *Moon in Leo:* An instinct for self-dramatisation characterises those with the Moon in this sign. Everything has to be played out as if on a big stage, with everybody drawn in as supporting players. It can be quite insufferable, except for the fact that it is at the same time entirely genuine: these people need to be admired, but they also need to love and be loved. They tend to dominate their children, insisting that they should be clean and well-behaved, and their homes are equally well-kept.

☿ *Mercury in Leo:* The combination of Leo and Mercury indicates a great deal of self-confidence in intellectual matters; combined with a forceful and persuasive way of putting things, this can easily establish a reputation as an authority on some special subject. But those with the indication should beware a tendency to be over-confident and to conceive things in broad and general terms, ignoring the essential details.

♀ *Venus in Leo:* People with this combination are the kind who give expensive parties; the women always like to be the centre of attention. They are ardent but faithful lovers, possessive and inclined to be jealous, but warmhearted, fond of children, and with a great love of art and some ability in painting or sculpture.

♂ *Mars in Leo:* This combination characterises the kind of personality that we think of as typifying the high Renaissance: the great dramatic actor, the lyric poet 'burning bright', the military leader, the patroness of the arts. All those with Mars in this sign are passionately attracted to the opposite sex, and are themselves strongly attractive. It is perhaps a great personal tragedy that they tend to lose their hair early in life.

♃ *Jupiter in Leo:* The steadfast, confident qualities of Leo, combined with the benign maturity of Jupiter, can prove to be almost overwhelming. A love of pomp and circum-

♄ *Saturn in Leo:* Saturn rules in Aquarius, the house opposite to Leo, and is 'in detriment' here. As a result, this planetary position means that Leo's ambition tends to turn into a lust for power, his faith into bigotry, his love of self into egotism, and his benevolence into strictness and discipline. People with this combination must examine their motives closely, and set themselves standards which they must maintain.

The lion is born to rule, and all those portrayed on these two pages have been leaders, whether in the field of letters like G. B. Shaw (far left) or in the more usual political field like Benito Mussolini, Napoleon, or President Castro of Cuba

stance, an abundance of benevolent energy: people with these indications are of the type who organise charity dinners, historical pageants and great religious festivals. They are likely to be comparatively wealthy, with plenty of opportunity to exercise their talent for organisation in this kind of activity, but they must avoid a tendency to become arrogant and self-important. Success in gambling or speculation may encourage them to become over-confident, with subsequent financial disaster and social disgrace.

♅ *Uranus in Leo:* New standards of sexual behaviour, new concepts in art and music – these are some of the characteristics associated with Uranus in Leo. Bad aspects with another planet indicate a tendency to unwise stubbornness, which may result in estrangement from a loved one or a serious illness.

♆ *Neptune in Leo:* Talent in music or the arts may be expected of people with Neptune in Leo; even if they are not practitioners, they will take a very positive interest in the subject and encourage its development.

Virgo

♍ VIRGO *day house of Mercury*

The analytical mind is what characterises Virgoans above all else. They may at times be thought reserved and lacking in feeling, but this is because, diplomatically, they conceal their nervous and contradictory nature behind a matter-of-fact front. At heart they are sympathetic, but they often find it necessary to hide their kinder feelings, even to suppress them, because they are afraid of appearing too emotional and unworldly, not sufficiently business-like. As a result, they may make rather exacting employers, although they are invariably just in their demands.

Virgoans can cut through a tangled web of words to reach the exact meaning of a statement; their shrewdness also enables them to make sense of the most complex situations.

A comparison of the writer D. H. Lawrence (right) with Ernest Hemingway shows how different they were. Hemingway, as a native of Cancer, developed a new style of objective journalism; Lawrence's writing reveals the analytical yet functional character of his mind

They work methodically and logically through a problem, and they can produce a clear tabulation of the most involved schemes. They have an excellent eye for detail, and they are genuinely inventive; they are good technicians and practical with their hands, and they do well in a career such as engineering drawing. However, their questioning natures make them more fitted to work in an office or library than in a workshop. They have a deep interest in history and statistics, and a good memory for quotations from well-known writings.

When material circumstances permit them to exercise their shrewdness and subtlety to the full, Virgoans can be very unscrupulous, particularly in business; but usually they have sufficient moral sense to keep any such tendencies under strict control, and they are then the most reliable and conscientious of people. Their principal failings are vacillation and lack of self-confidence; appreciating so many different points of view, they find it difficult to make up their minds. For this reason they often shirk responsibility and prefer to work under someone else's direction; with the Moon in a Fire sign, however, they make capable leaders.

Virgoans make excellent book-keepers and statisticians, editors and analytical chemists. If they are able to keep themselves healthy, they may show great skill in ministering to others less fortunate.

Ascendant in Virgo: The physical characteristics represented by Virgo are a well-knit, and possibly even plump, body, of above

average stature; an oval face with a ruddy or dark complexion, dark hair and eyes, and an unusual nose with pronounced curves at the nostrils. Virgoans should be careful about their diet, as they are inclined to worry and this affects their bowels. Drugs and patent foods have a strange fascination for them, but they should be particularly careful in their use.

☽ *Moon in Virgo:* Virgo is known as the sign of service, and the Moon in this sign indicates a shy and retiring personality, one that prefers to work quietly behind the scenes. There is a great insistence on neatness, which can degenerate into an obsession, or a preoccupation with unnecessary detail. Diet and health in general are a matter of constant concern.

☿ *Mercury in Virgo:* As Mercury rules Virgo, its influence in this sign is particularly strong. As with Gemini, the other sign ruled by Mercury, the outcome is that type of mind known as 'scientific'; but where Mercury in Gemini indicates a preoccupation with ideas for their intellectual quality, Mercury in Virgo suggests a concern for the practical application of these ideas. Those with this combination insist on accuracy and attention to detail, which at times can appear unnecessarily pedantic; they generally acquire a good education and put it to use.

♀ *Venus in Virgo:* The analytical nature of Virgo can be a great drawback for lovers: they tend to examine their emotions and be over-critical of their partners. Say Frances Sakoian and Louis Acker: 'These people try to understand the beauty of a rose by dissecting it petal by petal'.

Those with Venus in Virgo may, in fact, never marry, either because they persist in subjecting every motive to close analysis, or because they are too shy and are repelled by the physical side of love. The coolly calculating exterior they show to the world effectively inhibits romantic relationships, and in the end they find themselves alone, with only a small dog or cat for company.

♂ *Mars in Virgo:* Mars can add the necessary practical element to the method and precision of the typical Virgoan personality: this is a good indication for success at such work as engineering modelmaking, calligraphy or precision surgery. There is a tendency to be fussy and over-critical, and this can lead to bad relations with employers or employees; there is, however, a danger of accidents at work if the concentration on detail is relaxed at any time.

♃ *Jupiter in Virgo:* Jupiter rules in Pisces, the sign diametrically opposite to Virgo, and is therefore 'in detriment'. The unhappy outcome is a conflict between the attention to detail of a Virgoan with the broad expansiveness of Jupiter. People with this combination may be found to war with themselves, avoiding attention to some small detail that they

know to be important, or driving themselves into overwork to escape the temptation to relax.

There are good indications as well, however. The wealth of Jupiter can be put to good use in furthering the Virgoan interest in medical matters, by contributing to medical charities or by supporting hospital appeals.

♄ *Saturn in Virgo:* The cold and withdrawn nature symbolised by Saturn does not improve the coolness and shyness of Virgo. People with this combination tend to take on a great deal of responsibility with their

work, becoming austere and depressed as it gradually overwhelms them. They may suffer ill-health, particularly in the digestion or the urino-genital system.

♅ *Uranus in Virgo:* The generation with Uranus in Virgo will conceive new and ingenious approaches to contemporary problems in labour relations, ecology and child care. They are prepared to work hard and resourcefully, but they are likely to experience changes and upsets in employment.

♆ *Neptune in Virgo:* Neptune is in its detriment in Virgo, indicating a generation in which poverty and bad economic conditions prevent the exercise of imagination and creative abilities. With bad aspects, there is a tendency to psychosomatic illnesses.

From the cool beauty of Greta Garbo (left) and the clear intelligence of Elizabeth I, the 'virgin queen', to the Machiavellian gaze of Cardinal Richelieu and the calm appraisal of Goethe (below), the most remarkable point about all four faces is the unusual nose structure that is so characteristic of Virgo

Libra

≏ LIBRA *day house of Venus*

Where Aries represents a new beginning, Libra represents the point of culmination of the year, the mid-point of the seasons where effort has been crowned with success. All the hard work that has gone into the first half of the year is balanced by the produce of the harvest and its gradual consumption through the winter months. When the harvest is in, it is the time to relax for a short while, enjoying the last of the sun and fruits of the earth.

So Librans are lovers of pleasure and beauty, elegance and harmony. They have the ability to compare things and reach an impartial judgment on them; at the same time they dislike argument, considering that the true merits of whatever is being discussed are obvious.

In excess, the Libran urge to compare and criticise can lead them into undesirable habits: as A. E. Waite put it, 'their curiosity seems insatiable, and they will be found in their element at every sale, bazaar, church service, wedding or funeral of note, observing and comparing every detail . . . fashion, ceremony, convention, family histories and social scandal seem to be the breath of life to the . . . Libran'.

Librans show great talent as fashion designers or interior decorators; they also have ability in the management of all sorts of public entertainment. Other suitable careers are lawyer or antique dealer.

Ascendant in Libra: The Libran body is well-formed and beautiful, of average stature or above; the face is rounded and the complexion is good; the hair is often flaxen, long and smooth, and the eyes generally blue and full of feeling. The constitution is fundamentally strong, but the health can be impaired by excessive eating and drinking, with trouble for the kidneys and bladder.

☽ *Moon in Libra:* With the Moon in Libra, the native shows an inherent tendency to be easily swayed by the advice of others; there is an intense dislike of extravagant behaviour, or of unfriendly relationships, and the innate courtesy of the Libran leads to the

Sun in Libra. Brigitte Bardot (right) epitomises the Libran physical type of western European, with her long blonde hair and blue eyes full of feeling

acceptance of attitudes that are not always wisely thought-out. However, the positive side of this combination is most attractive: people with the Moon in Libra are gracious and charming, and sensitive to the reactions of others, because their emotional wellbeing is dependent on others' approval; they entertain often in their delightful homes.

☿ *Mercury in Libra:* This combination denotes an intense interest in human relationships and in thought and behaviour patterns. Natives like to work with others in some intellectual pursuit; but the partner must also be physically acceptable, without unattractive personal habits and idiosyncrasies. Careers in psychology, public relations or sociology are particularly suited to those with Mercury in this sign.

♀ *Venus in Libra:* Venus rules in Libra, and the outcome is a type of person who enjoys companionship, who understands other people's feelings, and who therefore considers social relations of the greatest importance. Marriage is a preoccupation to those with this indication and, since they are likely to be themselves very attractive physically, they seldom have much difficulty in finding a partner. At the same time, their inherent distaste for excess in any form may cause them to find the physical aspects of love less attractive than the intellectual companionship they seek.

♂ *Mars in Libra:* Mars rules in the opposite sign, Aries; the obvious antipathy between the extrovert energy of Mars and the discriminating refinement of Libra is intensified as a result. With good aspects, Mars brings a positive quality to the equivocating nature of Libra, initiating all sorts of social activity; but the conflict between the two types of temperament – and Libra abhors conflict at all times – leads to confusion and to a resultant narrowing of outlook.

♃ *Jupiter in Libra:* This is the planet of mature justice, in the sign of balanced judgment; at its best, there is a strong indication of the ability to make wise decisions, both for oneself and for other people. Judges, marriage counsellors, diplomats, these represent the kind of people who can apply the outcome of years of experience to the solution of social problems. Of course this tendency can be carried too far: when there are bad aspects it represents an urge to make moral judgments on behalf of others.

♄ *Saturn in Libra:* Discipline and responsibility are represented by Saturn in Libra; the native's concern may well be with contracts, whether in business matters or in the arranging of marriages. Saturn is in a powerful position in this sign, and if the aspects are good natives may become wealthy and of high standing in the community. With bad aspects, there may be a tendency to demand too much of employees.

♅ *Uranus in Libra:* New attitudes to marriage, new ideas in community living, these developments are characteristic of Uranus in Libra. There may also be some development of telepathic communication.

♆ *Neptune in Libra:* This is the planetary position of Neptune for those born between 1942 and 1957. It represents a shift in the relative importance of different aspects of social relationships, and at the same time an increase in the sense of mutual responsibility.

Mahatma Gandhi, the architect of Indian independence, is a good example of the Libran's capacity for judgment. Having weighed all arguments and reached a logical conclusion, he was so confident of his case that no alternative seemed worthy of discussion

35

Scorpio

♏ SCORPIO *day house of Mars*

This is a water sign, and the smooth surface can conceal unfathomable and treacherous depths. It has been said that Scorpians have the most powerful natures, whether for good or evil. Calm and watchful, and yet with a magnetic intensity about them, they seem to exert a strange hypnotic influence over other people.

They are very strong-willed, determined yet cautious, shrewd and self-confident,

although perhaps somewhat too direct in their manner when they do speak out. They can be very quick to take offence, and very critical of something they dislike. They can quite easily make lifelong enemies by the destructiveness of what they have to say.

Yet at the same time Scorpians make excellent friends, and possessive and passionate lovers; frequently tragic love-stories, even tales of violence, are to be told of them.

For all the tenacious quality of their characters, and the appearance they give of being withdrawn from the centre of activity, Scorpians are at the same time deeply sensitive, and easily moved by their emotions. They can be hurt so readily, and frequently it is their own fault: they are too demanding, sceptical and unforgiving of faults in others, usually because they cannot excuse the same faults in themselves.

Scorpio is the symbol of sex, and here it is governed by Mars: debauchery and perversion are always dangers to be watched for.

Some of the most influential public speakers and diplomats may be found among Scorpians, as well as those practised in the occult. They also make excellent research scientists, detectives and doctors: the combination of Sun in Scorpio and Moon in Cancer is a particularly strong indication for the medical profession.

Ascendant in Scorpio: Scorpio represents a strong thick body, of average stature, and generally rather hairy; the hair is frequently coarse, thick and curling; the top of the head tends to be bullet-shaped, and the face somewhat square with an aquiline nose. Scorpians have considerable resistance to disease, and a generally strong constitution, but may suffer from ailments of the bladder and genitals.

☽ *Moon in Scorpio:* This is not a good position for the Moon, which here represents strongly partisan feelings derived from desire. Personal affairs will be taken very seriously; jealousy, brooding, the irrational lust for revenge – all these attitudes are characteristic. There is a stubborn adherence to selfish principles, but this can be turned to good advantage in the pursuit of a worthwhile objective.

☿ *Mercury in Scorpio:* The combination of Mercury in Scorpio can produce a mind that is acutely penetrating, ruthless and intolerant in its methods, and yet intuitively capable of the most profound insights. It will be a mind that operatives secretively but shrewdly, working out ways of overcoming obstacles that others may already have given up hope of conquering. At its best it will be enquiring and analytical; at its worst, scheming and destructive.

♀ *Venus in Scorpio:* Venus rules in Taurus and so is in detriment in Scorpio. The effect is an intense and perhaps unhappy preoccupation with sex and sensuality; emotional relationships are likely to be passionate, with jealous quarrels and much display of selfishness. In women, this can lead to the development of that particularly possessive yet self-sufficient character known as the *femme fatale.*

♂ *Mars in Scorpio:* Mars is in the sign of his rulership, and his influence is particularly strong. The powerfulness of the sexual energy can be manifested in many ways, and it need not be in making love: the young soldier who dies gallantly, fighting alone to the last, because he will not give up his post, is just as characteristic of this influence.

♃ *Jupiter in Scorpio:* The secret nature of Scorpio wars unhappily with the urbanity of Jupiter. Those with Jupiter in this sign will have large-scale involvement in all kinds of finance and legal undertaking, but may find themselves distracted by lawsuits, tax demands and foolish ventures in partnership.

♄ *Saturn in Scorpio:* Taking on responsibilities with great seriousness and emotional dedication, people with Saturn in Scorpio may find that they have accepted too great a burden. They are near-perfectionists in their work, and they expect too much of others. They can become resentful on a minor matter of principle, and may well plot some revenge out of all proportion to the (often imagined) injury.

♅ *Uranus in Scorpio:* As well as sex, Scorpio represents death and regeneration, and the combination with the principle of upheaval represented by Uranus is a potent one. Uranus is in Scorpio from 1975, and some astrologers regard it as signalling a great period of change which must take place before the 'age of Aquarius' is ushered in.

♆ *Neptune in Scorpio:* Neptune symbolises the mysterious and the occult, and the influence upon Scorpio's love of secrecy may be interpreted in many ways. Perhaps the spiritual movements that began between 1956 and 1970, when Neptune was last in Scorpio, will gradually reveal themselves as Neptune passes through Sagittarius.

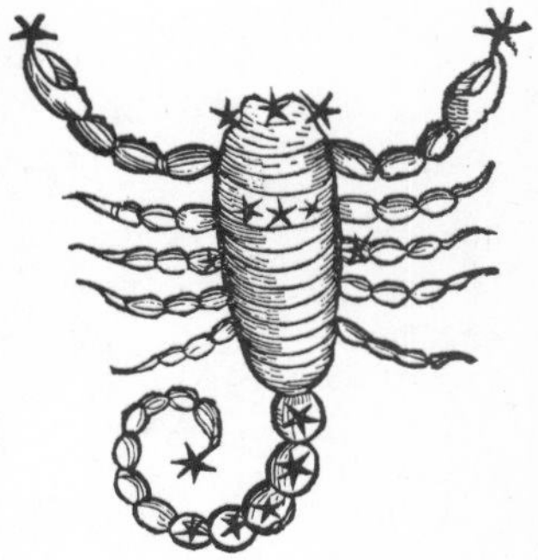

It is no coincidence that all three Scorpians portrayed on these two pages should be women. The Scorpian qualities of cautious determination and shrewd self-consciousness are outstandingly exemplified by the writer George Eliot (far left), the actress Katherine Hepburn (left) and the scientist Marie Curie (below)

Sagittarius

♐ SAGITTARIUS *day house of Jupiter*

Honesty and truth are of the greatest importance to Sagittarians: this is a Fire sign and, like Aries and Leo, it represents very positive and forward-moving qualities. Sagittarians are optimistic, trustworthy, enterprising, loyal yet independent, and very active. Yet, as A. E. Waite put it, 'It is by the Law that the Sagittarian comes into his heritage, and he has to learn through rebelliousness, diffusiveness, and other abuses of his higher nature'.

They are natural teachers and philosophers, and find their greatest pleasure in revealing to others the many laws by which the whole universe is governed; true revolutionaries are inevitably of this type, as their intention is always to replace unnatural laws by natural ones. But there is another side to the coin: Sagittarians may very easily become the worshippers of the law they preach, the slaves of ritual and convention. They may be rebels simply for the sake of rebellion; hypocrites in religious belief because the form of practise satisfies them; or even political turncoats where flattery and deceit may help to achieve ambition.

Yet Sagittarians seldom betray a personal trust, and remain good friends and companions, although their tendency to be straightforward and outspoken on any subject can cause a good deal of pain to those close to them.

They have strong will-power, and are excellent organisers, but they are nevertheless better suited to partnership or co-operation with others. Their outspokenness, and their somewhat impulsive anger, can cause difficulties in this connection; they understand very easily how to wound people at their weakest points. But give them a just cause to fight for, and they will doggedly defend it without fear for themselves. They can be generous, but are for ever on their guard, and may therefore seem mean.

Sun in Sagittarius fits the native for the higher professions, such as politics, teaching, the law or religion. There is, however, a tendency to be somewhat restless, and this may result in changes of career. Other careers indicated are the armed forces, advertising, horse-dealing, and bookmaking.
Ascendant in Sagittarius: Sagittarius suggests stature a little above average, with a wiry body; handsome appearance and dignified carriage; open and expressive eyes, oval face, somewhat bronzed, and a high forehead; an inclination to baldness; and somewhat large front teeth in a narrow jaw.

The constitution is sound, but Sagittarians are inclined to be highly-strung, and may suffer nervous breakdowns. Physically, the hips and thighs are susceptible to disease, such as sciatica and rheumatism.

☽ *Moon in Sagittarius:* In Sagittarius, the Moon symbolises a personality of a lofty and idealistic nature. There may be a dedication to conventional religious or philosophic tenets, perhaps derived from childhood education; with bad aspects, this can lead to narrow-minded bigotry and a self-centred, 'holier-than-thou', attitude.

Two very different, yet comparable, Sagittarians: Winston Churchill (left) and Maria Callas (below). Strong-willed and outspoken, to the point where their just anger can often give offence, Sagittarians will doggedly defend a cause without fear for themselves or for the injuries they may suffer as a result

☿ *Mercury in Sagittarius:* Mercury is in detriment in Sagittarius, and this indicates a tendency to be concerned with attitudes and opinions rather than with the facts behind them. This can give the native a deep insight into the way in which social trends are likely to move, and he may gain a reputation as a prophet; but he should never lose sight of the truth, and should always adhere to his belief in the freedom of speech.

♀ *Venus in Sagittarius:* Those with Venus in this sign are frank and unsecretive about their feelings, and so emotions such as jealousy are foreign to their nature. They tend to be somewhat conventional in their attitudes, and their emotional relationships will be affected by their beliefs: they are likely to marry within their own religious group, or will certainly try to persuade a loved one to accept their well thought out moral standards.

♂ *Mars in Sagittarius:* The crusader, the moral reformer, the missionary or – at a more humdrum level – the boy scout leader: these are the types represented by Mars in Sagittarius. They like outdoor sports, particularly hunting; travel; and military parades and tattoos. But their quest for adventure can lead them to ignore important matters that need their attention at home.

♃ *Jupiter in Sagittarius:* This is a good indication. Jupiter rules in Sagittarius, and the sense of law and fair play is very strong; deep consideration is given matters of philosophy and religion, and there is almost certainly bound to be a desire to convert others to the beliefs that have been adopted.

♄ *Saturn in Sagittarius:* The presence of Saturn lends Sagittarius a deep sense of serious purpose; people with the planet in this sign have strongly-held moral principles and will continue the search for truth throughout the major part of their lives. But at the same time they are likely to suffer from intellectual pride, being afraid of criticism.

♅ *Uranus in Sagittarius:* New concepts in religion and philosophy, particularly in matters concerning the occult, or a growing interest in the beliefs of foreign peoples – these are what may be expected of the presence of Uranus in Sagittarius.

♆ *Neptune in Sagittarius:* This represents the considered acceptance of mystical and occult subjects into the broad structure of conventional philosophy. There is also the danger of attraction to false prophets and valueless religious cults.

Capricorn

♑ CAPRICORN *day house of Saturn*
Ruled by Saturn and symbolised by the goat,
the type of person represented here is
usually described as 'economical, practical,
persevering, shrewd, diplomatic, reserved,
cautious . . . essentially a plodder'. But it is
not for nothing that the word 'capricious'
has become a part of everyday language, for
this essentially goat-like characteristic is
just as typical of the plodding Capricornian.
At the moment when he most needs to be
shrewd and cautious, he will be seized by the
urge to ruin everything with an outbreak of
irresponsible flippancy, and only the strongest self-control will prevent him from giving
way to temptation.

Average Capricornians are confident and
rather self-centred, strong-willed, suspicious
and capable of waiting a long time to secure
their goal. They tend to be very ambitious,
and frequently succeed in becoming wealthy;
but their lives are not altogether happy, and
they may attract a considerable amount of
enmity from people who do not understand
or trust them. When their ambitions remain
unfulfilled, they tend to become surly and

The martyrdom of Jeanne
d'Arc, born with Sun in
Capricorn. The
unpredictable character of
Capricorn showed itself at
numerous times in her
career, and most
dangerously at her trial,
where she could not
control the desire to bandy
arguments with her judges

melancholy, avaricious and complaining.

They are good managers, and are never happy until they are exercising authority; they ask their associates to perform exactly what they have undertaken, no more and no less, and they are strict but fair judges. They have a clever and subtle intellect, and delight in winning arguments; they make good friends within a relatively small circle, and bitter revengeful enemies.

A. E. Waite had something very perceptive to say: 'If all the world consisted of Capricornians it would be a hive of industry and order; but we should be offering up human sacrifices to wooden gods as of old and doing much as we did thousands of years ago; for Capricorn does not *create*, at most it improves, organises, and sacrifices'.

Capricornians make good financiers and speculators, particularly when the Moon is in Leo; politicians, when the Moon is in Sagittarius; or managers, estate agents and brokers, farmers or contractors.

Ascendant in Capricorn: Capricorn indicates a stature generally slightly below average, with a dry and rather bony body; a long and angular face, with thin neck, and sparse hair; narrow chest and possibly weak knees, resulting in a slightly odd carriage. Although the constitution is fairly strong, Capricornians frequently complain of ill-health and are subject to melancholia and depression. Physical troubles generally affect the legs, and skin disorders also occur.

☽ *Moon in Capricorn:* The Moon is in detriment in this sign, and signifies a cold and cautious disposition. There is ambition, but it is directed solely to material self-interest and a dedicated pursuit of status, without consideration of spiritual matters.

☿ *Mercury in Capricorn:* The serious side of Capricorn is lightened by the mercurial disposition, and the outcome is a shrewd mind capable of long concentration, and producing practical and well organised ideas. But when the light-footed satyr takes over, and begins his capers, the combination with Mercury can produce wild ideas and soaring, impractical schemes; it is just as well that this phase does not last for long. Those with Mercury in Capricorn make good mathematicians; if there are bad aspects, this ability may be put to the service of avarice.

♀ *Venus in Capricorn:* When those who have Venus in Capricorn marry young, they generally choose someone older than themselves, often someone relatively wealthy who can help them to improve their material status; if they marry later in life, they are more likely to choose a partner considerably younger, whom they hope to be able to develop to suit their demands. In the side of their nature that they expose to public view they are undemonstrative and dignified in behaviour; but they can be very sensual in private, and may indulge their wildness in all sorts of secret love affairs, even while professing (and, indeed, intending) loyalty to their partner. In music and in art their taste inclines to the classical and well-established.

♂ *Mars in Capricorn:* The energy of Mars is well employed in Capricorn in the attainment of everything necessary for material success and social standing. Those with this combination are proud at a job well and properly done, and respect others with the same ability. They are typical of the parents who struggle to do well for their children, and who are filled with contempt and despair when these children disdain 'the opportunities they have been given'.

♃ *Jupiter in Capricorn:* Maturity brings good sense to Capricorn, representing high integrity, good judgment and the ability to accept responsibility in important positions. There is not surprisingly a preference for conservative, traditional values and, as a result, a rather rigid and intolerant attitude to movements for social change. The native tends to be strict and unemotional with his family, and may be guilty of neglecting them.

♄ *Saturn in Capricorn:* The restrictive influence of Saturn is intensified in the house that he rules. Those with this combination

Capricornians like Sir Isaac Newton (below, left), Benjamin Franklin (below) and the film actor Humphrey Bogart (bottom), all showed themselves leaders in their chosen professions. They exemplified the Saturnine characteristic of driving inexorably for their goal; the delight in winning arguments, and the capacity to make bitter enemies

are pillars of the community, outstanding examples of moral rectitude, but cold and unapproachable. Disaster may strike if the capricious streak in their nature suddenly emerges; they may 'kick over the traces' and behave in a way that they will soon regret – but the rest of the world will be relieved.

♅ *Uranus in Capricorn:* In Capricorn, Uranus signifies a generation dedicated to sweeping changes in government and business structure. Yet at the same time, because of the conservative aspects of Capricorn, they are somewhat reluctant to give up everything that they have inherited from former organisations.

♆ *Neptune in Capricorn:* This is a combination of great uncertainty. The materialistic aspects of Capricorn do not mix well with the spiritual and indeed mystical qualities represented by Neptune, while the effects of a sudden outbreak of capriciousness must be completely unpredictable.

Aquarius

♒AQUARIUS *night house of Saturn*

Aquarians have much the same intensely magnetic characters as Scorpians, but the impression they make is very different: where Scorpio reveals the darkly shifting depths of water, Aquarius has the aetherial, electric, qualities of air. Aquarians have an open, forthcoming personality, quite unlike the secretive watchfulness of Scorpians.

Refinement and humanity are the leading characteristics of the Aquarian; quietness, independence and idealism tempered with practicality. But in a way appearances are deceptive; for they are also very strong and forceful people, although nervous and highly-strung. To complete the enigma, they may frequently conceal all these characteristics behind a facade of frivolity.

They are quick and active, and are capable of enormous temporary resistance to fatigue, although they may injure their health by devoting themselves totally to some demanding work. They are adamant that they must be left quite alone at times; that the help of others can only be tolerated when they are in command; and that they only can decide when the time is right to discuss any matter.

Sometimes Aquarians suffer outbreaks of unexpected temper, generally marked by a tense and threatening silence, with fits of eccentricity and simmering anger; at others, they appear to be 'the life and soul of the party', loving intellectual and artistic pleasures such as the theatre and other public entertainments. There is often a marked ability in impersonation; and, although

Aquarians may seem to ignore or condescend to others, they respect philanthropy.

They may suffer emotional disappointments, because they sometimes expect more of others than is reasonable, but at the same time they are tenacious and faithful friends and lovers, so long as they do not believe themselves to be deceived in anything. Their principal faults are a wayward egotism, a tendency to be very dogmatic in their opinions, and the ability to sustain dislike and hatred for those who deceive them.

Good careers for those with Sun in Aquarius include everything connected with the electrical and radio industries, as well as poets, astronomers and entertainers.

Ascendant in Aquarius: This signifies a stature tending to be slightly below average, thick-set or even plump; a good complexion, with flaxen or sandy hair in youth, darkening at a later age; a somewhat long face, but good looking, with hazel or blue eyes with a certain magnetic quality. The constitution is not over strong, and the legs and ankles are particularly susceptible to trouble.

☽ *Moon in Aquarius:* When the Moon is in Aquarius, it symbolises humanitarianism, but without much emotional involvement. There may well be some direct intuitive sympathy, but at the same time there is insistence upon individual freedom; where this takes place in a family relationship it can lead to some unusual, domestic situations. Moon in Aquarius also indicates some trouble with the eyes.

☿ *Mercury in Aquarius:* This planetary

position represents the ability to observe and record objectively and without prejudice; for those with this combination the truth comes above everything else, and they scorn tradition or convention wherever it conflicts with the truth as they know it. They are seldom if ever surprised by events, however bizarre, and they are capable of accepting equally all sorts of things that others might find disconcerting or incomprehensible. At its highest, this ability enables them to penetrate the physical facade of reality; they may well show clairvoyance or telepathy.

♀ *Venus in Aquarius:* Rather like those with Venus in Gemini, people with this planetary position want to be friends with everybody, but their relationships are likely to be cooler, more impersonal, although they are popular and well-liked generally. At the same time, the attitudes of these people toward conventional sexual morality are likely to be dismissive: they prefer to establish their own standards according to their own well-considered principles. Many partnerships are likely to be of a temporary nature, because those with Venus in Aquarius are attracted to intellectuals and eccentrics, and abhor possessiveness in the loved one.

♂ *Mars in Aquarius:* The energy of Mars is well-directed in Aquarius: independence of thought directed to practical ends, combined with high intelligence, can result in the development of new inventions, new ways of doing things, new ways of living. Unfortunately the native can become contemptuous of established authority, and throw out everything old before the new has become properly established.

♃ *Jupiter in Aquarius:* Those with Jupiter in Aquarius recognise no distinctions in class, race or creed. They are very tolerant, and appreciate that very many different kinds of people must each live their lives their own way, and that there is not one single set of moral and social standards. At the same time, in the pursuit of some universal yardstick that can be applied to everybody, they may involve themselves in all sorts of idealistic causes.

♄ *Saturn in Aquarius:* With good aspects, Saturn in Aquarius signifies an ambitious, well-organised, intellectual person, capable of concentration on a single project and evolving new concepts from it. People with this position do not shut themselves up in an ivory tower, however: they have a good sense of responsibility in human relationships, and make loyal friends and associates. When the aspects are bad, they tend to exhibit insensitivity and selfishness toward their friends.

♅ *Uranus in Aquarius:* Where Saturn in Aquarius indicates a mind capable of good scientific enquiry, Uranus indicates one capable of going further, and penetrating the frontier of the occult world. There is also

more than a trace of the idealistic revolutionary, dedicated to making a better world for his fellow men and women.

♆ *Neptune in Aquarius:* Uranus enters Aquarius in 1996 and Neptune in 1998; according to some astrologers, 'this will mark the beginning of a thousand years of peace, which was spoken of in the Book of Revelation'. Any attempt to link this with the 'Age of Aquarius' is, however, doomed to failure: if the spring equinox were recognised as entering Aquarius, then the part of the zodiac occupied by Uranus and Neptune would be, in fact, Sagittarius. It is only because we persist in calling the equinoctial point 0° Aries that these planets can be imagined as 'entering' Aquarius.

Aquarians make excellent research scientists, as exemplified here by Charles Darwin (far left), Galileo Galilei (left) and the inventor Thomas Edison (below). For those with Sun in Aquarius, good careers include astronomy and everything connected with the radio and electrical industries

Pisces

♓ PISCES *night house of Jupiter*

Subtlety, sympathy and tact characterise Pisces; the average Piscean has a ready understanding of the problems of others, a willingness to listen and learn, and a capacity for patience and persistence when dealing with all sorts and conditions of men. However, Pisceans can often be over-sensitive and emotional: fretting, peevish, lacking initiative, they may become deceitful, hypocritical, maybe alcoholics.

In general Pisceans are good-natured and friendly, kind and easy-going. Although ambitious, they lack concentration, and so seem to go forward from point to point without any overall plan to their careers. They generally do best in a subordinate position, because they know that if they were forced to work on their own initiative they would be tormented by worry and would almost certainly fail.

They show a quick understanding and a readiness to learn, and they have a vivid imagination and first-rate powers of expression. For this reason they frequently show marked literary powers, and they also have a great interest in music, art, archaeology and the occult. Such faults as they have are easily – too easily, in terms of the effect upon their character – forgiven; but they themselves are soon made despondent, and they tend to think of themselves as unappreciated, unencouraged, martyrs to others' caprices.

Charity or nursing seems to play an important part in the lives of those born with the Sun in this sign; as a career it is perhaps not the best choice. Other possible occupations are librarian, secretary, manager of a department, book-keeper, or caterer. Because of their lack of fixity of purpose, combined with their lively and ordered minds, Pisceans quite frequently follow two or more occupations at the same time.

Ascendant in Pisces: The Piscean physical type is of stature slightly below average, with a fleshy body and short thick limbs; the face is usually somewhat large, and the complexion pale, the hair light to dark brown and the eyes prominent and droopy, perhaps with inflammation of the lids; there is often some peculiarity in the feet. The constitution is seldom very strong, and boils, ulcers and other skin swellings occur with somewhat painful frequency.

☽ *Moon in Pisces:* The emotional nature of those born with the Moon in Pisces is well described by Frances Sakoian and Louis Acker as 'a psychic sponge, soaking up the thoughts and emotions of others'. The effect can be so strong that the native feels desperately vulnerable, and retreats to some hideout away from it all. Such people are very easily hurt, and may develop feelings of paranoia.

☿ *Mercury in Pisces:* As with the Moon, Mercury in Pisces signifies a mind absorbing influences from all directions; but the effect is upon the intellect rather than the personality. People with this combination have intensely imaginative minds, and photographic memories, and they seem to reach conclusions intuitively rather than by conscious logic. Many are telepathic.

♀ *Venus in Pisces:* Artistic inspiration results from a combination such as this: many great composers, poets and painters have been found to have Venus in Pisces. Such people have a marked understanding of the feelings of others. They marry for love and for no other reason, and they expect others to give them love and affection in return. Because of their sensitivity they may hide their feelings to avoid being hurt by a rebuff, and miss the romance of a lifetime.

♂ *Mars in Pisces:* Those with Mars in this sign find themselves easily hurt, and they react to injury with intense resentment. But, lacking self-confidence and decision, they are unlikely to express their feelings openly; they may sulk or take underhand action.

♃ *Jupiter in Pisces:* In Pisces, Jupiter represents emotional maturity and compassion. Those who have this combination are very active in supporting and helping those who are more unfortunate than themselves – sometimes with unhappy results, when they find that the others have taken advantage of them. There is a tendency toward involvement with religious movements which appear to offer emotional security or spiritual illumination.

♄ *Saturn in Pisces:* This is not a good indication, because those with this combination suffer from a tendency to live almost totally in the past, reliving experiences in their imagination and indulging in vain regrets for days that are gone. When aspects are good these people can show understanding and humility; but with bad aspects there is a marked tendency to persecution complex and other neuroses.

♅ *Uranus in Pisces:* Where so many Pisceans have a tendency to live in the past,

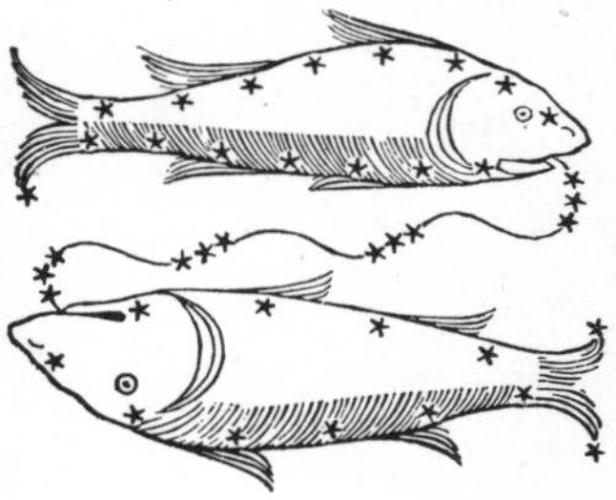

As many Virgoans show a marked peculiarity of nose structure, so Pisceans may be known for their large, rather hooded eyes. This characteristic is clearly visible in Elizabeth Barrett Browning (far left), George Washington (left), Georg Frederick Handel (below left) and Elizabeth Taylor (below right)

Uranus in this sign represents a positive effort to break with this influence. Since the past cannot be changed, and memory should certainly not be repressed, it becomes essential to draw on it for creative purposes, through dreams and subconscious thought.

♆ *Neptune in Pisces:* Neptune was just entering Pisces at the time of its discovery. In this sign it represents the most highly advanced occult powers, and a breakthrough in psychic communication.

·SOL·

Il sole ad honor luhomo et gloria spzona
Et vognj leggiadoza si dilecta
Si sapienza porta la cozona

3
WORKING OUT THE DETAILED HOROSCOPE

Now that we have looked at the basic scientific meaning of the horoscope as a map of the solar system at any given time, and considered the traditional significance attached to the positions of the different planets, it is time to describe in detail how the horoscope can be drawn.

It is possible, as I have already shown, to use a nautical almanac; but this does not provide us with the positions of the planets Mercury, Uranus, Neptune or Pluto. Also, it gives the planetary positions in terms of degrees along the celestial equator ('right ascension' or RA). Since the ecliptic is at an angle to the equator, a mathematical correction must be applied: at $0°\Upsilon$, $0°\varpi$, $0°\simeq$ and $0°\text{VS}$, degrees of the ecliptic will be the same as degrees of the equator, but at points in between it is necessary to correct for 'latitude'.* Astrologers have made all these corrections in the past, and incorporated them in a set of tables called an 'ephemeris'; it is really rather pointless to go through the process again, and so on pages 76–88 an abbreviated ephemeris for the years between 1880 and 1980 is provided. Working examples from this, you can learn how to use the much more detailed tables which can be bought in bookshops.

Sidereal Time

Because Earth does not take exactly 24 hours to revolve once on its axis – in fact it takes 23 hours 56 minutes 4.09 seconds – it has not quite completed its orbit round the sun in 365 days. This is why we have to add one day to the year every four years: each 'Leap Year' has 366 days. (Adding one whole day every four years is a little too much, which is why the first year of every century is not a Leap Year.) But for each revolution of Earth the celestial sphere appears to revolve once, and we are concerned, not with the position of the planets in relation to Earth, but with their apparent position against the background of the stars. So all the times in an ephemeris are given in star time or, to give it its astronomical name, Sidereal Time. Astronomers, who want to be able to point their telescopes at the right part of the sky to observe a particular star at a particular time, also use Sidereal Time, and it is measured, as usual, from 0° Aries.

Sidereal Time at midnight on the night of 31 December/1 January is given in the following table:

1880–1891:	Leap Year	06 40
	next year	06 43
	next year	06 42
	next year	06 41
1892–1899:	Leap Year	06 41
	next year	06 44
	next year	06 43
	next year	06 42
1900:		06 41
1901:		06 40
1902:		06 39
1903:		06 38
1904–1923:	Leap Year	06 37
	next year	06 40
	next year	06 39
	next year	06 38
1924–1955:	Leap Year	06 38
	next year	06 41
	next year	06 40
	next year	06 39
1956–	: Leap Year	06 39
	next year	06 42
	next year	06 41
	next year	06 40

To find the Sidereal Time at any time in the year, we use the next set of tables:

Addition for month

	FEB h m	MAR h m	APR h m	MAY h m	JUNE h m	JULY h m
Common year	2 2	3 52	5 55	7 53	9 55	11 54
Leap year	2 2	3 56	5 59	7 57	9 59	11 58

	AUG h m	SEPT h m	OCT h m	NOV h m	DEC h m
Common year	13 56	15 58	17 56	19 59	21 57
Leap year	14 0	16 2	18 0	20 2	22 1

Addition for day

2nd	4m	8th	28m	14th	51m	20th	1h 15m	26th	1h 39m
3rd	8m	9th	32m	15th	55m	21st	1h 19m	27th	1h 42m
4th	12m	10th	35m	16th	59m	22nd	1h 23m	28th	1h 46m
5th	16m	11th	39m	17th	1h 3m	23rd	1h 27m	29th	1h 50m
6th	20m	12th	43m	18th	1h 7m	24th	1h 31m	30th	1h 54m
7th	24m	13th	47m	19th	1h 11m	25th	1h 35m	31st	1h 58m

Addition for hours

1	2	3	4	5	6	7	8	9	10	11	12
0m	0m	1m	1m	1m	1m	1m	1m	1m	2m	2m	2m

Each planet 'rules' a house of the horoscope, as well as those aspects of human life to which it particularly applies. In this illumination from the fifteenth-century Italian manuscript *De Sphaera*, Sun rules only by day, and his house is Leo. The human occupations over which he exerts a particular influence are all concerned with power and the victory of domination over others

* For those of a mathematical turn of mind, the correction is very straightforward. It is given by the formula: log. cos 23° 27′ + log. cotangent RA from Υ or $\simeq$ = log. cotangent of angle from Υ or $\simeq$.

These tables apply for an astronomer at Greenwich: looking at his tables, he may calculate that a particular star will just come above the eastern horizon at, say, 22.50, but an astronomer further westward would not see the star until several minutes later, while an astronomer in the east will have seen the star earlier. So we have to make a final correction for longitude:

For each degree longitude W, subtract 4m
For each degree longitude E, add 4m

These are the corrections to change Greenwich Mean Time (GMT) into Sidereal Time (ST). But, of course, only people living in Britain and parts of West Africa have their clocks set to GMT – and in Britain, and many other countries, there is Summer Time (and, during the 1939–45 war, even Double Summer Time). So first of all, before calculating the ST, it is essential to convert local time (LT) to GMT.

Let us take a specific example and work it out; when we have the ST we can turn to the ephemeris and draw the horoscope.

Converting LT to ST

Our example is a woman born at 09.09 local time in Los Angeles on 1 June 1926. Long. 118°W.

There was no Summer Time (Daylight Saving Time) in Los Angeles in 1926, so the GMT is 09 09 + 08 00 hours = 17 09 GMT. Sidereal time for 1 Jan 1926 (that is, two years after Leap Year 1924):

Sidereal time for 1 Jan 1926:	06 40
Addition for month:	09 55
Addition for day:	none
Addition for 17 hours:	00 03
Add GMT	17 09
	33 47
Subtraction for longitude	− 07 52
	25 55

As we are concerned only with the time, and not with the day, we can subtract 24 hours, to give ST = 01 55.

This may seem complicated and cumbersome, but working out two or three more examples will make the operation quite a simple one – and it is, after all, essential!

Drawing the horoscope

What follows is a simplified scheme, and one that many astrologers would dismiss because it does not conform to their very complicated theories. There are almost as many theories as there are astrologers, and the arguments between them are concerned with how we can divide the heavens into twelve 'houses', and what is the precise meaning of the 'ascendant'.

Astrology developed in countries that were not very far from the tropics, and it was easy to see that the sun always rose approximately in the east, spent approximately twelve hours in the heavens, and set

approximately in the west. It was only when astrology was brought into northern Europe – and when renaissance mathematicians began to study the science of navigation – that difficulties emerged. People living north of the Arctic Circle do not see the sun at all during the winter, and all 24 hours of the day at midsummer: what does the ascendant mean to them? When the mathematics of spherical trigonometry had been worked out, astrologers spent years in complicated calculations. They computed the degree of the zodiac that would be rising over the horizon for every few minutes of the day, but they marked this on their charts as if it were always due east. We shall follow the system used in chapter 1, and draw the horoscope as a circular map showing the positions of the planets within the circle of the zodiac, and leave the matter of the ascendant and the houses until later.

What we need to know is the degree of the zodiac which lies on the meridian: that is, due south; astrologers call this the *medium coeli* (MC), which means 'midheaven'. The following table gives the MC for each 12 minutes of the sidereal 'day', and for times in between it is quite easy to calculate the difference.

ST	MC	ST	MC	ST	MC	ST	MC
00·00	0 ♈	06·00	0 ♋	12·00	0 ♎	18·00	0 ♑
00·12	3 ♈	06·12	3 ♋	12·12	3 ♎	18·12	3 ♑
00·24	7 ♈	06·24	6 ♋	12·24	7 ♎	18·24	6 ♑
00·36	10 ♈	06·36	8 ♋	12·36	10 ♎	18·36	8 ♑
00·48	13 ♈	06·48	11 ♋	12·48	13 ♎	18·48	11 ♑
01·00	16 ♈	07·00	14 ♋	13·00	16 ♎	19·00	14 ♑
01·12	20 ♈	07·12	17 ♋	13·12	20 ♎	19·12	17 ♑
01·24	23 ♈	07·24	19 ♋	13·24	23 ♎	19·24	19 ♑
01·36	26 ♈	07·36	22 ♋	13·36	26 ♎	19·36	22 ♑
01·48	29 ♈	07·48	25 ♋	13·48	29 ♎	19·48	25 ♑
02·00	2 ♉	08·00	28 ♋	14·00	2 ♏	20·00	28 ♑
02·12	5 ♉	08·12	1 ♌	14·12	5 ♏	20·12	1 ♒
02·24	8 ♉	08·24	4 ♌	14·24	8 ♏	20·24	4 ♒
02·36	11 ♉	08·36	7 ♌	14·36	11 ♏	20·36	7 ♒
02·48	14 ♉	08·48	10 ♌	14·48	14 ♏	20·48	10 ♒
03·00	17 ♉	09·00	13 ♌	15·00	17 ♏	21·00	13 ♒
03·12	20 ♉	09·12	16 ♌	15·12	20 ♏	21·12	16 ♒
03·24	23 ♉	09·24	19 ♌	15·24	23 ♏	21·24	19 ♒
03·36	26 ♉	09·36	22 ♌	15·36	26 ♏	21·36	22 ♒
03·48	29 ♉	09·48	25 ♌	15·48	29 ♏	21·48	25 ♒
04·00	2 ♊	10·00	28 ♌	16·00	2 ♐	22·00	28 ♒
04·12	5 ♊	10·12	1 ♍	16·12	5 ♐	22·12	1 ♓
04·24	8 ♊	10·24	4 ♍	16·24	8 ♐	22·24	4 ♓
04·36	11 ♊	10·36	7 ♍	16·36	11 ♐	22·36	7 ♓
04·48	13 ♊	10·48	11 ♍	16·48	13 ♐	22·48	11 ♓
05·00	16 ♊	11·00	14 ♍	17·00	16 ♐	23·00	14 ♓
05·12	19 ♊	11·12	17 ♍	17·12	19 ♐	23·12	17 ♓
05·24	22 ♊	11·24	20 ♍	17·24	22 ♐	23·24	20 ♓
05·36	25 ♊	11·36	23 ♍	17·36	25 ♐	23·36	23 ♓
05·48	27 ♊	11·48	27 ♍	17·48	27 ♐	23·48	27 ♓
06·00	0 ♋	12·00	0 ♎	18·00	0 ♑	24·00	0 ♈

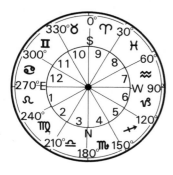

(Above) Drawing up the horoscope circle for sidereal time 01.55

(Right) Another view of the rulership of Sun, from a sixteenth-century series of woodcuts by Hans Sebald Beham. Sun's chariot is drawn across the sky by horses, while in the palace below men engage in aristocratic sports such as fencing and wrestling

To return to our example, therefore, we need to find the MC for a Sidereal Time of 01 55. The table gives us:

01 48 : MC = 29 ♈
02 00 : MC = 2 ♉

01 55 is 7 minutes after 01 48, and the difference for 12 minutes is 3° (remember there are 30° in each sign, so Aries changes to Taurus after 1 degree). The difference for 7 minutes is therefore approximately 2°:

01 55 : MC = 1 ♉

We can therefore draw up our horoscope circle as we did in chapter 1 (see left).

Now we can look up the planetary positions in the ephemeris.

The abbreviated ephemeris to be found on pages 76–88 gives the position of each planet at noon GMT on the first day of the month. Our example is for 1 June 1926, so we can make the calculations easily; later other examples will show how to calculate planetary positions for any time in the month.

Looking therefore at the appropriate table in the ephemeric we get the noon positions for the ten planets in terms of the number of degrees by which they have

Sonn.

49

entered each sign. We can write these down as follows:

Sun: 10 ♊   Moon: 16 ♒
Mercury: 6 ♊   Venus: 29 ♈
Mars: 21 ♓   Jupiter: 27 ♒
Saturn: 21 ♏   Uranus: 29 ♓
Neptune: 22 ♌   Pluto: 13 ♋

We have to make some corrections to these figures, because GMT is some 5 hours after noon, and several of the planets move quite quickly through the zodiac.

The Sun moves 1° per day, and so its position does not have to be corrected.

The Moon moves about 13° per day, and so should be corrected by $5/24 \times 13° = 3°$ approx. Its position will therefore by 19 ♒

During the previous month, Mercury has moved through 52°, which is a rate of more than 1·5° per day, and so 5 hours represents nearly 0·5°, and we should correct its position to 7♊. Venus is moving only at about 1° per day, and so we do not make a correction, nor for any of the slower planets.

Inspection of the position of Saturn at other times of the year shows that it is 'retrograde' between March and August – that is, it appears to be going backward along its track through the zodiac. This apparent motion, which is also shown by other planets at various times during the year, and is responsible for the noticeable changes in speed of Mercury and Venus, will be considered later in detail.

We can now insert all these planetary positions into our circular horoscope. There are one or two points that will give you a quick check on the accuracy of your plotting. First of all, since you know the local time, you know the position of the sun in the sky; here it is just about halfway between the horizon and the zenith, as you would expect it to be at 9 in the morning. Secondly, Mercury is *never* more than 28°, and Venus 48°, away from the Sun.

Another example
As a further exercise in calculating sidereal time, let us draw up one other horoscope, before subjecting both to analysis. This time we choose a man born at 06 22 pm on 20 April 1889, in Braunau-am-Inn, on the Austro-German border, longitude 13°E. Although standard time was not adopted in Austria and Germany for another two years, it is fairly certain that the local time was equivalent to 17 22 GMT.

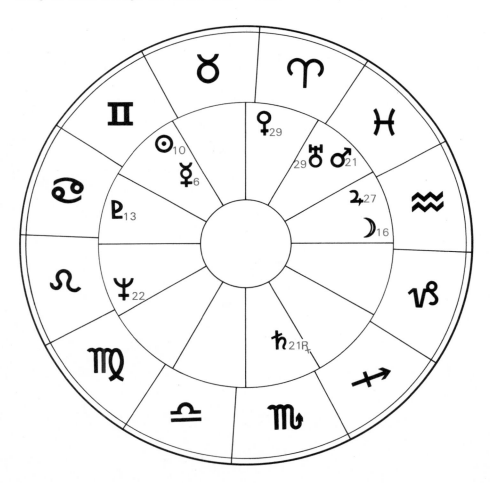

(Right) The completed horoscope for a woman born at 09 09 local time in Los Angeles on 1 June 1926

ST at midnight on 1 January 1889 was:

	06 43
Addition for month	05 55
Addition for day	01 15
Addition for 17 hours	00 03
Add GMT	17 22
	31 18
Addition for longitude	+00 52
	32 10
Subtract 24 hrs	08 10

From the midheaven table, we get:

08 00: MC = 28° ♋
08 12: MC = 1° ♌

At 08·10, therefore, the MC will be so close to 1 ♌ that we can approximate to this value.

When we look at the abbreviated ephemeris for 1889, we find that we have to make an extra calculation, because these tables only give planetary positions for the first day of each month. However, it is not too difficult to work out positions for intervening dates. For instance:

1 April 1889: Sun 12 ♈
1 May 1889: Sun 11 ♉

In thirty days, therefore, the sun moves 29°; in nineteen days it will move nearly 19°, and be in ♉ on 20 April. And because we are considering some 6 hours after noon, no further correction need be made.

It is a little more difficult to be quite sure about the position of the moon. We start from its positions at the beginning of each month:

1 April 1889: Moon 24 ♈
1 May 1889: Moon 27 ♉

In the course of these thirty days the Moon has made more than one complete circle of the zodiac, at the rate of about 13° per day. Calculating forward from 1 April, we would expect 19 days to advance the moon by 19 × 13° = 247°, to 1♑. Calculating backward from 1 May, we would expect 11 days to retard the moon by 11 × 13° = 143°, to 4♑. On 20 April, therefore, we would expect the moon to be 2–3° into Capricorn at midday, and a good 3♑ by 17 00 GMT.

Calculating the position of Mercury is fairly simple. On 1 March, Mercury is in 18♒, on 1 April 21♓, and on 1 May 19♉. That is, in 61 days it has passed through 91° of the zodiac. On 1–2 April, therefore, it will be moving at about 1½° per day, and at

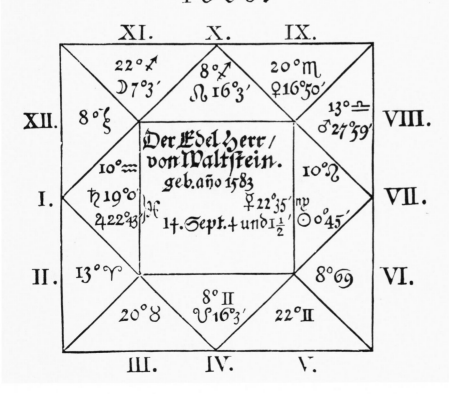

(Left) a typically sixteenth-century way of drawing up a horoscope, as a square rather than a circle. The horoscope is divided into twelve 'houses' which are exactly the same in scope and significance as in a circular horoscope, but it is rather more difficult to perceive the 'aspects' of the various planets. This horoscope is a particularly famous one drawn by the astronomer Johannes Kepler for count Waldstein (later to become Duke Albrecht von Wallenstein) in 1608. The horoscope has been drawn for a sidereal time of approximately 16 26 at 52°N latitude. The ascendant is 10 ♒ and the MC is 8 ♐. The system of house-division (see chapter 5) is that of Regiomontanus. From his interpretation of this chart, Kepler predicted the count's future military successes and the year of his murder

over 2° per day by the end of the month. Calculate 19 days at 1·75° per day: that is a total of 33·25°, so at midday on 20 April Mercury will be at 24·25♈. By 1700 GMT we can place Mercury at 25♈ with confidence.

The calculation for Venus is complicated by the fact that this planet, as we can see from the data below the table, is retrograde from 10 April, and does not return to forward ('direct') motion until 22 May. This would in any case be apparent from the monthly positions: 18♉ on 1 April, 11♉ on 1 May, and 5♉ on 1 June.

On 10 April, therefore, Venus appears to be stationary at 19♉, before beginning to move backward for six weeks to 3♉. At the beginning and end of this period the planet will be moving quite slowly, and over the first ten days it is unlikely to regress by more than 2°. So we write the position of Venus as 17♉R. (The astronomical explanation of why planets appear to move backward through the zodiac will be fully explained at the end of this chapter.)

By exactly analogous processes, we obtain the positions of the remaining planets:

Mars 16	Jupiter 8♑
Saturn 14♌	Uranus 19♎R
Neptune 1♊	Pluto 4♊

Planetary aspects

When we submit a horoscope to analysis, we do not consider only the significance of the positions of the planets in the zodiac, we also consider the possible effects of two or more planets in combination. Much as spring tides are produced by the Sun and Moon, either in conjunction or in opposition, while neap tides are attributable to the gravitational pulls of the two bodies being at right angles to one another, the other planets can be envisaged as exerting some kind of gravitational force which can be enhanced or diminished according to their positions in relation to one another.

Conjunction and opposition

Two or more planets can be in conjunction – that is, in the same part of the heavens together – or in opposition, on opposite sides of Earth; and their influence will be correspondingly enhanced.

Planets in conjunction will obviously combine their influences, and the effect will be strongly felt; but whether the effect is good or bad will depend upon the significance of the individual planets. So, a combination of the Sun's gravitational pull with that from Venus or Jupiter is generally considered to be good; but the conflict between

(Left) Completed horoscope for a man born at 06 22 pm on 20 April 1889 in Braunau-am-Inn. (Right) Another illumination from *De Sphaera*. Moon rules by night in Cancer, and extends her influence over the tides and all watery things

· LVNA ·

La luna al nauigar molto conforta
Et in peschare et ucellare et caccia
A tutti i suoi figliuoli apre la porta
Et anche al solazzare che ad altri piaccia

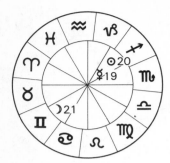

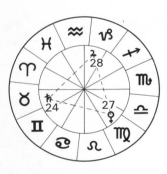

the force of the Sun and that of Mars or Saturn can only result in a reduction of the good effects of the Sun.

Opposition between planets can be interpreted in much the same way, but since the pulls are inevitably in opposite directions the effect must be discordant.

Square
Two planets 'in square' – like Sun and Moon at neap tide – result in a diminishment of each other's effects, but when there is a third planet at another corner of the square, so that two are in opposition, the effect is strongly disruptive.

Trine
Two planets 120° apart, that is at two points of a triangle, similarly reduce each other's influence, but when the triangle is completed by a third planet the pulls are balanced, and the result is great stability. These planets are said to be 'in trine'.

These are the most important 'aspects' of the planets. Some astrologers insist that the 'sextile' aspect – when planets are 60° apart – is also strongly effective for good, but this is only so when there are altogether four planets involved, two 60° apart being each in opposition to a similar pair.

Other aspects, such as the 'semi-sextile' (30° apart), the 'semi-square' (45° apart), the 'sesqui square' (135° apart) and the 'inconjunct' (150° apart) are all uniformly weak in their effects.

Obviously, the combined influences of two planets in conjunction are only really strong when the planets are very close together, and the effect reduces rapidly as they separate. The same is true of any other aspect, and the question arises – how many

degrees may separate the positions of planets in assessing their aspects? This margin of difference is called the 'orb' of the aspect, and in general it should not exceed 3° – so two planets may be 6° apart and still within each other's orb.

We are now in a position to begin interpreting the two horoscopes.

A note on retrograde motion
The accompanying diagram shows very clearly how and why retrograde motion of the planets appears to take place. The orbit of Earth lies within the orbit of Mars, and the sight-lines of five successive observations of Mars are drawn from Earth toward the background of the zodiac. It is obvious how Mars appears to move backward between observations 2 and 4. The same phenomenon occurs, less frequently but for a longer period of time, with every one of the outer planets. The retrograde motion of the inner planets, Venus and Mercury, is produced in a similar way: but in this case they are the faster planets, and are observed from Earth as their orbits round the Sun appear to make them wander from side to side.

Finally, here is a useful checklist of the typical retrograde motion for each planet:

	occurrence	length of retrogression
Mercury	every 3½ months	20–24 days
Venus	about every 19 months	5–7 weeks
Mars	about every 26 months	10–12 weeks
Jupiter	irregular	4 months
Saturn	once a year	4–8 months
Uranus	once a year	5–7 months
Neptune	once a year	about 5 months
Pluto	once a year	5–8 months

(Above) Examples of conjunction and opposition, square, and trine aspects. (Near right) How and why retrograde motion appears to take place. It is obvious how Mars appears to move backward between observations 2 and 4. (Far right) Moon, her chariot drawn by maidens, exerts her influence over wells, streams and the sea, fishing and boating of all kinds, and – remarkably – over the activities of the travelling mountebank who is performing the cup-and-balls trick on the table in the distance

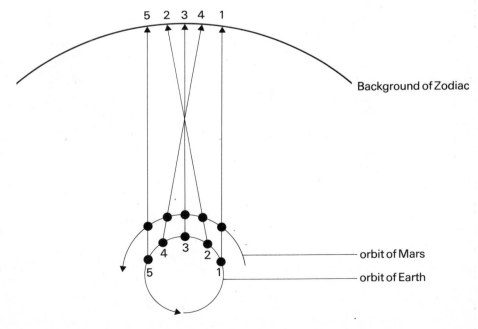

Luna.

Lewis 16th King of France
Born 23 Augt 3 H 30 Mt
P.M.
1754.

Marie Antoinette Queen of France
Born 2 Novr 7 H 23 Mt
P.M.
1755.

Crown'd
11 June
1775.

Lewis Capet Executed 21 Jan
10 H 20 Mt in the Morning
1793.

Marie Antoinette of Lorrain & Austria
Widow of Lewis Capet
Executed 16 Octr 11 H
30 Mt in the Morning
1793.

4 INTERPRETING THE HOROSCOPE

(Above) The first horoscope example, ready for interpretation. (Left) Another historically-famous horoscope – or, rather, set of horoscopes – cast by the English astrologer Ebenezer Sibley for the birth, coronation and death of Louis XVI of France and his queen Marie-Antoinette. The system of house division is by Placidus (see chapter 5)

There are certain difficulties in demonstrating the interpretation of a horoscope. As was explained in chapter 1, one is faced, in making a detailed interpretation, with a wide range of possibilities from which one makes a deliberate choice. What determines this choice is an instinctive *feel* about the character and potentialities of the person whose horoscope is being inspected. Obviously, this aspect of horoscope interpretation cannot be communicated in print, and therefore the examples to be given will only take into consideration the most obvious indications. With this reservation in mind, let us look first of all at the horoscope of the woman born on 1 June 1926, and analyse it 'by the book'.

What sort of a person is she? The Sun, the ascendant and the Moon may tell us something about her physical appearance and her personality.

The ascendant sign is Leo – that is, the sign rising above the eastern horizon. This would lead us to expect a woman slightly taller than the average for her sex, with a well-built body, fairly lean in her youth but inclining to plumpness as she grows older; a woman with an upright, almost stately carriage, blonde hair, a big round head and blue or grey eyes – eyes which might give trouble later in life.

Sun in Gemini suggests an elusive, contradictory nature: happy and pessimistic, charming and sullen, intellectual and stolid. This woman is easily adaptable, inherently versatile: she will find it very difficult to remain devoted for long to anyone, and in her career she will constantly seek change. Gemini is an Air sign, and so too is Aquarius, where the Moon is to be found: as air moves more freely near fire, so the personality of this woman, with the ascendant in the Fire sign of Leo, will develop its qualities of reason, humanity and refinement.

At the same time, Moon in Aquarius suggests that this is a person who tends to avoid too much emotional involvement and who, although she can be full of sympathy, will always insist on her personal freedom of action. There is also a reinforcement of the suggestion that there may be trouble with the eyes.

Sun and Mercury are always very close to one another, but in this horoscope they are well within each other's orb, and therefore we should pay close attention to the significance of Mercury in Gemini. The analytical intelligence represented by Mercury exerts a restraining influence on the mutability of Gemini, resulting in an original and inventive person, an excellent speaker with the ability to see both sides of the argument; but the versatility that Gemini represents will be an over-riding influence. Gemini is the night house of Mercury, and there is no planet in his day house, Virgo; and since Mercury is the symbol of communication, of writing and the performing arts, we may assume that our subject is more likely to be involved in the theatre than in literature – a night-time rather than a daytime activity. Combined with the strong indications of almost unmanageable versatility, this will suggest that the horoscope is that of an actress.

Venus high in the midheaven indicates a very womanly woman, sensual and generous. The planet lies on the dividing line (the 'cusp') between Aries and Taurus, and we would therefore expect the subject to show the bad, rather than the good, qualities of both: she will be passionately romantic and fond of luxury, her possessiveness warring with her generosity.

Mars in Pisces, on the other hand, indicates a sensitive nature easily hurt, with a certain lack of self-confident openness.

Jupiter in Aquarius is a good indication for a socially tolerant person, who recognises no distinctions of class, race or creed, and who feels that people should live their lives according to their own code. This may, of course, lead them to involve themselves in some sort of idealistic cause.

However, the position of Saturn in Scorpio should fill us with foreboding. People who have Saturn in this position are likely to take on too much responsibility, involving themselves with great seriousness and emotional dedication, but discovering eventually that they demand more of themselves than they are able to give. After trying to drive themselves to near-impossible perfection, they may end by reproaching themselves bitterly, and may even attempt self-destruction. The retrograde motion of Saturn, taking this planet back into the sign from which it had nearly escaped, may be

· MERCVRIVS ·

Mercurio di ragion lucida stella
Produce deloquenza gran fontana
Subtili ingiegni et ciaschunarte bella
Et e inimico dogni cosa uana :·

read as a reinforcement of all the bad indications of this position.

As for Uranus in Pisces, we can read this as a sign suggesting the effort to break with the past, perhaps by exploiting it for creative purposes; and Neptune in Leo may be interpreted as indicating a positive ability in the arts.

The question of 'houses' is still to be put off to a later chapter, but the influence of Pluto can only be considered in terms of the house that he occupies. The ascendant is always taken to mark the first house and therefore, in this horoscope, Pluto is in the twelfth house. This is, as it were, the 'dark cupboard' of the subject's life, full of hidden things, and here Pluto sits, balefully projecting his sense of uncertainty and the fickleness of fate.

So much for the positions of the planets; now we must consider their aspects to one another.

The aspect that dominates this horoscope is the square composed of Neptune in Leo, Saturn R in Scorpio, and Jupiter in Aquarius. Saturn is at the dominant apex of this grouping, drawing the other planets' influences toward himself, and distorting

(Left and right) Mercury rules in Virgo and in Gemini; his chariot is drawn by two cockerels, and in his left hand he holds the caduceus. Among the activities upon which he exerts his influence are those which require a quick intelligence and an adept hand, such as wood-carving, cooking, painting, the performance of music, and astrology

Vaughan sculp:

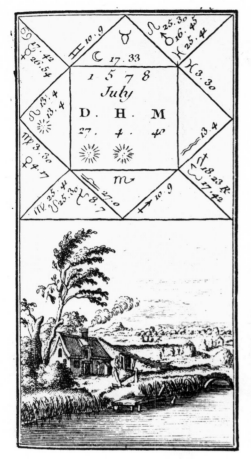

Ancient astrologers associated each of the seven planets with one of the seven metals: Saturn with lead, Jupiter with tin, Mars with iron, Venus with copper, Mercury with mercury, Moon with silver, and Sun with gold. To the alchemists, therefore, who strove to transmute metals step by step into pure gold, it was clear that each step should be under the influence of the appropriate planet. (Left) A page from the *Ordinall* of the fifteenth century alchemist Thomas Norton, copied for the 1652 edition of Elias Ashmole's *Theatrum Chemicum Britannicum*. Astrology could also be used to determine the right time at which to search for the different metals. The two pages (above) are from *La Physique Occulte, ou Traité de la Baguette Divinatoire*, of 1762, and are supposed to be astrological schemes for discovering gold, diamonds and sapphires under the influence of the Sun (left), and silver and crystal under the influence of the Moon (right). All house divisions in the horoscopes on these pages are by the Regiomontanus system (see chapter 5)

them: the toleration, and the happy and contented middle-life, represented by Jupiter, and the artistic creativity of Neptune, are warped and nullified by this dark planet in the sign of self-destruction.

The malefic influence of this square is at least partially redeemed by three planets which lie nearly in trine: Mars in Pisces, Saturn in Scorpio, and Pluto in Cancer. Here the great energy represented by Mars can be envisaged as drawing out the best of Saturn, his patience and sense of justice, and neutralising the uncertainty of Pluto. This concentration of power toward Pisces suggests a quick understanding and a willingness to learn, a good imagination and excellent powers of expression.

Mars is definitely the dominant planet of this trine, and his effect is strengthened by the closeness of Uranus; but Uranus is the symbol of disruption, and the near conjunction of these two planets in the mid-afternoon sky is traditionally interpreted as indicating a sudden unexpected end to life.

Jupiter and the Moon, close together on the western horizon, and in opposition to Neptune in the first house, suggest many uncertainties in married life; and the fact that the two strongly male planets, Sun and Mars, are both in dual signs indicates that there are likely to be several attempts at marriage.

Venus in Aries and Neptune in Leo form two points of a trine. Some astrologers treat this aspect as if there were an invisible planet at the third point of the triangle, in Sagittarius. This planet would be in opposition to the Sun in Pisces; the 'gravitational' effect of Venus and Neptune is to reduce the influence of the Sun and its conjunction with Mercury, and so this trine must be interpreted as having an adverse effect.

What, then, do we make of this horoscope? It would appear to be of a handsome blonde actress, well-built and a little above average in height. Her childhood is not the happiest, but she will manage to break away from the past and establish herself with considerable success in her profession. However, there may be several unsuccessful marriages; in spite of her innate intelligence she finds it difficult to fulfil her intellectual ambitions, and may drive herself too hard; in a frenzy of despair, she may well commit suicide.

The horoscope is that of Marilyn Monroe.

* * * *

Now for the horoscope of the man born on 20 April 1889.

The ascendant sign is Scorpio – only just, but it is Scorpio rising, and this indicates the physical type we should expect: a strong and sturdy body of average height, inclined to be hairy; a rather bullet-shaped head

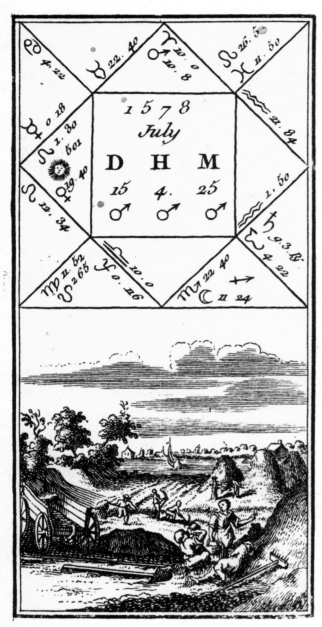

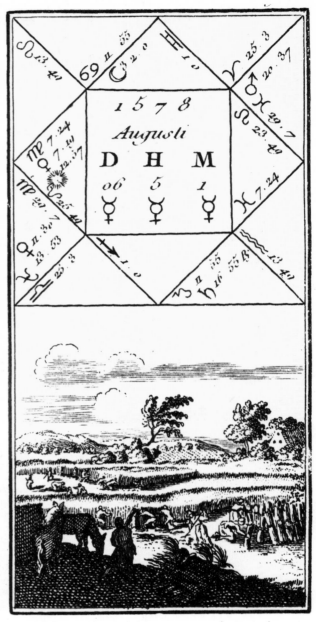

Astrological schemes for discovering (left to right, respectively) iron and emerald under the influence of Mars, quicksilver under the influence of Mercury, tin and cornelian under the influence of Jupiter, and copper and amethyst under the influence of Venus. The times given (in hours and minutes) are in some cases taken from midday, and in other cases from midnight, which accounts for some apparent inconsistencies

covered with thick coarse hair; a rather square face but with a sharp nose. This man will show considerable resistance to disease, but may suffer from ailments of the bladder and genitals.

The Sun is down on the western horizon, and on the cusp between Aries and Taurus. The subject is likely to be full of ambition and impossible to divert from his purpose; opposition to his plans will bring about a fit of uncontrollable rage, and he may well harbour resentment for a long time until he can find an opportunity for revenge. Those with the Sun on a cusp are likely always to show the bad aspects of both signs: the most pleasant characteristics of this subject would be the enthusiasm with

which he can enter into new projects, and the way in which he can communicate this enthusiasm to others. He is probably very persuasive in his talk, although given to unforgiveable exaggeration.

Moon in Capricorn is 'in detriment', signifying a cold and emotionally-cautious disposition. The ambition denoted by the Sun's position is reinforced, but there are strong indications that it is entirely selfish and materialistic.

Mercury in Aries represents a combination of two streams of energy, generally resulting in a person who is quick-thinking and fond of constructive argument. However, he is likely to be carried away by the plausibility of his own proposals, to the

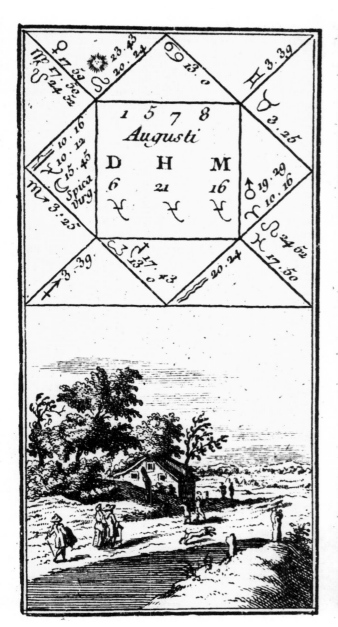

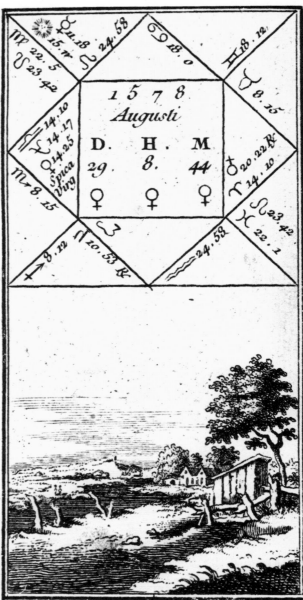

extent that he cannot endure opposition or delay and will drive ahead with his own ideas, without proper consideration of their ultimate effect.

Venus and Mars are in conjunction in Taurus, and Venus is retrograde. This part of the sky, just on the western horizon, is traditionally associated with marriage, and the conjunction of these two planets, representing the male and female principles, may be read as indicating a sexual relationship in which the male is the dominant partner, possibly given to displays of violence in his lovemaking, and excessively jealous. Mars is in detriment in Taurus, and the male is likely to prove an unsuccessful lover, either physically (and the ascendant in Scorpio must be remembered here), or emotionally.

Traditionalism, the opposition toward any movements for social change, is the indication of Jupiter in Capricorn; the subject is likely to be relatively strict and unemotional with his family, and may neglect them.

Saturn is in detriment in Leo, and represents the worst part of all that Leo stands for. So we may expect a lust for power, bigotry, egotism and a taste for strictness and discipline. In combination with the indications of Jupiter in Capricorn, and of Uranus retrograde in Libra, this leads us to expect someone of strongly conservative tastes and beliefs, who is determined to impose them

(Below) The second horoscope for interpretation

(Below and opposite)
Venus rules in Libra and in Taurus. Her car is drawn by doves, and she is the patroness of all pleasurable activities

on others, irrespective of whether they are willing, or not.

Neptune is on the cusp of Taurus and Gemini; his influence in this horoscope, representing the more spiritual aspects, is negligible. But the position of Pluto, darkly foreboding in that part of the western sky associated with death, suggests that the subject of this horoscope, also, could meet an unexpected end.

The dominant aspect in this horoscope is the square made up of Saturn in Leo, and Venus conjunct with Mars in Taurus. Like Sun and Moon at the time of neap tide, these planets will tend to cancel out each other's effects: we may expect the violence and jealousy of the subject's sex-life on the one hand, and his lust for power on the other, to conflict with one another.

Apart from the conjunction of Mars and Venus, which has already been dealt with, there is also a conjunction between Moon and Jupiter in Capricorn. We would expect this to result in an augmentation of the emotional coldness already indicated for this subject. The opposition between Mercury and Uranus may be read as indicating the kind of brusque intolerance that results when a good intelligence is frustrated by his inability to balance his desire for change against his desire to keep everything the same.

The only good aspect in the whole horoscope is the near-trine between Mercury in Aries and Saturn in Leo: here Saturn imposes his better influence on the restless intellectual energy of Mercury, making for seriousness of thought and intention.

Our second horoscope, therefore, indicates a man of average height, with a sturdy body, and a bullet-shaped head covered with thick hair. He is filled with ambition, entirely dedicated to self-interest, and obstinately sticks to his plans against all opposition. If countered, he is likely to fly into an uncontrollable rage.

He will be a persuasive speaker, and will readily communicate his enthusiasm for his proposals to others; but these proposals are likely to be of a strongly traditionalist and conservative nature, suggesting a return to a more disciplined society in which the subject is to play a dominant part.

Emotionally, the subject will be undemonstrative; he is likely to prove a poor lover, and this may be partly attributable to some disease of the genitals. And there is a strong possibility that his death may be violent and unexpected.

The reader, no doubt, has by now identified the subject of this horoscope: it is, of course, Adolf Hitler.

Rectification

Hitler's horoscope has been drawn and interpreted here on the basis of a birth time of 06.22 pm. In fact, his time of birth is not recorded, and this time was calculated by the German astrologer Elsbeth Ebertin by the technique known as 'rectification'.

This consists in assigning an approximate birth time, drawing up the horoscope for this time, and then comparing it with the horoscopes for known significant events in the subject's later life. By gradually approximating one to the other (generally by the process of 'progression' described in chapter 5) it is possible to reach a point at which the prognostications of the birth horoscope agree with the times at which the subsequent events took place. The time of this horoscope is then taken as the birth time.

Elsbeth Ebertin attracted the attention of Hitler by her forecasting his involvement in the Munich *putsch* of 1923, which she published in *A Glimpse of the Future* in the summer before.

Venus.

· VENVS ·

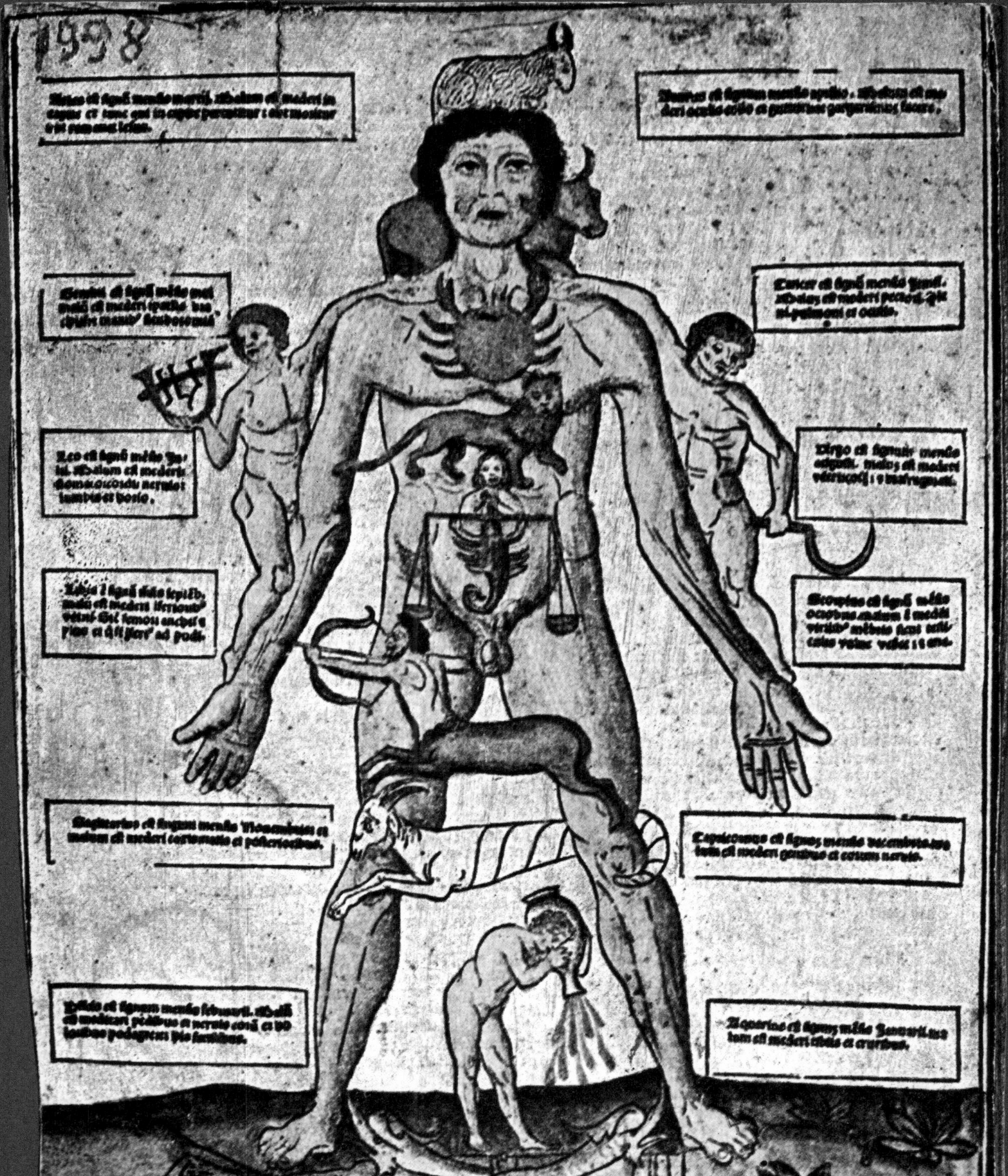
1998

5 THE VEXED QUESTION OF HOUSES

A fifteenth-century chart indicates the relationship of each sign of the zodiac to an appropriate part of the body. Medieval physicians believed that the parts of the body were affected by the planets present in the relevant sign, both at birth and throughout the life of the native. By analogy, certain times of the year were particularly good for treatment of diseases: Venus well-aspected in Scorpio, for example, augured well for the treatment of venereal disease

Reference has already been made in previous chapters to the way in which the zodiac can be divided into houses; and the rather evasive quality of this reference should have prepared the reader for the news that this is perhaps the hardest part of astrology to explain and justify. Over the centuries a great deal of confusion has developed about the subject, and many astrologers, losing sight of what a horoscope represents, have added to the confusion by proposing new, and even more confusing, systems of their own.

Astrology began in Mesopotamia, in India, and in the southern provinces of China – all places that lie very near to the Tropic of Cancer. Within the tropics, the midday sun is very nearly directly overhead every day of the year; it rises nearly due east every day, and sets nearly due west. By a strange (and, in some ways, fortunate) coincidence, Babylon, the great Indian observatory outside Delhi, and the southern Chinese observatory at Chungking all lie not very far from latitude 23° 27', where the zodiac appears to turn as a great circle almost directly about Earth.

So it seemed very appropriate to represent the horoscope as a circle, divided across its centre by a line representing the horizon, with the eastern horizon to the left, and the western horizon to the right.

But as we move away from the tropic and toward the pole, the situation changes. In summer the sun rises over the northeastern horizon, and sets in the northwest; north of the Arctic Circle at midsummer, the sun does not set at all, but is visible throughout a complete circle in the sky. Conversely, in winter, the sun rises and sets south of east and west, and above the Arctic Circle it is invisible for some part of the winter.

In the same way, throughout each day, the zodiac does not appear as a circle running through the east and west points. Some signs of the zodiac, known as signs of 'short ascension' – Capricorn to Gemini – appear to rise south of the eastern point; the signs of 'long ascension' – Cancer to Sagittarius – appear to rise north of the eastern point. And the point of the zodiac which is highest in the sky will be found correspondingly east or west of the southern meridian. This is where the confusion began.

The astronomers of Babylon divided the sky into twelve 'houses'. They did this to account for the fact that the planets were not always exactly in the ecliptic, but appeared to wander a certain number of degrees either side of it; they therefore had to assume that each sign of the zodiac extended its influence through a fixed 'slice' of the sky, which they thought of as a house to which a planet could return when it had completed one of its journeys about the sky. The Sun, the great god of the day, had his house in Leo, where he ruled at the height of his splendour; the Moon ruled in Cancer, at the right hand of the Sun. The other five planets were given two houses, one for day and one for night. And since the zodiac divided the sky into twelve equal parts, each of these houses was also equal, comprising 30°, one-twelfth of the 360° circle.

Ptolemy, the great mathematician and geographer of the second century AD, devised the way of drawing the horoscope that we have used in this book. It is not meant to be an exact representation of the heavens; it is a kind of map to show the relative positions of the planets, and the houses of the zodiac in which they are situated at the particular time for which the horoscope is drawn.

These are the 'planetary houses', but Ptolemy complicated the matter further by introducing the concept of 'mundane houses'. He assumed that every birthplace possessed its own 'framework' of twelve houses, and that a horoscope could be divided among these twelve houses, each representing some part of the character and fate of the person whose horoscope it was. The first house was marked by the ascendant, and represented the person himself; the second, which lay below the eastern horizon (and was called a succeedent house because it followed the first) denoted money and possessions; and the third (a 'cadent' house) represented thought and communication. The fourth house was marked by the north point – the nadir or *imum coeli* – and represented the home; the fifth, another succeedent house, represented creation; and the cadent sixth stood for servants and for health.

The seventh house, in the west, was called the 'descendant', and denoted partnership;

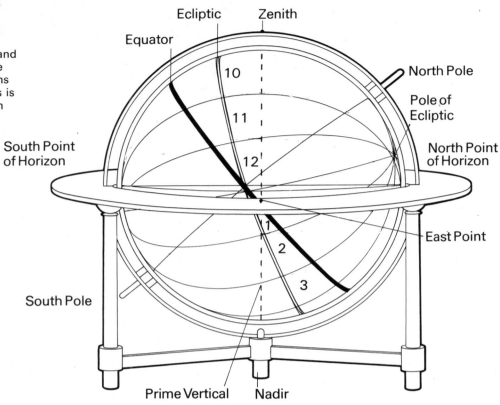

(Right) A model of the celestial sphere, such as can be seen in many scientific museums. The thick horizontal ring represents the horizon, and the mundane houses are marked as equal divisions of the zodiac circle. This is the 'equal house' system proposed by Ptolemy

the eighth, succeedent of the seventh, represented deaths and inheritances; the ninth, cadent, represented distant journeying. The tenth house was marked by the midheaven, and stood for fame; the succeedent eleventh was for social position; and the cadent twelfth represented secrecy and concealment.

To Ptolemy, who after all had devised the drawing of the horoscope as a circle and understood that it was a conventionalised map, it seemed perfectly logical to divide this circle into twelve equal houses of 30° each, which might or (most usually) might not coincide with the twelve planetary houses of the zodiac: as the wheel of the zodiac turned through the sky, the planetary houses passed one by one in and out of the mundane houses of the individual whose horoscope had been drawn.

Ptolemy's writings have provided us with most of what we know about ancient astrology, and it is not quite clear – and has remained a point of argument with astrologers for many years – whether he regarded the ascendant and midheaven as making the beginnings of the first and tenth houses respectively, or whether he thought of them as the mid-points. Nevertheless, there is no doubt that he thought of each house comprising 30° of the circle of the zodiac, and

his system is therefore known today as the 'equal house' system. A modification of this system has been employed in drawing up the horoscopes considered in the previous two chapters.

As time went on, and the mathematics of astronomy and navigation was developed by the Arabs, astrologers began – quite unnecessarily – to make the system more complicated. First of all, Ibn Ezra, who flourished in the eleventh century, calculated a set of twelve mundane houses which were equal divisions of the celestial equator. He imagined the heavens divided into six 'slices' above the earth, and six below; the lines dividing these slices ran from the north point of the horizon to the south point, passing through equal division points on the celestial equator. Long and complicated trigonometrical calculations had to be made to determine at what points these lines cut the ecliptic; and since the north and south points moved relative to the celestial equator with every change of latitude, a different set of figures was required for every birthplace. Arabs of the middle ages were intoxicated with the excitement of this sort of calculation, and it is easy to excuse them, but there is absolutely no reason why systems of this kind should have been perpetuated and elaborated. This system is

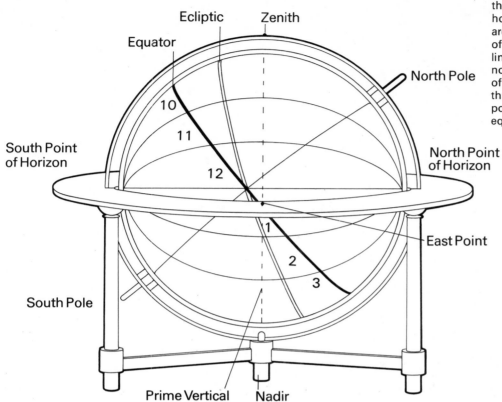

Ecliptic Zenith
Equator
10
11
12
North Pole
South Point of Horizon
North Point of Horizon
1
East Point
2
3
South Pole
Prime Vertical Nadir

(Left) The same model of the celestial globe, showing how the mundane houses are obtained by the method of Regiomontanus: the lines of division run from north point to south point of the horizon, passing through equal division points on the celestial equator

known also as the *modus rationalis*, although there is no rational justification for it.

Before going any further, it is important to understand why latitude is of such significance in the calculation of house divisions – after all, we succeeded in drawing convincing horoscopes for both Marilyn Monroe and Hitler without being concerned with the latitude of their birthplace. For this purpose we must return to the idea of the celestial sphere we considered in chapter 1.

If we imagine a model of our celestial sphere supported in a framework rather like that used for terrestrial globes, it would look like the diagram above left – models like this can be seen in many scientific museums. The big thick circular ring represents the horizon for the observer, wherever he might be in the world, and the whole sphere can be pivoted about the east-west line. The angle between the line joining the poles and the plane of the horizon can be changed from 0° to 90°, and it is this angle that we use in defining latitude. For someone at the equator, the north polar star will lie on the northern horizon, and so the angle of latitude will be 0°; at the North Pole the star will be directly overhead, and the angle of latitude is 90°.

In the diagram, the eastern horizon coincides with the point of intersection of the celestial equator and the ecliptic – that is 0° Aries. As the celestial globe turns about the north-south polar axis, the ecliptic will appear to be turning about a different centre: some signs of the zodiac will rise north of the east point, and others to the south; some will appear to take longer than average to reach their highest point in the sky, and others will take less. The degree of the zodiac just on the horizon will therefore not change steadily, but in a periodic way. And it is obvious that this effect will become more pronounced as the latitude is increased until, above latitude 66° 33', many signs will be permanently above the horizon. As mathematicians became aware of the phenomenon of latitude, they began to calculate 'tables of ascendants': these gave the degree of the zodiac on the eastern horizon for every interval of the sidereal day, and for many different geographical latitudes. And from these figures it was possible to make further calculations of the house divisions.

The method of Ibn Ezra has been known in Europe since the fourteenth century, under the name of Regiomontanus, but Europe already had another method, that of Campanus, which dates from the thirteenth century. This is similar in some ways to that of Regiomontanus: the heavens are

· MARS ·

Il bellicoso marte sempre infiama
Li animi alteri al guerreggiare et sforza
Hor questo hor quello ne satia sua brama
In lacquistar: ma piu sempre rinforza :

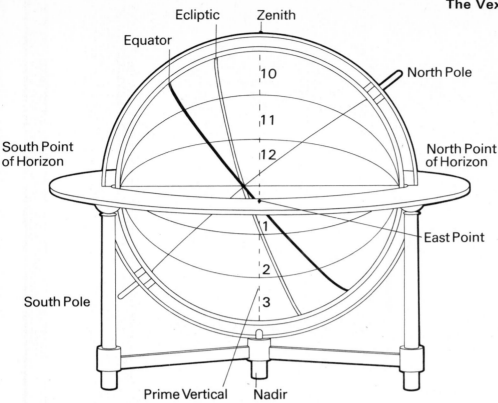

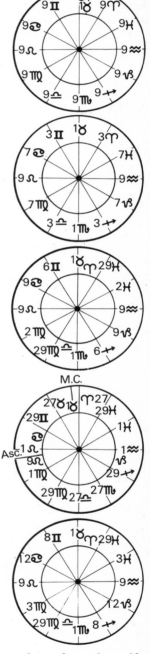

(Left) The Campanus system of house division, based on the great circle overhead. (Below) House divisions by five different methods for the horoscope of Marilyn Monroe

divided into comparable slices running from the north point to the south point, but in this system the lines divide equally the great circle that passes directly overhead from east to west. The ecliptic passes overhead only at latitude 23° 27', and at other latitudes it is at an angle to the overhead circle (see diagram above); more complicated trigonometrical calculations were therefore necessary to discover what divisions of the ecliptic these mundane houses made.

But this was only the beginning. As mathematics became more sophisticated, every major astrologer attempted to devise a method of his own. The Frenchman Morin de Villefranche, known as Morinus, proposed a compromise, based on Regiomontanus, in which the slices run from the *ecliptic* pole to divide the celestial equator equally. The advantage of this system is that the houses remain the same, whatever the latitude – but they bear no relationship to the position of the midheaven or the ascendant.

There is one system of house-division that is still used more than any other: this is the method of Placidus. It is by far the most complicated and least logical system, being based upon a division of the *time* taken by any degree of the zodiac to rise from the *imum coeli* to the midheaven. Above the Arctic Circle, many degrees of the zodiac remain always above the horizon, and so, in polar regions, some signs of the zodiac do not appear in the horoscope at all. Nevertheless, the system is widely employed, for one very good reason: *Raphael's Ephem-*

eris, which was the first to be regularly published and which is still published every year, has always contained tables of houses according to Placidus, and until recently it was almost impossible to obtain any others. Fortunately, the system works fairly well at lower latitudes, but even so it is common to find as much as one-sixth of the horoscope given up to degrees of one sign.

To exemplify the way in which these different systems divide up the houses, let us look at the two birth-dates for which we have drawn up horoscopes in the previous chapters, and see how the house divisions lie. We shall assume for this purpose that the ascendant marks the beginning of the first house (except in the case of the Morinus system), the midheaven the beginning of the tenth (except in the case of Equal House and Morinus systems), and that the houses are equal divisions of the horoscope circle, so that the beginning of the eleventh house lies (as it were) at eleven o'clock, the twelfth house at ten o'clock, the second house at eight o'clock, and the third house at seven o'clock.

Marilyn Monroe was born at sidereal time 01 55. From the published tables of houses, we obtain the following figures for latitude 34°N (the latitude of Los Angeles):

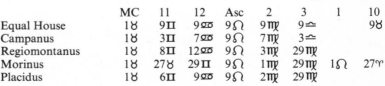

	MC	11	12	Asc	2	3	1	10
Equal House	18♉	9♊	9♋	9♌	9♍	9♎		9♉
Campanus	18♉	3♊	7♋	9♌	7♍	3♎		
Regiomontanus	18♉	8♊	12♋	9♌	3♍	29♍		
Morinus	18♉	27♉	29♊	9♌	1♍	29♍	1♌	27♈
Placidus	18♉	6♊	9♋	9♌	2♍	29♍		

(Below) House divisions by five different methods for the horoscope of Adolf Hitler

These house divisions will be found plotted on to horoscope circle diagrams on the previous page.

For Adolf Hitler, born at sidereal time 08 10, latitude 47° 30'N, we get the following house divisions:

We can now mark these on to a series of horoscope circles, as in the accompanying diagrams. The first thing we discover is that, at these latitudes, there is not a great deal of difference between the various systems. Nevertheless, there are certain anomalies. In the Regiomontanus houses for Hitler, for instance, 40° of the zodiac – 10° of Gemini and the whole of Cancer – must be packed into 30° of the horoscope in the ninth house; and in the Placidus system it is 36°. In the eighth house both systems include only 22° of Aries. For Marilyn

	MC	11	12	Asc	2	3	1	10
Equal House	1♌	24♌	24♍	24♎	24♏	24♐		24♋
Campanus	1♌	27♌	24♍	24♎	29♏	1♑		
Regiomontanus	1♌	6♍	2♎	24♎	18♏	20♐		
Morinus	1♌	5♍	2♎	24♎	0♐	3♑	1♏	5♌
Placidus	1♌	5♍	2♎	24♎	21♏	24♐		

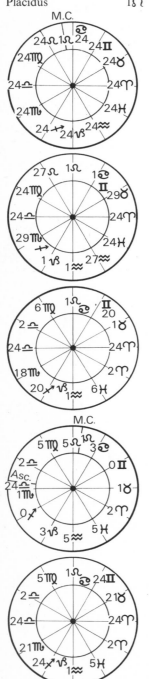

Monroe, born somewhat nearer the equator of Earth, the differences are not so great.

It is when we look at the figures for more northerly latitudes that the anomalies become more apparent. Consider the house divisions for sidereal time 12 00 at lat. 60°:

	MC	11	12	Asc	2	3	1	10
Equal House	0♎	25♍	25♎	25♏	25♐	25♑		
Campanus	0♎	15♎	29♏	25♏	21♑	8♓		
Regiomontanus	0♎	24♎	9♏	25♏	21♐	12♒		
Morinus	0♎	28♎	28♏	25♏	2♒	2♓	0♑	0♎
Placidus	0♎	26♎	13♏	25♏	28♐	18♒		

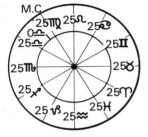

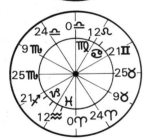

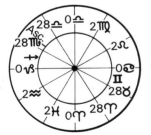

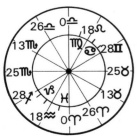

And as for latitudes above the Arctic Circle, as Alan Leo, the most forceful twentieth century exponent of the Placidus system, put it: 'Horoscopes calculated for such latitudes shown many curious features'. So much so that by latitude 70°N Gemini and Cancer do not appear in the horoscope at all!

What is important to remember is that all these systems are *only* ways of defining the mundane houses, and have nothing to do with the relative positions of the planets and the signs of the zodiac. What these astrologers have lost sight of in all their abstruse calculations is that their circular horoscope is a symbolic map of the heavens; they have tried to turn it into a map of the circular horizon, at the same time distorting their geography· so that the ascendant degree of the ecliptic is always drawn as if it were due east.

The most important part of a horoscope is to show the positions of the planets: these house orientated horoscopes merely make it more difficult to see the planetary aspects. Traditional astrology has never suggested that the degree of the ascendant is of great importance; it is the area of the zodiac in which the planets are situated that is of the most significance.

Nothing exemplifies this more clearly than the horoscope of someone born just as the Sun is rising. Let us list the zodiacal position of the sun at sunrise for the first day of each month in 1974, and compare this with the data given in a table of ascendants. The figures given in the Nautical Almanac are for Greenwich, 51° 30′N.

Date	Sunrise	ST	Ascendant	Sun
Jan 1	08 08	14 50	9♑	11♑
Feb 1	07 41	16 25	9♒	12♒
Mar 1	06 47	17 21	7♓	11♓
Apr 1	05 36	18 23	14♈	11♈
May 1	04 31	19 06	8♉	11♉
June 1	03 46	20 22	8♊	11♊
July 1	03 44	22 20	7♋	9♋
Aug 1	04 21	00 59	7♌	9♌
Sept 1	05 11	03 51	6♍	9♍
Oct 1	06 00	06 38	7♎	8♎
Nov 1	06 54	09 35	7♏	9♏
Dec 1	07 45	12 24	8♐	9♐

The figures for the position of the Sun correspond closely with what one would expect for long and short ascension; the figures from the table of ascendants are completely inconsistent, and would suggest that Pisces is a sign of long ascension, leaving Taurus and Gemini rather indeterminate. Moreover, we would naturally expect the rising sun to be just on the eastern horizon, and in no single case is this so when the ascendant is taken as the horizontal.

What, then, ought we to make of the idea of mundane houses? Modern astrologers tend to make more of the significance of these houses than of any other part of the horoscope, but they are all so confused, and disagree so violently, about how the house divisions are to be defined, that they throw the whole concept into disrepute. Mundane houses represent the fate of the individual: no two persons have ever been born at exactly the same time on exactly the same spot, and so everybody possesses a unique 'frame of reference' which intersects the space of the universe in which the planets move. This framework, therefore, should be superimposed upon the horoscope after it has been drawn. What could be simpler or more logical than to divide that horoscope into twelve equal segments as Ptolemy did? Remember, although there are rules concerning the interpretation of astrological data, that in the end you depend upon your intuitive faculties and nothing else.

More importantly, this chapter has thrown some light upon the meaning of the ascendant. It is clearly illogical to try to impose the mathematical calculation of the ascendant degree upon a chart that is intended to be only a symbolical representation of the position of the planets against the background of the sky. An accurate and completely workable horoscope can be drawn and interpreted by erecting the midheaven and dividing twelve houses equally from it, as those of Marilyn Monroe and Adolf Hitler have shown. This method does away with the need to have a table of ascendants for each latitude, with the accompanying complications in the horoscopes of people born above the Arctic Circle. And, since Earth must be regarded as an infinitely

(Facing page) The war-chariot of Mars is drawn by a pair of dogs. The activities upon which he exerts his influence are above all the arts of war, but they also include all those trades and professions which demand discipline and a certain aggressiveness: inventors and pioneers, butchers, iron-workers and surgeons are among those who come under the influence of Mars. (Left) House divisions by five different methods for sidereal time 12 00 at latitude 60°N

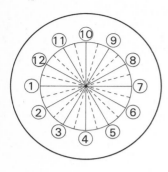

(Below and opposite) Jupiter rules in Pisces and in Sagittarius, and his chariot is drawn by peacocks. Wealth and splendour characterise the areas in which he exerts his influence

small speck at the centre of the celestial sphere, the planets *must* be in exactly the same spatial positions, whatever the position of the observer.

Modification for southern latitudes

This discussion of latitude can be appropriately concluded by a brief consideration of how to draw a horoscope for someone south of the Earth equator. Standing looking northward to the ecliptic, they will see the zodiac rising over the eastern horizon on the right hand. It would be possible, therefore, to draw a horoscope in this form, which would be a mirror image of a corresponding northern horoscope and, in order to make it easily comparable we must 'turn it over', as it were, from right to left. Since the only starting point we require is the midheaven, the resultant horoscope is the same as one for the northern hemisphere.

The Significance of the Houses

As mentioned earlier, there is considerable disagreement over whether the midheaven marks the beginning or the middle of the tenth house – and so on, round the circle of the horoscope. The most logical would be for it to be situated in the middle of the house: in this way, a planet situated at or near the midheaven would exert its powerful influence in the tenth house for 15° on either side. If you decide to add houses to your interpretation of the horoscope, the best way is to insert dotted lines to mark the house divisions, as in the diagram.

The significance of each house is usually taken as follows:

House 1: The individual whose horoscope it is, his outward appearance and personality – in fact, what is normally signified by his ascendant sign, which will almost invariably be the dominant sign of the first house.

House 2: Money and portable possessions, income, finances.

House 3: Intelligence, communications, near relationships.

House 4: The home, and the mother.

House 5: Creation and procreation, love affairs, children and sexual compatibility. May also be concerned with amusements and pleasures, gambling or speculation.

House 6: Servants, conditions of employment, illness and recovery.

House 7: Marriage and other partnerships. This house is opposite to the first house, and signifies the individual's 'opposite number'.

House 8: Death and inheritance.

House 9: Foreign travel, exploration of distant places (both geographical and spiritual), the law and the church.

House 10: Fame, notoriety, professional career; also the father.

House 11: Social position, friends and acquaintances, societies and organisations.

House 12: Secrecy, the subconscious, the psychic faculties, unknown enemies, and also places of concealment and confinement.

These interpretations are directly related to the significance of the various signs of the zodiac; it is assumed that the first house is under the influence of Aries, the second under the influence of Taurus, and so on. Further information can be found under the individual signs in chapter 2.

Progressions and Prediction

Present-day astrology has developed from an ancient magical principle which, in its

Benegno e ioue e de mirti pianeta
Produce mathematici e doctori
Theologi er gransauij ne dineta
Alchuna gentil cosa o grandi honori :·

· SATVRNVS ·

Saturno huomini tardi et rei pduce
Rubadur et buxiardi et assasini
Villani et uili et senza alchuna luce
Pastor et zoppi et simili meschini :·

(Left) Saturn has come to represent old age, and his scythe has become a crutch; but in this illumination from *De Sphaera* he also holds a sickle. He rules in Aquarius and Capricorn, and exerts his influence over activities requiring mature judgment, such as government, law, and games of skill

briefest form, may be expressed as 'As above, so below'. The old magicians saw man's body and soul (the 'microcosm') as a miniature working model of the whole of creation (the 'macrocosm'), and so they saw the movement of the great cosmic clock mirrored in the history and fate of man. By an analogous argument, observing how the Sun returned to the same part of the heavens each year, they suggested that the planetary movements for each day in between foreshadowed the planetary movements of the years to come.

This means that there are two ways in which we can determine the astrological forecast for some time in the future: we can draw a horoscope for that particular time, or we can 'progress' the birth horoscope on the basis of 'a day for a year', one hour for two weeks, four minutes for a day, and so on.

Suppose, for instance, that having drawn the horoscope for a person born at 12 00 noon on 30 June 1960, we wish to discover what the cosmic clock indicates for them at 06 00 on the morning of 15 May 1978. Drawing up a horoscope for this time will take no account of what planetary aspects existed at the time of their birth, and it is a long and complicated business to compare the horoscope with their birth chart. As an alternative, we can calculate a progressed horoscope, allowing 17 days for the years, plus 20 hours for 10 months, plus 56 minutes for 14 days, plus 3 minutes for 18 hours. We draw the horoscope for 08 59 on 18 July 1960, and interpret this as a direct progression from the birth horoscope of the subject.

Astrology also recognises what are called 'horary questions'. Anyone who has a problem on which he requires advice may frame a question, and erect a horoscope for the time at which he asked it; the interpretation of the horoscope, hopefully, supplies the answer. James Wilson, the author of the best *Dictionary of Astrology*, puts the situation very succinctly:

'If the artist be skilful, and the querent sincere, and really anxious respecting the result, there is little reason to doubt but the answer will in general be true and satisfactory, not in those minute particulars which some pretend to discover, but in the real and essential circumstances which ought alone to be the end and design of such a question; namely, the final conclusion of the business and its ultimate consequences. . . . There is nothing in it either celestial or diabolical, meritorious or criminal, good or evil; a person is equally justifiable in making an inquiry into one thing as another, and to propose an horary question is an act as indifferent in itself as to ask what it is o'clock; it contains nothing supernatural, for it is nature itself, operating in its usual way.'

Few astrological predictions have provoked as much political investigation as the one made by William Lilly in 1648, and again in 1651. In 1648, he wrote that 'in the year 1665 . . . or near that year . . . more or less of that time, there will appear in this kingdom so strange a revolution of fate, so grand a catastrophe . . . as never yet appeared . . . it will be ominous to London . . . to all sorts of people . . . by reason of sundry fires and a consuming plague.' He returned to the subject with a broadsheet illustrated with various woodcuts, including the one below. Gemini is the sign of the zodiac which represents the City of London.

In 1665, the great outbreak of bubonic plague occurred in London, and the following year came the disastrous fire. It seemed possible, to some members of Parliament, that Lilly himself might have started the fire when he saw that the first part of his prediction had come true. It was only after a long inquiry that Lilly was exonerated – and his reputation was made for ever.

6 A CONDENSED PLANETARY EPHEMERIS
1880-1980

Each table gives the positions of each planet at midday on the first day of each month throughout the year. Below the main table are given the dates and planetary positions from which Mercury, Venus and Mars begin their retrograde motion, and the dates and positions from which they commence their direct (forward) motion again. Approximate positions between these dates should be found by the method detailed in chapter 3. Retrograde motion of the other planets lasts for several months at a time, and can be found from the figures given in the monthly tables. Thus, for instance, Uranus can be seen to commence retrogression during December 1880, and to begin forward motion again in May 1881. In calculating positions during these periods, remember that planets appear to remain stationary for a day or more at the position where they change direction, and that they are moving most rapidly midway between these 'stations'.

1880	☉	☽	☿	♀	♂	♃	♄	♅	♆	♇
JAN.	11♑	24♌	18♐	26♏	15♉	9♓	9♈	9♍	9♉	26♉
FEB.	12♒	14♎	3♒	2♑	24	15	11	8	9	25
MAR.	11♓	9♏	25♓	7♒	8♊	22	14	7	10	25
APR.	12♈	2♑	6♈	15♓	24	0♈	18	6	11	26
MAY	11♉	10♒	15♈	22♈	11♋	7	22	5	12	26
JUNE	11♊	0♈	10♊	0♊	0♌	13	25	5	13	27
JULY	10♋	4♉	5♌	7♋	18	17	28	6	14	28
AUG.	10♌	18♊	16♌	15♌	7♍	19	29	8	14	28
SEPT.	9♍	2♌	25♌	23♍	27	19	29	9	14	28
OCT.	9♎	5♍	19♎	0♏	16♎	15	27	11	14	28
NOV.	9♏	24♎	3♐	8♐	7♏	11	24	13	13	28
DEC.	10♐	1♐	24♏	15♑	28	10	23	14	12	27

☿ ℞ Mar. 20-14♈ D. Apr. 12-2♈ ℞ July 23-20♌ D. Aug. 16-8♌
℞ Nov. 14-10♐ D. Dec. 4-24♏

1881	☉	☽	☿	♀	♂	♃	♄	♅	♆	♇
JAN.	11♑	24♑	27♐	23♒	21♐	11♈	22♈	14♍	12♉	27♉
FEB.	13♒	17♓	17♒	28♓	14♑	15	23	13	12	26
MAR.	11♓	25♓	26♓	27♈	5♒	21	26	12	12	26
APR.	12♈	14♉	15♓	19♉	29	28	29	11	13	27
MAY	11♉	17♊	24♈	14♉	22♓	5♉	3♉	10	14	27
JUNE	11♊	1♌	27♊	6♉	15♈	12	7	10	15	28
JULY	10♋	3♍	1♌	25♉	7♉	18	10	11	16	29
AUG.	9♌	19♎	22♋	25♊	28	23	12	12	17	29
SEPT.	9♍	8♐	10♍	29♋	18♊	26	12	14	17	29
OCT.	8♎	16♑	0♏	5♍	3♋	26	11	16	16	29
NOV.	9♏	10♓	23♏	13♎	14	23	9	17	15	29
DEC.	9♐	18♈	21♏	20♏	14	19	7	18	15	28

☿ ℞ Mar. 3-26♓ D. Mar. 25-13♓ ℞ July 5-1♌ D. July 29-21♋
℞ Oct. 29-24♏ D. Nov. 18-9♏ ♀ ℞ Apr. 13-21♉ D. May 25-5♉
♂ ℞ Nov. 18-16♋

1882	☉	☽	☿	♀	♂	♃	♄	♅	♆	♇
JAN.	11♑	7♊	8♑	29♐	4♋	16♉	6♉	19♍	14♉	28♉
FEB.	13♒	23♋	29♒	8♒	27♊	17	6	18	14	27
MAR.	11♓	2♌	27♒	13♓	1♋	20	8	17	14	27
APR.	12♈	17♍	16♓	22♈	12	26	11	15	15	28
MAY	11♉	20♎	10♉	28♉	26	2♊	15	15	16	28
JUNE	11♊	6♐	4♋	6♋	13♌	9	19	14	17	29
JULY	9♋	13♑	5♋	12♌	0♍	16	22	15	18	0♊
AUG.	9♌	6♓	25♋	19♍	19	23	25	17	19	0
SEPT.	9♍	0♉	24♍	24♎	9♎	28	26	18	19	0
OCT.	8♎	7♊	4♏	25♏	29	1♋	26	20	18	0
NOV.	9♏	24♋	23♎	18♐	20♏	1	24	22	18	0
DEC.	9♐	27♌	1♐	18♐	12♐	29♊	21	23	17	29♉

☿ ℞ Feb. 14-10♓ D. Mar. 8-25♒ ℞ June 16-11♋ D. July 10-2♋
℞ Oct. 12-8♏ D. Nov. 1-23♎ ♀ ℞ Nov. 17-22♐ D. Dec. 28-7♐
♂ D. Feb. 3-27♊

1883	☉	☽	☿	♀	♂	♃	♄	♅	♆	♇
JAN.	11♑	10♎	20♑	7♐	5♑	24♊	20♉	23♍	16♉	28♉
FEB.	12♒	24♏	22♒	26♐	29	22	19	23	16	28
MAR.	11♓	2♐	14♒	24♑	21♒	22	21	22	16	28
APR.	11♈	19♑	27♓	29♒	15♓	25	24	20	17	29
MAY	11♉	26♒	27♉	4♈	8♈	29	27	20	18	29
JUNE	11♊	19♈	20♊	11♉	2♉	6♋	1♊	19	19	0♊
JULY	9♋	28♉	18♊	17♊	24♋	12	5	20	20	1
AUG.	9♌	20♋	12♌	25♋	15♊	19	8	21	21	1
SEPT.	9♍	8♍	4♎	3♍	5♋	26	10	23	21	1
OCT.	8♎	11♎	19♎	11♎	23	1♌	10	25	21	1
NOV.	9♏	25♏	24♎	20♏	9♌	4	9	26	20	1
DEC.	9♐	28♐	12♐	27♐	19	4	6	28	19	0

☿ ℞ Jan. 29-23♒ D. Feb. 19-8♒ ℞ May 28-21♊ D. June 21-13♊
℞ Sept. 25-22♎ D. Oct. 16-7♎ ♂ ℞ Dec. 24-22♌

1884	☉	☽	☿	♀	♂	♃	♄	♅	♆	♇
JAN.	11♑	16♒	29♑	6♒	21♌	2♌	4♊	28♍	18♉	29♉
FEB.	12♒	6♈	21♑	14♓	12	28♋	3	28	18	29
MAR.	11♓	1♉	19♒	19♈	3	25	4	27	19	29
APR.	12♈	24♊	14♈	25♉	5	25	6	25	19	0♊
MAY	11♉	2♌	0♊	27♊	14	27	9	24	20	0
JUNE	11♊	21♍	23♉	22♋	28	2♌	13	24	22	1
JULY	10♋	24♎	27♊	26♋	14♍	8	17	24	23	1
AUG.	10♌	8♐	28♌	12♋	3♎	14	21	26	23	2
SEPT.	9♍	22♑	5♎	25♋	23	21	23	27	23	2
OCT.	9♎	25♒	22♍	23♌	13♏	27	24	29	23	2
NOV.	10♏	14♈	7♏	27♍	5♐	2♍	24	1♎	22	1
DEC.	10♐	21♉	24♐	3♏	27	5	22	2	21	1

☿ ℞ Jan. 12-7♒ D. Feb. 1-21♑ ℞ May 6-1♊ D. May 30-23♉
℞ Sept. 6-6♎ D. Sept. 28-21♍ ℞ Dec. 26-21♑
♀ ℞ June 20-28♋ D. Aug. 3-12♋ ♂ D. Mar. 12-2♌

1885	☉	☽	☿	♀	♂	♃	♄	♅	♆	♇
JAN.	11♑	15♋	17♑	11♐	21♑	6♍	19♊	3♎	21♉	0♊
FEB.	13♒	7♍	19♑	20♑	15♒	3	18	3	21	0
MAR.	11♓	15♍	1♓	25♒	7♓	0	17	2	21	0
APR.	12♈	4♏	29♈	3♈	2♈	26♌	19	0	22	1
MAY	11♉	7♐	6♉	10♉	25	26	22	29♍	23	1
JUNE	11♊	21♑	18♉	19♊	18♉	28	26	29	24	2
JULY	10♋	24♒	14♋	25♋	9♊	2♍	29	29	25	2
AUG.	9♌	10♈	6♍	3♍	0♋	8	3♋	0♎	25	3
SEPT.	9♍	0♊	12♍	11♎	20	15	6	2	26	3
OCT.	8♎	9♋	27♍	17♏	9♌	21	8	4	25	3
NOV.	9♏	2♍	19♏	23♐	26	27	8	6	25	2
DEC.	10♐	10♎	1♑	27♑	11♍	2♎	7	7	24	2

☿ D. Jan. 15-5♑ ℞ Apr. 18-12♉ D. May 12-3♉ ℞ Aug. 21-19♍
D. Sept. 12-5♍ ℞ Dec. 10-5♑ D. Dec. 30-19♐

1886	☉	☽	☿	♀	♂	♃	♄	♅	♆	♀
JAN.	11♑	28♏	20♐	26♒	22♍	5♎	4♋	8♎	23♉	1♊
FEB.	13♒	14♑	27♑	8♓	25	6	2	8	23	1
MAR.	11♓	23♑	15♓	24♒	18	4	1	7	23	1
APR.	12♈	7♓	24♈	0♓	7	0	2	5	24	1
MAY	11♉	9♈	16♈	25♓	7	27♍	4	4	25	2
JUNE	11♊	27♉	28♉	28♈	16	26	8	4	26	3
JULY	10♋	4♋	0♌	2♊	0♎	28	12	4	27	3
AUG.	9♌	27♌	1♍	8♋	17	3♎	16	5	28	4
SEPT.	9♍	20♎	21♌	15♌	7♏	8	19	6	28	4
OCT.	8♎	27♏	11♎	22♍	27	15	22	8	28	4
NOV.	9♏	14♑	29♏	1♏	20♐	21	23	10	27	3
DEC.	9♐	17♒	14♐	9♐	12♑	27	22	12	26	3

☿ ℞ Mar. 31-24♈ D. Apr. 23-13♈ ℞ Aug. 3-1♍ D. Aug. 27-18♌
℞ Nov. 24-19♐ D. Dec. 14-3♐ ♀ ℞ Jan. 30-8♓ D. Mar. 11-22♒
♂ ℞ Jan. 27-25♍ D. Apr. 17-6♍

1887	☉	☽	☿	♀	♂	♃	♄	♅	♆	♇
JAN.	11♑	0♈	21♐	18♑	6♒	2♏	20♋	12♎	25♉	2♊
FEB.	12♒	14♉	9♒	27♒	1♓	5	17	12	25	2
MAR.	11♓	23♉	28♓	2♈	23	6	16	12	25	2
APR.	11♈	10♋	24♓	10♉	17♈	3	16	10	26	2
MAY	11♉	18♌	17♈	16♊	9♉	0	17	9	27	3
JUNE	11♊	11♎	17♊	22♋	2♊	27♎	20	8	28	4
JULY	9♋	20♏	5♌	24♌	23	26	24	8	29	4
AUG.	9♌	11♑	3♌	23♍	13♋	28	28	9	0♊	5
SEPT.	9♍	28♒	0♍	6♎	3♌	3♏	2♌	11	0	5
OCT.	8♎	1♈	23♎	23♍	22	8	5	13	0	5
NOV.	9♏	15♉	2♐	27♍	11♍	15	6	15	29♉	4
DEC.	9♐	19♊	19♏	22♎	27	21	6	16	28	4

☿ ℞ Mar. 13-6♈ D. Apr. 5-24♓ ℞ July 15-12♌ D. Aug. 8-1♌
℞ Nov. 8-4♐ D. Nov. 28-18♏ ♀ ℞ Sept. 1-6♎ D. Oct. 12-20♍

1888	☉	☽	☿	♀	♂	♃	♄	♅	♆	♇
JAN.	11♑	7♌	0♑	26♏	13♎	28♏	5♌	17♎	28♉	3♊
FEB.	12♒	28♍	22♒	3♑	25	3♐	2	17	27	3
MAR.	11♓	23♎	16♓	8♒	0♏	6	0	17	27	3
APR.	12♈	16♐	14♓	16♓	25♎	6	0	15	28	3
MAY	12♉	23♑	1♉	22♈	15	4	0	14	29	4
JUNE	11♊	11♓	3♋	0♊	13	0	3	13	0♊	5
JULY	10♋	14♈	22♋	7♋	21	27♏	6	13	1	5
AUG.	10♌	28♉	20♋	15♌	5♏	27	10	14	2	6
SEPT.	9♍	12♋	17♍	24♍	24	29	14	15	2	6
OCT.	9♎	15♌	3♏	1♏	14♐	3♐	17	17	2	6
NOV.	10♏	5♎	8♏	9♐	7♑	9	20	19	2	5
DEC.	10♐	12♏	25♏	16♑	0♒	16	20	21	1	5

☿ ℞ Feb. 24-19♓ D. Mar. 17-5♓ ℞ June 26-23♋ D. July 20-13♋
℞ Oct. 20-18♏ D. Nov. 11-2♏ ♂ ℞ Mar. 5-0♏ D. May 22-12♎

1889	☉	☽	☿	♀	♂	♃	♄	♅	♆	♇
JAN.	11♑	6♑	14♑	23♒	24♒	23♐	19♌	22♎	0♊	4♊
FEB.	13♒	28♒	1♓	29♓	18♓	29	17	22	0	4
MAR.	11♓	6♓	18♒	27♈	9♈	4♑	15	21	0	4
APR.	12♈	24♈	21♓	18♉	2♉	7	14	20	0	4
MAY	11♉	27♉	19♉	11♉	24	8	14	19	1	5
JUNE	11♊	11♋	2♋	5♉	16♊	6	15	18	2	5
JULY	10♋	14♌	24♊	24♉	6♋	3	18	18	3	6
AUG.	9♌	1♎	2♌	25♊	26	29♐	22	18	4	7
SEPT.	9♍	22♏	29♍	0♌	16♌	29	26	20	5	7
OCT.	8♎	1♑	1♏	5♍	5♍	1♑	29	21	4	7
NOV.	9♏	24♒	21♎	13♎	24	5	2♍	23	4	6
DEC.	10♐	2♈	6♐	21♏	12♎	11	4	25	3	6

☿ ℞ Feb. 7-3♓ D. Feb. 28-18♒ ℞ June 8-3♋ D. July 1-24♊
℞ Oct. 4-2♏ D. Oct. 25-16♎ ♀ ℞ Apr. 10-19♉ D. May 22-3♉

1890	☉	☽	☿	♀	♂	♃	♄	♅	♆	♇
JAN.	11♑	19♉	25♑	0♑	0♏	18♑	4♍	26♎	2♊	5♊
FEB.	13♒	4♋	6♒	9♒	17	25	2	27	2	5
MAR.	11♓	13♋	15♒	14♓	0♐	1♒	0	26	2	5
APR.	12♈	26♌	4♈	22♈	11	7	28♌	25	2	5
MAY	11♉	29♍	1♊	29♉	13	11	27	24	3	6
JUNE	11♊	17♏	7♊	7♋	5	12	28	23	5	7
JULY	10♋	24♐	19♊	13♌	28♏	11	0♍	23	6	7
AUG.	9♌	18♒	19♌	19♍	3♐	7	4	23	6	8
SEPT.	9♍	11♈	6♎	24♎	17	3	8	24	7	8
OCT.	8♎	17♉	5♎	25♏	5♑	2	11	26	7	8
NOV.	9♏	4♋	29♎	17♐	26	4	14	28	6	7
DEC.	9♐	6♌	17♐	14♐	18♒	8	17	0♏	5	7

☿ ℞ Jan. 21-17♒ D. Feb. 10-1♒ ℞ May 18-13♊ D. June 11-4♊
℞ Sept. 17-15♎ D. Oct. 8-0♎ ♀ ℞ Nov. 13-20♐ D. Dec. 24-4♐
♂ ℞ Apr. 24-13♐ D. July 5-28♏

1891	☉	☽	☿	♀	♂	♃	♄	♅	♆	♇
JAN.	11♑	20♍	0♒	6♐	12♓	15♒	17♍	1♏	5♊	6♊
FEB.	12♒	4♏	17♑	26♐	5♈	22	16	1	4	6
MAR.	11♓	13♏	23♒	25♑	25	28	14	1	4	6
APR.	11♈	2♑	20♈	0♓	17♉	6♓	12	0	5	6
MAY	11♉	10♒	23♉	5♈	8♊	12	10	29♎	6	7
JUNE	11♊	3♈	17♉	12♉	29	16	11	28	7	7
JULY	9♋	12♉	2♋	18♊	18♋	18	12	27	8	8
AUG.	9♌	2♋	2♍	26♋	8♌	17	15	28	9	9
SEPT.	9♍	18♌	28♍	4♍	28	14	19	29	9	9
OCT.	8♎	21♍	21♍	11♎	17♍	10	23	0♏	9	9
NOV.	9♏	6♏	12♏	20♏	7♎	8	26	2	8	8
DEC.	9♐	9♐	27♐	28♐	26	9	29	4	8	8

☿ ℞ Jan. 5-0♒ D. Jan. 25-14♑ ℞ Apr. 30-23♉ D. May 22-14♉
℞ Aug. 30-29♍ D. Sept. 23-14♍ ℞ Dec. 20-14♑

1892	☉	☽	☿	♀	♂	♃	♄	♅	♆	♇
JAN.	11♑	28♑	2♑	6♒	15♏	14♓	0♎	5♏	7♊	7♊
FEB.	12♒	20♓	21♑	15♓	5♐	20	0	6	6	7
MAR.	11♓	14♈	7♓	20♈	23	26	28♍	6	6	7
APR.	12♈	7♊	1♉	26♉	11♑	4♈	26	5	7	7
MAY	12♉	14♋	24♈	27♊	27	11	24	4	8	8
JUNE	11♊	1♍	21♉	21♋	11♒	17	23	3	9	8
JULY	10♋	4♎	22♋	23♋	17	22	24	2	10	9
AUG.	10♌	17♏	7♍	10♋	13	25	27	2	11	9
SEPT.	9♍	1♑	29♌	25♋	7	24	0♎	3	11	10
OCT.	9♎	5♒	4♎	23♌	12	21	4	5	11	10
NOV.	10♏	25♓	24♏	28♍	26	17	8	7	11	9
DEC.	10♐	3♉	29♐	4♏	13♓	15	11	8	10	9

☿ D. Jan. 9-28♐ ℞ Apr. 10-4♉ D. May 4-24♈ ℞ Aug. 11-11♍
D. Sept. 5-28♌ ℞ Dec. 3-29♐ D. Dec. 23-13♐ ♀ ℞ June 18-26♋
D. July 31-10♋ ♂ ℞ July 6-17♒ D. Sept. 3-7♒

1893	☉	☽	☿	♀	♂	♃	♄	♅	♆	♇
JAN.	11♑	27♊	19♐	12♐	3♈	16♈	12♎	10♏	9♊	8♊
FEB.	13♒	18♌	2♒	21♑	23	20	13	11	9	8
MAR.	11♓	27♌	22♓	25♒	12♉	25	12	11	9	8
APR.	12♈	14♎	11♈	4♈	2♊	2♉	9	10	9	8
MAY	11♉	17♏	15♈	11♉	22	9	7	9	10	9
JUNE	11♊	1♑	7♊	19♊	12♋	16	6	7	11	9
JULY	10♋	5♒	4♌	26♋	1♌	22	6	7	12	10
AUG.	9♌	23♓	21♌	4♍	20	28	8	7	13	10
SEPT.	9♍	14♉	23♌	11♎	10♍	1♊	11	8	14	11
OCT.	9♎	23♊	17♎	17♏	29	1	15	9	14	11
NOV.	9♏	16♌	2♐	24♐	20♎	29♉	19	11	13	10
DEC.	10♐	23♍	29♏	27♑	9♏	25	22	13	12	10

☿ ℞ Mar. 23-16♈ D. Apr. 15-5♈ ℞ July 26-23♌ D. Aug. 19-11♌
℞ Nov. 16-13♐ D. Dec. 6-27♏

1894	☉	☽	☿	♀	♂	♃	♄	♅	♆	♇
JAN.	11♑	10♏	25♐	25♒	0♐	22♉	24♎	14♏	11♊	9♊
FEB.	13♒	24♐	15♒	5♓	22	22	25	15	11	9
MAR.	11♓	3♑	28♓	21♒	11♑	25	25	15	11	9
APR.	12♈	16♒	17♓	29♒	3♒	0♊	23	15	11	9
MAY	11♉	19♓	22♈	25♓	24	6	20	13	12	10
JUNE	11♊	7♉	25♊	28♈	16♓	13	19	12	13	10
JULY	10♋	15♊	3♌	2♊	5♈	20	18	11	14	11
AUG.	9♌	9♌	24♌	9♋	23	27	20	11	15	11
SEPT.	9♍	2♎	7♍	16♌	4♉	2♋	22	12	16	12
OCT.	8♎	7♏	28♎	23♍	3	5	26	13	16	12
NOV.	9♏	24♐	27♏	9♏	24♈	6	29	15	15	11
DEC.	9♐	26♑	20♏	10♐	22	4	3♏	17	15	11

☿ ℞ Mar. 6-29♓ D. Mar. 28-16♓ ℞ July 7-4♌ D. July 31-24♋
℞ Oct. 31-27♏ D. Nov. 20-11♏ ♀ ℞ Jan. 27-6♓
D. Mar. 10-20♒ ♂ ℞ Sept. 16-5♉ D. Nov. 22-21♈

1895	☉	☽	☿	♀	♂	♃	♄	♅	♆	♇
JAN.	11♑	10♓	6♑	19♑	0♉	0♋	6♏	19♏	14♊	10♊
FEB.	12♒	25♈	28♒	27♒	15	27♊	7	20	13	10
MAR.	11♓	4♉	2♓	2♈	0♊	26	7	20	13	10
APR.	12♈	24♊	15♓	10♉	18	29	6	19	13	10
MAY	11♉	2♌	7♉	16♊	6♋	3♋	3	18	14	11
JUNE	11♊	26♍	4♋	22♋	24	9	1	17	15	11
JULY	9♋	4♏	10♋	25♌	13♌	16	1	16	16	12
AUG.	9♌	23♐	23♋	22♍	2♍	23	1	16	17	12
SEPT.	9♍	9♒	22♍	4♎	22	29	3	17	18	13
OCT.	8♎	11♓	4♏	20♍	11♎	5♌	6	18	18	13
NOV.	9♏	26♈	26♎	26♍	2♏	8	10	20	18	12
DEC.	9♐	0♊	29♏	22♎	23	9	13	21	17	12

☿ ℞ Feb. 17-21♓ D. Mar. 11-28♒ ℞ June 19-15♋ D. July 13-5♋ ℞ Oct. 15-11♏ D. Nov. 4-25♎ ♀ ℞ Aug. 30-4♎ D. Oct. 11-18♍

1896	☉	☽	☿	♀	♂	♃	♄	♅	♆	♇
JAN.	11♑	19♋	18♑	27♏	14♐	7♌	17♏	23♏	16♊	11♊
FEB.	12♒	12♍	26♒	3♑	7♑	3	19	24	15	11
MAR.	11♓	5♎	15♒	8♒	29	0	19	25	15	11
APR.	12♈	28♏	26♓	16♓	22♒	29♋	18	24	16	11
MAY	12♉	4♑	26♉	23♈	15♓	1♌	16	23	16	11
JUNE	11♊	21♒	24♊	1♊	8♈	6	14	22	18	12
JULY	10♋	23♓	19♊	8♋	0♉	11	13	21	19	13
AUG.	10♌	7♉	11♌	16♌	21	18	13	20	20	13
SEPT.	9♍	22♊	4♎	24♍	9♊	24	14	21	20	14
OCT.	9♎	26♋	23♎	1♏	23	1♍	17	22	20	14
NOV.	10♏	16♍	24♎	10♐	29	6	20	24	20	13
DEC.	10♐	25♎	11♐	16♑	24	9	24	26	19	13

☿ ℞ Feb. 2-25♒ D. Feb. 22-11♒ ℞ May 30-24♊ D. June 23-16♊ ℞ Sept. 27-25♎ D. Oct. 18-10♎ ♂ ℞ Nov. 2-29♊

1897	☉	☽	☿	♀	♂	♃	♄	♅	♆	♇
JAN.	11♑	18♐	29♑	24♒	13♊	10♍	27♏	27♏	18♊	12♊
FEB.	13♒	9♒	24♑	29♓	13	8	0♐	29	18	12
MAR.	11♓	18♒	18♒	27♈	21	4	1	29	18	12
APR.	12♈	4♈	11♈	16♉	5♋	1	0	29	18	12
MAY	11♉	7♉	2♊	7♉	21	0	29♏	28	19	12
JUNE	11♊	22♊	16♉	3♉	8♌	2	26	26	20	13
JULY	10♋	26♋	24♊	24♉	26	6	25	25	21	14
AUG.	9♌	14♍	26♌	25♊	15♍	12	24	25	22	14
SEPT.	9♍	6♏	6♎	0♌	4♎	18	25	25	22	14
OCT.	9♎	16♐	24♍	6♍	24	25	27	26	23	14
NOV.	9♏	8♒	5♏	14♎	15♏	1♎	1♐	28	22	14
DEC.	10♐	14♓	22♐	21♏	7♐	6	4	0♐	21	14

☿ ℞ Jan. 14-10♒ D. Feb. 4-24♑ ℞ May 10-5♊ D. June 3-26♉ ℞ Sept. 10-8♎ D. Oct. 2-24♍ ℞ Dec. 29-24♑ ♀ ℞ Apr. 8-17♉ D. May 21-1♉ ♂ D. Jan. 17-12♊

1898	☉	☽	☿	♀	♂	♃	♄	♅	♆	♇
JAN.	11♑	0♉	22♑	0♑	0♑	9♎	8♐	2♐	21♊	13♊
FEB.	13♒	14♊	18♑	9♒	23	10	10	3	20	13
MAR.	11♓	22♊	28♒	14♓	15♒	8	12	4	20	13
APR.	12♈	6♌	27♈	23♈	9♓	5	12	3	20	13
MAY	11♉	9♍	11♉	0♊	2♈	1	11	2	21	13
JUNE	11♊	28♎	17♉	8♋	26	0	9	1	22	14
JULY	10♋	6♐	11♋	13♌	18♉	2	7	0	23	15
AUG.	9♌	0♒	5♍	20♍	9♊	6	6	0	24	15
SEPT.	9♍	22♓	17♍	24♎	29	12	6	0	25	16
OCT.	8♎	27♈	25♍	24♏	16♋	18	8	1	25	16
NOV.	9♏	14♊	17♏	15♐	1♌	25	11	2	24	15
DEC.	9♐	16♋	0♑	10♐	8	1♏	14	4	24	15

☿ D. Jan. 18-8♑ ℞ Apr. 21-15♉ D. May 15-6♉ ℞ Aug. 24-21♍ D. Sept. 26-8♍ ℞ Dec. 13-8♑ ♀ ℞ Nov. 12-17♐ D. Dec. 23-2♐ ♂ ℞ Dec. 11-9♌

1899	☉	☽	☿	♀	♂	♃	♄	♅	♆	♇
JAN.	11♑	0♍	22♐	4♐	5♌	6♏	18♐	6♐	23♊	14♊
FEB.	12♒	16♎	25♑	26♐	24♋	9	21	7	22	14
MAR.	11♓	26♎	12♓	25♑	19	10	23	8	22	14
APR.	12♈	16♐	27♈	0♓	25	8	24	8	22	14
MAY	11♉	25♑	17♈	5♈	7♌	5	23	7	23	14
JUNE	11♊	18♓	26♉	12♉	22	1	21	6	24	15
JULY	9♋	26♈	27♋	19♊	9♍	0	19	5	25	16
AUG.	9♌	14♊	3♍	27♋	27	2	17	4	26	16
SEPT.	9♍	29♋	22♌	5♍	17♎	6	17	4	27	17
OCT.	8♎	1♍	8♎	12♎	7♏	12	18	5	27	17
NOV.	9♏	16♎	27♏	21♏	29	18	21	7	27	16
DEC.	9♐	20♏	20♐	28♐	21♐	25	24	8	26	16

☿ D. Jan. 1-22♐ ℞ Apr. 3-27♈ D. Apr. 26-16♈ ℞ Aug. 6-4♍ D. Aug. 29-21♌ ℞ Nov. 27-22♐ D. Dec. 17-6♐ ♂ D. Feb. 28-19♋

1900	☉	☽	☿	♀	♂	♃	♄	♅	♆	♇
JAN.	11♑	10♑	20♐	7♒	14♑	1♐	28♐	10♐	25♊	15♊
FEB.	12♒	3♓	6♒	15♓	8♒	7	1♑	12	25	15
MAR.	10♓	11♓	26♓	19♈	0♓	10	4	12	24	15
APR.	11♈	4♉	28♓	25♉	25	11	5	12	24	15
MAY	11♉	11♊	15♈	26♊	18♈	9	5	12	25	15
JUNE	11♊	28♋	13♊	20♋	11♉	5	3	10	26	16
JULY	9♋	1♍	5♌	20♋	3♊	2	1	9	27	17
AUG.	9♌	15♎	8♌	8♋	24	1	29♐	9	28	17
SEPT.	9♍	29♏	27♌	24♋	15♋	3	28	9	29	18
OCT.	8♎	3♑	21♎	22♌	3♌	7	29	9	29	18
NOV.	9♏	23♒	2♐	27♍	20	13	1♑	11	29	17
DEC.	9♐	2♈	20♏	3♏	3♍	19	4	12	28	17

☿ ℞ Mar. 16-9♈ D. Apr. 8-27♓ ℞ July 19-15♌ D. Aug. 12-4♌ ℞ Nov. 10-6♐ D. Nov. 30-20♏ ♀ ℞ June 17-24♋ D. July 30-8♋

1901	☉	☽	☿	♀	♂	♃	♄	♅	♆	♇
JAN.	10♑	25♉	28♐	11♐	12♍	26♐	8♑	14♐	28♊	16♊
FEB.	12♒	16♋	19♒	20♑	10	3♑	11	16	27	16
MAR.	10♓	26♋	21♓	25♒	0	8	14	17	26	16
APR.	11♈	13♍	13♓	3♈	23♌	12	16	17	27	16
MAY	10♉	16♎	26♈	11♉	27	13	16	16	27	16
JUNE	10♊	0♐	29♊	19♊	8♍	12	15	15	28	17
JULY	9♋	3♑	26♋	25♋	23	8	13	14	29	18
AUG.	9♌	22♒	19♋	3♍	11♎	5	11	13	0♋	18
SEPT.	8♍	14♈	13♍	11♎	0♏	3	10	13	1	19
OCT.	8♎	23♉	0♏	17♏	21	5	10	14	1	19
NOV.	8♏	16♋	16♏	23♐	13♐	9	12	15	1	18
DEC.	9♐	22♌	22♏	26♑	6♑	15	14	17	1	18

☿ ℞ Feb. 27-22♓ D. Mar. 21-8♓ ℞ July 2-26♋ D. July 25-16♋ ℞ Oct. 25-20♏ D. Nov. 14-4♏ ♂ ℞ Jan. 14-13♍ D. Apr. 5-23♌

1902	☉	☽	☿	♀	♂	♃	♄	♅	♆	♇
JAN.	10♑	8♎	10♑	24♒	0♒	22♑	18♑	18♐	0♋	17♊
FEB.	12♒	22♏	0♓	2♓	24	29	21	20	29♊	17
MAR.	10♓	0♐	21♒	18♒	16♓	5♒	24	21	29	17
APR.	11♈	13♑	17♓	28♒	10♈	11	27	21	29	17
MAY	10♉	16♒	13♉	24♓	3♉	15	28	21	29	17
JUNE	10♊	5♈	3♋	27♈	26	17	27	20	0♋	18
JULY	9♋	12♉	28♊	1♊	17♊	16	26	18	1	19
AUG.	8♌	6♋	27♋	8♋	8♋	13	23	18	3	19
SEPT.	8♍	29♌	26♍	16♌	28	9	22	17	3	20
OCT.	7♎	5♎	2♏	23♍	17♌	7	21	18	4	20
NOV.	8♏	21♏	20♎	1♏	5♍	9	22	19	4	19
DEC.	8♐	24♐	2♐	9♐	21	13	25	21	3	19

☿ ℞ Feb. 10-5♓ D. Mar. 4-21♒ ℞ June 12-6♋ D. July 6-27♊ ℞ Oct. 8-4♏ D. Oct. 29-19♎ ♀ ℞ Jan. 25-3♓ D. Mar. 8-18♒

1903	☉	☽	☿	♀	♂	♃	♄	♅	♆	♇
JAN.	10♑	8♒	21♑	18♑	5♎	18♒	28♑	23♐	2♋	18♊
FEB.	11♒	24♓	14♒	27♒	15	25	2♒	24	1	18
MAR.	10♓	4♈	13♒	2♈	16	2♓	5	25	1	18
APR.	11♈	24♉	29♓	10♉	6	9	7	26	1	18
MAY	10♉	2♋	28♉	16♊	28♍	16	9	25	2	18
JUNE	10♊	26♌	13♊	22♋	0♎	21	9	24	3	19
JULY	8♋	4♎	17♊	24♌	11	23	8	23	4	20
AUG.	8♌	22♏	14♌	21♍	27	23	6	22	5	20
SEPT.	8♍	7♑	4♎	1♎	16♏	20	4	22	6	21
OCT.	7♎	9♒	12♎	17♍	6♐	16	3	22	6	21
NOV.	8♏	23♓	26♎	25♍	29	14	3	23	6	20
DEC.	8♐	27♈	14♐	21♎	22♑	14	5	25	5	20

☿ ℞ Jan. 25-19♒ D. Feb. 15-4♒ ℞ May 23-16♊ D. June 16-8♊ ℞ Sept. 21-18♎ D. Oct. 13-3♎ ♀ ℞ Aug. 28-2♎ D. Oct. 10-16♍ ♂ ℞ Feb. 19-16♎ D. May 10-27♍

1904	☉	☽	☿	♀	♂	♃	♄	♅	♆	♇
JAN.	10♑	16♊	29♑	26♏	16♒	18♓	8♒	27♐	4♋	19♊
FEB.	11♒	9♌	18♑	3♑	10♓	24	12	28	4	19
MAR.	10♓	2♍	21♒	8♒	3♈	0♈	15	29	3	19
APR.	11♈	25♎	17♈	16♓	26	8	18	0♑	3	19
MAY	11♉	1♐	26♉	23♈	18♉	15	20	0	4	19
JUNE	11♊	18♑	19♉	1♊	10♊	21	21	29♐	5	20
JULY	9♋	21♒	29♊	7♋	1♋	26	20	28	6	21
AUG.	9♌	4♈	0♍	15♌	21	0♉	18	26	7	21
SEPT.	9♍	20♉	1♎	24♍	11♌	0	16	26	8	22
OCT.	8♎	25♊	20♍	1♏	0♍	27♈	15	26	8	22
NOV.	9♏	16♌	9♏	9♐	19	23	15	27	8	21
DEC.	9♐	24♍	26♐	16♑	7♎	21	16	29	8	21

☿ ℞ Jan. 9-3♒ D. Jan. 29-17♑ ℞ May 3-26♉ D. May 26-17♉ ℞ Sept. 3-1♎ D. Sept. 25-17♍ ℞ Dec. 23-17♑

1905	☉	☽	☿	♀	♂	♃	♄	♅	♆	♇
JAN.	10♑	17♏	8♑	23♒	24♎	21♈	19♒	1♑	7♋	20♊
FEB.	12♒	8♑	19♑	28♓	9♏	24	22	2	6	20
MAR.	10♓	17♑	3♓	26♈	20	29	25	4	5	20
APR.	11♈	3♓	0♉	14♉	25	5♉	29	4	5	20
MAY	10♉	6♈	28♈	4♉	20	12	1♓	4	6	20
JUNE	10♊	20♉	18♉	2♉	10	20	3	3	7	21
JULY	9♋	24♊	17♋	23♉	10	26	3	2	8	22
AUG.	9♌	13♌	6♍	25♊	20	2♊	1	1	9	22
SEPT.	8♍	5♎	4♍	0♌	6♐	6	29♒	0	10	23
OCT.	8♎	14♏	29♍	5♍	26	6	27	0	10	23
NOV.	8♏	7♑	21♏	13♎	18♑	4	26	1	10	22
DEC.	9♐	12♒	0♑	21♏	10♒	0	27	3	10	22

☿ D. Jan. 12-1♑ ℞ Apr. 14-7♉ D. May 8-27♈ ℞ Aug. 17-14♍ D. Sept. 9-1♍ ℞ Dec. 7-1♑ D. Dec. 27-15♐ ♀ ℞ Apr. 7-15♉ D. May 19-28♈ ♂ ℞ Apr. 4-15♏ D. June 18-8♏

1906	☉	☽	☿	♀	♂	♃	♄	♅	♆	♇
JAN.	10♑	28♓	18♐	0♑	4♓	27♉	29♒	5♑	9♋	21♊
FEB.	12♒	12♉	28♑	9♒	27	27	3♓	6	8	21
MAR.	10♓	19♉	18♓	14♓	18♈	29	6	8	8	21
APR.	11♈	3♋	17♈	22♈	11♉	4♊	10	8	8	21
MAY	10♉	7♌	14♈	29♉	2♊	10	13	8	8	21
JUNE	10♊	26♍	1♊	8♋	23	17	15	8	9	22
JULY	9♋	4♏	1♌	13♌	13♋	24	15	6	10	23
AUG.	8♌	28♐	26♌	19♍	3♌	0♋	14	5	11	23
SEPT.	8♍	20♒	20♌	24♎	23	6	12	5	12	24
OCT.	7♎	25♓	13♎	23♏	12♍	10	10	5	13	24
NOV.	8♏	12♉	0♐	14♐	1♎	11	8	5	13	23
DEC.	8♐	14♊	5♐	6♐	20	9	9	7	12	23

☿ ℞ Mar. 27 18♈ D. Apr. 19-8♈ ℞ July 30-26♌ D. Aug. 23-14♌ ℞ Nov. 21-15♐ D. Dec. 10-28♏ ♀ ℞ Nov. 21-15♐ D. Dec. 10-29♏

1907	☉	☽	☿	♀	♂	♃	♄	♅	♆	♇
JAN.	10♑	29♋	22♐	2♐	9♏	5♋	10♓	9♑	11♋	22♊
FEB.	11♒	15♍	11♒	25♐	28	2	13	10	10	22
MAR.	10♓	25♍	28♓	24♑	14♐	1	17	12	10	22
APR.	11♈	16♍	19♓	29♒	0♑	3	20	13	10	22
MAY	10♉	25♐	18♈	5♈	12	7	24	13	10	22
JUNE	10♊	18♒	20♊	12♉	19	13	26	12	11	23
JULY	8♋	25♓	4♌	18♊	15	19	27	11	12	24
AUG.	8♌	13♉	27♋	26♋	7	26	27	10	13	24
SEPT.	8♍	27♊	2♍	4♍	11	3♌	25	9	14	25
OCT.	7♎	29♋	25♎	12♎	23	8	23	9	15	25
NOV.	8♏	13♍	29♏	20♏	12♒	12	21	10	15	24
DEC.	8♐	17♎	18♏	28♐	2♓	14	21	11	14	24

☿ ℞ Mar. 9-2♈ D. Apr. 1-19♓ ℞ July 12-7♌ D. Aug. 5-26♋ ℞ Nov. 4-0♐ D. Nov. 24-14♏ ♂ ℞ June 6-19♑ D. Aug. 10-7♑

1908	☉	☽	☿	♀	♂	♃	♄	♅	♆	♇
JAN.	10♑	6♐	2♑	6♒	23♓	12♌	22♓	13♑	14♋	23♊
FEB.	11♒	29♑	24♒	15♓	15♈	8	25	14	13	23
MAR.	11♓	22♒	8♓	20♈	5♉	5	28	16	12	23
APR.	11♈	15♈	14♓	25♉	26	4	2♈	17	12	23
MAY	11♉	21♉	3♉	26♊	16♊	5	5	17	13	23
JUNE	11♊	8♋	3♋	19♋	6♋	9	8	16	13	24
JULY	9♋	10♌	15♋	16♋	26	14	10	15	14	25
AUG.	9♌	25♍	21♋	6♋	16♌	21	10	14	16	25
SEPT.	9♍	10♏	19♍	23♋	5♍	28	9	13	16	26
OCT.	8♎	16♐	3♏	23♌	24	4♍	7	13	17	26
NOV.	9♏	7♒	0♏	28♍	14♎	9	4	14	17	26
DEC.	9♐	17♓	27♏	4♏	4♏	13	3	15	17	25

☿ ℞ Feb. 21-15♓ D. Mar. 14-1♓ ℞ June 22-18♋ D. July 16-8♋ ℞ Oct. 18-14♏ D. Nov. 7-28♎ ♀ ℞ June 15-22♋ D. July 28-5♋

1909	☉	☽	☿	♀	♂	♃	♄	♅	♆	♇
JAN.	10♑	9♉	15♑	12♐	24♏	15♍	4♈	17♑	16♋	24♊
FEB.	12♒	29♊	28♒	21♑	15♐	13	6	18	15	24
MAR.	10♓	8♋	15♒	26♒	4♑	9	9	20	14	24
APR.	11♈	24♌	22♓	4♈	24	6	13	21	14	24
MAY	10♉	26♍	21♉	11♉	14♒	5	17	21	15	24
JUNE	10♊	10♏	28♊	19♊	4♓	6	20	21	15	25
JULY	9♋	14♐	20♊	26♋	21	10	22	20	17	25
AUG.	9♌	3♒	5♌	4♍	4♈	15	23	18	18	26
SEPT.	8♍	27♓	1♎	11♎	6	21	23	17	19	27
OCT.	8♎	6♉	27♎	17♏	29♓	28	21	17	19	27
NOV.	8♏	27♊	21♎	23♐	26	4♎	18	18	19	27
DEC.	9♐	2♌	8♐	26♑	4♈	10	17	19	19	26

☿ ℞ Feb. 3-29♒ D. Feb. 24-13♒ ℞ June 3-28♊ D. June 27-19♊ ℞ Oct. 2-27♎ D. Oct. 22-12♎ ♂ R. Aug. 24-7♈ D. Oct. 24-25♓

1910	☉	☽	☿	♀	♂	♃	♄	♅	♆	♇
JAN.	10♑	18♍	26♑	23♒	18♈	13♎	17♈	21♑	18♋	26♊
FEB.	12♒	1♏	29♑	29♒	5♉	15	18	22	17	25
MAR.	10♓	9♏	15♒	15♒	22	13	21	24	17	25
APR.	11♈	23♐	6♈	27♒	11♊	10	24	25	17	25
MAY	10♉	27♑	1♊	24♓	0♋	6	28	25	17	25
JUNE	10♊	17♓	0♊	28♈	19	5	2♉	25	18	26
JULY	9♋	26♈	20♊	2♊	8♌	6	5	24	19	27
AUG.	8♌	19♊	22♌	9♋	27	10	6	23	20	27
SEPT.	8♍	11♌	5♎	16♌	17♍	15	6	22	21	28
OCT.	7♎	16♍	28♍	23♍	6♎	21	5	21	21	28
NOV.	8♏	2♏	1♏	2♏	27	28	3	22	22	28
DEC.	8♐	4♐	19♐	10♐	17♏	4♏	1	23	21	27

☿ ℞ Jan. 18-12♒ D. Feb. 8-27♑ ℞ May 15-8♊ D. June 8-29♉ ℞ Sept. 14-11♎ D. Oct. 6-26♍ ♀ ℞ Jan. 23-1♓ D. Mar. 5-15♒

1911	☉	☽	☿	♀	♂	♃	♄	♅	♆	♇
JAN.	10♑	19♑	26♑	19♑	8♐	10♏	0♉	24♑	20♋	27♊
FEB.	12♒	7♓	16♑	28♒	0♑	13	1	26	20	26
MAR.	10♓	16♓	24♒	2♈	21	15	3	28	19	26
APR.	11♈	7♉	23♈	10♉	14♒	13	6	29	19	26
MAY	10♉	16♊	17♉	16♊	6♓	10	10	29	19	26
JUNE	10♊	9♌	16♉	22♋	29	6	14	29	20	27
JULY	9♋	16♍	5♋	24♌	20♈	5	17	28	21	28
AUG.	8♌	3♏	3♍	21♍	11♉	6	19	27	22	28
SEPT.	8♍	17♐	23♍	28♍	28	10	20	26	23	29
OCT.	7♎	19♑	21♍	14♍	9♊	15	20	25	24	29
NOV.	8♏	3♓	13♏	24♍	9	21	17	26	24	29
DEC.	8♐	7♈	28♐	22♋	0	28	15	27	23	28

☿ ℞ Jan. 2-26♑ D. Jan. 22-10♑ ℞ Apr. 25-18♉ D. May 19-9♉ ℞ Aug. 27-24♍ D. Sept. 19-10♍ ℞ Dec. 16-10♑ ♀ ℞ Aug. 25-29♍ D. Oct. 7-13♍ ♂ ℞ Oct. 19-11♊ D Dec. 30-24♉

1912	☉	☽	☿	♀	♂	♃	♄	♅	♆	♇
JAN.	10♑	27♉	25♐	26♍	24♉	5♐	14♉	28♑	23♋	28♊
FEB.	11♒	20♋	22♑	3♑	1♊	10	14	0♒	22	27
MAR.	11♓	14♌	10♓	8♒	12	14	15	2	21	27
APR.	11♈	6♎	29♈	16♓	28	15	18	3	21	27
MAY	11♉	12♏	19♈	23♈	14♋	14	22	3	21	27
JUNE	12♊	28♐	23♉	1♊	2♌	11	26	3	22	28
JULY	9♋	1♒	25♋	8♋	20	7	29	2	23	29
AUG.	9♌	15♓	5♍	16♌	10♍	6	2♊	1	24	29
SEPT.	9♍	1♉	24♌	24♍	29	7	4	0	25	0♋
OCT.	8♎	8♊	6♎	1♏	19♎	11	4	0	26	0
NOV.	9♏	0♌	26♏	10♐	10♏	16	2	0	26	0
DEC.	9♐	9♍	24♐	16♑	2♐	23	0	1	26	29♊

☿ D. Jan. 5-14♐ ℞ Apr. 6-0♉ D. Apr. 29-19♈ ℞ Aug. 9-7♍ D. Sept. 2-24♌ ℞ Nov. 29-25♐ D. Dec. 19-8♐

1913	☉	☽	☿	♀	♂	♃	♄	♅	♆	♇
JAN.	10♑	1♏	19♐	23♒	23♐	0♑	28♉	2♒	25♋	29♊
FEB.	12♒	20♐	4♒	28♓	16♑	7	27	4	24	28
MAR.	10♓	29♐	24♓	26♈	8♒	12	28	6	24	28
APR.	11♈	14♒	3♈	12♉	2♓	16	1♊	7	23	28
MAY	10♉	16♓	14♈	0♉	25	18	4	8	23	28
JUNE	10♊	0♉	10♊	1♉	18♈	17	8	7	24	29
JULY	9♋	4♊	4♌	23♉	11♉	13	12	7	25	0♋
AUG.	9♌	24♋	14♌	25♊	2♊	10	15	5	26	0
SEPT.	8♍	18♍	25♌	0♌	22	8	17	4	27	1
OCT.	8♎	26♎	19♎	6♍	8♋	9	18	4	28	1
NOV.	9♏	17♐	2♐	14♎	21	13	17	4	28	1
DEC.	9♐	22♑	23♏	21♏	24	18	15	5	28	0

☿ ℞ Mar. 19-12♈ D. Apr. 11-0♈ ℞ July 22-18♌ D. Aug. 14-7♌ ℞ Nov. 13-9♐ D. Dec. 3-23♏ ♀ ℞ Apr. 4-12♉ D. May 16-26♈ ♂ ℞ Nov. 27-25♋

1914	☉	☽	☿	♀	♂	♃	♄	♅	♆	♇
JAN.	10♑	7♓	27♐	0♑	16♋	25♑	13♊	6♒	27♋	0♋
FEB.	12♒	21♈	17♒	9♒	7	3♒	11	8	26	29♊
MAR.	10♓	29♈	25♓	14♓	7	9	12	9	26	29
APR.	11♈	14♊	14♓	23♈	16	15	13	11	25	29
MAY	10♉	19♋	23♈	0♊	0♌	20	16	12	26	29
JUNE	10♊	9♍	27♊	8♋	16	22	20	12	26	0♋
JULY	9♋	18♎	29♋	13♌	3♍	22	24	11	27	1
AUG.	8♌	11♐	20♋	20♍	22	19	28	10	28	1
SEPT.	8♍	2♒	10♍	24♎	11♎	15	1♋	9	29	2
OCT.	7♎	7♓	29♎	23♏	1♏	13	2	8	0♌	2
NOV.	8♏	22♈	21♏	12♐	23	13	2	8	0	2
DEC.	8♐	25♉	20♏	2♐	15♐	17	0	9	0	2

☿ ℞ Mar. 2-25♓ D. Mar. 24 11♓ ℞ July 4-29♋ D. July 27-19♋ ℞ Oct. 28-23♏ D. Nov. 17-7♏ ♀ ℞ Nov. 8-12♐ D. Dec. 18-27♏ ♂ D. Feb. 13-6♋

1915	☉	☽	☿	♀	♂	♃	♄	♅	♆	♇
JAN.	10♑	10♋	8♑	1♐	8♑	22♒	28♊	10♒	0♌	1♋
FEB.	12♒	28♌	29♒	25♐	2♒	29	26	12	29♋	0
MAR.	10♓	6♍	25♒	24♑	24	6♓	25	13	28	0
APR.	11♈	28♎	16♓	0♓	18♓	13	26	15	28	0
MAY	10♉	7♐	10♉	5♈	11♈	20	29	16	28	1
JUNE	10♊	0♒	3♋	12♉	5♉	25	2♋	16	28	1
JULY	9♋	6♓	2♋	19♊	27	28	6	15	29	2
AUG.	8♌	23♈	24♋	27♋	18♊	28	10	14	0♌	3
SEPT.	8♍	7♊	24♍	5♍	8♋	26	14	13	2	3
OCT.	7♎	8♋	3♏	12♎	26	22	15	12	2	3
NOV.	8♏	23♌	21♎	21♏	13♌	19	17	12	3	3
DEC.	8♐	27♍	0♐	28♐	25	19	16	12	3	3

☿ ℞ Feb. 13-8♓ D. Mar. 6-23♒ ℞ June 14-9♋ D. July 8-0♋
℞ Oct. 10-7♏ D. Oct. 31-21♎

1916	☉	☽	☿	♀	♂	♃	♄	♅	♆	♇
JAN.	10♑	18♏	19♑	7♒	0♍	22♓	13♋	14♒	2♌	2♋
FEB.	11♒	11♑	19♒	15♓	23♌	28	11	15	1	2
MAR.	11♓	5♒	13♒	20♈	13	4♈	10	17	0	1
APR.	11♈	27♓	28♓	26♉	11	12	10	19	0	1
MAY	11♉	2♉	28♉	26♊	19	19	12	19	0	2
JUNE	11♊	18♊	17♊	18♋	2♍	25	15	20	1	2
JULY	9♋	21♋	18♊	13♋	17	1♉	19	19	2	3
AUG.	9♌	5♍	13♌	4♋	6♎	4	23	18	3	4
SEPT.	9♍	23♎	4♎	23♋	25	5	26	17	4	4
OCT.	8♎	0♐	16♎	23♌	15♏	3	29	16	5	4
NOV.	9♏	22♑	25♎	28♍	8♐	29♈	1♌	16	5	4
DEC.	9♐	1♓	13♐	4♏	0♑	26	0	16	5	4

☿ ℞ Jan. 27-22♒ D. Feb. 18-6♒ ℞ May 25-19♊ D. June 18-11♊
℞ Sept. 23-21♎ D. Oct. 14-5♎ ♀ ℞ June 12-20♋ D. July 25-3♋
♂ ℞ Jan. 1-0♍ D. Mar. 22-10♌

1917	☉	☽	☿	♀	♂	♃	♄	♅	♆	♇
JAN.	11♑	23♈	0♒	13♐	24♑	26♈	28♋	18♒	4♌	3♋
FEB.	12♒	11♊	20♑	21♑	18♒	28	26	19	3	3
MAR.	11♓	19♊	19♒	26♒	10♓	3♉	24	21	3	2
APR.	11♈	4♌	14♈	5♈	4♈	9	24	22	2	2
MAY	11♉	5♍	29♉	12♉	27	16	25	23	2	3
JUNE	10♊	20♎	21♉	20♊	20♉	24	27	24	3	3
JULY	9♋	24♏	26♊	27♋	12♊	0♊	1♌	23	4	4
AUG.	9♌	15♑	28♌	5♍	3♋	6	5	22	5	5
SEPT.	8♍	8♓	3♎	12♎	23	10	9	21	6	5
OCT.	8♎	17♈	20♍	18♏	12♌	12	12	20	7	5
NOV.	8♏	8♊	7♏	24♐	29	10	14	20	7	5
DEC.	9♐	12♋	24♐	26♑	15♍	6	15	20	7	5

☿ ℞ Jan. 10-6♒ D. Jan. 31-20♑ ℞ May 6-29♉ D. May 30-21♉
℞ Sept. 6-4♎ D. Sept. 28-20♍ ℞ Dec. 25-20♑

1918	☉	☽	☿	♀	♂	♃	♄	♅	♆	♇
JAN.	10♑	27♌	15♑	22♒	27♍	3♊	13♌	21♒	6♌	4♋
FEB.	12♒	11♎	18♑	25♒	3♎	2	11	23	6	4
MAR.	10♓	19♎	0♓	13♒	29♍	3	9	25	5	3
APR.	11♈	5♐	28♈	26♒	18	8	8	26	4	3
MAY	10♉	10♑	3♉	24♓	14	14	8	27	4	4
JUNE	10♊	1♓	17♉	28♈	21	20	10	28	5	4
JULY	9♋	11♈	14♋	3♊	4♎	27	13	27	6	5
AUG.	8♌	4♊	5♍	9♋	21	4♋	17	26	7	6
SEPT.	8♍	23♋	9♍	17♌	10♏	10	21	25	8	6
OCT.	7♎	28♌	27♍	24♍	0♐	14	24	24	9	7
NOV.	8♏	12♎	19♏	3♏	23	16	27	24	9	6
DEC.	8♐	15♏	0♑	10♐	15♑	15	28	24	9	6

☿ D. Jan. 14-3♑ ℞ Apr. 17-10♉ D. May 10-0♉ ℞ Aug. 19-17♍
D. Sept. 12-3♍ ℞ Dec. 9-4♑ D. Dec. 29-18♐ ♀ ℞ Jan. 21-28♒
D. Mar. 3-13♒ ♂ ℞ Feb. 4-3♎ D. Apr. 26-14♍

1919	☉	☽	☿	♀	♂	♃	♄	♅	♆	♇
JAN.	10♑	0♑	18♐	19♑	10♒	11♋	28♌	25♒	9♌	5♋
FEB.	12♒	18♒	26♑	28♒	4♓	7	26	27	8	5
MAR.	10♓	27♒	15♓	3♈	26	6	24	28	7	5
APR.	11♈	19♈	22♈	11♉	20♈	7	22	0♓	7	5
MAY	10♉	28♉	14♈	17♊	12♉	11	21	1	7	5
JUNE	10♊	20♋	28♉	22♋	4♊	17	23	2	7	5
JULY	9♋	26♌	29♋	24♌	25	23	25	1	8	6
AUG.	8♌	12♎	29♌	20♍	16♋	0♌	29	1	9	7
SEPT.	8♍	26♏	20♌	25♍	6♌	6	3♍	29♒	10	7
OCT.	7♎	28♐	11♎	11♍	25	12	6	28	11	8
NOV.	8♏	13♒	28♏	24♍	13♍	16	9	28	12	8
DEC.	8♐	18♓	12♐	22♎	1♎	18	11	28	11	7

☿ ℞ Mar. 29-22♈ D. Apr. 22-11♈ ℞ Aug. 2-29♌ D. Aug. 25-17♌
℞ Nov. 23-18♐ D. Dec. 13-2♐ ♀ ℞ Aug. 23-27♍ D. Oct. 4-11♍

1920	☉	☽	☿	♀	♂	♃	♄	♅	♆	♇
JAN.	10♑	9♉	20♐	27♏	17♎	17♌	12♍	29♒	11♌	7♋
FEB.	11♒	2♋	8♒	4♑	0♏	13	10	1♓	10	6
MAR.	11♓	27♋	28♓	9♒	8	10	8	2	9	6
APR.	11♈	18♍	22♓	17♓	7	8	6	4	9	6
MAY	11♉	23♎	18♈	24♈	27♎	9	5	5	9	6
JUNE	11♊	8♐	19♊	2♊	21	13	5	6	9	7
JULY	9♋	11♑	5♌	9♋	27	18	7	6	10	7
AUG.	9♌	26♒	1♌	17♌	10♏	24	10	5	11	8
SEPT.	9♍	14♈	1♍	28♍	28	1♍	14	3	12	9
OCT.	8♎	22♉	24♎	2♏	18♐	7	18	2	13	9
NOV.	9♏	15♋	1♐	10♐	10♑	13	21	2	14	9
DEC.	9♐	24♌	19♏	17♑	3♒	17	24	2	14	8

☿ ℞ Mar. 11-5♈ D. Apr. 3-22♓ ℞ July 14-10♌ D. Aug. 7-29♋
℞ Nov. 6-2♐ D. Nov. 26-16♏ ♂ ℞ Mar. 15-9♏ D. June 2-21♎

1921	☉	☽	☿	♀	♂	♃	♄	♅	♆	♇
JAN.	11♑	14♎	2♑	24♒	27♒	19♍	25♍	3♓	13♌	8♋
FEB.	12♒	1♐	23♒	29♓	21♓	18	24	4	12	7
MAR.	10♓	9♐	14♓	25♈	12♈	14	22	6	12	7
APR.	11♈	23♑	14♓	10♉	5♉	11	20	8	11	7
MAY	11♉	25♒	0♉	27♈	27	9	18	9	11	7
JUNE	10♊	10♈	2♋	0♉	18♊	10	18	10	11	8
JULY	9♋	14♉	19♋	23♉	8♋	13	19	10	12	8
AUG.	9♌	5♋	20♋	25♊	29	19	22	9	13	9
SEPT.	8♍	29♌	17♍	1♌	19♌	25	26	8	14	10
OCT.	8♎	8♎	2♏	6♍	8♍	1♎	29	7	15	10
NOV.	9♏	28♏	6♏	15♎	27	8	3♎	6	16	10
DEC.	9♐	2♑	25♏	22♏	15♎	13	6	6	16	10

☿ ℞ Feb. 22-18♓ D. Mar. 16-3♓ ℞ June 25-21♋
D. July 19-11♋ ℞ Oct. 20-16♏ D. Nov. 9-0♏ ♂ ℞ Apr. 2-10♉
D. May 14-24♈

1922	☉	☽	☿	♀	♂	♃	♄	♅	♆	♇
JAN.	10♑	17♒	13♑	1♑	4♏	17♎	7♎	7♓	15♌	9♋
FEB.	12♒	1♈	0♓	10♒	21	19	7	8	15	8
MAR.	10♓	10♈	16♒	15♓	5♐	18	6	10	14	8
APR.	11♈	26♉	20♓	24♈	18	14	4	11	13	8
MAY	10♉	2♋	18♉	1♊	25	11	2	13	13	8
JUNE	10♊	24♌	0♋	8♋	22	9	1	13	14	9
JULY	9♋	3♎	22♊	14♌	13	10	1	14	14	10
AUG.	8♌	25♏	2♌	20♍	13	13	4	13	15	10
SEPT.	8♍	14♑	29♍	24♎	24	18	7	12	17	11
OCT.	8♎	18♒	0♏	23♏	11♑	25	10	11	17	11
NOV.	8♏	2♈	20♎	10♐	1♒	1♏	14	10	18	11
DEC.	9♐	5♉	6♐	29♏	23	8	17	10	18	11

☿ ℞ Feb. 5-1♓ D. Feb. 27-16♒ ℞ June 6-1♋ D. June 30-22♊
℞ Oct. 3-0♏ D. Oct. 24-15♎ ♀ ℞ Nov. 5-10♐ D. Dec. 16-25♏
♂ ℞ May 8-25♐ D. July 17-11♐

1923	☉	☽	☿	♀	♂	♃	♄	♅	♆	♇
JAN.	10♑	20♊	25♑	0♐	15♓	13♏	19♎	10♓	18♌	10♋
FEB.	12♒	9♌	4♒	25♐	8♈	17	20	12	17	10
MAR.	10♓	17♌	14♒	25♑	28	19	19	13	16	9
APR.	11♈	10♎	3♈	0♓	20♉	18	17	15	16	9
MAY	10♉	19♏	0♊	6♈	10♊	15	15	16	15	9
JUNE	10♊	11♑	5♊	13♉	1♋	11	14	17	16	10
JULY	9♋	16♒	18♊	19♊	21	9	14	18	16	11
AUG.	8♌	2♈	19♌	27♋	11♌	10	15	17	18	11
SEPT.	8♍	16♉	5♎	6♍	0♍	13	18	16	19	12
OCT.	7♎	18♊	3♎	13♎	20	19	21	15	20	12
NOV.	8♏	4♌	29♎	22♏	9♎	25	25	14	20	12
DEC.	8♐	9♍	17♐	29♐	28	2♐	28	14	20	11

☿ ℞ Jan. 20-15♒ D. Feb. 10-29♑ ℞ May 18 11♊ D. June 10-2♊
℞ Sept. 16-14♎ D. Oct. 82-9♍

1924	☉	☽	☿	♀	♂	♃	♄	♅	♆	♇
JAN.	10♑	1♏	28♑	8♒	18♏	8♐	1♏	14♓	20♌	11♋
FEB.	11♒	25♐	16♑	16♓	8♐	14	2	16	19	11
MAR.	11♓	19♑	24♒	21♈	27	18	2	17	18	10
APR.	11♈	9♓	22♈	26♉	16♑	20	0	19	18	10
MAY	11♉	14♈	21♉	26♊	4♒	19	28♎	20	18	11
JUNE	11♊	29♉	17♉	16♋	20	16	26	21	18	11
JULY	9♋	1♋	4♋	9♋	2♓	12	26	22	19	12
AUG.	9♌	17♌	3♍	3♋	5	10	27	21	20	13
SEPT.	9♍	5♎	26♍	23♋	28♒	11	29	20	21	13
OCT.	8♎	13♏	21♍	23♌	26	14	2♏	19	22	13
NOV.	9♏	7♑	13♏	29♍	5♓	20	6	18	22	13
DEC.	9♐	15♒	28♐	5♏	20	26	9	18	23	13

☿ ℞ Jan. 4-29♑ D. Jan. 24-13♑ ℞ Apr. 27-21♉ D. May 21-12♉
℞ Aug. 29-27♍ D. Sept. 21-13♍ ℞ Dec. 18-13♑ ♀ ℞ June 10-18♋
D. July 23-1♋ ♂ ℞ July 24-5♓ D. Sept. 22-25♒

1925	☉	☽	☿	♀	♂	♃	♄	♅	♆	♇
JAN.	11♑	5♈	29♐	13♐	8♈	3♑	12♏	18♓	22♌	13♋
FEB.	12♒	21♉	22♑	22♑	27	10	14	19	21	12
MAR.	10♓	29♉	7♓	27♒	16♉	16	14	21	21	12
APR.	11♈	13♋	0♉	5♈	5♊	20	13	23	20	11
MAY	11♉	15♌	22♈	13♉	25	22	11	24	20	12
JUNE	10♊	0♎	21♉	21♊	14♋	22	9	25	20	12
JULY	9♋	5♏	23♋	27♋	3♌	19	8	25	21	13
AUG.	9♌	26♐	5♍	5♍	23	15	8	25	22	14
SEPT.	9♍	20♒	27♌	13♎	12♍	13	10	24	23	14
OCT.	8♎	28♓	3♎	18♏	2♎	13	12	23	24	15
NOV.	9♏	18♉	24♏	24♐	22	17	16	22	25	15
DEC.	9♐	22♊	27♐	26♑	12♏	22	20	22	25	14

☿ D. Jan. 7-27♐ ℞ Apr. 8-3♉ D. May 3-22♈ ℞ Aug. 12-9♍
D. Sept. 4-26♌ ℞ Dec. 2-27♐ D. Dec. 22-11♐

1926	☉	☽	☿	♀	♂	♃	♄	♅	♆	♇
JAN.	10♑	7♌	18♐	21♒	3♐	29♑	23♏	22♓	24♌	14♋
FEB.	12♒	21♍	2♒	22♒	25	6♒	25	23	24	13
MAR.	10♓	0♎	22♓	10♒	14♑	13	26	25	23	13
APR.	11♈	17♏	9♈	26♒	7♒	19	26	26	22	13
MAY	10♉	23♐	14♈	25♓	28	24	24	28	22	13
JUNE	10♊	16♒	6♊	29♈	21♓	27	21	29	22	13
JULY	9♋	25♓	3♌	3♊	11♈	27	20	29	23	14
AUG.	8♌	17♉	19♌	10♋	0♉	24	19	29	24	15
SEPT.	8♍	5♋	22♌	17♌	14	20	21	28	25	16
OCT.	8♎	8♌	17♎	25♍	19	18	23	27	26	16
NOV.	8♏	22♍	1♐	3♏	12	18	26	26	27	16
DEC.	9♐	25♎	27♏	11♐	5	21	0♐	26	27	16

☿ ℞ Mar. 22-15♈ D. Apr. 14-3♈ ℞ July 25-21♌ D. Aug. 18-9♌
℞ Nov. 16-11♐ D. Dec. 5-25♏ ♀ ℞ Jan. 28-26♒
D. Feb. 28-10♒ ♂ ℞ Sept. 29-19♉ D. Dec. 7-5♉

1927	☉	☽	☿	♀	♂	♃	♄	♅	♆	♇
JAN.	10♑	10♐	25♐	20♑	8♉	26♒	3♐	26♓	27♌	15♋
FEB.	12♒	0♒	14♒	29♒	20	3♓	6	27	26	14
MAR.	10♓	8♒	27♓	4♈	4♊	10	7	28	25	14
APR.	11♈	1♈	15♓	12♉	21	17	8	0♈	25	14
MAY	10♉	10♉	21♈	17♊	8♋	24	6	2	24	14
JUNE	10♊	1♋	24♊	23♋	27	29	4	3	24	15
JULY	9♋	6♌	1♌	24♌	15♌	3♈	2	3	25	15
AUG.	8♌	22♍	22♋	19♍	5♍	3	1	3	26	16
SEPT.	8♍	6♍	7♍	22♍	24	1	2	2	27	17
OCT.	7♎	8♐	27♎	9♍	14♎	27♓	4	1	28	17
NOV.	8♏	24♑	25♏	23♍	4♏	24	7	0	29	17
DEC.	8♐	1♓	19♏	22♎	25	23	10	0	29	17

☿ ℞ Mar. 4-28♓ D. Mar. 27-14♓ ℞ July 6-2♌ D. July 31-22♋
℞ Oct. 30-26♏ D. Nov. 19-10♏ ♀ ℞ Aug. 20-25♍ D. Oct. 3-9♍

1928	☉	☽	☿	♀	♂	♃	♄	♅	♆	♇
JAN.	10♑	23♈	5♑	27♏	17♐	27♓	14♐	0♈	29♌	16♋
FEB.	11♒	16♊	27♒	4♑	10♑	2♈	17	2	28	16
MAR.	11♓	11♋	29♒	10♒	2♒	8	19	2	27	15
APR.	12♈	0♍	16♓	18♓	25	15	19	4	27	15
MAY	11♉	4♎	9♉	24♈	18♓	23	18	5	26	15
JUNE	11♊	19♏	4♋	3♊	12♈	29	16	7	27	16
JULY	9♋	21♐	6♋	9♋	4♉	5♉	14	7	27	17
AUG.	9♌	7♒	24♋	18♌	25	9	13	7	28	17
SEPT.	9♍	27♓	23♍	26♍	14♊	10	13	6	29	18
OCT.	8♎	5♉	4♏	3♏	29	9	14	5	0♍	18
NOV.	10♏	28♊	24♎	11♐	9♋	5	17	4	1	18
DEC.	9♐	6♌	0♐	17♑	7	1	20	4	1	18

☿ ℞ Feb. 16-11♓ D. Mar. 9-26♒ ℞ June 17-12♋ D. July 11-3♋
℞ Oct. 13-10♏ D. Nov. 2-24♎ ♂ ℞ Nov. 12-9♋

1929	☉	☽	☿	♀	♂	♃	♄	♅	♆	♇
JAN.	11♑	26♍	19♑	24♒	25♊	1♉	24♐	4♈	1♍	17♋
FEB.	12♒	11♏	23♒	29♓	21	3	27	5	0	17
MAR.	10♓	19♏	13♒	25♈	27	7	29	6	0	16
APR.	11♈	2♑	26♓	8♉	9♋	13	0♑	8	29♌	16
MAY	11♉	4♒	26♉	24♈	24	20	0	9	29	16
JUNE	10♊	20♓	22♊	29♈	11♌	27	28♐	11	29	17
JULY	9♋	26♈	18♊	24♉	28	4♊	26	11	29	18
AUG.	9♌	18♊	10♌	26♊	17♍	10	24	11	0♍	18
SEPT.	9♍	11♌	3♎	1♌	7♎	15	24	11	1	19
OCT.	8♎	19♍	21♎	7♍	27	16	25	9	2	20
NOV.	9♏	9♏	23♎	15♎	18♏	15	27	8	3	20
DEC.	9♐	12♐	11♐	23♏	9♐	12	0♑	8	4	19

☿ ℞ Jan. 29-24♒ D. Feb. 20-9♒ ℞ May 28-22♊ D. June 21-14♊
℞ Sept. 26-23♎ D. Oct. 17-8♎ ♀ ℞ Mar. 30-8♉ D. May 12-22♈
♂ D. Jan. 27-21♊

1930	☉	☽	☿	♀	♂	♃	♄	♅	♆	♇
JAN.	10♑	27♑	29♑	2♑	2♑	8♊	4♑	8♈	3♍	19♋
FEB.	12♒	12♓	22♑	11♒	26	6	7	8	3	18
MAR.	10♓	21♓	17♒	16♓	18♒	8	10	10	2	18
APR.	11♈	8♉	11♈	24♈	12♓	12	12	11	1	17
MAY	10♉	15♊	0♊	1♊	5♈	17	12	13	1	18
JUNE	10♊	8♌	24♉	9♋	29	24	11	14	1	18
JULY	9♋	17♍	23♊	15♌	21♉	1♋	9	15	1	19
AUG.	8♌	8♏	26♌	20♍	12♊	8	6	15	2	20
SEPT.	8♍	26♐	4♎	24♎	3♋	14	5	15	4	20
OCT.	8♎	28♑	22♍	22♏	20	18	6	14	5	21
NOV.	8♏	12♓	5♏	7♐	5♌	20	7	12	5	21
DEC.	9♐	14♈	22♐	25♏	15	20	10	12	6	21

☿ ℞ Jan. 13-8♒ D. Feb. 3-22♑ ℞ May 9-3♊ D. June 3-24♉
℞ Sept. 9-7♎ D. Oct. 2-22♍ ℞ Dec. 28-22♑ ♀ ℞ Nov. 2-7♐
D. Dec. 13-22♏ ♂ ℞ Dec. 19-17♌

1931	☉	☽	☿	♀	♂	♃	♄	♅	♆	♇
JAN.	10♑	0♊	20♑	29♏	16♌	16♋	14♑	12♈	6♍	20♋
FEB.	12♒	20♋	17♑	25♐	5	12	17	12	5	19
MAR.	10♓	29♋	28♒	25♑	28♋	11	20	13	4	19
APR.	11♈	22♍	27♈	1♓	1♌	11	22	15	3	19
MAY	10♉	0♏	8♉	6♈	11	15	23	17	3	19
JUNE	10♊	21♐	16♉	14♉	25	20	23	18	3	19
JULY	9♋	26♑	10♋	20♊	12♍	27	21	19	4	20
AUG.	8♌	12♓	4♍	28♋	0♎	3♌	19	19	5	21
SEPT.	8♍	26♈	15♍	6♍	20	10	17	19	6	22
OCT.	7♎	28♉	24♍	14♎	10♏	16	17	18	7	22
NOV.	8♏	16♋	17♏	22♏	1♐	20	18	17	8	22
DEC.	8♐	23♌	29♐	0♑	24	23	20	16	8	22

☿ D. Jan. 17-6♑ ℞ Apr. 20-13♉ D. May 14-4♉ ℞ Aug. 22-20♍
D. Sept. 14-6♍ ℞ Dec. 12-6♑ ♂ D. Mar. 9-27♋

1932	☉	☽	☿	♀	♂	♃	♄	♅	♆	♇
JAN.	10♑	16♎	20♐	8♒	17♑	22♌	24♑	15♈	8♍	21♋
FEB.	11♒	9♐	25♑	16♓	11♒	18	27	16	7	21
MAR.	11♓	3♑	14♓	21♈	4♓	15	1♒	17	7	20
APR.	12♈	21♒	25♈	26♉	29	13	3	19	6	20
MAY	11♉	25♓	16♈	26♊	22♈	13	5	21	5	20
JUNE	11♊	9♉	27♉	15♋	15♉	17	5	22	5	21
JULY	9♋	11♊	29♋	6♋	6♊	22	3	23	6	21
AUG.	9♌	28♋	2♍	1♋	28	28	1	23	7	22
SEPT.	10♍	18♍	21♌	23♋	18♋	5♍	29♑	23	8	23
OCT.	8♎	26♎	10♎	24♌	6♌	11	28	22	9	23
NOV.	9♏	20♐	28♏	29♍	24	17	29	21	10	23
DEC.	9♐	27♑	17♐	6♏	8♍	21	1♒	20	10	23

☿ D. Jan. 2-20♐ ℞ Mar. 31-25♈ D. Apr. 24-14♈ ℞ Aug. 4-2♍
D. Aug. 27-19♌ ℞ Nov. 25-21♐ D. Dec. 14-4♐ ♀ ℞ June 8-15♋
D. July 21-29♊

1933	☉	☽	☿	♀	♂	♃	♄	♅	♆	♇
JAN.	11♑	16♓	20♐	14♐	18♍	23♍	4♒	19♈	10♍	23♋
FEB.	12♒	1♉	8♒	23♑	19	22	8	20	10	22
MAR.	10♓	8♉	27♓	28♒	11	19	11	21	9	21
APR.	11♈	22♊	26♓	6♈	2	16	14	23	8	21
MAY	11♉	24♋	16♈	13♉	3	13	16	24	7	21
JUNE	11♊	11♍	15♊	21♊	13	14	16	26	7	22
JULY	9♋	17♎	5♌	28♋	27	17	15	27	8	23
AUG.	9♌	9♐	5♌	6♍	15♎	22	13	27	9	23
SEPT.	9♍	3♒	29♌	13♎	4♏	28	11	27	10	24
OCT.	8♎	11♓	22♎	19♏	24	5♎	10	26	11	24
NOV.	9♏	29♈	2♐	24♐	17♐	11	10	25	12	25
DEC.	9♐	3♊	19♏	26♑	9♑	17	12	24	12	24

☿ ℞ Mar. 14-7♈ D. Apr. 6-25♓ ℞ July 17-13♌ D. Aug. 10-2♌
℞ Nov. 8-5♐ D. Nov. 28-19♏ ♂ ℞ Jan. 21-20♍
D. Apr. 12-1♍

1934	☉	☽	☿	♀	♂	♃	♄	♅	♆	♇
JAN.	10♑	17♋	0♑	20♒	3♒	21♎	14♒	23♈	12♍	24♋
FEB.	12♒	2♍	21♒	18♒	28	23	18	24	12	23
MAR.	10♓	11♍	19♓	8♒	20♓	22	21	25	11	23
APR.	11♈	29♎	13♓	26♒	14♈	19	25	26	10	23
MAY	10♉	7♐	28♈	25♓	7♉	16	27	28	10	23
JUNE	10♊	0♒	0♋	29♈	29	13	28	0♉	10	23
JULY	9♋	9♓	24♋	4♊	20♊	14	28	1	10	24
AUG.	9♌	29♈	19♋	10♋	11♋	17	26	1	11	25
SEPT.	8♍	16♊	14♍	18♌	1♌	22	24	1	12	25
OCT.	8♎	18♋	1♏	25♍	20	28	22	0	13	26
NOV.	8♏	2♍	12♏	4♏	8♍	5♏	22	29♈	14	26
DEC.	9♐	4♎	23♏	12♐	25	11	23	28	15	26

☿ ℞ Feb. 25-20♓ D. Mar. 19-6♓ ℞ June 28-24♋
D. July 22-14♋ ℞ Oct. 23-19♏ D. Nov. 12-3♏ ♀ ℞ Jan. 15-24♒
D. Feb. 26-8♒

Condensed Ephemeris

1935	☉	☽	☿	♀	♂	♃	♄	♅	♆	♇
JAN.	10♑	21♏	11♑	21♑	10♎	17♏	25♒	28♈	15♍	25♋
FEB.	12♒	11♑	0♓	0♓	21	21	28	28	14	25
MAR.	10♓	19♑	19♒	4♈	25	23	2♓	29	13	24
APR.	11♈	13♓	18♓	12♉	18	23	5	0♉	12	24
MAY	10♉	22♈	15♉	18♊	8	20	8	2	12	24
JUNE	10♊	12♊	2♋	23♋	7	16	10	4	12	24
JULY	9♋	17♋	25♊	24♌	16	14	10	5	12	25
AUG.	8♌	1♍	29♋	18♍	2♏	14	9	5	13	26
SEPT.	8♍	16♎	27♍	19♍	20	17	7	5	14	27
OCT.	7♎	19♏	2♏	7♍	10♐	22	5	5	15	27
NOV.	8♏	7♑	20♎	23♍	3♑	28	4	3	16	27
DEC.	8♐	15♒	3♐	22♎	26	5♐	4	2	17	27

☿ ℞ Feb. 8-4♓ D. Mar. 2-19♒ ℞ June 9-4♋ D. July 3-25♊
℞ Oct. 6-3♏ D. Oct. 27-17♎ ♀ ℞ Aug. 18-23♍ D. Sept. 30-7♍
♂ ℞ Feb. 27-25♎ D. May 18-6♎

1936	☉	☽	☿	♀	♂	♃	♄	♅	♆	♇
JAN.	10♑	8♈	23♑	28♏	20♒	12♐	6♓	2♉	17♍	27♋
FEB.	11♒	1♊	10♒	5♑	14♓	18	9	2	16	26
MAR.	11♓	24♊	14♒	10♒	6♈	22	13	3	16	25
APR.	12♈	12♌	2♈	18♓	0♉	24	16	4	15	25
MAY	11♉	15♍	1♊	25♈	22	24	19	6	14	25
JUNE	11♊	29♎	9♊	3♊	13♊	21	22	8	14	26
JULY	9♋	1♐	19♊	10♋	4♋	17	23	9	14	26
AUG.	9♌	18♑	18♌	18♌	24	15	22	10	15	27
SEPT.	9♍	8♓	6♎	26♍	14♌	15	20	9	16	28
OCT.	8♎	17♈	7♎	3♏	3♍	18	18	9	17	29
NOV.	9♏	11♊	28♎	11♐	22	24	16	8	18	29
DEC.	8♐	17♋	16♐	18♑	10♎	0♑	16	6	19	29

☿ ℞ Jan. 23-18♒ D. Feb. 13-2♒ ℞ May 20-14♊ D. June 13-6♊
℞ Sept. 18-16♎ D. Oct. 10-1♎

1937	☉	☽	☿	♀	♂	♃	♄	♅	♆	♇
JAN.	11♑	6♍	0♒	22♒	28♎	7♑	17♓	6♉	19♍	28♋
FEB.	12♒	20♎	18♑	29♓	14♏	14	20	6	18	27
MAR.	11♓	28♎	22♒	25♈	26	20	23	7	18	27
APR.	11♈	12♐	19♈	5♉	5♐	24	27	8	17	26
MAY	11♉	15♑	24♉	21♈	4	27	1♈	10	16	27
JUNE	11♊	2♓	18♉	28♈	24♏	27	3	11	16	27
JULY	9♋	9♈	1♋	24♉	20	24	5	13	17	28
AUG.	9♌	1♊	1♍	26♊	27	20	5	14	17	29
SEPT.	9♍	25♋	0♎	2♌	12♐	18	3	14	18	29
OCT.	8♎	2♍	20♍	8♍	1♑	18	1	13	19	0♌
NOV.	9♏	20♎	11♏	16♎	22	21	29♓	12	20	0
DEC.	9♐	23♏	27♐	23♏	15♒	26	28	11	21	0

☿ ℞ Jan. 6-2♒ D. Jan. 26-15♑ ℞ May 2-24♉ D. May 24-15♉
℞ Sept. 2-0♎ D. Sept. 24-15♍ ℞ Dec. 21-16♑ ♀ ℞ Mar. 28-6♉
D. May 9-19♈ ♂ ℞ Apr. 15-6♐ D. June 27-20♏

1938	☉	☽	☿	♀	♂	♃	♄	♅	♆	♇
JAN.	10♑	7♑	5♑	2♑	8♓	3♒	29♓	10♉	21♍	29♋
FEB.	12♒	23♒	20♑	11♒	1♈	10	2♈	10	21	29
MAR.	10♓	1♓	4♓	16♓	22	17	5	10	20	28
APR.	11♈	20♈	0♉	25♈	14♉	23	8	12	19	28
MAY	10♉	28♉	26♈	2♊	5♊	28	12	14	19	28
JUNE	10♊	21♋	19♉	9♋	26	2♓	15	15	18	28
JULY	9♋	0♍	19♋	15♌	16♋	2	17	17	19	29
AUG.	9♌	20♎	6♍	21♍	6♌	0	18	18	19	0♌
SEPT.	8♍	6♐	1♍	24♎	26	26♒	17	18	20	1
OCT.	8♎	8♑	1♎	22♏	15♍	23	15	18	22	1
NOV.	8♏	21♒	22♏	5♐	5♎	23	13	16	23	2
DEC.	9♐	24♓	29♐	21♏	23	25	11	15	23	1

☿ D. Jan. 10-29♐ ℞ Apr. 12-6♉ D. May 6-25♈ ℞ Aug. 15-12♍
D. Sept. 7-29♌ ℞ Dec. 5-0♑ D. Dec. 24-13♐ ♀ ℞ Oct. 31-5♐
D. Dec. 11-20♏

1939	☉	☽	☿	♀	♂	♃	♄	♅	♆	♇
JAN.	10♑	11♉	18♐	28♏	13♏	1♓	12♈	14♉	23♍	1♌
FEB.	12♒	2♋	0♒	25♐	2♐	7	13	14	23	0
MAR.	10♓	11♋	19♓	25♑	19	14	16	14	22	0
APR.	11♈	4♍	14♈	1♓	6♑	21	20	16	21	29♋
MAY	10♉	13♎	13♈	7♈	21	28	23	17	21	29
JUNE	10♊	3♐	3♊	14♉	2♒	4♈	27	19	21	0♌
JULY	9♋	7♑	2♌	21♊	4	8	0♉	21	21	0
AUG.	8♌	22♒	23♌	29♋	27♑	9	1	22	21	1
SEPT.	8♍	6♈	21♌	7♍	24	7	1	22	23	2
OCT.	7♎	10♉	14♎	14♎	3♒	3	29♈	22	24	3
NOV.	8♏	29♊	0♐	23♏	19	0	27	20	25	3
DEC.	8♐	7♌	2♐	0♑	8♓	29♓	25	19	25	3

☿ ℞ Mar. 25-18♈ D. Apr. 17-6♈ ℞ July 28-24♌ D. Aug. 21-12♌
℞ Nov. 19-14♐ D. Dec. 8-28♏ ♂ ℞ June 23-5♒ D. Aug. 24-24♑

1940	☉	☽	☿	♀	♂	♃	♄	♅	♆	♇
JAN.	10♑	1♎	23♐	9♒	28♓	1♈	24♈	18♉	26♍	2♌
FEB.	11♒	22♏	12♒	17♓	19♈	6	26	18	25	2
MAR.	11♓	16♐	29♓	22♈	9♉	12	12	19	25	1
APR.	12♈	2♒	17♓	27♉	0♊	19	1♉	20	24	1
MAY	11♉	5♓	21♈	26♊	20	27	5	21	23	1
JUNE	11♊	19♈	23♊	13♋	10♋	4♉	9	23	23	1
JULY	9♋	21♉	3♌	2♋	29	9	12	25	23	2
AUG.	9♌	8♋	25♋	0♋	18♌	14	14	26	24	3
SEPT.	9♍	29♌	6♍	23♋	8♍	15	15	26	25	4
OCT.	8♎	8♎	27♎	24♌	27	14	14	26	26	4
NOV.	9♏	1♐	28♏	0♎	17♎	11	11	25	27	4
DEC.	9♐	8♑	19♏	6♏	7♏	7	9	24	27	4

☿ ℞ Mar. 6-0♈ D. Mar. 29-17♓ ℞ July 9-5♌ D. Aug. 2-25♋
℞ Nov. 2-28♏ D. Nov. 21-12♏ ♀ ℞ June 5-13♋
D. July 19-27♊

1941	☉	☽	☿	♀	♂	♃	♄	♅	♆	♇
JAN.	11♑	25♒	5♑	15♐	28♏	6♉	8♉	23♉	28♍	4♌
FEB.	12♒	10♈	27♒	23♑	19♐	7	8	22	27	3
MAR.	11♓	18♈	4♓	28♒	8♑	11	10	23	27	2
APR.	11♈	2♊	15♓	7♈	29	17	13	24	26	2
MAY	11♉	5♋	5♉	14♉	20♒	24	17	25	25	2
JUNE	11♊	23♌	4♋	22♊	11♓	1♊	21	27	25	3
JULY	9♋	0♎	11♋	29♋	0♈	8	24	29	25	3
AUG.	9♌	24♏	22♋	6♍	15	14	27	0♊	26	4
SEPT.	9♍	17♑	21♍	14♎	24	19	28	0	27	5
OCT.	8♎	23♒	3♏	19♏	20	21	28	0	28	6
NOV.	9♏	10♈	28♎	25♐	12	21	26	29♉	29	6
DEC.	9♐	13♉	28♏	26♑	14	17	24	28	0♎	6

☿ ℞ Feb. 17-13♓ D. Mar. 12-29♒ ℞ June 20-16♋
D. July 14-6♋ ℞ Oct. 15-12♏ D. Nov. 5-26♎ ♂ ℞ Sept. 7-24♈
D. Nov. 10-11♈

1942	☉	☽	☿	♀	♂	♃	♄	♅	♆	♇
JAN.	10♑	28♊	17♑	19♒	25♈	13♊	22♉	27♉	0♎	5♌
FEB.	12♒	13♌	27♒	14♒	11♉	11	22	26	0	4
MAR.	10♓	22♌	14♒	6♒	27	12	23	27	29♍	4
APR.	11♈	11♎	23♓	25♒	15♊	16	26	28	28	4
MAY	10♉	19♏	23♉	25♓	3♋	21	29	29	27	4
JUNE	10♊	13♑	26♊	29♈	22	28	3♊	1♊.	27	4
JULY	9♋	21♒	19♊	4♊	11♌	5♋	7	3	27	5
AUG.	9♌	10♈	7♌	11♋	0♍	12	10	4	28	5
SEPT.	8♍	26♉	2♎	19♌	20	18	12	5	29	6
OCT.	8♎	28♊	26♎	26♍	9♎	23	12	4	0♎	7
NOV.	8♏	11♌	22♎	5♏	0♏	25	11	4	1	7
DEC.	9♐	14♍	9♐	12♐	20	25	9	2	2	7

☿ ℞ Feb. 2-27♒ D. Feb. 23-12♒ ℞ June 2-26♊ D. June 25-17♊
℞ Sept. 29-26♎ D. Oct. 20-11♎ ♀ ℞ Jan. 13-21♒
D. Feb. 23-6♒

1943	☉	☽	☿	♀	♂	♃	♄	♅	♆	♇
JAN.	10♑	1♏	27♑	21♑	12♐	22♋	7♊	1♊	2♎	7♌
FEB.	12♒	23♐	26♑	0♓	4♑	18	6	1	2	6
MAR.	10♓	3♑	16♒	5♈	25	15	6	1	1	5
APR.	11♈	26♒	8♈	13♉	18♒	16	8	2	0	5
MAY	10♉	4♈	1♊	18♊	11♓	19	11	3	0	5
JUNE	10♊	23♉	27♉	24♋	4♈	24	15	5	29♍	5
JULY	9♋	27♊	21♊	24♌	25	0♌	19	7	29	6
AUG.	8♌	12♌	23♌	17♍	16♉	7	23	8	0♎	7
SEPT.	8♍	27♍	5♎	15♍	5♊	14	25	9	1	8
OCT.	7♎	1♏	25♍	5♍	18	20	27	9	2	8
NOV.	8♏	21♐	3♏	22♍	22	24	26	8	3	9
DEC.	8♐	29♍	20♐	22♎	14	27	24	7	4	9

☿ ℞ Jan. 16-11♒ D. Feb. 6-25♑ ℞ May 13-6♊ D. June 5-27♉
℞ Sept. 12-9♎ D. Oct. 4-25♍ ℞ Dec. 31-25♑ ♀ ℞ Aug. 16-21♍
D. Sept. 27-4♍ ♂ ℞ Oct. 28-22♊

1944	☉	☽	☿	♀	♂	♃	♄	♅	♆	♇
JAN.	10♑	23♓	25♑	28♏	5♊	27♌	22♊	6♊	4♎	8♌
FEB.	12♒	14♉	16♑	5♑	8	23	20	5	4	8
MAR.	11♓	6♊	27♒	11♒	18	20	20	5	3	7
APR.	12♈	23♋	26♈	19♓	2♋	17	21	6	3	6
MAY	11♉	25♌	13♉	26♈	18	18	24	7	2	6
JUNE	11♊	8♎	17♉	4♊	6♌	21	28	9	2	7
JULY	9♋	11♏	9♋	11♋	24	25	1♋	11	2	7
AUG.	9♌	28♐	5♍	19♌	13♍	1♍	5	12	2	8
SEPT.	9♍	20♒	19♍	27♍	2♎	8	8	13	3	9
OCT.	8♎	28♓	24♍	4♏	22	14	10	13	4	10
NOV.	9♏	22♉	16♏	12♐	13♏	20	11	12	5	10
DEC.	9♐	28♊	0♑	18♑	4♐	25	9	11	6	10

☿ D. Jan. 20-9♑ Apr. 22-16♉ D. May 16-7♉ ℞ Aug. 24-22♍
D. Sept. 16-9♍ ℞ Dec. 14-9♑ ♂ D. Jan. 10-5♊

1945	☉	☽	☿	♀	♂	♃	♄	♅	♆	♇
JAN.	11♑	15♌	23♐	25♒	27♐	27♍	7♋	10♊	6♎	10♌
FEB.	12♒	0♎	24♑	29♓	20♑	27	5	9	6	9
MAR.	11♓	8♎	11♓	24♈	12♒	24	4	9	6	8
APR.	11♈	22♏	28♈	3♉	6♓	20	4	10	5	8
MAY	11♉	26♐	18♈	18♈	29	18	7	11	4	8
JUNE	11♊	15♒	24♉	27♈	23♈	18	10	13	4	8
JULY	9♋	23♓	26♋	24♉	14♉	21	14	15	4	9
AUG.	9♌	16♉	4♍	27♊	6♊	25	18	16	4	10
SEPT.	9♍	8♋	22♌	2♌	26	1♎	21	17	5	11
OCT.	8♎	15♌	7♎	8♍	13♋	8	24	17	6	11
NOV.	9♏	1♎	27♏	17♎	27	14	25	17	7	12
DEC.	9♐	4♏	22♐	24♏	3♌	20	24	16	8	12

☿ D. Jan. 3-23♐ ℞ Apr. 4-28♈ D. Apr. 27-17♈ ℞ Aug. 7-5♍ D. Aug. 30-22♌ ℞ Nov. 27-23♐ D. Dec. 17-7♐ ♀ ℞ Mar. 25-4♉ D. May 7-17♈ ♂ ℞ Dec. 5-3♌

1946	☉	☽	☿	♀	♂	♃	♄	♅	♆	♇
JAN.	10♑	18♐	19♐	3♑	28♋	25♎	22♋	14♊	9♎	11♌
FEB.	12♒	4♒	5♒	12♒	17	27	20	14	8	11
MAR.	10♓	12♒	25♓	17♓	14	27	18	13	8	10
APR.	11♈	2♈	0♈	26♈	22	24	18	14	7	10
MAY	11♉	10♉	15♈	3♊	4♌	20	20	15	6	9
JUNE	10♊	3♋	12♊	10♋	20	18	20	17	6	10
JULY	9♋	11♌	5♌	16♌	6♍	18	26	19	6	10
AUG.	9♌	0♎	11♌	21♍	25	21	0♌	20	6	11
SEPT.	8♍	15♏	26♌	25♎	15♎	25	4	22	7	12
OCT.	8♎	17♐	20♎	21♏	5♏	1♏	7	22	8	13
NOV.	8♏	1♒	2♐	2♐	26	8	9	21	9	13
DEC.	9♐	4♓	21♏	18♏	18♐	14	9	20	10	13

☿ ℞ Mar. 17-10♈ D. Apr. 9-28♓ ℞ July 20-16♌ D. Aug. 13-5♌ ℞ Nov. 11-7♐ D. Dec. 2-21♏ ♀ ℞ Oct. 28-3♐ D. Dec. 8-17♏ ♂ D. Feb. 22-14♋

1947	☉	☽	☿	♀	♂	♃	♄	♅	♆	♇
JAN.	10♑	22♈	28♐	27♏	11♑	20♏	7♌	19♊	11♎	13♌
FEB.	12♒	14♊	18♒	25♐	5♒	25	4	18	11	12
MAR.	10♓	25♊	23♓	26♑	27	27	3	18	10	12
APR.	11♈	18♌	14♓	2♓	22♓	27	2	18	9	11
MAY	10♉	26♍	25♈	8♈	15♈	24	3	20	9	11
JUNE	10♊	14♏	28♊	15♉	8♉	20	5	21	8	11
JULY	9♋	18♐	27♋	21♊	0♊	18	8	23	8	12
AUG.	8♌	2♒	19♋	29♋	22	18	12	25	9	13
SEPT.	8♍	17♓	11♍	8♍	12♋	21	16	26	9	14
OCT.	7♎	22♈	0♏	15♎	0♌	26	19	26	10	14
NOV.	8♏	13♊	18♏	24♏	17	2♐	22	26	12	15
DEC.	8♐	21♋	21♏	1♑	0♍	8	23	25	12	15

☿ ℞ Feb. 28-23♓ D. Mar. 22-9♓ ℞ July 2-27♋ D. July 26-17♋ ℞ Oct. 26-21♏ D. Nov. 15-6♏

1948	☉	☽	☿	♀	♂	♃	♄	♅	♆	♇
JAN.	10♑	15♍	9♑	10♒	7♍	15♐	22♌	23♊	13♎	14♌
FEB.	12♒	5♏	29♒	18♓	4	21	20	22	13	14
MAR.	11♓	27♏	22♒	22♈	23♌	26	18	22	12	13
APR.	12♈	12♑	18♓	27♉	18	29	16	23	12	13
MAY	11♉	14♒	14♉	26♊	24	29	16	24	11	13
JUNE	11♊	28♓	4♋	11♋	6♍	26	18	25	10	13
JULY	10♋	1♉	29♊	29♊	21	22	20	27	10	14
AUG.	9♌	19♊	28♋	29♊	9♎	19	19	29	11	14
SEPT.	9♍	11♌	27♍	23♋	29	20	28	0♋	12	15
OCT.	8♎	20♓	3♏	24♌	19♏	22	1♍	1	13	16
NOV.	9♏	12♏	21♎	0♎	11♐	27	4	0	14	16
DEC.	9♐	18♐	3♐	7♏	4♑	3♑	6	29♊	15	16

☿ ℞ Feb. 11-7♓ D. Mar. 4-22♒ ℞ June 11-7♋ D. July 6-28♊ ℞ Oct. 8-5♏ D. Oct. 29-20♎ ♀ ℞ June 3-11♋ D. July 16-25♊ ♂ ℞ Jan. 9-8♍ D. Mar. 30-18♌

1949	☉	☽	☿	♀	♂	♃	♄	♅	♆	♇
JAN.	11♑	5♒	22♑	15♐	27♑	11♑	6♍	28♊	15♎	16♌
FEB.	12♒	20♓	15♒	24♑	22♒	18	4	27	15	15
MAR.	11♓	28♓	14♒	29♒	14♓	23	2	27	15	15
APR.	11♈	13♉	0♈	8♈	8♈	29	0	27	14	14
MAY	11♉	17♊	29♉	15♉	1♉	2♒	29♌	28	13	14
JUNE	11♊	6♌	14♊	23♊	24	2	0♍	0♋	13	14
JULY	9♋	15♍	18♊	29♋	15♊	0	2	1♋	12	15
AUG.	9♌	8♏	15♌	7♍	6♋	26♑	6	3	13	16
SEPT.	9♍	0♑	5♎	14♎	27	23	8	4	14	17
OCT.	8♎	6♒	13♎	20♏	15♌	23	13	5	15	18
NOV.	9♏	21♓	26♎	25♐	3♍	25	17	5	16	18
DEC.	9♐	23♈	14♐	26♑	19	0♒	19	4	17	18

☿ ℞ Jan. 25-20♒ D. Feb. 15-5♒ ℞ May 24-17♊ D. June 16-9♊ ℞ Sept. 22-19♎ D. Oct. 13-4♎

1950	☉	☽	☿	♀	♂	♃	♄	♅	♆	♇
JAN.	11♑	8♊	0♒	17♒	2♎	7♒	19♍	3♋	17♎	18♌
FEB.	12♒	24♋	19♑	10♒	10	14	18	2	17	17
MAR.	11♓	2♌	20♒	5♒	9	21	17	1	17	16
APR.	11♈	22♍	15♈	25♒	28♍	27	14	1	16	16
MAY	11♉	0♏	27♉	25♓	22	3♓	13	2	15	16
JUNE	10♊	24♐	19♉	0♉	27	6	13	4	15	16
JULY	9♋	2♒	28♊	5♊	8♎	7	14	5	15	17
AUG.	9♌	20♓	29♌	12♋	25	6	17	7	15	18
SEPT.	8♍	5♉	2♎	19♌	14♏	2	21	9	16	19
OCT.	8♎	7♊	20♍	27♍	4♐	28♒	25	9	17	19
NOV.	9♏	21♌	8♏	5♏	26	28	28	9	18	20
DEC.	9♐	25♌	25♐	13♐	19♑	0♓	1♎	9	19	20

☿ ℞ Jan. 9-4♒ D. Jan. 30-18♑ ℞ May 4-28♉ D. May 28-19♉ ℞ Sept. 4-2♎ D. Sept. 27-18♍ ℞ Dec. 24-18♑ ♀ ℞ Jan. 11-19♒ D. Feb. 22-3♒ ♂ ℞ Feb. 13-11♎ D. May 5-22♍

1951	☉	☽	☿	♀	♂	♃	♄	♅	♆	♇
JAN.	10♑	14♎	12♑	22♑	14♒	5♓	3♎	7♋	19♎	20♌
FEB.	12♒	7♐	19♑	1♓	8♓	11	2	6	20	19
MAR.	10♓	17♐	2♓	6♈	0♈	18	1	5	19	18
APR.	11♈	10♒	29♈	14♉	23	26	28♍	6	18	18
MAY	10♉	17♓	27♈	19♊	16♉	2♈	26	6	17	17
JUNE	10♊	5♉	17♉	24♋	8♊	8	26	8	17	17
JULY	9♋	8♊	16♋	24♌	28	13	27	10	17	18
AUG.	9♌	22♌	6♍	16♍	19♋	14	29	11	17	19
SEPT.	8♍	8♍	6♍	12♍	9♌	13	2♌	13	18	20
OCT.	8♎	13♎	28♍	3♍	28	9	6	14	19	21
NOV.	8♏	4♐	20♏	23♍	17♍	6	10	14	20	22
DEC.	9♐	13♑	0♑	23♎	4♎	4	13	13	21	22

☿ D. Jan. 14-2♑ ℞ Apr. 15-9♉ D. May 8-29♈ ℞ Aug. 17-15♍ D. Sept. 10-2♍ ℞ Dec. 7-2♑ D. Dec. 26-16♐ ♀ ℞ Aug. 14-19♍ D. Sept. 26-2♍

1952	☉	☽	☿	♀	♂	♃	♄	♅	♆	♇
JAN.	10♑	6♓	18♐	28♏	21♎	6♈	15♎	12♋	22♎	21♌
FEB.	12♒	26♈	28♑	6♑	6♏	11	15	11	22	21
MAR.	11♓	17♉	18♓	12♒	15	16	14	10	21	20
APR.	12♈	2♋	19♈	20♓	18	23	12	10	21	19
MAY	11♉	4♌	14♈	27♈	10	1♉	10	11	20	19
JUNE	11♊	18♍	2♊	5♊	1	8	9	12	19	19
JULY	10♋	21♎	2♌	12♋	4	14	9	14	19	20
AUG.	9♌	9♐	27♌	20♌	16	19	10	16	19	21
SEPT.	9♍	2♒	21♌	28♍	3♐	21	13	17	20	22
OCT.	8♎	11♓	14♎	5♏	23	20	17	18	21	23
NOV.	9♏	3♉	0♐	13♐	15♑	17	21	19	22	23
DEC.	9♐	9♊	7♐	19♑	8♒	13	24	18	23	23

☿ ℞ Mar. 28-20♈ D. Apr. 20-9♈ ℞ July 31-27♌ D. Aug. 24-15♌ ℞ Nov. 21-16♐ D. Dec. 11-0♐ ♂ ℞ Mar. 26-18♏ D. June 11-1♏

1953	☉	☽	☿	♀	♂	♃	♄	♅	♆	♇
JAN.	11♑	25♋	23♐	25♒	1♓	11♉	27♎	17♋	24♎	23♌
FEB.	12♒	10♍	12♒	29♓	25	12	27	16	24	22
MAR.	11♓	18♍	29♓	24♈	16♈	16	27	15	24	22
APR.	12♈	3♏	20♓	0♉	9♉	22	25	15	23	21
MAY	11♉	8♐	19♈	15♈	0♊	28	23	15	22	21
JUNE	11♊	28♑	20♊	27♈	22	5♊	21	17	21	21
JULY	9♋	7♓	4♌	24♉	11♋	12	21	18	21	22
AUG.	9♌	1♉	28♋	27♊	2♌	19	22	20	21	23
SEPT.	9♍	22♊	3♍	3♌	22	24	24	22	22	24
OCT.	8♎	26♋	26♎	9♍	11♍	26	28	23	23	24
NOV.	9♏	11♍	1♐	17♎	1♎	26	1♏	23	24	25
DEC.	9♐	13♎	19♏	25♏	19	23	5	23	25	25

☿ ℞ Mar. 10-3♈ D. Apr. 1-20♓ ℞ July 13-9♌ D. Aug. 6-28♋ ℞ Nov. 5-1♐ D. Nov. 25-15♏ ♀ ℞ Mar. 24-2♉ D. May 5-15♈

1954	☉	☽	☿	♀	♂	♃	♄	♅	♆	♇
JAN.	11♑	27♏	3♑	4♑	7♏	19♊	8♏	22♋	26♎	25♌
FEB.	12♒	14♑	25♒	13♒	25	17	9	20	26	24
MAR.	10♓	22♑	11♓	18♓	11♐	17	10	19	26	23
APR.	11♈	13♓	14♓	26♈	26	20	8	19	25	23
MAY	11♉	21♈	2♉	3♊	6♑	25	6	20	24	23
JUNE	10♊	15♊	3♋	11♋	8	2♋	4	21	24	23
JULY	9♋	22♋	16♋	16♌	1	9	3	23	23	23
AUG.	9♌	10♍	20♌	22♍	25♐	15	3	24	24	24
SEPT.	9♍	25♎	18♍	26♎	3♑	22	4	26	24	25
OCT.	8♎	27♏	3♏	27	19	27	8	27	25	26
NOV.	9♏	11♑	3♏	29♏	7♒	0♌	12	28	26	27
DEC.	9♐	16♒	26♏	15♏	28	0	15	27	27	27

☿ ℞ Feb. 21-16♓ D. Mar. 15-2♓ ℞ June 24-19♋ D. July 18-10♋ ℞ Oct. 19-15♏ D. Nov. 9-29♎ ♀ ℞ Oct. 27-0♐ D. Dec. 7-15♑ ♂ ℞ May 23-8♑ D. July 29-24♐

1955	☉	☽	☿	♀	♂	♃	♄	♅	♆	♇
JAN.	10♑	6♈	15♑	26♏	20♓	27♋	19♏	26♋	28♎	27♌
FEB.	12♒	29♉	29♒	25♐	12♈	23	21	25	28	26
MAR.	10♓	10♊	15♒	26♑	2♉	20	21	24	28	25
APR.	11♈	2♌	21♓	2♓	24	20	20	24	27	25
MAY	10♉	9♍	21♉	8♈	14♊	23	18	24	26	24
JUNE	10♊	25♎	29♊	16♉	4♋	28	16	25	26	24
JULY	9♋	28♏	20♊	22♊	24	4♌	15	27	26	25
AUG.	9♌	12♑	4♌	0♌	14♌	11	15	29	26	26
SEPT.	8♍	28♒	0♎	8♍	4♍	17	16	1♌	26	27
OCT.	8♎	4♈	29♎	16♎	23	23	19	2	27	28
NOV.	8♏	25♉	20♎	24♏	13♎	28	22	3	28	29
DEC.	9♐	4♋	7♐	2♑	2♏	1♍	26	2	29	29

☿ ℞ Feb. 5-0♓ D. Feb. 26-14♒ ℞ June 4-29♊ D. June 28-21♊
℞ Oct. 1-29♎ D. Oct. 22-13♎

1956	☉	☽	☿	♀	♂	♃	♄	♅	♆	♇
JAN.	10♑	27♌	26♑	10♒	22♏	1♍	29♏	1♌	0♏	28♌
FEB.	12♒	16♎	1♒	18♓	12♐	28♌	2♐	0	1	28
MAR.	11♓	7♏	16♒	23♈	2♑	25	3	29♋	0	27
APR.	12♈	22♐	7♈	27♉	22	22	2	28	0	26
MAY	11♉	23♑	2♊	25♊	11♒	22	1	29	29♎	26
JUNE	11♊	8♓	1♊	9♋	29	25	29♏	0♌	28	26
JULY	10♋	11♈	21♊	26♊	13♓	29	27	1	28	27
AUG.	9♌	0♊	22♌	29♊	23	5♍	26	3	28	28
SEPT.	9♍	23♋	6♎	23♋	21	11	27	5	29	29
OCT.	8♎	2♍	29♍	25♌	13	18	29	6	29	0♍
NOV.	9♏	24♎	2♏	1♎	16	24	2♐	7	1♏	0
DEC.	9♐	29♏	20♐	7♏	27	29	6	7	2	0

☿ ℞ Jan. 18-13♒ D. Feb. 8-28♑ ℞ May 16-9♊ D. June 8-1♊
℞ Sept. 14-12♎ D. Oct. 6-27♍ ♀ ℞ June 2-9♋ D. July 15-23♊
♂ ℞ Aug. 10-22♓ D. Oct. 9-12♓

1957	☉	☽	☿	♀	♂	♃	♄	♅	♆	♇
JAN.	11♑	15♑	28♑	16♐	14♈	1♎	9♐	6♌	2♏	0♍
FEB.	12♒	0♓	17♑	25♑	2♉	1	12	5	3	0
MAR.	11♓	9♓	25♒	0♓	19	29♓	14	4	2	29♌
APR.	12♈	24♈	23♈	8♈	9♊	25	14	3	2	28
MAY	11♉	29♉	18♉	15♉	28	22	13	3	1	28
JUNE	11♊	20♋	16♉	23♊	18♋	22	11	4	0	28
JULY	9♋	29♌	6♋	0♌	6♌	25	9	6	0	29
AUG.	9♌	23♎	3♍	8♍	26	29	8	8	0	29
SEPT.	9♍	13♐	24♍	15♎	16♍	5♎	8	9	1	1♍
OCT.	8♎	17♑	22♍	20♏	5♎	11	10	11	1	2
NOV.	9♏	1♓	14♏	25♐	25	18	13	12	3	2
DEC.	9♐	3♈	29♐	26♑	15♏	24	16	12	4	2

☿ ℞ Jan. 2-27♑ D. Jan. 23-11♑ ℞ Apr. 26-20♉ D. May 20-10♉
℞ Aug. 28-25♍ D. Sept. 20-11♍ ℞ Dec. 17-11♑

1958	☉	☽	☿	♀	♂	♃	♄	♅	♆	♇
JAN.	11♑	17♉	27♐	15♒	7♐	29♎	20♐	11♌	4♏	2♏
FEB.	12♒	4♋	23♑	6♒	28	1♏	23	10	5	1
MAR.	11♓	12♋	9♓	3♒	19♑	1	25	8	5	1
APR.	11♈	4♍	0♉	25♒	10♒	29♎	26	8	4	0
MAY	11♉	13♎	20♈	26♓	4♓	25	25	8	3	0
JUNE	11♊	5♐	22♉	0♉	26	22	23	9	2	0
JULY	9♋	12♑	24♋	5♊	17♈	22	21	10	2	0
AUG.	9♌	0♓	5♍	13♋	7♉	25	19	12	2	1
SEPT.	9♍	15♈	25♌	20♌	23	29	19	14	3	2
OCT.	8♎	17♉	5♎	27♍	2♊	5♏	20	15	4	3
NOV.	9♏	2♋	25♏	6♏	27♉	12	23	16	5	4
DEC.	9♐	7♌	26♐	11♐	18	18	26	17	6	4

☿ D. Jan. 6-25♐ ℞ Apr. 8-1♉ D. Apr. 30-20♈ ℞ Aug. 11-8♍
D. Sept. 3-25♌ ℞ Dec. 1-26♐ D. Dec. 21-9♐ ♀ ℞ Jan. 9-17♒
D. Feb. 20-1♒ ♂ ℞ Oct. 11-2♊ D. Dec. 21-16♉

1959	☉	☽	☿	♀	♂	♃	♄	♅	♆	♇
JAN.	10♑	28♍	18♐	23♑	17♉	24♏	0♑	16♌	7♏	4♍
FEB.	12♒	21♏	3♒	2♓	26	29	3	15	7	4
MAR.	10♓	2♐	23♓	6♈	9♊	2♐	6	13	7	3
APR.	11♈	24♑	6♈	14♉	25	2	7	13	6	2
MAY	10♉	0♓	14♈	20♊	12♋	29♏	7	12	5	2
JUNE	10♊	16♈	8♊	24♋	0♌	26	6	13	5	2
JULY	9♋	18♉	4♌	24♌	18	23	4	14	4	2
AUG.	9♌	2♋	16♌	14♍	8♍	23	1	16	4	3
SEPT.	8♍	19♌	23♌	8♍	27	25	0	18	5	4
OCT.	8♎	24♍	18♎	2♍	17♎	29	1	20	6	5
NOV.	8♏	16♏	2♐	22♍	8♏	5♐	3	21	7	6
DEC.	9♐	25♐	24♏	23♎	29	12	6	21	8	6

☿ ℞ Mar. 20-13♈ D. Apr. 12-1♈ ℞ July 23-20♌ D. Aug. 16-8♌
℞ Nov. 14-10♐ D. Dec. 4-24♏ ♀ ℞ Aug. 12-16♍ D. Sept. 24-0♍

1960	☉	☽	☿	♀	♂	♃	♄	♅	♆	♇
JAN.	10♑	17♒	26♐	29♏	21♐	19♐	10♑	21♌	9♏	6♍
FEB.	12♒	6♈	16♒	7♑	14♑	25	13	20	9	6
MAR.	11♓	27♈	26♓	12♒	6♒	0♑	16	18	9	5
APR.	12♈	11♊	15♓	20♓	29	3	18	17	9	4
MAY	11♉	13♋	24♈	27♈	23♓	4	18	17	8	4
JUNE	11♊	27♌	28♊	5♊	16♈	1	17	18	7	4
JULY	10♋	2♎	0♌	12♋	8♉	27♐	15	19	7	4
AUG.	9♌	22♏	21♋	20♌	0♊	24	13	21	7	5
SEPT.	9♍	15♑	10♍	28♍	19	24	12	23	7	6
OCT.	8♎	24♒	0♏	5♏	5♋	26	12	24	8	7
NOV.	9♏	15♈	23♏	13♐	16	2♑	13	26	9	8
DEC.	9♐	20♉	21♏	20♑	17	7	16	26	10	8

☿ ℞ Mar. 3-26♓ D. Mar. 25-12♓ ℞ July 5-1♌ D. July 29-20♋
℞ Oct. 29-24♏ D. Nov. 18-8♏ ♂ ℞ Nov. 21-19♋

1961	☉	☽	☿	♀	♂	♃	♄	♅	♆	♇
JAN.	11♑	6♋	8♑	26♒	8♋	14♑	20♑	26♌	11♏	8♍
FEB.	12♒	20♌	0♓	0♈	0	22	23	24	11	7
MAR.	11♓	29♌	26♒	23♈	3	27	26	23	11	7
APR.	12♈	15♎	17♓	26♈	14	3♒	28	22	11	6
MAY	11♉	20♏	10♉	13♈	28	6	0♒	22	10	6
JUNE	11♊	12♑	4♋	26♈	14♌	7	29♑	22	9	6
JULY	9♋	21♒	3♋	24♉	2♍	5	28	23	9	6
AUG.	9♌	14♈	25♋	28♊	20	1	26	25	9	7
SEPT.	9♍	3♊	24♍	3♌	10♎	28♑	24	27	9	8
OCT.	8♎	7♋	4♏	10♍	0♏	27	23	29	10	9
NOV.	9♏	21♌	22♎	18♎	21	0♒	24	0♍	11	10
DEC.	9♐	22♍	1♐	25♏	13♐	4	26	1	12	10

☿ ℞ Feb. 14-9♓ D. Mar. 8-25♒ ℞ June 16-11♋ D. July 10-2♋
℞ Oct. 12-8♏ D. Nov. 1-22♎ ♀ ℞ Mar. 22-29♈ D. May 3-12♈
♂ D. Feb. 6-0♋

1962	☉	☽	☿	♀	♂	♃	♄	♅	♆	♇
JAN.	11♑	7♏	20♑	5♑	6♑	11♒	0♒	0♍	13♏	10♍
FEB.	12♒	25♐	21♒	14♒	0♒	18	3	29♌	14	10
MAR.	11♓	3♑	14♒	19♓	22	25	7	28	14	9
APR.	11♈	25♒	27♓	27♈	16♓	1♓	9	27	13	8
MAY	11♉	4♈	27♉	4♊	9♈	7	11	26	12	7
JUNE	11♊	27♉	19♊	11♋	3♉	11	11	27	11	7
JULY	9♋	3♋	17♊	17♌	25	13	10	28	11	8
AUG.	9♌	20♌	12♌	22♍	16♊	11	8	0♍	11	9
SEPT.	9♍	5♎	4♎	25♎	6♋	8	6	2	11	10
OCT.	8♎	7♏	19♎	20♏	24	4	5	3	12	11
NOV.	9♏	23♐	24♎	26♏	10♌	3	5	5	13	12
DEC.	9♐	29♑	12♐	12♏	21	5	7	5	14	12

☿ ℞ Jan. 29-23♒ D. Feb. 19-7♒ ℞ May 28-21♊ D. June 21-12♊
℞ Sept. 25-22♎ D. Oct. 16-7♎ ♀ ℞ Oct. 25-28♏ D. Dec. 5-13♏
♂ ℞ Dec. 27-25♌

1963	☉	☽	☿	♀	♂	♃	♄	♅	♆	♇
JAN.	10♑	20♓	29♑	26♏	24♌	9♓	10♒	5♍	15♏	12♍
FEB.	12♒	14♉	21♑	25♐	16	15	13	4	16	11
MAR.	10♓	24♉	19♒	27♑	7	22	17	3	16	11
APR.	11♈	15♋	12♈	3♓	8	29	20	2	15	10
MAY	11♉	21♌	0♊	9♈	16	6♈	22	1	14	10
JUNE	10♊	6♎	21♉	16♉	29	13	23	2	14	10
JULY	9♋	8♏	25♊	23♊	15♍	17	22	2	13	10
AUG.	9♌	22♐	27♌	1♌	3♎	19	21	4	13	11
SEPT.	9♍	9♒	6♎	9♍	23	19	18	6	13	12
OCT.	8♎	14♓	21♍	16♎	13♏	15	17	8	14	13
NOV.	8♏	7♉	6♏	25♏	5♐	11	17	9	15	14
DEC.	9♐	15♊	23♐	2♑	27	10	18	10	16	14

☿ ℞ Jan. 12-7♒ D. Feb. 1-21♑ ℞ May 6-1♊ D. May 30-22♉
℞ Sept. 6-5♎ D. Sept. 28-21♍ ℞ Dec. 26-21♑ ♂ D. Mar. 15-5♌

1964	☉	☽	☿	♀	♂	♃	♄	♅	♆	♇
JAN.	10♑	8♌	18♑	11♒	21♑	11♈	20♒	10♍	17♏	14♍
FEB.	12♒	26♍	18♑	19♓	15♒	15	24	9	18	14
MAR.	11♓	17♎	1♓	23♈	9♓	20	27	8	18	13
APR.	12♈	1♐	29♈	28♉	3♈	28	1♓	7	17	12
MAY	11♉	3♑	4♉	25♊	25	5♉	3	6	17	12
JUNE	11♊	18♒	17♉	7♋	19♉	12	5	6	16	12
JULY	10♋	23♓	14♋	23♊	10♊	18	4	7	15	12
AUG.	9♌	14♉	6♍	28♊	1♋	23	3	9	15	13
SEPT.	9♍	7♋	10♍	23♋	21	26	1	10	15	14
OCT.	8♎	16♌	27♍	25♌	10♌	26	29♒	12	16	15
NOV.	9♏	6♎	20♏	1♎	27	22	28	14	17	16
DEC.	9♐	11♏	1♑	8♏	12♍	19	29	15	18	16

☿ D. Jan. 15-5♑ ℞ Apr. 18-12♉ D. May 12-2♉ ℞ Aug. 21-18♍
D. Sept. 12-4♍ ℞ Dec. 10-5♑ D. Dec. 30-19♐ ♀ ℞ May 31-6♋
D. July 13-20♊

1965	☉	☽	☿	♀	♂	♃	♄	♅	♆	♇
JAN.	11♑	26♐	20♐	17♐	24♍	16♉	1♓	15♍	19♏	16♍
FEB.	13♒	10♒	27♑	25♑	28	17	5	14	20	16
MAR.	11♓	19♒	16♓	0♓	21	20	8	13	20	15
APR.	12♈	5♈	23♈	9♈	11	26	12	12	20	15
MAY	11♉	11♉	15♈	16♉	9	2♊	14	11	19	14
JUNE	11♊	3♋	29♉	24♊	18	9	17	11	18	14
JULY	10♋	12♌	0♌	1♌	2♒	16	17	12	17	14
AUG.	9♌	5♎	0♍	8♍	18	23	16	13	17	15
SEPT.	9♍	24♏	21♌	16♎	8♏	28	14	15	18	16
OCT.	8♎	27♐	11♎	21♏	28	1♋	12	17	18	17
NOV.	9♏	10♒	29♏	25♐	21♐	1	11	18	19	18
DEC.	9♐	12♓	14♐	25♑	13♑	29♊	11	19	20	19

☿ ℞ Mar. 31-23♈ D. Apr. 23-12♈ ℞ Aug. 3-0♍ D. Aug. 27-18♌
℞ Nov. 24-19♐ D. Dec. 14-3♐ ♂ ℞ Jan. 30-28♍ D. Apr. 20-9♍

1966	☉	☽	☿	♀	♂	♃	♄	♅	♆	♇
JAN.	11♑	27♈	21♐	13♒	7♒	24♊	12♓	20♏	21♍	19♍
FEB.	12♒	15♊	9♒	2♒	2♓	23	15	19	22	18
MAR.	11♓	24♊	28♓	4♒	24	21	19	18	22	18
APR.	11♈	16♌	23♓	25♒	18♈	25	23	17	22	17
MAY	11♉	25♍	17♈	26♓	10♉	29	26	16	21	16
JUNE	11♊	18♏	17♊	1♉	3♊	6♋	28	16	20	16
JULY	9♋	24♐	5♌	6♊	24	12	0♈	16	20	17
AUG.	9♌	10♒	2♌	13♋	14♋	19	29♓	18	19	17
SEPT.	9♍	25♓	0♍	22♌	5♌	26	28	19	20	18
OCT.	8♎	28♈	24♎	28♍	23	1♌	25	21	20	19
NOV.	9♏	14♊	2♐	7♏	12♍	4	23	23	21	20
DEC.	9♐	20♋	19♏	14♐	29	5	23	24	23	21

☿ ℞ Mar. 13-6♈ D. Apr. 5-23♓ ℞ July 15-12♌ D. Aug. 8-0♌
℞ Nov. 8-3♐ D. Nov. 28-17♏ ♀ ℞ Jan. 7-14♒ D. Feb. 18-20♑

1967	☉	☽	☿	♀	♂	♃	♄	♅	♆	♇
JAN.	10♑	12♍	1♑	23♑	14♎	2♌	24♓	25♍	24♏	21♍
FEB.	12♒	6♏	22♒	2♓	27	28♋	26	24	24	20
MAR.	10♓	16♏	16♓	7♈	3♏	25	0♈	23	24	20
APR.	11♈	7♑	13♓	15♉	29♎	25	3	22	24	19
MAY	11♉	11♒	29♈	21♊	19	27	7	21	23	19
JUNE	10♊	26♓	1♋	25♋	16	2♌	10	20	22	18
JULY	9♋	28♈	21♋	24♌	22	7	12	21	22	19
AUG.	9♌	12♊	19♋	13♍	7♏	14	12	22	22	19
SEPT.	9♍	29♋	16♍	5♍	25	21	11	24	22	20
OCT.	8♎	5♍	2♏	0♍	14♐	27	9	26	22	21
NOV.	8♏	28♎	9♏	22♍	7♑	2♍	7	28	23	22
DEC.	9♐	6♐	24♏	22♎	0♒	5	6	29	25	23

☿ ℞ Feb. 24-19♓ D. Mar. 17-5♓ ℞ June 26-22♋ D. July 20-13♋
℞ Oct. 20-17♏ D. Nov. 11-2♏ ♀ ℞ Aug. 10-14♍
D. Sept. 22-27♌ ♂ ℞ Mar. 8-3♏ D. May 25-15♎

1968	☉	☽	☿	♀	♂	♃	♄	♅	♆	♇
JAN.	10♑	28♑	12♑	29♏	24♒	6♍	6♈	29♍	26♏	23♍
FEB.	12♒	16♓	0♓	7♑	18♓	3	8	29	26	23
MAR.	11♓	7♈	18♒	13♒	10♈	0	11	28	27	22
APR.	12♈	21♉	21♓	21♓	3♉	27♌	15	27	26	21
MAY	11♉	23♊	19♉	28♈	25	26	19	26	26	21
JUNE	11♊	9♌	1♋	6♊	17♊	28	22	25	25	20
JULY	10♋	14♍	23♊	13♋	7♋	3♍	24	26	24	20
AUG.	9♌	6♏	2♌	21♌	27	8	26	27	24	21
SEPT.	9♍	29♐	0♎	29♍	17♌	15	25	29	24	22
OCT.	8♎	8♒	1♏	6♏	6♍	21	23	0♎	25	23
NOV.	9♏	27♓	21♎	14♐	25	28	21	2	26	24
DEC.	9♐	2♉	7♐	20♑	13♎	3♎	19	4	27	25

☿ ℞ Feb. 7-2♓ D. Feb. 28-17♒ ℞ June 8-2♋ D. June 30-24♊
℞ Oct. 4-1♏ D. Oct. 25-16♎

1969	☉	☽	☿	♀	♂	♃	♄	♅	♆	♇
JAN.	11♑	16♊	26♑	26♒	1♏	6♎	19♈	4♎	28♏	25♍
FEB.	13♒	0♌	6♒	0♈	18	6	20	4	29	25
MAR.	11♓	9♌	15♒	22♈	2♐	4	23	3	29	24
APR.	12♈	26♍	4♈	23♈	13	0	26	2	28	23
MAY	11♉	2♏	1♊	11♈	17	27♍	0♉	1	28	23
JUNE	11♊	24♐	6♊	26♈	10	26	4	0	27	23
JULY	10♋	3♒	19♊	25♉	3	28	7	0	26	23
AUG.	9♌	25♓	20♌	28♊	6	3♎	9	1	26	24
SEPT.	9♍	14♉	7♎	4♌	19	8	9	3	26	24
OCT.	8♎	16♊	4♎	10♍	6♑	15	7	5	27	25
NOV.	9♏	0♌	0♏	18♎	28	22	5	7	28	26
DEC.	9♐	2♍	18♐	26♏	20♒	27	3	8	29	26

☿ ℞ Jan. 21-16♒ D. Feb. 10-0♒ ℞ May 18-12♊ D. June 11-4♊
℞ Sept. 17-15♎ D. Oct. 8-0♎ ♀ ℞ Mar. 20-27♈ D. May 1-11♈
♂ ℞ Apr. 27-16♐ D. July 8-1♐

1970	☉	☽	☿	♀	♂	♃	♄	♅	♆	♇
JAN.	11♑	17♎	29♑	5♑	13♓	3♏	2♉	9♎	0♐	27♍
FEB.	12♒	6♐	18♑	14♒	6♈	6	3	9	1	27
MAR.	11♓	15♐	23♒	19♓	26	6	5	8	1	27
APR.	11♈	8♒	20♈	28♈	18♉	4	8	7	1	26
MAY	11♉	17♓	22♉	5♊	10♊	0	12	6	0	25
JUNE	11♊	9♉	17♉	12♋	0♋	27♎	16	5	29♏	25
JULY	9♋	15♊	3♋	17♌	19	26	19	5	29	25
AUG.	9♌	1♌	2♍	23♍	9♌	28	22	6	28	26
SEPT.	9♍	15♍	28♍	25♎	29	3♏	23	8	28	26
OCT.	8♎	18♎	21♍	19♏	18♍	8	22	9	29	28
NOV.	9♏	5♐	12♏	23♏	8♎	15	20	11	0♐	29
DEC.	9♐	12♑	28♐	10♏	27	21	18	13	1	0♎

☿ ℞ Jan. 5-0♒ D. Jan. 25-14♑ ℞ Apr. 30-23♉ D. May 22-14♉
℞ Aug. 30-28♍ D. Sept. 23-14♍ ℞ Dec. 20-14♑
♀ ℞ Oct. 23-26♏ D. Dec. 3-10♏

1971	☉	☽	☿	♀	♂	♃	♄	♅	♆	♇
JAN.	10♑	4♓	2♑	25♏	16♏	28♏	16♉	14♎	2♐	0♎
FEB.	12♒	28♈	21♑	26♐	6♐	3♐	16	14	3	29♍
MAR.	10♓	7♉	6♓	27♑	23	6	17	13	3	28
APR.	11♈	27♊	0♉	3♓	12♑	7	20	12	3	28
MAY	11♉	1♌	23♈	10♈	29	4	24	10	2	27
JUNE	10♊	15♍	20♉	17♉	14♒	1	28	10	1	27
JULY	9♋	17♎	21♋	23♊	21	27♏	2♊	10	1	27
AUG.	9♌	2♐	6♍	1♌	19	27	4	10	0	28
SEPT.	9♍	19♑	29♌	10♍	13	29	6	12	1	29
OCT.	8♎	25♒	2♎	17♎	15	3♐	6	14	1	0♎
NOV.	8♏	19♈	23♏	26♏	27	9	5	16	2	1
DEC.	9♐	27♉	28♐	3♑	14♓	16	3	17	3	2

☿ D. Jan. 9-28♐ ℞ Apr. 10-4♉ D. May 4-24♈ ℞ Aug. 11-11♍
D. Sept. 5-27♌ ℞ Dec. 3-28♐ D. Dec. 23-12♐ ♂ ℞ July 9-20♒
D. Sept. 6-10♒

1972	☉	☽	☿	♀	♂	♃	♄	♅	♆	♇
JAN.	10♑	18♋	18♐	11♒	4♈	23♐	0♊	18♎	4♐	2♎
FEB.	12♒	6♍	1♒	19♓	24	29	29♉	18	5	2
MAR.	11♓	26♍	23♓	24♈	13♉	4♑	0♊	18	5	2
APR.	12♈	11♏	10♈	28♉	4♊	8	3	17	5	1
MAY	11♉	13♐	15♈	25♊	23	8	6	15	5	0
JUNE	11♊	0♒	7♊	5♋	13♋	6	10	15	4	29♍
JULY	10♋	6♓	4♌	20♊	2♌	3	14	14	3	29
AUG.	9♌	28♈	20♌	27♊	21	29♐	17	15	3	0♎
SEPT.	9♍	22♊	23♌	24♋	11♍	28	19	16	3	1
OCT.	9♎	0♌	18♎	26♌	0♎	1♑	21	18	3	2
NOV.	9♏	19♍	2♐	2♎	20	5	20	20	4	3
DEC.	10♐	22♎	29♏	9♏	10♏	11	18	22	5	4

☿ ℞ Mar. 23-16♈ D. Apr. 15-4♈ ℞ July 26-23♌ D. Aug. 19-11♌
℞ Nov. 16-12♐ D. Dec. 6-26♏ ♀ ℞ May 29-5♋ D. July 11-18♊

1973	☉	☽	☿	♀	♂	♃	♄	♅	♆	♇
JAN.	11♑	6♐	26♐	17♐	1♐	18♑	15♊	23♎	6♐	5♎
FEB.	13♒	21♑	15♒	26♑	23	25	14	23	7	4
MAR.	11♓	29♑	28♓	1♓	12♑	1♒	14	23	8	4
APR.	12♈	16♓	16♓	10♈	4♒	7	16	21	7	3
MAY	11♉	22♈	22♈	17♉	26	11	19	20	7	2
JUNE	11♊	15♊	25♊	25♊	17♓	12	22	19	6	1
JULY	10♋	24♋	2♌	1♌	7♈	11	26	19	5	1
AUG.	9♌	16♍	23♋	9♍	25	7	0♋	20	5	2
SEPT.	9♍	4♏	8♍	16♎	7♉	3	3	21	5	3
OCT.	8♎	6♐	28♎	21♏	8	2	5	22	5	4
NOV.	9♏	20♑	27♏	26♐	28♈	4	5	25	6	5
DEC.	9♐	22♒	20♏	25♑	25	8	3	26	7	6

☿ ℞ Mar. 6-29♓ D. Mar. 28-15♓ ℞ July 7-4♌ D. July 31-23♋
℞ Oct. 31-27♏ D. Nov. 20-11♏ ♂ ℞ Sept. 19-8♉ D. Nov. 25-24♈

1974	☉	☽	☿	♀	♂	♃	♄	♅	♆	♇
JAN.	11♑	8♈	6♑	11♒	1♉	14♒	1♋	27♎	8♐	7♎
FEB.	12♒	27♉	28♒	28♑	16	22	29♊	28	9	6
MAR.	11♓	7♊	1♓	1♒	2♊	28	28	28	10	6
APR.	11♈	0♌	15♓	25♒	19	6♓	29	26	9	5
MAY	11♉	10♍	7♉	26♓	7♋	12	1♋	25	9	5
JUNE	11♊	0♏	4♋	2♉	26	16	5	24	8	4
JULY	9♋	6♐	8♋	7♊	14♌	18	9	24	7	4
AUG.	9♌	21♑	23♋	14♋	3♍	17	13	24	7	4
SEPT.	9♍	5♓	22♍	22♌	23	13	16	25	7	5
OCT.	8♎	8♈	4♏	29♍	12♎	10	18	27	7	6
NOV.	9♏	26♉	26♎	7♏	3♏	8	19	29	8	7
DEC.	9♐	3♋	29♏	15♐	24	9	18	1♏	9	9

☿ ℞ Feb. 17-12♓ D. Mar. 11-27♒ ℞ June 19-14♋ D. July 13-5♋
℞ Oct. 15-11♏ D. Nov. 4-25♎ ♀ ℞ Jan. 5-11♒ D. Feb. 16-26♑

Condensed Ephemeris

1975	☉	☽	☿	♀	♂	♃	♄	♅	♆	♇
JAN.	10♑	26♌	18♑	24♑	15♐	13♓	15♋	2♏	10♐	9♎
FEB.	12♒	19♎	26♒	3♓	8♑	19	14	3	11	9
MAR.	10♓	28♎	14♒	8♈	29	26	12	2	12	8
APR.	11♈	18♐	25♓	15♉	22♒	3♈	12	1	12	8
MAY	11♉	21♑	25♉	21♊	15♓	11	14	0	11	7
JUNE	10♊	5♓	23♊	25♋	8♈	17	17	29♎	10	6
JULY	9♋	7♈	18♊	24♌	0♉	22	21	28	10	6
AUG.	9♌	21♉	9♌	11♍	22	24	25	29	9	7
SEPT.	9♍	9♋	3♎	1♍	11♊	24	28	0♏	9	8
OCT.	8♎	16♌	23♎	29♌	25	21	1♌	1	10	9
NOV.	8♏	10♎	22♎	22♍	3♋	17	3	3	10	10
DEC.	9♐	18♏	10♐	24♎	28♊	15	3	5	11	11

☿ ℞ Feb. 1-26♒ D. Feb. 22-10♒ ℞ May 30-24♊ D. June 23-15♊
℞ Sept. 27-24♎ D. Oct. 18-9♎ ♀ ℞ Aug. 8-12♍
D. Sept. 20-26♌ ♂ ℞ Nov. 5-2♋

1976	☉	☽	☿	♀	♂	♃	♄	♅	♆	♇
JAN.	10♑	9♑	28♑	0♐	17♊	15♈	1♌	6♏	13♐	12♎
FEB.	12♒	26♒	24♑	8♑	16	19	29♋	7	13	11
MAR.	11♓	17♓	18♒	14♒	23	25	27	7	14	11
APR.	12♈	1♉	11♈	22♓	7♋	2♉	26	6	14	10
MAY	11♉	4♊	1♊	29♈	22	9	27	5	13	10
JUNE	11♊	21♋	24♉	7♊	9♌	16	0♌	4	13	9
JULY	10♋	28♌	24♊	14♌	27	22	3	3	12	9
AUG.	9♌	20♎	26♌	22♌	16♍	27	7	3	11	10
SEPT.	9♍	14♐	6♎	0♎	5♎	1♊	11	4	11	10
OCT.	9♎	21♑	23♍	7♏	25	1	14	6	12	11
NOV.	9♏	9♓	6♏	14♐	16♏	29♉	16	8	12	12
DEC.	10♐	12♈	23♐	21♑	8♐	24	17	9	14	13

☿ ℞ Jan. 14-9♒ D. Feb. 4-23♑ ℞ May 10-4♊ D. June 3-25♉
℞ Sept. 10-8♎ D. Oct. 2-23♍ ℞ Dec. 29-23♑ ♂ D. Jan. 20-15♊

1977	☉	☽	☿	♀	♂	♃	♄	♅	♆	♇
JAN.	11♑	26♉	22♑	27♒	0♑	21♉	16♌	11♏	15♐	14♎
FEB.	13♒	11♋	18♑	29♓	24	22	14	12	16	14
MAR.	11♓	19♋	29♒	21♈	16♒	25	12	12	16	14
APR.	12♈	6♍	27♈	19♈	10♓	0♊	10	11	16	13
MAY	11♉	13♎	10♉	9♈	3♈	6	10	10	16	12
JUNE	11♊	6♐	16♉	26♈	27	13	12	9	15	12
JULY	10♋	15♑	11♋	25♉	19♉	20	15	8	14	11
AUG.	9♌	6♓	6♍	29♊	10♊	26	19	8	14	12
SEPT.	9♍	23♈	16♍	5♌	0♋	2♋	23	9	13	13
OCT.	8♎	26♉	25♍	11♍	18	5	27	10	14	14
NOV.	9♏	10♋	17♏	19♎	3♌	6	29	12	15	15
DEC.	9♐	12♌	0♑	27♏	12	4	1♍	14	16	16

☿ D. Jan. 18-7♑ ℞ Apr. 21-15♉ D. May 15-5♉ ℞ Aug. 24-21♍
D. Sept. 16-7♍ ℞ Dec. 13-7♑ ♀ ℞ Mar. 18-25♈ D. Apr. 29-8♈
♂ ℞ Dec. 14-12♌

1978	☉	☽	☿	♀	♂	♃	♄	♅	♆	♇
JAN.	11♑	29♍	24♐	6♑	9♌	0♋	0♍	15♏	17♐	17♎
FEB.	12♒	19♏	25♑	15♒	27♋	27♊	28♌	16	18	17
MAR.	11♓	29♏	13♓	20♓	21	26	26	16	18	16
APR.	11♈	23♑	26♈	28♈	27	29	24	16	18	15
MAY	11♉	2♓	16♈	5♊	8♌	3♋	24	15	18	14
JUNE	11♊	22♈	26♉	13♋	23	9	25	13	17	14
JULY	9♋	26♉	28♋	18♌	10♍	16	27	13	16	14
AUG.	9♌	11♋	3♍	23♍	28	23	1♍	13	16	14
SEPT.	9♍	26♌	22♌	25♎	17♎	29	4	13	16	15
OCT.	8♎	29♍	9♎	18♏	8♏	5♌	8	15	16	16
NOV.	9♏	17♏	28♏	18♏	0♐	8	11	16	17	17
DEC.	9♐	25♐	19♐	8♏	22	9	13	18	18	18

☿ D. Jan. 2-21♐ ℞ Apr. 3-26♈ D. Apr. 26-15♈ ℞ Aug. 6-3♍
D. Aug. 29-20♌ ℞ Nov. 27-21♐ D. Dec. 17-6♐
♀ R Oct. 21-27♏ D. Dec. 1-8♏ ♂ D. Mar. 3-22♋

1979	☉	☽	☿	♀	♂	♃	♄	♅	♆	♇
JAN.	11♑	18♒	20♐	25♏	15♑	7♌	14♍	20♏	19♐	19♎
FEB.	12♒	10♈	7♒	26♐	9♒	3	13	21	20	19
MAR.	10♓	19♈	26♓	28♑	1♓	0	11	21	20	19
APR.	11♈	8♊	27♓	4♓	26	29♋	8	21	21	18
MAY	11♉	11♋	15♈	10♈	19♈	1♌	7	19	20	17
JUNE	10♊	25♌	13♊	18♉	12♉	5	8	18	20	17
JULY	9♋	27♍	5♌	24♊	4♊	11	10	17	19	16
AUG.	9♌	12♏	8♌	2♌	25	18	13	17	18	17
SEPT.	9♍	0♑	28♌	11♍	16♋	24	16	18	18	17
OCT.	8♎	8♒	22♎	18♎	4♌	1♍	20	19	18	19
NOV.	8♏	1♈	2♐	26♏	21	6	24	21	19	20
DEC.	9♐	10♉	20♏	4♑	5♍	9	26	23	20	21

☿ ℞ Mar. 16-9♈ D. Apr. 8-26♓ ℞ July 19-15♌ D. Aug. 12-3♌
℞ Nov. 10-6♐ D. Nov. 30-20♏

1980	☉	☽	☿	♀	♂	♃	♄	♅	♆	♇
JAN.	10♑	0♋	29♐	12♒	14♍	10♍	27♍	24♏	21♐	22♎
FEB.	12♒	16♌	20♒	20♓	14	8	26	25	22	22
MAR.	11♓	7♍	20♓	24♈	4	5	25	26	23	21
APR.	12♈	21♎	14♓	28♉	26♌	1	22	25	23	20
MAY	11♉	25♏	28♈	24♊	29	0	20	24	22	20
JUNE	11♊	12♑	1♋	2♋	10♍	2	20	23	22	20
JULY	10♋	20♒	25♋	17♊	25	6	22	22	21	19
AUG.	9♌	13♈	20♋	26♊	13♎	12	24	22	20	20
SEPT.	9♍	6♊	15♍	24♋	2♏	18	28	22	20	20
OCT.	9♎	13♋	2♏	26♌	23	25	1♎	23	20	21
NOV.	9♏	0♍	14♏	2♎	15♐	1♎	5	25	21	22
DEC.	10♐	2♎	24♏	9♏	7♑	6	8	27	22	23

☿ ℞ Feb. 27-22♓ D. Mar. 21-8♓ ℞ July 1-25♋ D. July 25-16♋
℞ Oct. 25-20♏ D. Nov. 14-4♏ ♀ ℞ May 27-2♋ D. July 9-16♊
♂ ℞ Jan. 17-16♍ D. Apr. 8-26♌

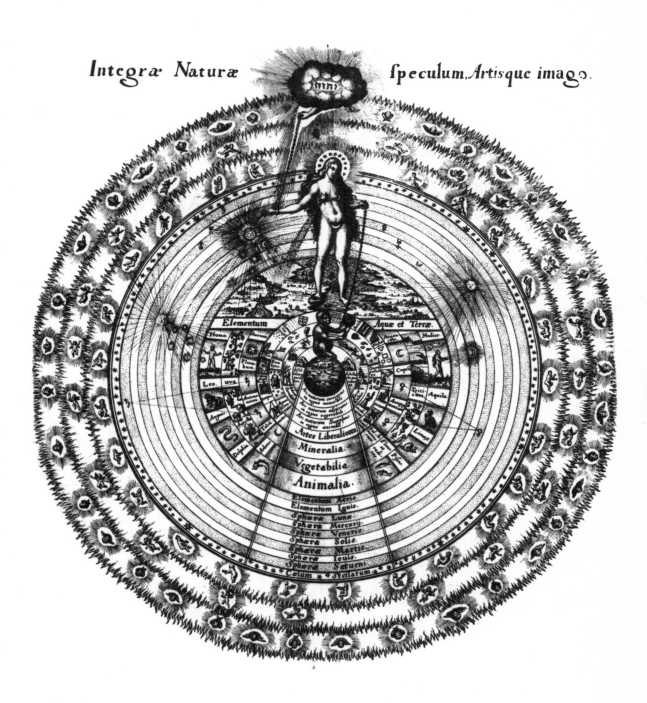

PART 2

THE BOOK OF CHANGE
The I Ching

Neil Powell

Contents

1

Tao: the Chinese way

Three great religions flourished in pre-communist China. The first was Confucianism, an austere doctrine of 'doing the proper thing', an aristocratic philosophy which had great appeal for many intellectuals, particularly the Mandarins who made up the Imperial Civil Service, but had little to offer the ordinary Chinese, were he townsman or peasant.

The second was Buddhism, divided into a large number of diversive and often competing schools, from those concerned with rationalist logical systems to others preaching the severe anti-intellectualism which later gave birth to the Zen Buddhism of Japan – now so popular in the western world. Some of these Buddhist sects had almost totally departed from the simplicity and anti-ritualism of the original Buddhism of India and practised a variety of magical techniques largely concerned with the placation of demons and the achievement of 'good luck'.

Such magical varieties of Buddhism tended to blend with the more popular aspects of Taoism, the faith of the great mass of the Chinese people. But Taoism was much more than a variety of folk magic. It had something for everybody – it provided not only simple charms and ceremonies for the use of the peasant, but a lofty philosophy of 'the Way of Heaven' for those who could understand its scriptures and the many abstruse commentaries upon them, a complex system of magical rites for those drawn towards what westerners usually call 'the occult', and a technique of exercises involving physical sexuality for those who sought spiritual illumination through the channels of the senses.

The most sacred and basic of the Taoist scriptures was (and is, for the faith still flourishes among the Chinese of South-East Asia) the *Tao-te-Ching*, the Book of the Tao. This work, attributed to Lao-Tse, a sage born in 604 BC, is the shortest of the world's great scriptures. In the original Chinese version only some five thousand characters are employed and, even in the more long-winded languages of the west, translations are usually only some four to ten thousand words in length. Yet, in spite of its brevity, the *Tao-te-Ching* expresses doctrines of such depth and complexity that it has spawned a great mass of commentaries and explanatory treatises; as early as the seventh century AD there were no less than 4,500 of these.

What exactly is the 'Tao' of the book's title? The word is usually translated as 'Way', meaning Way in its religious sense as used by Christ ('I am the Way, the Truth and the Life'), but no English word provides a really satisfactory equivalent, and even in Chinese the word has more than one meaning and different schools of Taoist thinking have used the word in different ways.

The Tao is, says one inscription, 'the ancestor of all doctrines, the mystery beyond mysteries'; it cannot be put into words, only understood on an instinctive level – 'the Tao that can be put into words is not the Everlasting Tao'.

Perhaps the best way that the ordinary westerner can come to some understanding of the inner meaning of the Tao is to immerse himself in the *Tao-te-Ching* and other Taoist scriptures or to examine the practical techniques, from acupuncture to the Chinese martial arts, that are ultimately derived from Taoism.

Neither of these courses of action is easily performed, for the values and ways of thought which find expression in Taoist writings and techniques are alien to those dominant in the science- and technology-based cultures of Europe and North America. Taoist values are opposed to action and material achievement, 'power and learning is adding more and more to oneself, Tao is subtracting day by day'. Passivity is seen as a desirable quality, 'rigour is death, yielding is life'. Law and Order, the twin gods of the policeman and the lawyer, are seen as obstacles to the Tao: 'as laws increase, crimes increase'.

At their most extreme these attitudes make the Taoist into a sort of pacifist anarchist who totally rejects not only all laws and governments as enemies of the Tao but even

Confucius, one of the greatest of Chinese philosophers, was nearly 70 years old when, in 481 BC, he said: 'If some years were added to my life, I would give fifty to the study of the I Ching, and might then escape falling into great errors'

the simplest mechanical aids to the everyday business of living. Just how far this rejection of material things can go is illustrated by a popular Taoist story:

An intelligent young man observes an elderly peasant irrigating his crops by the tedious process of raising water from a well, one bucket at a time, and taking it to the fields. The young man describes a simple mechanism that would deliver water directly from the well to the crops. 'I know of this apparatus', says the old man, 'but those who use cunning machines soon begin to practise cunning ways. Thus their hearts become cunning, and a cunning heart prevents one from being pure in thought. Those whose thought is impure have troubled spirits, and these cease to be fit vehicles for the Tao'.

With such curious ways of thought as those expressed in this story go equally alien modes of regarding time, space and the material objects that make up the world as the ordinary man knows it.

In the western world we think of time and space as made up of separate things. Thus time is regarded as a flow of separate units – seconds, minutes and hours – each one divided from the others although, in a sense, identical with them. Similarly space is viewed as divided into separate elements, some of them alive, like people and animals, others, such as tables and chairs, inanimate.

To the Taoist adept this displays a vulgar and incomplete understanding of the true nature of reality. For him, or her – for many of the great Taoist sages have been women – everything is part of everything else. Reality is not hard and fixed, it is ceaseless change. The river one stepped into yesterday is not the same river one bathes in today, the universe is a moving pattern, nothing is permanent. All the separations of objects and moments of time which we take for granted in the west are no more than philosophical fictions which are themselves mere elements in the everchanging web of reality. Only by being conscious of his own everfluctuating nature, only by abandoning the myth of a unique and unchanging 'self', can man attain the spiritual liberation of being a fit vehicle for the Tao.

This acceptance of the changing nature of reality, this refusal to look upon anything as being altogether alien to humanity, has made Taoism the most tolerant of all the world's religions. In Taoist temples one can find images of Christ beside those of Lao-Tse, terrifying pictures of demons beside those of the tender Goddess of Mercy – all are seen as aspects of the constant flux of existence: all the gods are 'real'. In view of this tolerance it is not surprising that Taoism, alone of the great religions, has flatly refused to condemn 'the black arts' – magical and occult practices – but has instead absorbed them into itself.

This concern with magic has been seen by Christian missionaries and other hostile observers as evidence of the degeneracy of Taoism, an indication that the lofty philosophy of Lao-Tse had become corrupted by 'heathen supersition'. In fact Lao-Tse, who was not the founder of Taoism but only its reviver and expositor, never condemned the performance of ritual magic and there is evidence that occult theories and techniques have been an integral part of the faith since the days of the Yellow Emperor, its mythical founder, who is supposed to have flourished somewhere about 2500 BC.

A Chinese coin, impressed with the eight trigrams that are the basis of the I Ching. The order in which these symbols are arranged is that attributed to King Wen, and is known as the Sequence of Later Heaven, or Inner World Arrangement

Taoist magic exists on many different levels. At its lowest there are the rites employed by peasants to ensure good luck and a rich harvest or to cure sick animals. Such rites are no more, or course, than Chinese equivalents of the charms used for similar purposes by the European 'cunning men' (white witches) and Pennsylvanian hexdoctors of the last century. On a somewhat more intellectual level are the practices associated with such a Taoist school as the 'Pervading Unity Tao'. Such schools teach abstention from alcohol, tobacco and other stimulants, are rigidly vegetarian, worship the gods of all religions, use magic charms in attempts to obtain their desires, and endeavour to communicate with supernatural beings through the use of what is called 'the flying spirit pencil'. This last is no more than a Chinese variant of the planchette used by European spiritualists – a writing instrument is placed within a holder mounted upon small wheels, and each of the group using it places a finger upon the holder, which then moves about writing meaningful messages supposedly transmitted by spirits of one kind or another acting through the motionless bodies of the sitters.

Such activities may appear futile to westerners unattracted to occultism, but it must be admitted that members of such Taoist groups seem to find their practices meaningful and valuable on both a psychological and spiritual level. In addition to this there is no doubt that such cults have sometimes preserved and transmitted Taoist literature which has exerted an influence outside the culture which gave it birth. Thus *The Secret of the Golden Flower*, a treatise which deeply affected the late C. G. Jung and the whole school of western psychology derived from him, was from just such a school.

On the highest level of Taoist magic are the practices of those adepts which, so it is believed, can lead the practitioner to the ultimate attainment desired by Taoists of every level of sophistication – joining the ranks of the *hsien*; the legendary immortals who can fly on dragons, perform miracles such as feeding multitudes on boiled stones and bringing the dead to life, converse with the gods, and produce legions of spirit-soldiers from thin air.

There are many varieties of technique, it is held, which can lead the adept towards immortality and the powers which accompany it. But the best known and most widely practised are concerned with sexual magic, sometimes called sexual alchemy, processes which transform sexuality from a mere channel of physical pleasure into a supernatural rite.

Some of these processes involve the suppression of ordinary physical sexuality, others its almost frenzied expression, but all are based on the idea that the energies of the universe can be classified under two headings, Yin and Yang. The first is passive, watery, pertaining to the moon – female energy. The latter is active, fiery, pertaining to the sun – – the energy of the male. While immortality is essentially a masculine (yang) quality no man can attain it without some element of the yin essences and the converse is true for women.

In full-blooded Taoist sexual magic, therefore, joyous physical intercourse between man and woman plays an essential part, for the visible sexual secretions are regarded as only the gross by-products of the male and female energies which are transmitted from one partner to the other in the course of orgasm and the events leading up to it. The energies of yin and yang are first stimulated by foreplay, then raised to a higher pitch by the use of particular sexual postures – many of them, such as 'the seagull's wing over the cliff edge', given symbolic names – and particular rhythms of penetration, for example a pattern of deep and shallow penile thrusts such as three shallow, five deep, seven shallow, nine deep.

Intercourse carried on in such complex postures and rhythms, it is supposed, greatly stimulates the production of the pure essences

of yin and yang. As the act proceeds towards its climax the male adept is enabled to extract yin from the breasts and under the tongue of his partner. Finally comes orgasm; the male and female energies are liberated and exchanged between the lovers, the man absorbing the female energies from the woman's womb through the channel of the penis while, at the same time, he transmits the male energy through the penis and into the womb.

In the past, and possibly still at the present day, some Taoist magicians, both male and female, practised a curious and perhaps selfish variant of this rite. They held that it was desirable totally to conserve one's own energy, be it male or female, but to extract as much as possible from members of the opposite sex. They therefore had intercourse with as many partners as they could, bringing those partners to full orgasm but avoiding it themselves until the desire to achieve a climax was uncontrollable. Preferably the partners employed in this practice were as young as possible, for those who had only just achieved puberty were considered to be pariicularly rich in yin and yang, but this was not essential. When orgasm was finally achieved by those who used this technique, it was, of course, explosive – but some adepts deliberately avoided this culmination by methods of physical and psychological desensitization of the sexual organs, although more than one Taoist school regarded this as a dangerous practice.

What purpose is supposedly forwarded by such sexual antics, by the dynamic interchange of yin and yang? Or is there no real purpose behind Taoist sexual magic, is it just an excuse for debauchery? The answer to the latter question is a very definite no. Throughout most of its history Chinese culture has been far more sexually liberated than that of the western world. China, it is true, suffered periods of puritanism and sexual repression, usually imposed by some fanatically Confucian ruler, but on the whole those Chinese who have wanted to indulge in sexual athletics have been able to do so without incurring any penalties (save for being the butt of vulgar jokes), or even any marked disapproval.

Far from being intended as an excuse for immortality the interchange of yin and yang has always had a deeply serious purpose, 'the transmutation of lead into gold'. In other words, the raising of the sexual energy of an individual to a level at which it approximates to the pure and undifferentiated Tao.

This transformation is achieved in 'crucibles'. These are not, for Taoists, the containers used in the chemistry of both west and east, but centres of psycho-spiritual activity which exist in the subtle body – roughly the equivalent of the Christian 'soul' – which underlies the physical body of each and every man and woman. The exact nature of the process used to employ the yin and yang in this spiritual transmutation is too complex to be outlined in a brief article and it suffices to say that the Taoist adept uses meditative, physical and visually imaginative exercises somewhat similar to those employed by the Tantric (sexo-religious) yogis of India.

Almost identical exercises are employed by those Taoists, usually male, who give their adherence to another variety of sexual magic in which there is no partner of the opposite sex. The basis of this practice is the deliberate arousal of the sexual instincts, often by masturbation, but the avoidance of 'earthing' them by orgasm. Instead the physical and emotional energies are sent 'up' from the genitals into the psycho-spiritual crucibles where they are transformed, by similar exercises to those mentioned above, into the spiritual gold of the Tao.

While, as has been described, Taoist magic appears to exist on several levels, it is wise to remember that such a differentiation comes from thinking in a western, not a Taoist, manner. To the genuine Taoist, who refuses to make any real separation between one thing and another, all varieties of magic are essentially one, no more than aspects of the ever-changing pattern of reality. In the last analysis it is impossible to separate the village magician with his charms and hocus-pocus from the practitioner of the most intellectually subtle variety of sexual magic, or even from the lofty Taoist philosopher who does naught but meditate on the lofty words of the *Tao-te-Ching* and its commentaries.

Nothing illustrates this Taoist refusal to divide reality better than the *I Ching,* the Chinese *Book of Change*, an oracle book – that is, a book which provides answers to questions – now widely known in Europe and America, particularly through the medium of the translation, introduced by the eminent psychologist C. G. Jung.

The world has had many oracle books and almost all the world's religious scriptures have been at times employed as such; it used, for example, to be a common Christian practice to open the Bible at random, let one's finger fall upon a text and, should that text prove meaningful, apply it as an answer to the question one wished to ask.

The I Ching differs from all other oracle books, however, in that, instead of regarding the present and the future as fixed and unchanging and giving instructions of the 'do this, do that' variety, it regards both past and present as dynamic, flowing, never the same from one moment to the other. Instead, therefore, of imposing a definite course of action it lists possibilities – if you do so-and-so it will be productive of such-and-such a result.

A similar concern with dynamism and change can be seen in acupuncture, a traditional system of Chinese medicine derived from Taoism. Acupuncture, once derided in the west but now being seriously investigated by medical scientists, differs from orthodox medicine not only in the

methods it employs – largely the insertion of gold or silver needles into the skin of the patient – but in the way it views the individual human being.

The orthodox physician regards the sick man as a biological machine quite separate from the rest of the universe. There is some sort of mechanical fault, he feels, and this must be corrected by drugs or surgery. The

acupuncturist, on the other hand, sees his patient as an aspect of the one underlying reality, his sickness no more than an artificial separation from the life-giving and abundant energies of the universe. What is needed is to restore the harmony and connection of those energies with the currents of the same energies in the individual. Whether this belief is true or false, whether or not acu-

A Chinese vase of the sixth century AD, with a circular decoration of animals representing the constellations of the zodiac

Tao: the Chinese way

The founders of the three great Chinese religions: Confucius, Buddha and Lao-tse, seen here seated within the petals of a lotus flower

puncture is effective, it is clear that its underlying philosophy is unquestionably Taoist and, as such, alien to western ways of thought.

At the present day Taoism is nominally tolerated in China. In practice, however, it has been subjected to a severe persecution. Its temples and other holy places have been turned into museums, storage space and granaries, or even pulled down; its adepts and magicians have been forced to perform 'useful work' in the fields and the factories; at times many copies of its scriptures have been destroyed as 'counter-revolutionary'.

And yet, paradoxically enough, many of the practical techniques derived from Taoism are actively encouraged. Thus T'ai Chi, a Taoist system of physical culture, is practised by millions of Chinese, acupuncture is used in some of China's most modern hospitals, and the herbal remedies of Taoist healers are beginning to be scientifically investigated.

In the west there is also a widespread interest in such techniques, but in this case concern with the practical aspects of Taoism is accompanied by a growth of interest in the religious and philosophical ideas that gave birth to them. Today the Taoist scriptures and sexo-magical techniques are studied far more in Europe and North America than they are in China itself.

The I Ching

The I Ching is one of the oldest and most respected oracles in the world. In its present form it can be traced back three thousand years, and even then it was old, being based on more primitive oracles.

It has survived intact through the centuries because wise men in every age have held it in high esteem as a source of profound wisdom and valuable guidance, both in the search for spiritual enlightenment and in the conduct of material affairs.

Its elusive magic has captivated some of the greatest minds the world has known, from that corner-stone of traditional Chinese society, Confucius, down to C. G. Jung. Today it is probably more widely known and more frequently consulted by people in all walks of life than at any previous time.

The I Ching is constructed around 64 six-line figures whose English name is hexagrams. These are made up of all the possible permutations of a broken line and an unbroken line in combinations of six.

All phenomena are the result of the interaction between positive, creative, masculine yang forces, and negative, passive, feminine yin forces. Yang is represented by the unbroken lines and yin by the broken lines which go to make up each hexagram. In this way the 64 hexagrams can be said between them to symbolise all the stages of change and flux operating in the universe, and the texts of the I Ching describe these changes and apply them to the pre-occupations of mankind.

The hexagrams that follow on pages 22 to 87 are each accompanied by several texts. The first text, called *The Judgment*, is the oldest. It was composed by King Wên, founder of the Chou dynasty, after he had been imprisoned by the last Shang Emperor, Chou Hsin.

The second text, the *Commentary*, is one of the later interpretations attributed to Confucius, though he is unlikely to have written it himself.

The third text, *The Image*, is another Confucian commentary. It is intended to explain how the sensible person who follows the I Ching's advice – generally referred to as the 'superior man' – would act at such a time.

The final group of texts, one attributed to each of the six lines of the hexagram, were composed by King Wên's son, the Duke of Chou, who destroyed the Shang dynasty in 1027 BC. These short and often enigmatic lines were written about forty years after King Wên's text.

To each of these groups of texts, the author has appended some explanation.

2
How to consult the I Ching

The I Ching can be consulted in three ways. The first involves the use of a bundle of fifty sticks, the second requires three coins, and the third uses six specially marked wands. Of these three methods the oldest and most venerated is the fifty sticks technique.

You need fifty narrow wooden sticks, each about one foot in length. Traditionally these are dried yarrow stalks, because the yarrow plant grows profusely on wild common land in China where sacrifices were held in the old days. Over the years it assumed a magical significance and at least until the present century was planted on the graves of Confucius and Meng-tse, the two most honoured sages of China.

Due to the popularity of the I Ching in Western countries at the present day, bundles of yarrow stalks can be bought in many book-shops specialising in occult subjects, but if you are unsuccessful in locating these narrow pieces of bamboo or even wooden dowel will serve.

Your copy of the *Book of Change* should be kept, when it is not in use, on a shelf fairly high above the floor, and wrapped in a clean piece of cloth, preferably silk. When you wish to consult it, it should be placed on a clear table and unwrapped, so that the book lies on the silk. The yarrow stalks or bamboo sticks should be kept in a simple closed box on the same shelf.

In ancient China, the seat of wisdom and judgment lay in the north, and those giving audience always faced south. You should therefore place your table in the northern part of the room, and approach it from the south. In front of the Book of Change lay the sticks, and place beside them a small incense burner.

Traditionally, before consulting the I Ching, you should make three kowtows to the floor and then, while still kneeling, pass the fifty sticks three times through the smoke of the incense.

Then compose yourself quietly and think of the question you want to put to the oracle. Try to phrase it in your mind as clearly as possible, and make sure that it is a question which is of real importance to you. Remember that the I Ching does not tell the future, but offers advice on how you should conduct yourself in the present in order to make the best of what the future holds in store.

Next, turn your attention to the sticks. The instructions that follow may seem complicated at first, but work slowly and they will soon seem quite simple.

(1) Take one of the fifty sticks and put it completely aside. It will not be used again but is included in the bundle to make the total up to the magically significant number of fifty.

(2) Using your right hand, divide the heap of sticks into two heaps, separating them by a few inches.

(3) Take one stick from the heap on your right and place it between the ring finger and little finger of your left hand.

(4) Remove sticks four at a time from the heap on your left until there are four or less left. Place these remaining sticks between the left hand middle finger and ring finger.

(5) Remove sticks four at a time from the heap on your right until there are four or less left. Place these remaining sticks between the index finger and middle finger.

You will now find that the sticks held between the fingers of your left hand total either 5 or 9 ($1 + 1 + 3$, $1 + 3 + 1$, $1 + 2 + 2$, or $1 + 4 + 4$). Put these sticks to one side.

A street fortune-teller in Japan, holding the fifty bamboo sticks. His paraphernalia also includes charts for palmistry and astrology

Gather together all the discarded sticks (totalling 49 less the 5 or 9 you have just laid aside) and work through the process of dividing again, starting with stage (2).

When you have done this you will find a total of either 4 or 8 sticks between the fingers of your left hand ($1 + 1 + 2$, $1 + 2 + 1$, $1 + 4 + 3$, or $1 + 3 + 4$). Put these sticks aside.

Gather the discarded sticks together once more, omitting the two small heaps of 5 or 9 sticks and 4 or 8 sticks. Now work through the process of dividing the sticks a third time, starting with stage (2).

At the end of all this you will have, in addition to the discarded sticks, three small heaps. The first will contain 5 or 9 sticks; the second will contain 4 or 8 sticks, and the third will also contain 4 or 8 sticks. Look up the three numbers you have, in the table on the following page.

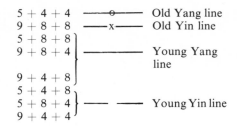

5 + 4 + 4	Old Yang line
9 + 8 + 8	Old Yin line
5 + 8 + 8	
9 + 8 + 4	Young Yang line
9 + 4 + 8	
5 + 4 + 8	
5 + 8 + 4	Young Yin line
9 + 4 + 4	

Note down the line that corresponds to your three numbers. This is the bottom line of your hexagram. To arrive at the second line up from the bottom you must gather together your 49 yarrow sticks once more and work through the stages of dividing and counting again.

This must be done a further four times in order to arrive at the six lines of a complete hexagram, reading from bottom to top.

If you look at the above table you will see that there are not just two lines, broken and unbroken, yin and yang, but four lines – young and old yin, and young and old yang.

If your hexagram is made up of just Young Yin (—— ——) and Young Yang (————) lines, turn to the appropriate text and read the *Judgment, Commentary,* and *Image.* Ignore the rest, as it is not appropriate.

If your hexagram contains one or more Old Yin (—x—) or Old Yang (—o—) lines, look up the text and read the *Judgment, Commentary,* and *Image,* and then read the passage relating to the special Old lines appearing in your hexagram.

Each of the four types of line is given a Chinese 'Ritual Number':

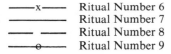

——x——	Ritual Number 6
————	Ritual Number 7
—— ——	Ritual Number 8
——o——	Ritual Number 9

This is why the short passage referring to each of the six lines of a hexagram begins 'In the third line SIX . . . ', or 'In the fifth line NINE . . . .'. Six and Nine are the Ritual Numbers of Old Yin and Old Yang lines.

If one or more of these especially significant lines is found in your hexagram you can take your consultation a stage further. The Old lines are also known as moving lines, because they are thought to be in a state of change and about to become their opposites.

So, an Old Yin line can be changed into a Young Yang line, and an Old Yang line can be changed into a Young Yin line, thus giving you a second hexagram. Read the *Judgment, Commentary,* and *Image* of this hexagram and it will throw extra light on your original question.

This ancient method of consulting the I Ching may seem extremely complicated at first glance, but it is a lot easier to do than to read about, and once you have practised a little and learned the few simple rules it will all appear very straightforward.

Whenever possible, the I Ching should be consulted by the method employing yarrow stalks. This is time-consuming and, although the true I Ching enthusiast will always contrive to make time to use it, there are two other methods which are somewhat quicker: these are the methods using three coins (undoubtedly the most convenient of all methods for westerners), and six wands.

The Three Coins Method

The three coins are tossed and, according to the way they fall, the lines of the hexagram can be obtained. As with the yarrow stalks, the first toss gives the bottom line, and so on upward. Chinese coins traditionally have an inscribed face and a blank face, and the inscribed side is given a value of 2 and the blank side a value of 3.

If you cannot obtain Chinese coins, you can use any western coins; but in this case 'heads' is valued at 3, and 'tails' at 2. So a toss of three coins can give you totals of 6, 7, 8 or 9, indicating respectively Old Yin, Young Yang, Young Yin, and Old Yang.

The Six Wands Method

This is the simplest way of consulting the oracle. Unlike the fifty sticks technique described previously, it is not necessary to perform a complicated sequence of operations before you can learn the answer to your question from the oracle.

Here is how you begin. First you need a set of six special wands. These should be about 8 inches (20 cm) long and 1 inch (2·5 cm) wide, and about ⅛ inch (3 mm) thick. Each wand should be coloured plain black on one side and plain black on the other side with a 1½-inch wide band of white painted across it in the middle.

When a wand falls with the all-black side uppermost this counts as an unbroken yang line (————). When a wand falls with the side showing the white stripe uppermost this counts as a broken yin line (—— ——).

So all you need to do to get a quick answer to your question is shuffle the six wands together behind your back as you concentrate on the question, then roll them smoothly onto a table in front of you as if you were unrolling a small mat.

Arrange them into the form of a hexagram, starting with the wand closest to you, which will represent the bottom line. The second closest will be the second line up, and so on.

When you can see which hexagram you have cast, look it up in the text. The *Judgment, Commentary,* and *Image* will give you the answer to your question.

However, there is obviously a limitation to this method of consulting the oracle. By casting the six wands you cannot obtain 'moving lines', so the texts given to the lines of the hexagram cannot be taken into account, and you cannot obtain a further hexagram which might throw extra light on your problem.

The six wands method is a useful way of first approaching the I Ching, but once you are fairly familiar with the oracle you should

endeavour to learn the fifty sticks technique. This will enable you to make the most of what the Book of Change has to offer.

In old China sets of wands were made from materials such as tortoiseshell inlaid with ivory, or from rare and valuable woods. But you can easily make a set for your own use from strips of ordinary wood of the right size.

Interpreting the Moving Lines

When you have obtained a hexagram without 'moving' lines, only the *Judgment,* the *Commentary* and the *Image* have any meaning for you, but the occurrence of moving lines does not only add significance to the original hexagram but carries you on to a second hexagram.

Here is an example. Assume you divided and counted the yarrow sticks as instructed and came up with this result:

```
5 + 4 + 8   ——  ——
9 + 8 + 4   ————————
5 + 4 + 8   ——  ——
9 + 4 + 4   ——  ——
5 + 8 + 4   ——  ——
5 + 4 + 8   ——  ——
```

This gives you Hexagram No 8, *Pi.* You should turn to Hexagram No 8 and read the *Judgment, Commentary,* and *Image.*

But suppose you came up with this result:

```
5 + 4 + 8   ——  ——
9 + 8 + 4   ————————
9 + 8 + 8   ——x——
9 + 4 + 4   ——  ——
5 + 8 + 4   ——  ——
9 + 8 + 8   ——x——
```

This will still give you Hexagram No. 8, *Pi,* but it includes two 'moving' lines – the bottom line and the fourth line up. Read the *Judgment, Commentary,* and *Image* accompanying Hexagram No 8, then read the texts given to the first line (reading from the bottom up) and the fourth line. These are important.

Now, change the two moving lines into their opposites. In both cases here an Old Yin line will become a Young Yang. You now have a second hexagram, No 17, *Sui:*

```
——  ——
————————
————————
——  ——
——  ——
————————
```

Read the *Judgment, Commentary,* and *Image* attached to this hexagram for more advice on your problem.

It may also be worthwhile discovering what happens if the moving lines are changing at different times. If the Old Yin in the bottom line changes into a Young Yang first, you will obtain hexagram No 3, *Chun.* But if the Old Yin in the fourth line changes first, you will obtain hexagram No 45, *Ts'ui.*

The advice given by the I Ching can be expressed as one of four simple injunctions: advance confidently; advance cautiously; stay where you are; retreat. But the texts of no two hexagrams are identical and the advice given in each is both subtle and precise.

You should always bear in mind that the I Ching is the product of a philosophy which was not at all concerned with achieving short-term material advantages, but was rather preoccupied with the problem of acting in a 'correct' way which harmonised with the cosmic rhythms of life. So the advice you receive from the oracle may not take very much account of your hopes for worldly success and comfort – its real concern is your spiritual welfare.

The construction of the hexagrams

To the ancient Chinese, observation of the world around them revealed three factors that were ever-present:

First, the cycle of events – day following night and season following season.

Second, the process of growth and decay – revealed, for example, in the waxing and waning of the moon, and in the life cycles of plants, animals and men.

Third, the polarity of the universe – everything has its opposite, and opposites are complementary to each other.

The positive and negative poles of existence were labelled yang (positive) and yin (negative). Yang included everything in the universe which was masculine, active, creative, hard, bright and strong. Yin included everything which was feminine, passive, destructive, soft, dark and yielding.

Yang and yin were not viewed as permanent and irreconcilable opposites, but as principles that were being constantly attracted to each other, finally to merge but then draw apart again in a ceaseless rhythmic cycle.

One of the ancient Confucian commentaries on the I Ching says: *The sun goes and the moon comes: the moon goes and the sun comes, sun and moon succeed each other, and their radiance is the outcome.*

Cold goes and heat comes; heat goes and cold comes; by this cycle of the cold and heat the year is completed.

That which is past becomes less and less, and that which lies ahead grows more and more; this contraction and expansion influence each other and advantageous progress is made.

The interplay of yang and yin give rise to all the phenomena of the universe, and these phenomena are classified in a 'Table of Elements.' This table is similar to the ancient Aristotelian classification in which everything is composed of various amounts of one of the

Ch'ien ☰	heaven	sky	ice cold	early winter	creative active strong firm light	father	head	horse	purple	metal	northwest
Tui ☱	pool	marsh	mist rain	autumn	joyful pleasurable	youngest daughter concubine	mouth	sheep	blue	flesh	west
Li ☲	fire	lightning	sun	summer	clear beautiful depending clinging	middle daughter	eye	pheasant	yellow	fire	south
Ch'en ☳	thunder		thunder	spring	active moving arousing	eldest son	foot	dragon	orange	grass	east
Sun ☴	wind	wood		early summer	gentle penetrating	eldest daughter	thigh	cock	white	air	southeast
K'an ☵	water	cloud a pit the abyss	moon	winter	labouring enveloping dangerous melancholy	middle son	ear	boar pig	red	wood	north
K'en ☶	mountain		thunder	early spring	stubborn immovable perverse	youngest son	hand fingers	dog	green	stone	northeast
K'un ☷	earth		heat	early autumn	receptive passive weak dark	mother	belly	cow mare	black	soil	southwest

four elements – air, fire, water or earth. In the Chinese system, however, there are five elements – fire, water, earth, metal and wood. These are known as the five *hsing*.

These are assigned rulership of the points of the compass, the seasons of the year, sacred animals, and parts of the human body in particular. Like their counterparts in the west, Chinese sages saw man as a microcosm, a miniature reflection of the universe who contained all its elements within him.

But there was one important difference between the world-view of the Chinese and that of Western man. This was in the Chinese acceptance of humanity as an integral part of the realm of nature, not as a species set apart. The aim of Chinese spiritual disciplines was not the emancipation of man from the world, but rather the breaking down of the barriers that separated him from it. Not union with a supernatural creator who existed apart from his creation, but union with Tao, the all-embracing energy of the cosmos, the underlying ground of yang and yin.

The I Ching was designed to mirror the universe, and could therefore be used to chart the fluctuating fortunes of this miniature universe, man, by reflecting the interacting flow of yang and yin through space and time by use of an ingenious set of symbols.

The positive current of yang is symbolised by the unbroken line —————, and the negative current of yin is symbolised by the broken line ——— ———. These two lines combined in pairs are called the greater and lesser yang and the greater and lesser yin to show the basic interactions of the two opposites.

A third line is then added to each digram to represent the three powers operating in the universe: Heaven, Earth, and – between the two – Man. These three-lined figures, or trigrams, symbolise all the basic stages in the processes of change. There are eight of them, showing all the possible combinations of yang and yin lines in groups of three, and they are frequently represented, in Chinese art, as turning in a circle around the interlocking dark and light symbols of yang and yin.

The eight trigrams are viewed as a family, and each is given a name and a number of attributes, as listed in Table 1.

Finally, each of the eight trigrams is paired with itself and all of the others, resulting in a total of sixty-four six-lined figures, the hexagrams. Each hexagram relates to one phase in the cycle of change throughout all levels of the universe and, as every event in the universe in some way affects the whole, the person consulting the I Ching automatically obtains a response which is relevant to his situation.

One of the Confucian commentaries on the I Ching, the Great Commentary, states: *When the superior man is about to take action of a private or a public nature he refers to the oracle, making his enquiry in words. It receives his message, and the answer comes as if it were an echo. Whether the subject be far or near, mysterious or profound, he knows forthwith what its outcome will be.*

The I Ching teaches that events do not happen arbitrarily, but follow precise rhythms and cycles of change. By deducing which stage in a cycle your particular situation has reached, according to the ancient theory, you can predict which stage is about to follow.

The philosophy of the I Ching

In China, as in the West, correspondences between parts of the human body and parts of the universe were carefully worked out and applied to divination and medicine.

The head was associated with heaven, and the hair with the stars. The eyes corresponded to the sun and the ears to the moon. The breath was linked with the wind and the blood was the equivalent of rain, running through veins and arteries which represented streams and rivers. The bones were thought of as mountains and the orifices of the body as valleys.

Five vital internal organs took their nature from the five elements – the lungs (wood), heart (fire), kidneys (earth), spleen (metal) and liver (water).

By observing the workings of nature, the oracle teaches, it becomes possible to understand the secret rhythms that rule the destiny of man, and learn to use them as a guide in the conduct of life. This is explained in one of the Confucian commentaries on the I Ching, which states:

The sage gazes up and contemplates the phenomena of the heavens, then looks down and examines the patterns of the earth; thereby he learns the causes of darkness and light.

He traces things to their beginning and follows them to their end; therefore he knows the significance of life and death.

The yin-yang symbol surrounded by the eight trigrams. This arrangement is known as the Sequence of Earlier Heaven, or Primal Arrangement

A delicate sense of humour is apparent in even the most serious manifestations of Chinese philosophy, and Chinese artists throughout the centuries have delighted in making puns — literal and visual — based on Taoist beliefs and the fundamentals of the I Ching. This painting, entitled 'Passing the summer at the thatched hall of the Inkwell', is by the artist Wu Li; and the painter has made play with his own name, for the trigram associated with summer is Li, the fire. The view is southward to the source of yang, and the artist has used a palette rich in yellow, the colour that is the attribute of summer and of Li itself. And the way in which each part of the picture is closed in on itself by walls or fences recalls the actual form of the trigram

He observes how the union of essence and breath form things, and how the disappearance of the spirit produces their dissolution; therefore he knows the constitution of the lower and higher souls.

Being so closely attuned to nature, the I Ching was used by the Chinese as a useful addition to their lunar calendar. Twelve hexagrams, known as the 'sovereign' hexagrams, were allotted to the twelve months.

The titles given to the component trigrams in the lunar calendar reflect the weather to be expected during each season of the year in North China (Table 2).

The annual cycle was divided into two halves; the first half, which commenced in February prior to the spring equinox, being ruled by the outgoing, positive, masculine forces of yang; and the second half of the year, which commenced in August prior to the autumn equinox, being ruled by the inward-turning, negative, feminine forces of yin.

If, when you consult the I Ching, you find you have obtained one of the twelve sovereign hexagrams, this may serve as a pointer to the time of the year when certain events might be expected to come to pass.

The nature of the I Ching and the superior man's use of the oracle are described thus in the Confucian 'Great Appendix.'

The sages set forth the hexagrams, examined their symbolism, and added explanations. In this way good fortune and bad were made clear.

The strong and the weak lines displace each other, producing changes and transformations in the hexagrams.

Therefore the good and evil fortune mentioned in the texts refer to the rights and wrongs in the affairs of men. The repentance and regret mentioned in the texts refer to men's sorrows and anxiety.

The changes and transformations of the lines symbolise the advance and retreat of the powers of nature. Thus strong and weak lines symbolise day and night. The movements taking place within the six lines of a hexagram reveal the progress of the three powers (i.e. heaven, man and earth).

Therefore the superior man follows the advice of the oracle. He studies the explanations of the lines with greatest pleasure.

The superior man, living quietly, contemplates the symbols and studies their explanations. When starting anything he consults the oracle and studies its advice. In this way he gains the help of heaven, which brings good fortune and advantage in everything he does.

The reverence in which the I Ching was held by Chinese scholars is well summed up in the words of Confucius:

What is it that the I does? It makes known the outcome of things, brings about the accomplishments of men, and gathers within itself all things under heaven. This and nothing more its function. Therefore the sages, by consulting it, would properly direct the aims of

all under heaven, would give stability to their undertakings, and resolve their doubts.

When you have manipulated the yarrow stalks, tossed three coins, or thrown the six wands and arrived at a hexagram, read the whole text through several times, paying particular attention to any moving lines that occur. The moving lines are the essence of the I Ching's message, and though they seem obscure at first, are of real importance.

THE ANCIENT CHINESE CALENDAR

	Sovereign Hexagram	Names of the fortnights	Commencing		Sovereign Hexagram	Names of the fortnights	Commencing
1.	T'AI	Beginning of Spring The Rains	5 Feb. 20 Feb.	7.	P'I	Beginning of Autumn End of Heat	8 Aug. 24 Aug.
2.	TA CHUANG	Awakening of Creatures Spring Equinox	7 March 22 March	8.	KUAN	White Dews Autumn Equinox	8 Sept. 24 Sept.
3.	KUAI	Clear and Bright Grain Rain	6 April 21 April	9.	PO	Cold Dews Descent of Hoar Frost	9 Oct. 24 Oct.
4.	CH'IEN	Beginning of Summer Lesser Fullness	6 May 22 May	10.	K'UN	Beginning of Winter Lesser Snow	8 Nov. 23 Nov.
5.	KOU	Grain in Ear Summer Solstice	7 June 22 June		FU	Greater Snow Winter Solstice	7 Dec. 22 Dec.
6.	TUN	Lesser Heat Greater Heat	8 July 24 July	12.	LIN	Lesser Cold Greater Cold	6 Jan. 21 Jan.

The art of Tao

All Taoist art is full of symbolism and allusion. In this silk painting (right) the giant peach is the symbol of long life; the stag represents fortune and honours; the bats are for happiness; and the pine-tree, spreading its protection over all, stands for tenacity. In the porcelain dish (below, far right) the shepherdess, a yin symbol, is surrounded by two male and one female sheep. These sheep represent the trigram Tui, the pool of water.

(Below, left) A jade 'Pi' disc, representing the enclosed, yet infinite, nature of the universe.

(Below, right) A jade amulet, with the yin-yang symbol of the Great Ultimate and the twelve Earthly Branches, guarded by a dragon and a phoenix

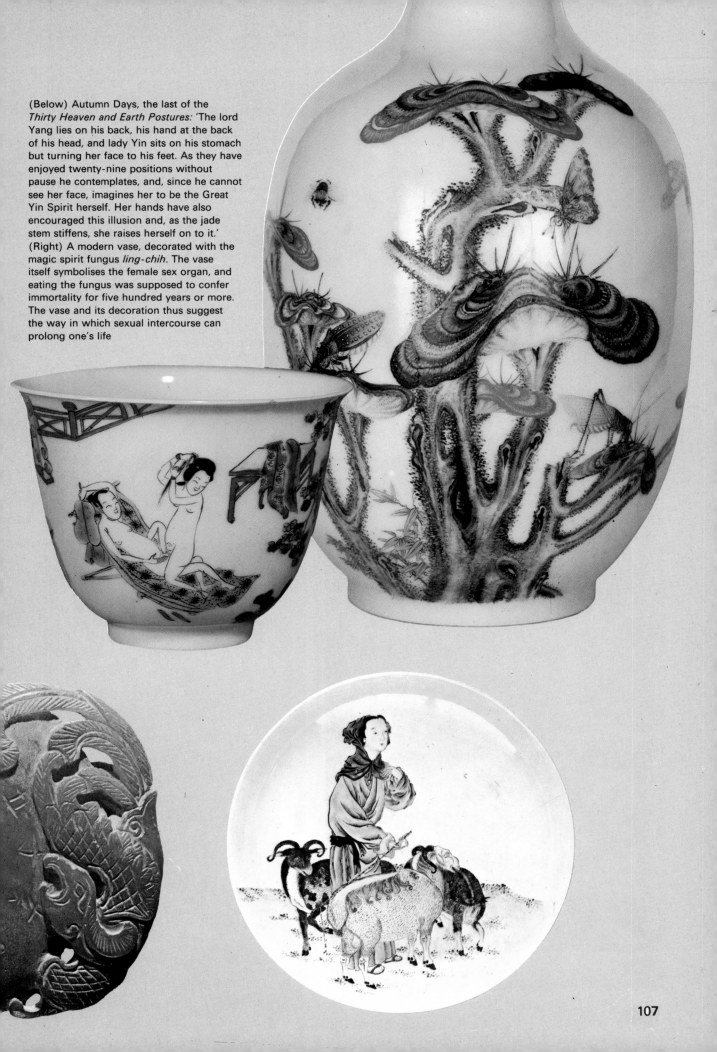

(Below) Autumn Days, the last of the *Thirty Heaven and Earth Postures*: 'The lord Yang lies on his back, his hand at the back of his head, and lady Yin sits on his stomach but turning her face to his feet. As they have enjoyed twenty-nine positions without pause he contemplates, and, since he cannot see her face, imagines her to be the Great Yin Spirit herself. Her hands have also encouraged this illusion and, as the jade stem stiffens, she raises herself on to it.' (Right) A modern vase, decorated with the magic spirit fungus *ling-chih*. The vase itself symbolises the female sex organ, and eating the fungus was supposed to confer immortality for five hundred years or more. The vase and its decoration thus suggest the way in which sexual intercourse can prolong one's life

'Among green mountains I build a house' (left) is dated the first day of the tenth month 1663. The house faces south, toward the height of yang vitality; behind it, the sharp phallic peaks of summer are yielding place to the rounded yin shapes of winter and darkness, water and the north. Water flows everywhere, symbolising change, wreathing behind the house in clouds of mist that reflect the veins of 'dragon energy' writhing through the rocks. The pine trees and the crane before the house represent the long life to be won by sexual practices and meditation

There are many stories of the *hsien,* Taoist adepts who achieved immortality by diet or alchemy. One of the most familiar is Li T'ieh-kuai (below left) in the form of a lame beggar with an iron crutch. The story goes that once, when his spirit left his body to visit Lao-tse, his own body was burnt by accident, and he was compelled to return to the body of a beggar who had starved to death nearby. On his back he carries a gourd, filled with magic potions capable of reviving the dead

THE BOOK OF CHANGE

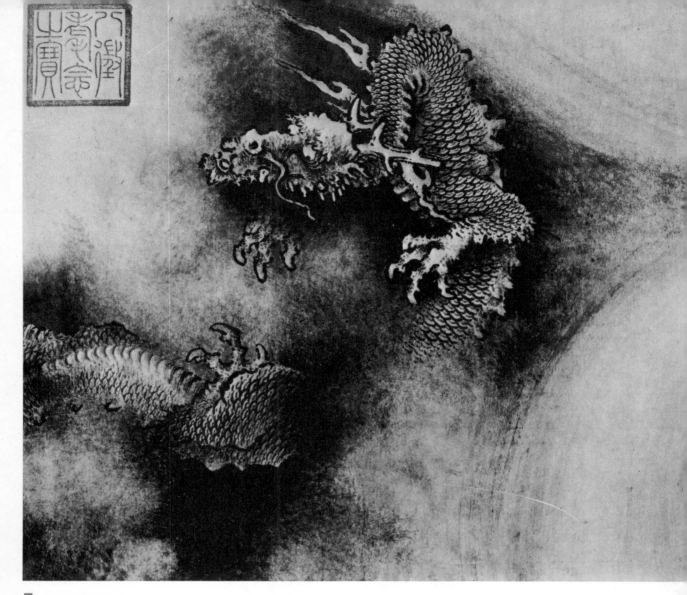

I CH'IEN

乾

The Creative Principle

The trigrams:
     above: Ch'ien Heaven, the creative
     below: Ch'ien Heaven, the creative
Ch'ien represents what is great, penetrating, advantageous, correct and firm. It is the originator, the creative. The hexagram consists entirely of yang lines, with the qualities of creativity, virility, activity and strength. There is no weakness or yielding. It is a double image of the trigram named heaven, or origination. It embodies the inner creative power of the lower trigram, representing that of man, and the outer creativity of the upper trigram, that of heaven.

The Judgment
Ch'ien works sublime success. Perserverance brings favourable results to he who is firm and unyielding.

Commentary
Vast is the great originator. All things owe their beginning to it, and it contains all the meanings embodied in its name: the clouds move and the rain falls everywhere; all things appear in their developed form.
     The initiated comprehend the relationship between beginning and end, and how each of the six lines reaches its accomp-

lishment at the appointed time. They mount the chariot drawn by these six dragons at the proper hour, and drive across the sky.
     Ch'ien transforms everything, developing its true nature as heaven determines, preserving great harmony in union. The initiate appears, high above all things, and everything under heaven enjoys true repose.

The Image
The movement of the heavens reveals transcendent power. The superior man, therefore, nerves himself to untiring activity.

The Lines
In the bottom line, NINE signifies:
     The dragon lies concealed in the deep.
     Action at such a time would be unwise.
In China the dragon is a symbol of the dynamic energy of nature, manifested in the lightning of the storm. The superior man himself is represented as the dragon, and when the dragon flies, the time of action is near; but the wise man, having drawn this line, bides his time for the propitious moment.

In the second line, NINE signifies:
     The dragon appears in the field.
     It is a favourable time to see the great man.
The beneficial forces of nature begin to

manifest themselves. It is time for the superior man to embark upon his chosen field of activity: though he may begin in a subordinate position his innate seriousness of purpose, his sense of responsibility and the influence he exerts will ultimately raise him to a position of power, where all who observe him will benefit by it.

In the third line, NINE signifies:
    The superior man is active all day long.
    At nightfall his mind is still full of care.
    Danger, but no reproach.
The great man increases in his importance; his fame spreads, and crowds flock to him. But he must beware of ambition destroying his integrity. He who can remain aware of what still lies ahead will avoid all pitfalls, and suffer no blame.

In the fourth line, NINE signifies:
    The flight across the abyss is not sure
    He who is resolute suffers no reproach.
The dragon seems to be leaping up, but is still in the deep. The time of decision has come for the great man: he can go forward and upward, making an important place for himself in the world, or he can retire again into solitude and contemplation. Whichever way he acts, so long as it is true to his nature, there will be no blame attached to what he does.

In the fifth line, NINE signifies:
    The dragon flies across the heavens.
    It is a favourable time to see the
        great man.
All nature is in accord: water flows to what is wet, fire turns to what is dry. Clouds follow the dragon, wind follows the tiger. The great man has made his choice, and everyone follows him with their eyes as he reaches the height of his achievement.

In the sixth line, NINE signifies:
    The dragon flies too high.
    There will be cause for repentance.
Here is a warning not to aspire too high, allowing arrogance to isolate the great man from the rest of mankind.

'The dragon flies across the heavens' The dragon is a symbol of dynamic energy, manifested in the lightning of the storm. Clouds follow the dragon, as the wind follows the tiger

2 K'UN

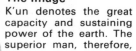

The Passive Principle

The trigrams:
above: K'un Earth, the passive
below: K'un Earth, the passive
K'un represents also what is great, penetrating, advantageous, correct, and having the firmness of the mare. The hexagram consists entirely of yin lines, feminine, yielding and shaded. It is the diametrical opposite of Ch'ien in structure but its complement in character. Male and female, heaven and earth, spirit and matter, the creative and the passive principle, are nothing but two aspects of the same whole.

The Judgment
K'un brings supreme success through steadfast acceptance. When the superior man takes the initiative in action he will go astray; if he follows, he will find his true leader. It is advantageous to find friends in the west and south, and to relinquish friends in the north and east. Quiet perseverance brings good fortune to the superior man.

Commentary
The creativity of K'un is complete: all things owe their birth to it, and it obediently accepts the influences of heaven, supporting and containing all things. The mare is an earthly creature: she moves about the earth without restriction, mild and docile, strong and well-favoured. So should the superior man behave.

The Image
K'un denotes the great capacity and sustaining power of the earth. The superior man, therefore, employs his virtue in supporting all men and all things.

The Lines
In the bottom line, SIX signifies:
He treads only on hoarfrost,
But solid ice is near.
Just as the earth prepares for life in the spring, so it makes ready in the autumn for death. When the first frost appears, the ice of winter is not far away. In life, signs of decay and death make their appearance, but these warnings can be heeded. The wise man, finding that his steps take him on to newly-frozen water, retraces his path and bides his time until the ice is strong enough.

In the second line, SIX signifies:
Straight, square, great; line, plane, solid—
Purposeless, the work still goes forward.
Creation moves in a straight line, generating the first dimension; at right angles it generates the plane, defining the second dimension. Movement in the third dimension generates the cube, the form that the Chinese believed to be the shape of the earth. Allowing himself to be carried forward by the inexorable progress of nature, the superior man proceeds toward his destiny.

In the third line, SIX signifies:
Although the line is hidden, it persists;
Who serves a king should do his work and not seek fame.
The wise man happily leaves fame to others. He does not try to impose his ideas on others, but perseveres at his set tasks, confident that true virtue will be recognised.

In the fourth line, SIX signifies:
A tightly tied sack.
No praise, but no reproach.
The sack keeps its secrets, but it is also a place of darkness and danger. Great caution is necessary: powerful antagonists should not be challenged, but undeserved praise will later turn to one's disadvantage. The wise man keeps himself to himself, whether in solitude or in the midst of the world's turmoil.

In the fifth line, SIX signifies:
A yellow undergarment:
Supreme good fortune.
Yellow is the colour of the earth and of the middle way: it symbolises sincerity and reliability. As an undergarment it is not shown off ostentatiously, it is the sign of noble reserve. One in a high but subordinate position should be discreet.

In the sixth line, SIX signifies:
Dragons fight in the field.
Their blood is black and yellow.
The black or dark blue dragon signifies heaven; the yellow dragon symbolises the false inflation of the earth principle. When one attempts to fight a way into a position higher than that to which one is entitled, both sides will suffer injury.

(Right) 'A yellow undergarment . . .' A funerary figure of the T'ang period. (Far right) The yellow dragon represents the false inflation of K'un the passive principle

An eighteenth century fan painting of rocks and bamboo in the snow. Chun represents a shoot bursting its way through the soil in the first days of spring

3 CHUN

Initial Difficulties

The trigrams:
above: K'an deep dangerous water
below: Chen thunder and awakening
The sign for Chun represents a new shoot, struggling to burst its way through the soil in the first days of spring. The lower trigram, Chen, represents upward movement, and its image is thunder. The upper trigram, K'an, has a downward movement and its image is rain. There is chaotic confusion: the air is filled with thunder and rain; but the thunderstorm brings release from tension, and everything is calm again.

The Judgment
Initial difficulties are followed by supreme success, the result of acting firmly and correctly. Nothing should be attempted without appointing those who can provide appropriate assistance.

Commentary
In Chun we see the intercourse begin of Ch'ien the strong and K'un the weak, and the difficulties that arise. Motion in the midst of danger leads on to success. By the action of the thunder and rain, all the space between heaven and earth is filled up. But the time is still full of disorder and obscure: nothing can be predicted with confidence. It is advantageous to appoint deputies and helpers, but it is unwise to suppose that the storm is at an end and that rest and peace are at hand.

The Image
Clouds and thunder represent the idea of initial difficulty. The superior man busies himself with creating order out of confusion.

The Lines
In the bottom line, NINE signifies:
Obstacles and hesitation before action.
Perseverance is rewarding.
It is advantageous to appoint assistants. When obstacles are met with at the beginning of an enterprise, the best course may well be inaction. But this is not the avoidance of action; it is a time to persevere and calculate how best to overcome the obstacle. The wise man chooses those who are to help him in a spirit of humility.

In the second line, SIX signifies:
Difficulties increase.
One of the horses breaks free from her wagon.
But he is not a highwayman,
He is one who wishes her to be his wife.
The chaste maiden rejects his advances,
And waits ten years before she bears children.
As the hindrances multiply, as the horses drag the wagon through the mud of a stormy night — suddenly, here is a mounted man trotting to and fro. But this is not an enemy, it is a friend who comes to offer help; yet his offer must not be accepted, because it will conflict with the freedom of decision. Only after a long time will the right moment present itself.

In the third line, SIX signifies:
He hunts deer in the forest without a guide,
And loses his way.
The superior man, understanding the situation,
Gives up the chase.
To continue brings humiliation.
Obstinately pursuing a goal without seeking advice to result in failure. The wise man, realising the difficulties into which his impulsiveness has led him, retires to reconsider his actions.

In the fourth line, SIX signifies:
The horses break from the wagon.
She seeks the assistance of her suitor.
The time is auspicious
For going forward.
There is a wrong time, and a right time, to accept offered help. It may mean that pride must be swallowed, and that assistance must be sought from one who was previously rejected. There is no shame in accepting help in a difficult and dangerous situation.

In the fifth line, NINE signifies:
Obstacles to generosity.
A little perseverance brings success.
Much perseverance brings misfortune.
The individual is in a position where even his most generous gestures are misinterpreted. But he must not try to force the outcome; it is only through firm and confident actions, carried out unobtrusively, that he will succeed in overcoming the obstacles.

In the sixth line, SIX signifies:
The horses drag the wagon back.
Tears of blood are wept.
The difficulties have been too great: the only way is back to the beginning. But success is not achieved by giving up; the bloody tears will not flow for long, and another way will be found.

Youthful Inexperience

The trigrams:
above: Ken   mountain, stillness
below: K'an   dangerous deep water

As Chun represents the infant plant struggling to break the surface, so Meng represents its undeveloped appearance. The water bubbling up at the foot of the mountain is the image of inexperienced youth. When the spring firsts bursts out, it has no idea where it is going; but its determined flow eventually fills up the deep, and it goes on its way.

The Judgment
There will be progress and success. I do not seek out the young and inexperienced; he comes to find me. When he first asks my advice, I instruct him. But if he comes a second or a third time, that is troublesome, and I do not advise the troublesome. Firm and correct action brings favourable results.

Commentary
Uncultivated growth. The dangerous pit lies at the foot of the mountain, and to stay on the edge of the abyss is youthful folly. There are perils and obstacles in the way of progress, but the young and inexperienced should be nurtured like a new plant. The intention of the initiate is accomplished.

The Image
As the spring gushes out at the foot of the mountain, so the superior man improves his character by diligent thoroughness in all his actions.

The Lines
In the bottom line, SIX signifies:
The ignorant youth should be
    disciplined,
But remove his fetters lest he be
    humiliated.

Firmness and severe treatment, even punishment, are of great help in dispelling ignorance and folly. But going on in this way will give cause for regret, for discipline will degenerate into tyranny.

In the second line, NINE signifies:
To suffer fools kindly brings good
    fortune.
Understanding of women brings good
    fortune.
The son can take charge of the
    household.

The young man who begins to develop and to understand the importance of tolerance, as it is shown to him by his elders, will soon himself be able to take on their responsibilities.

In the third line, SIX signifies:
No good will come of a maiden who
    loses control
When she sees a man of bronze. Do not
    cherish her.

The 'man of bronze' may represent a wealthy suitor, or a figure of heroic appeal. The weak and inexperienced man is compared to a girl throwing herself at such a person; as he struggles to improve himself, he may lose all individuality by trying to imitate a stronger personality.

In the fourth line, SIX signifies:
Bound in the chains of his ignorance,
He suffers humiliation and regret.

The inexperienced youth can so easily entangle himself in fantasies, and only confusion will result, followed by shame. If he persists, no teacher can aid him: he must be left to return to reality by his own efforts, no matter how much humiliation he suffers as a result.

In the fifth line, SIX signifies:
The simplicity of the child
Brings good fortune.

Inexperience is best overcome by seeking the teacher in a spirit of humility, and learning without arrogance.

In the sixth line, NINE signifies:
Punishing the inexperienced youth,
One should not injure him.
The purpose of punishment is to prevent
    injury.

As the first line says, 'the ignorant youth should be disciplined'. But the punishment should not be imposed in anger; it should be measured, objective, never an end in itself. It is for the good of the ignorant, not to relieve the conscience of the teacher.

(Below) 'Bound in the chains of his ignorance, he suffers humiliation and regret.' Scene from a fifteenth century silk scroll

5 HSÜ

Patient anticipation

The trigrams:
above: K'an   dangerous deep water
below: Ch'ien Heaven, the creative
Water is seen in the heavens in the form of clouds. But clouds, though they give promise of rain, also indicate that we must wait for that promise to be fulfilled. The trigrams, symbolising danger above but strength within, also draw attention to the importance of biding one's time until that time is right.

The Judgment
Waiting. With sincerity, there will follow brilliant success. Perseverance brings good fortune. It is advantageous to cross the great water.

Commentary
The dangerous deep of K'an lies ahead, and though the creative power of Ch'ien drives him forward, he must show patience. Only then will the time come when he can go forward and achieve his goal with success. A journey — but not necessarily across water, indeed it may be a spiritual one — will be rewarding at this time.

The Image
Clouds rise up to heaven, representing patient anticipation. The superior man, accordingly, spends the time in eating and drinking, satisfying himself and remaining cheerful.

The Lines
In the bottom line, NINE signifies:
> He waits at the edge of the meadow
> And furthers his plans by remaining still.
> No reproach.

Danger is still far off: the prudent man does not take cover, but he does not make himself vulnerable by advancing into the open. He employs the time in preparing himself for future action.

In the second line, NINE signifies:
> He waits on the sandy bank of the
>   mountain stream.
> There are rumours of scandal,
> But, in the end, good fortune.

The sand is soft, and does not afford a good footing. Danger shows itself only in gossip and malicious whispers, and a steadfast calmness in the face of calumny will bring success at last.

In the third line, NINE signifies:
> He waits in the mud,
> Expecting the arrival of the enemy.

The flood waters are very near, and the ground underfoot is slippery and treacherous. It is not a good place to stand and meet the onrush of danger. With resolution, it would have been possible to clear the stream at a bound, and reach the farther bank, but now the peril must be faced with as much preparation as possible.

In the fourth line, SIX signifies:
> He waits standing in blood,
> But he will escape from the pit.

Disaster threatens; it is now a matter of life or death. There is no going forward, there is no going back. One stands as in a pit, waiting with fortitude and brave composure for fate to take its course. This is the only way of escaping from the pit.

In the fifth line, NINE signifies:
> He waits at the table.
> Perseverance brings good fortune.

This is the still eye of the storm, the quiet water at the heart of the rushing rapids. The wise man employs the time in recovering his strength, eating and drinking as he can, in order to meet the struggles to come with strength of body and mind.

In the sixth line, SIX signifies:
> He falls into the pit.
> Three unexpected guests arrive:
> Receive them with respect and all will
>   be well in the end.

All seems lost. All the restraint, all the husbanding of resources and building of strength, seems of no avail. But in the deepest despair, help comes from an unexpected and unsought source. At first it may not be recognised for what it is, but the wise man will welcome it and accept the assistance that rescues him from his predicament.

Conflict

The trigrams:

above: Ch'ien Heaven, the creative
below: K'an dangerous deep water
The upper trigram represents heaven, which tends to move upward; while the lower trigram, representing water, moves ever downward. So the two halves of Chun pull away from one another, producing a situation of tension and incipient conflict. The attribute of the male Ch'ien is strength, that of K'an is subtlety and intrigue; a character combining outward determination with inward cunning will be a quarrelsome one.

The Judgment

Conflict. Confidence is obstructed, and a cautious halt at the halfway stage will bring good fortune. But obstinate determination to go forward against all obstacles can only end in misfortune. It is a favourable time to see the great man, but it is unsafe to cross the great water.

Commentary

No matter what the sincerity of a man's motives, it is impossible to avoid the conflict, but the danger can be mitigated by a cautious approach. The prudent man remains clear-headed and inwardly strong, recognising that his only course lies in meeting his opponent halfway, and that the conflict must not be allowed to become permanent. Advice from the great man strengthens his position, but if he attempts to go forward across the water he will fall into the abyss.

The Image

Heaven and water moving in opposite ways are the image of conflict. The superior man therefore appraises the beginning of any venture with great care.

The Lines

In the bottom line, SIX signifies:
If the conflict is not prosecuted,
There will be some gossip;
But, in the end, good fortune.
The prudent man desists in advancing his views in the face of opposition, and peace is quickly restored. This may give rise to scurrilous talk, but once the conflict has been resolved the enterprise will be carried through eventually to a satisfactory conclusion.

In the second line, NINE signifies:
He cannot continue the conflict,
But yields and returns home.
His fellow townsmen,
Three hundred households,
Suffer no reproach.
The Chinese have always believed that to retreat in the face of superior strength is no disgrace. A man, from a false sense of honour, may try to prosecute the struggle; but in doing so he involves the honour of his kinsmen and may bring disaster upon a whole community. 'He who fights and runs away may live to fight another day'.

In the third line, SIX signifies:
He nourishes himself on the
ancient virtues,
And remains firm and constant.
There is danger, but good fortune at last.
Who serves a king should do his work
and not seek fame.
He who adheres to the established code of conduct may find himself in danger of losing his position, but success will come in the end. Whatever a man possesses through the strength of his character cannot be taken away from him, but if he is working for a superior he can only avoid conflict by doing his duty and letting undeserved fame and prestige go to others.

In the fourth line, NINE signifies:
He cannot continue the conflict,
But gives way and submits to fate;
Changing his disposition,
He finds peace in perseverance.
Good fortune.
The man, unsatisfied with his situation, attempts to improve it by struggle, since he is now the stronger contender. But his is an unjust cause, and only by accepting his destiny, and adhering to the laws of the universe, does he find peace and success.

In the fifth line, NINE signifies:
To engage in conflict before a just judge
Brings supreme success.
The moment has come for conflict, for the cause is good, and the judgment of an impartial man will bring great good fortune.

In the sixth line, NINE signifies:
Though he gain the leather belt,
Three times before noon it will be taken
from him.
The leather belt is the trophy of the victor, the honourable girdle of the great fighter. But although he has won his battle his success does not last: others assail him again and again, and the result is unending conflict.

Two wrestlers, a bronze from the time of the Chou dynasty, the sixth century BC

7 SHIH

A Troop of Soldiers

The trigrams:
above: K'un Earth, the passive
below: K'an dangerous deep water
Water lies beneath the earth, like a subterranean stream about to rise to the surface as a spring. So the soldiers lie hidden when they are not needed, but ready to burst into action whenever it is necessary. The trigrams, combining inner danger with outer devotion, are also symbolic of military organisation.

The Judgment
With firm and correct action, and a leader of age and experience, there will be resultant good fortune without reproach.

Commentary
The name of Shih describes the multitude of the host. The firmness and correctness indicated by the hexagram refer to moral strength. The man who can lead the army aright is fit to be king, for the strong line in the lower trigram holds the whole together and everything responds to his control. Proceeding with a dangerous task is a means to winning the allegiance of the people and the control of the kingdom. The results may distress the whole countryside, but in the face of good fortune how can any error arise?

The Image
Water hidden in the earth is the image of the army. The superior man, accordingly, wins followers by his generosity.

The Lines
In the bottom line, SIX signifies:
The soldiers must set out in good order;
If there is disorder, there will be
misfortune.
Discipline is the essential of all military organisations, and the secret of victory. The troop that goes into battle in disarray is certain to be defeated, and this applies to any venture. The man who begins any undertaking without carefully considering his strategy is doomed to failure; he must not fail to take into account, also, the good faith of those who support him in his various enterprises.

In the second line, NINE signifies:
He stands surrounded by his forces.
There is good fortune, and no reproach.
Three times the king awards battle
honours.
The leader should always be in the midst of his army: he should not be in the van, ex-

posing himself to unnecessary dangers, nor at the rear, where he will lose the loyalty of his men. He who draws this line is assured of success if he follows this principle; he will earn his reward as part of his forces, sharing his honours with his men. Whatever the enterprise. the leader is only ensured of success if he plans to share the profits with his associates.

In the third line, SIX signifies:
The army that carries corpses in its
wagons
Is assured of failure.
This is an image with several interpretations. An army must be able to move quickly and easily, to give way where the enemy force is superior, and to regroup its men where they can be most effective: the army that carries its dead with it is already defeated. It was also the custom in China to carry a young boy in place of the corpse at funerals, who was honoured as his family's representative. Many corpses would therefore each be represented, and none would stand out as the leader. In an army where all are generals, who will fight?

In the fourth line, SIX signifies:
The army retreats
But there is no disgrace.
There is no shame is withdrawing in the face of superior force; even if defeat is certain it is better to preserve the strength one still still posses.

In the fifth line, SIX signifies:
When wild beasts roam the field
There is no disgrace in capturing them.
The eldest son is in command
The youngest carries away the dead:
Persistence brings misfortune.
The enemy occupies the battlefield, looting and triumphing. Now is the time to attack and destroy them. But the fight must not be allowed to degenerate into unthinking slaughter. A strong leader is necessary, who knows when to call a halt to the slaughter before the enemy can mount a counterattack.

In the sixth line, SIX signifies:
The king issues his commands,
Grants estates and titles of nobility;
But power should not be given to the
inferior.
After victory in battle, the leader of the army and his officers are rewarded with honours. But the rank and file should be given only material reward, not land and authority, for their inexperience may mean that they will rule badly.

(Above) Liu Pang, founder of the Han dynasty, with his soldiers, entering a city in triumph. A detail from an eleventh century scroll

Seeking Unity

The trigrams:
      above: K'an   dangerous deep water
      below: K'un   Earth, the passive

This is the reverse of the previous hexagram, Shih, where the water lay beneath the earth. Now the water lies upon the earth, flowing toward other water, forming streams that unite into rivers, rivers that flow into the seas. All the lines of this hexagram, except the fifth (the place of the ruler), are feminine and yielding. It is the fifth line that holds them together as they flow.

The Judgment
Unity brings good fortune. Consult the oracle again to discover whether you possess true grace, constancy and perseverance; then there is no reproach. Those who are irresolute will gradually come to him; but delaying too long will lead to misfortune.

Commentary
The hexagram represents inferiors docilely following the lead of the superior man. Indeed, his equals and his superiors will also follow him, for a strong man is needed to hold the people together. Those who first join him will take part in the forming of organisations and the laws that bind them together; latecomers will be unable to share in the good fortune of the community.

The Image
Water upon the earth is the image of holding together. So the kings of old made grants of land to their principal followers, and maintained friendly relations with their princes.

The Lines
In the bottom line, SIX signifies:
    True loyalty is without reproach.
    When the breast is as full of sincerity as a
      flowing bowl
    Good fortune comes from far away.
The whole is greater than the parts: the content of the earthenware bowl is everything, and the empty bowl symbolises the nothingness of form. The truth in a man's heart speaks louder than his words. The inner strength of the sincere man will attract unexpected good fortune from without.

In the second line, SIX signifies:
    The movement to unity comes from
      within.
    Righteous persistence brings good
      fortune.
When a man understands his true nature, he will join with others not as a servant but as an equal. But if he obsequiously seeks preferment, he is wasting himself. Only the superior man, who acts with dignity and firmness, will find success.

In the third line, SIX signifies:
    He joins with those who are unfit.
We must beware of entering into associations with people who surround us, but who are not of our way of thinking; the superior man does not spurn those below or above him, but opens his heart only to those who are his equals.

In the fourth line, SIX signifies:
    Join with the leader.
    Righteous persistence brings good
      fortune.
When the leader emerges, the wise man throws in his lot with him. But he must still remain constant and not allow himself to be led astray.

In the fifth line, NINE signifies:
    This is the sign of union.
    The king hunts with beaters on three
      sides only,
    Losing the game that runs before him.
    The people need no threats,
    And there is good fortune.
In the royal hunts of ancient China the game was driven only from three sides, so that some had an opportunity to escape. Those who did not were driven towards a fence with a gate behind which the king stood ready to fire his arrows. A well-governed citizenry needs no coercion: they should join in voluntary union, free to express themselves while recognising the authority of their rulers.

In the sixth line, SIX signifies:
    There is no leader, no union.
    Great misfortune.
No enterprise can succeed without strong leadership. The right moment for unity has passed; now hesitation will only bring regrets when it is too late.

8 PI

Pi signifies inferiors docilely following the lead of a superior man. The illustration is from a stone-rubbing and represents Confucius with a disciple

9
HSIAO CH'U

The Power of the Weak

The trigrams:
above: Sun wind, gentleness, penetration
below: Ch'ien Heaven, the creative
This hexagram represents the ability, even of the weak, to restrain and impede. The five strong yang lines are held in check by the yin line in the fourth place, the position of the minister. The concept of exercising power by yielding is one that has been developed by the Taoists, who were also only too aware of the weakness inherent in a show of strength.

The Judgment
Success lies in the power of the weak. Dense clouds gather, but there is no rain from the western borders.

This hexagram reflects the situation in China at the time when King Wen, who came from the western marches of the kingdom, was at the court of the ruling tyrant Ti-Hsin: the moment for overthrowing the tyrant had not yet come, and Wen could only keep the more powerful man in check by means of friendly persuasiveness.

Commentary
Hsiao Ch'u combines the symbols of strength and flexibility. The weak line in the fourth position occupies its proper place, and the strong lines above and below it show that there will be progress and success, at the same time conferring freedom upon their subjects. 'Dense clouds but no rain' indicate a strong forward movement, but a movement that has not yet reached its culmination.

The Image
The wind drives across the sky, crowding the clouds together. The superior man, accordingly, reveals his virtuous qualities to all.

The Lines
In the bottom line, NINE signifies:
How could there be reproach
In returning to the true way?
Success lies in this.
The 'true way' is here the Tao: not only the path of correctness, but the way in which one finds this path. The superior man follows the path on which he can advance or retreat as he wishes. It is wise and sensible to avoid obtaining anything by force, and so good fortune must result.

In the second line, NINE signifies:
Persuaded to retrace his steps,
He finds success.
He who can accept that the best course is to retreat in the face of inauspicious events will bring good fortune in the end, but he does not endanger himself unnecessarily.

In the third line, NINE signifies:
The spokes of the wagon wheel are broken,
Husband and wife stand glowering at each other.
In trying to force a way ahead in spite of the obstacles in the way, the man suffered a serious accident: he has ignored the advice of the weaker party, and conditions beyond his control have proved him wrong. But the result is to no-one's advantage, and, quarrelling with his companion, he sacrifices his dignity.

In the fourth line, SIX signifies:
If he shows confidence,
Fear and bloodshed are avoided.
There is no reproach.
Confident that he is pursuing the correct course, the wise man, even though he may appear to give way in the face of opposition, steers a way that avoids catastrophe. Disinterested truth will overcome all obstacles, and the end will be achieved.

In the fifth line, NINE signifies:
Sincerity and loyalty
Make for good neighbours.
In the weaker person loyalty means devotion, in the stronger, sincerity breeds trust. Both result in stronger ties, because either member of a partnership complements the other: the outcome is success for both.

In the sixth line, NINE signifies:
The rains come, and there is rest at last
For he has followed his way.
But persistence puts the women in danger,
For the moon is nearly full,
And if the superior man goes forth
There is misfortune.
The wind, continually driving the clouds together, finally brings the rain. But this success has been achieved by cautious advance, not precipitate action, and it is not wise to pursue matters further. The moon represents the darker powers, and when it reaches fullness it is already on the wane. One must be content with what has already been attained.

Treading wisely

The trigrams:

above: Ch'ien Heaven, the creative
below: Tui a pool of water, joy

Lü means both the proper conduct and, literally, treading upon something. Here the strong, the father principle of Ch'ien, stands upon Tui, which represents the youngest daughter; but, at the same time, the lower trigram Tui stands upon its own firm base and (as it were) treads upward against the weight above. This is a symbol of the love and joy that exist between a father and his favourite daughter.

The Judgment

He treads upon the tail of the tiger, but it does not bite him. Success.

The youngest daughter is the representation of the wild and uncontrollable; the father is the stronger, and attempts to impose his will, and it is his love and correct conduct that will triumph. In more general terms, this means that the stronger, though troubled by the weaker, will acquiesce and do no harm, because the relationship is friendly and without rancour.

Commentary

Weakness treads upon strength. But pleasure and satisfaction respond to strength, so there is no danger. He is raised to a high position, responding to heaven's will, and cannot be harmed or distressed. He shines in glory.

The Image

Heaven above, the pool below: the image of treading. The superior man, consulting both high and low, knows his proper place and gains the approbation of the people.

The Lines

In the bottom line, NINE signifies:
He goes forward in simplicity.
There is no reproach.

Common conventions have little meaning for the man who takes simplicity and truth as his guidelines. He who asks nothing of others may act as he thinks best.

In the second line, NINE signifies:
The man in darkness
Treads a smooth and level path,
And finds good fortune.

The 'man in darkness' is not one in ignorance or who does not know his way, but one who goes forward without attracting attention. He keeps to the middle path of Tao, asking nothing of anyone, and not diverted from his course by attractions of only superficial worth. Alone and self-sufficient, he is content and does not challenge fate; and therefore fortune smiles upon him.

In the third line, SIX signifies:
Even a one-eyed man can see,
A lame man can walk;
He treads on the tail of the tiger
And is bitten. Misfortune.

The champion plays the part of the king. Though the one-eyed man can see, he cannot see well enough: like a lame man he stumbles on to the tiger's tail, inviting danger which it is beyond his power to combat. So the king's champion, boasting the strength of his lord, may be tempted to think himself a powerful ruler when he is only a man of muscle. No-one should attempt to push ahead beyond the limit of his abilities.

In the fourth line, NINE signifies:
He treads on the tail of the tiger,
But caution and circumspection
Bring good fortune in the end.

In a dangerous enterprise, inner power must be combined with cautious understanding of the situation, and final success will only be achieved by circumspection. Only the man who knows what he is doing and proceeds carefully dare tread upon the tiger's tail with impunity.

In the fifth line, NINE signifies:
He treads with care.
Persistence.
But consciousness of danger.

One must be resolute and firm in conduct, but there is still danger, and obstinate perseverance is perilous unless the danger is well understood.

In the sixth line, NINE signifies:
Watching his step,
And the length of the path that he treads,
Heeding the favourable omens
Brings great good fortune.

The enterprise nears completion. The wise man examines the way he has come, and what lies before him. Only by comprehending the consequences of all his actions can he know what he can expect.

(Left) 'Watching his step and the length of the path that he treads . . .' A Chinese traveller returning from a pilgimage to India, and carrying sacred Buddhist scriptures

II T'AI Peace

The trigrams:
above: K'un Earth, the passive
Ch'ien Heaven, the creative

The feminine creative, which moves downward, is above; the male creative, which moves upward, is below. Thus they combine their influences and produce harmony, so that all things flourish. This is the hexagram that represents the first month of spring.

The Judgment
The small declines, and the great and good is coming. Good fortune and success.

Commentary
Celestial and terrestrial forces are in communion with one another, and all things move freely without restraint. High and low, superiors and inferiors, are combined in social harmony and, sharing the same aims, are in harmony with one another. Yang, representing strength, lies within; yin, representing joyous acceptance, lies without. The superior man is at the centre of things, his fortune steadily increasing, while those of mean nature are at the edges, declining in their influence.

The Image
Heaven and earth unite, forming T'ai, the symbol of peace. In such a way a mighty ruler regulates the separate ways of heaven and earth, marking the seasons and the divisions of space. So he brings assistance to people on every side.

The Lines
In the bottom line, NINE signifies:
When the grass is pulled up
Roots and the sod come with it.
Each in his own way
Finds success in his enterprise.
In favourable times, the man who is called to public service brings like-minded people with him, whose common aim will be the welfare of the people. Going forward according to a well-defined plan will result in accomplishment.

In the second line, NINE signifies:
He deals gently with the uncultured,
Crosses the river without a boat,
Is undismayed by the distance,
And does not favour his companions,
This is the way to tread the middle path.
The superior man can find a use for everything, and is not dismayed by the shortcomings of others, for the great can make use even of the imperfect. Particularly in prosperous times we must not hesitate to undertake dangerous but necessary enterprises; at the same time taking care not to join forces with others for mere personal advantage.

In the third line, NINE signifies:
There is no plain not followed by a hill,
No departure not followed by a return.
He who persists in the face of danger
Is without reproach.
Do not despair at the inevitability of
change;
A setback may be a blessing.
Bad things may be conquered, but they are not destroyed, and may return at any time. We should enjoy our good fortune when we have it, but remain mindful of danger, so that we may persevere against it. As long as a man remains superior to what fate may bring him, fortune will not desert him.

In the fourth line, SIX signifies:
He flutters down,
Not boasting of his riches.
Joins with his neighbours,
Frank and sincere.
In times of peace and prosperity, those in high places mix with the more lowly as equals. This is not pretended for reasons of expediency, but is genuine unaffected spontaneity which is based upon inner conviction.

In the fifth line, SIX signifies:
I am the emperor I
Giving his daughter in marriage.
This brings blessings
And great good fortune.
The emperor's daughter, though of higher rank than her husband, had to defer to him like any other wife. So the emperor's benign action, bestowing his most precious possession upon one of his subjects, brings fortune by its wise and modest combination of high and low.

In the sixth line, SIX signifies:
The city wall tumbles into the moat.
Now is not time for an army.
Give orders to your own people.
Though this is the correct course
Reproach cannot be avoided.
Peace is at an end: the setback signalled in the third line of the hexagram has come to pass. There is no advantage in trying to hold off the evil moment by vain resistance; it is better to try to organise a passive resistance within one's immediate circle. Nevertheless, no matter how correct this behaviour may be, there will still be cause for regret.

'The city wall tumbles into the moat. Now is not the time for an army.' An illustration from The Water Margin, *a picaresque romance about brigands of the thirteenth century. For many centuries the precepts of the* Tao-te-Ching *were followed by secret societies which combined sorcery with banditry, the chiefs of which virtually ruled large areas of China*

Stagnation

The trigrams:
above: Ch'ien Heaven, the creative
below: K'un Earth, the passive

This hexagram is the opposite of the pre-ceding T'ai: heaven is above, moving further and further away, and earth sinks below into the depths. P'i is associated with the seventh month, when the year is already in decline, and the decadence of autumn is everywhere.

The Judgment
Stagnation. Evil doers work against the perseverance of the superior man. The great and good withdraws, and the inferior advances.

Commentary
Heaven and earth are not in proper com-munion with one another; and so there is lack of understanding between all kinds of men, matters do not have free course, and conditions are unfavourable to the firm and correct behaviour of the superior man. The inner trigram is made up of weak yin lines, and the outer of strong yang lines. So the way of the inferior appears to be increasing, and that of the superior waning.

The Image
Heaven and earth stand divided, the image of stagnation. The wise man withdraws into himself and conceals his true quality. In this way he avoids the calamities that threaten him; but he will not be rewarded or honoured.

The Lines
In the bottom line, SIX signifies:
When the grass is pulled up
Roots and the sod come with it.
Each in his own way
Finds success by perseverance.

This text is almost exactly the same as for the first line of T'ai, the preceding hexagram, but it has a very different meaning. In place of the word 'enterprise' we find 'persever-ance', and the implication is not of a man drawing others with him into public service, but of one who persuades others to join him in retirement.

In the second line, SIX signifies:
They suffer and obey;
Thus inferior people find good fortune.
But the superior man uses the time of stagnation
To achieve success.

Those in lower positions would gladly be instructed by the wise man, hoping that he could put an end to their confusion. But he, since he cannot improve matters, does not try: he keeps himself to himself and pre-serves his spiritual strength.

In the third line, SIX signifies:
He conceals the shame in his breast.

One of inferior standing has seized power, but, realising that he has no dominion over the people from amongst whom he has

'The wise man withdraws into himself and conceals his true quality.' A stone figure of a savant, from the time of the Sui

risen, he feels the first stirrings of shame. He may not admit his doubts in himself to others, but the beginning of self-realisation is the first step to recovery.

In the fourth line, NINE signifies:
He who answers a call from on high
Is without reproach.
Those who follow him will benefit.

The period of stagnation is near its end, and conditions are about to change for the better. The man who leads the people out of the slough of despond must feel the call like the prophets of old.

In the fifth line, NINE signifies:
Stagnation is coming to an end.
There is great fortune for the great man.
What if we fail? what if we fail?
Then bind it to a clump of mulberry shoots.

When a mulberry bush is cut back, strong shoots sprout from the base: so the image of tying something to the shoots symbolises a way of making success certain.

In the sixth line, NINE signifies:
Stagnation is ended.
Stagnation began it, but now there is good fortune.

This standstill in the affairs of men does not come to an end of its own accord. the right man is necessary to lead the people out of the morass and confusion in which they find themselves. This is the difference be-tween a condition of stagnation and a state of peace: constant effort is needed to main-tain peace, and if left to itself it will decline into decadence and stagnation again.

13
T'UNG JEN

同
人

Companions

The trigrams:
    above: Ch'ien Heaven the creative
    below: Li   fire, brightness

It is the nature of the fire to burn upward into heaven, symbolising the concept of fellowship or love. The yin line in the second place gives the hexagram its central character, its yielding quality serving to hold together the five yang lines that surround it. This hexagram is the complement of hexagram number 7, Shih, the Troop of Soldiers. Shih has danger within and obedience surrounding it, the image of the unquestioning army; but T'ung Jen is clarity within and strength without, the image of a brotherhood held together by its own firmness.

The Judgment
Fellowship and openness mean success. It is advantageous to cross the great water. Persevering in all things, the superior man advances.

Commentary
T'ung Jen appears in the distant parts of the country, indicating progress and success, 'crossing the great water' symbolising an important journey of any kind. Someone weak comes to a position of power, taking the centre of the stage and responding fully to the creative power. Such a one may well be known as the beloved. The central yang line in the upper trigram represents the superior man, the only one who can comprehend and affect the thinking of all the people.

The Image
Heaven and fire together symbolise companionship. The superior man, accordingly, organises the people and distinguishes things according to their kinds and classes.

Heaven moves upward, just as fire does, but it is very different from fire. As the stars in the sky mark the divisions of time, so human society and all things that belong together must be ordered. Companionship is not just a gathering together of like-minded people: there must be organisation of the diversity.

The Lines
In the bottom line, NINE signifies:
    Companionship begins with those at
      the gate.
    No reproach.

The beginning of union among many very different people should occur in the open, where all can see and be seen, and all are on an equal footing. They start out as friends, with high hopes, and are agreed upon their aims.

In the second line, SIX signifies:
    The family bands together.
    Humiliation.

Forming factions within the broader brotherhood of man is the first sign of a coming struggle for power. Out of this will come failure and disgrace.

In the third line, NINE signifies:
    He hides his weapons in the thicket,
    Watching from the top of a high hill.
    For three years he does not show himself.

When factions are formed, no man trusts another. Each plans a secret ambush, hiding his true feelings, spying upon the actions of his fellows. For a long time he waits, hoping to catch his opponents by surprise, but there is no joy in this.

In the fourth line, NINE signifies:
    He climbs upon his battlements
    For he cannot fight.
    But good fortune is near.

The first steps are taken toward reconciliation. The wise man still holds aloof in a place of safety, but he does not make the mistake of attacking those whom he thinks of as his opponents, and soon all will be well.

In the fifth line, NINE signifies:
    Lovers begin by weeping and lamenting
    But in the end they laugh.
    The struggles of many bring them
      together.

Any association will begin with troubles that may cause grief, but when these have been resolved the companions will find happiness. The troubles endured and overcome by others will serve as example, and the help and understanding of their fellow companions will bring them together in due course.

In the sixth line, NINE signifies:
    The beloved is in a distant place.
    No regrets.

The companions trust one another, even when they are far apart. But the fact that the beloved is in a distant place means that the association is still not fulfilled: the time of true brotherhood of man has not yet arrived. But there is hope and no occasion for self-reproach.

'He climbs upon his battlements . . .' A pottery model of a watchtower, from the time of the Han dynasty, second century AD

Abundant Possessions

The trigrams:

above: Li   fire, brightness
below: Ch'ien   Heaven, the creative

Here the flame burns in the highest heaven, revealing all things in its light. The weak yin line is in the place of the ruler, indicating that wealth comes to the man who is modest and benevolent, even though he occupies a high position.

The Judgment

Ta Yu indicates wealth in abudance, and great success.

Commentary

As in the preceding hexagram, T'ung Jen, it is the weak yin line that holds the hexagram together, and it occupies the most important position. The virtues of the hexagram are strength and vigour combined with elegance and brightness. Because it responds to heaven, performing all things at the proper time, it indicates great progress and success.

The Image

Fire in the heavens above is the image of possession in abundance. The superior man, obeying the benevolent will of heaven, supresses evil and advances the virtuous.

The Lines

In the bottom line, NINE signifies:
> He has no communion with evil,
> Remaining blameless;
> Keeping conscious of difficulty
> He averts reproach.

The man who is beginning to amass possessions is so far without blame; he has not attracted envy and dislike because he has not yet been forced to compromise with his principles. But wealth can be utterly destructive if a wealthy man is led astray. Only an awareness of the obstacles he has yet to overcome can keep him on the path of righteousness.

In the second line, NINE signifies:
> Big wagons are for loading.
> He may attempt any enterprise
> Without reproach.

There is no fear of failure for lack of resources. The big wagon is ready to be loaded with possessions, and can transport them wherever they may be needed. The man who intends to undertake a great venture must be ready for any eventuality, and must be prepared to entrust his wealth to others who will take a share in the responsibility.

In the third line, NINE signifies:
> A prince offers all to the emperor.
> But this is not in a small man's power.

The truly magnanimous man should not regard all that he possesses as his exclusive property, but should devote it to the good of the people at large. A petty man attempts to keep everything for himself, to the detriment both of himself and of the common good.

In the fourth line, NINE signifies:
> He distinguishes himself from his
> neighbours.
> No blame.

A rich and powerful man among other rich and powerful men must remain aloof. But provided he does not do this from a false sense of pride, or show envy and attempt to compete with them, he remains without reproach.

In the fifth line, SIX signifies:
> He who is sincere and accessible
> But maintains his dignity
> Will gain great honours.

This indicates a very favourable situation. The hearts of the people are won, not by force and repression, but by benevolence and philanthropy. But when the benevolent man is too readily accessible, he may well be treated with insolence; and insolence can only be kept in check by careful maintenance of dignity at all times.

In the sixth line, NINE signifies:
> Giving and receiving
> Blessed by the heavens
> He enjoys great good fortune.

The relationship between the great and good man and those around him is one of reciprocal benevolence: he gives from his wealth and receives their thanks; they give their love and receive his protection.

14 TA YU

(Above) 'A prince offers all to the emperor'. The emperor T'ai Tsung receiving ambassadors: a painting on silk of the T'ang epoch, from the Imperial Palace in Pekin

15 CH'IEN

'The superior man is recognised, but maintains his humility.' Figure of a court dignitary from the time of the Han dynasty

Humility

The trigrams:

above: K'un   Earth, the receptive
below: Ken   mountain, stillness

In this hexagram Ken, the mountain, is the youngest son of the creative principle: it dispenses the gifts of heaven, the rain that falls from the clouds around its peak, and shines in the clear air with the light of heaven itself. Ken represents the modesty of great and strong men. K'un, the earth, is exalted, symbolising the way in which simple men are in their turn raised up by true modesty.

The Judgment

Humility engenders success. The superior man, understanding this, enjoys a satisfactory outcome to his undertakings.

Commentary

Ch'ien symbolises progress and success, for it is heaven's way to send down its good influences and shed radiance, and it is earth's way to send its influences upward from below. So it is also heaven's way to reduce the over-full and augment the modest; as it is earth's way to throw down the full and raise up the humble. The demons and gods abominate the over-full and bless the modest, as it is the way of men to hate the full and love the humble. Modesty in a high position shines still more brilliantly; there is nothing higher. As the mountain is hidden by the earth, so the wise man hides his abilities and wealth with proper humility.

The Image

Within the earth, there is a mountain, the image of humility. The superior man reduces that which is too much, and increases that which is too little, setting one in the scale to balance the other.

The Lines

In the bottom line, SIX signifies:
  The superior man
  Is even modest about his modesty.
  He may cross the great water
  And find good fortune.

Any major undertaking is increased in difficulty when the participants insist upon their individual contributions being suitably recognised; but those who approach a problem without pride or concern for their personal standing will solve it quickly and simply.

In the second line, SIX signifies:
  Modesty itself achieves recognition.
  Persistence brings good fortune.

He who is seen to be truly modest will be honoured for it, and success will be his if he adheres to his path.

In the third line, NINE signifies:
  The superior man is recognised
  But maintains his humility.
  He brings all matters to conclusion.
  Good fortune.

Success now begins to be apparent, but the wise man is not dazzled by fame: he remains humble, endearing himself to the people about him and working steadily to win their loyalty and support for his future enterprises.

In the fourth line, SIX signifies:
  Proper humility
  And nothing that is not proper humility
  In all his actions.

This is the line representing the minister, the intermediary who transmits the orders of the ruler above, and represents the desires of the people below. True modesty is the sign of confidence in one's position; it should not be permitted to degenerate into servility.

In the fifth line, SIX signifies:
  Employ your neighbours
  Without boasting of your riches.
  Attack with vigour
  All is propitious.

He who occupies a position of responsibility, modest though he be, must engage the help of others at times to carry out his plans.

In the sixth line, SIX signifies:
  Modesty achieves recognition.
  He sets his army on the march
  But only to punish his own city and land.

It is often the hardest thing of all for a truly modest man to recognise the moment at which he should impose his will upon those around him. But, provided the discipline is just and necessary, he will be honoured for his actions.

Anticipation

The trigrams:
    above: Chen thunder and awakening
    below: K'un Earth, the receptive
The attributes of the upper trigram, Chen, are movement and danger; the attributes of the lower, K'un, are passivity and obedience. The movement, meeting devotion, inspires enthusiasm. The strong yang line in the fourth place, the place of the minister, demands obedience from all the weak yin lines; but there is an inherent danger in this arrangement.

The Judgment
It is advantageous to establish a number of tributary princes, and place the army in a state of readiness.

Commentary
The thunder awakes in heaven, and the earth is docile below. The sun and the moon keep their courses, and the four seasons do not change their appointed times. So action according to the will of heaven gives rise to anticipation and calm confidence. The sage also follows heaven's will, and the people follow his judgment with little need for punishment or for any form of penalty. Great indeed are the moment and the meaning of Yü!

The Image
Thunder bursts from the earth into heaven. In such a way did the ancient kings do honour to heaven and its supreme lord with solemn music and appropriate sacrifice, remembering also in this way their revered ancestors.

The Lines
In the bottom line, SIX signifies:
    He proclaims his anticipation of pleasure
    An evil omen.
Here the lowly person looks forward selfishly to his own satisfaction; he boasts arrogantly of what he desires the near future to bring him, and so invites his own misfortune.

In the second line, SIX signifies:
    He is firm as a rock
    But not the whole day.
    Persistence brings success.
The wise man is not led away by illusion: he sees what is to come without dissipating his energies in unnecessary actions, and knows exactly the right moment at which to move. Adherence to this way will bring him good fortune.

In the third line, SIX signifies:
    Ignorant anticipation brings regrets.
    Hesitation leads to repentance.
The inferior man looks upward, placing his reliance upon those above him without understanding that he too should take action. If he does not appreciate the right moment for movement he will regret it.

In the fourth line, NINE signifies:
    He is the source
    Of harmony and satisfaction,
    And achieves great things.
    Have no doubts.
    Gather friends around you
    As the clasp gathers the hair.
The superior man is an inspiration to all, and inspires joyful anticipation through his own confidence and freedom from hesitation. He gathers and holds men together by the support he affords them.

In the fifth line, SIX signifies:
    He is constantly sick
    But does not die.
Continuing to look forward, he finds himself obstructed at every turn. But provided he does not expend his hopeful anticipation in empty enthusiasm he will survive.

In the sixth line, SIX signifies:
    His anticipation is deluded,
    Devoted to self-satisfaction;
    But if he changes his course,
    Even when all seems completed,
    There is no blame.
It is easy to be led astray by foolish enthusiasm, but even at the last moment a sober awakening can save the situation.

'It is advantageous to . . . place the army in a state of readiness.' A terracotta relief from the Han dynasty

17 SUI

Allegiance

The trigrams:
above: Tui   a pool of water, joy
below: Chen   thunder and awakening
Above is joy, the youngest daughter; below is awakening, the eldest son. So the awakening interest of the older man is excited by the joyous movement of the young girl; he defers to her and shows her consideration, but in due course she will follow him.

The Judgment
Compliance in the beginning leads to ultimate success. Firmness and rectitude are advantageous, and there is no blame.

Commentary
In Sui the strong trigram places itself below the weak; in the two we see the combination of movement and pleasure. The whole universe complies with what the hour dictates: a leader must adjust his actions to the situation; a follower must adjust his actions to those of his leader. But just as the leader should not ask others to follow him unless his path is the right one, so his followers must assure themselves of his rectitude.

The Image
Thunder rumbles below the surface of the pool. As darkness falls, the superior man goes into his house to rest.

The Lines
In the bottom line, NINE signifies:
    He changes the object of his pursuit.
    Persistence brings good fortune.
    Going forth from his door
    And meeting with those outside
    He attains achievement.
The wise man will not maintain his allegiance to a belief that is no longer supportable: when the time is right, confidence in his judgment will lead on to success. He must be prepared to listen to the opinions of others, and so form his own, deciding whether he will throw in his lot with a leader, or whether he himself will lead.

In the second line, SIX signifies:
    He who clings to the little boy
    Loses the strong man.
The 'little boy' represents the first allegiance, which may have been to principles that were not properly thought out, or which were applicable to a situation that no longer exists. It is a time to make more mature decisions, and transfer allegiance to a new leader or moral system.

In the third line, SIX signifies:
    He who clings to the strong man
    Loses the little boy,
    But gains what he desires.
    Persistence is advantageous.
In giving up an old allegiance, one naturally loses something: the joy of first experiencing a belief in a cause, the excitement of a first love that can never be recaptured. With maturity, one gives up the unmixed happi-ness of youth, the pleasure of the absence of responsibility. But the wise man is satisfied within himself as his personality develops and he begins to understand what he wants.

In the fourth line, NINE signifies:
    Allegiance brings success,
    But persisting in the same course
    Brings misfortune
    Taking his own way with sincerity
    How can he be blamed?
There are dangers in blind allegiance, both for the followers and for the followed. Those who follow are often not honest in their intentions, seeking personal advancement and maintaining their positions by flattery and subservience; and their leader, becoming accustomed to their insincere attentions, will suffer misfortune and eventually lose both his followers and his own position. His only hope is to pursue his own course sincerely and with conviction.

In the fifth line, NINE signifies:
    Trusting in goodness.
    Good fortune.
This line reiterates the significance of the line before. He who knows in his heart what is right must follow it without deviation.

In the sixth line, SIX signifies:
    Sincere, he secures allegiance
    And is himself more firmly bound.
    The emperor makes sacrifices
    Upon the Western Mountain.
In the days of the Chou dynasty, the rulers honoured great sages by affording them, at their death, a place in the royal family's temple of ancestors. The first part of the interpretation is usually taken to mean that the sage, although he himself has reached the furthest stages of his development, is constrained by the demands of his followers; it can also mean that one who becomes the unchallenged leader will still be bound to his followers by the responsibility he has assumed.

Arresting Decay

The trigrams:
>   above: Ken   mountain, stillness
>   below: Sun   wind, gentleness

The Chinese character *ku* is said to represent 'a bowl in whose contents worms are breeding'. This is because the gentleness and indifference of the lower trigram Sun has been covered by the unmoving solidity of the upper trigram Ken; in these enclosed conditions the expected result is stagnation, fermentation and decay. But just as natural decay can be controlled to provide desirable fermentation products, such as soy sauce or rice wine; so the condition of decay represented by Ku can be arrested and exploited.

The Judgment
Proper control of decay affords progress and success. It is advantageous to cross the great water. Three days before the beginning; three days after.

As has already been pointed out, 'crossing the great water' symbolises any important undertaking, whether it involves a journey or not. The passage 'three days before the beginning; three days after' has provoked much discussion among commentators. In any properly controlled fermentation, there is an initial period before the process really begins to 'work', and another period at the end of which it is important to arrest fermentation before unwelcome decomposition products are formed. The inception and growth of some new idea may therefore be likened in many details to the process of fermentation.

Commentary
In Ku we have the strong and immovable above, the weak and pliant below. But control of the processes of decay leads to good order everywhere under heaven, so that he who goes firmly forward will come to business that must be dealt with. The ending of confusion marks the beginning of order.

The Image
The wind blows at the foot of the mountain.

The superior man, addressing himself to the people, rouses them up and strengthens his resolve.

The Lines
In the bottom line, SIX signifies:
>   A son repairs the errors of his father.
>   A good son, redeeming the reputation of his father.
>   At first, danger
>   But in the end, good fortune.

The father is the representative of convention and tradition, perhaps the ruler of a state, who has allowed the vitality of himself and his country to degenerate into mere form and custom. The son symbolises the vigour of youth, a new leader who is able to revitalise the state: but before he emerges, there is great danger that the existing system will destroy itself.

In the second line, NINE signifies:
>   A son repairs the errors of his mother.
>   But he should not be too inflexible.

Here the errors have not been committed by a strong man, but out of weakness. In setting things right, a degree of kindness and consideration is necessary.

In the third line, NINE signifies:
>   A son repairs the errors of his father.
>   There will be some remorse
>   But no great blame.

Here the young man has been too precipitate in arresting the processes of decay, like one who stops the fermentation of a wine prematurely. But too much energy is better than too little, and so, although his hasty actions may cause him certain regrets, he is free of reproach.

In the fourth line, SIX signifies:
>   The son condones the errors of his father.
>   Persisting, he falls into disgrace.

The significance of Ku lies in recognising the processes of decay, and in understanding the right moment at which to bring them to a stop. The indulgent son who is not confident enough to put right the mistakes of the past will bring humiliation upon himself as well as on his father.

In the fifth line, SIX signifies:
>   The son repairs the errors of his father
>   And wins praise.

The fifth line is the position of the ruler: the true leader receives acclaim for his actions in arresting the process of decay, particularly in that he also accepts responsibility for the previous shortcomings of others.

In the sixth line, NINE signifies:
>   He does not serve the emperor
>   But seeks higher goals.

There are some who do not feel themselves obliged to concern themselves with worldly affairs, but who prefer to withdraw into their private thoughts. This withdrawal is justified when the superior man turns his mind to spiritual matters; for the purpose of the sage is not to redeem the present but to create the values of the future.

(Above, left) 'He does not serve the emperor but seeks higher goals.' An immortal in meditation; a watercolour of the Yüan epoch

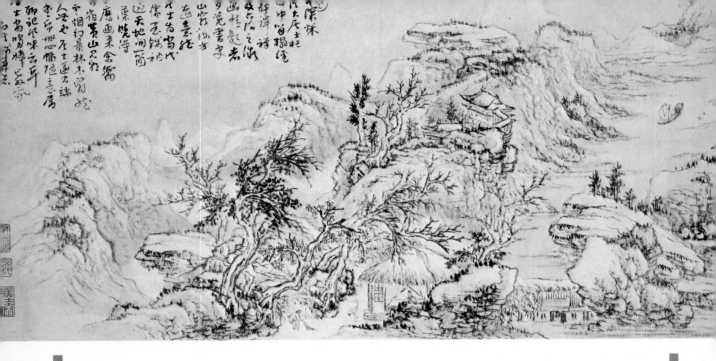

19 LIN

Approaching

The trigrams:

above: K'un Earth, the passive
below: Tui a pool of water, joy

This hexagram is associated with the twelfth month of the year, from January to February, when the days gradually begin to lengthen once again, and the word *lin* has a number of different meanings that are only roughly encompassed by the word 'approaching'. Fundamentally it may be translated as 'becoming great', with an extension of meaning to include the idea of something strong and superior approaching something of lower standing, and from this to the idea of a man in high position condescending toward those below him.

The Judgment

Lin indicates great progress and success; persistence will be advantageous. But in the eight month there will be misfortune.

Commentary

In Lin we see the strong yang lines moving upward into the compliance of the upper yin lines. It is a time of joy and hopeful progress as spring approaches; determination and perseverance help us to attain success. But spring and summer are succeeded by autumn, the time of decay, and the next hexagram shows the reversal of this one.

The Image

The earth above the lake is the image of approaching. The superior man, accordingly, is inexhaustible in his desire to teach, and his tolerance and care for the people are unlimited.

(Above) Winter landscape, a painting by Ts'an dated 1666. All the shapes of the landscape and the trees are rounded in yin forms. Apart from the earth above the lake, 'the image of Lin', the only other predominant material is wood, the 'element' associated with winter

The Lines

In the bottom line, NINE signifies:
They approach together.
Persistence means good fortune.

The reference here is to the first and second yang lines, which are both moving upward. Good influences begin to exert themselves, and likeminded men of goodwill cooperate. Nevertheless, although it is wise to follow the general trend, only adherence to what is right will bring final success.

In the second line, NINE signifies:
They approach together.
Good fortune:
Everything is favourable.

The situation is still full of promise: everybody is cooperating, and all matters are going forward. But this is on a material level: although success shines on everything there is no true spiritual basis to people's actions.

In the third line, SIX signifies:
He approaches in comfort
But gains no advantage.
If there is remorse
There is no reproach.

When a man achieves power and influence he may become over confident, slacken his efforts, and lose all the advances he has made. But if he recognises his errors in time, he will be free from blame.

In the fourth line, SIX signifies:
They come together.
There is no reproach.

While the three lower lines represent a man rising to power and influence, the three upper lines of the hexagram represent the attitude of persons of higher rank to those below them. Here a rich and successful man draws a man of acknowledged ability into his own circle.

In the fifth line, SIX signifies:
Wisdom approaches.
This is the way of the great prince.
Good fortune.

The great ruler must have about him men of ability; his personal wisdom lies in how he selects the right people to advise him. And in allowing those he has chosen to exercise their powers of decision, he appropriately attains success.

In the sixth line, SIX signifies:
Magnanimity approaches.
Good fortune. No reproach.

The great initiate returns to the world, for his desire to teach, and his care for his disciples, are without limit. This means great good fortune for all the men whom he gathers about him; and for himself, there is no blame.

Contemplation

The trigrams:
above: Sun wind, gentleness,
penetration
below: K'un Earth, the passive

The word *kuan* possesses two related but opposed meanings in Chinese; by a slight change in tonal stress it can be made to mean both contemplating and being contemplated. The dual implications can perhaps be better understood if the hexagram is seen as a representation of one of those scenic gateways that were formerly erected on high hills in China. Such an erection formed a landmark that could be seen for miles around, but it also afforded a vantage point commanding a wide view of the countryside. In the same way, someone who raises himself to a position in which he is able to contemplate the rest of humanity at the same time puts himself up for inspection by the crowd.

The Judgment
Kuan represents the worshipper who has washed his hands, but not yet made the offering. Impressed by his sincerity, all look up to him.

Commentary
Kuan combines the trigrams representing docility and flexibility; the hexagram is ruled from on high by the yang lines in fifth and sixth place, and the weak yin lines look up from below. When we contemplate the transcendental ways of heaven, we observe how the four seasons follow one another without deviation. The sages, pursuing the same way, have given their instructions, and all under heaven submit to them.

The Image
The wind moves over the earth. So did the kings of old visit all parts of the kingdom, to see their people and give them instruction.

The Lines
In the bottom line, SIX signifies:
Contemplation like a child
Brings no reproach to the inferior man;
But for the superior man, humiliation.
The child watches from a distance, innocently but without understanding. There is a wise man at hand, not understood by the ordinary people; they do not suffer from their lack of understanding because he brings them benefits. But for the superior man such lack of comprehension is shameful.

In the second line, SIX signifies:
Contemplation through the crack of the door
Is sufficient only for a housewife.
Watching through the door-crack, looking outward from within, one sees a great deal but it is always the same view: it is related always to one's personal domestic needs. A man (or a woman) who intends to take part in public life must have a much broader outlook than this.

In the third line, SIX signifies:
Contemplation of ourselves
Determines the choice
Between advance and retreat.
The third line is the point of transition. It is no longer sufficient to observe the world with the innocent eye of the child, or from a self-centred viewpoint. One must strive to acquire objectivity by looking inward and observing one's feelings and emotions, and learning from these, one begins to plan the future development of one's life.

In the fourth line, SIX signifies:
Contemplating the condition of the kingdom,
He decides to seek a place at court
And flourishes.
A man who understands the ways in which a kingdom is ruled should be given a position of authority; but he will be there more as a guest, acting on his own initiative, than as a minister of the king.

In the fifth line, NINE signifies:
Contemplating his life,
The superior man is without reproach.
The man in a position of authority over others should be ready at all times to examine his motives and his past record. But he will not be brooding over past mistakes: he will be examining his influence upon others and, if this influence is good, he will enjoy the satisfaction of a career without blame.

In the sixth line, NINE signifies:
Contemplating himself,
The superior man is without reproach.
This is the highest type of man who, after the deepest self-examination, has finally excluded all selfish interests. Liberated from his ego, he can contemplate the transcendental ways of heaven.

Lao-tse, the author of the Tao-te-Ching, *and founder of the Taoist religion*

21 SHIH HO

噬嗑

▦▦ (hexagram)

Biting Through

The trigrams:
above: Li   fire, brightness
below: Chen thunder and awakening
This hexagram is thought of as representing a mouth; the yang line in fourth place is something through which the teeth are biting. When this something has been bitten through, the mouth will be closed, obstacles cleared away and problems resolved.

The Judgment
Shih Ho signifies successful progress. It is advantageous to seek justice.

Commentary
Union is brought about by biting through the intervening obstacles, and the hexagram indicates successful progress. Yang and yin lines are equally divided in the figure: thunder and movement are denoted by the lower trigram, brightness and intelligence by the upper. Thunder and lightning are the manifestation of the sudden release of built-up tension in nature. A yin line occupies the fifth place, the place of the ruler; although this is not its proper position, it is advantageous for the processes of law.

The Image
Thunder and lightning are the symbol of biting through. The kings of old, therefore, framed their laws with care, making the punishment fit the crime.

The Lines
In the bottom line, NINE signifies:
    His feet are locked in the stocks
    His toes are gone.
    No reproach.
The intrepretation of this line has provoked much disagreement among Chinese scholars. The first and sixth lines are considered to represent the man who suffers punishment, the rest represent those who impose the penalties. For western readers the stocks is only a mild form of punishment, and they have interpreted 'his toes are gone' as meaning the toes are hidden by the wooden beam of the stocks; on the other hand, cutting off a man's toes was a specific Chinese punishment, and the penalty described here may be a rather more severe one than is generally supposed. But no matter whether the punishment is light or severe, this line indicates plainly that it is fully justified.

In the second line, SIX signifies:
    Biting through tender meat
    His nose is gone.
    No reproach.
Again this line is open to different interpretations. Some commentators translate it as meaning that the subject is so concerned to see justice done that he 'cuts off his nose to spite his own face'. Others merely see the nose hidden by the depth of the meat into which he has bitten, meaning that he loses sight of clemency in his pursuit of the wrong-doer. Again, however, it is worth remembering that cutting off a felon's nose is a specific punishment, and the verse makes it clear that, although this may be too severe a penalty, it is nevertheless without blame.

In the third line, SIX signifies:
    Biting through dried meat
    He injures himself.
    There is some humiliation
    But no reproach.
Here the punishment is being carried out by someone without sufficient power and authority, and in performing it he does harm to himself. However, since the punishment was necessary, and he was performing his duty, he will soon recover and will not be blamed.

In the fourth line, NINE signifies:
    Biting through dried gristle and bone
    He receives the arrows demanded.
    It is advantageous to realise the difficulties
    For perseverance brings good fortune.
In a civil law case in ancient China, it was customary for the litigants to bring to court a bundle of arrows. The case is a hard one to judge, and it is only by recognising all the difficulties involved that one can find the persistence to reach a just conclusion.

In the fifth line, SIX signifies:
    Biting through dried lean meat.
    He receives the gold required.
    Aware of danger
    He perseveres without reproach.
In a criminal case, it was customary for the parties to deposit a sum in gold before the hearing. The fifth line represents the 'lord of judgment': in his powerful position he is in-inclined to be lenient, and although the case is a difficult one it is not too difficult. If the judge remains conscious of the dangers involved in making the wrong decision, his judgment will be just. The yellow of gold is the colour of correctness in the middle way.

In the sixth line, NINE signifies:
    His neck is locked in the wooden cangue
    His ears are gone.
    Misfortune.
Deaf to good counsel, the felon is locked in the great block of the cangue, which he must carry about his neck until his crime has been expiated; it may even be that he has suffered the severest punishment of having his ears cut off.

(Right) The cangue, the Chinese equivalent of the pillory

Grace

The trigrams:
    above: Ken mountain, stillness
    below: Li   fire, brightness
A fire breaks out from the depths of the earth, blazing up to illuminate the heavenly heights of the mountain. The outer stillness of the mountain, lit from within by the inspiration of intelligence, is the symbol of grace.

The Judgment
Pi indicates that grace, impelled by brightness, should be given a free course. Even in minor matters it is advantageous to go forward.

Commentary
The weak yin line rises between the two yang lines of the lower trigram, adorning them with its brilliance. The alteration of firmness and yielding is the pattern of heaven itself; by contemplating the patterns of heaven we begin to understand the changing seasons. As the earth adorns heaven, and heaven the earth, so do the different levels of society adorn one another, and by observing them we can learn to live in grace.

The Image
Fire below the mountain is the symbol of grace. The superior man, observing this, throws light upon the processes of government, but does not dare to intervene in the processes of law.

The Lines
In the bottom line, NINE signifies:
> He adorns his feet
> Leaves his carriage
> And walks in grace.

He who begins in a subordinate position must learn to progress by his own labours — to 'walk on his own two feet'. He does not accept the easy assistance offered by the carriage, but at the same time he makes sure that he is properly shod for his undertaking.

In the second line, SIX signifies:
> He wears his beard with elegance.

A beard is the sign of age and sagacity, and he who wishes to associate with his elders should conform to their customs. At the same time, it must be remembered that a fine beard on the chin of a young and inexperienced man is nothing but adornment, and may indicate only vanity.

In the third line, NINE signifies:
> Adorned
> He glistens with grace.
> Righteous perseverance brings good
>   fortune.

This is a very pleasant situation: life is good, there is every material comfort, and the phrase 'gracious living' exactly describes it. But such a state of affairs can only be maintained by perseverance in the true way.

In the fourth line, SIX signifies:
> He is adorned
> But only in white;
> A white horse with wings.
> One comes, not as a robber
> But for a betrothal.

White is the colour of simplicity, but also of funerals; the winged white horse is the symbol of innocent belief, transcending the limits of time and space. The fourth line is the bottom line of the upper trigram, and finds its correlate in the bottom line of the lower trigram, from which it is separated by the strong third line. This is the 'robber', who is really a man of good reputation, anxious to ensure that the adornment of the fourth line by the first is carried out according to proper form.

In the fifth line, SIX signifies:
> There is grace in hills and gardens.
> His silk girdle is thin and small.
> Disgrace, but in the end good fortune.

The Chinese loved gardens, and to own, or even to visit, one was a great privilege. To be invited to walk in a great man's garden, and then to appear poorly dressed, could bring nothing but humiliation and disgrace. Nevertheless, it is a relatively small fault and, even though it may be attributed to meanness rather than poverty, in the end all will be well.

In the sixth line, NINE signifies:
> Nothing but grace in white.
> No reproach.

At the highest stage of development, true grace is to be found without adornment. Simplicity is all.

(Above, left) 'He is adorned, but only in white.' A detail from an eighth century representation of eight officials of the T'ang court

23 PO

Disintegration

The trigrams:
above: Ken   mountain, stillness
below: K'un   Earth, the passive

Po means disintegration in the sense of the breaking away of unnecessary encumbrances, and the first four lines of the hexagram symbolise a succession of losses which appear at the time to be misfortunes, but which in the long run are resolved in the fifth line, leading to recognition of virtue in the sixth.

The Judgment
Disintegration. There is no direction in which to move with advantage.

Commentary
In Po we see the weak yin lines threatening to shatter the last remaining yang lines and make it like themselves. (Po should be compared with hexagram 20, Kuan: what was a strong tower, with its two strong yang lines at the top, is now in danger of collapse, like a house with a weak ridge beam.) Small men are increasing; the superior man, therefore, remains where he is and accepts the situation. He contemplates the ebb and flow of society about him, as the tides are moved by the heavenly bodies.

The Image
The mountain stands upon the earth, and symbolises disintegration: those above can only maintain their position by strengthening those below them.

The Lines
In the bottom line, SIX signifies:
The leg of the bed is broken.
Persistence brings disaster.
Failure.

Inferior men stealthily undermining the position of the superior man; even those who remain loyal to him are threatened with misfortune. There is nothing to do but accept the situation and await its outcome.

In the second line, SIX signifies:

The side of the bed is broken.
Persistence brings disaster.
Failure.

The situation deteriorates, the danger is drawing nearer. The superior man begins to mistrust even those who call themselves his friends. His only course is to adjust himself to his conditions, not to maintain his position stubbornly against those who are out to destroy him.

In the third line, SIX signifies:
He breaks with them.
No reproach.

The individual severs all his ties, both with friends and with enemies. Relying on his own integrity, he is without blame.

In the fourth line, SIX signifies:
The bed is overturned.
His skin is split:
Great misfortune.

The worst has happened: disaster has struck. The superior man is brought down, and his personal safety is threatened.

In the fifth line, SIX signifies:
A string of fishes
Symbolising favour
For the ladies of the court.
Advantage in every way.

The worst is over. Now the strong yang line in sixth place begins to exert its influence, and the yin lines submit to it, just as the empress leads her ladies in waiting like a line of fishes. The time of remaining still is past: it is advantageous to move in any direction.

In the sixth line, NINE signifies:
The largest fruit
Is uneaten on the tree.
The superior man rides in his carriage.
Inferior men throw down their houses.

On the topmost branches, the unattainable fruit grows and ripens but is not plucked: at the right time it will fall and plant a seed to grow anew. The superior man once more has influence, and he is surrounded by those who respect him, as if he rode in a carriage. But the inferior men, by their own actions, have brought destruction upon themselves.

Po represents the autumn of 'cold dews' and 'descent of hoar frost'. This painting by Kuo Hsi (1025–1090) is entitles 'Autumn light on mountains and valleys' and it effectively portrays that time of year in which the sharp yang forms of summer continue their disintegration into the softer yin forms of approaching winter

24 FU The Turning Point

The trigrams:
above: K'un Earth, the passive
below: Chen thunder and awakening
This hexagram is linked with the eleventh month, the time of the winter solstice, the turning point between a year gone and a year yet to come. The Chinese believed that natural forces, of which the thunder is the representative, rested in the earth at wintertime.

The Judgment
In Fu there is free going out and coming in, no-one to hinder. Friends arrive without blame, returning to their homes on the seventh day. Advantage in all directions.

Commentary
This hexagram indicates success, because the strong yang line is rising from the bottom, returning to its natural starting point. Motion and acceptance of motion are combined in the two trigrams making up the hexagram; that is why there is going out and coming in without hindrance. This movement, with its return after seven days, is a natural motion in accord with the movements of heaven; and the very workings of heaven and earth are represented in the return to the turning point of the year.

The Image
Thunder within the earth is the very symbol of the turning point. So, at the time of the winter solstice, the kings of old closed the passes, so that merchants and strangers were unable to travel abroad, and the kings themselves did not progress through their dominions.

The Lines
In the bottom line, NINE signifies:
Returning from a short distance:
No regrets
And great good fortune.
Small deviations from the way are often unavoidable, but he who turns back before he has gone too far, knowing the error he has made, is not to be blamed. Indeed, in acknowledging his mistake, he brings good fortune on himself.

In the second line, SIX signifies:
Turning back with heaven's blessing.
Good fortune.
All turning back requires an act of conscious decision, and wins the approbation of heaven. If one can put pride aside and follow the example of others, there will be good fortune.

In the third line, SIX signifies:
Turning back many times
Brings danger
But no reproach.
This represents those who lack constancy, who wander from the way of righteousness, turn back, and then are diverted again. There is danger that they may eventually find themselves lost in evil ways but, provided they recognise this danger, there is no blame.

In the fourth line, SIX signifies:
Walking with the others
But returning alone.
This is perhaps the hardest of all: to be associated with companions, to realise that they are going in the wrong direction and to leave them.

In the fifth line, SIX signifies:
Turning back in nobleness
Brings no remorse.
This represents a man of high principle who, recognising that he has gone astray, immediately turns back whatever it may cost him.

In the sixth line, SIX signifies:
He turns back too late.
Misfortune.
Evil causes, evil effects.
Armies sent into battle in this way
Are sure to suffer defeat
Disastrous to their emperor.
Even for ten years
There will be no redress.
When a man persists, pursuing the wrong path in blind obstinacy, there comes a point at which he cannot turn back. Nothing but disaster can ensue, and it will be a very long time before he can attempt to right matters.

'Turning back with heaven's blessing. Good fortune.' A painting from the T'ang period

Innocence

The trigrams:

 above: Ch'ien Heaven, the creative
 below: Chen thunder and
  awakening

Wang is the symbol of recklessness and in-sincerity; Wu Wang comprises meanings that are almost the opposite of this. But the innocence that is symbolised is so ingenu-ous, so unsophisicated, that it retains one aspect of the significance of Wang — a trace of the unexpected.

The Judgment

Wu Wang indicates integrity, and resultant success. Persistence in righteousness brings its reward; but one who is not as he should be will suffer misfortune, and none of his undertakings will have a favourable out-come.

Commentary

The strong first line becomes part of an outer trigram of three yang lines, forming Ch'ien, and enclosing an inner trigram which is itself ruled by a strong line; the hexagram is full of power and movement and strength. The fifth line is a yang line, in the place of the ruler, and the weak second line responds to it: he whose movement follows the laws of heaven will be innocent and without guile.

But incorrect action on the part of the subject will lead to errors that cannot easily be put right. In what direction should he move, even though he sincerely and inno-cently believes in all he does? What can he achieve if it is not in accordance with the will of heaven?

The Image

The thunder rolls below the heavens, and all things find their true nature, free from all insincerity. So the kings of old, filled with virtue, made their laws according to the seasons and the ways of nature, bringing abundant nourishment to all mankind.

The Lines

In the bottom line, NINE signifies:
 Protected by his innocence and his in-integrity
 He achieves good fortune.
The noble impulses of the innocent heart are always good; we may follow them with confidence. But one who is devious by nature, and who justifies his actions by false appeals to honour, may flourish for a while but will suffer failure in the end.

In the second line, SIX signifies:
 Count not upon the harvest while still ploughing,
 Nor upon the third year's crop
 Before the first is in.
 It is favourable to embark upon an undertaking.
As thou sowest, so shalt thou reap; count not your chickens before they are hatched. Each task has its own time and appointed place, and, as each turns out well, so the next can be undertaken; but unwise antici-pation can only bring disappointment.

In the third line, SIX signifies:
 An unexpected misfortune:
 An untethered cow is her master's loss,
 The gain of the passer-by.
Carelessness or over-confidence is soon followed by calamity. He who innocently places his trust in the honesty of others may find himself the loser.

In the fourth line, NINE signifies:
 Correct and resolute
 He suffers no loss.
The open and candid man of integrity must know when to call upon his strength and resist the persuasion of others.

In the fifth line, NINE signifies:
 Though he is ill
 The fault is another's.
 Without medicine
 He will find joy in his recovery.
The difficulty in which he finds himself is not of his own making, but the result of some other's mistake. He should not try to remedy matters by external means, or ex-periment with some untried panacea: quietly and innocently he should let nature take its course. Then the problem will solve itself.

In the sixth line, NINE signifies:
 Unplanned, out of season,
 A journey can bring only misfortune.
 The time is only favourable
 For those with no destination in mind.
When, in any situation, the time and condi-tions are not right, the wisest course is to wait quietly, making no plans for the future. Trying to push ahead, opposing oneself against fate, can only result in failure.

26 TA CH'U The Restraining Force

The trigrams:
above: Ken mountain, stillness
below: Ch'ien Heaven, the creative
The creative power is subjugated to Ken, which imposes stillness. This should be contrasted with hexagram 9, Ch'u, the Power of the Weak, in which the creative power is tamed by gentleness. Here four strong lines are restrained by two weak lines, in the positions of both the prince and the minister.

The Judgment
Perseverance brings favourable results. Subsisting away from the home and family, without taking service at court, will bring good fortune. It is favourable to cross the great water.

Commentary
This hexagram symbolises strength and magnanimity, glory and honour, a daily renewal of character. The firm rises, paying respect to the worthy. Restraint in the exercise of power is praiseworthy. He who dines away from home is, by implication, entertaining other worthy people. Great and difficult undertakings, such as crossing the wide river or the sea, are successful because they accord with heaven's will.

The Image
Heaven beneath the mountain is the symbol of the restraining force of the great; at the same time we glimpse the sky among the mountain peaks. The superior man studies the sayings of antiquity and the deeds of heroes of the past, strengthening his innate virtue and learning to understand what is to come.

The Lines
In the bottom line NINE signifies:
    Danger threatens.
    Avoid all action.
The man who wishes to go forward boldly, but who sees that circumstances oppose him, is wise not to attempt to overcome them. Waiting patiently, he will find that the situation is bound to change.

In the second line, NINE signifies:
    The springs of the wagon are broken.
There is no virtue in trying to fight the force which is holding one back. This line is central to the lower trigram, indicating that there is no blame.

In the third line, NINE signifies:
    A good horse will gallop with the others.
    Go forward, aware of the dangers.
    Practise chariot driving and armed
        defence daily.
    It is favourable to have a destination.
A strong horse follows the others: it is good to follow the example of a strong man. But one should still go forward cautiously, conscious of surrounding hazards and preparing oneself against unexpected attack. Above all, it is important to have a definite goal toward which one struggles.

In the fourth line, SIX signifies:
    The headboard of a young bull.
    Great good fortune.
In China, it was the custom to attach a board to the head of young bull, before his horns began to sprout, so that they would not be damaged, but also that they would grow in such a way that they could not do harm to others. By forestalling wild force it is most easily controlled: the safest way to deal with problems is to meet them in advance.

In the fifth line, SIX signifies:
    The tusks of a gelded boar.
    Good fortune.
The strength of forward advance is now even more impetuous, likened to the charge of a savage boar. But if the nature of the boar is changed by gelding, his tusks are no longer a danger. This is a more indirect and subtle way of meeting danger in advance.

In the sixth line, NINE signifies:
    Reaching command of heaven.
    Success.
There are no more obstructions: the creative power throws off the weight of the mountain. Following the way of heaven, honoured by all, the wise man achieves all that he desires and nothing stands in his way.

'Practice chariot driving and armed defence daily.' A rubbing from a clay tablet found in a Han dynasty tomb in Changtu

Nourishment

The trigrams:
    above: Ken   mountain, stillness
    below: Chen thunder and
                        awakening

The form of this hexagram is readily seen as a picture of a mouth wide open to receive sustenance. The lower three lines represent nourishment of oneself, and the upper trigram represents the nourishment of others, more particularly nourishment in a spiritual sense.

The Judgment
I indicates that perseverance brings good fortune. Pay heed to those who nourish others, and observe how they seek to nourish themselves.

Commentary
Take and give the right kind of nourishment, and good fortune is assured. Observe the needs of others, both those who nourish themselves and those whom you would wish to nourish, but do not neglect your own sustenance. As heaven and earth nourish all things, so the wise man nourishes men of talent and virtue, and through them reaches out to all the people, nourishing them both physically and spiritually.

There is a reference here to the words of Meng-tse (c. 371-288 BC): 'One who nourishes his smaller self becomes a small man, and one who nourishes his greater self becomes a great man . . . The man who only eats and drinks is counted mean by others, for he nourishes what is little to the neglect of what is great.'

The Image
Below the mountain the thunder rolls, the image of nourishing. The superior man is careful of everything that he says, and he observes due moderation in his eating and drinking.

The Lines
In the bottom line, NINE signifies:
    You let your magic tortoise go.
    Your mouth hangs open.
    Misfortune.
The tortoise was regarded as a magic animal because it appeared to live on air and required no earthly sustenance; the shells of tortoises were used for divination. The man with his mouth agape may be taken as symbolising either personal greed or envy of others: he has abandoned his self-reliance for empty discontent and jealousy of those who find themselves in better circumstances than himself.

In the second line, SIX signifies:
    Turning from the path
    To seek nourishment in the high hills.
    Persisting in such ways brings misfortune.
Here the man has sought sustenance from those in high places, living on the charity of others. In this, he behaves unworthily, succeeding only in bringing misfortune upon himself.

In the third line, SIX signifies:
    Nourishment that nourishes not
    Brings great misfortune.
    Avoid such ways for ten years
    For there is no favourable destination.
Wandering from gratification to gratification brings no satisfaction. Ten years is a complete cycle of time, and signifies forever. Seeking nourishment in this way is like taking no nourishment at all; the lord Buddha gave up sustenance on the advice of his teachers, and soon came to regret such an empty method of self discipline.

In the fourth line, SIX signifies:
    Good fortune comes
    From seeking nourishment in the high hills.
    Staring about with hungry eyes like a tiger
    Brings no reproach.
At first this seems to contradict the second line, but we have now reached the upper trigram, and the line no longer refers to a man bent on seeking his own advantage but to one who searches about him for others to help him attain his high ideal.

In the fifth line, SIX signifies:
    Turning away from the path.
    Perseverance brings good fortune.
    But success does not lie in crossing the great water.
Here is a man conscious that his own nourishment is not complete: to continue his nourishment of others he must seek help in developing his own strength. Now is not the time for him to embark on any great undertaking, for he is still dependent upon the assistance of others.

In the sixth line, NINE signifies:,
    The fountain of nourishment.
    Watching for dangers brings good fortune.
    Now is the time to cross the great water.
This describes one who has become at last a great sage, with a profound influence upon spiritual sustenance of others. Such a man, who takes note of all the pitfalls that surround and remains conxcious of the responsibilities, can undertake the most difficult labours.

'Staring about with hungry eyes like a tiger . . .'

28 TA KUO

Excess

The trigrams:
above: Tui a pool of water, joy
below: Sun wind, gentleness, penetration

In this hexagram the four strong lines are held from without by two weak lines. Where the strong holds the weak all is well and nothing is out of balance, but here the reverse is the case. The hexagram is like a beam, thick and heavy in the middle, but weak at its ends.

The Judgment

The weight is excessive. The ridgepole of the roof sags and is near to breaking point. It is favourable to have a destination,

Commentary

This is a condition that cannot last: the weight of the strong lines is too much for the weak ones. The situation must be changed: an extraordinary state of affairs demands extraordinary measures to deal with it. But although the tasks to be carried out are great, nothing is to be gained by violent movement. The gentle penetration of the wind is the example to follow, and full consideration should be given to the direction in which the desired change is to be made.

The Image

The forest is submerged in the water, the pool rises above it. The superior man, though he stands alone, is free from fear; if he has to withdraw from the world he is undaunted.

The Lines

In the bottom line, SIX signifies:
Spread white rushes upon the floor.
No error.

If the roof is to be lowered, then a mat of rushes should be spread to take the weight. White rushes are much rarer than ordinary ones, signifying the care of a valuable object, and due caution in planning for its preservation.

In the second line, NINE signifies:

(Above) 'The withered tree puts forth flowers'. A painting on silk by an anonymous artist of the Ch'ing epoch

The withered tree sprouts from its roots.
An old man takes a young wife.
Everything is favourable.

The old tree standing in the water puts forth new shoots: an unusual symbol of a rare re-awakening. This is the situation when an old man takes a new young wife, but in this case all is well.

In the third line, NINE signifies:
The ridgepole sags.
Misfortune.

This refers to a man who insists on driving ahead, taking no advice from others, and trying to force his companions to go along with him. Resenting this, they refuse to give him their support: the burden steadily increases, and catastrophe is the only outcome.

In the fourth line, NINE signifies:
The ridgepole is shored up.
Good fortune.
But if there is insincerity
Humiliation.

A leader emerges who, by his good relations with those of lower rank, succeeds in becoming master of the situation. But if he does not work for the good of all, misusing his position for personal advancement, nothing but disgrace will ensue.

In the fifth line, NINE signifies:
The withered tree puts forth flowers.
An old woman takes a young husband.
No blame. No praise.

Blossoming, the old tree exhausts its powers and only brings its death nearer. An old woman may marry again, but she is barren and no children will result. There is no evil in such a situation, but equally no successful outcome.

In the sixth line, SIX signifies:
Wading through the water
It rose above his head.
Misfortune, but no blame.

Here the man goes forward courageously, trying to complete his task whatever the danger. But although he meets with misfortune the fault is not his, and he is not to blame.

The Abyss

The trigrams:
above: K'an dangerous deep water
below: K'an dangerous deep water
This is one of only eight hexagrams in which the trigram is doubled. In each trigram a strong yang line has plunged into the deep between two yin lines, and is closed in by them, as deep water lies in a ravine. The trigram K'an represents the soul of man enclosed within the body, the light of human reason locked up in the dark of animal instinct.

The Judgment
Abyss upon abyss, danger piled on danger. But if you are sincere there is success locked up within you, and whatever you undertake will be successful.

Commentary
There is grave danger, but, as water flows without flooding over, so a man can cross the abyss without loss of confidence. Employing his reason he will succeed, and setting his eye upon a goal to be attained he will win respect and achieve results. The dangers sent from heaven none can escape, but earthly dangers are but mountains, rivers, hills and precipices. So, too, are the ominous means that are employed by kings and princes to protect their realms, both from without and within.

The Image
The water flows ever on and so reaches its destination: the image of the abyss upon the abyss. So the superior man walks in eternal virtue, instructing others in the conduct of affairs.

The Lines
In the bottom line, SIX signifies:
    Abyss upon abyss.
    He falls into the depths.
    Misfortune.
Growing accustomed to danger, a man can become hardened to it, and his familiarity may turn to evil ways. He is bound to be caught, and misfortune is the natural result of his error.

In the second line, NINE signifies:
    The abyss is dangerous and deep.
    Taking small steps
    He only slowly climbs out.
Beset by dangers, one cannot quickly overcome them. It is best first to become accustomed to the situation and then, by gradual means, to overcome it. A spring at first flows slowly, moving forward and gathering its strength until it flows out into the open.

In the third line, SIX signifies:
    Forward and backward, abyss beneath
      abyss.
    He falls deeper into the pit
    Unable to help himself.
Any attempt to escape from the danger only increases it, and escape is impossible. Wasting one's energies on fruitless attempts, one finds oneself in greater danger.

In the fourth line, SIX signifies:
    A flagon of wine
    And with it a bowl of rice
    Handed in through a hole in the rock.
    There is certainly no blame.
Help is at hand, but although the fault is not one's own, very little can be done about it. The available relief is rough and ready, for this is not the time to stand on ceremony.

In the fifth line, NINE signifies:
    The water does not overflow the abyss,
    Rising only to the brim.
    There is no blame.
The way out of danger is to follow the line of least resistance, as the water flows away out of the ravine. In normal times a man might give thought to what he was doing, carefully considering every step: in great danger it is enough to escape from it by any means.

In the sixth line, SIX signifies:
    Bound with black ropes
    Hedged in by thorns
    For three years he cannot find the way.
    Great misfortune.
Here is a man so hemmed in by danger that he cannot find any way out of it. But although his perilous situation will persist, it is finite, and he can plan for his eventual release.

30 LI

离住

Flaming beauty

The trigrams:
above: Li fire, brightness, beauty
below: Li fire, brightness, beauty
This is another doubled hexagram. The trigram Li means both 'clinging. and 'brightness', as the flame clings burning bright, with no certain form of its own except as it is defined by the object on which it burns. Where K'an represents the soul shut up within the darkness of the body, Li represents the radiant beauty of nature.

The Judgment
Li is the clinging flame. Persistence brings great good fortune. Nurturing cows brings rewards and blessings.

The cow is the symbol of docility, indicating that the wise man submits to the will of heaven. One should make oneself as dependent upon the principle of righteousness as animals are upon nature.

Commentary
The sun and moon depend from heaven, as living things depend upon earth. Clear bright consciousness of what is right results in the transforming and perfecting of all things under heaven. The weak yin lines in the second and fifth positions between the strong yang lines indicate success and the fact that docility like that of a cow will lead to good fortune.

The Image
Fire rises in two tongues of flaming beauty. So the wise man sheds his light over every quarter of the earth.

The Lines
In the bottom line, NINE signifies:
  First light: tracks run in all directions.
  But approaching with respectful steps
  He suffers no blame.
As day dawns, people awake and, still sleepy, may set off in the wrong direction. But one who remains calm can accommodate all the different impressions that flood into his newly awakened consciousness, and set about his tasks without confusion.

In the second line, SIX signifies:
  Bright yellow sunlight.
  Great good fortune.
It is now full daylight. Yellow is the colour of moderation; in China it was the prerogative of the upper classes, often being reserved for the royal family and the highest nobles. The middle way, the golden mean, brings success.

In the third line, NINE signifies:
  In the light of the setting sun
  He does not strike his *ch'ing* and sing
  But mourns his lost youth.
  Misfortune.
The *ch'ing* is a stone chime which, struck with a heavy stick, produced a musical note. As Meng-tse said: 'A concert is complete when the large bell proclaims the com-

mencement of the music, and the ringing stone proclaims its close.' At the end of the day, the man who does not celebrate the pleasure of his past life, and what is still to come, will bring only sadness and misfortune upon himself.

In, the fourth line, NINE signifies:
  It comes so suddenly,
  Flames up, dies, and is cast away.
A man who rises suddenly to success will as suddenly vanish again from view. Unexpected good fortune may burst upon us, but it will have passed away before we have had time to enjoy it. Real success comes slowly.

In the fifth line, SIX signifies:
  His tears flow in torrents
  He groans in sorrow.
  Good fortune.
Here the man has reached the high point of his life: at last understanding the vanity of all things, he reviews his situation and soberly regrets whatever he had done wrong in the past.

In the sixth line, NINE signifies:
  The king sends him forth
  To punish and set things right.
  Victorious, he kills the rebel leader
  But takes his followers captive.
  No reproach.
Punishment should not be distributed indiscriminately. In public life, revolution is best treated by rooting out evil in the person of the rebel leader, but sparing the followers. In the spiritual life, the same moderation should apply.

(Above) Meng-tse, otherwise known as Mencius. He was a disciple of Confucian doctrine who believed in the essential goodness of human nature

Influence

The trigrams:

above: Tui   a pool of water, joy
below: Ken   mountain, stillness

Ken, the lower trigram, represents the youngest son; Tui, the upper, represents the youngest daughter. Thus this hexagram signifies the persuasive influence that exists between the sexes, representing wooing and marriage.

The Judgment

Influence, attraction, success. Righteous perseverance furthers one's desires. Taking a maiden for a wife brings good fortune.

Commentary

The yielding trigram Tui is above, the firm trigram Ken is below. Although they are opposite in nature, their mutual attraction draws them together. In many of the most auspicious of Taoist positions for sexual intercourse the man is below the woman. All nature owes its existence to the influence of earth upon heaven, and heaven upon earth. In the same way, the wise man exerts his influence upon men's hearts, observing what causes them pleasure and what causes pain, and bringing the whole world to peace.

The Image

The lake is high upon the mountain. So the superior man welcomes those who approach him, humbly and without selfishness.

The Lines

In the bottom line, SIX signifies:
    He feels the influence in his big toe.
Even before a man begins to move, he reveals his activity in a flexing of the toes of his foot, but this intention is not apparent to others. As long as it has no visible outcome, it has no importance to the rest of the world, and is neither good nor evil.

In the second line, SIX signifies:
    The influence shows itself in the legs.
    Misfortune.
    It is better not to venture forth.
An ill thought-out movement, a sudden movement of the legs, may easily result in a fall. It is better to remain where one is until the persuasive influence is analysed and understood.

In the third line, NINE signifies:
    He feels the influence in his loins.
    Clinging to his wife in this way
    Is shameful.
Here is a man who follows the dictates of his heart or of his animal instincts rather than of his head.

In the fourth line, NINE signifies:
    Righteous perseverance brings good
        fortune.
    There are no regrets.
    But when a man is agitated in mind,
    His thoughts flying to and fro,
    Only his closest friends
    Will be influenced by him.
The influence to move comes from within; there are no regrets at having delayed until the moment is right. But the man who acts without due consideration will find it difficult to persuade more than his nearest companions to follow him.

In the fifth line, NINE signifies:
    The influence is felt in the nape of the
        neck.
    No regrets.
Resolution shows itself in a stiffening of the back and the neck. But even though the man will experience no remorse at this strengthening of his resolve, he may still find it difficult to persuade others.

In the sixth line, SIX signifies:
    The influence shows itself in the jaws and
        tongue.
Trying to persuade others by talk alone is a superficial way of doing things, particularly if there is no profound thought behind what is said. Its influence is of little importance, bringing neither good nor bad fortune.

'The yielding Tui is above, the firm Ken below.' A nineteenth century album painting representing the union of yin and yang

32 HENG

Endurance

The trigrams:
above: Chen thunder and awakening
below: Sun wind, gentleness, penetration

This hexagram, with the strong trigram Chen above the weak trigram Sun, is the exact inverse of Hsien, the preceding hexagram, and represents the bonds of an enduring marriage.

The Judgment
Endurance signifies steady progress, with success and freedom from error. Righteous persistence brings its reward; and it is certainly favourable to have a destination in view.

Commentary
Thunder and wind work together, representing gentleness combined with arousal. The interplay of strong and weak lines makes for endurance, and success, freedom from error and the rewards of righteous persistence all indicate that the established way can be pursued for a long time; for the way, as it is followed by heaven and earth, sun and moon, endures for ever, and the four seasons, continuing their ceaseless cycle of transformation, extend their influence for eternity. The wise man keeps steadfastly to his chosen path, succeeding in transforming all things under heaven and rendering them perfect. The true nature of everything in heaven and earth can be discovered in contemplating what it is that makes them endure.

The Image
Thunder and wind, the one influencing the other, are the image of endurance. The superior man stands firm, his direction unaltered.

The Lines
In the bottom line, SIX signifies:
Lasting success is not attained hastily
By digging a burrow for oneself.
Persistence in this course brings misfortune,
For one is without destination.
Whatever is to endure must be developed slowly, and after careful consideration. The man who attempts to establish a lasting position by entrenching himself in his present circumstances shows no thought for the future, or for the direction in which he should go.

In the second line, NINE signifies:
There are no regrets.
Although forward movement is necessary, one should avoid taking action before the time is ripe. To preserve the continuity of one's life, it is important to hold to one's principles. The man who realises that he is not yet ready, who does not attempt anything beyond his present powers, will have no regrets.

In the third line, NINE signifies:
Lacking persistence in his virtuous conduct
He meets with disgrace
And lasting humiliation.
A man who changes with the wind, leaving his emotions at the mercy of what happens in the world around him, sacrifices the inner endurance of his character. Friends and supporters will desert him, and he will end his life in shame.

In the fourth line, NINE signifies:
There is no quarry in the field.
Persistence itself is not enough. A man who takes his bow to the field, hunting where there is no game to be shot at, is foolish. In the same way, the trader who persists in attempts to sell where there are no customers, the politician who speaks without an audience, the general who pursues a non-existent foe, is not seeking out his true goal.

In the fifth line, SIX signifies:
Obstinate constancy is favourable for a woman
But not for a man.
The Chinese held that a wife should follow her man for the whole of her life; but a man should decide upon his duty as the circumstances determined it. Adhering blindly to tradition and conformity, he loses sight of his ultimate destination.

In the sixth line, SIX signifies:
Persisting in ceaseless activity
Brings misfortune.
Impatience is as much to be deplored as conservatism, for insisting upon immediate action a man will not give himself time to see and avoid errors into which he is hurrying himself. Headstrong endurance can only lead to misfortune.

Withdrawal

The trigrams:
above: Ch'ien Heaven, the creative
below: Ken mountain, stillness
The dark power of Ken rises from below, and the spiritual light retreats before it to safety. This hexagram is associated with the sixth month of the year, in which the power of the sun first begins to decline before the power of winter. So retreat is not a matter to be decided wilfully by man, but a natural process, and withdrawal in these circumstances is proper.

The Judgment
Withdrawal means success. Persistence in small matters is nevertheless to one's advantage.

Commentary
In certain situations a retreat is in effect an advance. A strong yang line is in the fifth place, the place of the ruler, and all the other lines respond to it: all actions take place in accordance with the times. As young plants grow when properly watered, so persistence in small matters brings advantage. A with-withdrawal at the proper time presages success.

The Image
The mountain stands below heaven. The superior man, keeping his distance from men of inferior character, is not angry but dignified.

The Lines
In the bottom line, SIX signifies:
Withdrawing with the rearguard.
This is dangerous.
It is no time to choose a destination.
The rearguard of a retreating army is designed for sacrifice: few survive. It is obviously better to be in the van; but whatever one's position, there is no time, in the disorder of a retreat, to seek out a direction of one's own.

In the second line, SIX signifies:
He binds him with yellow rawhide thongs.
None can untie them.
Yellow is the colour of the middle way, the correct line of duty; and rawhide thongs are very strong and not to be torn or unknotted. With a powerful will, the inferior man is bound to the superior, so that he cannot be shaken loose; in this way he intends to achieve his goal.

In the third line, NINE signifies:
Delay in withdrawal
Is frightening and dangerous.
But retaining the servants and concubines
Brings good fortune.
It is the retainers and their lack of initiative that occasions the delay, and the most obvious course is to abandon them to their fate. But the superior man who engages them in his service, taking the initiative and leading them out of danger, has made a step in the right direction.

In the fourth line, NINE signifies:
Choosing withdrawal, the superior man benefits,
But the inferior man is destroyed.
The man who makes a calculated retreat from a dangerous situation, not allowing himself to be burdened with an inferior, escapes; but the inferior man, deprived of the counsel of the other, will suffer great misfortune. The wise man is not to be blamed for this; he is not compelled to link his fate with that of another.

In the fifth line, NINE signifies:
Withdrawal by agreement.
Perseverance brings good fortune.
When the time is right for retreat, the wise man recognises it, and there is no need for discussion and disagreement. But he must still adhere firmly to his decision, modifying it only as circumstances change.

In the sixth line, NINE signifies:
Happy withdrawal.
Everything is favourable.
The sense of the word 'withdrawal' is now subtly altered, for there is no further danger in retreat. The superior man has reached a spiritual state free from doubt, and there are now no obstacles to his retiring from the world into contemplation.

33 TUN

'A Taoist temple in the mountains' by the tenth century painter Dong Yuan. The hexagram Tun is associated with the sixth month of the year, when the mists begin to form after the days of high summer

34
TA CHUANG

Strength of Greatness

The trigrams:
above: Chen   thunder and awakening
below: Ch'ien Heaven, the creative
The four strong yang lines have entered from below and are ascending; the combination of the strength of Ch'ien with the powerful movement of Chen is what gives meaning to the name of this hexagram. In appearance it is reminiscent of the horned head of the goat, an animal renowned for rapid powerful movement. The hexagram is also linked with the second month of the Chinese year. the time when everything is springing strongly to life.

The Judgment
Ta Chuang is the strength of the great. Perseverance in a course of righteousness brings reward.

Commentary
The strength of righteousness and greatness combined brings full understanding of the inner nature of everything in heaven and on earth. The lower trigram, signifying strength, controls the upper, which signifies movement, and from this results great vigour. Righteous persistence is duly rewarded because, in the context of this hexagram, what is great and what is right are synonymous.

The Image
Thunder above the heavens is the image of the strength of greatness. The superior man does not lead a path that is not in accord with established order.

The Lines
In the bottom line, NINE signifies:
  Strength in the toes.
  But going forward brings misfortune,
  This is certainly true.
  Have confidence.
The feet are the lowest part of the body, and furthest from the brain. Trying to advance by sheer brute strength, like someone who possesses ambition but no intelligence, is bound to lead to disaster. The wise man restrains his violent impulses, but retains confidence in his future advancement.

In the second line, NINE signifies:
  Righteous persistence brings good
    fortune.
There are now opportunities for advancement, but it is wise still not to plunge unheedingly ahead. Only by maintaining the true inner equilibrium of Tao, without excessive use of strength, is good fortune achieved.

In the third line, NINE signifies:
  The inferior man exploits his strength
  But the superior man is restrained,
  For persistence is dangerous:
  The goat butts obstinately against the
    hedge
  And his horns are caught.
The inferior man who comes to power

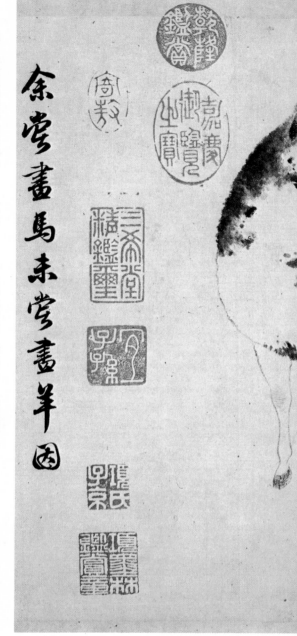

glories in it and abuses it, but the wise man is conscious at all times of the danger inherent in thrusting ahead regardless of circumstances; he will renounce or limit his power when there is no purpose in an empty display of strength.

In the fourth line, NINE signifies:
  Righteous persistence brings good
    fortune,
  Regrets vanish.
  The hedge falls apart,
  The goat frees himself.
  In a big wagon, the axle is very strong.
Obstacles are best overcome by calm and intelligent perseverance. The goat does not

子昂常畫馬仲
信壽得羊三百
羣姿富一雙惟
具良逼真靈字不
妙援萃有誰方
疏凱畜中稠伊
人家意長
甲辰新正月
滌翁

'The goat butts
obstinately . . .' From
a thirteenth century
scroll by Chao
Meng-fu

free himself by fruitless struggling, but by
slowly working his horns free from the
branches as they part. The power of the
superior man does not show itself openly
but, as the wagon is borne forward dependent entirely upon the strength of its axle, so
he is able to bear the great load of his responsibilities.

In the fifth line, SIX signifies:
    The goat is lost too easily
    But there is no cause for regret.
The goat is renowned for its outward
aggressiveness and its inward docility. The
situation has been resolved, perhaps too
easily, so that one gives up the struggle to
rest; nevertheless, abandoning one's obstinate position at this point will bring no
misfortune.

In the sixth line, SIX signifies:
    The goat butts obstinately against the
        hedge
    There is no advantage in going on,
    But taking due note of the mistake
    Brings good fortune.
Going too far, one comes to a deadlock, in
which it is impossible to advance or retreat.
The more one struggles, the more one is
ensnared. But by coming to an understanding of the obstacle one is enabled to find the
solution.

35 CHIN

Progress

The trigrams:
    above: Li   fire, brightness, beauty
    below: K'un   Earth, the passive
This hexagram represents the sun rising over the earth, a symbol of steady and unimpeded progress.

The Judgment
The great prince is honoured with many horses, and in a single day the emperor grants him three audiences.

Commentary
The Chinese character Chin itself means progress. The combination of the passive trigram K'un with the beauty of Li represents the earth radiant with bright light. The weak yin lines ascend to the fifth and ruling line of the hexagram, signifying a great prince, splendid steeds, and royal favour.

    The effect of progress comes from the prince, a man subservient to his emperor but at the same time a leader of others. He does not abuse his influence, but dedicates it to the service of his ruler who, enlightened and free from jealousy, showers favours upon him.

The Image
Chin is the image of progress, the sun rising above the earth. The superior man reflects in himself the brightness of heavenly virtue.

The Lines
In the bottom line, SIX signifies:
    Going forward, then hindered;
    But persistence brings good fortune.
    He meets lack of confidence with
      tranquillity.
    No error.
Even when everything seems to be going forward, one may be brought to a halt by influences over which one has no control. It may be that those with whom one is dealing have no confidence in oneself; but the only wise course is not to attempt to arouse confidence, or try to force one's way forward, but to remain cheerfully untroubled by the delay.

(Above) 'The great prince is honoured with many horses . . .' A gift of horses for the emperor Ch'ien-lung

In the second line, SIX signifies:
    Progress in sorrow.
    Persistence brings good fortune.
    And great happiness comes
    From the honoured grandmother.

The sorrow arises from the fact that the progress envisaged receives no recognition; but there is no alternative to perseverance, even though present circumstances bring nothing but unhappiness, for in due course someone, man or woman, will bestow gentle affection and instruction.

In the third line, SIX signifies:
    All are in accord.
    Sorrow vanishes.
This is the moment at which one realises that one is making true progress, for the backing of others is encouraging.

In the fourth line, NINE signifies:
    Making progress like a squirrel.
    Persistence is dangerous.
The squirrel builds up large stores of food; some of them are in places that the squirrel subsequently forgets. The squirrel in a cage constantly runs forward on its wheel, making for a destination that it can never reach. So the man who amasses great possessions (often by dubious means) seems to have a goal in view but seldom reaches it, and often loses not only his gains but everything that he has.

In the fifth line, SIX signifies:
    All sorrow vanishes.
    Care not for loss or gain.
    It is advantageous to have a destination.
    All things are favourable.
A man who finds himself in an important position in an era of progress should keep himself gentle and impassive, and not regret any past mistakes. He should look forward in confidence that all his ventures will succeed.

In the sixth line, NINE signifies:
    He butts onward with lowered horns
    Only to subdue his own people.
    Consciousness of his danger
    Brings no blame.
    But persistence results in humiliation.
Making progress by means of attack is only permissible in a situation where it is necessary to correct the mistakes of one's own followers; but to pursue punishment for its own sake is a sign of a lack of enlightenment. One who remains aware of the danger he risks is able to avoid mistakes, however, and succeed in what he set out to do; perseverance in aggressive behaviour can only lead to shame and misfortune.

Sinking Light

The trigrams:

above: K'un   Earth, the passive
below: Li   fire, brightness, beauty

The sun has sunk beneath the earth: the name of the hexagram, Ming I, literally means 'wounding of the bright'. This hexagram comprises not only a transposition of the trigrams of the previous hexagram, but is in fact its inversion. In Chin, a wise man, assisted by competent helpers, made steady progress; in Ming I, the wise man is in peril from a malevolent man in authority.

The Judgment

The light is sinking. Righteous persistence in the face of adversity brings advancement.

Commentary

As the sun declines into the earth, so its light is extinguished. Meet adversity like King Wen, attiring your inner self in refinement and intelligence, displaying gentleness and compliance in your outward behaviour. Determined to triumph over all difficulties, hide your light under a bushel. Be like Prince Chi who, with his troubles locked within his heart, fixed his whole being upon righteousness with rigid determination.

The Image

The light sinks into the earth, the image of Ming I. The superior man, walking among the people, keeps his light hidden. But still it shines.

The Lines

In the bottom line, NINE signifies:
The light sinks as he flies through the sky
His wings droop.
For three days, busy about his occasions,
The superior man goes without food or
      rest.
Though his lord whispers about it,
He has a goal in view.

The Emperor Yü, busied with the problems of controlling the floods, frequently passed the door of his family home without stopping to greet his relations; Confucius himself is reported to have gone several days without stopping for food. Nevertheless, one who concerns himself too much with mundane matters will be forced to withdraw from obstacles too great to be surmounted. In spite of everything, however, if he has a true goal in view, he will be honoured, even though those above him in authority criticise him for persistence.

In the second line, SIX signifies:
The light sinks.
Wounded in the thigh,
He saves himself by the strength of a
      horse.
And brings assistance.
Good fortune.

Though the superior man conceals his light, he is harmed by the actions of one in authority. But striving with all his strength, he brings relief to the distress of others in a similar plight.

In the third line, NINE signifies:
The light sinks
As he searches in the south
And captures the prince of darkness.
But foolish persistence must be avoided.

By good chance, and not by design, the wise man encounters and vanquishes his principal enemy. But, no matter how good his intentions and right his cause, he was vulnerable and showed excessive zeal that amounted almost to madness. Though it is praiseworthy to struggle against adversity. it is foolish to endanger oneself unnecessarily.

In the fourth line, SIX signifies:
Leaving his gate and courtyard,
He thrusts into the left of the belly
And exposes the heart
Of the prince of darkness.

The wise man has exposed the true nature of his adversary. But, performing this deed as he sets out from his place of safety, and realising that the evil is too great to cope with, he withdraws even further from the scene.

In the fifth line, SIX signifies:
The light sinks.
As it sank for Prince Chi.
But righteous persistence is rewarded.

Prince Chi lived at the court of the tyrant Ti-Hsin, who is clearly the 'prince of darkness' referred to. But although Prince Chi could not withdraw physically from the court, he hid his true feelings and feigned insanity. Treated as little more than a slave, he did not allow his misery to deflect him from his belief that the true light can never be extinguished.

In the sixth line, SIX signifies:
No light in the darkness.
After ascending to the heavens
He plunged into the depths of earth.

The prince of darkness is triumphant. But the darkness brings its own destruction, and in the end evil will be overcome.

The emperor Yü sometimes known as 'the engineer': he is traditionally credited with having confined the rivers of China within their banks after thirty years of labour

37
CHIA JEN

The four beauties,
sisters of a great
Chinese family,
depicted by the
fifteenth century
painter T'ang-yin

The Family

The trigrams:
above: Sun   wind, gentleness,
              penetration
below: Li   fire, brightness, beauty

This hexagram represents the strength of the family. The strong yang line at the top represents the father, the strong bottom line the son. The strong line in the fifth place may also represent the father, the weak yin line in second place the wife: alternatively, the strong lines in fifth and third place are two brothers, the weak second and fourth lines their wives. Each individual line possesses the character in accordance with its position.

The Judgment

It is the woman's persistence that brings good fortune. Women who cast this hexagram should take it as a favourable omen, but for men it does not have a successful significance.

Commentary

It is the place of women to keep within; men stand without. Keeping to their appointed places, men and women act in accordance with the laws of heaven; when the family is in order, then all the social relationships of mankind are also in order. When father, mother, sons and brothers take their proper positions within the structure of the family, when husbands play their proper part and wives are truly wifely, all is well.

The Image

The wind rises from the fire. The words of the superior man are full of meaning, his life is constant and endures.

The Lines

In the bottom line, NINE signifies:
  The family circle is closed
  And in good order.
  Regret vanishes.

The family is a well-defined unit, and every member knows his place. From his earliest years, each child must be treated with kind and loving firmness, so that he learns discipline; if he is allowed to exercise his whims and passions, he and his parents will eventually regret the indulgence.

In the second line, SIX signifies:
  She should not indulge her whims
  But attend to the needs of the household.
  Peristence brings good fortune.

Although this line refers directly to the position of a wife in the home, it has a much wider application. One who is in a position of service, whether to a single household or to the state, should not follow his own selfish desires but should devote himself to his proper duties.

In the third line, NINE signifies:
  When there are quarrels in the family
  Too much strictness brings regret,
  But nevertheless good fortune.
  When women and children mock,
  Disgrace.

Discipline tempered with tenderness is the best means of preserving concord, and too great severity is to be avoided; nevertheless, in case of doubt, strictness is to be preferred to indulgence, and brings happiness.

In the fourth line, SIX signifies:
  She is the treasure of the house.
  Great good fortune.

The fourth line represents the daughter-in-law, who can prove to be the greatest treasure of the family, but this verse also refers to any woman of the house who nourishes the family and supervises its economy. The fourth line can also represent the faithful minister of a kingdom.

In the fifth line, NINE signifies:
  He is a king in his own house.
  Fear not;
  Good fortune.

When a husband governs his family as a king governs his kingdom (or conversely) all is well. Ruling justly and kindly, evoking love and banishing fear, he brings prosperity to all.

In the sixth line, NINE signifies:
  His sincerity and confidence
  Bring him honour.
  Good fortune in the end.

The man who subjects his actions to constant self-examination will bring good fortune to himself and to all his dependants, earning himself honour and universal acclaim.

Opposites

The trigrams:
above: Lui   fire, brightness, beauty
below: Tui   a pool of water, joy
Li, the flame, burns upward, while Tui, the pool of water, soaks downward — two movements that are opposite to one another. Moreover, Li represents the second daughter and Tui the youngest daughter: though they may live in the same house their attentions are directed to two different men, and therefore their desires will run in opposite directions.

The Judgment
Opposites — but in small matters, good fortune.

Commentary
Fire moves upward, water moves downward, like two women under one roof whose wills do not accord. But if joy is joined to beauty, there is radiance. The weak yin lines ascend, responding to the strong yang lines and indicating good fortune in minor matters. For, although heaven and earth may be separate and apart, they work to the same end; men and women are opposite, but they desire union; all things are individual, but each accomplishes its purpose in accordance with its kind.

The Image
Fire above, and the pool below: the image of K'uei. The superior man remains himself, even in the midst of the crowd.

The Lines
In the bottom line, NINE signifies:
> There are no regrets.
> He loses his horse, but should not run
>> after it.
> For it will return of itself.
> Meeting with evil men
> He avoids condemnation.

When a man begins to encounter opposition, he should not attempt to bring about reconciliation by force, for he will only evoke greater opposition; just as a horse that is pursued will continue to run ever further away. With evil men, one should be particularly cautious: it is impossible to dismiss them forcibly, or ignore them, and so one should endure their company until they leave of their own accord.

In the second line, NINE signifies:
> He meets his lord in a narrow street.
> No blame.

This is an accidental encounter, possibly between people who have not been on speaking terms for some time; but, the street being narrow, there is no way in which they can avoid one another, and so friendly relations are re-established.

In the third line, SIX signifies:
> He sees his wagon halted,
> The oxen reined back.
> His hair and his nose are cut off.
> An ominous beginning
> But an auspicious end.

Everything is going wrong: there are obstacles at every turn. One is hindered and dragged back, insulted and dishonoured in the most terrible way. K'uei is different by only the second line from hexagram 21, Shih Ho, 'biting through'; and the texts of the third and fifth lines of K'uei are reminiscent of the texts of Shih Ho, and clearly have a related significance.

In the fourth line, NINE signifies:
> Solitary and estranged
> One meets a like-minded person
> With whom to live in confidence.
> There is danger, but no mistake.

Holding oneself aloof from the crowd because one cannot agree with their standards and beliefs, one becomes lonely. One is then particularly vulnerable, and an encounter with someone who seems to share one's isolation can assume an exaggerated significance. However, if one is aware of the dangers inherent in the situation it can be turned to the best advantage and there will be no regrets.

In the fifth line, SIX signifies:
> Regrets vanish.
> He cleaves to his companion
> As if he bit through the thin skin.
> Going forward,
> What error can there be in this?

At first, one does not recognise the true friend; then it is as if a veil had been torn away. One should go forward to meet such a friend; all obstacles will be removed.

In the sixth line, NINE signifies:
> Wandering solitary and estranged
> He sees a pig caked with mud,
> A wagonload of devils.
> First he draws his bow against them,
> Then lays it aside;
> For this is no assailant
> But a close relative.
> He goes forward in soft rain;
> Good fortune comes.

Here one has kept oneself aloof so long that one cannot recognise one's true friends: they appear as treacherous and unclean as a pig in his sty, or as menacing as a wagon full of devils. One's first reaction is to defend oneself; only in due course does one realise that the apparent enemy is in reality a friend. As the soft rain of summer cleans dirt and dust from everything, so one's doubts are swept away and one advances toward a successful outcome. This text is often quoted as an example of the obscurity of the I Ching.

39 CHIEN

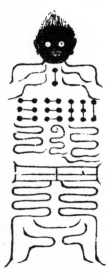

Obstacles

The trigrams:
above: K'an water, dangerous pit
below: Ken mountain, stillness
This hexagram represents a perilous abyss in front, with a precipitous mountain rising behind. Whichever way one turns one is beset with obstacles.

The Judgment
There is advantage to the south and west; obstacles to the north and east. It is advantageous to see and meet with a great man. Righteous persistence brings good fortune.

Commentary
Chien denotes difficulty, for danger lies in front of one. Wisdom lies in perceiving the danger and successfully avoiding it: the southwest is the direction of retreat, and that way leads to the middle course, but the northeast is the direction of advance, and nothing favourable lies that way. The strong yang line in the fifth position indicates that righteous persistence will be of great value to the community or the state; visiting a great man is bound to result in significant achievements.

The Image
Water upon the mountain, the image of Chien. So the superior man turns back in order to examine himself and cultivate his virtue.

The Lines
In the bottom line, SIX signifies:
  Going forward means obstacles,
  Standing still earns praise.
Encountering obstacles, threatened with danger, one should not attempt to go blindly forward; one should consider the nature of the obstacles and how to deal with them.

In the second line, SIX signifies:

The servant of the king
Encounters obstacle after obstacle,
But the fault is not his.
This is the path of duty: when a man may not act upon his own responsibility but must continue to struggle in the service of others, or for a higher cause, then he should not be reproached.

In the third line, NINE signifies:
  Going forward leads only to obstacles
  And he turns back.
This line reiterates the message of the first line: a man who acts as the father of his family must think not only of himself but of those in his care. It would be foolish to push forward into danger, and if he turns back he will be joyfully welcomed by his kin.

In the fourth line, SIX signifies:
  Going forward leads to obstacles.
  Remaining still he allies himself
  With those who are on their way.
This is a situation in which a man cannot overcome obstacles by himself; he must wait until others join him in an alliance.

In the fifth line, NINE signifies:
  He struggles against all obstacles
  But friends are coming to help him.
The man is called upon to give assistance in an emergency, and even though the dangers he faces may be too much for him, he bravely opposes himself to them. His example attracts others whom he effectively organises so that the obstacles may be finally overcome.

In the sixth line, SIX signifies:
  Going forward leads to obstacles
  Remaining still brings great good fortune. Now is the time to see the great man.
This is the sage who may move spiritually as he pleases. But his own practical nature constantly draws him back to the world, where his example and his teaching can bring good fortune both to himself and to others.

The Masters of the Four Directions: north, west, south and east. From a thirteenth century talisman

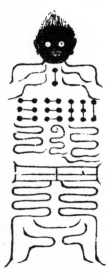

Deliverance

The trigrams:
above: Chen   thunder and
            awakening
below: K'an   water, dangerous pit
This hexagram represents deliverance from the dangers of the previous hexagram. The obstacles have been removed, troubles are resolved. However, deliverance is only beginning, and the lines of the hexagram represent its progressive stages.

The Judgment
There is advantage to the south and west. Those who have no good reason to go forward will gain good fortune by turning back. Those who have a destination in view should hasten forward to be sure of success.

Commentary
Hsieh represents deliverance from danger by activity. South and west are favourable, for those who go in this direction, that of retreat, will be loved by all; and turning back brings good fortune and makes it possible to follow the middle way. But those with a good reason to go forward should hurry on their way. When heaven and earth are released from the clutch of winter as thunder and rain, the buds of fruit trees and every sort of plant burst open. Great indeed are events in the time of Hsieh!

The Image
Thunder and rain begin, the image of deliverance. The superior man forgives mistakes and pardons crimes.

The Lines
In the bottom line, SIX signifies:
   No error!
The obstacles have been removed, the barriers lifted. There is nothing to be said at this moment, nothing to be done except to rest and be thankful.

In the second line, NINE signifies:
   Taking the yellow arrow,
   He kills three foxes in the field.
   Righteous persistence brings success.
Commentators disagree upon the precise significance of this text. The foxes are sly and devious animals; the arrow is yellow, the colour of moderation and honour. Does the hunter kill three foxes with a single arrow — as one might say, 'three birds with one stone' — or does he receive the arrow as recognition for his qualities?

In the third line, SIX signifies:
   Carrying his baggage on his back
   Yet riding in a carriage
   He tempts robbers to attack him.
   Persistence in this course
   Brings nothing but shame.
This text refers to a man who has risen from poverty, in which he was compelled to carry his belongings on his back, to a new-found wealth to which he is not used. As Confucius says: 'A man who is insolent

'The prince draws his bow'. From a ninth century life of Buddha

toward those above him, and unyielding to those below him, tempts robbers to plot an attack upon him . . . Rich ornaments worn by a virgin are an enticement to others to despoil her.'

In the fourth line, NINE signifies:
   Release yourself with your toe.
   Then friends will come
   In whom you can put your trust.
Here deliverance is difficult and fumbled: it is as if a man were struggling to release himself from bonds by attempting to untie them with his toes rather than his fingers. He has encumbered himself with inferior people, and must break with them before he can join with friends who truly share his beliefs.

In the fifth line, SIX signifies:
   The superior man can deliver himself
   And enjoys good fortune.
   Proving his worthiness to inferior men.
The inferior men are difficult to rid oneself of; the superior man must first break with them in his mind, and only then will they give up their attempts to hold him back, as they perceive that he is in earnest.

In the sixth line, SIX signifies:
   The prince draws his bow
   And slays the falcon on the high wall.
   Everything is favourable.
Still hindered from deliverance by the machinations of an inferior who is, however, in a position of importance, the superior man must make his plans, get ready the means of his release, and then act with resolve.

41 SUN

Decrease

The trigrams:
above: Ken   mountain, stillness
below: Tui   a pool of water, joy

This hexagram is regarded as having been formed by a change in hexagram 11 (T'ai, Peace), the strong yang line in the third place having been replaced by the weak yin line from the top place; so that what is below has been decreased to the advantage of what is above. It is as if the foundations of a building had been weakened while the upper walls were strengthened.

The Judgment
One who effects decrease with sincerity will bring about great good fortune without blame. Righteous persistence is correct, and there is advantage in every move made toward a destination. If there is doubt about how to proceed, two small bowls are sufficient for the sacrifice.

Commentary
There is loss below, but gain above, and the way leads ever upward. The line in the text concerning the use of two small bowls means that one should use whatever comes to hand. At times it is right to decrease the strong and increase the weak. Decrease and increase, filling and emptying — there is an appointed time for each.

The Image
The lake lies at the foot of the mountain, the image of Sun. The superior man controls his anger and suppresses his desires.

'A man going forth alone . . .' Painting of the Yüan epoch by Chao Meng-fu

The Lines
In the bottom line, NINE signifies:

When work is done, hurry away:
This is not wrong.
Consider, however, how you decrease others.

When a man has completed his own business, it is unselfish and praiseworthy for him to hurry to the aid of others; but he must calculate carefully how much additional burden he can accept, and whether the limited responsibility he can assume is really a help to them.

In the second line, NINE signifies:
Righteous persistence brings reward.
But going forward brings misfortune.
One can bring increase to others
Without decreasing oneself.

A man who wishes to be of service to others must possess a serious self-awareness and preserve his essential dignity, for someone who sacrifices his principles at the insistence of another diminishes not only himself.

In the third line, SIX signifies:
If three set out together
One is lost by the way.
But a man going forth alone
Finds company.

A group of three is not an ideal working unit, for jealousy is bound to arise. A man who begins on his own is sure to find someone who will join with him.

In the fourth line, SIX signifies:
Decreasing his faults
He finds another hurrying to rejoice.
No blame.

If a man does not recognise his own faults he will often find that even friendly people are not disposed to join with him. But as he begins to recognise his shortcomings his friends will flock round him, and there is happiness on both sides.

In the fifth line, SIX signifies:
He is increased
By many — ten pair or more — of tortoise shells.
Great good fortune.

Tortoise shells were used in divination, and were of considerable value. To someone destined for good fortune, it will come without fail, and all the oracles will give him favourable omens.

In the sixth line, NINE signifies:
Increasing without reducing others
He is without blame.
Righteous persistence brings good fortune.
It is favourable to have a destination.
He hires servants
But has no family or home.

Those who rise to high position without harming others bring benefits to everyone. Perseverance and hard work bring success, and the successful man is in a position to enlist the help of others. But these others are not those who will aid him in marrying or setting up a home: his actions will be devoted to public service and will be for the good of all.

Increase

The trigrams:
> above: Sun   wind, gentleness, penetration
> below: Chen   thunder and awakening

This hexagram represents increase because it is a development from hexagram 12, P'i, Stagnation: the strong yang line of the upper trigram has sunk to the bottom, and is rising through the lower trigram. This expresses the fundamental conception that to rule truly is to serve.

The Judgment
It is favourable to have a destination; now is the time to cross the great water.

Commentary
There is loss above and gain below, and the joy of the people is boundless, for when those placed above behave virtuously to those below them without pride their ways are brilliantly illuminated. It is favourable to have a destination, for the way is straight and lies in the middle, leading to unexpected good fortune. Finding a wooden bridge or a boat, you may cross the great water. Increase comes at once and constantly, every day brings unhindered progress. Heaven dispenses its blessings and earth brings forth its fruits. At the appointed time, increase is everywhere.

The Image
Wind and thunder, the image of I. The superior man, seeing what is good, imitates it; recognising his faults, he corrects them.

The Lines
In the bottom line, NINE signifies:
> Now is the time for great undertakings.
> Great good fortune.
> No blame.

He who is favoured by fate with great ability must use it to achieve something great, and those below him will willingly assist him, provided too much is not demanded of them.

In the second line, SIX signifies:
> There is someone who indeed increases him.
> With many pair of tortoise shells
> And will not accept refusal.
> Persistence brings good fortune.
> The king presents his offerings to the lord of heaven.
> Good fortune.

When destiny smiles on a man, everything for which he strives will come inevitably to him. But only a virtuous man, who observes all the proper forms of behaviour, will enjoy such a fate.

In the third line, SIX signifies:
> He is increased by evil means
> But, acting in all sincerity
> He is not to blame.
> Walking confidently in the centre
> Bearing his jade seal of office
> He reports to his prince.

The man who walks the middle way will prosper even in the midst of adversity. The jade seal that he bears is the symbol of his faithfulness.

In the fourth line, SIX signifies:
> Walking in the centre
> He advises the prince
> And is followed.
> He is the man to be used
> In moving the place of government.

When it is necessary for the government to show its strength to all, the seat of the capital may be moved; in the time of the emperor Shang it was moved five times. Great trust must be placed in the man charged with the responsbility of moving it; he should be above all a virtuous man who has the wellbeing of all the people truly at heart.

In the fifth line, NINE signifies:
> Be sincere and kind
> Ask no questions
> And great good fortune will result.
> All will recognise your confidence and virtue.

This is the position of the ruler, benevolently bestowing good things upon his people without demanding their allegiance; for his kindness and goodness will be recognised by all.

In the sixth line, NINE signifies:
> He brought increase to no-one
> And someone sought to strike him.
> He is not constant in his heart.
> Misfortune.

Those in high places who neglect their duty of bringing increase to those below them will soon find themselves alone, and perhaps even attacked by those they have abandoned.

(Above) 'Walking in the centre, he advises the prince . . .' A minister in his scarlet robe, from the eighth century painting 'Eight officials' by Ch'eng Hung

43 KUAI

Resolution

The trigrams:
above: Tui   a pool of water, joy
below: Ch'ien Heaven, the creative
Ch'ien represents the father, and Tui the youngest daughter; the strong yang lines are rising resolutely upward through the hexagram, and cannot be restrained by the weak yin line at the top. The result will be a breakthrough, like a cloudburst, or a flooded river bursting its banks. And the outcome of such a breakthrough will be a *resolution* of the state of tension that produced it. Kuai is associated with the third month of the year, when frequent rainstorms burst upon the land.

The Judgment
Everything should be reported in full at the king's court, even though frankness is dangerous. When reporting to one's own city, it is not proper to be armed. It is good to have a destination in view.

Commentary
Kuai is the symbol of displacing with determination, for the strong resolve the affairs of the weak; strength is combined with cheerfulness and determination with placidity. Reporting — possibly the guilt of a criminal —at the king's court is indicated by the single weak line above the five strong lines; the importance of a known destination is also indicated by the way in which the movement of these strong lines is brought to an end.

The Image
The lake has risen above the heavens, the image of Kuai. The superior man, accordingly, bestows his gifts upon those below him; he does not rest upon his virtues.

The Lines
In the bottom line, NINE signifies:
Mighty and proud in his strength
He advances his feet.
But he is unequal to the task
And suffers humiliation.
In the Chinese, the text employs much the same words as in the text for the bottom line of hexagram 34, Ta Chuang: there is a reference to advancing with the toes, representing an attempt to go forward by sheer brute strength, without giving proper consideration to the means or to the outcome.

In such circumstances, one is likely to suffer a setback at the most damaging moment.

In the second line, NINE signifies:
Shouts in the night.
But he who is forearmed
Is forewarned
And has no fear.
The superior man is always on his guard and so, when there is an alarm, he does not become excited and flustered. When reason triumphs over fear, he treats difficulties as though they did not exist; as he develops his strength of character, so others submit to him without argument.

In the third line, NINE signifies:
Setting the jaw and advancing straight forward
Brings misfortune.
The superior man determines on interception.
Walking alone in the rain
He is spattered with mud
And his friends murmur against him.
No blame.

In the struggle against evil, the most obvious course is to set one's jaw firmly and nobly and plunge forward. But this is not wise. The wise man, although his resolve is firm, takes a way that will enable him to cut off the criminal, even though it may appear to be devious. Because of this he will be misjudged and thought to be inferior. But remaining true to himself and his faith, he will make no mistake.

In the fourth line, NINE signifies:
His haunches are flayed
And he walks with difficulty.
Letting himself be led like a sheep
He could put an end to his pain.
But though he hears this advice
He believes it not.
Obstinately, the man pushes forward, even though he suffers; he has an inner drive that will not let him rest. This is not the way: he should desist from his foolish course and take the advice of others. But obstinacy deafens a man to all good counsel.

In the fifth line, NINE signifies:
Like a bed of weeds,
Tenacious but shallow-rooted,
Inferior men cling to the earth.
The superior man, determined to uproot them,
Treads the middle way
And suffers no reproach.
The inferior man in a high position holds desperately to his place, and it takes dangerous determination to remove him. But one must not be deflected from the true path.

In the sixth line, SIX signifies:
There is no warning.
The end is misfortune.
At the very moment when victory appears to be in one's grasp, a moment of inattention can bring disaster.

Coming Together

The trigrams:

above: Ch'ien   Heaven, the creative
below: Sun   wind, gentleness,
                 penetration

This hexagram is linked with the fifth
month, the time of the summer solstice,
when the first whisper of the darkness of the
coming winter is heard, intruding upon the
days of joy. This is the weak yin line, driven
from the top of the preceding hexagram,
furtively and unexpectedly reappearing at
the bottom: it represents the female principle
advancing of its own accord to meet the
male. Although it signifies the pleasure of
sexual intercourse, it also contains elements
of danger.

The Judgment

Coming together, meaning the woman is in
power. A marriage in such circumstances
would be unfavourable.

Commentary

The yielding confronts the firm. A marriage
with such a woman would not last long.
Nevertheless, it is from such an intercourse
that heaven and earth give birth to all things,
and when strength is properly controlled
and correctly used, everything in the world
goes well. And great indeed is the importance of what is done at the right time indicated by Kou.

The Image

The wind is below the heavens, the image of
Kou. Accordingly, the prince gives out his
orders, proclaiming them to the four quarters of the kingdom.

The Lines

In the bottom line, SIX signifies:
    The wheel is checked with a brake of
      bronze;
    Righteous persistence brings good
      fortune.
    It is not fortunate to have a destination.
    A lean pig still struggles.
A bad influence must be constantly checked,
and its ill effects will be avoided. But if the
restraints are relaxed, as if allowing a
chariot to move forward again toward its
destination, only misfortune can result. A
pig should be fat, and so it must not be
allowed to run about, however hard it
struggles.

In the second line, NINE signifies:
    The fish is in the bag.
    No error.
    But it is not for the guests.
There is a difference of opinion about the
interpretation of this text. The fish can be
seen as a wily, untrustworthy influence that
must be kept confined; but it can also be a
desirable catch that should be shared with
others. Not to share it can be unwise.

In the third line, NINE signifies:
    His haunches are flayed
    And he walks with difficulty.
    Mindful of his danger
    He makes no great mistake.
Going forward obstinately, even though one
is suffering, is unwise. But the man who
knows what he is doing will suffer no misfortune.

In the fourth line, NINE signifies:
    There is no fish in the bag.
    Misfortune.
It is necessary to make use of inferior people
in furthering one's aims. The man who does
not do so will lose them by his indifference,
just when he most needs them.

In the fifth line, NINE signifies:
    The medlar leaves shade the melon,
    Hiding its beauty.
    Then it drops as if from heaven.
The melon on the vine must be shaded with
leaves so that it does not ripen too quickly
and spoil. The superior man protects those
below him, but does not let them know that
they are in his control. Then power comes to
him like a ripe fruit from the vine.

In the sixth line, NINE signifies:
    He meets them with his horns.
    Regrets, but no blame.
This is a man who holds himself aloof from
encounters with others, rebuffing their advances from a noble sense of pride. He will
be reproached for his aloofness, but he does
not care about his contemporaries' opinions.

*'Coming together,
meaning the woman is in power . . .'
A porcelain incense holder decorated
in the eighteenth century by Ch'ien-lung*

45 TS'UI

Congregation

The trigrams:
above: Tui   a pool of water, joy
below: K'un   Earth, the passive

This hexagram is related, both in its form and its significance, to hexagram 8, Pi, Seeking Unity. In Pi, dangerous deep water is over the earth; in Ts'ui, the water has gathered together into a pool, fulfilling the search for unity represented in Pi.

The Judgment
Congregation brings success. The king makes his way to the temple of his ancestors, and it is favourable to see the great man: progress and success. Righteous persistence brings its reward. Important sacrifices are made, bringing good fortune. It is favourable to have a destination in view.

Commentary
Ts'ui symbolises congregation, assembling together, union. The trigram Tui, representing willing acceptance, is joined with Tui, meaning joy. A strong yang line occupies the fifth position, the place of the ruler; hence the meaning of union. The king makes his way to the ancestral temple to make his offerings to the spirits of his forbears and so secure the prosperity of his people. Congregation is implied in the meeting with a great man, and persistence is necessary for the purpose of putting matters to right. Sacrifices must be made in accordance with the rules of heaven; and by observing the way in which all things congregate together, we learn to understand the inner nature of all things in earth and in heaven.

The Image
Above the earth, a pool of water gathering: the image of Ts'ui. The superior man, accordingly, makes ready his weapons, forearmed against the unlooked-for.

The Lines
In the bottom line, SIX signifies:
Sincerity, but without pertinacity,
Brings sometimes disorder,
At times union.
He cried out
And a grasping hand made him laugh
  again.
No regrets; go forward without blame.
People congregate, seeking a leader; but there are so many of them that they cannot make a common decision, each being influenced by the opinions of the others. But if they recognise their dilemma, their cry for help will be heard, and reassurance from their prospective leader is sufficient to bring unity.

In the second line, SIX signifies:
Let yourself be drawn forward
Assuring good fortune and no blame.
If you are sincere
Even a small sacrifice is acceptable.
There are subliminal forces that bring men together, and by accepting and yielding to these forces, we gain fortune and avoid all blame. Those who congregate in this way understand one another, without any necessity for explanations or formalities; just as the supreme being is satisfied with the smallest offering from a man whose heart is true.

In the third line, SIX signifies:
The congregation is sad,
For no destination seems favourable.
Yet going forward brings no blame,
Only a little regret.
Sometimes a man discovers that the group with whom he had hoped to join is without any sense of direction. It is better for him then, even though he may suffer some pain, to advance in his own way, as long as he is convinced that it is right.

In the fourth line, NINE signifies:
Great good fortune.
No blame.
This is the fourth line, the place of the minister. It represents a man who gathers people around him in the service of his prince. He is striving, not for himself but for the good of the people, and so his work is crowned with success.

In the fifth line, NINE signifies:
In his high position he gathers people
  together.
No blame.
If some have no confidence in him
Let him persevere in virtue
And dispose of all regrets.
There may be those who gather about a man solely because of his influential position, and not from any innate confidence in him. His only course is to gain their confidence by his example of unswerving devotion to duty.

In the sixth line, SIX signifies:
Sighing and weeping,
But no blame.
When the honourable intentions of a man are misunderstood, he will be sad that he has not brought others together. But the fault is not his, and he is not to be blamed.

Moving upward

The trigrams:
above: K'un   Earth, the passive
below: Sun   wind, gentleness,
             penetration

The lower trigram, Sun, also symbolises wood. This hexagram represents (rather like hexagram 3, Chun) the action of a shoot in the earth pushing upward with effort.

The Judgment
Moving upward with effort against restraint brings success. Seek out the great man and have no fears. There is advantage to the south.

Commentary
The weak line moves upward at the proper time. In this hexagram, gentleness and willing acceptance are joined together. The strong line in the central position of the lower trigram wins response from the upper trigram, indicating great progress and success. Unexpected good fortune will result from the desire to see the great man and the concomitant freedom from fear or anxiety that will result. Southward lies the way to fortune, and all desires will eventually be fulfilled.

The Image
In the bottom line, SIX signifies:
    Move upward
    Welcomed by those above.
    Great good fortune.
This hexagram represents the unimpeded rise from obscurity and inferior origins to a position of power, and this line is the beginning of such a rise. Good fortune comes from the acceptance and confidence of those in higher positions.

In the second line, NINE signifies:
    Sincere,
    Though he made only a small sacrifice
    He suffers no blame.

A man of strong character, secure in his convictions, will not be criticised even if he is out of tune with his surroundings and impatient with formalities.

In the third line, NINE signifies:
    He moves upward
    Into an unoccupied city.
The obstacles are removed: the man of ambition ascends unimpeded, like a liberator entering a city that has been abandoned by the enemy. But the text adds no promise of good fortune: perhaps the unoccupied city is only a trap to lead him into disaster.

In the fourth line, SIX signifies:
    The king makes offerings on Mount Ch'i:
    Good fortune and no blame.
This text refers to the time when the Chou dynasty was coming into power in China; it was prince Chou, the son of king Wen, who provided the texts for the individual lines. Wen made sacrifices at the shrine on Mount Ch'i, in his homeland district in western China, and honoured his assistants by including them in the ceremony.

In the fifth line, SIX signifies:
    Righteous persistence brings good
        fortune
    But one moves upward step by step.
As a man moves ever higher, it is essential that he should not be carried away by his continuing success. He must go steadily onward, step by step, almost hesitantly, patiently making his way without haste, overlooking nothing.

In the sixth line, SIX signifies:
    Moving upward in darkness.
    Unremitting persistence is favourable.
Blind ambition can lead one onward not to success but to failure. Now it is more important than ever to know exactly what one means to do and where one means to go: the outcome may still be material loss, but some advantage will be gained.

Sheng represents a new shoot pushing upward with effort, as the bamboo bursts out of the soil in this painting by Li K'an.

47 K'UN

Exhaustion

The trigrams:
above: Tui   a pool of water, joy
below: K'an   water, dangerous pit

This hexagram represents a pool which has drained away into the deep pit; the water of the pool is exhausted. Within the joyousness of Tui there is an abyss, an emptiness.

The Judgment
Though there is exhaustion and adversity, righteous persistence will lead to eventual success. There is good fortune for the truly great man, and no blame. Even though he has something to say, however, his words will not be heeded.

Commentary
Joy and danger are joined together: adversity comes from something that lies hidden. He who succeeds in spite of the difficulties that face him is certainly one of the truly great; the strong line in the fifth place indicates that righteous persistence will bring good fortune to such a man. But since his words will not be heeded, it is most sensible of him not to speak at all.

The Image
The water of the pool has drained away; the image of K'un. The superior man will risk even his life to achieve the result that he wishes.

The Lines
In the bottom line, SIX signifies:
Exhausted by the bare branches that
    entangle him
He strays into a gloomy valley
And for three years meets no-one.
A man who is overwhelmed by adversity may lose all initiative, caring nothing for his material condition and fixing his attention soley upon his problems rather than upon their solution. Until he can begin to think constructively about his situation, there will be no way out for him.

In the second line, NINE signifies:
Exhausted, even with a meal before him.
A minister in his scarlet sash arrives;
Now is the moment to make sacrifice.
Going forward brings misfortune
But no blame.
Sitting at the table, apparently well-fed and content, one is still exhausted and oppressed by care from which there seems to be no escape. But the minister is a messenger from the prince, who is seeking able men; it is an appropriate moment to make an offering, and pray for the removal of difficulties. Nevertheless, the time is not yet ripe for setting out; all must first be prepared.

In the third line, SIX signifies:
Exhausted by the rocks that face him
He finds nothing to lean on but thistles
    and briars.
Returning to his house
He finds his wife has gone.
Misfortune

This represents a man who is too easily discouraged by adversity. Although it is possible that the rocks may be climbed, or even passed by, he exhausts himself almost at the sight of them, and finds nothing reliable on which he can depend. Turning back from the obstruction to seek rest in his home, he finds that even there he can depend on nothing.

In the fourth line, NINE signifies:
He advances very slowly
Delayed by the golden carriage in front.
There are regrets, but not for long.
Here is a man who is wealthy and successful in all material things; but he has only recently come into wealth and the ways of the rich prove an obstruction to his desire to press forward spiritually. However, the underlying strength of his nature overcomes the drawbacks, and he reaches his goal.

In the fifth line, NINE signifies:
His nose and feet are cut off;
Oppression at the hands of the scarlet-
    sashed minister.
Slowly, however, joy comes to him.
Now is the time for sacrifice.
The man is obstructed both above and below, and receives no assistance from those whose duty it should be to render aid to the people. Gradually, however, matters will take a turn for the better; in the meantime, offerings and prayer should be made.

In the sixth line, SIX signifies.
Exhausted by the clinging creepers,
Tottering on the edge of a cliff,
He tells himself
'If I move I shall regret it.'
But repenting former mistakes
He can go forward to good fortune.
The difficulties are slight, the clinging creepers should be easily broken; but the man is still without resolution, racked with fear that whatever he does may prove to be wrong. If only he can make up his mind, come to a decision on the basis of recognising his errors, then all will be well.

The Well

The trigrams:
above: K'an — water, dangerous pit
below: Sun — wind, gentleness, penetration

The trigram Sun is also associated with wood, and this hexagram, with water above and wood below, represents the well — perhaps lined with wooden boards — in which the water is lifted up in clay or wooden pitchers attached to wooden poles.

The Judgment
In Ching, we are reminded that though the place of a town may be moved, the places of its wells cannot be changed. A well neither increases nor decreases; people come and go and draw water to their satisfaction. But sometimes, just when one is almost down to the water, the rope is not quite long enough, or the pitcher breaks — misfortune.

Commentary
It is the combination of wood with water, the wood raising the water up, that gives the symbolism of the well. It is the strong yang line in the centre of the upper trigram that implies the unmoving nature of the well and its unchanging contents. The shortness of the rope indicates that we may fail to achieve what appears to be within our grasp; the breaking of the pitcher warns of certain misfortune.

The Image
Water above wood, the image of Ching. The superior man encourages people as they work, advising them how they may best help one another.

The Lines
In the bottom line, SIX signifies:
When the well is muddy
None drink from it;
When the well is old
No creatures come to it.

If a man has no spiritual qualities, he is like someone sunk in mud, and has no significance for others. In the end, he will be alone.

In the second line, NINE signifies:
Fish dart in the well water
The pitcher is broken and leaks.

The water in the well is clear, but it is not used; there are fish there to be caught, but the pitcher cannot be used for drawing water out. This represents a man who possesses good qualities that he makes no use of; he associates with inferiors, and gradually deteriorates until he can no longer accomplish anything.

In the third line, NINE signifies:
The well is cleansed, but still,
To my heart's sorrow,
No-one comes to drink from it.
Yet the water could be drawn.
If the king were wise
Many could share his good fortune.

This indicates that a capable man is at hand, but that his abilities are not recognised and no use is made of him. If only someone in high position could appreciate his talents he could do much to help the people.

In the fourth line, SIX signifies:
The well is being lined.
No error.

The well is being repaired, and it cannot be used until the work is completed. Sometimes one must devote one's energies to one's own spiritual improvement, and at this time it is impossible to help others.

In the fifth line, NINE signifies:
The well water is cool
From an icy spring
And all may drink.

A virtuous man in a position of authority is an example to everyone; he offers the water of life to all who come to him.

In the sixth line, SIX signifies:
The well is uncovered
All may draw without hindrance.
Have confidence. Great good fortune.

The really great man is like a dependable well, never running dry, forbidden to none, supplying all who come to him with spiritual nourishment; and the more people take from him, the greater his spiritual wealth becomes.

A print derived from a T'ang engraved stone of the tenth century, depicting a peasant raising water in wooden buckets

49 KO

Throwing Off

The trigrams:
    above: Tui   a pool of water, joy
    below: Li   fire, brightness, beauty

In its original sense, Ko means an animal's pelt that moults every year, or a skin that is sloughed. By extension, it can be taken to mean a great political change, a throwing off of government, or revolution; retaining at the same time the original sense of 'revolution', a turn in the wheel of time or of fate. The two trigrams making up the hexagram are the same as in K'uei (hexagram 38, Opposites), but now they are reversed, the younger daughter being above and the elder below, so that the opposites are in direct conflict like water over fire.

The Judgment
When there is revolution, none will believe in it before the day of its completion, but then there is complete success. Righteous persistence brings reward, regrets vanish.

Commentary
Water and fire extinguish each other, like two women who share the same household but whose wills are in constant conflict. The revolution must come first, before the faith of the people in it will be established. An enlightened attitude, both to the change itself and to the means by which it is brought about, will bring joy in success, making it possible to put everything to rights. It is the power of the forces of heaven and earth to bring about the renewal that is revealed in the progress of the four seasons. Tang and Wu (Ch'eng T'ang, 'the completer', the first of the Shang emperors, and Wu Wang, the son of king Wen) revolted in accordance with the will of heaven, and the people answered their call. Great indeed are the events of the time of throwing off.

The Image
Fire below water, the image of Ko. The superior man makes observations of the calendar, and determines the days and seasons.

The Lines
In the bottom line, NINE signifies:
    He is wrapped in the skin of a yellow ox.
Yellow is the colour of the middle way, and the ox is the symbol of docility. The hour for change has not yet come, and the wise man will refrain from making changes until the time is ripe.

In the second line, SIX signifies:
    When the day comes
    Throw off.
    Go forward with good fortune.
    No blame.
One should always attempt first to secure reform by moderate means, but when these are unsuccessful revolution becomes necessary. Proper preparation is essential; the time must be right; and a man with the necessary abilities, and the support of the people, is required.

In the third line, NINE signifies:
    Action brings misfortune.
    Persistence brings danger.
    But when throwing off has been three
      times discussed
    One may commit oneself
    And be believed.
This is a warning against haste and ruthlessness in initiating change, as well as against delay in the name of righteousness. The concepts should be discussed with care, and the plans given mature consideration; only then is it wise and proper to set matters in motion.

In the fourth line, NINE signifies:
    Regrets vanish.
    One is accepted by the people.
    Throwing off brings good fortune.
He who brings about a revolution of any kind must have the necessary authority, as well as the inner strength. Because in the end the people will only support undertakings that they know to be good.

In the fifth line, NINE signifies:
    The great man makes his changes
    As the tiger moults his pelt.
    Even before he consults the oracle
    He is believed.
The tiger, a symbol of brilliance and majesty, moults his coat every year; but the stripes, even though they may change, remain as clear and visible as ever. In the same way, when a great man leads a revolution, the reasons for the changes that he makes are apparent to all. He is so confident of his actions that he does not need to seek advice by divination.

In the sixth line, SIX signifies:
    The superior man makes his changes
    As the leopard moults his pelt.
    The inferior man changes his face.
    Beginning brings misfortune.
    Righteous persistence brings good
      fortune.
When repression has been thrown off, or when a new direction has been established, the superior man continues to make smaller changes necessary to establish the new order. The leopard is the symbol of beauty, whose moult makes only small changes in its spotted coat. Lesser men easily adapt to the new conditions; but to attempt to continue with radical changes will bring disaster. Success lies in perseverance along the middle way.

The Cauldron

The trigrams:

above: Li   fire, brightness, beauty
below: Sun   wind, gentleness,
             penetration

The hexagram is the image of a cauldron: at the bottom are the legs, above them the rounded belly, then the handles like ears, and at the top the rim. The cauldron is the symbol of the nourishment it contains, and it is also the sacrificial vessel. It stands in the fire, fanned by the wind.

The Judgment

Great good fortune and success.

Commentary

The cauldron represents the peace and beauty indicated by its two component trigrams, as wood (represented by Sun) and fire combine to cook the sacrificial offering. The sages of old cooked their sacrifices in order to make them more acceptable to the supreme being, and made lavish feasts to nourish their wise and capable helpers. Ting is the symbol of flexible obedience: ears are make quick of hearing, and eyesight is sharpened. The weak yin line enters and ascends to the fifth place, where it responds to the strong yang lines below. All these things indicate great progress and success.

The Image

Fire upon wood, the image of Ting. The superior man, assuming a righteous posture, holds firmly to the decrees of heaven.

The Lines

In the bottom line, SIX signifies:
    The cauldron is turned over.
    To empty it of decaying meat.
    Taking a concubine to bear sons
    Brings no blame.
Reversing the normal order of things is acceptable when the reason for the action is good. Although a concubine is regarded as a lowly person, she should be honoured for the sons she bears. Every person, no matter how inferior his station, can gain recognition for his accomplishments if he acts in a honourable way to better himself.

In the second line, NINE signifies:
    The cauldron is filled
    And my friends are envious.
    But they cannot harm me.
    Good fortune.
'My cup runneth over' says the psalmist. The man who has obtained some solid achievement will be the envy of everyone, even his friends. But, armed with his spiritual strength, he is unassailable.

In the third line, NINE signifies:
    The handles of the cauldron are broken
    It cannot be moved.
    The fat pheasant goes uneaten.
    When sudden rains come
    Regret fades away
    And good fortune comes in the end.
This represents a man whose abilities go un-recognised, and who is therefore rendered ineffectual; all his good qualities are going to waste. But the unexpected rainstorm, which cools the fire and the pot standing on it, is an omen of good fortune.

In the fourth line, NINE signifies:
    The legs of the cauldron are broken.
    The prince's dinner is spilled
    And his garments splashed.
    Misfortune.
Here is a man not fit for his responsibilities. He is careless and brings misfortune not only upon himself but upon his superiors.

In the fifth line, SIX signifies:
    The cauldron has yellow handles
    And a golden rim.
    Righteous persistence brings its reward.
The problems indicated in the last two texts have been resolved: the man in authority is unpretentious and approachable. As a result he finds competent helpers; but he must remain resolutely virtuous.

In the sixth line, NINE signifies:
    The cauldron has a rim of jade
    Great good fortune.
    Everything is favourable.
In the preceding text, the rim of gold denotes strength and purity; jade is hard, but at the same time luminously lustrous. The sage represented in the top line gives good advice to all, finding favour in the eyes of the supreme being, and bringing good fortune to everyone without concern for his personal advantage.

A ritual cauldron in the courtyard of a Chinese temple

51 CHEN

Thunderclap

The trigrams:
> above: Chen thunder and awakening
> below: Chen thunder and awakening

The trigram Chen, repeated here, represents the eldest son, one who is likely to take over the leadership with energy and strength. Twice a strong yang line develops below two yin lines, its energy pushing it forcibly upward; like thunder, which bursts out with a terrifying clap, the movement produces surprise and terror.

The Judgment
Chen portends success. First comes the shock, evoking apprehension and fear, then the aftermath of laughter. For a hundred miles around people are terrified, but the sincere worshipper does not let his sacrifical cup and spoon drop.

Commentary
Thunder indicates success: but the initial terror is followed by happiness. The thunder itself is like what it provokes: shouts and laughter, fearful glee. Those who are a hundred miles away are startled, and those who are close at hand are terrified. Nevertheless, someone makes his appearance who can guard the ancestral temple and the shrines of the rural gods, one who is fit to preside at the sacrifical ceremonies.

The Image
Thunder repeated is the image of Chen. The superior man, in fear and trembling, develops his virtues and examines his faults.

The Lines
In the bottom line, NINE signifies:
> The thunderclap comes: oh! oh!
> Laughter and cheer follow.
> Good fortune.

First comes the shock and the surprise, bringing fear and trembling. One finds oneself at a disadvantage. But after the ordeal there is relief: fear teaches us a lesson from which we can learn to our advantage.

In the second line, SIX signifies:
> Thunder comes closer.
> Danger is at hand.
> He loses every one of his possessions
> And flees into the nine hills.
> He should not go in search of them
> For after seven days he will recover them.

On this occasion the shock is so great that one is actually in danger, and suffers crippling loss. At this time resistance to fate is foolish; the only course is to retreat to some isolated spot where the danger cannot penetrate, and within a reasonable time all will be well again.

In the third line, SIX signifies:
> Thunder is everywhere,
> Driving one to distraction.
> Acting impetuously now
> Will bring no misfortune.

When one is overwhelmed by shock, it is easy to lose one's presence of mind. But there are times when it is wise to act upon the spur of the moment: this is one of them and, even though the act of impetuousity may bring little advantage, it will certainly do no harm.

In the fourth line, NINE signifies:
> After the thunderclap
> The ways are deep in mud.

This is the situation in which shock has produced dazed confusion, so that one seems to move as if deep in the mire. There is little to do but wait for conditions to improve.

In the fifth line, SIX signifies:
> Thunder rolls about the heavens,
> Danger is at hand.
> With care, nothing is lost
> But there are matters for attention.

Successive shocks seem to come from all sides. Nevertheless, by maintaining a position at the centre of the disturbance, one avoids loss and is even able to accomplish something.

In the sixth line, SIX signifies:
> Thunder brings chaos
> People gaze around in terror.
> Taking action brings misfortune,
> For though we are not ourselves touched
> Our neighbours are harmed.
> No blame
> Although our nearest speak against us.

When the shock is one suffered by a community, it is enough to keep one's head and be unaffected by the general fear: to attempt any action at this time would be foolish. Those around one, who suffer misfortune as much through their own panic as through the direct effects of the incident, will be quick to accuse and reproach, but the man who keeps his head clear in such a situation will be able to rise above all calumny.

Inaction

The trigrams:
above: Ken　mountain, stillness
below: Ken　mountain, stillness

In this hexagram the male principle, represented by the yang lines, is striving upward, and the female principle, represented by the yin lines, moves downward. The inaction results from the fact that these movements have come to a conclusion in each trigram.

The Judgment
Keeping the back unmoving so that one no longer feels one's body; walking out into the courtyard without noticing the people there – there is no blame.

This alludes to the practice of Taoist meditation. In what has come to be known as the 'spiritual alchemy' of Tao, the spine is thought of as a sort of still connecting three 'crucibles': one at the base of the spine, one at the level of the solar plexus behind the stomach, and the third in the head. By meditation and breathing, the sexual energy of the pelvic region is gradually distilled, ever upward, until the initiate is filled with nothing but spiritual energy and is in a state of oneness with the energies of the universe, and finally achieves immortality.

Commentary
Ken signifies resting, desisting, coming to a stop. When it is the time for inaction, that is the time to stop; when the time comes for action, then act! By action and inaction, each at its appointed time, man makes glorious progress. The inaction represented by Ken means inaction in its proper place and time. The upper and the lower trigrams exactly correspond to each other, but do not interact; hence the wording of the Judgment.

The Image
The mountains stand together, the image of Ken. The superior man, accordingly, does not move in his thoughts beyond the position in which he finds himself.

The Lines
In the bottom line, SIX signifies:
His toes are still.
No blame
Righteous persistence is advantageous.

As in the texts for hexagram 31, Hsien, and hexagram 34, Ta Chuang, the toes represent the simplest sort of movement: by keeping the toes still one stops even before one has begun to move. A man who knows the importance of inaction at the beginning will eventually find the right way, but perseverance is essential to keep him from drifting without purpose.

In the second line, SIX signifies:
His calves are still.
He cannot aid the one he follows
And is disquieted.

The feet and legs have begun a movement, as in the instinct to follow someone more powerful than oneself. But the movement is suddenly halted: he who is moving may fall, like one who discovers almost too late that the course he is pursuing is wrong, the man he is following is evilly disposed.

In the third line, NINE signifies:
His loins are still.
His spine is stiff.
Danger.
The heart is suffocated.

He who endeavours to stifle sexual desire when his mind is not prepared for it will suffer painful results. But he who understands the true purpose of Taoist meditation and practices it correctly will feel inspiration in his heart.

In the fourth line, SIX signifies:
His trunk is still.
No blame.

Inaction at this time is appropriate: the initiate is well on the way to spiritual enlightenment, even though he is not yet free from all dangers of doubt that he is right in his policy of inaction.

In the fifth line, SIX signifies:
His jaws are still.
His speech being ordered,
He has no cause for regret.

To know when to speak and when not to speak is the way to true wisdom.

In the sixth line, NINE signifies:
He is noble in his inaction.
Good fortune.

This is the goal of inaction: spiritual nobility, which brings nothing but good fortune in its train.

(Below) 'He is noble in his inaction. Good fortune.' From a painting attributed to the thirteenth century artist Ma Yuan

53 CHIEN

漢

Gradual progress

The trigrams:
above: Sun　wind, gentleness
below: Ken　mountain, stillness
In this hexagram Sun also represents wood, as a tree on a mountain, caressed by the wind, grows slowly according to the laws of nature.

The Judgment
The maiden is given in marriage, bringing good fortune. Righteous perseverance is advantageous.

Commentary
The gradual progress symbolised by Chien is like the marriage of a young woman; there is good fortune for herself and for the man she marries, and in the dowry that she brings with her. The lines move upward, each in its correct place, to the strong yang line in the fifth position, the position of the ruler. Gradually progressing in righteousness, a man becomes fit to rule his land. The un-moving quality of the mountain, conjoined with the gentleness of the wind, gives rise to inexhaustible activity.

The Image
Upon the mountain stands a tree, the symbol of gradual progress. The superior man, accordingly, abides in dignity and virtue, inclining the people to good behaviour.

The Lines
In the bottom line, SIX signifies:
　The wild geese gradually approach the
　　shore.
　The younger son is in danger,
　And spoken against.
　But there is no blame.
The wild goose, in Chinese mythology, flies toward the sun, which represents the male principle, like a young maiden who seeks a husband; it is also a symbol of marital fidelity, for it is said that it never takes a second mate. As they approach the shore, the geese are leaving the danger of the open water for the safety of land: a young man who has set out on his way through life feels his danger greatly, and is sensitive to any criticism. But the trouble which he may suffer is through no fault of his own. (More than two thousand years after this text was written, the 'wild geese', the sons of the out-lawed Irish nobility, fled from their lands to settle in Portugal.)

'Upon the mountain stands a tree, the symbol of gradual progress.' Painting by the thirteenth century artist Kao Che-bo

In the second line, SIX signifies:
　The wild geese gradually approach the
　　cliff.
　They eat and drink in peace and joy.
　Good fortune.
The high cliff is a place of safety where the geese can rejoice that the danger is past. In terms of the marriage referred to in the Judgment and Commentary, this line represents material success.

In the third line, NINE signifies:
　The wild geese gradually approach the
　　dry plains.
　The husband goes forth
　And does not return.
　The wife is with child
　But does not give birth.
　Misfortune.
　Now is the time to drive away robbers.
The dry plains are no safe place for geese; there is no food and no hiding place. The marriage represented is unsuccessful and barren; the husband risks his own life and endangers his family. But this is un-necessary: if he can avoid provoking con-flict, and remain to protect his home, mis-fortune will be avoided.

In the fourth line, SIX signifies:
　The wild geese gradually approach the
　　trees.
　Perhaps they will find a branch to perch.
　No blame.
Trees, also, are unsuitable places for geese, but they may find a safe branch on which to take refuge. In marriage, one of the part-ners may bring stability by kind and thought-ful acts.

In the fifth line, NINE signifies:
　The wild geese gradually approach the
　　high ground.
　For three years the wife is without child
　But in the end all will be well.
　Good fortune.
In a high position a man can very easily become isolated, perhaps from his family, perhaps from his colleagues. His relation-ships are sterile, and nothing is accomplish-ed. But as progress continues misunder-standings will be cleared away, and there will be a happy reconciliation.

In the sixth line, NINE signifies:
　The wild geese gradually approach the
　　summits.
　Their feathers are used in sacred rites.
　Good fortune.
There is nowhere further to advance: the geese fly ever upward to heaven, as the superior man rises far beyond the reach of ordinary mortals. But still his blessings fall like the feathers of the geese, which are gathered and used in the temple rituals.

The Marriageable Maiden

The trigrams:

      above: Chen thunder and awakening
      below: Tui   a pool of water, joy

Chen represents the eldest son and Tui the youngest daughter; the hexagram represents the older man leading a young girl through the door of his house. But the girl is not his first wife; she is his second wife or perhaps the first of his concubines. For this reason Kuei Mei is not a very fortunate omen, even though it should not be taken as referring in every case to marriage.

The Judgment

Kuei Mei is the marriageable maiden. Going forward brings misfortune, and no destination is at present favourable.

Commentary

This hexagram symbolishes the proper relationship between heaven and earth; for if heaven and earth had no intercourse, nothing would come into existence and flourish. The marriage of the younger sister is both her end and her beginning. Joy and movement together (represented by the two trigrams) — this is the image of a maiden marrying. But the inappropriate positions of the third and fifth lines indicate that going forward will bring misfortune, for the weak yin lines are mounted upon the strong yang lines.

The Image

Thunder over the water, the image of Kuei Mei. The superior man, accordingly, understands the mischief that may be made at the beginning in order to reach a lasting conclusion.

The Lines

In the bottom line, NINE signifies:
    The maiden marries as a concubine.
    The lame man can still walk.
    Going forward brings good fortune.

The girl who enters a family in the position of first concubine is in much the same position as a man who is appointed adviser to a high minister; he has no power of his own, but although this hampers his activities he is still able to advance both himself and the matters for which he is responsible.

In the second line, NINE signifies:
    The one-eyed man can still see.
    The hermit can still advance himself
    By righteous perseverance.

A man who neglects the affections of his concubine is like a man with one eye: he is concerned only with his own interests. But even the solitary person, man or woman, is not without virtue.

In the third line, SIX signifies:
    The maiden was but a slave
    And rose to become a concubine.

Desperate to improve one's position, one can take the first opportunity that offers itself. But it is likely to be only a small advance, one still implying subservience.

In the fourth line, NINE signifies:
    The maiden remains unwed
    Beyond the proper day.
    But a late marriage comes in time.

A girl may delay her marriage, in expectation of finding the right husband, until it seems too late. But her intentions are correct, and in the end all will be well.

In the fifth line, SIX signifies:
    The emperor I gave his daughter in
      marriage.
    Her garments were not as fine
    As those of her bridesmaid.
    The moon is near full
    And brings good fortune.

The emperor I is T'ang the Completer. He decreed that his daughters, though of highest rank, should be subordinate to their husbands (see the fifth line of hexagram 11, T'ai). The compliant modesty of the princess is shown in the simplicity of her clothes compared with that of her younger sister, the bridesmaid. She is like the moon which, shortly before it is full, shines brightly but does not yet oppose its face directly to the sun.

In the sixth line, SIX signifies:
    The woman holds the basket
    But there is nothing in it.
    The man sacrifices the sheep
    But no blood flows.
    Having no destination is favourable.

The empty basket, and the sacrificed sheep that does not bleed, signify ritual form without sincerity. In such circumstances, there is no advantage to be gained from proceeding further.

54
KUEI MEI

歸
妹

A copy of a fourth century painting on a silk scroll by Ku K'ai-chih

55 FENG

Abundance

The trigrams:
above: Chen thunder and awakening
below: Li fire, brightness

Chen, symbolising movement, is above Li, symbolising clarity: this combination produces abundance. However, here the height of development has been reached, suggesting that such a situation will not endure indefinitely.

The Judgment
Abundance means great success: the greatness of the king is an inspiration. Do not be downhearted, for the bright sun is now at its zenith.

Commentary
Brilliance conjoined with movement signifies abundance. The king has still greater possibilities before him: he inspires his people and they respect him, he shines like a sun before the whole world. But the sun at its zenith begins to decline; the moon that has waxed begins to wane. So all that is in heaven and earth grows and diminishes according to the season; and how much truer indeed is this of men, as well as of the gods.

The Image
Thunder and lightning come together, the image of Feng. The superior man, accordingly, hears law suits, judges and inflicts the necessary penalties.

The Lines
In the bottom line, NINE signifies:
    Meeting his equal
    Accepting his hospitality for ten days
    There is no error.
    Going forward earns respect.
Those who represent the attributes of brilliance and movement are well matched; even if they spend a complete cycle of time together, the total period of affluence, the time is well spent. Nevertheless, accepting the hospitality of equals is only a temporary respite, and very soon the time comes when it is essential to one's intellectual wellbeing to go forward again.

In the second line, SIX signifies:
    The shadows close in,
    The polestar can be seen at noonday.
    Going forward now invites mistrust and
      hate.
    But sincere devotion
    Brings good fortune.
From the depths of a mine shaft or a well, where the scattered light of the sun has been dissipated, it is possible to see the stars even at midday; the same phenomenon is visible during an eclipse. When the machinations of a powerful party obscure the brilliance of the ruler, it is a time for the wise man to give up any ideas of energetic advance, which would only earn him mistrust and envy. Nevertheless he should maintain his loyalties and his principles, for in the end all will be well.

In the third line, NINE signifies:
    The shadows are thick as a great banner
    And at noonday the smallest stars are
      visible.
    Though he break his right arm
    There is no blame.
All is now in eclipse: even the most insignificant persons seem like bright stars in the gloom and confusion. Even the right-hand man of the ruler is without power to undertake anything.

In the fourth line, NINE signifies:
    The shadows are like a huge tent
    The polestar can be seen at noonday.
    He meets his prince, an equal.
    Good fortune.
Even though the darkness is still unrelieved, the eclipse is beginning to pass. Meeting with a prince of equal rank indicates that the time for action is almost arrived.

In the fifth line, SIX signifies:
    Light begins to appear in the sky
    As after a storm.
    Unexpected good fortune
    And fame draw near.
The dominance of the adversary's party is waning, and the ruler is surrounded by wise and able men who propose a modest course of action.

In the sixth line, SIX signifies:
    His house is full of abundance
    And there is a wall about it.
    Peeping out through the gate
    He sees no-one
    For three years — nobody.
    Misfortune.
The subject of this text has gone too far: in devoting his attentions solely to material success he has cut himself off not only from his friends and associates but from his closest family.

The Wayfarer

The trigrams:

above: Li   fire, brightness
below: Ken   mountain, stillness

The mountain, Ken, is unmoving; while the fire, Li, burns upward. The two trigrams have nothing to hold them together, and so represent the separation that is the fate of the wayfarer.

The Judgment

Lu, the wayfarer, signifies success in small matters. Perseverance brings good fortune to the travelling man.

Commentary

The weak yin line in the centre of the upper trigram is freely subservient to the yang lines on either side of it. The obstinacy represented by the mountain, conjoined to the beauty of fire, indicates success in small matters, and the good fortune that will eventually come to determined wayfarers. Great is the time and great the right course indicated by Lu.

The Image

Fire upon the mountain is the image of Lu. The superior man, accordingly, is wise and cautious in imposing penalties, and does not allow lawsuits to drag on.

The Lines

In the bottom line, SIX signifies:

The wayfarer concerns himself with trifles
And so attracts calamity.

The traveller upon the way should not demean himself, or bother with unimportant matters; he is himself humble and defenceless, and so it is even more important to preserve his spiritual dignity, and avoid the disputes he finds along the road.

In the second line, SIX signifies:

The wayfarer reaches an inn,
His valuables safe in his bosom,
And finds a young servant loyal to him.

The wayfarer is well-behaved and keeps to himself; preserving his spiritual dignity, he finds a suitable resting place. In this way, he not only retains the respect of others and his own material prosperity, but he wins the allegiance of a trustworthy follower.

In the third line, NINE signifies:

Careless,
He burns down the inn,
And loses his loyal servant.
Though firm and correct,
He is in danger.

The wayfarer is rude and ill-mannered; entirely by his own fault he loses his lodging, possibly his belongings, and the loyalty of those who follow him. Whatever his plans, it would be folly to attempt to proceed with them at this moment.

'The bird burns its own nest'. A representation in porcelain of the legendary phoenix, which to the Chinese was a symbol of high virtue

In the fourth line, NINE signifies:

The wayfarer finds a roadside shelter,
He earns his living
And acquires an axe.
But still he laments
That his heart is not glad.

The traveller modestly restricts his ambition to what he can immediately achieve. He makes a living and is, at least temporarily, established in the community where he finds himself. But he is nonetheless a stranger, and must defend himself; he has not found a home.

In the fifth line, SIX signifies:

He shoots at a pheasant
But loses his arrow.
However, in the end,
He wins praise and gains high office.

The wayfarer, who has arrived near the court of the prince, tries to shoot a pheasant as a gift for his host. But although he is unsuccessful in this, and suffers a minor loss as a result, he eventually receives great benefits.

In the sixth line, NINE signifies:

The bird burns its own nest.
As first the wayfarer laughs
And then he cries and weeps.
Careless,
He loses his cow.
Misfortune.

The bird burning its own nest is the phoenix, a symbol to the Chinese of high virtue. Yet at the same time there is a suggestion in this text that carelessness is responsible for the burnt nest. The wayfarer who sees it at first behaves irresponsibly, laughing at what he conceives to be the misfortune of another; but then he experiences his own misfortune. The Chinese commentators imply that the loss of a cow through carelessness means that no news will ever be received of something lost.

57 SUN

'He consults a confusion of magicians and diviners'. Two magicians in the middle of performing their esoteric rites

Submission

The trigrams:
    above: Sun   wind, gentleness
    below: Sun   wind, gentleness

This is one of the eight double trigrams; Sun represents the eldest daughter and gentleness, but like the wind — or like wood, with which it is also identified — it has also the property of penetration. In the natural world, the wind penetrates the clouds, bringing clarity and serenity; in human affairs, it is the penetrating clarity of intelligence that uncovers the darkness of intrigue and perversity. It took the subtle philosophy of Tao to recognise that the concomitant of such penetration was willing submission — not submission to an external fate, but the 'giving way' which is the first step to victory.

The Judgment
Submission and gentleness lead to success in many minor matters. It is advantageous to have a destination in view and to visit a great man.

Commentary
Willing submission is necessary in carrying out the will of heaven. The strong yang line is correctly in the fifth place, indicating that what is willed will be fulfilled. The weak yin lines in first and fourth place are both obedient to the yang lines above them, indicating moderate success, and the advantage of movement in any direction.

The Image
Winds follow one upon the other the image of Sun. The superior man, accordingly, makes his commands known once more, and performs his tasks according to the will of heaven.

The Lines
In the bottom line, SIX signifies:
    Coming and going like the wind.
    He should seek advantage
    In righteous persistence like a brave
        soldier.
Indecisiveness is often the outcome of submissiveness: this is wrong, for only the persistence shown by someone who behaves like a bold military commander can bring advance.

In the second line, NINE signifies:
    He creeps beneath the bed.
    And consults a confusion of magicians
        and diviners.
    But there is good fortune and no error.
Everything is unsure. When motives are hidden and their outcome cannot be decided, it is not blameworthy to make use of any means of determining what is to come.

In the third line, NINE signifies:
    He penetrates repeatedly
    And must give way.
    Humiliation.
It is better to reach a decision quickly than to come eventually to an impasse as a result of constant questioning.

In the fourth line, SIX signifies:
    The time for regret is past.
    Three kinds of game
    Are found in the hunt.
The three kinds of game are appropriate especially for sacrifices to the gods, for feasting guests, and for everyday nourishment. When one occupies an important administrative position in which experience, innate modesty and decisive action can be combined, success is assured.

In the fifth line, NINE signifies:
    Righteous persistence brings good
        fortune.
    Regrets vanish,
    And everything is favourable.
    There is no good beginning
    But a good end.
    Three days before the change
    And three days after
    Bring good fortune.
This text promises good fortune, but it is important to make plans for there is only a limited period during which advantage can be taken of it. The beginning may not have been propitious, but almost unexpectedly the right time will make itself apparent.

In the sixth line, NINE signifies:
    He creeps beneath the bed.
    He loses his living and his axe.
    Persistence brings misfortune.
The subject of this text is too submissive, showing humility amounting to servility. This does him no good, for as a result he loses not only his material wealth but his very means of survival.

Joy

The trigrams:
> above: Tui a pool of water, joy
> below: Tui a pool of water, joy

This hexagram is another of the eight which are made up of doubled trigrams. Tui is the youngest daughter, whose gentleness brings joy through the strength of the strong yang lines in the fourth and fifth place.

The Judgment
Joy means success. Righteous perseverance brings its just reward.

Commentary
Tui signifies satisfaction in gladness. In each of the trigrams there is a strong yang line in the centre, with a weak yin line above it. This shows that seeking joy through righteous persistence is the right way to accord with the will of heaven and to reach concordance with the feelings of one's fellow men. When the people are led with gladness, they forget their burdens; as they wrestle in joy with their difficulties, they even forget that they must die. The great power of joy lies in the encouragement that it can give to all.

The Image
The waters resting one upon the other, the image of joy. The superior man, accordingly, joins with his friends in discussion and practises with them.

The Lines
In the bottom line, NINE signifies:
> Contented joy.
> Good fortune.

Very little need be said in explanation of the texts for the lines of this hexagram, for they are very clear in their meaning. This line signifies the quiet, undemonstrative strength that contented joy confers: wordless, self-contained and free from all envy.

In the second line, NINE signifies:
> Sincere joy.
> Good fortune,
> No regrets.

Confident in his integrity, the sincerely joyous man will not be drawn from his path by doubtful pleasures offered him by inferior companions.

In the third line, SIX signifies:
> Coming joy.
> Misfortune.

There is disagreement in the interpretation of this text, but it seems probable that it means that misfortune is experienced at a time when a happy event is expected; it may be that the coming joy is only postponed by temporary setback.

In the fourth line, NINE signifies:
> Calculating joys to come
> He is restless.
> Close to misfortune
> He nevertheless is happy.

Faced with the choice of a variety of pleasures, some high and some low, a man will enjoy no inner peace. But if he is aware of the danger of indulgence, and makes his decision accordingly, he will experience true joy.

In the fifth line, NINE signifies:
> Putting one's trust in crumbling things
> Means danger.

One may not be aware that something is beginning to crumble away; it may be an article of faith, a political system, a business enterprise, or a relationship with another person. It is important to be very much on one's guard, so as to be able to draw back when the first signs of disintegration become apparent.

In the sixth line, SIX signifies:
> Joy in seduction.

This is the weak yin line at the top of the hexagram, and it represents one who gets his pleasure, both by attracting and persuading others and by succumbing himself to all kinds of meretricious attraction. He has abandoned his spiritual advancement to give himself over to the joys of the flesh and of material things.

Joy in seduction: the man desired by three sisters, a drawing from a nineteenth century album page

59 HUAN

汉

Dispersal

The trigrams:
  above: Sun wind, gentleness
  below: K'an water, dangerous pit
The wind blows across the water, dispersing it into spume, mists, and eventually drying it up. So a man's energy, which is dangerously dammed up within him, may be released by gentleness.

The Judgment
Huan indicates progress and success. The king approaches his ancestral temple; and it is advantageous to cross the great water, and to be righteously persistent in all.

Commentary
Successful progress is symbolised by the strong yang line in the second place, which is not exhausted there. The weak yin line in fourth place is appropriately outside the lower trigram, and the fifth line above, representing the king, responds to it. The king approaching his ancestral temple, and occupying the centre of the upper trigram, is maintaining his position without any change of mind. One of the additional attributes of Sun, the upper trigram, is wood; the advantage of crossing the great water derives from mounting upon a vessel of wood, and great success is the result.

The Image
The wind blows over the water, the image of Huan. So the kings of old built temples in which to sacrifice to the supreme being.

'So the kings of old built temples': a block-print of the early seventeenth century

The Lines
In the bottom line, SIX signifies:
 He brings assistance with the strength of a horse.
 Good fortune.
The wind over the water can bring clouds, and if they are not dispersed by a constant wind they will bring rainstorms. At such a time it is important to join together in vigorous action, before concealed divisions of opinion bring about misunderstanding.

In the second line, NINE signifies:
 In the midst of dispersal
 He hastens to the altar.
 Regrets vanish.
The symbolism of the upper trigram is of a temple in which one can find shelter from the dangers of the pit below. The implication is that one should find some spiritual means of protection from the evil; and the altar represents the means that one has established to protect oneself.

In the third line, SIX signifies:
 All self-interest is dispersed.
 No regrets
Only by a great renunciation can a man obtain the strength to achieve great things. He must put aside all personal desires that may come between him and the welfare of others and set his sights on a goal outside himself.

In the fourth line, SIX signifies
 He disperses his followers.
 Great good fortune.
 Dispersal leads to accumulation,
 Good men standing like a mound.
 Something that ordinary people
 Would not have thought of.
The followers who are dispersed are those who have not proved themselves equal to their tasks. 'Cast thy bread upon the waters, for thou shalt find it after many days': the man of good intent who rids himself of incompetent companions and who continues on his self-appointed path of service to the community will soon be joined by others of a like mind.

In the fifth line, NINE signifies:
 He issues his proclamations
 As sweat flows from the body.
 The king scatters his stores
 Among the people
 Without blame.
Just as a high fever is dispersed in perspiration, so the king may relieve his anxieties by dispersing his possessions among the needy. Great and generous ideas are necessary for success at this time.

In the sixth line, NINE signifies:
 He disperses bloodiness
 Keeping evil at a distance.
 Departing without blame.
All the commentaries upon this text disagree upon the precise meaning of the words, but it seems clear that 'dispersing bloodiness' means the avoidance of bloodshed, removing oneself from the danger of injury.

Restraint

The trigrams:
above: K'an   dangerous deep water
below: Tui   a pool of water, joy

The word Chieh really means the joints of the bamboo, or the joints of the human frame, or the natural regular divisions of the year; thus it represents the voluntary limitations that may be set upon growth or expenditure in order to maintain matters in due moderation. The pool of water can only occupy a limited space; the movement of more water from above must be strictly restrained, or the pool will overflow.

The Judgment
Restraint brings success and progress. But restrictions that are severe and difficult should not be perpetuated.

Commentary
Chieh signifies success because the strong yang lines and the weak yin lines are equal in number, and there is a yang line in fifth position. Severe and difficult restrictions should not be allowed to continue because they produce exhaustion. Even in the midst of danger we experience pleasure and satisfaction in following the proper course. It is by the restraint exercised between terrestrial and celestial forces that the four seasons arrive each at its appointed time; so, when due restraint is shown in the duties of government, the state suffers no injury, and the people no hurt.

The Image
Water above the pool, the image of Chieh. The superior man, accordingly, creates his system of number and measure, and discusses the nature of virtue and proper conduct.

The Lines
In the bottom line, NINE signifies:
He restricts himself
To the outer gates and courtyard.
No blame.
The man who knows rightly how to limit his undertakings in the face of insuperable obstacles can accumulate an energy that, at the right moment, will enable him to act positively. Confucius says: 'Where disorder develops, words are the first steps. If the prince is not discreet, he loses his servant. If the servant is not discreet, he loses his life . . . . Therefore the superior man is careful to maintain silence and does not go forth.'

In the second line, NINE signifies:
He restricts himself
To the courtyard within his gate.
Misfortune.
When the time for action arrives, it is essential to act at once. As water flows into a pool, so there comes a moment when it must find an outlet.

In the third line, SIX signifies:
He places no restraint upon himself:
Lamentations
But no blame.
Those who give themselves up to indulgence may well have cause to regret it, but provided they are prepared to accept the responsibility for their actions they are not to be condemned.

In the fourth line, SIX signifies:
He restrains himself
Contentedly.
Success.
This text needs no further elucidation: its meaning is unambivalent.

In the fifth line, NINE signifies:
He restrains himself
Sweetly and voluntarily.
Good fortune.
Going forward brings approbation.
This is a very important line, for the strong yang line is in the position of the ruler. When a man in an important position applies necessary restraints to his own actions, without demanding too much from his associates, then his modesty will bring good fortune and it will be possible to advance with general approval.

In the sixth line, SIX signifies:
Troublesome restraint.
Persistence brings misfortune
But there is no regret.
Restrictions that are too severe will not be endured for long; even the ascetic's body will eventually rebel against self-torture. Nevertheless, on occasions a certain ruthlessness toward oneself is the only way to salvation.

61 CHUNG FU

中孚

'The crane calls in the shadows'. A detail from an embroidered coat, representing a crane with peaches to symbolise the longevity to be attained by suitable sexual practices

Inner Truth

The trigrams:

above: Sun   wind, gentleness, penetration

below: Tui   a pool of water, joy

The wind blows over the water, revealing its invisible movement in visible disturbance of the surface. The strong yang lines above and below, and the yielding yin lines in the centre, indicate a heart free from prejudice and open to the truth. At the same time, the strong line at the centre of each trigram indicates the strength of inner truth.

The Judgment

Inner truth and sincerity: the pig with the fish. This leads to good fortune. It is advantageous to cross the great water. Righteous persistence brings its just reward.

Commentary

The lines reveal joy and gentleness conjoined: confidence and sincerity will ensure the development of the kingdom. The combination of the pig with the fish may be identified as the dolphin, known in all ancient mythologies as a friendly guide upon a journey, and as one who can save a sailor from drowning: so good fortune attends any undertaking that involves crossing the great water. Persistence accompanied by confidence is always advantageous, for it accords with the will of heaven.

The Image

Wind over the water, the image of Chung Fu. The superior man, accordingly, gives thought to matters of law and delays the sentence of death.

The Lines

In the bottom line, NINE signifies:

Be prepared

As he who fishes or hunts the boar.

Good fortune.

Other intentions bring disquietude.

The angler, or the huntsman waiting in ambush for his prey, must be patient and unmoving, but ready for any emergency. But if he is unsure about his place of concealment, or finds himself in argument with others about tactics, the only result will be unease and anxiety.

In the second line, NINE signifies:

The crane calls in the shadows;

And the young ones answer.

I have a cup of contentment

And I will share it with you.

The parent crane does not reveal itself when it calls: it cries from its place of concealment, but its young still hear it and reply. This is like the response of all men of good intent when they hear the clear expression of truth. When we become aware of an important truth, we should communicate it to others.

In the third line, SIX signifies:

He finds his equal.

Now he strikes his drum,

Now he stops.

Now he weeps, and now he sings.

The equal may be an honest companion, or a worthy adversary. But one is unsure how to proceed: whether to announce the truth boldly to everyone, or to keep it to oneself; whether to rejoice in the revelation vouchsafed to one, or sorrow that it is not apparent to all.

In the fourth line, SIX signifies:

Like the moon near its fullness,

Or a team-horse whose companions have broken away.

No blame.

When the moon is at the full it stands in opposition to the sun, but at that very moment it begins to wane: so must one be modest and reverent in the face of enlightenment.

The horse pulling the carriage must continue on its way, even when its companions break free. Only in this way can one retain one's inner confidence.

In the fifth line, NINE signifies:

He seems drawn forward by his truth

And draws other with him.

No error.

The fifth line is the position of the ruler: only when his inner strength is sufficient can he carry others with him.

In the sixth line, NINE signifies:

Cockcrow rises to heaven.

Perseverance brings misfortune.

Every day at dawn the cock crows in its pride; but it cannot fly, and only its cry rises into the skies. Over-confidence in one's abilities and good fortune is followed by evil consequences.

The Small Persist

The trigrams:
above: Chen thunder and awakening
below: Ken mountain and stillness
This hexagram represents a most unusual situation: weak yin lines enclose it on both sides, and preponderate; but the two strong yang lines are at the centre. These yang lines exert their influence, creating conflict and exceptional conditions; but it is the yin lines which must relate to the external world. A man who attains a position of authority for which he is not really adequate must exercise unusual prudence.

The Judgment
The small persist. Success. Righteous perseverance brings its just reward. Small things may be accomplished, but the time is not right for great things. Birds fly high, singing, but lose their tune. It is better not to strive upward, but to stay below.

Commentary
This hexagram indicates success for the small; their persistence will be rewarded, and their deeds fit the times. The yin line in fifth place signifies success in small affairs, and good fortune. The yang line in fourth place has not succeeded in reaching a ruling position, indicating that it is not the moment for great matters. The symbol of a bird denotes that it is better to descend than to ascend; this is the way to good fortune.

The Image
Thunder upon the mountain, the image of Hsiao Kuo. The superior man, accordingly, shows excess in his reverence, too much grief in his bereavement, and too much economy in his husbandry.

The Lines
In the bottom line, SIX signifies:
    The bird flies upward
    And meets misfortune.
The young bird that flies too soon, before it is fully fledged, is courting disaster. Exceptional measures should only be taken when there is nothing else left.

In the second line, SIX signifies:
    Passing by the ancestor
    And meeting the ancestress:
    Failing to see the prince
    But encountering a minister.
    No blame.
In the temple, the grandson stands on the same side as the grandfather. To pass by the tablets of the male ancestor, going toward those of the ancestress, is unusual, but it still shows proper reverence and humility. In the same way it is proper, having failed to secure a meeting with the prince, to make an appointment with one of his ministers.

In the third line, NINE signifies:
    Take unusual precautions
    For subordinates may come from behind
    To strike you.
    Misfortune.

At certain times extraordinary caution is necessary. There are many who, conscious of their righteousness, think it petty to keep on their guard against the subterfuges of their subordinates; but the wise man is vigilant at all times.

In the fourth line, NINE signifies:
    No blame.
    He meets him in his path
    And does not slip by.
    Going forward brings danger
    Be on your guard.
    Now is not time for action
    But for constant determination.
The yang line is not in a dominant position, and although it tries to exert its force, there is no blame if the correct course is taken. Nevertheless, all opposition and obstacles in the path must be met face-on; but it is not the time for pushing forward.

In the fifth line, SIX signifies:
    Dense clouds
    But no rain from the western marches.
    The prince shoots his arrow
    Hitting the man in the cave.
The image of the bird has become that of high flying clouds. But though they are dense, no rain falls, suggesting that what is to come from the west is not misfortune. The fifth line represents the prince, but the two yin lines at the top represent a cave; a man in authority exercises the powers that have been given to him, but in doing so he exceeds his abilities, and injures another who represents no threat to him.

In the sixth line, SIX signifies:
    He passes by
    Not facing him.
    The bird flies away,
    Meaning misfortune.
    Calamity and injury.
To go by, not acknowledging the existence of obstacles, is arrogant. Overshooting the target, one misses it: the bird escapes, but only to encounter a more successful hunter. Small things prosper, but pushing forward only brings down upon oneself misfortune and pain.

(Right) Ancestral commemorative tablet of painted wood

63 CHI CHI   Climax and After

The trigrams:
above: K'an   dangerous deep water
below: Li   fire, brightness

This hexagram represents an evolutionary phase of hexagram 11, T'ai, Peace. The strong yang lines have moved upward into their appropriately strong positions, displacing the yin lines into their proper weak positions. Everything is in its proper place. But although this is a very favourable hexagram, it still gives grounds for caution: for it is when equilibrium has been reached that any sudden movement may cause order to revert to disorder.

The Judgment
After the climax there is success in small matters. Righteous persistence brings its reward. Good fortune in the beginning, but disorder in the end.

Commentary
Chi Chi indicates progress in small matters. The proper position of the yang and yin lines shows that righteous persistence will be rewarded; the weak line at the centre of the lower trigram indicates good fortune in the beginning, but the way peters out, efforts come to an end, and disorder returns.

'It is the neigbour in the west, with his small spring sacrifice . . .' From a fifteenth century block-print

The Image
Water over the fire, the image of Chi Chi. The superior man, accordingly, gives due thought to the misfortunes to come, and takes precautions in advance.

The Lines
In the bottom line, NINE signifies:
Like a driver who brakes his chariot,
Or a fox with a wet tail.
No blame.
When all things are pressing forward, the wise man does not allow himself to be carried away by the general fever of enthusiasm. He may not be entirely unaffected by the disasters that overwhelm his companions, but he is like a fox who, having safely crossed the water, has got only his tail wet.

In the second line, SIX signifies:
She loses her carriage curtain.
Do not run after it
For in seven days it will be recovered.
In China it was a breach of propriety for a woman to drive in a carriage without a curtain. This hexagram represents someone who does not have the confidence of those in authority above him, although he feels that he deserves it. His first thought will be to try to draw attention to himself, to seek further promotion; this is wrong, for he should wait patiently until he is recognised for what he is.

In the third third line, NINE signifies:
The Illustrious Ancestor
The emperor Wu Ting
Attacked the country of devils.
Three years he took in subduing it.
Small men are not fit for such enterprises.
Wu Ting, one of the ablest of the Shang dynasty, led an expedition against the barbarous tribes on his northern borders about 1324BC. When peace and stability have been achieved, there is almost always some rebellious influence which must be overcome: frequently a tedious and bitter struggle ensues, and only a great man is suitable for the task.

In the fourth line, SIX signifies:
The finest clothes turn to rags.
Be careful all day long.
The wise man is not deceived by present prosperity: he knows that even the best things deteriorate and must be renewed, and so he is constantly on his guard against misfortune.

In the fifth line, NINE signifies:
The neighbour in the east sacrifices an ox:
But it is the neighbour in the west,
With his small spring sacrifice,
Who is blessed for his sincerity.
The neighbour in the west does not make ostentatious gestures; at the right moment, he makes his offering with proper sincerity, and so gains good fortune.

In the sixth line, SIX signifies:
His head is in the water.
Misfortune.
The man who has safely crossed water, and then gets his head wet, can only have done so by turning back; if he goes forward without looking back, however, he will escape misfortune.

Before Climax

The trigrams:
above: Li   fire, brightness
below: K'an   dangerous deep water
This hexagram is the reverse of the previous one: the transition from disorder to order is not yet complete. Chi Chi is associated with autumn, when the year's growth is complete, but Wei Chi is associated with the burgeoning of spring.

The Judgment
Success. The little fox has almost crossed the water, but gets its tail soaked. No destination is favourable at present.

Commentary
This hexagram indicates progress and success because the weak yin line in the fifth position occupies a central position in the upper trigram between the two yang lines. The little fox has crossed the stream, but he has not yet succeeded in getting past the middle of the danger. The fox's wet tail and the fact that no destination is favourable imply that there is no way at present of advancing one's affairs. Although the yin and yang lines are not in their proper places, they nevertheless accord suitably with one another.

The Image
Fire over the water, the image of Wei Chi. The superior man, accordingly, carefully distinguishes between the nature of things, and between the various places that they occupy.

The Lines
In the bottom line, SIX signifies:
His tail is soaked:
Disgrace.
When the times are in ferment, there may be a temptation to push one's way forward in order to achieve something while there is an opportunity. But such precipitancy can lead to failure and humiliation if the time is not ripe.

In the second line, NINE signifies:
The driver brakes his chariot.
Righteous persistence brings its reward.
The time for action is not yet here. The subject of this line shows his persistence in his determination to slow his chariot by applying the brake.

In the third line, SIX signifies:
The destination is not yet reached,
And going forward brings misfortune.
Nevertheless
It is advantageous to cross the great water.
Although the time to go forward to the climax has arrived, one is not yet properly prepared. However, it is essential to preserve one's determination to advance as soon as the conditions become sufficiently favourable.

In the fourth line, NINE signifies:

Righteous persistence brings good
fortune.
Regrets vanish.
To subdue the country of the devils
Took great effort
But after three years
Vast territories were won.
As in the previous hexagram, this is a reference to the campaign of Wu Ting. Only perseverance will bring success in times of struggle.

In the fifth line, SIX signifies:
Righteous persistence brings good
fortune
Regrets vanish
The superior man shines forth
In sincerity.
Success.
Victory has been won. All has gone well, perseverance has triumphed, and the successful outcome has justified the action. He who has achieved all this makes his influence felt amongst all men, and gains their confidence. But he should remember to be generous in sharing his good fortune with the followers who have contributed to his successful undertaking.

In the sixth place, NINE signifies:
Confident and trusted
He may drink in celebration.
No blame
But if he wet his head,
He loses all.
Now, at the moment of achievement before climax, is the time to celebrate success; and since the way forward may make many hard demands, there is no blame. But the man who carries his celebration to excess will lose the trust of others as quickly as he has won it.

'Confident and trusted, he may drink in celebration.' One of the earliest examples of a human figure in Chinese sculpture

INDEX TO THE HEXAGRAMS

Lower trigram	Upper trigram	Hexagram
☰	☰	1 CH'IEN
	☱	43 KUAI
	☲	14 TA YU
	☳	34 TA CHUANG
	☴	9 HSIAO CH'U
	☵	5 HSÜ
	☶	26 TA CH'U
	☷	11 T'AI

Lower trigram	Upper trigram	Hexagram
☲	☰	13 T'UNG JEN
	☱	49 KO
	☲	30 LI
	☳	55 FENG
	☴	37 CHIA JEN
	☵	63 CHI CHI
	☶	22 PI
	☷	36 MING I

Lower trigram	Upper trigram	Hexagram
☱	☰	10 LÜ
	☱	58 TUI
	☲	38 K'UEI
	☳	54 KUEI MEI
	☴	61 CHUNG FU
	☵	60 CHIEH
	☶	41 SUN
	☷	19 LIN

Lower trigram	Upper trigram	Hexagram
☳	☰	25 WU WANG
	☱	17 SUI
	☲	21 SHIH HO
	☳	51 CHEN
	☴	42 I
	☵	3 CHUN
	☶	27 I
	☷	24 FU

Lower trigram	Upper trigram	Hexagram
☴		44 KOU
		28 TA KUO
		50 TING
		32 HENG
		57 SUN
		48 CHING
		18 KU
		46 SHENG

Lower trigram	Upper trigram	Hexagram
☶		33 TUN
		31 HSIEN
		56 LÜ
		62 HSIAO KUO
		53 CHIEN
		39 CHIEN
		52 KEN
		15 CH'IEN

Lower trigram	Upper trigram	Hexagram
☵		6 SUNG
		47 K'UN
		64 WEI CHI
		40 HSIEH
		59 HUAN
		29 K'AN
		4 MENG
		7 SHIH

Lower trigram	Upper trigram	Hexagram
☷		12 P'I
		45 TS'UI
		35 CHIN
		16 YÜ
		20 KUAN
		8 PI
		23 PO
		2 K'UN

PART 3

Palmistry

Francis King

Contents

1
Palmistry: a prophetic science?

Louis Hamon, better known to his many fashionable and wealthy clients as 'Cheiro', the society palmist

Palmistry – the working out of personal character and destiny on the basis of the lines upon, and the shape of, the hand – has been studied, praised, abused, and been the subject of much argument, for many hundreds of years. Rarely, however, has the matter been the centre of a legal action.

One such case, however, not only came up in the English High Court but led directly to a series of occurrences which showed how palmistry may provide amazingly accurate prophecies of future events. The legal case in question was a libel action launched by a woman palmist who called herself 'Satanella' against the magazine *Society*.

Society specialised in gossipy stories about the rich, the famous and the notorious – and it had slipped up badly. What had happened was that two palmists, Mr and Mrs Keighley, had set up a joint fortune-telling practice in London's fashionable Bond Street under the somewhat dramatic name of 'Saturn and Satanella'. After a time husband and wife fell out with one another and a separation took place, Mrs Keighley leaving her husband in full possession of the Bond Street premises and taking up business elsewhere.

Soon Mr Keighley took a new female partner – a woman with an extremely dubious reputation who had previously been closely involved with a man who had been both a notorious blackmailer and mixed up in an attempted murder.

Information about the woman's past reached *Society* and she was written up as 'The Notorious Satanella'. Mrs Keighley, who still practised her art under that name, sued for libel. Through their lawyer, Marshall Hall, who was later to become perhaps the finest defence counsel ever to practise at the English Bar, the defendants pleaded that their words referred not to Mrs Keighley but to her successor.

One of the witnesses called to show that the words were generally thought to refer to Mrs Keighley was the society palmist Louis Hamon, better known by his pseudonym of 'Cheiro'. Cheiro was an excellent witness, unshaken in a searching cross examination by Marshall Hall – and Mrs Keighley won her case, obtaining £1000 damages.

That evening, purely by chance, Marshall Hall encountered Cheiro in a hotel. He approached him, congratulated the palmist on his skill as a witness, and made an appointment for a professional consultation – presumably wanting to test for himself the skill of which Cheiro had boasted in Court. Hall made notes of the interview and Cheiro's prophecies:

'The left hand, which denotes the inherited qualities, does not give nearly as much promise as the indications by the right, which shows the development of the individual. Judge, therefore, that by your own efforts and determination you have carved out your own career, and must stand out as the one really distinguished member of your family. The commencement of your line of destiny being so uncertain, as it starts from the wrist, shows that in early life you were very undecided as to the career you should adopt . . . . . . There is no sign of any success whatever until . . . . . your twenty–fifth year . . . . from . . . thirty years of age to the last moment of your life, your success will steadily be on the increase until . . . you are fated to become one of the most prominent men in your profession. Your line of head indicates that you are endowed with more eloquence than logic. . . . . The worst feature of your hand has to do with the affectionate side of your character. The line of heart under the base of the fingers shows that you will be singularly unlucky in connection with such matters. You will be idolised by women but they will bring you little happiness. There are two marriages distinctly indicated; the first will cause you to pass through some bitter ordeal that will affect the whole of your life . . . . In length of life you will reach the average span. You will die in harness at the very zenith of your career'.

Every single character trait singled out, every prophecy made, in the above notes was fulfilled in Marshall Hall's later career.

But most astounding was a seemingly minor prophecy made by Cheiro towards the end of the consultation. Cheiro said 'I see something so vividly that I feel bound to tell you of it, though at the same time it seems to be of such small importance, and so impossible that I hesitate'. Marshall Hall begged the palmist to continue and Cheiro went on: 'I see you standing on the balcony of what looks like a large country house with a big garden below and big trees all in front. But the strange thing is that the grounds seem lighted up with a very vivid electric light; and even the trees are lighted up with coloured lamps. What makes it still stranger is that there are thousands of people trampling down the flower-beds, and looking up to the balcony, and you are apparently trying to speak or actually speaking. There are several people on the balcony, men and women, and the faces of the crowd are very white in the strong light. Beside you on the left, is a woman, much shorter than you are, waving a white handkerchief in her left hand, and the people below are shouting. That is what I see, but what it

Cheiro's 'Indian' consulting room was decked out in an exotic style, reflecting both his taste for luxury and his love of the mysteries of the occult

means is more than I can tell you.'

Sixteen months after his interview with Cheiro, Marshall Hall fought a General Election as Conservative candidate for Southport. The counting took place in the Town Hall at night, and Marshall Hall was elected with a majority of 209. Before the result was announced to the waiting crowd the Returning Officer made a request; it had been customary for the wife or a lady supporter of the winning candidate to anticipate the Returning Officer's official announcement by waving a red or blue handkerchief from the Town Hall balcony. This old custom, he said, should be abandoned.

Marshall Hall, together with his wife and other supporters then went out onto the balcony. The lawyer looked down at the cheering crowd, their faces white from the brilliant lighting, behind them the trees illumined with coloured lanterns. 'Where have I seen all this before?' he asked himself – and then remembered Cheiro's prophecy. Then, looking round, he saw that his wife, who had taken the Returning Officer's request literally, was waving a *white* handkerchief to the crowd. Cheiro's vision had been reproduced in every particular.

This was by no means the only prediction of almost incredible accuracy made by Cheiro. Men and women of unimpeachable honesty confirmed that Cheiro prophesied, for example, the exact dates of death of Queen Victoria and King Edward VII. Indeed, the list of events he seems accurately to have foreseen is almost endless.

But palmistry existed, of course, long before Cheiro; the subject is mentioned in ancient Indian manuscripts of 3000 years ago and in Chinese writings of much the same date. It is even referred to in the Old Testament, for a verse of the Book of Job asserts that God 'sealeth up the hand of every man; that all men may know his work'.

Palmistry is also mentioned in Western European manuscripts of the Middle Ages, often in connection with astrology. Some of the stories told in these manuscripts recount the traditional legend of how palmistry reached Europe. According to this legend the philosopher Aristotle visited Egypt, found a gold-lettered manuscript dealing with palmistry on the altar of Hermes, and forwarded it to Alexander the Great. Without accepting the literal truth of this tale it can be accepted that palmistry made its way to the west from Asia by way of the ancient Greeks.

Cheiro's 'Indian' consulting room was decked out in an exotic style, reflecting both his taste for luxury and his love of the mysteries of the occult

Palmistry: a phophetic science?

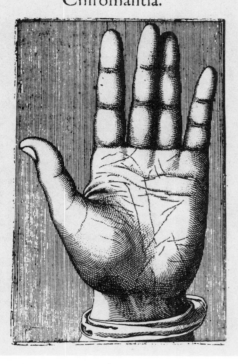

140 TRACT. I SECT. II. PORT. VI. LIB. I.

TRACTATUS PRIMI.

SECTIONIS II.

PORTIO VI.

De Scientia animæ naturalis cum vitali,
seu aftrologia chiromantica
feu
Chiromantia.

Before outlining the beliefs and practices of modern palmistry it is worth asking whether modern developments uphold this ancient art. Indeed they do.

The German psychologist Julius Spier, who spent many years gathering classifying and studying thousands of palm prints, found that palmistry accurately indicated what he called the 'true dispositions' of his subject. Furthermore, he found that the hands of children accurately indicated the psychological problems that were likely to trouble them in future life. Through the knowledge thus gained he was often able to forestall mental illness in his young patients.

Spier was no crank; his only book, *The Hands of Children*, had an introduction by no less a person than C. G. Jung, believed by many to have been the greatest psychologist of the present century.

Another indication of modern scientific interest in palmistry has been the growth of a discipline which its practitioners call 'dermatoglyphics'. Practitioners of this have found a close relationship between abnormal lines on the hands and abnormal physical conditions that are inborn. Such conditions notably include heart defects and abnormal chromosome conditions and usually are indicated by the so-called 'simian line' where the Head and Heart lines (see p 19) run as one. In traditional palmistry the simian line – so called because it is frequently found amongst the larger apes – is held to be a sign of 'degeneracy' and it is of great interest that recent research by a group of New York doctors has proved that this line often occurs in mongoloid children and in those adversely affected by an attack of German measles (rubella) during the mother's pregnancy.

Needless to say this does not mean that *everyone* who has the simian line is a 'degenerate', a mongol, or suffering from some major defect acquired in the womb. But it does show that at least one dogma of traditional palmistry is supported by the findings of modern medicine.

Palmistry has long been the subject of learned treatises, as evidenced in these pages from a fifteenth century manuscript (right) and Robert Fludd's *History of Two Worlds*, published at the beginning of the seventeenth century (above)

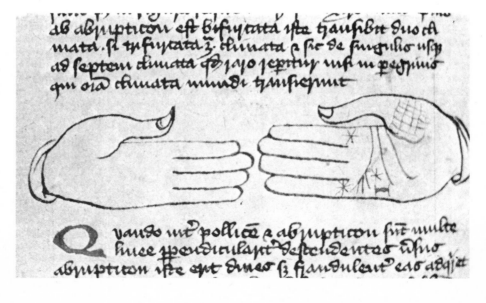

2
The shape of the hand

There is a common misconception that palmistry is concerned only with the lines *upon* the hand. This is not so – the first thing a palmist looks at is the *general shape* of the hands of his subject.

There are several ways of classifying the shapes of hands. Some palmists for example, use the fourfold classification of the German palmist Carl Carus. Carus's classification begins with the 'elementary' hand – the crude, thick hand of the heavy manual worker. The second type of hand for Carus was what he called the motoric; this he characterised as fairly large, flexible and strong, found largely among businessmen, technicians and skilled craftsmen, and indic-

ative of a lively, extrovert and practical nature.

The sensitive hand, said Carus, is also flexible, but neither so large or strong as the motoric hand. It is associated with energy, a strongly emotional nature and adaptability. It is usually found among writers, artists and all those whose main interests in life are those concerned with the many problems of creativity.

Carus' last shape classification is the psychic hand – slim, long, pointed and soft and supposedly indicating a sensitive, intuitive, sometimes vague, personality which is often insufficiently conscious of the material things of life.

Below: the four types of hand according to the classification proposed by the German palmist Carl Carus. These are the 'elementary' hand (1), the 'motoric' (3), the 'sensitive' (2) and the 'psychic' (4)

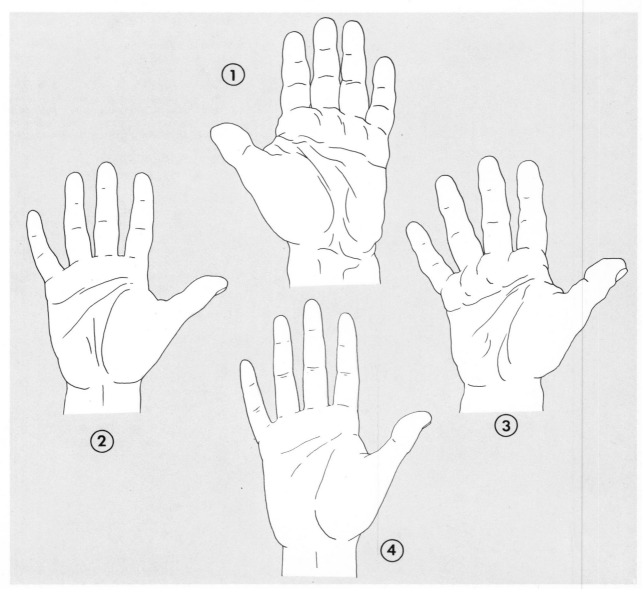

The shape of the hand

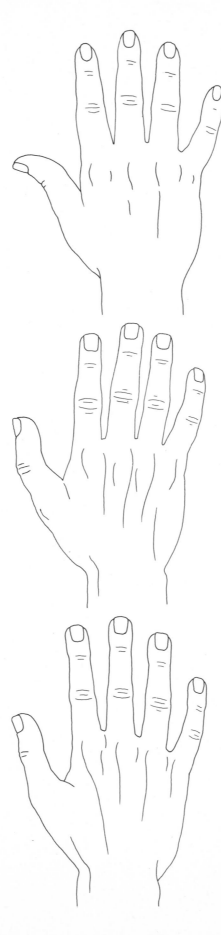

A more complex seven-fold classification of hand shapes was made by the 19th century French palmist Casimir D'Arpentigny. This was the system used by Cheiro and still adhered to by many present day palmists.

The seven types of hand in this classification are

I   The elementary hand
II   The square, sometimes called the 'useful' or 'practical' hand
III The spatulative or 'nervous active' hand.
IV The philosophic, or 'knotty' hand.
V   The conic, artistic hand.
VI The psychic or 'idealistic' hand.
VII The mixed hand.

I The Elementary Hand
According to D'Arpentigny and his followers this clumsy, large-palmed, short-fingered hand represents the lowest type of humanity – passionate, short tempered and destructive. Cheiro referred to this sort of personality in scathing terms; 'these are people without aspirations', he said, 'they but eat, drink, sleep and die'.

II The Square Hand
This is believed to indicate a logical, practical nature, orderly habits and considerable tenacity. On the debit side possessors of this type of hand tend to be over-sceptical and lacking in imagination and originality.

III The Spatulative Hand
This is somewhat crooked with the tips of the fingers ending in a blunt rounded way – similar to the shape of the spatula used by cooks and chemists. This type of hand may be either extremely firm or soft and flabby. The first case is supposed to show an excitable nature, full of energy and enthusiasm but sometimes lacking staying-power; the second type – the soft and flabby – indicates a restless nature and its possessors tend to be discontented personalities with erratic modes of conduct.

IV The Philosophic Hand
Heron Allen, one of D'Arpentigny's most devoted disciples, wrote: 'The great characteristics indicated by this type of hand are – analysis, meditation, philosophy, deduction . . . and the search after, and love of, the abstract and absolute truth . . . . . They are just (from an intuitive sense of justice and a discriminating instinct of ethics), unsuperstitious, great advocates of social and religious freedom and moderate in their pleasures . . . . . '

V The Conic Hand
This type of hand is sub-divided into three varieties:

(a) The supple hand with a small thumb and a medium–sized palm. The owner of this type of hand, said D'Arpentigny, is always drawn to the beautiful in art.

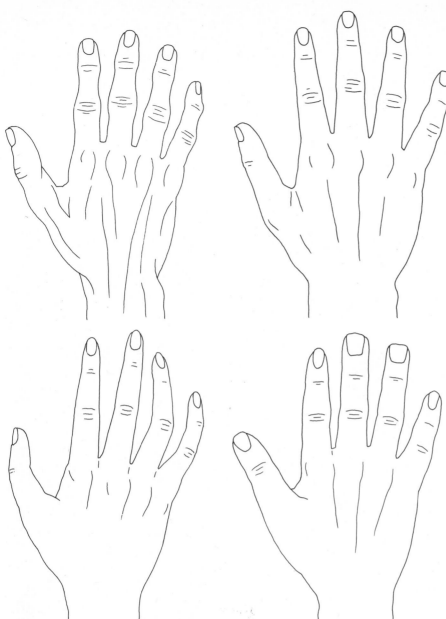

(b) A thick, short, large hand with a proportionately large thumb. Those with this type of hand are believed to be endowed with a burning desire for wealth, fame and fortune.

(c) A large and very firm hand with a strongly developed palm. Possessors of this formation tend to be highly sensual.

All three types are believed to indicate the type of personality which prefers beauty to usefulness, pleasure to work, and imagination to thought.

VI The Psychic Hand

Cheiro referred to this as the most beautiful but most unfortunate type of hand. Those possessed of it tend to be idealistic, neurotic dreamers guided only by their own idealism.

VII The Mixed Hand

In practice few people have hands the forms of which is confined to one of the above six categories. They have a 'mixed' hand, which combines characteristics from two, three or even more of the basic types. This is the main disadvantage of D'Arpentigny's system and as a result many contemporary palmists, Fred Gettings for example, have adopted a fourfold classification based on the traditional astrological 'elements' of Earth, Air, Fire and Water. This classification was originated in the 16th and 17th centuries.

The Elemental Hands

Fred Gettings has given an excellent description of the psychological types indicated by the possession of these hands.

'The Water hand was predominately of a phlegmatic disposition, extremely sensitive, and easily influenced by environment. The Air hand was predominately of a sanguine disposition, hopeful, confident and intellectual. The Fire hand was predominately of a choleric disposition, passionate, active,

The shape of the hand

The first of the four types of hand according to the classification adopted by Fred Gettings: the 'Earth' hand. It is a practical hand, with a square palm and short, strong fingers, and with relatively few, but deep, lines

warm and intuitive. The Earth hand was predominately of a melancholic disposition, practical, rather gloomy and given to rhythmic expression. The first two are regarded as essentially 'feminine', the latter two as 'masculine', so that a female with a Water hand would be particularly feminine, strongly of the Water type, while a male with a Water hand would have a marked feminine streak in the temperament but would not manifest so strongly the Water characteristics as would the female. The descriptions of these four types are of real value in the relationship between hand and temperament . . . . . . '

The Earth hand is characterised by its structural heaviness, its square palm, its short fingers and the depth and strength – although often paucity – of the lines inscribed upon the palm. It is sometimes called the 'practical hand' and its possessors are usually honest, notable for their inclination towards effort and hard work, and inclined to be physically productive – building workers, for example, tend to have such a hand. The Earth hand is, of course,

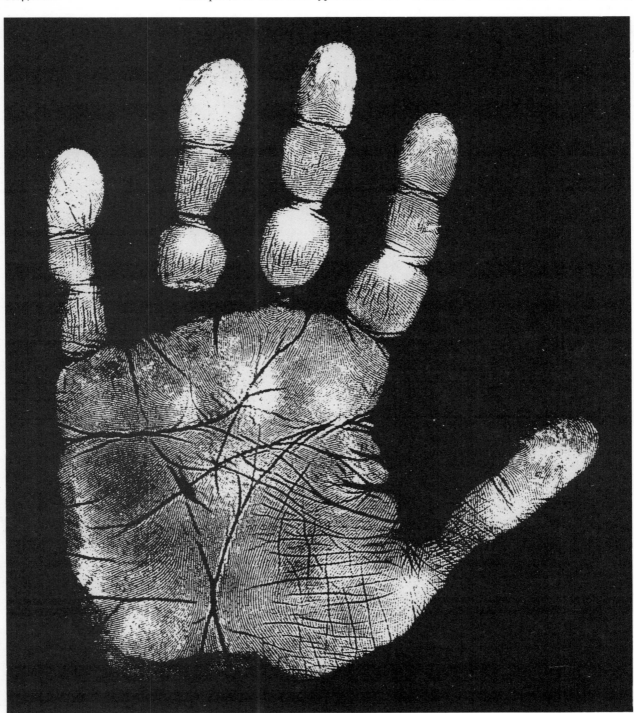

powerfully masculine and women who possess it have a strong streak of what is usually regarded as 'typical masculinity' in their psychological make-up. There is, as with all the elemental types, a darker side to the Earth hand; beneath the outward stolidity lurk forces which, given the right circumstances, can break out in a thoroughly destructive way. The comparison to be made here is a physical one – the earth on which we stand is stable, but beneath the stability are the strains and stresses which, if released, bring the destruction of the earthquake.

The Air hand is structurally strongly built, with long fingers and a square palm, with well defined lines inscribed upon it. It has often been called the 'intellectual hand' and its possessors usually have intellect rather than emotion as the main driving-force in their lives – indeed, they are often strongly contemptuous of activities engaged in, or judgments made, upon the basis of intuition or emotion. It is a feminine hand and is often found in women engaged in creative work, and those who have it are always conscious of a strong need to

The 'Air' hand is also structurally strong, but with longer fingers than the Earth hand. The lines, although well-defined, are finer than in the Earth hand

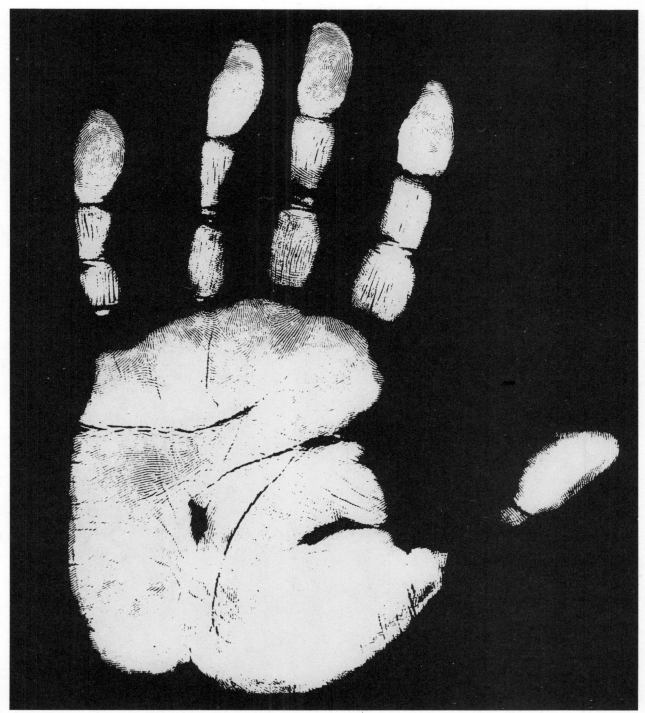

The shape of the hand

Compared with the length of the oblong palm, the fingers of the 'Fire' hand are relatively short. There are numerous lines, many of them quite deeply inscribed

communicate. Women journalists and broadcasters are often found with this type of hand and men who possess it frequently have a strongly feminine element in their personalities.

The Fire hand, also called the 'intuitive hand' has short fingers and a long, oblong palm with fairly prominent lines inscribed upon it. This is very much the extrovert's hand, the combination of short fingers and a long palm indicating an emotional lack of balance combined with a tendency to engage in actions and judgments on the basis of pure intuition. As an extrovert the Fire type tends to be outgoing, creative, changeable, active – often too active – and a prey to sudden enthusiasms and equally sudden dislikes. It denotes an extremely masculine nature and women with a Fire hand will tend to reveal, of course, a strongly masculine element in their psychological makeup.

The Water hand is delicately structured with long fingers and a long palm which is inscribed with a fine mesh of lines. It is sometimes called the 'sensitive hand' and,

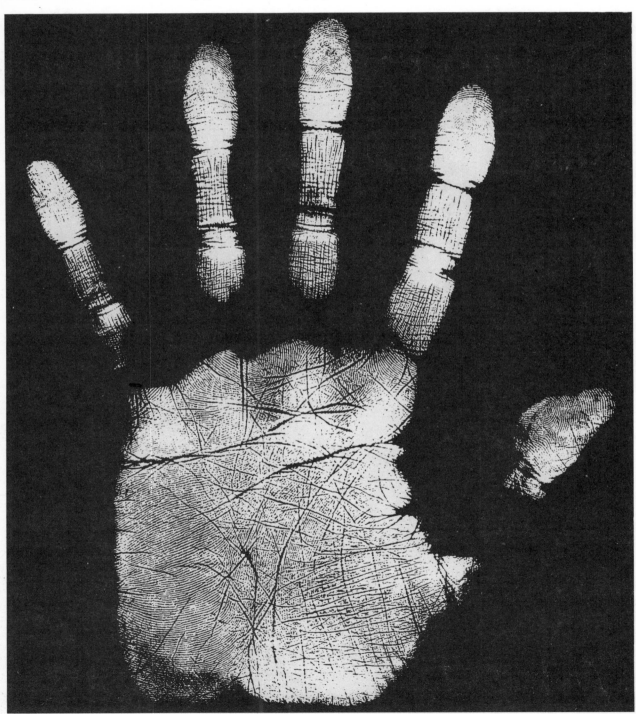

as this name indicates, its possessors are sensitive personalities, subject to ever–changing moods, their psychological state having its physical analogue in flowing water – running sometimes shallow, sometimes deep, ever changing and never utterly constant. It is above all a feminine form, its great characteristic being the traditional female attribute of receptivity – the owner of the Water hand tends to reflect the immediate environment in the same way that water reflects images of whatever overhangs it.

The division of the form of the hand into four elemental types has a correlation with astrology, which divides the twelve Signs of the Zodiac into four 'triplicities', which are themselves related in characteristics to the four elements.

There is also another method of astrological classification of the form of the hand, but as this is partially dependent upon the shape and form of the lines inscribed upon the palm, it is necessary to deal with the lines in some detail before it can be properly described.

The 'Water' hand is long and narrow and delicately structured, with a mesh of fine lines covering the palm. This hand is also frequently known as the 'sensitive' hand

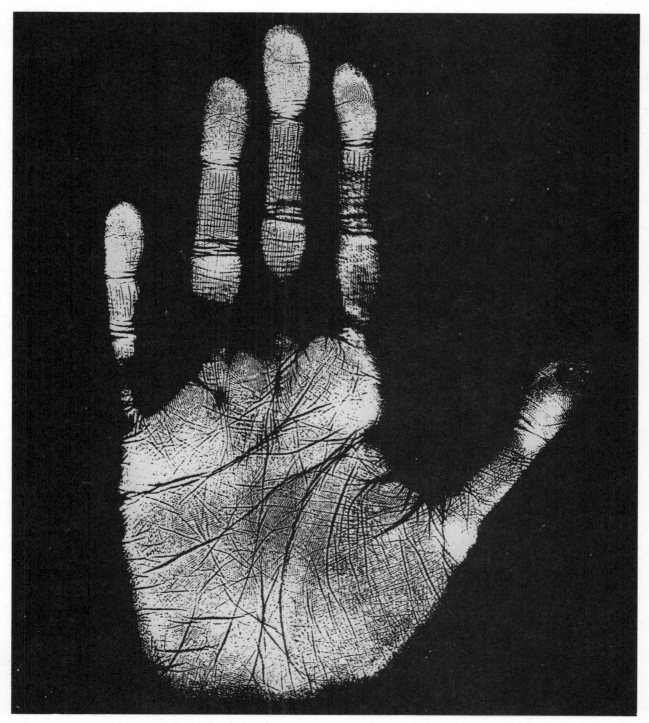

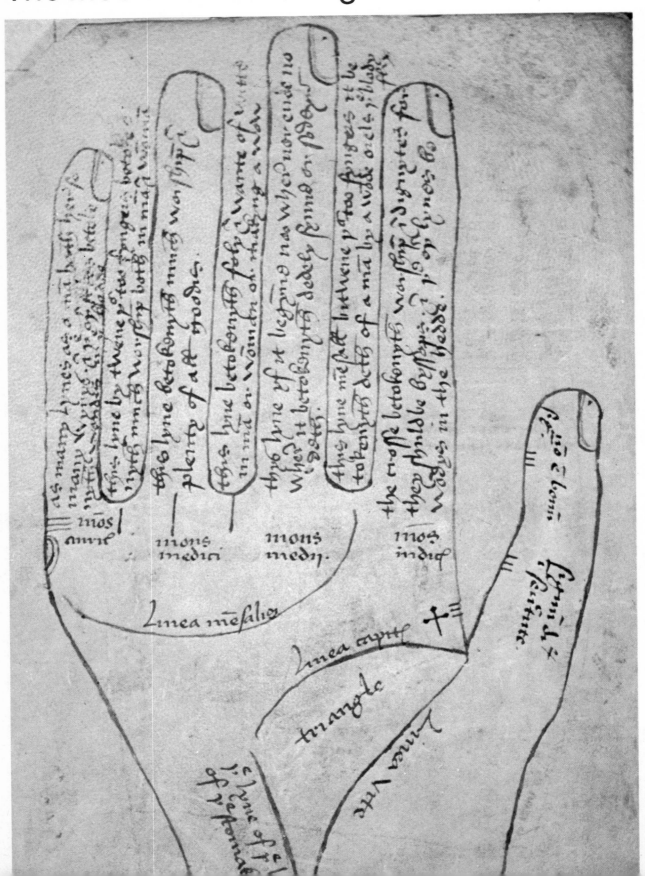

The fleshy areas of the hand around the central palm are called 'mounts' and, as will be seen from the diagrams and the accompanying text, they are attributed to the seven 'planets' of traditional astrology. These 'planets' include the sun and the moon which are not, of course, planets at all in the modern scientific sense but, for the sake of simplicity, are still given that nomenclature by modern astrologers and palmists. The name 'planet' means 'wanderer', and, from the viewpoint of the earth, all these bodies appear to move about the heavens.

It should be noted that there are in all eight mounts, not seven. This, it will be seen, is because Mars has a double – positive and negative – attribution.

The significance of the mounts is as follows:

A *The Mount of Venus* As might be expected from its attribution to the planet traditionally associated with love and beauty, a well-developed mount of Venus indicates a warm and sympathetic nature, a desire to love and be loved – both sexually and platonically – a strong feeling for beauty and an equally strong desire for the luxuries of life. If this mount is over-developed it is usually an indication that these qualities are excessively prominent in the psychological make-up and that the desires for admiration and sensual enjoyments are so strong that self-indulgence can lead to emotional disaster.

B *The Mount of Mars Positive* Astrologically the traditional martial virtues – courage, strength, vigour and a capacity to cope with the harder problems of life – are associated with the planet Mars, and a well developed mount of Mars indicates the same psychological strengths. Over-developed, the mount indicates a quarrelsome and aggressive personality – the sort of person who is perpetually finding cause for offence in the actions or sayings of others.

C *The Mount of Jupiter* In astrology Jupiter is the 'major benefic', the great bringer of good luck in any horoscope and, well-aspected, is an indication of material success in life. A well developed Mount of Jupiter is an indicator of a similar capacity for good fortune and success. Those who possess it are likely to obtain in life positions of responsibility in which they exert a good deal of influence over the actions of others. An overdeveloped mount of Jupiter indicates an altogether excessive desire for success combined with a love of power for its own sake.

D *The Mount of Saturn* Astrologers believe that a strongly emphasised Saturnian element in a horoscope indicates a quiet, prudent, character with a love of solitude who is unlikely to achieve success until late in life. A prominent Mount of Saturn

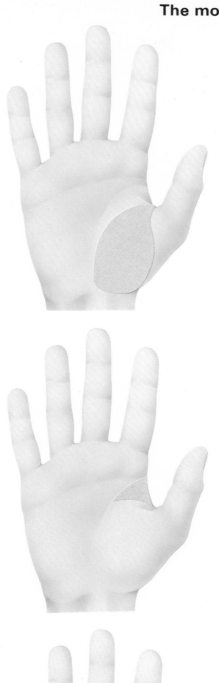

The Mount of Venus, the area of the hand associated with love and beauty. Over-development of this area can indicate a tendency to self-indulgence

The Mount of Mars Positive. It represents the martial virtues of strength and courage, but over-development indicates an aggressive personality

The Mount of Jupiter is situated below the forefinger; when it is well-developed it indicates good fortune and material success. Over-development, however, suggests a love of power for its own sake

(Facing page): The mounts below the fingers are clearly marked in this drawing from a fifteenth century manuscript in the Bodleian Library, Oxford. Notice the annotation to the cross on the Mount of Jupiter: 'the crosse betokenyth worship and dignytes for they shuld be Byshops . . ' (and see page 57)

The mounts and the fingers

The Mount of Saturn represents a love of solitude and an innate prudence together with some interest in occult matters

The Mount of the Sun – alternatively known as the Mount of Apollo – represents a love of beauty and the arts. When over-developed it indicates a personality principally concerned with outward show

The significance of the Mount of Mercury depends upon the nature of the rest of the hand. In general, however, it indicates a person who is witty and lively, and who loves change of all kinds

indicates the same qualities; it is also sometimes a sign of a strong interest in matters occult and philosophic. An overdeveloped Mount of Saturn indicates these qualities to excess – a depressive, and depressing, personality.

E *The Mount of the Sun (or Apollo)* A strongly developed Mount of the Sun indicates a love of beauty and art in all its forms. Everything that appeals to the aesthetic senses of man – painting, poetry, sculpture, landscape etc. – is important to the individual in whom this Mount is prominent. An overdeveloped Mount of the Sun indicates a personality to whom glory, show and an excessive floridity of taste are all-important.

F *The Mount of Mercury* Like the planetary influence of Mercury in astrology a strongly developed Mount of Mercury can be good or bad. On an 'ill aspected' hand a large Mount of Mercury makes the bad worse; on a 'well aspected' one it makes the good better. In general a prominent Mount of Mercury indicates a witty, lively person who loves travel, change and excitement. An overdeveloped Mount of Mercury indicates these characteristics in excess, sometimes disastrously so.

G *Mount of Mars Negative* This, like the Mount of Mars Positive, is indicative of the martial virtues when prominent – but these virtues tend to be present morally rather than physically. Overdeveloped it shows a personality which tends to be excessively conscious of its own rights and privileges and rather lax where those of others are concerned.

H *Mount of the Moon* A well-developed Mount of the Moon is associated with the type of personality which is both romantic and imaginative. If overdeveloped this Mount, indicates a dreamy, unrealistic character, often ill-fitted to handle the practical side of life.

The Fingers The fingers, like the mounts, are named after the planets. The index, or first, finger is the dominant one and is attributed to Jupiter – the 'major benefic' of astrology, the King of the Gods in Roman mythology. This finger is indicative of the individual's potential in the outer life of the world. Thus a strong finger of Jupiter, especially when matched by an equally strong thumb, indicates both success in worldly matters and a desire to dominate others. Carried to excess this particular formation shows a personality of the over-bearing sort, striving for domination and success and not caring in the least for the needs and feelings of others. A weak index finger, particularly if it is shorter than the third finger, is indicative of strong feelings of insecurity and is frequently allied with an inability to handle the practical aspects of

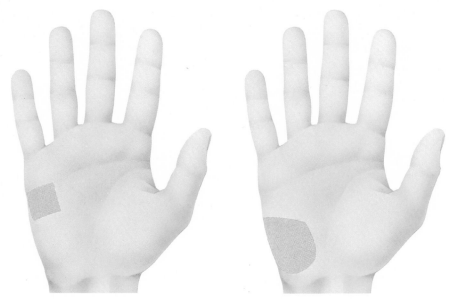

The Mount of Mars Negative (far left) is associated, like the positive mount (see page 15), with the martial virtues, but with their moral rather than their physical aspects
The Mount of the Moon (near left) is associated with romantic and imaginative natures

life. A person with this formation must guard against a tendency to be too easily dominated by others.

The second, or middle, finger is attributed to Saturn and the person with an extremely long Saturnian finger tends to coldness in personal relations but is extremely competent, in dealing with practical matters. An overly short finger of Saturn is associated with a somewhat impractical personality, but one which is often creative and can easily express a sympathy with the feelings of others.

The third finger pertains to the Sun and to the god Apollo. Its development indicates the emotional qualities of the personality; a well-developed, long finger of the Sun shows emotional stability, a short, ill-formed, one the opposite. Apollo, the god of the Sun, is traditionally associated

with medicine and music, and some palmists think that a strong Apollo finger is a sign that the individual's career will tend to be associated with one or other of these. There is an old folk belief, unsupported by modern medicine, that there is a vein running straight from this finger to the heart, and it is for this reason that wedding rings are placed upon this finger.

The fourth, or little finger is attributed to Mercury – both the planet and the Roman god. It is the finger of relationships, the interaction between the individual and other human beings. If the finger is markedly separated from the others it is a sign that the individual finds it difficult to achieve such interaction on a meaningful level. A long little finger is held to be sign of a powerful intellect; an extremely short one of stupidity.

From another fifteenth century manuscript in the Bodleian Library, showing the fingers of Jupiter, Saturn, Sun and Mercury clearly marked

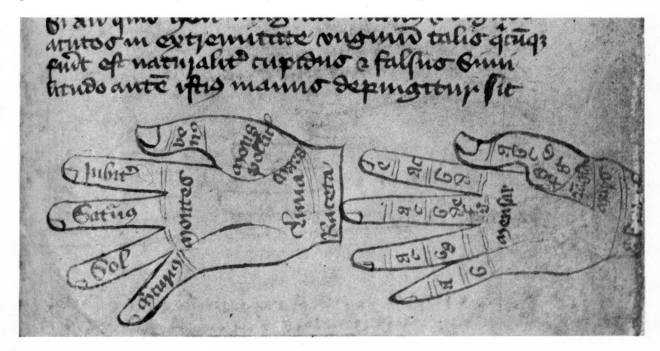

4
Principal lines of the hand

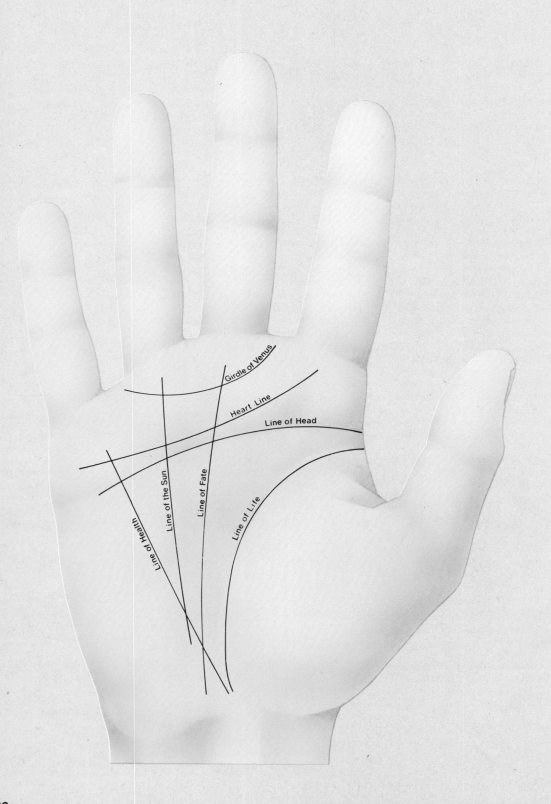

There are normally seven major and five minor lines on the hand. The seven major ones are:

(a) *The Line of Life* – a curved line outlining and surrounding the Mount of Venus.

(b) *The Line of Head* – which crosses, more or less diagonally, the centre of the palm.

(c) *The Heart Line* – running roughly parallel to the Line of Head below the base of the fingers.

(d) *The Girdle of Venus* – running nearer the base of the fingers than the heart line and usually encircling the Mounts of Saturn and Apollo.

(e) *The Line of the Sun* – which normally runs more or less straight down the palm to the Mount of Apollo.

(f) *The Line of Health* – which runs diagonally down the palm to the Mount of Mercury.

(g) *The Line of Fate* – which runs down the centre of the hand from or near the wrist to the Mount of Saturn.

Of these, the first three are the most important and are normally found in every hand. The five minor lines are:

(a) *The Line of Mars* – This is a curved line on the Mount of Mars which lies within, and roughly parallel to, the life line.

(b) *The Via Lasciva* – This runs roughly parallel to the health line

(c) *The Line of Intuition* – This curved line runs from the Mount of the Moon to that of Mercury.

(d) *The Line of Marriage* – A horizontal line on the Mount of Mercury.

(e) *The Bracelets* – These – one, two or three in number – are found on the wrist.

The above mentioned lines are usually found on both hands, but sometimes they are missing from one or both hands. A line present on one hand but very differently formed or missing altogether on the other hand is of great significance, for the right and left hands indicate different things; as the old palmists' saying has it: 'The left hand is the hand we are born with, the right hand is the hand we make'.

Literally this is not true; the hands change throughout life, an outer change reflecting an inner change. A particular hand marking might, for example, indicate neurosis, but after the appropriate treatment this marking would tend to disappear or, at any rate, become less conspicuous.

Nevertheless, palmists are agreed that there is a good deal of truth in the inner meaning of the old saying and believe that while the left hand indicates what Cheiro called the 'natural character' – in other words the personality traits and tendencies we were born with – the right hand reflects the effects of environment and personal effort on the life and psychological make-up of the personality. Interestingly enough, many palmists believe that in left-handed people the polarities are reversed – that the right hand indicates their inherited predispositions while the left shows how they have used their inborn potential.

The Line of Life

The length of the line of life, which, it will be remembered, encircles the Mount of Venus, was taken by old-fashioned palmists as an indication of the probable length of life. Thus the nineteenth century palmist Heron-Allen told a gloomy anecdote of how he informed a young man that 'a fatal illness would attack him at thirty-seven and kill him at forty-one' and how this prophecy was fulfilled to the letter. As the contemporary palmist Fred Gettings has pointed out, it is quite possible that Heron-Allen was this man's unwitting executioner: a prognostication of this sort can sink into the unconscious mind and, through the well-authenticated influence of the mind over the body, produce physical illness which makes the prophecy self-fulfilling.

Sensible modern palmists do *not* accept this approach, nor do they believe that the length of the Life line indicates the length of life – so if you have a very short Life line as many people have, there is no reason at all to anticipate an early death!

Modern palmists do not, however, think that the length of this line is of no importance; rather they say that its length correlates with the general physical vitality of the individual. Breaks in the line, it is said, *may* indicate illnesses, but, they may equally indicate a strong alteration in the direction or quality of the subject's life – a change of career in mid-life, for example.

Of great importance is the actual point from which the Life line arises. There are three main points of this sort:

(1) Its commencement – that is, the end of it nearest the fingers – may coincide with the beginning of the Head line. This is by far the most usual point of beginning.

(2) It may begin on the Mount of Jupiter, thus sometimes crossing the Head line as before proceeding towards the wrist.

(3) It may begin below the Head line (that is, further away from the fingers).

The first case, when it shares a beginning with the Head line, is an indication that the physical vitality is strongly controlled by the mind. This Head-Life joint beginning is also a sign of shrewdness of character. This shrewdness is particularly marked when there is a clear fork between the two lines. So much is this so that some palmists actually call this 'the typical businessman's mark'. The shrewdness indicated is in many ways a desirable quality, but sometimes it is overdone and the individual is too inclined to 'let his head rule his heart', to cramp the emotions and feelings by *always* taking the practical, hard-headed, course of action.

The principal lines of the hand

When the Line of Life shares a beginning with the Line of Head it indicates that physical activity is strongly controlled by the mind; a clearly-defined fork is known to many palmists as 'the business man's mark'

When the Line of Life begins on the Mount of Jupiter, it indicates physical energy devoted to the achievement of ambition

When the Line of Life originates below the Line of Head it denotes a relative lack of control of physical powers

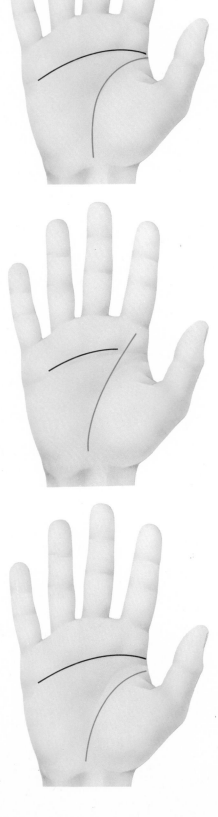

The second case, the Life line beginning on the Mount of Jupiter, is an indication that the individual's physical life will be powerfully influenced by Jupiterian tendencies. He or she will be ambitious, with the physical energies devoted to domination of the individual environment, the attainment of prestige and the fulfillment of ambition.

In the last case, when the Life line originates below the Head line, it is likely that there will be a comparatively unrestricted use of the physical vitality. This has its psychological dangers, for physical actions tend to be undertaken on the impulse of the moment, uncontrolled by practical considerations.

As will now be clear to the reader, palmistry has strong affinities with astrology and it is helpful to consider the Life line by the light of what has been called 'astro-palmistry'. According to this the Life line is attributed to the zodiacal sign of Gemini. Gemini stands for the essential duality of life, for the ever-present interaction between matter and spirit, between activity and passivity; an understanding of this enables the palmist to come to an intuitive understanding of the relationship between the Head and Life lines.

The Line of Head

There are three points from which the head line commonly arises:

(1) From the beginning of the Life line
(2) Within the life line, from the Mount of Mars.
(3) From the Mount of Jupiter – usually from its centre.

The significance of (1) – a coincidence of the beginnings of the Head and Life lines – has already been dealt with.

The second position of commencement, the line arising from the Mount of Mars, is not traditionally considered favourable. It supposedly indicates a worrying, somewhat neurotic personality subject to continually changing ideas. The strongly Martian element in the psychological make-up predisposes the individual with this hand towards a quarrelsome temperament.

The third commencing position (from the Mount of Jupiter and often from its centre) is a powerful position, particularly if it touches the Life line. A personality with this line formation is likely to be energetic, to be well-endowed with a variety of talents and have considerable ambition. Such a person is a born ruler, able to manage things and people justly but to his advantage.

As is clear from its name, the Head line is strongly linked with the mentality of the individual, and from its strength, its beginning and ending points, and its general formation the palmist measures the mental strengths and weaknesses of the personality.

When the line is straight throughout and strongly marked upon the palm its possessor is likely to be well endowed with common sense, somewhat over-concerned with material things, and both lacking in and contemptuous of the imaginative faculty.

A line that is straight in the first half but then inclines slightly is an indication of a well-balanced personality who will be both imaginative and practical in his or her mental approach to life. Such an alliance is, of cource, an extremely favourable one, for the individual concerned will be able to approach the things of the imagination in a way which is sympathetic yet level headed.

When the whole line is slightly inclined there is a strong imaginative element in the psychology; if the incline is very marked the imagination has full play and a somewhat 'bohemian' and unorthodox personality is indicated. This is particularly so if the line penetrates the Mount of the Moon.

Fred Gettings has given a splendid description of such a penetration:

'If the Head line penetrates the Mount of Moon, then it is tapping the undifferentiated energies which manifest as dreams and imagination, and a strange, imaginative view of reality must be expected. Such a termination may result in someone who is 'lost in dreams', but if the other signs in the hand indicate considerable executive power, then such a view of reality may be utilized and given form through one of the arts, especially through literature.'

This interpretation of the Mount of the Moon ending of the Head line is given strong support by surviving nineteenth century palm prints. Thus for example, both the great French author Dumas and the medium D. D. Home – strongly lunar and imaginative personalities – possessed this formation.

A similar imaginative tendency (but not such a marked one) is indicated when the line simply goes towards the Mount of the Moon without actually reaching it, or sends out a branch towards the Mount.

Such a branch or a movement towards other Mounts is sometimes observed, the significances of which are as follows:

(1) A movement or a branch towards the Mount of Jupiter is associated with an individual psychology which uses its mental strengths for ambitious – particularly ambitious for power – purposes.

(2) A movement or a branch towards the Mount of Saturn indicates an individual psychology which exerts its mental powers in the direction of religion, philosophy or music.

(3) A movement or a branch towards the Mount of the Sun indicates a fame – or even notoriety – seeking psychology.

(4) A movement or a branch towards the Mount of Mercury indicates that the intellectual powers are likely to be exerted in the fields of either business or science.

Sometimes a double Line of the Head is found. This rare formation traditionally indicates an extremely powerful mentality.

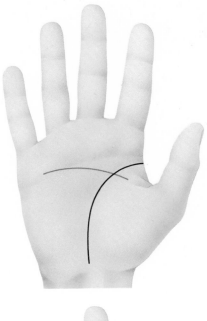

When the Line of Head originates from the Mount of Mars below the Line of Life, it is said to indicate a neurotic and somewhat quarrelsome person

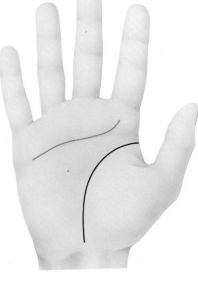

When the Line of Head originates on the Mount of Jupiter it is a particularly powerful indication. A person with this formation is a born ruler

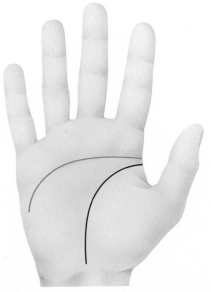

When the Line of Head penetrates the Mount of the Moon it denotes a person who places great importance upon dreams and the imagination

The principal lines of the hand

When the Line of Heart originates on the Mount of Jupiter, it denotes one who holds idealised views of the nature of love

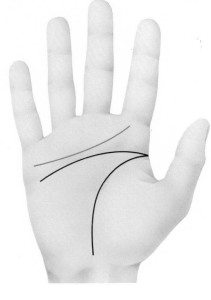

When the Line of Heart arises from between the fingers of Jupiter and Saturn, it represents a more common-sense approach to matters of the heart

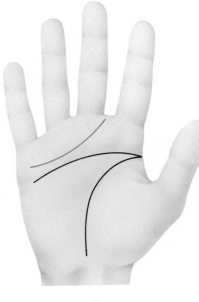

When the Line of Heart arises on or close to the Mount of Saturn, it indicates a person with a markedly powerful sexual drive, in whom personal satisfaction is more important than the feelings of others

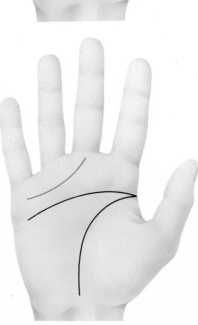

The Line of Heart

A good palmist always reads the Heart line in conjunction with the Head line, for when this procedure is followed it can be seen how mentality and emotions balance – or fail to balance – in the personality of the individual whose hand is being read.

There has always been a good deal of disagreement among palmists about the exact significance of the various formations of this line. Thus, for example, most palmists of the present day take a Heart line curving up strongly to the first finger as an indication of a healthy and vigorous emotional and sexual life; in the past, however, such a formation was given an altogether different and rather sinister significance – the 17th century palmist Richard Saunders actually wrote that the line:

'. . . *Naked*, without Branches, and touching the Root of the Index, Prognosticateth Poverty, Losses, Shipwrack for Fortune and Calamities.'

There are three important positions from which the Heart line may commence. They are:

(1) From the Mount of Jupiter, or from very near that Mount.
(2) From between the Mounts of Jupiter and Saturn, i.e., between the first and second fingers.
(3) From the Mount of Saturn, or from very near that mount.

The first formation – from the Mount of Jupiter – indicates a person whose emotional and sexual life approximates towards what the Victorians regarded as the highest type of love. That is to say a total idealisation of the loved one, who is put on a pedestal and worshipped as though he or she had no faults, no limitations, no human failings. Such a love *can* provide a lifetime of happiness, but it can also be dangerous and self-defeating. For should the idolised and worshipped turn out to have feet of clay, as is often the case, love turns to hatred and not even a shred of human affection is left behind.

The second formation, rising between the Mounts of Jupiter and Saturn, shows an altogether calmer approach towards the things of the heart. The nineteenth century palmist Benham, author of *The Laws of Scientific Hand Reading*, a book still studied at the present day, gave a fine description of the emotional psychology of the individual with this formation. Such a person, he said, would have a love life which would follow 'the common-sense, practical, middle ground', who would not allow him or herself to be carried away by sentiment, but would view love from a practical standpoint, inclined to think that 'love in a cottage' is a myth unless there is plenty of butter to put on the bread. A person, in short, whose affections are strong but always held within the bounds of what is considered sensible.

The third formation, with the line rising

from or close to the Mount of Saturn, is traditionally associated with a personality in which the sexual drive is extremely powerful. Love is never untinged with sex and the resulting sensuality often leads to a certain selfishness in matters of affection – as long as the person concerned is satisfied with the sensual pleasures, particularly the sexual pleasures, that are being obtained, he or she tends to be rather unconcerned about the feelings and emotional reactions of the partner.

The supposed significance outlined above, which although purely traditional in origin seems to be validated in a great number of cases, is confirmed by astro-palmistry, for Saturn is the Ruler of Capricorn, the leaping Goat who has always been strongly linked with sexuality.

Another common position for the beginning of the Heart line is in a swing upwards from the Life line or the Head line. This seems to be an indication of a certain coldness of attitude in emotional matters.

Perhaps the most important aspect of the Heart line is its tendency to be curved or straight. The more curved the line, the greater the wish to love and be loved; the straighter it is, the colder the personality – one which always lets its head rule its heart, its mental processes rule its emotional life.

Occasionally a hand is found in which the Heart line is so faint or so short that it can hardly be considered to be present at all – sometimes, indeed, it is altogether absent. Many of the palmists of the past took a very grim view of such a configuration. Said one:

'if in hand there be found *no* Line of Heart, it is an unfailing sign of treachery, hypocrisy, and the worst instincts, and, unless the Line of Health be very good, the subject will be liable to heart disease, and runs a grave danger of a sudden, early death'.

Such an interpretation would be regarded as rubbish by the overwhelming majority of present day palmists. Firstly, they see the line as being concerned purely with emotional and sexual life, not with the physical heart and a possibility of disease in that organ of the body; and secondly, they would interpret the absence of a Heart line as an indication of tightly-controlled – perhaps too tightly controlled – emotions; not of 'heartlessness' in the ordinary sense of the term and still less of 'treachery, hypocrisy, the worst instincts, and a sudden early death'.

The Line of Fate

The Line of Fate, which runs vertically down the centre of the palm to or towards the Mount of Saturn – sometimes extending as far as the second, or Saturnian, finger – is also sometimes referred to as the Line of Destiny, or the Line of Saturn.

Sometimes the line is found doubled. This is a splendid and desirable formation and indicates that the person involved will follow two quite distinct but associated careers. It is even more favourable if the two lines end on or near different Mounts; from the nature and rulership of these Mounts (see earlier chapter) the nature of the careers can be divined.

The palmist must not take the double line, described above, or any other formation of the line, as a sign that a certain career or destiny will inevitably be followed. The Line of Fate indicates not so much what will inevitably happen to us, what pursuits in life we may follow, as *the totality of influences brought to bear upon us by the world.* It relates to the people we will meet in the course of our careers, the influence they *may* have on us, either for good or ill, the intellectual and emotional conflicts and influences which *can* affect our worldly lives if we allow them to do so, and the ultimate endings of the careers we adopt *if we should decide to follow those careers through to the end.*

There are five positions from which the Fate line commonly arises:

(1) From the Life line.
(2) From the wrists, sometimes extending its position back to the bracelets.
(3) From the Mount of the Moon.
(4) From the Head line.
(5) From the Heart line. This is somewhat unusual.

The first formation, when the Fate line arises from the Life line, indicates that a successful career will be achieved through personal merit. This is particularly so if the Fate line is strong and well-marked upon the hand. Such success is unlikely to be achieved until fairly late in life, however, if the line's early length is 'tied down' to the Life line. This particular line-form is a strong indication that environmental factors, perhaps the influence of parents or other relatives, will be an obstacle in the earlier stages of the career.

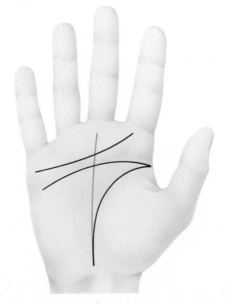

The Line of Fate, arising from the Line of Life, indicates the attainment of a successful career through personal merit

The principal lines of the hand

When the Line of Fate originates from the wrist, particularly if it extends to the Mount of Saturn, it is a sign of great good fortune (near right). When it arises from the Mount of the Moon (far right), it is an indication that material success is dependent on the unpredictable activities of others

When the Line of Fate originates from the Line of Head (near right) or the Line of Heart (far right) it is an indication that success will come relatively late in life

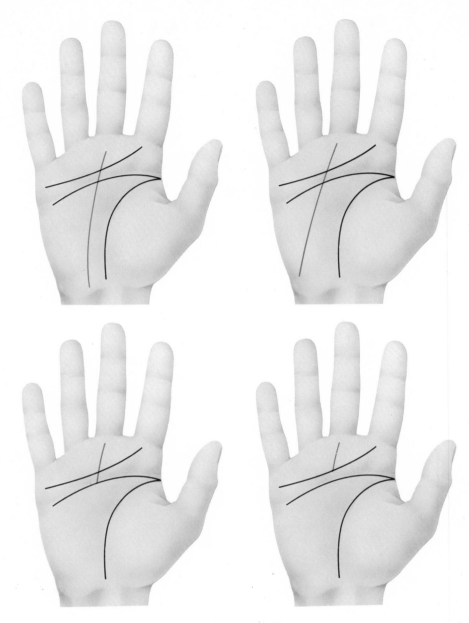

The second formation, that is, from the wrist, is a sign of career-satisfaction and great good fortune. This is particularly the case if the line extends as far as the Mount of Saturn.

The third formation, from the Mount of the Moon, is traditionally taken as an indication that 'success will be more or less dependent on the fancy and caprice of other people'. Such an interpretation would not be accepted by many contemporary palmists. Rather would they say that this is a sign that the subject would be well advised to make his career in some field which is in the public eye – journalism, radio, television, the arts and so on. If the line is straight but has a branch running up to the Mount of the Moon the significance is somewhat similar. It also raises a strong possibility that the influence of one person, or a number of people, will exert a considerable effect upon the career.

The fourth and fifth formations – from the Line of the Head or Heart – are indications that it will be comparatively late in life before success is achieved in the career.

The Fate line normally ends on or towards the Mount of Saturn. The significance of the line ending on or towards the other Mounts – or sending out a branch to other Mounts – is as follows:

(1) On, toward, or with a branch toward, the Mount of Jupiter; this indicates a strong, ambitious and efficient personality which will achieve success in its career, probably quite early in life.

(2) On, toward, or with a branch toward the Mount of the Sun; a successful career, with success probably being achieved towards middle life, which will bring the personality to the attention of others.

(3) On, toward, or with a branch toward, the Mount of Mercuty; success is

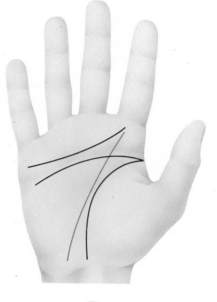

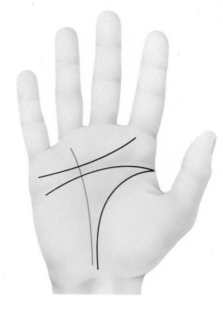

If the Line of Fate ends either on or toward the Mount of Jupiter (far left) it is a strong sign of a strongly ambitious personality who will achieve success quite early in life; when it ends on or towards the Mount of the Sun (near left) it indicates success achieved towards the middle of life; while if it ends on or towards the Mount of Mercury (below left) it suggests success in creation or travel

In this fifteenth century manuscript from the Bodleian Library collection, the Line of Fate can be seen rising from the wrist to the Mount of Jupiter, indicating great success early in life

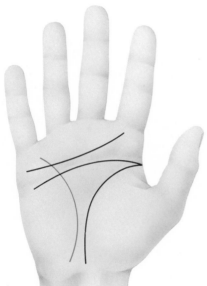

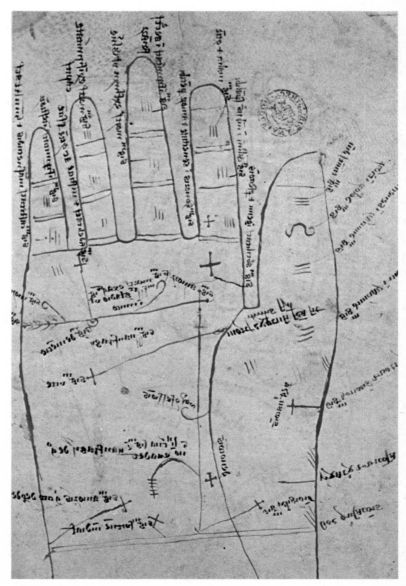

most likely to be achieved through careers involving travel, communications, books or science.

Some traditional interpretations

There are some traditional attributions of various formations of the Line of Fate which are of considerable interest, although they are indications of *trends* rather than of a fixed and unalterable destiny:

(1) When the Fate line extends beyond the palm, either into the finger of Saturn or (rarely) one of the other fingers, it is not a favourable signification. It is a sign that in career matters the person will be rather strongly inclined always to go too far. For instance, if the person's career leads him into a position where he manages others he will try to dominate them and will be regarded by them as a petty tyrant. If, on the other hand,

The principal lines of the hand

When the Line of Fate extends beyond the palm and into one of the fingers it is a sign that the person will tend to carry career matters too far

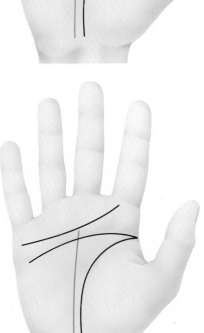

When a strong Line of Fate comes to a stop on the Line of Heart (near right) it is an indication that the person will allow the sexual side of life to interfere with a successful career. When the line stops on the Line of Head (far right) it is a sign that there will be intellectual mistakes

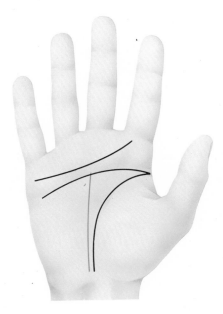

A Line of Fate full of breaks is an indication of many changes of career

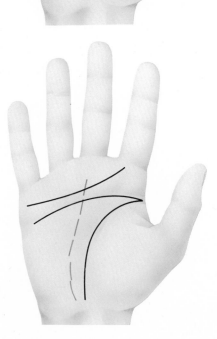

the person is in a subservient position he or she will tend to be over-obsequious and self-effacing in relations with superiors.

(2) When the line is strong but stops dead on the Heart line it is a sign that the sexual side of life obstructs a successful career; but if there is a harmonious joining of the two lines and they run together up to the Mount of Jupiter it is a sign of a highly successful career in which the emotions play a full part.

(3) When the Fate line stops dead on the Head line it is a sign that errors in thinking will hamper the development of the career.

(4) When the Fate line is full of breaks, continually stopping and starting, it is likely that the person's life will be marked by continual changes in career, the outcome of which will be sometimes successful, sometimes the reverse.

(5) When the Fate line does not commence until the central area of the palm – the area which the palmists of old called 'the Plain of Mars' – this indicates a troubled and difficult career. If, however, the line is a very long one, continuing through to a Mount or finger, these difficulties will be overcome, the troubles that have obstructed the first half of the career being conquered and success achieved.

When the Line of Fate is forked, one half of it coming from the base of the Mount of Venus and the other half coming from the base of the Mount of the Moon, the individual's whole career will swing from the extreme of the emotions on one side to the extreme of the occult, 'mystical' elements on the other.

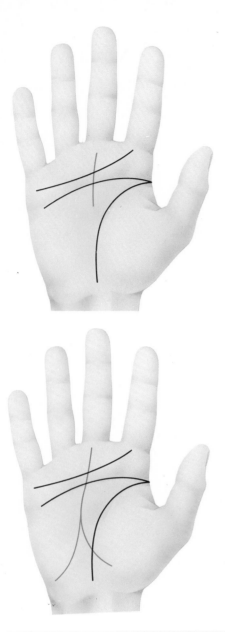

dirige vers l'hépatique, annonce des tribulations et adversités, surtout si cette ligne est inégale.

— Uue ligne partie de la rascette et montant directement vers l'index, annonce de longs voyages (tradition).

Quatre lignes à la restreinte semblables et bien colorées et placées en forme de bracelet, annoncent quatre-vingts à cent ans d'existence.

Si deux petits rameaux forment un angle aigu dans la rascette, ils annoncent un homme destiné a de riches héritages, honoré dans sa vieillesse, et cela plus encore, s'il se trouve une étoile ou une croix dans cet angle. Il sera en outre peu sujet aux maladies (tradition).

Nous donnons ci-contre l'exemple d'une MAIN HEUREUSE.

a. Double ligne de vie.

b. Bonheur absolu (saturnienne directe).

c. Luxe en amour et en bonté (rameaux au commencement et à la fin).

d. Union d'amour.

e. Anneau de Vénus.

f. Génie complet avec racines.

g. Réussite dans les arts, renommée.

h. Union de Mercure et de Vénus, perspicacité en affaires, amour et fortune.

i. Bon tempérament.

j. Triple bracelet magique, longue vie.

k. Amour unique.

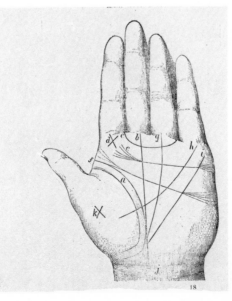

18

When the Line of Fate does not begin before the Plain of Mars (upper left) it is an indication of a troubled and difficult career. If it is forked (lower left) the person's career will be affected on one side by the emotions and on the other by mystical elements

In the fifteenth century manuscript above, the Line of Fate rises strongly from the wrist to an end between the mounts of Saturn and the Sun. In the diagram from Desbarolles's *Les Mystères de la Main* (left), the long and straight Line of Fate indicates 'total good fortune'

5
The subsidiary lines

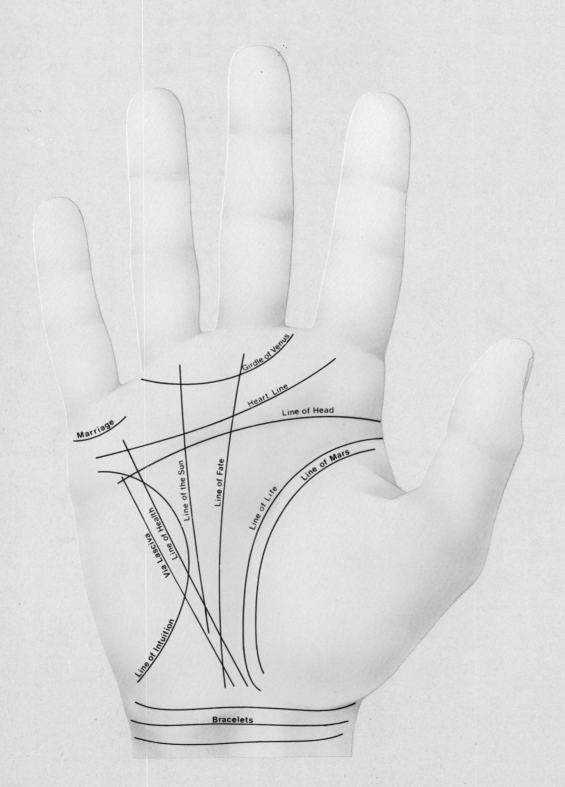

Girdle of Venus

Heart Line

Line of Head

Marriage

Line of Mars

Via Lasciva

Line of Health

Line of the Sun

Line of Fate

Line of Life

Line of Intuition

Bracelets

The Girdle of Venus

The girdle of Venus is a curved line running from the Mount of Mercury to the Mount of Jupiter or, sometimes, from between the third and fourth fingers to between the first and second fingers.

Early palmists believed that the existence of this line in the palm denoted a strongly sensual nature. Most modern palmists deny that this is so except when the line is found strongly marked on an exceptionally fleshy hand.

As a rule, far from being associated with exceptional sensuality, the line indicates a sensitive, intellectual psychology. Persons with this formation are likely to be notable for abrupt and irrational changes of mood – at one moment they are 'high', at the next they are gloomy, depressed and full of anxieties. In other words, they are typical cyclothymics.

Such personalities easily take offence, their temper flaring at the merest trifles. Fortunately for those who come into contact with them such outbursts of bad temper usually subside as quickly as they have arisen, unreasonable fury changing to profound repentance in a moment!

Obviously people cursed with this peculiar psychological make-up are extremely difficult to live with and this factor often creates great difficulties in all forms of partnership, particularly in marriage. According to the traditions of palmistry this is particularly so if the girdle of Venus touches the Line of Marriage.

Perhaps the whole problem of the person with this unfortunate marking was best summed up by Cheiro, who wrote that a man with this formation 'would want as many virtues in a wife as there are stars in the universe'.

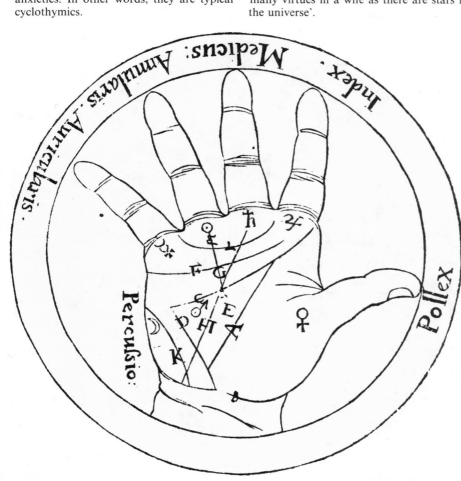

This diagram from Robert Fludd's *History of Two Worlds* (1617) shows a Line of the Sun originating from a point on the Line of Head at which it crosses the Line of Fate

The Line of the Sun

The Sun line, or line of Apollo, runs downwards from the Mount or the finger of the Sun (that is the third finger) towards the wrist, usually taking a course roughly parallel to the Fate line.

The appearance of this line in the hand increases the favourable potential of a good Fate line and, when it is in harmony with the other lines on the hand, ensures a life that will be crowned with success.

If it is not in harmony with the other lines on the hand (if, for example, there is a strong Sun line but a feeble Fate line) it merely indicates a personal psychology that is inclined towards the arts. Unless, however, a creative potentiality is indicated by the general formation of the other lines, such a personality is likely to be only a supporter and not a creative artist in his or her own right. In the words of Cheiro such a personality possesses 'the appreciation of art without the power of expression'.

Sometimes, it is interesting to note, the

The subsidiary lines

Sun line is completely missing on a hand that otherwise denotes a strongly artistic personality. This is an indication that such individuals, however dedicated they may be to the particular art form they pursue, will find it extremely difficult to achieve recognition. However hard they work, whatever their merits, success will rarely be obtained during their life time; they are more likely to gain posthumous recognition.

The Sun line may arise from one of the following positions:

  (1) The Life line
  (2) The Head line
  (3) The Heart line
  (4) The Fate line
  (5) The Mount of the Moon
  (6) The palm centre – the 'Plain of Mars'

The first formation, provided that the rest of the hand is in conformity with an artistic nature, indicates a personality who will follow a course of life in which the arts are of great importance. If the rest of the hand favours an artistic career such a person should attain success.

The second formation, rising from the Head line, denotes a personality whose artistic leanings will always be balanced by a strongly rational element in his or her psychology' If persons of this sort follow

A hand-print from Cheiro's collection, showing several strongly-marked parallel Lines of the Sun on the hand of A. J. Balfour

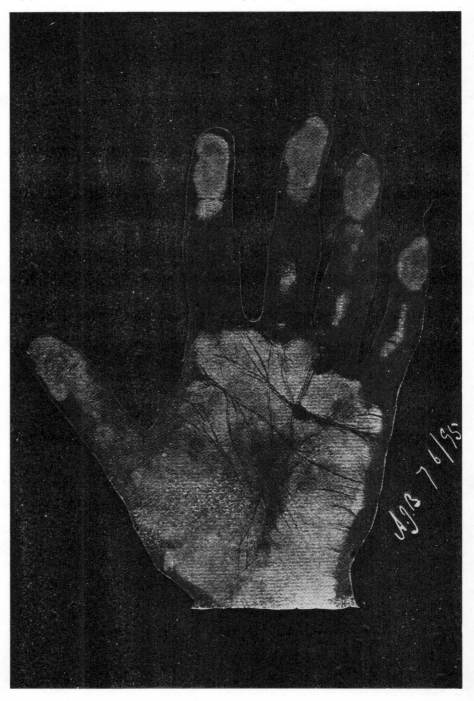

artistic careers they are unlikely to attain success (or failure) until fairly late in life.

The third formation, arising from the Heart line, indicates a strong taste for the arts and artistic things but little likelihood of success in a career devoted to them.

The fourth formation, arising from the Fate line, improves the indications of a weak Fate line. In the latter case a highly successful career is extremely probable although it may not be achieved until fairly late in life.

The fifth formation, arising from the Mount of the Moon, creates a strong possibility of success, but success arising from help received from others. Without such help fame will rarely be achieved. When, however, this Mount of the Moon commencement is combined with a strongly sloping Line of the Head it can be taken as a sign that success will be achieved in literature or some other art form in which imagination plays a large part.

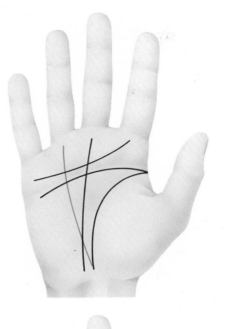

When the Line of the Sun rises from the Line of Life it is an indication of a successful personality

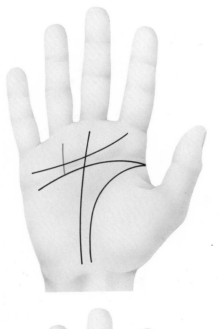

The Line of Sun arising from the Line of Head (far left) denotes someone whose artistic abilities may be balanced and to some degree inhibited by rational attitudes. If it arises from the Line of Heart (near left), it indicates a deep involvement in the arts that is unlikely to be crowned with much success

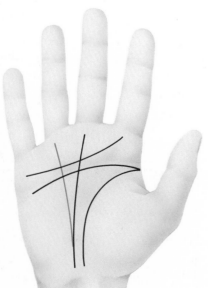

When the Line of the Sun arises from the Line of Fate (far left) it strengthens and improves the indications of the latter. When it arises from the Mount of the Moon (near left) it is a sign of success, but of success dependent upon the assistance of others

The subsidiary lines

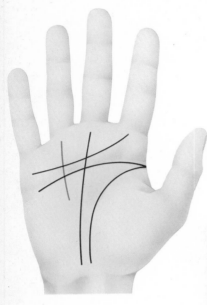

The Line of the Sun arising in the Plain of Mars indicates success eventually achieved in spite of early obstruction

The final formation, from the Plain of Mars, is a sign that success will ultimately be achieved in spite of many difficulties in the early part of life.

If the finger of the Sun (the third finger) is nearly equal in length to the finger of Saturn (the second finger) and if this formation is combined with a long Sun line the psychology indicated is that of the gambler. Such a personality will take chances on everything; on his emotional life, on his finances and on his career. Such a person, like one with the well-developed Girdle of Venus, is often extremely difficult to live with.

A well marked Sun line combined with a noticeably straight Head line indicates a love of power and wealth.

The Line of Health

The Health line, sometimes still called the 'hepatica', runs diagonally down the hand from the wrist, fairly near to the Mount of Venus, to or in the direction of the Mount of Mercury.

Old fashioned palmists believed that any point where the Health line met the Life line infallibly indicated the moment of death. Similarly, they believed that, however strong or well marked the Life line, a

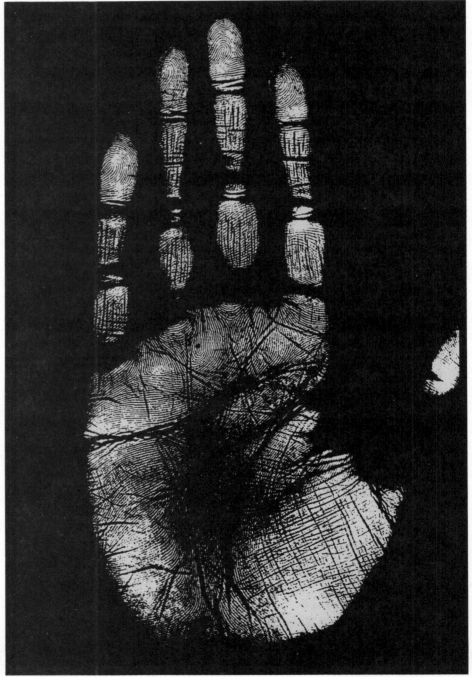

A well-defined Line of Health, sometimes known as the Line of Liver or Hepatica, on a female hand

feeble, or in any way abnormal Health line was a sure indication of an early death.

In contrast to these gloomy beliefs it was held that the absence of this line was an excellent sign, an indication of an extremely healthy and tough constitution. On the other hand the mere presence of the line was taken as denoting that there was a constitutional weakness of some sort.

Modern palmists take all this fatalistic gloom with more than a grain of salt. They say merely that the presence of the line indicates that the person who has this marking should devote more than usual care to his or her health.

The Line of Mars

The Line of Mars, sometimes called 'the inner life line', is a curved line running within and more or less parallel to the Life line.

The main significance of the presence of the Line of Mars on a hand is that it greatly strengthens the Life line. It gives energy to a weak Life line and increased power and energy to a strong and well marked Life line.

It does, however, have some less fortunate significations. As is clear from its name it is essentially martial in its nature and those who have it tend towards a choleric disposition. They quarrel easily, take offence at

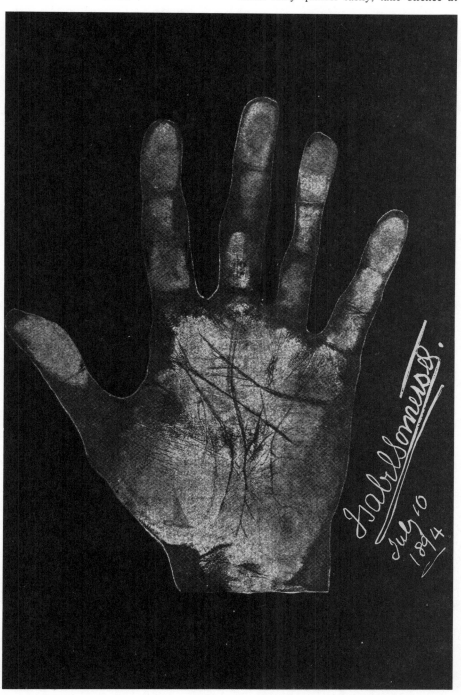

An unusually clear Line of Mars on the hand of Lady Isabel Somerset, a well-known temperance reformer of the late nineteenth century

The subsidiary lines

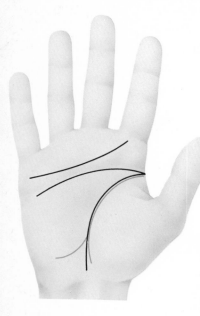

If the Line of Mars forks, with a branch running to the Mount of the Moon, it is an indication of continual craving for new sensations

trifles and often behave in a swaggering, overbearing and truculent manner. More positively the line equates with bravery and the virtues of the fighting man – it is an excellent line when found in the hand of a soldier or a professional boxer.

Another rather gloomy signification is given to this line by traditional palmistry. When it has a branch going down to the Mount of the Moon it is a sign that the man or woman who has it will have a continual craving for excitement, new experiences and powerful sensations. Such a person is quite likely to have a tendency towards alcoholism or drug addiction – the very danger of such courses is their fundamental attraction.

The Via Lasciva

The Via Lasciva, sometimes called the lesser health line, is rarely found. When it is, it runs parallel to and usually outside the Health line, with which it is often confused. Its presence in the palm is generally an indication of a strong, forceful personality with powerful and highly developed passions.

Considered, however, as a companion line to the Line of Health, it is believed by some palmists to repair many of the latter's defects.

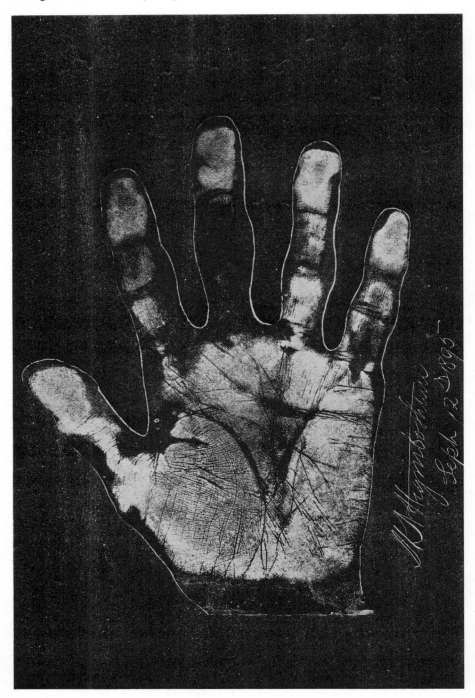

The Via Lasciva is not often found on the hand. Here, in another print from Cheiro's collection, it can be seen in the hand of H. N. Higinbotham, the President of the World's Columbian Exposition, 1895

The Line of Intuition

When found on the hand this line occupies a rough semi-circular position running from the Mount of Mercury to the Mount of the Moon. Sometimes, it cuts or runs along with the Health line, but normally if it is present at all it can easily be distinguished from it.

According to the traditions of palmistry it indicates, as its name suggests, a strongly intuitive psychology; a personality which is strongly receptive to 'vibrations' and emotional atmospheres. Such a person's perceptions always tremble on the verges of the unseen world. He or she can sense things that others cannot, can interpret the nuances of the behaviour of others without a word being spoken, and can make the right decisions on apparently irrational grounds. Such individuals have a tendency towards things psychic, can develop mediumistic powers and be influenced by forces – perhaps by entities – of whose very existence the ordinary person is generally quite unconscious.

In view of the old-established belief that women are the 'intuitive sex', it is interesting that this line is commoner in female hands than it is in male hands, as the palm print below shows.

A good example of the Line of Intuition on a female hand

The subsidiary lines

A strongly marked Line of Marriage extending upwards into the Line of the Sun is an indication of a wealthy marriage

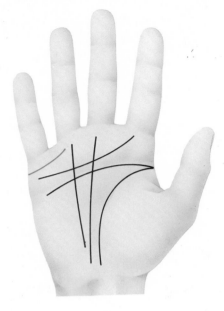

When the Line of Marriage runs alongside the Line of Heart it is a sign of happiness

A Line of Marriage that curves sharply upwards is an indication that a permanent liaison is unlikely

The Line of Marriage

The Line of Marriage consists of rather complicated markings found at the base of the finger of Mercury (the little finger) and sometimes actually extending onto the Mount of Mercury.

Its significance, of course, is concerned with marriage, but marriage in the broadest sense of the word. It is, in short, concerned with all our close relationships with other people. Marriage itself, or any other sexual relationship, is the closest and most common of such relationships.

The line (or, rather, marks) may begin at the side of the finger or not until the finger reaches the base of the Mount of Mercury. Only the long markings pertain to marriages or really close emotional relationships, the shorter markings referring to other personal relationships.

When the main marking is close to the Heart line, traditional palmistry takes this as an indication that marriage will take place or took place at a very early age, probably between the ages of sixteen and twenty-one. Similarly a main mark lying close to the centre of the Mount of Mercury supposedly indicates that a marriage will take place, or took place, between the ages of twenty-one and twenty-eight, while a mark three quarters across the Mount of Mercury – towards the Mount of the Sun – denotes one taking place between the ages of twenty-eight and thirty-five.

The tendency among modern palmists is not to take the Marriage line too seriously – the Heart line is usually considered a far better indication of emotional life of the present day.

However, for the sake of completeness and those studying palmistry who have a strong bent towards the traditional form of that art, the old beliefs about the Marriage line are given below.

When there is a strongly marked Marriage mark which rises straight on the Mount of Mercury, and when this mark extends upwards into the Sun line, it prognosticates a wealthy marriage or other form of permanent relationship. Such a marriage, however, may not be a happy one, as the strong influence indicates that there may be an element of caprice and imagination, rather than real love, in the affections.

The form of Marriage line which indicates happiness is when the line goes up to and runs along the side of the Heart line without actually joining it.

When the Marriage line curves sharply upwards it is a sign that the person concerned will be unlikely to get married or enjoy any permanent sexual liaison.

When the line forks at the end, and slopes downwards towards the centre of the hand, it is a sign of divorce or other form of permanent separation from the partner. Divorce or permanent separation are also indicated if a fine line crosses the marriage line to the centre of the palm.

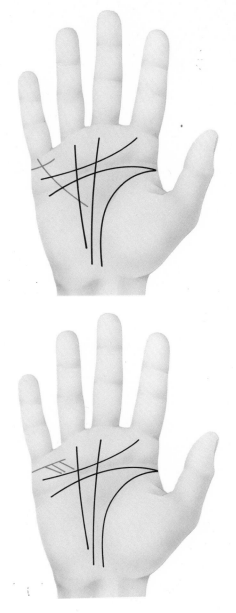

Divorce is indicated by a fork at the end of the Line of Marriage (far left) or by a fine line crossing the Line of Marriage towards the centre of the palm (near left)

When the Line of Marriage curves down towards the Line of Heart, it is said to be a sign that the beloved will die first (far left). Similarly fine lines sloping from the Line of Heart (near left) indicate a distressing state of health in one's partner

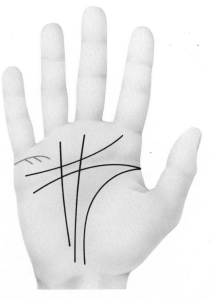

Some of these traditional beliefs are even gloomier than the one outlined in the previous paragraph. For instance, when the Marriage line curves downwards toward or even reaches the Heart line it is a sign that the beloved will die first. Similarly, when the Marriage line is well marked but with fine lines sloping from it to the Heart line it is a sign of past or approaching personal distress caused by the general state of health of the loved one.

If the Marriage line of a person's hand is full of little drooping lines shooting off from it, he or she would be unwise to establish any deep personal relationship, as such a relationship can only result in much unhappiness. A forked Line of Marriage has a similar significance and when the line is suddenly broken an equally sudden separation is likely to take place.

When the Marriage line goes downward and cuts the Sun line it signifies that the

A person with a Line of Marriage from which little drooping lines shoot off would be ill-advised to establish a lasting personal relationship with anyone

The subsidiary lines

A forked Line of Marriage (near right), or one that is broken, is a sign of sudden separation. When the line goes downward to cut the Line of the Sun (far right), it indicates loss of social status

When the Line of Marriage turns upwards and sends out a shoot towards the Mount of the Sun (near right), it suggests a rise in social status as the result of marriage. But a fine line running closely parallel with the Line of Marriage is an indication of adultery (far right)

A well-marked line from the Mount of the Moon that cuts the Line of Marriage is believed to indicate strong opposition to the match

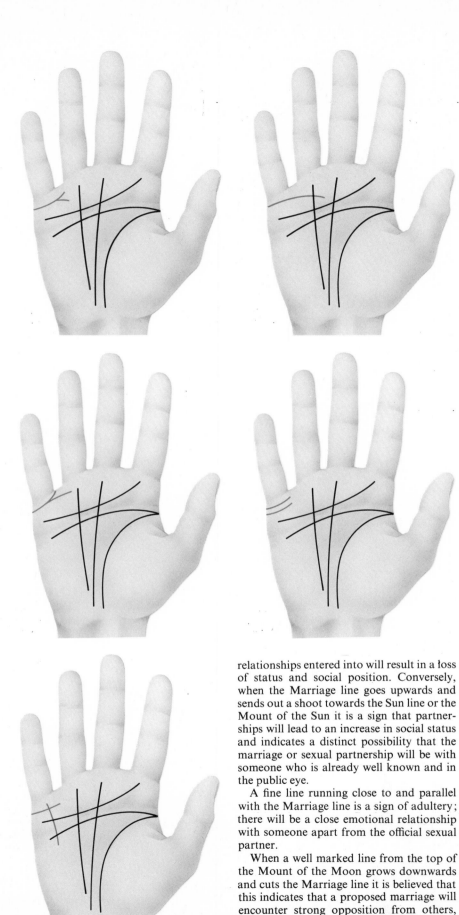

(Facing page) *The Palmist,* a painting by the eighteenth century artist Jean-Baptiste Le Prince (1734-1781)

relationships entered into will result in a loss of status and social position. Conversely, when the Marriage line goes upwards and sends out a shoot towards the Sun line or the Mount of the Sun it is a sign that partnerships will lead to an increase in social status and indicates a distinct possibility that the marriage or sexual partnership will be with someone who is already well known and in the public eye.

A fine line running close to and parallel with the Marriage line is a sign of adultery; there will be a close emotional relationship with someone apart from the official sexual partner.

When a well marked line from the top of the Mount of the Moon grows downwards and cuts the Marriage line it is believed that this indicates that a proposed marriage will encounter strong opposition from others, particularly from relatives and close associates of one party.

The subsidiary lines

The Bracelets (near right) are generally three in number, although two or even just one are not unusual. When the Line of Life extends into the Bracelets, it is taken as an indication of a long and healthy life. But when the first Bracelet is high on the wrist (far right) it is believed to be a sign of some weakness of the consitution

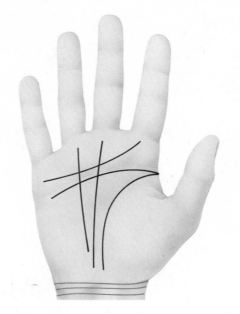

Breaks in the Bracelets (right) are said to indicate inordinate vanity and a tendency to lie

The Bracelets

After all the despondency associated with the Marriage line it is something of a relief to turn the attention towards the Bracelets.

There may be one, two or, most common, three of these encircling the front of the wrist, although not usually the back, rather like pieces of partially unravelled string.

When strongly and clearly marked the Bracelets indicate a particularly healthy and strong constitution. This is even more the case when the life line extends back to and runs into the Bracelets. Indeed, some palmists take this formation as an almost infallible indication of a long, healthy and happy life.

A less happy view of the significance of the Bracelets was taken by Cheiro and is still adhered to by some of his present-day followers. According to this belief when the first Bracelet – that is the one nearest the palm – is high on the wrist, almost rising to the palm, there is some internal weakness of the constitution. This is held to be particularly so when the Bracelet is arched. Breaks in the Bracelets are also of ominous significance. If all three Bracelets break in a point, one above the other, it is taken as an indication of inordinate vanity and untruthfulness, leading to disaster.

The Ring of Saturn

This rarely found formation, a semi-circular ring around the base of the Mount of Saturn, is supposed to be an unfavourable formation to find on the hand. It apparently leads to a lack of success in life and Cheiro and other palmists have asserted that it cuts the Mount of Saturn off so abruptly from the rest of the hand that those who have it tend to have the sort of personality that is unable to carry any matter through to a successful conclusion.

Alternatively, certain other palmists maintain that this ring indicates 'extraordinary occult powers'.

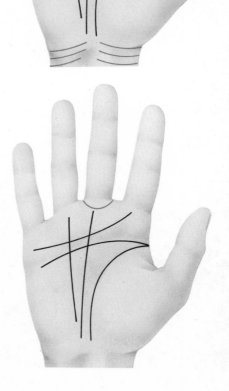

The rarely-found Ring of Saturn is supposed to denote lack of success in life

From a sixteenth century treatise attributed to Andreas Corvus of Mirandola: the Bracelets in the hand of an irrascible and evil man (above left) and a woman unsuited for motherhood (above right); an avaricious and thoughtless man (below left) and a stubborn man (below right)

6
The eight-fold classification of the hand

In an earlier chapter it was stated that there was another method of hand classification which could not be properly explained until the reader had some understanding of the general formation of the lines. The reader should by now have acquired such a general knowledge.

The form of classification is an eight-fold one. One type of hand is attributed to Earth and the other seven to the traditional 'planets' of Astrology (Moon, Mercury, Sun, Venus, Mars, Jupiter, Saturn).

The Hand of the Moon
The lunar hand is very soft, its lines weakly marked and many in number. On the Mount of the Moon a spiral often occurs, and this Mount is frequently set low with the Fate line springing from it.

The man or woman with a lunar hand is likely to be of a restless but easygoing temperament, to love travel and 'getting about', and to be somewhat extravagant in nature. This last trait tends to go with ever-fluctuating finances – although generally they seem to fluctuate for ill rather than good. The love of change and travel is likely to incline the lunar personality towards occupations in which these play a part – journalism or work in the tourist industry for example.

The adventurous and change-loving nature of this type of personality inclines him or her to gambling, speculation and other types of financial adventure. The same factor ensures that the lunar person-ality is one that is unwilling to stay in any one place for a long time and whose life will be marked by continual changes of job and career.

Astrologically the Moon rules the imagin-ation and the lunar psychology is, as might be expected, an imaginative one. The per-sonality is often one which enjoys peculiarly powerful and vivid dreams and is more in touch with the psychic images of the Unconscious mind than the overwhelming majority of people.

As might be expected, such people often have some psychic abilities, sometimes developing into mediumship, and many of them display a marked interest in the occult, the mystical and the 'night side of nature'.

The person with a lunar hand tends to be popular with those he meets; partly because he or she is a genuinely likeable person, partly because he or she has the reflective qualities of the moon, able to sense the emotional and mental moods of others and reflect them back in a thoroughly endearing way.

The main disadvantage of the lunar psychology is its tendency to changeability. Such people can be peculiarly irritating – one moment they are for stability in social affairs, the next moment for revolution – one day they argue hotly for the sacredness of the marriage bond, the next day they are equally hotly extolling the virtues of free love.

Such persons, it is clear, are difficult to enter into permanent emotional relation-ships with, but, nevertheless, many lunar personalities enjoy extremely happy marriages. What is essential is that the partner should realise that the lunar psy-chology is one of quickly changing moods and should learn to fall in with them and not to be swept away by the excitement of the moment.

The reflective, understanding, sympathetic nature of the Moon personalities makes them extremely effective at any form of social work, voluntary or professional. They make excellent nurses, prison visitors, child care officers and, where the imaginative strengths are allied with intellect, psychologists.

The Hand of Mercury
The Mercurial hand is distinguished by a fairly long little finger (that is, the finger of Mercury) and by a strong and well-marked Line of Intuition leading towards the Mount of Mercury, which will itself be fairly

The Lunar hand, soft and lightly marked with many lines, indicating a restless but easygoing nature

prominent. The four fingers tend to bend towards the thumb and the lower phalanges of the fingers are long and sometimes quite broad.

The primary characteristics of those with the Mercurial hand are quick wits and a marked intellectual ability. They love knowledge for its own sake, have a real devotion to learning and a strong interest in literature and science. An adaptability of thought and emotions is also found in the Mercurian. They have a calm and serene disposition combined with an optimistic outlook on life. This tends to be conducive to their love of study and to endow them with a faculty to deal with the practical things of life.

Their mentalities are so vigorous that they sometimes tend to overtax them – a 'nervous breakdown', a neurosis, a psychological disability arising from an overworked brain are the typical illnesses of the Mercurian psychology. They, like those with a lunar hand, have a marked love of travel, and if their environment, either at home or work, stifles this love of travel and/or learning, a psychological explosion is likely to follow. They also tend to worry and find a source of mental strain in their dealings with their subordinates, both at home and at work. Yet those with the Mercurial hand are likely to be popular with people they come into contact with, particularly if they move in literary or scientific circles.

Mercurians tend to 'marry well' and both marriage and other forms of partnership are likely to result in financial gain particularly when, as is often the case, the Mercurian shows marked business abilities – a strong capacity to deal with financial matters in a thoroughly sensible way.

The dangers indicated by the possession of a Mercurial hand are quite as apparent as its positive virtues. There is a tendency to overestimate the importance of the intellectual side of life at the expense of the emotions. This leads to a contemptuous attitude towards those not so well-endowed with intellect as the typical Mercurian. As a result, unless the Mercurians guard their tongues carefully, they can be overcritical about the shortcomings, particularly the mental shortcomings, of others.

Mercurians are also liable to over-worrying – making a fuss about trifles. At its worst this can lead to a thoroughly obsessional psychological profile – the sort of person who checks two or three times to see that all the gas taps are turned off, awakes in a rain storm to see whether there are any accidentally left-open windows or leaks in the roof, and even engages in continual hand washing for fear of contamination from bacteria.

Usually, however, the possessor of the Mercurial hand is a popular personality, sometimes a little aloof with those he or she regards as subordinates or intellectual inferiors, but often the life and soul of any social gathering.

The Mercurial hand, distinguished by its well-developed Finger of Mercury, a sign of quick wits and intellectual ability

The Hand of the Sun

In the Sun or solar hand the fingers are shorter than the palm – this, it should be noted, more or less equates it with the Fire hand in the elemental classification dealt with earlier in this book. The fingers are knotty, with the figure joints well marked and prominent. The fourth finger (that of the Sun) is as long or even longer than the third finger (that of Jupiter), while the Sun line is usually present, well marked and prominent in the hand.

Ambition, drive, a desire for power over others and a healthy constitution are the most notable attributes of those with a solar hand.

The Sun psychology is one that seeks the public eye, desires the recognition of others and longs for admiration. The solarian is prepared to work hard to achieve these objects and is often helped by his or her facility for accurate observation and enthusiasm for educational progress. In the field of education the solarian, like the person with a Mercurial hand, is often drawn to subjects connected with science and literature.

The attraction of power and glory for the solarian psychology is such that there is a love for any sort of social occasion in which the personality can come to the fore and gain attention and admiration – anything from a small party to a pageant or amateur dramatics. Consequently all types of social pleasures and amusements are of great importance to the solarian provided that he or she can play a central part in them.

The solarian psychology is such that it has considerable charms for the opposite sex. Marriage tends to be an important part of life and the solarian is more likely than not to marry someone who will bring him or her financial advantage. The solarian charm is such, however, that even the happiest and most stable of marriages is likely to be interspersed with a series of

The eight-fold classification

The Solar hand is similar to the Fire hand, with its strong fingers shorter than the palm; it denotes one with a love of public attention

The Hand of Venus

The hand of Venus is notable for the prominence of the Mount of Venus which is fleshy, shaped something like an inverted bowl, and has its central parts covered with 'rays' – fine but distinctly marked hair lines. The Line of Fate, which is sometimes called the Saturnian line, originates on the Mount of Venus. The thumb is short and thick and the whole hand somewhat small and out of proportion to the height and bulk of the person concerned.

The typical Venusian hand indicates a friendly and cheerful personality, popularity with others, and fondness for an active social life and the companionship of other people. Consequently, friends and friendship are a major factor in life and on the whole the influence, direct or indirect, of these friends exerts a beneficial effect on both the career and the more private side of life.

The popularity of the Venusian with the opposite sex is considerable and so strong that some Venusians tend never to settle down with a single partner but to flit like a bee from flower to flower. Such a tendency is incompatible with the long-term happiness of the Venusian and he or she would be well-advised to abandon this course of action and settle down into a permanent relationship. For once the man or woman with a Venusian hand *does* settle down he or she is likely to enjoy an exceptionally happy and harmonious relationship with the marriage partner. Curiously enough the Venusian marriage tends to go to one extreme or the other; usually, as described above, it is a source of happiness and emotional fulfilment, but in the comparatively few cases where it does go wrong it goes very wrong indeed and involves, besides much unhappiness, the possibility of heavy financial loss.

flirtations or, sometimes, more serious extra-marital affairs.

The solarian usually has strong relationships with parents, other older relatives and even older friends and acquaintances. There is a strong possibility of inheritance or some form of financial benefit from the former and career help from the latter.

This last mentioned factor is often important in the initial stages of the career and there may be, as a result, an early career success and achievement of ambitions.

The best careers for those with a solarian psychology are either those connected with land or property – possession of the Sun hand seems to give a natural tendency to success in dealing with either of these – or those which involve being in a position of trust. In the latter case the kindly intervention and friendliness of those in a superior position is likely to be of great value and, as a result of this, an early recognition of abilities may be attained.

As with all types of hand there is a darker side to the solarian nature. The major fault with the solarians is that they may be so desirous of glory, so ambitious for the limelight, that they become 'pushy' and antagonise both their superiors and those subordinate to them. When corrected for this they tend to be deeply offended and retire into sulky seclusion. All those with a Sun hand should guard themselves strictly against this anti-social tendency.

On the whole, however, the psychological make-up of the solarian is a pleasant one, in which an ambitious and idealistic nature is combined with the most desirable of the virtues – tolerance and an understanding of the thoughts and feelings of others.

Finally it must be noted that some people with the Sun hand share certain characteristics with people who have a Mercurial hand. This is particularly so when the Mount of Mercury is full, fleshy and prominent, indicating a tendency to be travel-loving and perpetually changing jobs.

In the more usual type of Venusian marriage, happy on both the physical and the emotional sides of life, the home environment does much to enrich the quality of life, which gets better and happier as the years go by. Venus is, of course, the 'ruler' of the beautiful things of this world and a beautiful, aesthetically attractive home is of great importance to those who have Venusian hands. The desire to live in an attractive and lovely environment also extends outside the home. The Venusian office worker, for example, will ensure that his office reflects his or her personality. The place of work will be beautified with flowers and pot plants, the 'tools of the trade' on the bench of office desk will be displayed to their best advantage, and the whole environment will be designed to stimulate and please.

The Venusian personality will be strongly interested in all the arts – dance, literature, painting, music – and there is a possibility that he or she will show a marked practical ability in one or other of them, particularly

if it is an art, such as dancing, which encourages social intercourse. Even if the Venusian does not make his living from the arts or in a field closely connected with them (interior design for example), they will always occupy an important place in his or her thoughts, feelings and individual philosophy of life.

It is a curious fact that accompanying the artistic flair of the Venusian hand there is often a marked ability for dealing with money matters and financial affairs in general. Along with this financial acumen goes a strong personal magnetism which ensures the active help and co-operation of others.

The Venusian hand has, as is the case with every sort of hand, its negative aspect. The Venusian makes no attempt to balance his or her love of beauty with common sense and a consideration for the feelings of others and becomes a totally selfish aesthete. All that such a person is concerned with is to make the personal surroundings as beautiful and ego-reflecting as possible. This goal is sought to the exclusion of all others and the negative Venusian does not worry who suffers – or who pays the bill – as long as the environment is a beautiful one. Such personalities were very common among the affected and intensely egotistic aesthetes of the 1890's – Oscar Wilde's associate Lord Alfred Douglas affords a fine example of just such a personality.

On the whole, however, the majority of Venusians do not follow such selfish paths. They are decent kindly people, with pleasant friends, living and working in pleasant surroundings.

The Hand of Mars
The Martial hand is characterised by a cross on what was traditionally called the 'Plain of Mars' – the centre of the palm. The thumb is particularly strong and well built, its first phalanx being particularly powerful and thick. The lines on the hand tend to be on the short side, but well marked, deeply graven into the palm.

Those who possess the Martial hand have all the martial virtues – and vices. They will be endowed with courage, both physical and moral, will have an adventurous and enterprising personality, and a real capacity for hard work. Everything they turn their hand to will be taken seriously and, once a project is started, it will be continued, whatever the difficulties, until it comes to a successful conclusion. Vast energy, sheer physical endurance and 'guts' ensure that even the most difficult plans are carried through to completion. It is the man or woman with the Martial hand who is most likely to launch a spare time business and, against all the odds, make a success of it. Similarly it is probably the Martial type who, in his or her leisure time, has the endurance to struggle on and take a degree or some other qualification which can be turned to practical use.

The psychological profile of the person with a Martial hand is notable for its mental alertness, being always 'on the ball', ready to adapt to changing circumstances and the vicissitudes of a roving existence.

The Martial personality is likely to acquire wealth in life, usually by his or her own efforts, although in some cases this is supplemented by money obtained through inheritance or by marriage.

Those endowed with the Martial hand are often enthusiasts for sport, and pleasure from this source, whether as participants or spectators, is likely to play an important part in their leisure activities.

The overflowing energy and hard working qualities of the Martial personality usually ensure a successful career, whatever its nature. This is the case whether the career is in a large or small organisation or whether the person is self-employed.

The vital force of the Martial personality is usually matched by a burning ambition.

The Venusian hand, with its prominent Mount of Venus, indicates a cheerful and extrovert personality

The Hand of Mars reveals a particularly powerful thumb. Those who have this hand possess both martial virtues and vices

The eight-fold classification

Characteristic of the Hand of Jupiter are the particularly heavy third phalanges of the fingers. Those with this hand are notable for their even temperament and generosity

The temperament is a masterful one and with this is often associated a marked executive ability. This powerful combination is usually sufficient to overcome all the obstacles that block the path to success. Social prominence is often achieved, those who work with them looking up to and admiring Martial personalities, but this prominence is seen as a tribute to success and is not cared for as a thing in itself.

The negative side of the Martial hand is all its virtues carried to excess – courage, for example, becomes pig-headedness and even cruelty toward subordinates.

The impetuosity of Mars leads to strange domestic situations – setting up house with a totally unsuitable partner, for example, or a very early marriage. On the whole the possessor of the Martial hand tends to marry either his or her complete opposite, a shy, withdrawn personality with very little vital energy of their own; or their complement, a forceful, dominant, independent personality. Marriages of both types tend to be either very happy or very unhappy. The shy and withdrawn personality is either totally crushed by the energy of the partner and becomes frail, repressed or neurotic, or becomes imbued with some of the forcefulness of the partner and is transformed into a more balanced personality. In the second instance happiness results when the powerful wills and personalities of the partners are turned in the same direction, when they both have a common goal in life. If their energies are directed to different ends, however, if one's drive is being exerted in a direction opposed to or at a tangent to the burning drive and ambition of the other, only unhappiness can result. Such marriages result in a miserable existence in which each partner resents the other's ambitions – or in separation or divorce.

The major fault of the person with a Mars hand is that he or she tends to be always sure of the complete rightness of his or her actions and outlook on life, and thus somewhat quarrelsome and aggressive with those who have a different philosophy of life. If, however, the Martial personality can keep this tendency in check he or she will prove a thoroughly pleasant companion – although inclined to be the dominant partner in any personal relationship.

The Hand of Jupiter
The Jupiterian hand is notable for the large, heavy and thick third phalanges of the fingers. The hand is also thick and large but usually surprisingly soft, almost flabby.

The home environment is of great importance to the psychological make-up of those with the Jupiterian hand and will play an enormous part in shaping the character. Always provided that the home influences are beneficial, success in life is practically assured. Even if the home environment is unfavourable the natural good luck that goes with the Jupiterian hand may well lead

to meetings with elders which will influence life for the better.

The outstanding characteristics of the man or woman blessed with the Jupiterian hand are a calm and equable temperament, a generous nature and an honourable disposition. The importance which the Jupiterian attaches to a life lived on honourable principles is enhanced by a natural good-will towards others, a philosophical outlook on life, and tolerance and broad-mindedness in regard to the foibles of others. Accompanying all these favourable indications is an inborn optimism and the type of mind which can greatly benefit from any and every educational opportunity.

The Jupiterian has an innate capacity to inspire respect and co-operation in those he comes into contact with, whether in the home or in the course of his work or leisure activities. This is an important factor in ensuring success in life, as is the robust Jupiterian constitution.

Those with Jupiterian hands often have a certain financial ability and the Jupiterian is usually highly successful in occupations such as accountancy and management finance, where this quality is important. Marriage and other forms of partnership are likely to prove of great psychological importance to the Jupiterian. There is also a strong possibility of material advantage.

To sum up, the man or woman with the Jupiterian hand is 'born lucky'. Everything they do, however irrational it may seem to others, will turn out well in the end. Jupiterians are generous. Their generosity will be repaid a hundred-fold. They are responsible, and they will be given responsibilities which will improve their status. Their high principles will bring them fortune and success.

The only negative aspect of the Jupiterian traits is that success can come so young and so easily to them that they are sometimes led to despise others who find success harder to attain.

The Hand of Saturn

On the Saturnian hand the second finger – that is the finger of Saturn – is long and the other fingers bear inwards towards it. The Mount of Saturn is usually prominent and rayed with fine hair-lines. There is almost always a line running from the Life line across the hand and into or towards the Mount of Saturn.

The Saturnian hand indicates a patient, self-controlled and persistent personality. A self-confident psychology – and one that is usually justified by marked practical ability – and a penetrating, shrewd and 'canny' nature are other Saturnian characteristics.

This latter quality is well indicated by the Saturnian's financial ability and by his or her abilities to engage in successful speculation, particularly in mines, houses and land.

The Saturnian is usually healthy and the possession of a Saturnian hand is almost

always an indication of a long and happy life.

With the cautious nature that is the hallmark of the Saturnian, marriage is often delayed until late in life and the partner chosen is often older. Loyalty and a deep, though often unexpressed, affection characterise such a marriage and material benefits may result from it.

The owner of the Saturnian hand tends to be ambitious – not for prominence in the public eye, not for the limelight, but for solid and well-based success. This ambition, allied with the Saturnian's marked business capacity, often leads to the attainment of positions of great responsibility and prominence.

Along with all these virtues goes a serious mind with, in spite of every success achieved, a definite inclination towards pessimism. This can lead to a somewhat solitary life – those with Saturnian hands find it difficult to make friends, although

once made their friendships are likely to be lifelong and to survive through good or ill. If the gloomy cast of mind to which Saturnians are always prone is given full rein they can become solitary individuals, getting a despondent satisfaction out of an isolated and almost hermit-like existence.

The Hand of Earth

This is a thick firm hand with the lines of the palm well marked and deeply graven. The line of head usually terminates upon or very near the Mount of Mercury and the head and life lines are generally abnormally close together. The thumb is usually square.

The possessor of the Earth hand is slow but sure. In astro-palmistry the Earth hand correlates with the zodiacal sign of Taurus and some palmists and astrologers have even gone so far as to suggest that those with this hand formation have a 'bullish' look about them – thick-necked and with wide nostrils.

The Earth personality has a strong taste for the good things of life, tackling every task with zest and enjoying food, drink and the material things of existence to the full.

The man or woman with the Earth hand combines self-centredness with a generous nature, and with this psychological make-up is capable of becoming an excellent husband or wife, a devoted father or mother.

Where the career is concerned those with Earth hands tend to be capable of following most types of work, but they are particularly good at manual jobs, at engineering, at geology, at pottery and, indeed, at anything that brings them into contact with the earth.

There is, needless to say, a negative side to the Earth personality. Sometimes the Earth person is stolid to the point of insensitivity or stupidity and sometimes beneath the outward mask an explosion of passion is building up which, once released, is capable of sweeping all before it.

A particularly long Finger of Saturn characterises the Saturnian hand. Those with this hand are likely to be patient, persistent and shrewd

The Earth hand is thick and firm, denoting a personality that is slow but sure, generous and indulgent

7
Triangle and quadrangle

The Triangle of Mars

The Triangle of Mars, sometimes called the Great Triangle, is outlined by the Head, Health and Life lines. Should the Health line be missing from the particular hand which is being examined the palmist must draw an imaginary line in the mind's eye to take its place. Alternatively, if the Hand line has a Sun line but no Health line the Sun line can be taken as representing that side of the triangle.

This latter formation is an extremely powerful one and can be taken as a strong indication of the achievement of success in life. Curiously enough, however, the same formation is traditionally taken as a sign of intolerance – it would seem that those with the Sun line forming one of the sides of the Triangle of Mars are less broad-minded than those in whom the Health line serves the same function.

The Triangle of Mars must be considered: (a) by itself, as an independent entity on the hand; (b) in connection with its upper and two lower angles; and (c) in connection with the area of the palm enclosed by the triangle.

Considered by itself the triangle should be as large as possible and clearly formed by the lines of Head, Health and Life. Such a formation strongly indicates a wide-ranging, tolerant and generous psychology. Persons of this sort are peculiarly unselfish, always taking their own personal interests as being of lesser importance than the general interests of the group to which they belong.

If the Triangle of Mars is small in area and not clearly formed, the lines of Head, Health and Life short, poorly marked and wavy, the opposite is strongly indicated. Such persons will have narrow and intolerant viewpoints, meanness in both the spiritual and physical meanings of the term, and will always be extremely egotistical, putting their own interests in front of those of both the group to which they belong and humanity in general. People of this sort always take care publicly to go along with the majority, however wrong that majority may be and even if they secretly agree with the principles of the minority.

When the last mentioned formation is present, but the health line is replaced by

The Triangle of Mars, formed by the lines of Head, Health and Life

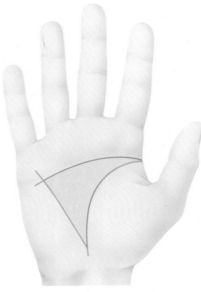

Alternatively (near right) the Triangle of Mars may be formed by the Sun, Head and Life Lines,denoting success in life. A small and poorly formed Triangle, on the other hand, indicates a narrow and egostistical personality (far right)

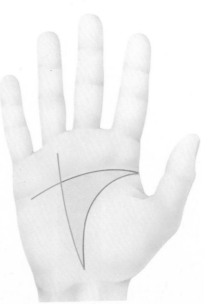

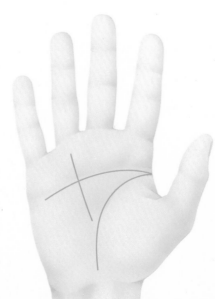

the Sun line, the individual concerned will have equally narrow, intolerant, egotistical, mean-spirited views. These will be combined, however, with a drive towards success and great firmness of purpose. This peculiar combination therefore indicates the possibility of marked success in a very limited sphere – finance or politics, for example.

The Upper Angle of the Triangle of Mars

This is formed by the junction of Life and Head lines. The angle should ideally be easy to see, well-pointed, and even. Such a formation indicates delicacy and clarity of mentality and thoughtfulness towards others.

When this upper angle tends towards the obtuse a commonsense psychology with very little emotional feeling is indicated. Such a person has little appreciation of the imaginative side of life and tends thoroughly to despise art, artists and those whose main pleasure in life comes from participation in, or observation of, the artistic aspects of human existence.

When the upper angle is extremely obtuse this denotes a character similar to the original John Bull so beloved of European satirists. Such a person will have a crude, blunt way of expressing himself or herself – sometimes verging on the coarse – which will probably give offence to others and create a great deal of unpopularity. A thoroughly impatient person is indicated, possessing all the negative and least likeable qualities of Mars; the man or woman will be aggressive and perpetually angry with what he or she considers the stupidity of others, will show little inclination to make a concerted application towards *anything* – from improving the home life to studying and trying to 'get on' in a career – and most of the time will be plunged into a thoroughly self-induced misery.

The Middle Angle of the Triangle of Mars

The 'middle' angle of the Martian triangle is formed by the junction, or near junction, of the Head and Health lines or the Head and Sun lines. When the middle angle is very acute it relates to a somewhat neurotic psychology and low physical and emotional vitality. Such a person often imagines that he or she is ill: this formation on the hand is often found in hypochondriacs.

When, on the contrary, the angle is somewhat or very obtuse, the person concerned tends to be slow in thought and lacking in perception. While the latter is undoubtedly a tendency which the person must guard against, deliberately making himself or herself as conscious as possible of the thoughts and emotions of others, the former is not necessarily an undesirable characteristic. For if the thought is slow, steady and thoroughly logical the person concerned tends to come up with the correct answer in the end and as a result the right course of action is eventually

A sharp angle between the lines of Life and Head, forming the upper angle of the Triangle of Mars, indicates delicacy and clarity of thought

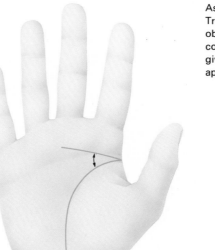

As the upper angle of the Triangle of Mars increases in obtusity, it indicates a bluff, commonsense personality, given to impatience with the apparent stupidity of others

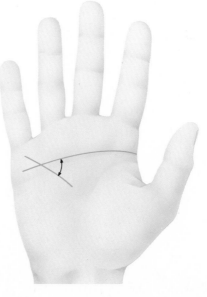

The angle between the lines of Head and Health is the middle angle of the Triangle of Mars. When it is acute it denotes a somewhat weak and neurotic personality

Triangle and quadrangle

When the middle angle of the Triangle of Mars is obtuse, it indicates a person who may be somewhat slow in thought and limited in perception

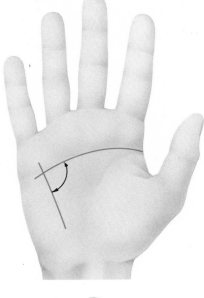

The lower angle of the Triangle of Mars is formed by the Line of Life and the Line of Health or of Sun. When it is acute it indicates a lack of all forms of vital energy

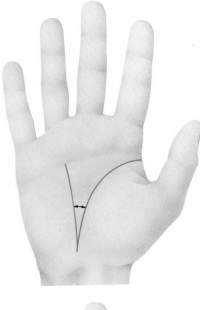

When the lower angle of the Triangle of Mars is obtuse it denote a powerful personality, generous and bursting with energy

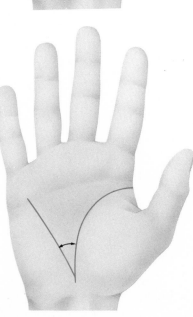

followed. The quick-witted person – the sort who shines in company – will have come up with his or her own answers long before the slow thinker, but the reaction of the mind is so fast that the wrong answer to a problem may have been given and an incorrect course of action already initiated.

The Lower Angle of the Triangle of Mars

This lower angle is formed by the junction, or near junction, of the Life and Health lines, or the Life and Sun lines. When the angle is somewhat acute – or worse, when it is very acute – and is formed by the Health line, not the Sun line, it indicates a lack of physical, emotional and spiritual energy.

Such people tend to find everything too much of an effort. They will commence a job – either a paid one or one in the home – or a course of academic or vocational training with real enthusiasm, but after a while the enthusiasm diminishes and then vanishes. What has been started is rarely finished.

If the angle formed is somewhat or very obtuse, a strong nature and a powerful psychology bursting with vitality is indicated. When such an angle is formed by the Sun line a particularly open-minded tolerant and generous personality with a great deal of vitality is indicated. As against this, if the Sun line is one of the lines forming an acute angle (see above), a narrow and intolerant mind is the most likely result.

The Quadrangle of the Palm

This is the roughly oblong space between the lines of the Heart and the Head. Some palmists of the present day attach little importance to this area but others, like their predecessors in the last and earlier centuries, affirm that it often provides useful hints about the character of the person whose palm is being examined.

Ideally the Quadrangle should be fairly wide at both ends and fairly even in shape so that its essential 'oblongness' is easily discerned. It should have a fairly smooth interior, not marked by the crossing of many fine lines: when such fine lines are found, incidentally, they usually arise from the lines which outline the Quadrangle, the Head and Heart lines.

Those who have this ideally formed Quadrangle are believed to have many virtues: calm, equable temperaments; the ability to take unbiased decisions on any matter which comes to their attention; marked intellectual ability and extreme loyalty both to friends and to people with whom there is a strong sexual or emotional attachment.

Such a Quadrangle will be fairly wide, – but it should not be *too* wide for in this case – besides the virtues mentioned above – the person concerned will be excessively broadminded. He or she will excuse and tolerate outrageous behaviour in others and will absolutely refuse to condemn the most

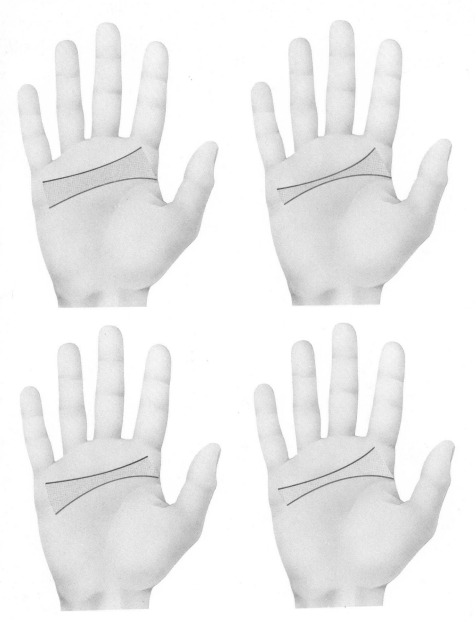

Ideally, the Quadrangle should be fairly wide at both ends and even in shape (far left). When it is quite wide at both ends but waisted in the middle (near left) it indicates a tendency to prejudice

When the Quadrangle is wide only at the end nearer the Mount of Mercury (far left) it denotes a person unconcerned with what others think; and conversely an excessive narrowness at this end indicates one who is over concerned about personal reputation. When the Quadrangle is noticeably wider at the end nearer the Finger of Saturn (near left) it indicates tolerance in the earlier years of life

unpleasant religious, political and philosophical outlooks, striving to be 'all things to all men'.

Such a person may also tend to think in a thoroughly disorganised and illogical way, will be attracted by almost any unconventional idea, and will be inclined to rashness in speech, speculation and action.

When the Quadrangle is reasonably broad at both ends but 'waisted' in the middle, an easily prejudiced mind likely to arrive at thoroughly unfair conclusions is indicated.

When the Quadrangle is wide at the end nearest the Mount of Mercury (i.e. the end nearest to the little finger) a personality who

is unconcerned about what others think of him or her is indicated. When, on the contrary, this end of the Quadrangle is extremely narrow a quite excessive concern about personal reputation and the thoughts and feelings of others concerning oneself is indicated.

When the Quadrangle is excessively wide at its end nearest the finger of Jupiter (i.e. the index finger) and very narrow at the

will be broad-minded and tolerant in the early years of life but which will become intolerant and very conventional in later years.

(Overleaf) Doctor Syntax and his man have their palms read by the gypsies. An illustration by Thomas Rowlandson for William Combe's *The Second Tour of Dr Syntax in Search of Consolation*, 1820

8
Star, cross, square and other signs

The star

The star is easy to recognize but difficult to describe. The best one can say is that it is a star-like formation, with five, six, seven or even more rays, which can be found anywhere on the palm, but usually on one of the Mounts. Traditional palmists attached great importance to it but, unfortunately, they could not agree on its significance. A minority considered it a sign of coming danger and crisis in relation to the particular aspects of life ruled by the Mount in question. Most of them, however, considered it a sign of exceptionally good fortune, and this is the position adopted by almost all contemporary palmists.

The Jupiterian Star

A star on the Mount of Jupiter has two meanings depending upon where the star is placed.

When the star is low down on the side of the Mount and faces the finger of Jupiter (that is, the first finger), an ambitious personality which will come into frequent contact with the famous is indicated. However, the person in question will not attain fame in his or her own right (unless this is indicated by other factors on the hand) but will merely reflect the fame and glory of others.

If the star is high up on the Mount of Jupiter, or on the side further away from the finger, it is not only a sign of great ambition but an indication that the man or woman concerned will acquire fame in his or her own right. This is particularly so when the lines of Head, Fate and Sun are strong and well marked. Such a combination is, in fact, one of the best that can be found on a palm and an almost infallible sign of success.

The Saturnian Star

At one time palmists looked upon the Saturnian star as a sign of some terrifying fate in store for the individual concerned. This is no longer the case. Modern palmists look upon it as a sign that the life will be distinguished and dramatic, not disastrous. Such a person will be ambitious and will gain fame and possibly fortune – but not to the same extent as those with the Jupiterian star.

The Solar Star

Like the Jupiterian star, the appearance of a star on the Mount of the Sun has two meanings.

When the Solar star is connected to the Sun line it implies that the person concerned will come to wide public attention through one of the arts. If, however, the star is fully on the Mount of the Sun the same thing is indicated, but not to so great an extent. However the fame will be accompanied by major financial success. If the star is placed very low on the Mount, near or on the finger of the Sun, the person concerned will have much contact with the rich and famous but will not necessarily share such fame and fortune.

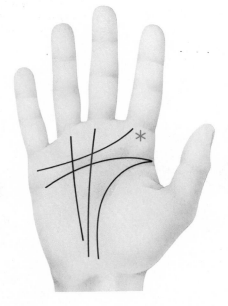 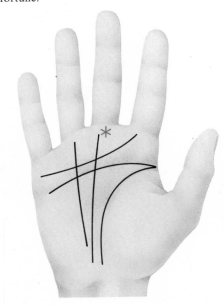

The Jupiterian Star (near right) is an ndication of fame according to the position in which it occurs; the Saturnian Star (far right) portends a dramatic life

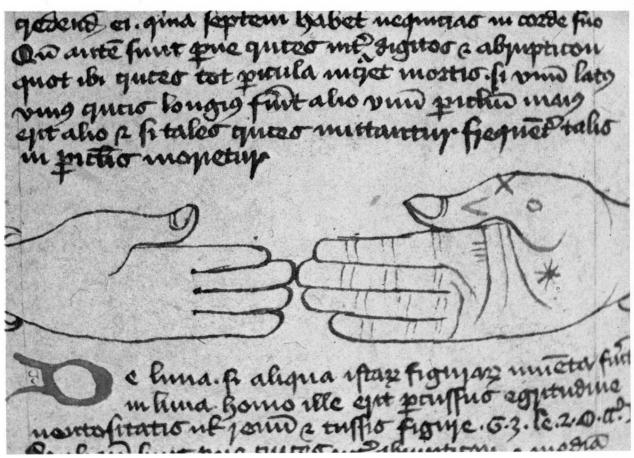

Star, circle and cross illustrated in a fifteenth century Bodleian Library manuscript

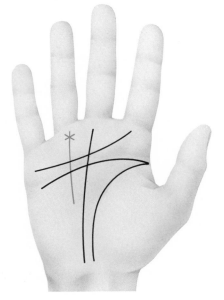

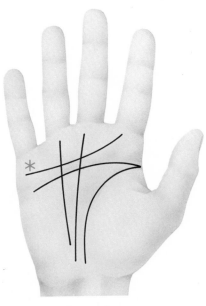

The Solar Star (far left), like the Jupiterian Star, has a significance dependent upon its position; the Mercurial Star (near left) indicates a brilliant career

The Mercurial Star
A star resting fully upon the Mount of Mercury indicates a brilliant career. Exactly in what field the subject's brilliance will show itself must be interpreted from the other factors present in the palm. It is most likely to occur, however, in some field connected with abstract learning, particularly in the physical sciences or in financial matters.

The Positive Martian Star
A star on the positive Mount of Mars – that is, the Mount *beneath* the Mount of Jupiter lying inside the Life line next to the Mount of Venus (see p. 56) – is taken as an indication of brilliant success in some martial activity. This need not be actual warfare – although such a star might be expected to be found on the hand of a brilliant military commander or a charismatic leader of men

233

Star, cross, square and other signs

The Positive Martian Star denotes success in a career under the astrological rulership of Mars

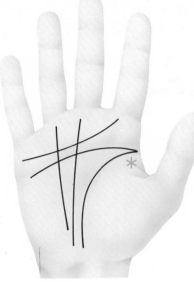

The Negative Martian Star suggests that success will come through patience and spiritual courage

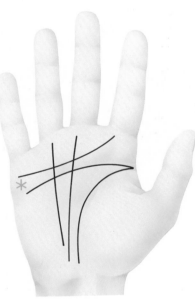

The Venusian Star (near right) is a sign of success in love or social life; the Lunar Star (far right) indicates success in matters concerned with the imagination

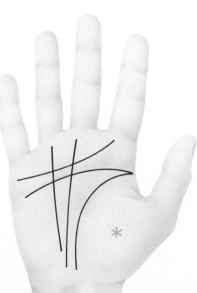
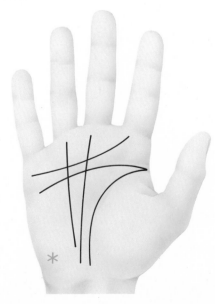

– but anything that falls under the astrological rulership of Mars; working in metal or organising great masses of men, for example.

The Negative Martian Star
A star on the negative Mount of Mars – that is, the Mount between the Mount of Mercury and the Mount of the Moon (see fig   ) – indicates that a brilliantly successful life will be attained through the 'passive' martial virtues of patience, moral courage, and sheer 'guts'.

The Venusian Star
The star on or towards the centre of the Mount of Venus is, like all the stars, an indication of brilliance and success. In this case, however, sex, love and human passion will play some part in the achievement of this success. It particularly indicates – and this applies whether the star is on hand of a man or a woman – a highly satisfactory love-life in which the opposition of any rival claimants to the loved one's affections will be easily overcome.

If the star lies low down on the Mount, or slightly off the Mount to one side or the other, it is an indication that the person concerned will come into much contact with those who themselves either achieve a brilliant career through the passions or are highly successful in their personal love-lives.

The Lunar Star
A star well placed upon the Mount of the Moon is a sign that success will be achieved in life through the use of the imagination, the power of lunar knowledge – that is, the instinctive knowledge which springs from the Unconscious – and those powerful qualities indicated by what those psychologically averse to them call 'dreaminess'. That is especially the case when the Head line ends well within the Mount of the Moon.

It is amusing to note that the palmists of the seventeenth and earlier centuries believed that a star on the Mount of the Moon indicated that the person concerned 'would meet his or her death by drowning'. It is unlikely that any reputable palmist of the present day would accept such an interpretation with all its implicit and explicit fatalism. The idea arose out of the astrological connection between the Moon and water and the astronomical relationship between the Moon and the ebb and flow of the tides.

The Star on the Tip of a Finger

This is traditionally taken to mean that anything 'touched' – that is, any project seriously undertaken – will be remarkably successful. In interpreting a star of this type (and the same holds true for all other varieties of stars), it must be remembered that the brilliance and success foreshadowed by the star in question will only be achieved if the other factors on the hand *indicate more favourable than unfavourable features*. If this is not indicated the star (or stars) can only be taken as mitigating in some measure the negative forces of an otherwise unfavourable hand.

The cross

The cross signifies absolutely the opposite of the star. The cross is always a sign of ill-fortune, thwarted hopes and troubles. As with the star, however, it must not be considered by the palmist in isolation but always in conjunction with the overall formation of the hand in general and the lines of the palm in particular. A favourable hand will mitigate or even totally cancel the unfavourable indications of the cross. Conversely, an unfavourable hand must be taken as strengthening the unfavourable characteristics that are generally indicated by a cross.

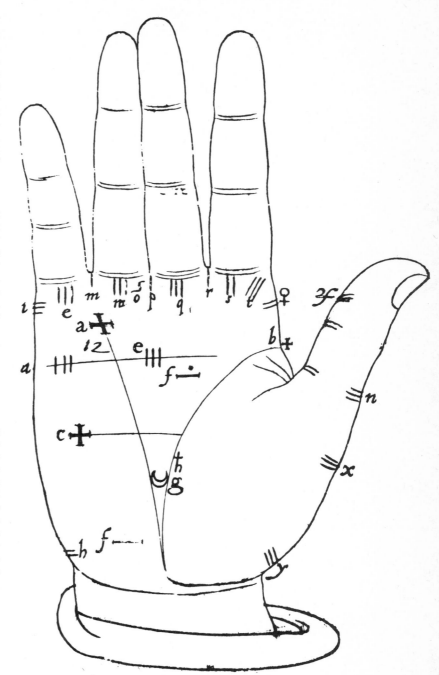

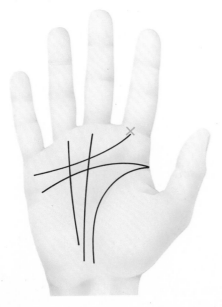

The Jupiterian Cross

In spite of its unfortunate general significance there is one position for a cross that is not only lacking in malign significance but is an indication of good fortune. This is when the cross is found on the Mount of Jupiter. In this position it prognosticates that at some time in the person's life a great and lasting affection will occur and that from this affection nothing but good will be derived. The significance and stength of the Jupiterian cross is greatly increased when the Fate line has its origin on, or from a position very near to, the Mount of the Moon.

Many palmists believe that the exact stage of life when the great affection will

The Solar and Lunar crosses, in an engraving from Robert Fludd's *History of Two Worlds*, 1617

The Jupiterian Cross is the one situation in which the cross is not a sign of ill-fortune. It indicates the occurrence of a great and lasting affection

Star, cross, square and other signs

The Saturnian Cross is a sign of a somewhat gloomy disposition and a tendency to withdraw from the world

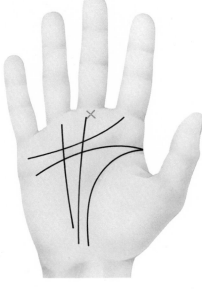

The Solar Cross indicates a lack of success in achieving one's ambitions in the arts

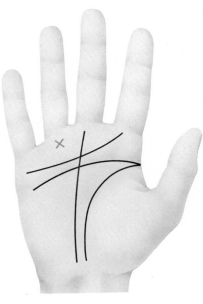

The Mercurial Cross denotes a lack of success in the sciences or in the world of communication

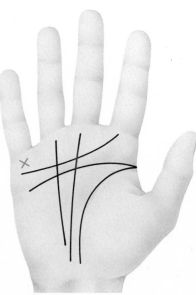

occur is foreshadowed by the position of the cross. When the cross is near the beginning of the Life line it will be in early life, when it is near the summit of the Mount it will be in middle life, and when it is on the base of the Mount near the finger of Jupiter it will be later – but these calculations can only be approximate.

The Saturnian Cross

A cross on the Mount of Saturn is an indication of a gloomy and depressive psychology which will frequently cause its possessor to withdraw from human contacts into silence and friendless isolation. Such a withdrawal from the rest of the world, such a self imposed denial of humanity's general need for friendship and love, will lead to disappointments and troubles.

When considering a Saturnian cross it must always be remembred, as with every other factor on the hand, that palmistry shows *tendencies*, not a fixed and unalterable fate. The palmist, then, who finds his subject with a Saturnian cross should explain to him or her the significance of that cross, point out the troubles that will follow if the indicated gloomy introspection is given free rein, and stress the importance of avoiding them by deliberately going out into the world, mixing with people and making friends. Similar considerations should be applied if any other form of cross is found in the subject's hand, as described in the paragraphs following.

The Solar Cross

This is an indication that success will be sought in fields connected with beauty and the arts but will prove totally impossible to achieve. The more the person concerned strives for the achievement of fame and financial success the worse will be the troubles and disappointments he or she undergoes.

The Mercurial Cross

The Mercurial Cross is another indication of failure, troubles and disappointments. These may come through an unsuccessful attempt to achieve success through the sciences or some other form of learning or, worse, 'sailing too near the wind' in an attempt to get easy financial success – something for nothing.

The Positive Martial Cross

This denotes a quarrelsome, violent and exceedingly choleric and argumentative individual who will experience many troubles arising out of his or her own aggressive psychology.

The Negative Martial Cross

A cross on the negative Mount of Mars is an indication of many troubles arising from the malignant and deliberate opposition of others.

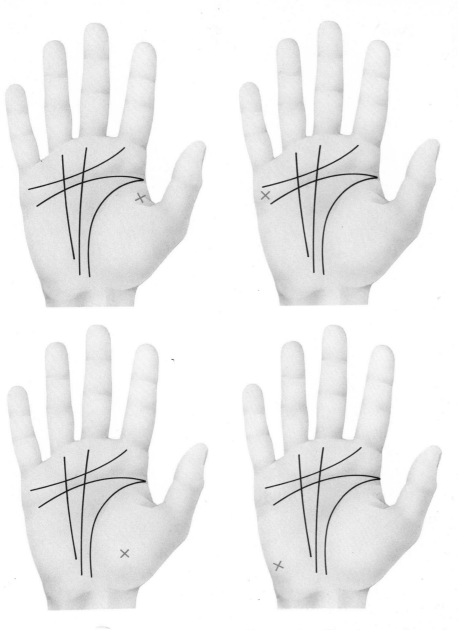

Both the Positive and Negative Martial Crosses (far and near left respectively) denote troubles arising from one's own behaviour or from the opposition of others

The Venusian Cross (far left) indicates troubles of an emotional nature; the Lunar Cross (near left) implies the possession of an over-active imagination

The Venusian Cross

A large and strongly marked cross on the Mount of Venus is an indication of troubles and difficulties arising out of that person's emotional feelings for another. Such troubles may come either from the miseries of unrequited love, from the opposition and rivalry of others, or from falling in love with a person who is either not free or quite unsuitable.

A smaller, less well-defined Venusian cross is held to refer to quarrels, difficulties and disappointments arising from a person's relationships with his close relatives.

The Lunar Cross

This is held to be the sign of an over-strong imagination. Such a person can find himself or herself lying to others for no good reason – lying for the sake of lying. Such persons not only deceive others but also themselves; they actually believe their own lies. Inevit-

ably enough reality, the true facts of a situation, eventually intrudes itself, the castles in the air dissolve into smoke and the usual troubles and difficulties follow.

The Cross on the Tip of a Finger

The person with this will tend to be always dabbling in things that do not really concern him or her, will be tempted to launch into new businesses while he or she is lacking in knowledge and experience and will be perpetually dropping one thing and starting another. If these tendencies are given free rein they will prove disastrous.

A cross on the tip of a finger indicates a tendency to dabble in all sorts of matters

Star, cross, square and other signs

A square on the Mount of Jupiter indicates the successful overcoming of danger resulting from too much ambition

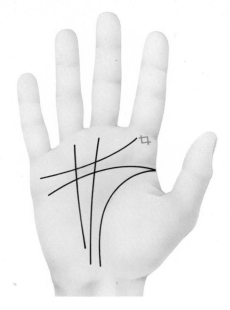

A square on the Mount of Saturn denotes the surmounting of tendencies to seek solitude

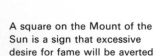

A square on the Mount of the Sun is a sign that excessive desire for fame will be averted

The square

The square was sometimes called 'the mark of preservation' by palmists of the last century, because it was and often still is believed to indicate danger, but danger overcome and turned to good opportunity.

The Jupiterian Square
A square on the Mount of Jupiter is a sign that dangers resulting from over-ambition, from an excessive lust for fame and/or riches, will be successfully overcome.

The Saturnian Square
A square on the Mount of Saturn indicates that difficulties arising from an over-introspective and solitude-seeking psychological make-up will be conquered.

The Solar Square
A square on the Mount of the Sun is a sign of danger arising from an excessive desire for fame or even notoriety. The dangers will be surmounted.

The Mercurial Square
A square on the Mount of Mercury is a sign of dangers arising from either the possession of too restless a temperament or too much concentration on some field of learning, probably concerned with one of the sciences. This square then, like other squares, indicates the sources of danger but makes it clear that the danger will be overcome.

The Martial Square
A square on either the negative of positive Mounts of Mars indicates that dangers arising from the opposition or ill temper of others will be triumphantly overcome.

The Venusian Square
A square on the Mount of Venus indicates that a danger in some way arising from the affections will be conquered.

The Lunar Square
A square on the Mount of the Moon indicates preservation from dangers resulting from an over-active imagination.

Squares are also of great significance when they are found on the major lines of the hand.

The Square on the Life Line
If there is a square on the Life line it is a sign that the person concerned will at some time of life be in danger of death but that the danger will pass and that the person will reach safety or be restored to health.

The Square on the Head Line
This is a signification that the individual will at some time be in danger on account of an over-emphasis on mental development or overwork which severely taxes the mind. The danger will, of course, as indicated by the square, be overcome.

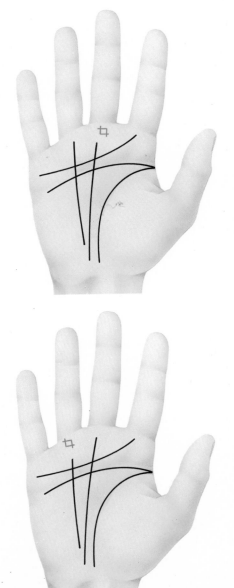

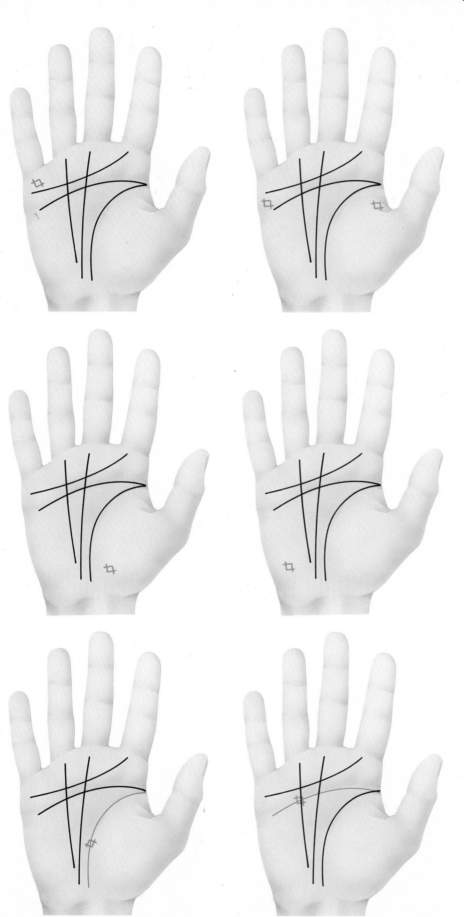

Squares on the Mount of Mars, negative or positive, mean the overcoming of ill-temper or malevolence

A square on the Mount of Venus (far left) indicates that troubles of the affections will be averted. On the Mount of the Moon (near left) a square denotes protection from the effects of an overactive imagination

A square on the Line of Life (far left) is a sign of deadly danger survived; a square on the Line of Head (near left) denotes mental dangers successfully averted

Star, cross, square and other signs

A square on the Line of Heart is a sign of emotional dangers overcome

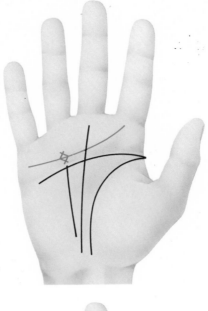

A square on the Girdle of Venus has a similar significance to a square on the Line of Heart

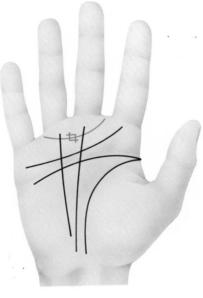

A square on the Line of Sun (near right) denotes the sweeping away of obstacles in the quest for fame. A square on the Line of Health (far right) indicates complete recovery from sickness

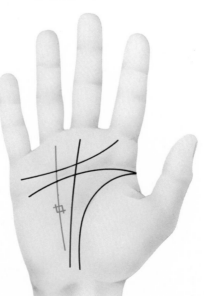
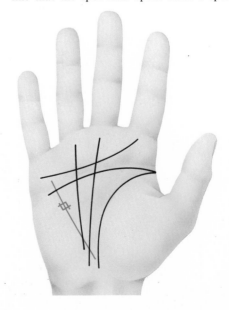

The Square on the Heart Line
This indicates troubles and dangers, both successfully surmounted, which arise out of the emotional life of the individual concerned.

The Square on the Girdle of Venus
This has a similar significance to a square on the Heart line.

The Square on the Sun Line
This indicates that the person concerned will meet with difficulties and obstacles in his or her search for fame. Eventually these obstacles will be swept away, these difficulties overcome.

The Square on the Health Line
The person concerned will pass through a period of ill health but his or her vital energies will ultimately be completely restored.

The Square on the Fate Line
The persons who have this unusual formation will find their 'drives' in desired directions obstructed through no fault of their own. Eventually such obstructions will be pushed aside and those who have been hampered by them will once again be able to go forward in life.

Islands, circles and spots

Islands, circles and spots are not usually fortunate signs; they are not regarded as being of great importance by many palmists of the present day. However for the sake of completeness and for those who wish to be acquainted with traditional palmistry in its entirety their supposed significance is given below.

A spot is held to be a sign of temporary ill-health. The exact nature of the illness concerned is sometimes indicated by the line that the spot falls upon. Thus a spot

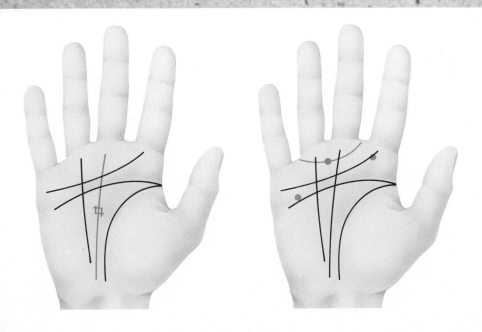

Circles on the wrists, and a Solar Cross, in another illustration from a fifteenth century manuscript in the Bodleian Library, Oxford

A square on the Line of Fate (far left) is a sign of outside obstructions eventually overcome. Spots (near left) are taken as signs of temporary ill-health

Star, cross, square and other signs

A circle on the Line of Heart or on the Mount of Venus signifies a lack of achievement in emotional matters

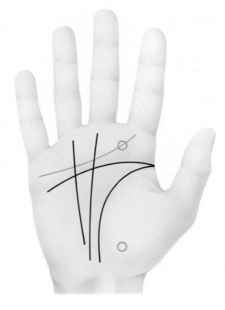

A circle on the Mount of the Moon indicates lack of success in any field involving the imagination

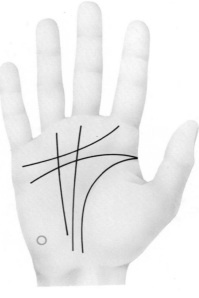

A circle on either Mount of Mars indicates lack of success in any of the careers supposed to be ruled by Mars

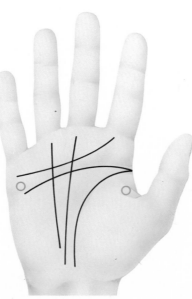

on the Head line would indicate either some psychological illness or, a more direct interpretation, some physical injury to the head. Similarly a spot on the Heart line or on the Girdle of Venus would indicate a period of emotional unbalance.

Importance is also sometimes attached to the colour of the spot. Thus a bright red spot is taken to indicate some feverish illness unless it is on the Head line, in which case it may either represent some form of delirium or psychological illness characterised by over-excitement or even mania. A blue, black, or blue-black spot supposedly indicates psychological illnesses ranging from mild neurosis to raging schizoprenia.

Readers should not be too worried if they find such spots on their own hands. Many palmists find them totally unreliable as a guide to the state of health and there are many people walking around with blackish spots on their palm who have never exhibited the slightest trace of mental illness.

A circle is usually held to indicate a notable lack of success in the particular field of activity ruled by the specific part of the hand on which it is found. Thus a circle on the Heart line or on the Mount of Venus would indicate a lack of achievement in the emotional life of the person concerned. Similarly, a circle on the Mount of the Moon would mean a lack of success in any field involving the imagination while a circle on either the positive or negative Mount of Mars would indicate that the person concerned would be unwise to try and make a career in soldiering, metal-working or any other field ruled by Mars. It would be tedious to continue to outline the significance of the circle on every specific line or Mount and, by this stage, readers should be able to work out such significations by themselves. However, it should be mentioned that there is one position in which a circle is not considered an unfortunate sign; that is when it is found on the Mount of the Sun, in which case it is believed to indicate outstanding success.

The island is also unfortunate in its signification; in this case it is believed to often appertain to genetic weakness, some undesirable feature which the person concerned inherited from his forebears. An island on the Head line, for example, is believed to indicate some inherited mental trouble or even inherited physical malformation of the head. In much the same way an island on the Heart line would be supposed to indicate an inherited emotional imbalance and an island on the Health line some inherited physical weakness.

Even when it does not refer to poor heredity the island is given gloomy significance by traditional palmistry. On the Life line it signifies a period of illness, more or less prolonged; on the Fate line heavy financial losses; and on the Sun line a loss of position and/or influence as a result of scandal. Any island on any of the Mounts is an indication of trouble:

On the Mount of Jupiter it shows a weakness of ambition.

On the Mount of Saturn it is a sign of general ill-luck.

On the Mount of the Sun it strangles any artistic impulses.

On the Mount of Mercury it indicates either restlessness or dishonesty.

On the positive Mount of Mars it indicates physical cowardice.

On the negative Mount of Mars it indicates moral cowardice.

On the Mount of the Moon it indicates a lack of imagination.

On the Mount of Venus it indicates a weakness and inconstancy in emotional life.

In short, the island is one of the gloomiest portents to be found upon the palm: fortunately, as previously indicated, most modern palmists take neither it, the circle nor the spot, as having a great deal of importance. So there is no need for despondency if you find one or other – or even all three – of these signs in your own palm or that of a friend.

Other minor signs sometimes found on the hand include the grill, the triangle and the mystic cross.

The grill is found quite often on a palm, almost invariably on one or other of the Mounts. Its significance, according to which Mount it is found upon, is as follows:

A grill on the Mount of Jupiter indicates over-ambition and egotism.

A grill on the Mount of Saturn indicates a solitary and gloomy personality.

A grill on the Mount of the Sun indicates a vain and limelight-seeking personality.

A grill on the Mount of Mercury indicates instability or even dishonesty.

A grill on the Mount of Moon indicates a bad tempered desire to dominate others.

A grill on the Mount of Venus indicates whose affections rarely stay fixed.

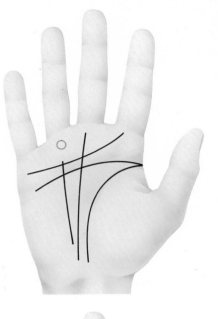

A circle on the Mount of the Sun has a very different significance from a circle in any other position, since it signals outstanding success

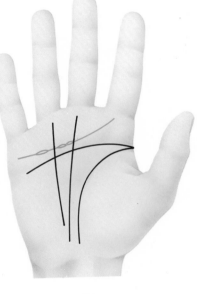

An islanded Line of Heart denotes an inherent emotional imbalance

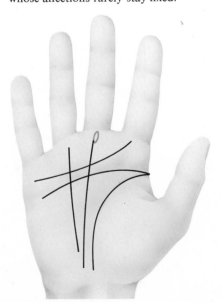

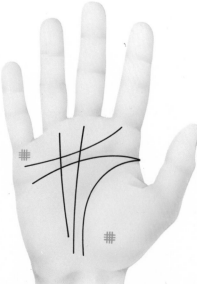

An island on the Mount of Saturn (far left) is a sign of general bad luck. A grill (near left), whatever position it appears in, is also a sign of marked faults of character

Star, cross, square and other signs

A triangle on the Mount of
Jupiter indicates a powerful
personality

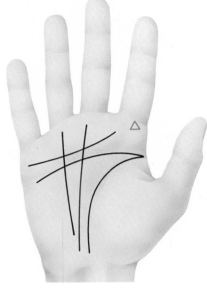

A triangle on the Mount of
Saturn has a special
significance in occult matters

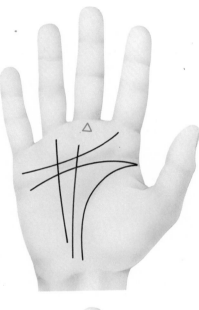

A triangle on the Mount of the
Sun is a sign of great aptitude
in the arts, particularly in
sculpture

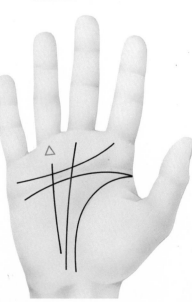

The triangle, a formation which, when encountered, is usually upon one or more of the Mounts, has an altogether happier significance than the grill. Its traditional meanings are as follows.

On the Mount of Jupiter it indicates a strong and forceful personality with a considerable talent for managing others and great ability as an organiser of all sorts of events.

On the Mount of Saturn it has an occult and mystical significance. Those with a triangle on this Mount tend to be occultists – or at least to have a great interest in the occult – and an ability to engage in the practical aspects of occultism, from divination and fortune-telling to alchemy and ritual magic. This sign was found on the Mount of Saturn of several well-known modern occultists, among them the theosophist Madame Blavatsky and the black magician Aleister Crowley.

On the Mount of the Sun the triangle indicates that the person who bears it will have great aptitude for the arts, particularly the plastic arts such as sculpture. The triangle, if the hand is otherwise favourable to an artistic career, indicates that the devotion to the arts will result in real success and that, in spite of this success, the artist concerned will remain modest, likeable and totally lacking in the peculiar arrogance that sometimes accompanies artistic eminence.

A triangle on the Mount of Mercury is a sure indication of financial success, such success frequently coming through devotion to some branch of learning, notably the sciences and literature, or one of the media of communication.

On either of the Mounts of Mars a triangle denotes courage, calmness under stressful situations and general cool-headedness. It is also a sure indication of success if the career chosen is soldiering or lies in some some other fields pertaining to the rulership of Mars.

A triangle on the Mount of the Moon indicates a personality which will achieve success through the controlled use of the imagination. Such a person might well be an imaginative writer – perhaps of science-fiction or that type of fantasy known as 'sword and scorcery'.

On the Mount of Venus the triangle denotes a happy emotional life.

Similar in significance to the triangle, but even more powerful in their effects, are the tripod and the spear head, illustrated in the diagram on the facing page.

The mystic cross is found somewhere in the quadrangle. It is a sign which shows a particular aptitude for, and interest in, the occult and the mystical. When it touches or is partly formed by the Line of Fate or a branch of that line, it is a sign that the life of the individual concerned could with advantage be devoted to the occult and the mystical.

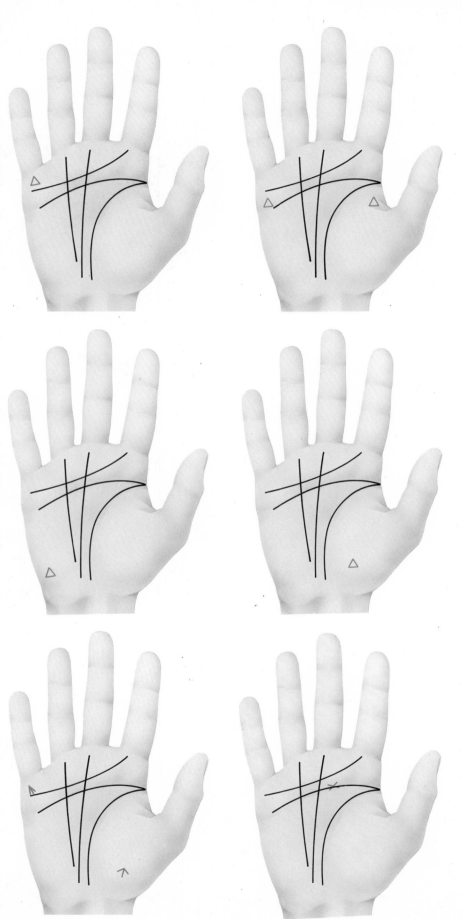

A triangle on the Mount of Mercury denotes financial success (far left). On either Mount of Mars (near left) a triangle signifies courage and calmness

A triangle on the Mount of the Moon (far left) suggests success in a career of imaginative writing; and one on the Mount of Venus (near left) means a happy emotional life

(Far left) The tripod and the spearhead, both signs even more powerful in their significance than the triangle. (Near left) The Mystic Cross

9
Taking palm prints

By this time readers of this book should be well qualified to read their own hands or those of friends and acquaintances. When doing so, ensure that plenty of light falls on the hand that is being examined: the ideal time of day for this is fairly early in the morning. This is not because of any special quality in the light of early day – indeed, strong artificial light is excellent for reading palms – but because the lines of the hand often appear more clearly, highlighted against the rest of the palm, in the earlier part of the day.

In many ways, however, it is easier to read palms from an imprint than directly from the hand itself; this is partly because it does not matter at what time of day the print is taken and partly because the sharp dark/light contrast of a palm print clearly show the finer lines which might be completely missed on an examination of a palm without such aid. Another advantage of palm prints is that they provide a permanent record of the hands at a particular moment in time; months or even years later, at the time of another examination of the hands, the changes and developments that may have taken place in the intervening period can be easily discerned. This is a matter of some importance, for most palmists believe that changes in the formations of the lines on the palm are outward reflections of inner changes. As a person develops the mind and soul he or she was born with, as the individual psychology is transformed or matures, as a person uses his or her free will to alter the life-style, so these alterations will be reflected in the 'psychic mirrors' of the hands.

Quite apart from this, anyone who has his or her hand read is almost always delighted to be asked to make two sets of palm prints – one for the palmist's records, another to take home, keep, and perhaps endeavour to interpret with the aid of a popular book on palmistry.

It is worth noting, as a peculiarity of the human psyche, that most people first react to the sight of their own palm prints very much as they do to first hearing their own voices on a tape recorder; just as in the latter case they usually say something of the nature of 'Do I *really* sound like that?' so, on seeing their palm prints for the first time they say 'Do my hands *really* look like that?'.

All that is needed to make palm prints are tubes of fingerprint ink, a roller, preferably large enough to ink a hand with one roll – one does not want to waste more time on the messy business of applying ink to the hand that one absolutely has to – and a supply of large-size fairly glossy paper. In

Britain the fingerprint ink and the roller can be bought from almost any shop dealing in artists' materials (the various branches of Reeves for example) and size A4 typing paper is ideal for making the prints upon.

Your only further requirement is something to squeeze the finger paint onto; a largish pane of old glass, an old plate or even an artist's palette are all ideal for this purpose.

Squeeze the paint out on to whatever 'palette' you are using, rub the roller back and forward over it until it is entirely, but lightly, covered with ink. While you are doing this get your subject to remove any objects from the hands and wrists which may interfere with the print – bracelets, watches, rings etc. – and to roll back the sleeves from the wrists.

Roll the ink-charged roller over the fingers and palm of your subject and far enough over the wrists for the print to include the bracelets. Place the inked hand, *as near flat as is possible*, upon a sheet of paper placed on a table or other firm support, and gently press down the entire hand, avoiding moving it sideways so that no smudging may result.

If the imprint is too faint repeat the process using a little more ink: if the imprint is too black and has obscured one or more of the

dust off the surplus powder, apply ink in the usual way and take your impression. This will almost invariably give a satisfactory result but if it doesn't it is better to do your reading from the subject's hands rather than make continual fruitless and embarras-

lines use less ink. It is best, in fact, to experiment with your own hands before you go on to those of other people: in this way you will quickly acquire the knack of always applying exactly the right amount of ink to get a clear, unsmudged and readable palm print.

The only exceptions to this are (a) when the subject whose print is desired has an excessively dry skin and (b) when the subject has an unusually hollow palm or a particularly large Mount of Venus.

In the former case the prints tend to be spotted – the ink clings to the driest part of the hand leaving irregular blank islands on the print. In the latter case the result is even worse, for there is apt to be an enormous blank area in the middle of the hand.

When the trouble is spotting the matter is easily adjusted. Get your subject to wash his or her hands with soapy and hot water, then dust the entire area of the hands with talcum powder or the sort of powder especially made for after-bath use on babies,

sing attempts to get a satisfactory print.

If the trouble is of the second type – that is, if a blank space appears in the middle of the palm because of excessive hollowness or an exceptionally well developed Mount of Venus – there are two ways of solving the problem.

The first is for the subject to place his or her hand on the glossy paper in the usual way and then for him or her to press the other hand down on the back of the hand from which the imprint is being taken with as much force as possible. It is preferable for the subjects to do this for themselves rather than for you to do it for them because the process can inflict a fair amount of pain if a heavy pressure is applied; your 'victims' know exactly how much pain they can stand, and you don't!

If this still doesn't work there is another process which some palmists find gives them the clear print they desire.

Get the subject, as before, to put his inked hand on the paper and to press down on the

In 1530, Henry VIII issued a decree against 'an outlandish people calling themselves Egyptians . . . who have come into this realm, and gone from shire to shire in great companies, and used great subtle and crafty means to deceive people, bearing them in hand that they, by palmistry, could tell men's and women's fortune, and so many times, by craft and sublety, have deceived the people of their money and have also committed many heinous crimes and robberies.' Despite continuing harassment, however, gypsies have continued to ply their trade, as shown in this seventeenth century painting

Taking palm prints

back of the hand with the other hand. Then slip *your* hand between the paper and the firm surface on which the paper is laid. This involves the co-operation of your subject in reducing the downward pressure on the hand, so be sure to explain to him or her exactly what you are trying to do. When your fingers have slipped under the hand to the middle of the palm gently press the paper up into the hollow of the hand, smoothing it into place with your fingertips. Remove the subject's hand from the paper and a perfect print should have been produced. It is worth adding, however, that (a) some palmists are unable to get good results by this method and that (b) the hollowness of some hands is of such depth that the print produced is distorted or smudged in such a way that it is impossible to discern it accurately enough to make a satisfactory reading. In either of these cases the only way out is to read directly from the palm in the traditional way.

If you are requested to take palm prints and make readings from them at an unexpected time, when you are far away from your apparatus of fingerprint ink and roller, a perfectly satisfactory print can be obtained by coating the hand either with theatrical grease-paint, or, usually more readily available, with lipstick, and pressing the hands downwards on pieces of paper in the usual way. The same procedure can be followed of course with your own hands, and indeed it is a great help in studying.

An alternative method is to make use of photographic paper, or any document copying paper that makes use of a liquid developer. The subject's hand is moistened all over with the developer, in the same way in which it would be inked, by means of a pad soaked in the liquid. The hand is then pressed down on to the paper. A darkroom is not necessary, since the paper must be exposed to light– as the image develops on the paper its intensity can be inspected and it can be 'fixed' in the usual way as soon as sufficient detail shows up.

An old gypsy reads a fashionable young man's hand: an illustration to *Les Devineresses*, one of the fables of La Fontaine, 1775

10
Travel, money and accidents

Travel and Long Journeys
Are there any indications of travels and long journeys to be found in the hands of people destined to undergo long journeys? The traditions of palmistry answer with an unequivocal 'yes'.

There are three sharply differentiated indications of these:

(1) From heavy lines on the face of the Mount of the Moon.

(2) From little fine lines leaving the Life line but travelling on with it.

(3) From a division in the Life line, one branch going towards the Mount of Venus, the other towards the Mount of the Moon. This indicates some great change in the subject's way of life and one such change can be emigration from one country to another – perhaps the greatest change any man or woman can make.

The changes indicated by (2) above – that is by fine lines leaving the Life line but following approximately the same course – are of a larger nature than those indicated by heavy lines on the Mount of the Moon, so they stand for major travels. The lines on the Mount of the Moon indicate shorter journeys, but if there are heavy lines running from the Bracelets into the Mount of the Moon longer journeys are indicated. When there are marked changes in the Fate line at a point paralleling the lines from the Bracelets, it is an indication that the journeys shown will lead to pronounced changes in the subject's personal destiny. When, however, the Fate line does not change at these points it is a sign that the journeys indicated will lead to no major changes in the way of life. If the travel line from the Bracelet ends in a small cross it is a sign that the journey in question will end somewhat disappointingly. If it ends in a square it signifies that some danger, from which the subject will escape unscathed, will be encountered during the course of the journey, while if the line ends in an island it is traditionally taken as an indication that the journey will result in some loss, probably financial in nature.

On those rare occasions when a travel line traverses the entire palm and ends on the Mount of Jupiter it is a signification that the journey will be a productive one resulting in great good fortune for the subject. Exactly the opposite can be expected when the travel line in question ends up on the Mount of Saturn. Similar 'mount rulings' indicate the nature of any travel line con-cluding on a particular mount. So a travel line concluding on the Mount of the Sun promises wealth and, even fame achieved through a journey, while one ending on the Mount of Mercury promises a surprising piece of good fortune attained through a journey.

When the heavy travel lines on the Mount of the Moon go on further than the Mount and encounter the Fate line, major journeys of great personal importance are indicated. This is particularly the case when these

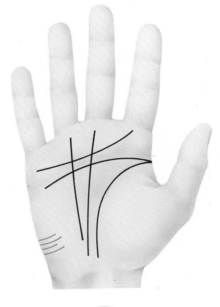

Heavy lines on the Mount of the Moon are an indication of short journeys, unless they run into the Mount of the Moon from the Bracelets

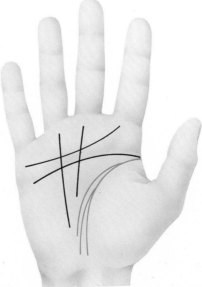

Fine lines leaving the Line of Life but travelling on with it generally denote major travels

Travel, money and accidents

A division in the Line of Life, one branch going towards the Mount of Venus, the other towards the Mount of the Moon, indicates a great change in life, and may mean emigration from one country to another

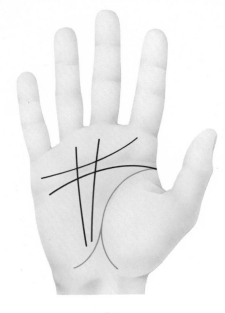

A line running from the Mount of Venus towards the Mount of Jupiter is a sign of good fortune in money matters

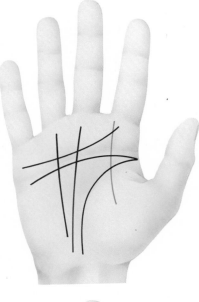

A line running from the Mount of Venus towards the Mount of Saturn is believed to be the sign of money from an inheritance

these travel lines come to an end by actually joining the Fate line; in this case they denote great benefits to be derived from travel.

Any square on a travel line is a sign of danger – but danger that will be successfully overcome (remember the general significance of a square as a sign of protection). Another type of danger is indicated when a travel line runs into the Head line; this foretells that the journey in question may lead to some psychological difficulty, probably temporary in nature.

Money

Money is the thing asked about most frequently by the clients of a palmist, be he or she an amateur or a professional. As we have seen when dealing with the general shape of the hand, the Mounts, the lines and other markings on the palm, there are all sorts of considerations affecting a subject's probability of attaining financial good fortune or the reverse. Sometimes, however, fairly quick answers to this question can be arrived at by a detailed consideration of the Mount of Venus.

A line running from the Mount of Venus toward the Mount of Jupiter and ending on or near the latter Mount is a sign of great good fortune in money matters. If such a line ends in a star this good fortune will be greatly increased.

A line running from the Mount of Venus toward the Mount of Saturn. If, however, near or actually upon Saturn is also a fortunate sign. In this case it is probable that the money concerned will either be obtained as the result of an inheritance or through the favourable actions of older relatives or friends.

If a line from the Mount of Venus connects up with and then travels along with the Sun line the indications are very much the same as in the case of a line travelling towards the Mount of Saturn. If, however, the line after touching the Sun line continues in its own way – that is, it cuts the Sun line into two – exactly the opposite is indicated: older relatives and friends will take actions liable to result in financial misfortune for the subject. The meaning of a line from the Mount of Venus cutting through the Fate and Life lines is somewhat similar.

A money line running from the Mount of Venus to the Mount of Mercury is an indication of financial success probably arising from devotion to some branch of learning, from financial business in the narrower sense of the term or from the study of books. It is also a sign that the activities of friends and relatives may result in good fortune.

Accidents

The traditions of palmistry assert that both past and coming accidents are shown in a trace upon the palm. There are several indications of these.

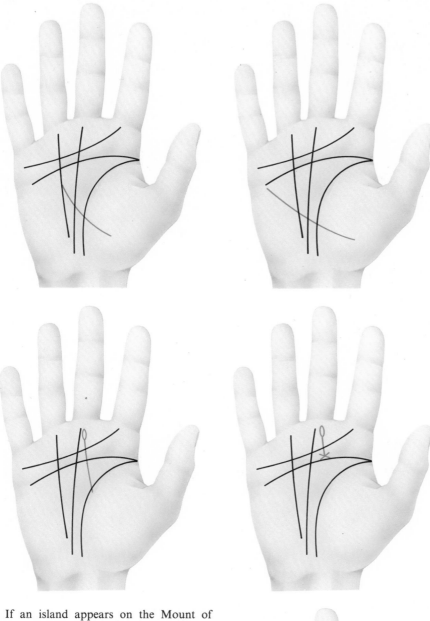

A line from the Mount of Venus that connects up with the Line of the Sun (far left) is also an indication of money by inheritance; but if it cuts the Sun line in two (near left) it means financial loss as the result of the actions of older relatives

An indication of serious danger from an accident is an island on the Mount of Saturn joined by a line to the Line of Life (far left). If the line ends in a small cross (near left) it means an accident nearby in which one is not hurt

If an island appears on the Mount of Saturn and from this island a line extends up the palm sufficiently far to join the Life line some serious danger has or will be undergone; for an approximation of the stage of life at which such an accident can be expected see the next section, *Time*.

When a line from an island on the Mount of Saturn ends in a small cross, either joined to the line or separated from it by a very small space, it foretells a serious accident taking place near the subject from which he or she escapes injury. When this line commences not on the Mount of Saturn but from its base it is traditionally believed that the accident in question has been caused by or connected with (or will be caused by or connected with) an animal or animals.

Any straight line from the Mount of Saturn to the Life line is indicative of an accident of some sort but it is most unlikely to be a serious accident unless the line

When the line begins from the base of the Mount of Saturn, it is believed that the accident will involve some animal

251

Travel, money and accidents

Any line from the Mount of Saturn is taken to represent an accident of some kind

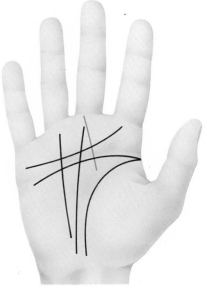

begins as an island on the Mount of Saturn.

Psychological accidents – that is both accidents which lead to some form of mental shock and those which originate in accident-proneness or other psychological difficulty – pertain to the Head line.

A line from an island on the Mount of Saturn which cuts the Head line indicates a serious shock to the mind or a serious accident resulting from psychological causes. When such a line ends in a cross it is a sign that the same accident will occur but that the subject will escape damage from it. Similarly a line from the Mount of Saturn cutting the Head line but not commencing on an island denotes a minor psychological shock or accident resulting from psychological causes.

Finally, in connection with accidents, it must be pointed out that many modern palmists do not agree that accidents are indicated in the palm and attach no im-

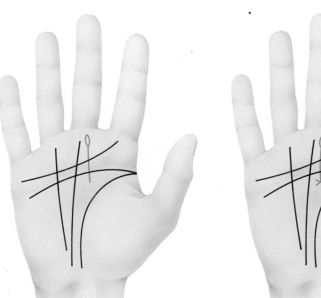

When a line from an island on the Mount of Saturn cuts the Line of Head it is a sign of severe shock (near right); but if it ends in a cross (far right) the subject will escape injury

Lines ending in a cross on the palms of both hands: an illustration from one of the earliest manuscripts on palmistry in the Bodleian Library

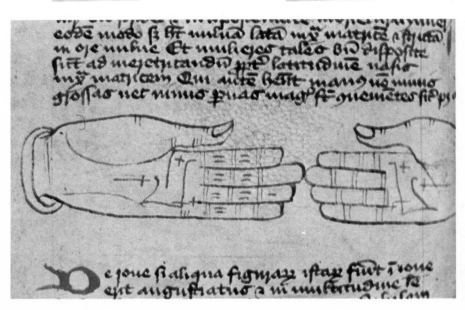

portance to lines from the Mount of Saturn – so there is no need to worry too much if you find such lines on your own hand.

Time

It must first be said that quite a few modern palmists deny that anything but very rough estimates of the time of a particular event can be read from the palm. They say, for example, that if a cross is on the first part of the Life line it indicates an event in early life, if on the middle part of the same line, an event in middle age, and so on. Other palmists, however, think that events past or future can be dated within a year or two of them actually happening. In spite of this insistence on the possibility of time-accuracy it has to be admitted that there is more than one method of computing time and that these methods often give widely differing results.

Two methods of time measurement are commonly in use. The first, used by Cheiro and his disciples past and present, is ultimately based on the supposed occult properties of the number seven. Devotees of this system refer to the 'law of seven' and point out how often the number appears in connection with matters occult and religious; they point, for example, to the seven Churches of the *Book of Revelation,* to the seven major deities of classical religion, the Seven Hells of the qabala, the seven days of the week and the seven visible colours of the spectrum.

This sevenfold system for arriving at a date can be applied to any line on the hand but it is most usually applied to the lines of Fate and Life. It will be seen from the diagram how this system works in practice for these lines; it can be easily adapted, of course, for other lines – the Sun line and the Heart line are the most notable of these.

The other system in common use is sixfold and was originated by the palmist Desbarolles. Its application to the Life line can be seen in the diagram; it can be easily adapted, as will be apparent, to any other line on the hand.

The present day palmist Jo Richardson uses this latter system and has given a most useful and informative description of how she applies it in practice.

Briefly, she uses a length of coarse white cotton thread to measure the Life line from the edge of the hand to its other end on the Bracelets; even if the Life line ends before the Bracelets the curve is carried on to a point where it would have met the Bracelet had it been long enough. The measured length of thread is then cut off with a pair of scissors.

The thread is then folded in two and a mark made at the half-way point. This point is taken as representing the thirtieth year of life and the ends of the thread as representing, respectively, the subject's birth and his or her seventieth birthday. The first half of the thread, representing the first thirty years of life, is marked off into five

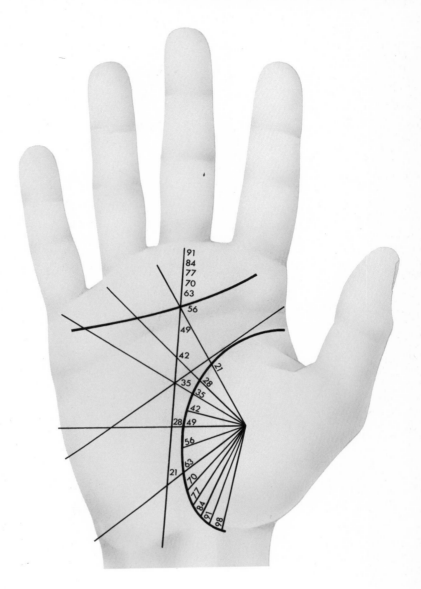

The sevenfold system of Cheiro for arriving at dates by means of the subdivision of the different parts of the palm. This method is usually applied to the Line of Fate, as in the diagram above, but is equally applicable to the Line of the Sun and the Line of the Heart, as shown in the diagram at the left

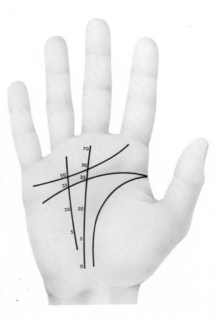

Travel, money and accidents

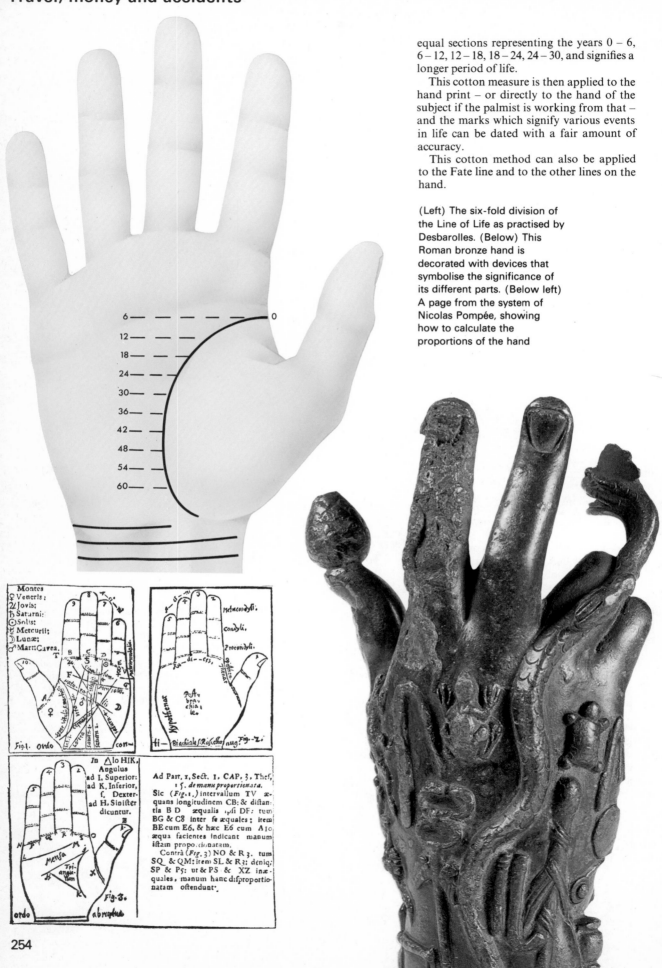

equal sections representing the years 0 – 6, 6 – 12, 12 – 18, 18 – 24, 24 – 30, and signifies a longer period of life.

This cotton measure is then applied to the hand print – or directly to the hand of the subject if the palmist is working from that – and the marks which signify various events in life can be dated with a fair amount of accuracy.

This cotton method can also be applied to the Fate line and to the other lines on the hand.

(Left) The six-fold division of the Line of Life as practised by Desbarolles. (Below) This Roman bronze hand is decorated with devices that symbolise the significance of its different parts. (Below left) A page from the system of Nicolas Pompée, showing how to calculate the proportions of the hand

11
Some case studies

Example 1

By the elemental classification of hands (see Chapter 2) this is a fine example of the type of hand attributed to Water. It is an exceptionally delicate and fine hand, and both the palm and the fingers are notable for their length and for their comparative narrowness. The fine mesh of lines which covers the entire hand should be noted; these are extremely characteristic of the Water hand.

One would expect a person with a hand such as this to be extremely sensitive and subject to rapid changes of mood, to be somewhat inconstant in both ideas and modes of behaviour and to be apt to reflect – always a quality of Water – the moods and behaviour of those with whom they come into contact. It is above all a female hand (and it is actually the hand of a woman), but one would expect a man with a similar hand to have a number of characteristics normally considered 'female', notably the quality of receptivity.

Such an analysis is supported by classifying the hand by the eight-fold planetary method dealt with in Chapter 6 of this book. By this mode of classification the hand comes nearest to the Venusian; that is, the Mount of Venus is prominent, it is covered with 'rays' – fine hair-lines – while the Fate line sends out branches into the Mount of Venus. It should also be noted that, in comparison to the rest of the hand, the thumb is somewhat short and thick, a characteristic Venusian formation.

The palmist would expect such a hand to indicate an exceptionally feminine person, who would vary from one extreme to the other, would have a number of romantic attachments, would dabble in the arts, and would have a marriage either notably successful or, if it went wrong, absolutely disastrous.

It will be noticed by the reader that the analysis of the hand by the eight-fold system produced nothing contradictory to the analysis of that same hand by the four-fold Elemental system. If anything the two analyses complement and strengthen one another. It is thus apparent that these modes of classification – and the same goes for other systems – are not so much rivals as brothers, supporting one another and throwing fresh light on the same problems.

Do the lines of the hand tend to support the conclusions drawn from the general shape of the hand? Unquestionably they do.

The position of the Sun line is interesting. This commences – as far as one can trace a commencement in such a mesh of lines – somewhere in the region of the Mount of the Moon, an indication of interest in one or other of the arts and particularly those in which imagination play a large part. This is a good beginning but the line is weak and poorly-formed and finally peters out on the Mount of Saturn. This is a gloomy formation and indicates that the person concerned will remain a mere dabbler in the arts and not acquire any lasting fame through them.

The reader should also note the way that the Fate line splits into numerous branches and weakens towards its ending – an indication of a life lived without any real direction, without any real aim in view, a life that is varied and lacking in ability to concentrate on any one thing.

Observe also the curious form taken by the Heart line, full of islands and 'chained' in a remarkable way; not an indication of a successful love-life. Note also how the Heart line rises from the Mount of Saturn; this is traditionally taken as an indication of a strong sexual drive, of a person whose

Example 1: the hand of a princess of the House of Bourbon

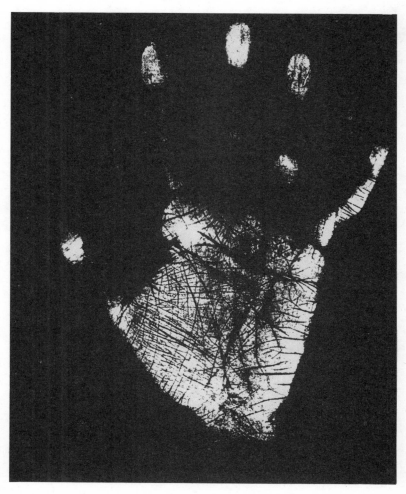

Some case studies

love is rarely untinged with sex, and of a certain selfishness especially noticeable in emotional affairs.

Other points of interest are the broken and distorted Girdle of Venus and the curiously drooping marriage line on the base of the finger of Mercury.

All the indications given above are in conformity with the life of the person concerned. She was a princess of the Spanish House of Bourbon, an aunt of King Alfonso XIII (1886–1941), and in her early life all looked well for her future. She had some talent for painting and imaginative literature (remember the Sun line arising from the Mount of the Moon) and a certain amount of musical ability, and inherited a large fortune in her own right. Throughout life, however, she never completed anything. She was totally unable to concentrate on any one thing and spent her time indulging in a series of ventures, some financial, some amatory, some artistic, which lost her much of her fortune, led to the failure of her marriage and disgraced her in the eyes of other European royalty.

In other words her life showed to the full the characteristics indicated by the shape of, and the lines upon, her hand.

Example 2: The hand of General Sir Redvers Buller

Example 2

On Carus' seven-fold classification of hands this comes closest to the 'square' (see Chapter 2). This is believed to indicate a practical plodding nature, orderly habits and a tenacity which approaches obstinacy combined with a psychological lack of imagination and little capacity for originality.

On the more modern, elementary classification this hand is closest to the type of elementary Earth. Its possessor would be expected to have strongly masculine traits – even if biologically female – and to make his or her career in a typically masculine environment. But the hand is not a *pure* Earth hand; there are elements in its structure which bear a resemblance to the Fire hand. So one would expect the psychology of the individual concerned to be of the extrovert type. There would also be a lack of emotional balance which might tend to lead to rash and impetuous action.

On the eight-fold classification of hand types (see Chapter 6) the hand approximates most closely to the Solarian hand – note that the fingers are knotty, that the finger of the Sun is longer than the finger of Jupiter and almost as long as that of Saturn, and that the Sun line is present on the hand. People with the Solarian hand tend to seek to gain power over others, to stand in the limelight and to achieve 'glory' in the widest sense of that word. This desire for the limelight tends sometimes to make for pushy persons who, if they feel they are not getting the attention and admiration they deserve, may retire into a fit of the sulks.

Putting the three classifications together and looking at the indications of each in the light shed by the other classifications, we can get some sort of composite picture of the person concerned.

Such a picture would denote a glory-seeking, admiration-craving, extroverted person. He or she would be anxious to dominate others, grimly tenacious of his or her ambitions, seeking a career in what would would be regarded as a typically masculine field, and apt to take rash action followed by sulkiness if thwarted in his or her desires. One further deduction could be made from the shape of the hand; the heavily knotted, almost deformed finger of Mercury indicates that the person concerned has little talent for vocal self expression. If the person did engage in it, he or she would not get out of any difficulties through the power of oratory.

The lines on the palm are in complete conformity with the indications given by the shape and the form of the hand discussed above.

Note first of all that the hand shows that very rare formation – a double Line of the Head. This is a sure indication of an intelligent person who has two very distinct sides to his or her psychology; the first side warm and loving, the second side cold, arrogant and self-seeking. One of these Head lines passes across the palm along with the Heart line: this is the line that gives a warmer side to the nature. The other begins high up on the Mount of Jupiter and slants across the palm. It is this line which shows cold calculating ambition.

The Fate and Sun lines are strong and well marked but a distinct weakness, some major setback in life, is indicated where a line crosses the Sun line towards Saturn. The fact that the Head and Heart lines run together across the palm is not, on the whole, a favourable indication; it usually shows a person with a one-track mind, totally convinced of his or her correctness, and unwilling or unable to follow the advice given by others.

The life of the subject whose hand this actually is confirms the correctness of the psychological portrait displayed by the shape of, and the lines upon, the hand. The subject was Sir Redvers Buller (1839–1908); his ambition, glory-seeking desire to dominate large masses of men, and his desire for a strongly masculine career, led him to become a soldier. He was brave – he won the Victoria Cross in 1879 – but obstinate, being convinced of the correctness of his own ideas and opposed to any form of original thought. As such he proved a thoroughly disastrous commander in the Boer War, sticking rigidly to the rule book and quite unable to adopt the new methods needed with the type of guerilla activity he encountered. Ultimately he was responsible for one disaster after another.

He was eventually returned to England, where he took command of the troops at Aldershot. The continuance in this office of one whose obstinacy had led to so many disasters resulted in a good deal of criticism from both politicians and the press. Instead of keeping quiet until the storm blew over he chose to make a speech in defence of himself. The speech was a disaster (remember that a deformed finger of Mercury; he was so outspoken, arrogant, and critical of superiors who did not share his ideas that it was regarded as a gross breach of discipline and he was retired on half-pay. He died, lonely, arrogant and embittered, in 1908.

Example 3

From the point of view of the fourfold Elemental classification of the hand (see Chapter 2) this sample is most curious, being a mingling of the Water and Fire types, of masculine and feminine characteristics. Thus while the strongly marked lines upon the palm, the long palm and the short fingers are typical of the Fire hand, the fine mesh of tiny lines upon the Mounts of Venus and the Moon (and to a lesser extent on the Mount of Mars positive) are more

typical of the Water hand. What exactly would one expect from this blending of characteristics? Probably the most likely result would be a sensitive individual, subject to wild and apparently almost motiveless changes of mood. Sometimes the person's mood would be more of a Water type, distinguished by receptivity and reflection of the environment. At other times it would be more of a Fire type, the person's behaviour being extroverted, outgoing and creative, and taking violent likes and dislikes to people and situations.

A similar mixture of contradictory characteristics is indicated when the hand is examined and analysed from the point of view of the eight-fold 'astrological' classification of the hand (see Chapter 6). Certain formations of the hand make one classify it as a Solarian hand, notably the fact that the fingers are shorter than the palm and that the finger of the Sun is notably well developed and as long as the finger of Jupiter. It is clear, however, that the hand is not exclusively Solarian *because there is no Sun line upon it*.

On another level there are indications

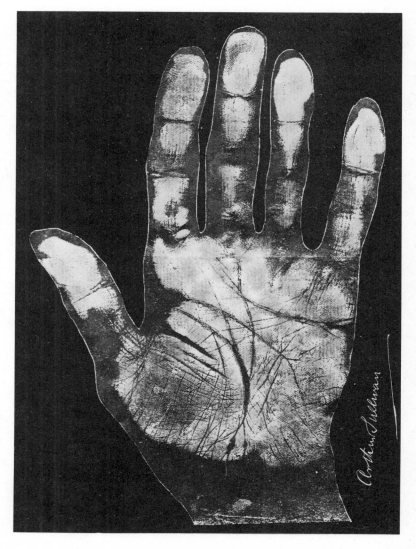

Example 3: The hand of Sir Arthur Sullivan

that the hand has strongly Venusian characteristics: note the prominence of the Mount of Venus and that it is covered by typically Venusian 'rays' – fine but distinctly marked hair lines.

This mixture of characteristics indicates a personality with as many contradictory aspects as those denoted by the Elemental classification. On the one side the Sun features denote a person who will desire success and public acclaim and probably achieve it – but not (remember the missing Sun line) in the field that he or she desired. The Venusian features indicate a person who desires friendship and companionship and longs to live in a beautiful and fulfilling environment, and for whom one or more of the arts, perhaps painting or music, are of great importance. Reconciling the latter feature with the Sun elements in the hand would probably indicate that it is through some art form that the desired success and fame are strived for.

Looking at the lines of the hand tends to confirm the above analysis. The head line curves up strongly into the Mount of the Moon, indicating a strong imagination and suggesting that the art form indicated by the Venusian characteristics would be of an imaginative nature. The Fate line, it will be noticed, swerves sharply into the Mount of Venus. This formation, it will be remembered, not only emphasises the hand's Venusian elements but denotes that the earlier part of the life was in some way adversely affected by close relationships.

Another point of interest is that there are two Fate lines, one rising from near the beginning of the Life line, the other from its middle. One peters out towards the middle of the hand, the other goes on to the Mount of Jupiter. This dual Fate line (and the ending of only one of them in a satisfactory way) is an indication of fame, yet perhaps not the fame which is desired but that which pertains to the Fate line with an unsatisfactory ending.

The hand print is in fact that of Sir Arthur Sullivan, the musician who won fame for his part in the world famous comic operas of Gilbert and Sullivan. Sullivan's life and character accord remarkably well with the picture arrived at on the basis of the hand and the lines upon it. He was born into a musical family – his father was a bandmaster and his mother an amateur singer – but his father lost his post when Arthur Sullivan was only fourteen years old and for many years the young composer had to make financial contributions towards the upkeep of his parents. Sullivan was a very friendly individual, devoted to those to whom he was close. He always surrounded himself with a crowd of admirers and reacted sharply to anything he considered an unfriendly action – all typically Venusian characteristics.

Sullivan found fame as a composer – the works he wrote with W. S. Gilbert were unquestionably the most popular English musical works of all time – but not the fame he desired. He wanted to be taken seriously as a composer of classical music and he burningly desired fame in this field, but all his serious music, the grand opera *Ivanhoe* for example, were comparative failures. He never achieved the public acclaim as a serious composer that he so badly wanted; instead he found fame as a composer of comic opera, a musical form he absolutely despised and regarded as totally beneath his talents. This failure in the field of real ambition combined with success in a musical form he despised amply explains the two Fate lines, one petering out, and the possession of numerous solar characteristics without a line of the Sun being present in the hand.

Example 4

On the Elementary classification this hand closely approximates the Water hand; it is delicately structured, both palm and fingers are long and inscribed with a fine mesh of lines. This type of hand, the reader will remember, has already been dealt with; the keywords in interpreting it are 'sensitivity' and 'receptivity' and so one would expect its owner to have a somewhat feminine psychology, whether or not this coincided with his or her biology.

The hand is clearly soft – there are no traces of callouses upon the print – and the lines upon it are large in number but somewhat soft and indistinct. The Line of Fate rises on the Mount of the Moon. Unquestionably this hand is of the Lunar type when its make-up is classified in accordance with the eightfold astrological classification dealt with in Chapter Eight.

The Lunar type of hand indicates both an adventurous and change-loving personality combined with a tendency towards the active use of the imagination and the powers of the Unconscious. People with this type of hand, it will be remembered, are sometimes drawn towards psychic matters; many of them display a marked tendency to be clairvoyant or gifted with some form of mediumship and are generally interested in the occult.

The Lunar personality is an attractive and popular one, partly because such a person genuinely likes other people and partly because he or she reflects the personalities of those encountered – a sure way of gaining favour. The main disadvantage of this personality is an excessive liability to change and a tendency to take up one wild theory or course of action after another.

The lines on this hand are of peculiar interest and give considerable support to the hand diagnosis of the eightfold classification. Their most notable characteristic is the double Head line. One of these Head lines, rising on the Mount of Jupiter and running almost straight across the palm, indicates a thoroughly extrovert psychology, a personality full of self-confidence, ambition and even a desire to achieve domination over others. The other Head line, closely joined to the Life line, denotes exactly the opposite psychology – an individual inclined to be shy, imaginative and apt to pull back under the pressure of any outside influences. One would expect such a person to be living a double life; not necessarily a double life in the bad sense of the term; perhaps the public and private lives of the individual are completely different from one another or perhaps two sharply differentiated careers are followed.

In fact the hand is that of Cheiro the palmist who, if not the best palmist of all time, was certainly the most widely known through the thousands of consultations he gave and the many books he wrote.

Cheiro's adventurous life – one moment a war correspondent, then a society palmist, then a public lecturer – fits in perfectly with the lunar classification of his hand. This lunar personality showed itself not only in Cheiro's adventurous life but in the characteristically hare-brained theories he sometimes espoused. This lunatic (in the proper sense of the word) theorising marred many of his books. In one of them, for example, he put forward the absurd theory that the hairs upon the human body are hollow safety-valves for the release of surplus electricity.

The double Head line's indications agree with what is known of Cheiro's life. For a start his public and personal lives were very different from one another – those who knew him as Louis Hamon, a lively and likeable _bon viveur_, rarely knew him as Cheiro the society palmist. This duality was shown in other ways; at times Cheiro could be shy and retiring, the author of sentimental religious poetry, at other times he was the complete extrovert, dominating his audiences from the lecture-platform.

Example 5

Using the fourfold Elemental classification this hand blends the characteristics of the Fire and Water hands. Thus the fingers are somewhat shorter than the long, oblong palm with its prominent lines – formations which make up the Fire hand. The fine mesh of lines inscribed upon the palm is, however, more typical of the Water hand.

From this dual nature of the hand it can be deduced that the person concerned has an extrovert, fiery temperament combined with a tendency to abrupt changes of mood and a capacity to reflect his or her surroundings.

On the eightfold astrological classification the hand is to some extent a Solarian type; note that the palm is longer than the fingers and that the finger of the Sun is well formed – both Solarian features. Note also, however, that the fingers lack the knottiness of the pure Solarian hand and that the mass of rays on the Mount of Venus indicates that some aspects of the personality pertain to Venus rather than the Sun.

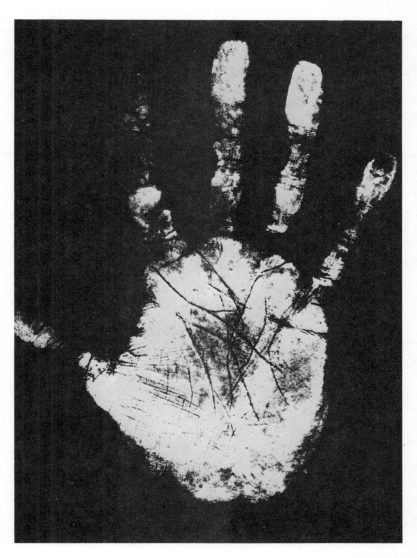

We have come across this combination of the Solarian and Venusian hand before in Sullivan's analysis. Unlike his palm, however, this example does have a line of the Sun and, what is more, a strongly marked and lengthy one. Thus in the present case one would expect the Solarian features to dominate and one can picture a personality to whom the arts are of great importance, who is strongly ambitious and is likely to achieve the desired fame, probably in some artistic field.

The lines on the hand give more evidence for the psychological profile based on the shape of the hand. Both the line of the Sun and that of Fate are exceptionally well marked. They are also of great length, beginning almost as far back as the Bracelets and continuing, parallel to one another, almost to the end of the palm. This denotes that success will be achieved early in life and will continue to the very end. The Fate line ends not on the Mount of Saturn but very clearly on the Mount of Jupiter, an indication that the success achieved will probably come in some field in which the

Example 4: The hand of Cheiro himself

Some case studies

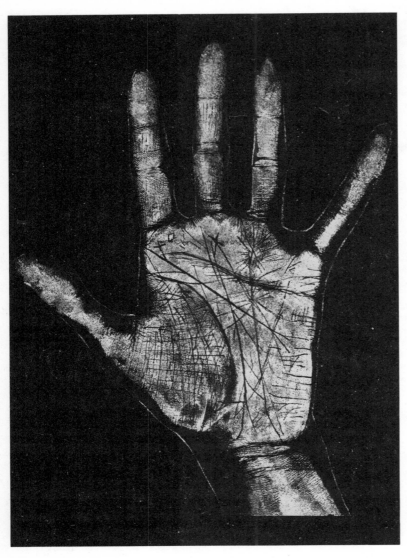

Example 5: The hand of the French actress Sarah Bernhardt

person concerned is very much in the public eye.

The Head line is remarkably straight, a sign of a controlled and determined personality. This control is partially mitigated by the fact that the line in question commences at a point quite separate from the Life line; such a formation probably indicates a certain impulsiveness at times when the rigid self-control indicated by the Head line temporarily breaks down.

The Life line is as strongly marked as the other lines on this fascinating hand and it must be observed that many of the rays on the Mount of Venus originate in the Life line and extend upwards. This is a strong indication of great bouts of energy in some artistic field.

The hand is that of Sarah Bernhardt, believed by many to have been the greatest actress of all time. She began her acting career at the early age of sixteen – remember how near the wrist the Fate and Sun lines had their beginnings – and ten years later she was famous throughout Europe. She retained this fame until her death over

fifty years later and even in old age she retained the power to make great spurts of energy in the dramatic field.

Everything known about her life correlates extremely well with the conclusions drawn from studying her palm.

Example 6

This thick, short, large hand provides a good example of one of Casimir D'Arpentigny's conic or artistic type of hands (see Chapter 2). People who have this particular variant of the conic hand are believed to be endowed with a strong desire for fame and fortune. In addition they are supposed to be individuals who prefer beauty to utility and imagination to logical thought.

A seemingly contradictory nature is indicated by the placing of this hand in one of the four Elemental categories – the Earth form. This Earth categorisation is based on the near-squareness of the palm, the shortness of the fingers and the depth and strength of the lines inscribed upon the palm. This classification is at first sight puzzling for, while D'Arpentigny's classification indicates an ultra-artistic personality, the possession of an Elemental Earth form would be expected to denote an individual who cared only for practical things, admired hard work and was physically productive.

On the eightfold astrological classification the hand is once more closest to the Earth type. Note that the beginnings of the Head and Life lines are actually joined – remember that any abnormal closeness of these lines is one of the characteristic formations of the Earth hand – and that the lines upon the palm are well marked and of obvious depth. Clearly, however, this is not a pure Earth hand because the Head line makes its way not to the Mount of Mercury but to the Mount of the Moon.

Putting this Earth hand together with the Lunar characteristics we can posit an individual who has a typically Earth-type psychology, enjoying the material things of life to the full and being very practical, but at the same time being gifted with a strong imaginative faculty.

To try to make a composite psychoportrait of this person with his or her artistic yet Earth-type hand and at least one Lunarian factor – the development of the Head line – is difficult but not impossible. One would expect to find either a practical man who has a strongly artistic side to his nature – perhaps, say, a master cabinet maker who produces furniture of great beauty – or an artist who is also businesslike and makes himself rich and well known through his art.

Except for the point already made about the relationship between the Head and Life lines, the most notable thing about this hand is the strong development of the Sun line. This begins near the wrist – a sign of fame being achieved in fairly early life – and continues strongly down the hand to its

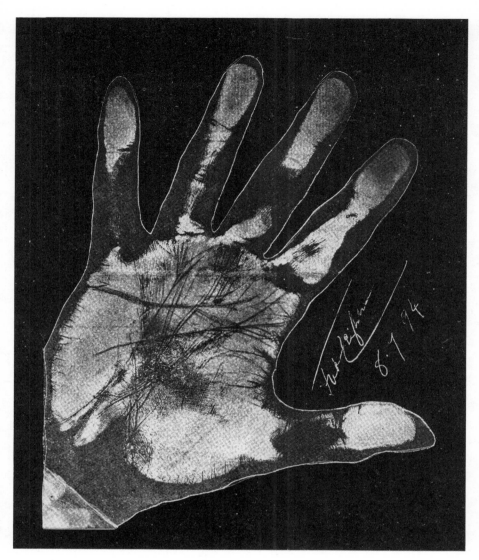

termination on the Mount of the Sun.

From this formation one would not only expect, as has already been pointed out, fame achieved early in life but also that this fame would persist throughout life and that the person concerned would enjoy much admiration and be the centre of much popular attention, both professional and social.

Summing up, one gets the portrait of a financially and socially successful individual who has achieved prominence either by making an art of their business or by making a business of their art. In fact the latter is correct. The hand is that of the Victorian academic painter Frederick Leighton whose works are once more, as they were in his lifetime, extremely fashionable in the world of art dealers and galleries. Leighton was enormously successful as a painter both socially – he had a peerage conferred upon him – and financially, for his works sold at prices which were enormous even by today's standards. He was also President of the Royal Academy, the very pinnacle of the English art establishment.

Example 7

On D'Arpentigny's sevenfold classification of hand types – and it is worth remembering that this mode of classification is the one used by the great majority of Cheiro's many contemporary disciples – this is a fine example of the psychic hand, which is considered the most beautiful and yet most unfortunate of all types of hand. Those possessing it are considered (see Chapter 2) to be over-idealistic and neurotic dreamers.

On the fourfold Elemental classification of hand types this is a perfect example of the Water hand. Note the meshed lines upon the palm and the extreme and near abnormal length of both the palm and fingers. Possessors of this type of hand are of course extremely sensitive, subject to wild swings of mood and, like water itself, ever-changing, sometimes deep and sometimes shallow.

The Line of Fate slopes strongly to the Mount of the Moon while the Head line swings up towards the same Mount and there is a strange short line on the Mount of the Moon near the end of the Head line: all things considered this hand approaches

Some case studies

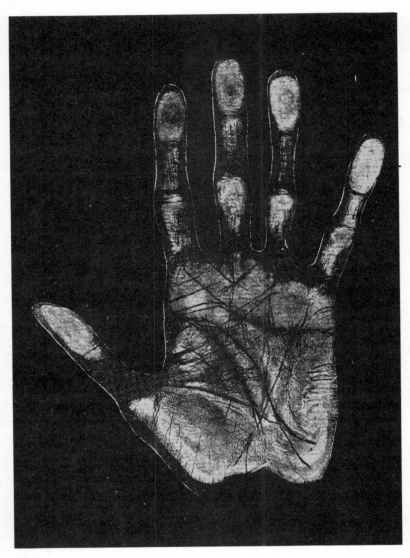

Example 7: The hand of a young woman who committed suicide

and the person him or herself – to cope with.

This shadowed psycho-portrait is made even darker when one considers the lines on the palm. Around the base of the fingers of Saturn are two crooked lines which join together to form a rough but probably potent Ring of Saturn. Traditionally this is regarded as a most unfavourable formation (see Chapter 5). It is believed to indicate a lack of success in life and the way it cuts off the Mount of Saturn from the rest of the hand indicates that the person concerned will rarely be able to bring any matter to a successful ending. Note also that from this Ring of Saturn springs a deeply etched line which cuts both the Head and Life lines at a very early stage of their development. This is a sign that something will go very wrong with the person's life, particularly its psychological aspect, at a comparatively youthful age.

Finally notice the previously mentioned and most unusual curve which the Head line takes as it slopes, first under and then onto, the base of the Mount of the Moon. Traditionally such a formation is believed to denote a tendency to powerful neurosis or even actual insanity. In fact, this is the hand of a girl who developed suicidal tendencies at the early age of eighteen years, made several attempts at suicide and finally took her own life at the age of twenty-eight.

Example 8

On D'Arpentigny's sevenfold classification of hand forms this hand most closely approximates to the square. One would expect a person possessed of this hand to be capable of clear and logical thought, to have a practical, order-loving and systematic psychology, and to have considerable 'grit' and tenacity. A less pleasant note is struck by the fact that such a person may have his logical sense so strongly developed that he or she has a contempt for the things of the imagination.

On the eightfold astrological classification this hand shows a mixture of 'planetary' characteristics, but it comes closest to the Solar type; in this connection it should be noted that the finger of the Sun is long and that the fingers are somewhat knotty. The presence of the Sun line in the hand is also of significance, as is the fact that this is a fairly prominent feature of a hand on which there are not a great many lines. We have already dealt with the Solarian hand in previous examples and it suffices to say that in its interpretation the key phrases are ambition, drive, hard work and a longing for public admiration.

On the fourfold elemental typology this hand has certain Fire elements – probably enough to overcome the lack of imagination indicated by the hand's squareness on the basis of the D'Arpentigny classification – but comes closest to the Earth type. Note particularly the hand's structural heaviness, its square palm, its

most closely the lunar type on the basis of the eightfold Elemental classification. The lunar psychology is a type subject to abrupt changes of mood (see Chapter 8). The Moon, of course, rules the imagination and an imaginative personality with a tendency to extreme vivid dreams is indicated. In addition to this it must be remembered that sometimes the Lunar personality goes too far in his or her tendency to changeability and, when this is the case, their fluid emotions are often difficult for other people to cope with.

So far the three methods of classifying the hand, carefully combining the indications of all three types into one composite picture, make it seem likely that the individual concerned is not altogether happy. The psychic hand is peculiarly unfortunate' and this makes one inclined to think that it is the darker side of the Water and Lunar hands, rather than their bright aspects, which will come to the fore. One senses an unhappy, unfortunate person subject to wild changes of mood whose inconstant emotions are difficult for others –

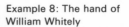

Example 8: The hand of
William Whitely

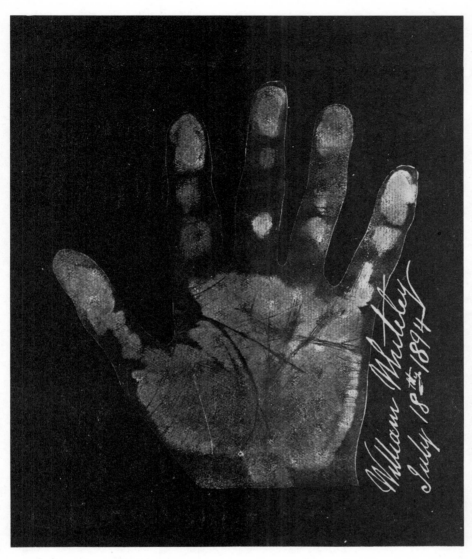

comparatively short fingers and, above all, the fact that although there are few lines marked upon the palm those that are present are strongly marked. Such a hand is indicative of a strongly masculine type of psychology.

Possessors of the Earth hand are normally honest, extremely hard working, intensely practical and physically productive. These indications tie in remarkably well with those given in the first paragraph above which are based on the sevenfold classification.

In conclusion we get a psycho-picture of a hard working, tenacious, ambitious and productive human being who has strongly marked psychological traits of the type normally considered masculine.

The lines on the hand are in no way remarkable except for the fact that there is a short line derived from the Fate line going towards the Mount of Sun which is suddenly cut short by a line arising from the plain of Mars towards the same Mount. Traditionally such a formation was often regarded as an indication that the person concerned would at some time be in intense peril of violence, or perhaps even violent death.

The hand was that of William Whitely, the founder of one of London's greatest department stores. He built his trading Empire up on the base of the practicality, hard work and tenacity so strongly indicated by the form of his hand. He died violently; shot by his own embittered and mentally disturbed illegitimate son.

12
Chinese palmistry

Today we live in a period in which there are strong interconnections and links between the various cultures of the world. No longer do we live in the environment of a hundred years ago when the western world concentrated almost exclusively on material things such as the steam engine and thoroughly despised the great philosphical and religious systems and texts of the east. Today westerners study yoga and the Hindu and Buddhist scriptures and the east, while not altogether neglecting this side of life, puts more and more emphasis on industrialisation.

No occult or religious book of eastern origin today influences westerners – particularly young westerners – more strongly than the *I Ching*, the ancient Chinese *Book of Change*. This book, which strongly attracted the great psychologist C. G. Jung, is regularly consulted by hundreds of thousands of Europeans and Americans. The *I Ching* details methods, involving either the manipulation of a bundle of sticks or the tossing up of three coins, by which answers to questions or advice regarding personal conduct can be obtained. The advice given by the book is based on which specific hexagram – a sixfold figure made up of whole and/or broken lines – is arrived at on the basis of the stick manipulation or the coin-tossing.

These sixty-four figures are composed of combinations of eight simple figures (trigrams) made up by three whole or broken lines. These eight trigrams are of incalculable antiquity, long pre-dating the *I Ching* itself and are as follows.

☷	☶	☵	☴
4	3	2	1

☳	☲	☱	☰
8	7	6	5

Running from right to left the western transliterations of the names of these symbols are as follows:
(1) Ch'ien (2) Tui (3) Li (4) Chen (5) Sun (6) K'an (7) Ken (8) K'un.

The eight trigrams form the basis of Chinese palmistry, an art very different in its rules and interpretations from western palmistry and yet, strangely enough, usually producing readings totally compatible with those arrived at by the western techniques.

The parts of the hand are classed as eight Palaces and are allocated to the trigrams as follows:

The Palace of Ch'ien correlates with the lower half of the Mount of the Moon and its development, or lack of development, is taken as an indication of whether or not the personality has spiritual force present in his of her psychological make-up. It is of interest to note that Ch'ien literally means

Heaven – the protective, spiritual influence in life.

The Palace of Tui is in the upper half of the Mount of the Moon. The word Tui can be roughly translated as pleasurable and joyful, and from the development of this Palace the Chinese palmist judges to what extent the person concerned will get joy from his or her sexual partners and children. It is also regarded as pertaining to the strength of the sexual desires and, as imagination plays a large part in these, it correlates in an interesting way to the western assignment of imaginative power to the Mount of the Moon.

The Palace of Li, which means beautiful, depending and clinging, corresponds roughly to the Mount of Saturn. The Chinese palmist reads the subject's social and financial position and the extent to which he or she will be successful in the chosen career, from the development of this Palace.

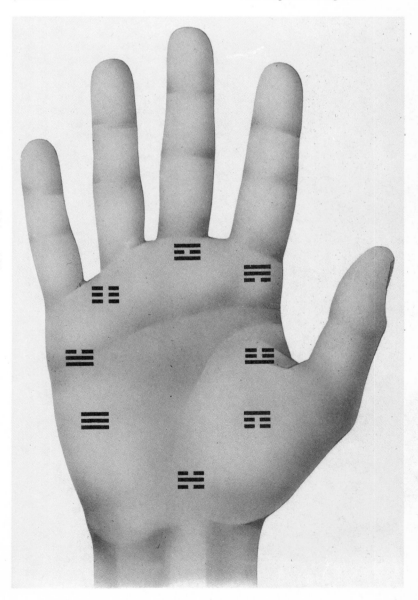

(Facing page) The symbols of the I Ching trigrams, and their names in Chinese, together with the Taoist *ying-yan* symbol, on the end of a cake of Chinese ink. These symbols are arranged in the Sequence of Earlier Heaven. On the hand below they are arranged in the Sequence of Later Heaven, or Inner World Arrangement, devised by King Wen, one of the earliest commentators on the original I Ching texts

(Facing page) A page from a manuscript dated 1466, indicating the significance of the different parts of the hand

The Palace of Chen, which literally means 'thunder' but conveys to Taoist Chinese the concepts of action, arousal and movement, coincides with the upper part of the Mount of Venus. From its development the physical and emotional vitality of the subject in regard to both the working and sexual lives is read.

The Palace of Sun, which in Chinese literally means 'wind' but conveys the ideas of gentleness and, paradoxically enough, the quality of being able to pierce other things, coincides in position with the Mount of Jupiter. The combination of gentleness and ability to penetrate is explained by the word 'wind': just as wind has the physical power of being sometimes gentle, sometimes piercing, and yet going steadily on its way, so Sun stands for these same qualities in a psychological sense. From the development of Sun the mental capacity and power of logical thought (a very penetrating quality) of the palmist's subject is deduced.

The Palace of K'an – literally water, but conveying the ideas of envelopment and danger, both qualities of large bodies of water – is situated between the bottom of the Mount of the Moon and the Life line. This area is held to rule the difficulties of life, particularly those which result from either heredity or from the early environment. The Chinese palmist assesses the amount of difficulties his subject has experienced or will experience on the basis of the development of this area.

The Palace of Ken more or less correlates with the lower part of the Mount of Venus.

Literally the word Ken means 'mountain' and the ideas conveyed by it are those associated with the everlasting mountains: immovability, obstinacy and, to some extent, a perverse going a certain way in defiance of the thoughts and actions of others. From its development the Chinese palmist reads to what extent his subject possesses these qualities.

The Palace of K'un literally means 'the Palace of Earth', and the latter element is given feminine qualities by Chinese Taoists. The word K'un, then, conveys what the Chinese regard as essentially feminine qualities – passivity, receptiveness and plasticity. On the hand the Palace of K'un is associated with the area beneath the fingers of the Sun and Mercury. From its development the Chinese palmist reads the amount of feminine elements present in the psychology of the subject and correlates this with his other interpretations.

Besides the eight Palaces there are two other parts of the palm that have some significance in the Chinese art. They are T'ien, which coincides almost exactly with the middle of the Mount of Venus, and Ming Tang, which correlates with the plain of Mars. The development of the first of these areas supposedly denotes the amount of purely material success, particularly the acquisition of property, the subject will meet with in his or her life. The development of the latter area is used to judge both good fortune in the wider sense of the term and the general respectability and capacity for self-discipline of the subject.

Short Bibliography

D'Arpentigny, *La Chirognomie*, France 1843
Cheiro, *The Language of the Hand*, numerous editions (eg Corgi Books, London 1968)
A. Desbarrolles, *Les Mysteres de la Main*, numerous editions since 1859
Henry Frith, *Practical Palmistry*, Ward Lock, nd
Fred Gettings, *The Book of the Hand*, Hamlyn, 1965
            The Book of Palmistry, Hamlyn, 1974
Mir Bashir, *The Art of Hand Analysis*, Muller, 1973
Jo Sheridan, *What Your Hands Reveal*, Mayflower, 1972

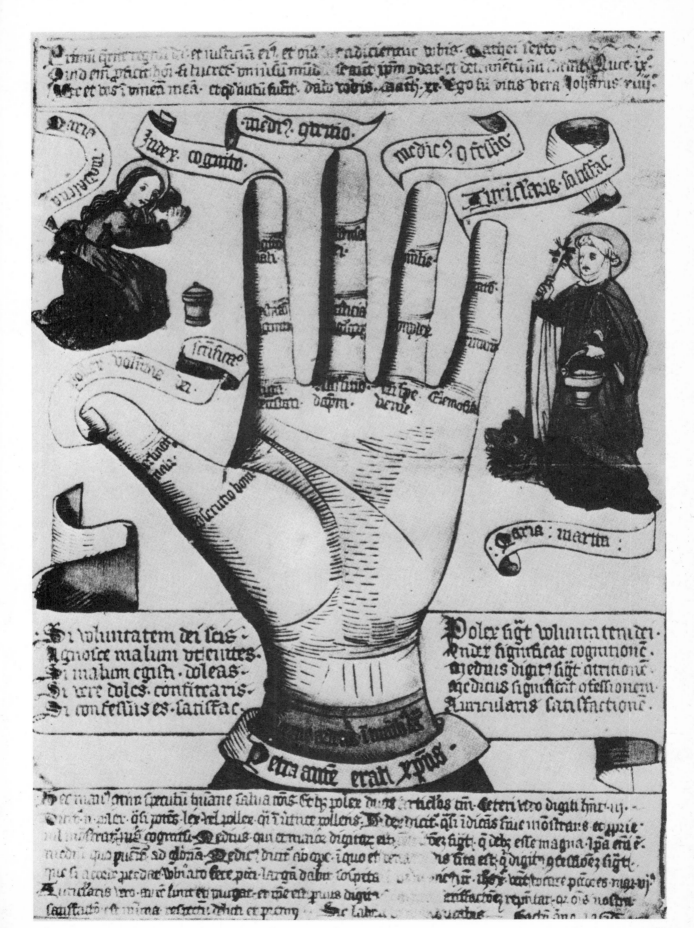

267

PART 4

The Tarot

Brian Innes

Contents

1
The origins of playing cards

Nobody can truly say where playing cards have come from. One of the most plausible theories is that they have developed from the same source as the game of chess: the Indian game of *Chaturange* (Four Kings), for instance, has four groups of pieces comprising King, General, Horseman and a phalanx of foot soldiers; and one Chinese card game has the same name as Chinese chess, *Keuma-Paou* (Chariots-Horses-Guns).

Another possibility is that the Chinese, who invented paper money very early, and who also were inveterate gamblers, eventually developed special pieces of paper which, while representing sums of money to be gambled, also represented different aspects of the gambling game.

Without doubt, however, cards have been used since the earliest times for divination. One of the most primitive ways of making decisions was to throw one or more arrows into a circle on the ground, to see which way they pointed; and it is significant that the Korean pack of eighty cards known as *Htou-Tjyen* still bears a stylised arrow on the back of each card.

How cards came to Europe is equally a mystery. It was long believed that they had been brought from the east, either by returning Crusaders or by gypsies, but both these theories would seem to be disproved by the date of the first definite reference to cards, which is 1377–79. We find a German monk named Johannes writing at Brefeld in Switzerland that 'a game called the game of cards has come to us in this year 1377'; and the chronicler Giovanni Covelluzzo, who wrote his history of the Italian town of Viterbo in 1480, is credited with the statement 'in the year 1379 the game of cards was brought into Viterbo from the country of the Saracens, where it is called *naib*'.

Now, the last crusade began in 1270, and the Christians were finally driven out of Asia Minor in 1291; there were several condemnations of gaming and dicing made during the next hundred years, but without any mention of cards, which seems unlikely if they had really been brought back by the Crusaders. Gypsies, on the other hand, did not appear in Europe until the fifteenth century; they undoubtedly adopted playing cards very quickly, but cards had certainly arrived before them.

The statement of Covelluzzo is particularly attractive, in the light of the fact that cards are known in Spain to this day as *naipes*. The Arabs brought many things to Europe through their occupation of Spain for six centuries, and some scholars believe the word *naib* to be of Arabic origin. There are certain other indications which suggest that cards may well have reached the rest of Europe through Spain, although few Spanish cards earlier than 1600 have survived.

The idea of the different suits is as old as the cards themselves: Korean cards are divided into eight suits, Chinese cards usually into four, and Indian cards into eight – or sometimes into ten, representing the ten incarnations of Vishnu.

There are a wide variety of packs of cards produced in Europe for all sorts of different games, but all comprise four suits. The total

number of cards in the four suits may vary, depending upon the game, between 32 and 56, but each suit will comprise some of the following cards: King, Queen, Knight and Squire or Valet (the 'court' or 'coat' cards), and the complete run of numbered cards from ten down to one (the Ace).

The first European suits, which have remained almost unchanged in Spain and Italy, were Cups, Batons, Swords and Gold Discs. The significance of these particular symbols goes very deep into history. The legend of the Holy Grail, for instance, suggests that these four suits represent the Grail itself, the sacred lance of Longinus that pierced the side of Christ on the cross, the legendary sword of King David, and the paten of the Last Supper. But these four 'Grail Hallows' are at least in part derived from an ancient Celtic tradition, which had survived in Ireland as the Four Treasures: the Cauldron of the Dagda, the Spear of Lug, the Sword of Nuada and the Stone of Fal. The connection between the Stone of Fal, the paten of the Last Supper, and the gold disc of the pack of cards may seem rather tenuous; it appears less so when it is remembered that the equivalent of this suit in a French pack is the *carreau*, or flooring tile – which in its turn has become the diamond of the English pack.

In Italian, the four suits are known as *coppe* (cups), *bastoni* (batons or clubs), *spade* (swords) and *denari* (coins); and in Spanish as *copas, bastos, espadas,* and *oros* (gold pieces). In the French pack, the symbol for the cup became distorted into a heart shape, *coeur*; the baton into a clover-leaf shape, *tréfle*; the sword into the broader shape of a pike-head, *pique*; and the gold disc was replaced by the *carreau*. These were adopted for the English pack, but in English the names of two suits, spades and clubs, clearly indicate their origin.

In Germany, the earliest cards known have suits of dogs, stags, ducks and falcons; but by 1460 what were to become the traditional suits were already established. Hearts remained the same, but the clover-leaf suffered a further distortion into an acorn, and the pikehead into a leaf; while the gold disc became a little round hawk bell.

One other feature of the 32 – 56 card pack is worthy of mention. From the late fifteenth century onward, the court cards of the French pack have borne the names of legendary or mythical characters. There have been various local variations, but the standard names have been, and still are, as follows:

King of Hearts: Charles
King of Spades: David
King of Diamonds: Caesar
King of Clubs: Alexander
Queen of Hearts: Judith
Queen of Spades: Pallas
Queen of Diamonds: Rachel
Queen of Clubs: Argine
Valet of Hearts: La Hire
Valet of Spades: Hogier
Valet of Diamonds: Hector
Valet of Clubs: Lancelot

In themselves, these names do not tell us very much about the history of playing cards: the kings are named after great military leaders of antiquity, the queens after prototypical female figures, and the valets after famous champions (Ogier the Dane was one of the legendary knights of Charlemagne; La Hire, on the other hand, was one of those who helped Joan of Arc liberate Orleans in 1429). But when we remember the possible connection of the four suits with the four Grail Hallows, the appearance of David as the King of Swords, and of Lancelot as the Valet of Clubs (supposed to represent the lance of Longinus), is significant. What is also important to remember is that each of these characters had a particular symbolism for medieval people; each was held up as an outstanding combination of certain virtues and abilities, and this is why there is no connection of religion, nationality or era, between the king, queen and knave of any suit.

The most remarkable thing about the playing cards we have been considering is that, within two generations of the date of 1377, they had not only spread all over Europe but had attained a standard of design that remained almost unchanged thereafter, even to the present day. Equally remarkable is the fact that another 22 cards were added to the pack, derived from a completely different source, that have also remained virtually unchanged over more than five hundred years. These are the cards that have received most attention from occultists and fortune-tellers alike, and that (not entirely correctly) we call today the Tarot.

Traditional symbols for the four suits of the playing card pack, as reproduced in the first book book to describe the occult significance of the Tarot, Court de Gebelin's *Monde Primitif*. From left to right: cups, rods, swords and *(above)* coins

ARITMETRICHA·XXV · 2Y

MVSICHA·XXVI · 26

POESIA·XXVII · 27

PHILOSOFIA·XXVIII · 28

ZINTILOMO·V · 5

CHAVALIER·VI · 6

DOXE·VII · 7

RE·VIII · 8

CALIOPE·XI · 11

VRANIA·XII · 12

ASTROLOGIA·XXXVIIII · 39

THEOLOGIA·XXX · 30

272

2
The history of the Tarot

'If one were to let it be announced that there survived to this day an ancient Egyptian work, a book that had escaped the flames which devoured their superb libraries, and which contained, unsullied, their teachings on important matters: everyone, no doubt would be in a hurry to acquaint themselves with such a precious and remarkable book. And if one added that this book was widely distributed throughout much of Europe, and that for many centuries it had been available to everybody, people's surprise would be vastly increased; and would it not reach its highest pitch when they were assured that nobody had ever imagined it to be Egyptian, that it was held to be nothing, that no-one had attempted ever to decipher a single page, and that the fruits of infinite wisdom were regarded as a collection of fantastic pictures without the least significance in themselves? Wouldn't it be thought that one was amusing oneself at the expense of the listeners' credulity? . . . . . Nevertheless, it is true: this Egyptian book, sole relic of their superb libraries, survives today. Indeed, it is so common, that no scholar has deigned to concern himself with it; before ourselves, nobody has ever suspected its illustrious origins. This book is composed of 77 or perhaps 78 leaves or pictures, divided into five classes, each presenting objects as varied as they are entertaining and instructive: this book is, in other words, the game of Tarot.'

With these words, the French writer Court de Gebelin began page 365 of the eighth volume of his book *Monde Primitif* in 1781. He was not a particularly eminent author – an obscure Protestant theologian from the South of France, he devoted some ten years to writing his vast pot-pourri of uninformed speculation on the survival of ancient myths, symbols and fragments of primitive tongues – and two-thirds of the way through volume 8 is not the most prominent position in any work, on no matter how fascinating a subject; nevertheless, it is solely for what he had to say about the Tarot that Court de Gebelin is remembered.

Tarot cards were almost unknown in Paris, but Court de Gebelin was familiar with them from his upbringing in the Languedoc, the Mediterranean region adjacent to the Spanish border. He was also aware of their popularity in Germany and Italy, where they were used in a game called *Tarocke* or *Tarocchi*. The pack of cards totalled 78: of these 56 were the standard pack, comprising four suits of 14 cards each, to which were added 22 picture cards or trumps, numbered from 1 to 21 with the last card un-numbered.

According to Court de Gebelin, 'the trumps, numbering 22, represent in general the temporal and spiritual leaders of society, the principles of agriculture, the cardinal virtues, marriage, death and resurrection or the creation; the many tricks of fortune, the wise and the foolish, time which consumes all, etc.. . . . ' As for the suits, he decided that they represented the four classes into which Egyptian society had been divided: the king and military nobility, symbolised by the sword; agriculture, symbolised by the club; the priesthood, symbolised by the cup; and commerce, symbolised by the coin.

He was also struck by the recurrence of the number seven: each suit comprised twice seven cards, and the numbered trumps made three times seven. All these things convinced Court de Gebelin that the cards were undoubtedly of Egyptian origin, and he claimed to be able to discern ancient Egyptian symbolism in the pictorial trumps.

Before we begin to discuss these pictures and what they represent, it is necessary to trace the career of some of the ideas first put forward in *Monde Primitif*.

Among those in Paris who were particularly struck with the ideas of Court de Gebelin was a certain wigmaker named Alliette, who had decided to practise as a fortune-teller, reversing the letters of his name to Etteilla for the purpose. Etteilla welcomed Court de Gebelin's theories, and elaborated upon them, declaring that the Tarot had been written on golden leaves in a temple near Memphis, 171 years after the flood; Hermes Trismegistos had planned the book, which should therefore properly be called *The Book of Thoth*, and it had been executed by seventeen magi working for four years. He even produced his own pack of 78 Tarot cards, which differed markedly in a number of respects from the traditional.

One of Etteilla's other interests was the Qabalah, the ancient Jewish mystical system, which expresses all creation in terms of ten concepts known as *sefiroth*. These ten sefiroth are arranged upon a symbolic Tree of Life: the meditating mystic, as he gains in experience, imagines himself traversing paths from sefiroth to sefiroth, beginning at Malkuth, the earthly kingdom, and finally reaching Kether, the supreme crown. And the total number of paths connecting the ten sefiroth is 22.

The French occultist Eliphas Lévi seized on this fact as proof that the Tarot cards were older, and of more universal significance, than even Court de Gebelin had suggested. Since the Hebrew alphabet contains 22 letters, he succeeded in relating each Tarot trump to a letter of the alphabet

Opposite: Twelve from the fifty cards known as the 'Mantegna' *tarocchi*. Others are illustrated with the individual Tarot cards to which they are related.
Above: the Magician, as engraved for Court de Gebelin. It is interesting that most of these illustrations, having been produced (presumably) by an amateur engraver, are reversed from left to right; however three – the Wheel of Fortune, Death and the Sun – are correct

From left to right, above: the Woman Pope, the Empress, the Emperor, the Pope, the Lovers and the Chariot; *below*: Justice, the Hermit, the Wheel of Fortune, Fortitude, 'Prudence' and Death. All are from Court de Gebelin, and the transformation of the Hanged Man into the portrait of the prudent man 'who, having put one foot forward, has lifted the other and now stands there examining the ground where he can place it safely' is very striking.

But Court de Gebelin did not explain how this man came to have one foot tethered to a stake

and to one of the 22 paths; and in his first book, *Dogme et Rituel de la Haute Magie*, he promised to make public the original designs from which the popular Tarot cards were derived. Although he described these designs, Lévi himself did not publish them – although the English freemason Kenneth Mackenzie wrote of having seen them in 1861 – and the nearest idea that we have of them is the pack of cards designed by Oswald Wirth to the specifications of Lévi's disciple Stanislas de Guaita, which was eventually made public in 1889. In fact, these cards are little more than a late nineteenth century prettification of the eighteenth century cards described by Court de Gebelin, with the addition of the letters of the Hebrew alphabet.

The next development came from another of Lévi's disciples, a librarian at the Ministry of Public Instruction in Paris named Jean-Baptiste Pitois, who wrote a *History of Magic* under the name of Paul Christian. Attributing his source (entirely without justification) to the ancient Roman philosopher Iamblichus, Christian describes the initiation rites of the Egyptian Mysteries, and the use of 22 paintings along the walls of a subterranean gallery in the Great Pyramid. His descriptions of these paintings are a strongly Egyptianised form of the traditional Tarot trumps, but there is no evidence that they are derived from anything but Christian's imagination, suitably inflamed by Lévi's theories.

After this, variations in Tarot pack design,

and in the interpretations to be attached to the different cards, proliferated thick and fast. A seminal work was the slim volume by the English occultist Macgregor Mathers, which was published in 1888; this was shortly followed by *The Tarot of the Bohemians: Absolute Key to Occult Science,* by the French physician Gerard Encausse, writing under the name of Papus. Then the translator of Papus's book, the Englishman A. E. Waite, designed another very different pack which was executed for him by Pamela Colman Smith. There was a Golden Dawn pack, similar to the Waite pack but with differences of detail; and Aleister Crowley's *Book of Thoth,* painted for him by Frieda Harris.

With the growing interest in the Tarot of

the past few years there have been a number of new designs, some attractive, some grotesque. But every new pack introduces details that were not present in the pack described by Court de Gebelin, and which have been added to exemplify some pet theory of the designer. The order of the cards is changed; some cards are discarded and replaced by entirely new ones; often the names of the individual trumps are altered in an attempt to make them conform to a more rigid system.

How 'genuine', however, was Court de Gebelin's pack? and what was its origin? He described each of the trumps, and also illustrated them, and there is no doubt that he was referring to the 22 trumps of the standard eighteenth century pack which is

The history of the Tarot

Right: the Court de Gebelin representation of Temperance. *Far right*: a fine example of a medieval memory image, from Thomas Murner's *Chartiludium logicae* (Strasbourg, 1509), which describes a card game for learning the processes of logic

now known as the 'Marseilles' pack. There are some inconsistencies in the drawings and descriptions in Court de Gebelin's work, but the 'standard' pack can be assumed to be as follows.

I	le Bateleur	The Magician
II	la Papesse	The Female Pope
III	l'Imperatrice	The Empress
IV	l'Empereur	The Emperor
V	le Pape	The Pope
VI	l'Amoureux	The Lovers
VII	le Chariot	The Chariot
VIII	Justice	Justice
IX	l'Ermite	The Hermit
X	la Roue de Fortune	The Wheel of Fortune
XI	la Force	Strength
XII	le Pendu	The Hanged Man
XIII	(untitled: represents Death)	
XIV	Temperance	Temperance
XV	le Diable	The Devil
XVI	la Maison Dieu	The Ruined Tower
XVII	l'Etoille	The Star
XVIII	la Lune	The Moon
XIX	le Soleil	The Sun
XX	le Jugement	(Last) Judgment
XXI	le Monde	The World

(either without number, or numbered 0):
le Mat   The Fool

Where do these pictures come from? Of one thing we can be quite sure: their source is not ancient Egypt. When Court de Gebelin published his book in 1781 Egypt was a place of mystery; hieroglyphic writing, in those years before the discovery of the Rosetta stone, appeared incapable of decipherment, and antiquarians were frustrated by the thought that they could never discover the secrets contained in papyri and on steles. It was fashionable to suggest that all the wisdom of the world might be concealed in a tantalising series of pictures that only those initiated into the mysteries could interpret.

In fact, there is plenty of evidence to show that the 22 Tarot trumps are the remnants of a late-medieval instructive card game. Much as we today teach our younger children with table games such as picture dominoes or Scrabble, the rich of the middle ages devised games which exploited the well-known memory images. Before the invention of printing a well-trained memory was essential to an intellectual, and all memory systems were based upon a repertoire of easily recognised images – saints with the symbols of their martyrdom, mythological characters, personifications of the cardinal virtues or of the parts of knowledge (Grammar, Rhetoric, etc). The introduction of printing sounded the death-knell of these memory systems, and it is perhaps no coincidence that the first card games employing memory images appeared almost coincidentally with the invention of printing in Europe.

There are, for instance, the *tarocchi* supposed to have been engraved by the artist Mantegna, which are made up of five sets of ten cards: numbers 1 to 10 represent the orders of society from the beggar to the Pope, numbers 11 to 20 comprise the nine Muses and Apollo, numbers 21 to 30 are the principal parts of knowledge, and numbers 31 to 40 are a rather mixed bag made up of three 'sciences' (astronomy, chronology and cosmology), the four cardinal virtues (temperance, prudence, fortitude and justice) and the three Christian virtues (faith, hope and charity); while numbers 41 to 50 comprise the seven planets, the stellar sphere, the prime mover and the first cause, as required by classical astronomy.

The 'Mantegna' cards seem to be the most complete, in the sense of comprising a range of images to represent just about everything that a fifteenth century educated person might be expected to know, but there are a number of other packs which are much closer in their constitution to today's full Tarot pack. The cards produced in Florence for the game of *minchiate*, for instance, included 42 trumps:

I	The Magician	XVIII	Faith
II	The Grand Duke	XIX	Charity
		XX	Fire
III	The Emperor	XXI	Water
IV	The Empress	XXII	Earth
V	Love	XXIII	Air
VI	Temperance	XXIV	Libra
VII	Fortitude	XXV	Virgo
VIII	Justice	XXVI	Scorpio
IX	The Wheel of Fortune	XXVII	Aries
		XXVIII	Capricorn
X	The Chariot	XXIX	Sagittarius
XI	The Hermit	XXX	Cancer
XII	The Traitor	XXXI	Pisces
XIII	Death	XXXII	Aquarius
XIV	The Devil	XXXIII	Leo
XV	The Tower	XXXIV	Taurus
XVI	Hope	XXXV	Gemini
XVII	Prudence		

Two further examples of medieval memory images, from Johannes Romberch's *Congestiorum Artificiose Memorie* (Venice, 1533) and from *Ars memorandi* (1470). The combination of a statuesque figure with a number of incongruous additions is strikingly like that of the traditional Tarot cards

After these 35 numbered trumps came a further six without numbers:

The Star, The Sun, The Moon, Fame, The World, and The Fool.

At least three other packs of the same period have survived (at least in part), which appear to have contained 22 trumps substantially the same as those in the Marseilles pack. All three are very similar in their graphic style: the trumps are un-numbered, painted in brilliant colours and illuminated with gold and silver leaf on thick pasteboard, and the subjects are recognisably the same as in the Tarot pack.

The first of these packs comprises a surviving 67 cards, of which eleven are trumps. It appears to have been painted sometime between 1428 and 1447 by Marziano da Tortona for Filippo Maria Visconti, duke of Milan, and was handed down in the Visconti family from generation to generation. The trumps are:

The Woman Pope, otherwise identified as
   Religion or Faith
The Empress
The Emperor
The Lovers
The Chariot
Fortitude
Death
The Judgment
The World

and two cards that must be identified as
Hope and Charity.

Three other packs are known to have been painted in 1484 by Antonio di Cicognara. One was presented to Cardinal Ascanio Sforza, the son of Francesco Sforza and Bianca Maria Visconti (the two families were united in 1432); the two others were presented to the cardinal's sisters, who were nuns at the Augustinian convent in Cremona founded by the Lady Bianca. Exactly what happened to these packs remains a bit of a mystery. Some of the cards certainly were in the possession of the Colleoni family of Bergamo; some are now in the museum at Carrara; some are in the Pierpont Morgan Library in New York; and there are a certain number in the Victoria & Albert Museum in London. At some time, however, they appear to have been mixed up with another pack painted by Bonifacio Bembo: the style is very similar although not identical, but an American bibliographer has contrived to identify a nearly complete pack from these remnants, which is now known as the 'Bembo' or Visconti-Sforza pack.

One other pack has survived in part, which is as old as – maybe even older than – the 'Bembo' pack. There is an entry in the account book of the treasurer to Charles VI of France for the year 1392, recording a payment to the painter Jacquemin Gringonneur for three packs of cards 'in gold and various colours, of several designs, for the amusement of the said king' Seventeen cards survive in the Bibliothèque Nationale that have long been believed to be the original Gringonneur cards, but it is now thought that they are probably fifteenth century, and of Italian origin. They are in a style similar to, although less sophisticated than, the Visconti and Sforza packs. None of the cards is named or numbered, but sixteen of the seventeen are unmistakably trumps:

l'Empereur	la Maison Dieu
le Pape	la Lune
l'Amoureux	le Soleil
le Chariot	le Jugement
Justice	le Monde (wrongly
l'Ermite	identified by all
la Force	commentators as
le Pendu	la Fortune)
la Mort	le Fou
Temperance	

It is clear, then, that the Tarot pack as we possess it today, with its 22 trumps and four suits of 14 cards, is a conglomeration from a variety of sources. It is certainly not, as Court de Gebelin believed, a single compilation of ancient symbolism – but this adds to, rather than detracts from, its value as a means of divination. Over the centuries the users of the Tarot trumps have consciously or unconsciously selected the medieval imagery that has the greatest significance for them, and the designers of the cards have modified their drawings in much the same way. Of course, the designs of some packs have suffered serious degradation in this process, but at their best the traditional packs have a defined strength of character that cannot be improved upon.

After having established the relatively unchanged designs of the 22 Tarot trumps, it is worth recalling that considerable variation is possible. We have dismissed the Etteilla Tarot as an artificial development, but it seems probable that Alliette derived his ideas from some traditional source, even if it were only a judicious blending of Tarot, *tarocchi* and *minchiate*. The Etteilla pack comprises the following cards:

I	Etteilla (The sun's light clearing the clouds)
II	Fire (A bright star above, two children wrestling below)
III	Water (Substantially the same as The Moon)
IV	Air (Substantially the same as The Stars)
V	Earth (Substantially the same as The World)
VI	Day and night
VII	Support and protection (The fifth day of creation: birds and fishes)
VIII	Etteilla (Eve by a tree)
IX	Justice
X	Temperance
XI	Fortitude
XII	Prudence
XIII	Marriage (Similarities to The Lovers)
XIV	The Devil
XV	The Magician
XVI	Judgment
XVII	Death
XVIII	The Capucin (The Hermit)
XIX	The Temple struck by Lightning
XX	The Wheel of Fortune (Fortune, blindfold, stands on her wheel; unusual as a medieval image, this is probably taken from the 'Gringonneur' World)
XXI	The Chariot
LXXVIII	The Fool

That Alliette must have had some external inspiration for his designs is shown by a pack of Spanish provenance in the author's possession, which is similar to, but significantly

Left: the Devil and the Ruined Tower, from Court de Gebelin. Although these illustrations are somewhat crudely engraved, they are of value in establishing the Tarot images as they were before occultists had modified them

different from, the Etteilla pack:

    I El Caos: La Nada — Chaos:
      Nothingness
    II La Luz — Light (The Sun)
    III Las Plantas — The Vegetable World
      (The Moon)
    IV El Cielo — The Heavens
    V El Cielo, el Hombre y los Animales
      Heaven, Man and the Animals
      (design resembles The World)
    VI Los Astros — The Stars
    VII Las Aves y los Peces — The Birds
      and the Fishes
    VIII Descanso o Repos — Rest or
      Repose
    IX La Justicia o La Paz — Justice or
      Peace
    X La Templanza — Temperance
    XI La Fuerza — Fortitude
    XII La Prudencia — Prudence
    XIII El Gran Patriarca — The Great
      Patriarch (design resembles The
      Lovers)
    XIV El Diablo — The Devil
    XV El Falso Adivino — The False
      Soothsayer (design resembles The
      Magician)
    XVI Juicio Final — The Last Judgment
    XVII La Muerte — Death
    XVIII El Ermitano — The Hermit
    XIX La Destruccion del Templo — The
      Ruined Tower
    XX La Rueda de la Fortuna — The
      Wheel of Fortune
    XXI Odio Africano: el Despota—The
      Tyrant (design resembles The
      Chariot)
      La Locura o el Alquimista — The
      Fool or the Alchemist

Although the designs of these cards obviously date from the nineteenth century, they retain quite a number of significant medieval symbols, and their relationship to the 'standard' Tarot can be clearly seen.

In Eastern Europe, Tarot trumps are common that bear little or no resemblance to those described in this book. They comprise 21 numbered cards, and one un-numbered. This un-numbered card is the Joker or Fool, in the travelling musician of trump 1 it is possible to guess at the Magician, and the Imperial eagle of the Habsburgs, perched on a cubic stone, can be found on trump 2. But all the cards are double-ended (like modern Italian Tarots) each bearing two scenes of folk-life in the Austro-Hungarian empire, and it is impossible to relate them in any way to the 'traditional' Tarot; neither do they seem to contain any element of medieval iconography. They can be used, as well as any other pack, for divination; but this book will be devoted to the 'traditional' pack and its historical relatives.

Left: some of the cards from the Florentine game of *minchiate*. They represent the Ruined Tower, the Star, the Moon, the Devil, the Chariot and Death. *Below and far left*: the completion of the Tarot illustrations from Court de Gebelin's *Monde Primitif*: the Stars, the Moon, the Sun, the Last Judgment, the World and the Fool . . . . . .

3
The Tarot and the Qabala

As we have seen, there is no secret wisdom concealed in the symbolism of the Tarot cards; the cards themselves have come down to us as the necessary equipment for a game called *tarok*, and they comprise the 56 cards of a four-suit pack combined with 22 trumps derived from another game called *minchiate*. The secret of the Tarot is what it symbolises for each individual, and those who want to become expert at divination by its use must become familiar with every little detail of each card, so that they know instinctively what the cards represent for them.

The nineteenth century occultists who wrote so many commentaries on the Tarot divided the 22 pictorial trumps from the rest of the pack, but regarded them all as repositories of secrets: they called the former the Major Arcana (from the Latin word *arca*, a chest in which secret things could be stored), and the latter the Minor Arcana. In the next chapter we shall look at the Major

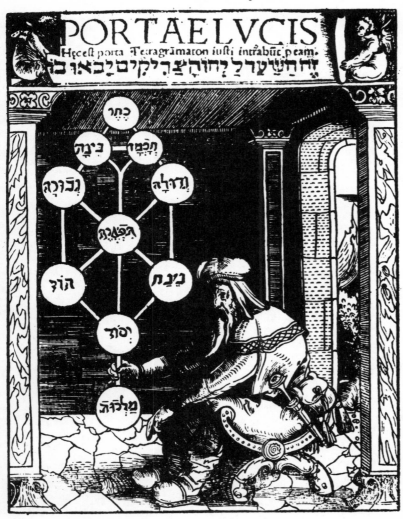

Arcana in detail, describing the images to be found on each card, and outlining the significance that has been attached to each.

Before beginning this survey, it is necessary to go a little deeper into the supposed connection between the Tarot and the Qabala that was suggested by Etteilla and developed by Eliphas Lévi and Papus.

The Qabala is a mystical system which sets out to provide answers to all the questions that confront religious thinkers. Although in principle it is applicable to any religious question, it is essentially Jewish in its derivation, and for its inspiration it relies heavily upon the Hebrew testament. The writers of the chronicles in the Bible made extensive use of word-play, not only in the sense of puns and allusions to similar-sounding words but in what is called *gematria*. This consists in giving numerical values to every letter of the Hebrew alphabet, and then totalling these values to obtain a value for any word made up of various letters. To Christian readers, by far the most familiar example of this is the statement in the Book of Revelations that 666 is 'the number of the Beast'.

The numerical values assigned to the 22 letters of the Hebrew alphabet are established by tradition. As an example of the kind of calculation performed by Qabalists, consider the passage from Genesis xlix:

> The sceptre shall not depart from Judah, nor a lawgiver from between his feet, until Shiloh come; and unto him shall the gathering of the people be.

The phrase IBA ShILH ('until Shiloh come') is totalled as follows:

I	=	10
A	=	2
Sh	=	300
I	=	10
L	=	30
H	=	5
B	=	2
Total		358

Now, the word Messiah, spelt MShICh, comes to the same total:

M	=	40
Sh	=	300
I	=	10
Ch	=	8
Total		358

and this was taken by the Qabalists as showing that the Messiah was prophesied in the passage concerning Shiloh. Moreover, the brazen serpent of Moses (Numbers, xxi, 9) is NaChaSh:

N	=	50
Ch	=	8
Sh	=	300
Total		358

It is clear that this *gematria* is dependent on the peculiarities of Hebrew orthography, in which the vowel sounds are generally omitted; but when works by Jewish mystics began to circulate in Europe in the late Middle Ages they were eagerly seized upon by western magicians, who not only found Christian significance in the Hebrew scriptures and the New Testament, but devised a similar system of their own, based upon the Arabic numerals 1 to 9. This latter system is known as numerology.

The Jewish mystics also developed an ancient concept which sought to explain the integral nature of God and his involvement with every aspect of the universe. This is not the place to go into a detailed description of the mystical Qabalai; very briefly, the Qabalists postulated a limitless something, a sort of 'prime cause', which they named the *En-Sof*. The En-Sof came before God the creator, who was manifested as ten lights, the *Sefiroth*, which might be compared to the internal psychic organs of God, and these ten lights were visualised as making up a kind of tree, from the lowest to the highest. At the top was *Kether*, the Crown, and at the bottom, *Malkuth*, the Kingdom.

A very ancient mystical tradition was that of the *Hekhaloth*, or heavenly palaces, through which the mystic must pass on his way to the *Merkabah*, the fiery chariot of God which Ezekiel saw in his vision. The Qabalists soon equated these Hekhaloth with the ten emanations of the Sefiroth, and imagined pathways linking each to each. Altogether, between the ten Sefiroth, there were 22 possible pathways.

It was the recurrence of this figure 22 that led Alliette to propose that the Tarot trumps represented a Qabalistic document. From here it was an easy step to imagine that each card represented one letter of the Hebrew alphabet and one path up the Sephirotic tree. Eliphas Lévi, and after him Gerard Encausse (Papus), elaborated the theory, and it was taken up by the English occultist Macgregor Mathers. Finally, Aleister Crowley published his *Liber 777* (stolen by him, says the contemporary English writer Ithell Colquhoun, from Mathers), which listed 194 sets of relationships (or 'correspondences') between Hebrew names and numbers of letters, parts of the body, colours, gods of all religions, drugs and perfumes, the planets and signs of the zodiac, and all sorts of other things – including, of course, the cards of the Tarot.

As will be seen in the next chapter, this theory gets off to a good start when card I, the Magician, is equated with the first letter of the Hebrew alphabet, *aleph*. But a similar symbolism cannot be found in any other card of the Tarot trumps, and European occultists soon began to disagree upon which letter should be assigned to which card. Where, for instance, should the Fool be put? Alliette assigned him to card 78, leaving only the first 21 to be allocated 22 letters; Mathers placed

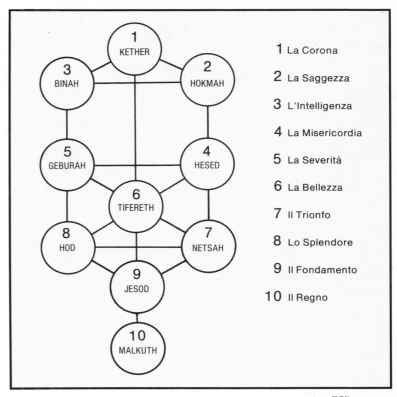

1 La Corona
2 La Saggezza
3 L'Intelligenza
4 La Misericordia
5 La Severità
6 La Bellezza
7 Il Trionfo
8 Lo Splendore
9 Il Fondamento
10 Il Regno

him between cards 20 and 21, equivalent to Sh; Crowley made him the first card. There were similar disagreements upon what the different Hebrew letters were themselves intended to symbolise: the ninth letter, *tet*, represents a roof, says Papus; Mathers (and Crowley) says it is a serpent. Oswald Wirth and Papus added a little serpent to card IX, the Hermit; but Crowley makes *tet* correspond to card VIII, Fortitude. It seems that there is little point in trying to force the Tarot into the Procrustean bed of the Qabala.

Joseph Maxwell, the French Procureur-General, attempted to apply European numerology to the cards. By the rules of numerology, all numbers are eventually reduced to single numerals between 1 and 9; this is done by successively adding the figures making up the number, until a single number is left. Thus, taking the number 358, we get:

$$3+5+8 = 16$$
$$1+6 = 7$$

Maxwell attempted to find significance in the numbers given to the Tarot trumps themselves. Numbers I to IX, of course, remained unchanged; X, by the equation $1+0 = 1$, reduced to unity, and the following cards to 2, 3, etc. One would therefore expect there to be some overt relationship between cards I and X, II and XI, etc; but no such relationship can be found. In fact, this system can be seen to be a numerical system based on the recurrent group of nine, rather than the decimal system of ordinary numbers, or the groups of seven that one might expect to find in the Tarot. As with the Hebrew alphabet, it presents more problems of interpretation than it solves.

Far left: the Tree of the Sefiroth and (*above left*) its translation into Roman characters. *Above*: qabalistic ideogram of the Hebrew letter *aleph*. The posture of the hands is reminiscent of that of the hands of the Magician, lending somewhat specious support to the suggestion that the Tarot is linked to the letters of the Hebrew alphabet

4
The significance of the Tarot trumps

In the chapter that follows, the images of the Tarot trumps are described, and their significance discussed. Many designs of Tarot pack are available nowadays, some of which have no connection whatsoever with the designs of the past. The packs described in this book are of three types:

(1) Packs of historical importance, which survive in museums and private collections, seldom complete.

(2) Packs of 'traditional' design, manufactured commercially by concerns which, in most cases, have made packs to the same design for two centuries or more.

(3) Packs designed by late-nineteenth and early-twentieth century occultists.

Specifically, the following are described:

Packs of historical importance:

The 'Gringonneur' pack, originally believed to be late fourteenth century French, but now thought to be fifteenth century Italian: Bibliothèque National, Paris

The so-called 'Bembo' pack described in *The Tarot Cards Painted by Bembo* (Gertrude Moakley, New York Public Library). These cards are to be found, some in the Pierpont Morgan Library, New York, and some in the Accademia Carrara, Bergamo. A modern reproduction set has been published. The 'da Tortona' cards, property of the Visconti family, described in the *Burlington Magazine*, 1903, were apparently lost during World War II

The 'Mantegna' *tarocchi*, specimens of which are owned by several different museums

Minchiate cards of various packs; the British Museum has an outstanding collection

Traditional packs:

The 'Tarot of Marseille' published by B. P. Grimaud in France

The Swiss 1JJ pack published by Müller in Switzerland

The pack designed by Claude Burdel, 1751, now redrawn and published by Müller

Italian double-headed pack, published by Modiano

Occultists' packs:

Pack described by Jean-Baptiste Pitois in *History and Practice of Magic*

Pack designed by Oswald Wirth, recently republished in its original coloration as companion to *The Wisdom of the Tarot* by Elisabeth Haich

Pack designed by A. E. Waite, and executed by Pamela Coleman Smith

The first thing that you must do is buy a full pack of Tarot cards. Familiarise yourself with every detail, by laying out the cards in small groups, studying each group, and deciding for yourself what significance each card has for you. You must learn to read them like the letters of the alphabet. But just as different alphabets – in Greek or Russian, for instance – have different letters, so each design of Tarot pack has certain meanings that were incorporated in it by its designer. There are the traditional meanings, which carry forward into every modern pack, and there are the particular significations of newer packs like the Etteilla or the Waite. By comparing these meanings, and understanding the source of the Tarot images, you will gradually build up a vast vocabulary of interpretation.

Full-page illustrations on the following pages set out representative cards from packs in the author's collection. In each case the order is as follows. *Left*: 'Bembo' pack, published in facsimile by US Games Systems. *Top centre*: 'Swiss' 1JJ pack published by Müller. *Top right*: Oswald Wirth pack, published in facsimile by Allen & Unwin. *Centre*: Italian modern pack published by Modiano. *Right centre*: 'Spanish' pack. *Centre bottom*: 'Ancien Tarot de Marseille' published by Grimaud. *Bottom right*: A. E. Waite pack, published by Rider & Co. Where appropriate, cards from the *tarocchi* have been included, *lower left*. *Above*: the Magician as described by Pitois

I The Magician
(French: *le Bateleur*   Italian: *il Bagatto*   German: *der Gaukler*)

A man wearing a broad-brimmed hat stands behind a table, on which are various pieces of the conjuror's equipment, such as dice, balls and cups. In some packs there appears to be a glue-kettle on the table, which has led some people to interpret this figure as a country craftsman, the other implements being perhaps a cobbler's knife and awl. In *minchiate* packs, the magician seems to be demonstrating a card trick to a man and a woman, who stand one behind each shoulder; in the 'Bembo' pack he is seated. Generally he holds a short wand in his left hand,

and a small ball in his right.

Wirth followed the traditional designs quite closely, but the implements on the table are replaced by chalice, sword and gold disc, and the conjuror's wand is increased in length.

Pitois describes the figure as 'the Magus, the type of the perfect man . . . he wears a white robe, his belt is a serpent biting its tail . . . The Magus holds in his right hand a golden sceptre; the index finger of his left hand points to the ground . . .' In front of the Magus, on a cubic stone, are a chalice, a

LE BATELEUR

1 LE BATELEVR

IL BAGATTO

IL BAGATTO

1 Diritto: IL RE THOT

Aleph

EL CAOS

1

LA NADA

1 Rovescio: IL CONSULTANTE

ARTIXAN · III ·

THE MAGICIAN

THE MAGICIAN.

Below: Hermes Trismegistos, in an inlaid pavement in Siena cathedral. He is described in the inscription as the 'contemporary of Moses'

sword and a golden coin.

The Waite pack pursues this concept, but the cubic stone is once more a table, and on it are all four of the symbols of the suits. The magus is bareheaded, with a gold band about his brow, but above his head the curly shape of the hat brim has been turned into the mathematical figure known as a lemniscate, the symbol for infinity, and roses and lilies bloom around him.

Interpretation: One of the grounds for controversy between different interpreters of the Tarot is whether the Fool – sometimes unnumbered, sometimes numbered 0 – should be considered as the first or last card of the 22. This will be discussed in detail when this card is described; but it will be clear that there are considerable problems for the qabalists. If the cards of the Tarot are to be related to the letters of the Hebrew alphabet, is the Magician *aleph* or *beth*? Most modern occultists, taking their lead from the esoteric traditions represented by the Golden Dawn. assign *beth* to this card; but Lévi, and after him Wirth and Papus, claimed to see the shape of the letter *aleph* in the poise of the magician's body and his arms.

What all are agreed, however, is that the Magician is the Egyptian god Thoth, or Tehuti, who was known to the Greeks as Hermes Trismegistos, 'thrice-great Hermes'. According to the Egyptian myth, Thoth was the god of all knowledge and the inventor of writing; medieval Christians believed him to have been a historical personage, of an age and standing with Moses and Zoroaster, and the possessor of all the secrets of the universe. Hermes is Mercury, messenger of the gods, patron of thieves and mountebanks, and so the simple conjuror that we see in the Tarot may well be Hermes in disguise.

This, like all the Tarot images, is an ambiguous one. It is man in search of knowledge but it is also the elusive source of that knowledge; in the Etteilla pack, card number 1 portrays creation in the void, but it signifies the man who is seeking an answer. Obviously its interpretation depends not only on the question being asked, but upon the relationship between this card and those around it.

One stands for God, and for man, and for the erect phallus. And infinity, like a figure 8 on its side, may represent the testicles; or should we see that broadbrimmed hat as the hat of the pilgrim, the seeker after truth?

II The Woman Pope

(French: *la Papesse*   Italian: *la Papessa*   German: *die Päpstin*)

A seated woman, wearing simple robes, but with the triple crown of the papacy. She carries an open book on her lap. The story of the woman pope can be traced back to 1282, when it appeared in two rather different forms. The legend of Pope Joan was reported in that year by Martin Polonus: according to this, a woman disguised as a man under the name of John Anglus was elected pope after the death of Leo IV (about 855 AD). She was eventually discovered after a period of two years, five months and four days, when she was found to be pregnant. The legend became very popular, although historical record shows that it is no more than a legend: it is known that only a month and a half elapsed between the death of Leo IV and the consecration of Benedict III.

The other story has some foundation in truth, as well as a direct connection with one of the earliest Tarot packs. The founder of an Italian religious sect, the Guglielmites, was Guglielma of Bohemia, and after her death in 1282 the rumour spread that she was to be resurrected in 1300 and usher in a new age in which women should be popes. Sister Manfreda Visconti was elected by the Guglielmites to be their papess, but was burnt at the stake in 1300, and is commemorated in one of the packs made for the Visconti family.

Tarot packs produced in Switzerland and southern France during the eighteenth century frequently replaced the Woman Pope by Juno, with her peacock, which symbolises immortality and the resurrection.

Oswald Wirth rather let his imagination run riot in his design for this card: the subject is still a seated figure wearing a triple crown, and in her left hand Wirth put the keys of St Peter, but the top of the crown is a crescent moon, the seat is a winged lion, and the book bears the Chinese *yin-yang* symbol on its cover.

In the Wirth pack this card is still called la Papesse, but the definitely non-Christian elements reflect the tendency to give this card another name, that of the High Priestess. This derives originally from Court de Gebelin, and was developed by Pitois, who described this figure as 'The Door of the Occult Sanctuary'. A woman is seated on the threshold of the temple of Isis, between a red and a black column. She wears a tiara surmounted by a crescent moon, and on her breast a solar cross. On her knees is an opened book.

The Waite pack, and several others that follow it more or less closely, conforms to this description, except that the crown takes on a very different shape, the crescent moon is placed below the priestess's foot, and the book bears the word 'Tora'. This is a transliteration of the Hebrew for 'law', but it is also an anagram of the letters 'taro'.

Interpretation: This is a card of knowledge, but of hidden knowledge; it represents the way in which understanding may be obtained intuitively rather than by enquiry. If we try to put ourselves in the position of medieval people interpreting this image, we can see

Above: the Woman Pope identified as the priestess of Isis, as described by Pitois

JUNON.

2   LA PAPESSE

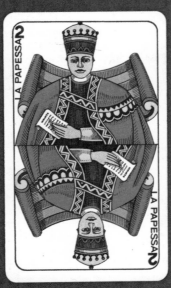

2 Diritto: OSIRIDE O LA GLORIA

LA LUZ

2 Beth

Beth 2

2 Rovescio: FUOCO - COLLERA

THE HIGH PRIESTESS

THE HIGH PRIESTESS

The significance of the Tarot trumps

Below: an unusual deviation from the traditional. The Spanish Captain, from an eighteenth century Belgian pack

that for them it represented the dangerous nature of secret knowledge. This enigmatic woman holds the keys of the kingdom and the book of the law, but she is not all that she seems: a woman disguised as the pope is both a sacrilege and an attack upon established order, yet at the same time she represents freedom and progress.

We must not forget her significance as the high priestess, perhaps of Isis; or as Juno or Hera, the queen of heaven – the name of Pope Joan herself is an anglicised form of Juno. For the Greeks identified Isis with Hera; and when Hera, alone and in secret, conceived and produced a child, it

was 'not a son who resembled gods or men, but the frightful, the terrible Typhon, scourge of mankind'. So must medieval man have thought of the child that Pope Joan conceived – indeed, perhaps the whole legend is a distorted memory of the myth of Hera, who herself wore a high cylindrical crown.

This card, then, represents a strongly feminine principle. It represents intuition, inspiration, the subconscious memory, perhaps also divination and prophecy. In certain contexts it is a subversive influence; and in detrimental situations it may signify emotional instability or lack of foresight.

III The Empress

(French: *l'Impératrice*   Italian: *l'Imperatrice*   German: *die Herrscherin*)

A fair-haired young woman wearing a crown is seated on a throne. In one hand, generally her left, she holds a sceptre supported by her shoulder, while her right arm nurses a shield bearing an imperial eagle. In some packs she has no shield and carries a spindle-shaped rod in her right hand.

The Wirth design is similar to the traditional designs, but the high back of the Empress's throne has been changed into an angel's wings, her head is surrounded with a halo of nine stars, and her left foot is on an inverted crescent.

In Pitois' description this card is a woman seated at the centre of a blazing sun, and crowned with twelve stars. She carries a sceptre, and on her other hand an eagle, and the moon is beneath her feet.

For Waite, this card was still the Empress, but she also reveals some of the attributes of Ceres or Demeter. Ripe wheat fills the foreground of the card; her shield, which stands by her feet, is heart-shaped and bears the symbol for Venus. She holds her sceptre in her right hand above her shoulder, and her crown is a diadem of twelve stars.

Interpretation: After the French Revolution, packs of cards were deprived of their royal connotations, and the name then given to the Empress was *la Grande Mère* – which means, not 'grandmother' but Great Mother. It seems that even as late as the end of the eighteenth century, cardmakers were aware of an ancient tradition that this card really represents the Great Goddess of antiquity.

Demeter, who was known to the Romans as Ceres, was the goddess of the Eleusinian mysteries; she represented the fertility of the earth, and she was often portrayed seated on her throne, crowned with ears of corn and holding a sceptre in her hand. In Arcadia, she was given a dove in one hand, and it is perhaps significant that the *minchiate* pack represents the Empress holding in one hand an orb with something very like a dove on top of it, and in the other a sceptre topped with what looks like an ear of corn.

Where the Woman Pope represented an

intellectual aspect of the feminine principle, the Empress may be interpreted as the body of woman, warm, yielding and maternal. In place of the hidden wisdom of the previous card, she offers human understanding and generous sensuality. She is the vegetable world, beauty and happiness – but perhaps with a hint of over-ripeness, even decadence. Deprived of the fire of intellect, she may sink into luxurious idleness, smothered by the richness that she herself has engendered.

Pitois' identification of this card as Isis-Urania is distinctly odd, since Urania was the muse of astronomy, and could hardly be coupled with the most important of the Egyptian goddesses. In any case, as we have seen, the connection between Isis and the Woman Pope is very much stronger. In fact, Pitois' description sounds much more like the goddess known as Ishtar to the Babylonians, Ashtoreth to the Hebrews, and Astarte to the Greeks; and although the Greeks identified Astarte with Aphrodite, her cult was in fact very similar to that of Demeter.

Above: Isis-Urania as described by Pitois. *Right*: statue of the goddess Demeter enthroned, from the National Museum, Naples. By Roman times, Demeter was largely identified with Cybele, the lover of Attis, who is represented in the Tarot by the Hanged Man

L'IMPERATRICE

3　L'IMPERATRICE　1

3 Diritto: GENIO BENEFICO

LAS PLANTAS

3 Rovescio: ISIDE - LA LUNA

THE EMPRESS

THE EMPRESS.

L'EMPEREUR

4   L'EMPEREVR   7

L'IMPERATORE

4 Diritto: RIFIUTO - SPOGLIAZIONE

4   Daleth

EL CIELO

4 Rovescio: INTELLIGENZA

IMPERATOR·VIIII·

THE EMPEROR

THE EMPEROR.

IV The Emperor

(French: *l'Empereur*   Italian: *l'Imperatore*   German: *der Herrscher*)

Here is an image that has changed very little in the past six hundred years. A crowned man sits in a chair, facing to his right. In his right hand he holds a sceptre, sometimes of an unusual shape, and by his feet is a shield bearing, like that of the Empress, an eagle.

This is the first surviving card in the 'Gringonneur' pack, and the subject is recognisably the same. In addition to his sceptre, the Emperor holds an orb in his left hand; and in place of the shield he is attended by two kneeling boys. Apart from these small differences the card is very similar to that described by Court de Gebelin nearly 400 years later. In the da Tortona pack, however, the Emperor (who is perhaps Frederick III of the Germans) faces directly outward, with two boys behind him and two more kneeling at his feet. The 'Bembo' card is rather different: the Emperor is turned to his left, and there are no attendants.

Oswald Wirth kept closely to the 'traditional' eighteenth century packs, even to the extent of following the strange helmet-like shape of the Emperor's crown; his only major change was in seating the Emperor on a cubic stone decorated with the imperial eagle, rather than a throne with a shield in front of it. He followed, but in a subdued way, the unnatural crossing of the legs in the traditional packs: in these, the Emperor's legs make a shape like the figure 4. The legs of Wirth's Emperor seem almost naturally crossed but Papus, in what purports to be a reproduction of Wirth's design, exaggerates the 4 even further. The significance of this gesture is that it reappears in two other cards.

Pitois calls this card 'The Cubic Stone'. A man wearing a helmet surmounted by a crown is seated on a cubic stone. 'His right hand holds a sceptre, and his right leg is bent and rests on the other in the form of a cross. . . .'

As for Waite, his Emperor sits four-square facing out from the card, on a throne decorated with rams' heads. In his left hand he holds an orb without a cross, and in his right a sceptre topped with the crux ansata. His legs are not crossed.

Interpretation: There is no doubt what the meaning of this card was in medieval times: the Emperor represented temporal power, fatherly protection, strength and leadership. Of course, he also represented the repressive power of the ruling class, and after the French Revolution he was replaced for some time by a figure named, by analogy with the Empress, *le Grande Père*. But this Great Father is not Zeus (Jupiter), any more than the Empress is Hera (Juno); this, the god of plenty and of civilisation, is Dionysos. A bas-relief of Dionysos from the Roman city of Herculaneum makes this very clear: the

Above: the Cubic Stone described by Pitois. *Left*; the first surviving card of the 'Gringonneur' pack. The boy attendants appear only in this and the da Tortona pack. *Below*: relief of Dionysos from Herculaneum

pose on the throne is identical, he holds a sceptre (tipped probably with a pinecone), and his legs are crossed in exactly the same peculiar way as in the traditional Tarot card.

Although we tend to think of Dionysos, whom the Romans called Bacchus, as the god of wine and festivity, in the Orphic religion he finally became, in the words of Plutarch, 'the god who is destroyed, who disappears, who relinquishes life and then is born again'.

We may think of this card as representing the principle of everlasting life, the breath that God breathed into the clay when he made man, the divine inspiration that causes some to rise above the rest. It is the spirit of renewal; it is the idea of persistence in the face of continuing opposition.

So, although this may be the spirit that makes men and women leaders, or captains of industry, it is also the spirit that fills great artists, mystics and saints. It is a source of energy and a source of power; it initiates action, and it then keeps it in continuing motion.

This card is the counterpart to the Empress: masculine as she is feminine, independent as she is all-embracing, creative as she is interpretative.

JUPITER.

5   LE PAPE   ⊓

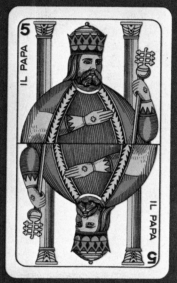

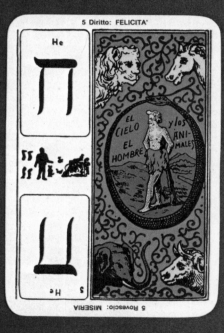

5 Diritto: FELICITA'

EL CIELO EL HOMBRE y los ANIMALES

5 Rovescio: MISERIA

E · PAPA · X · 10

THE POPE

THE HIEROPHANT

V The Pope

(French: *le Pape*   Italian: *il Papa*   German: *der Papst*)

There is no reason to suppose that this card, in medieval packs, symbolised anything other than the Pope: the same subject occurs in the *tarocchi*, and possibly in *minchiate* packs. Without doubt, this card in the 'Gringonneur' pack represents the Pope: in full papal robes, he sits clutching the keys of St Peter, with a cardinal sitting each side of him. In the 'Bembo' pack, he raises his right hand in benediction.

In the 'traditional' designs, this figure is even more clearly the Pope. He wears the triple papal crown, and carries the triple-barred papal cross upright in his left hand. Before him kneel two or three figures with tonsured heads, whom he appears to be blessing.

As with the Woman Pope this figure, in the Swiss and southern French packs, is replaced by Zeus or Jupiter. In the *tarocchi* Jupiter has his own card: he sits, dressed as a crowned king, with an arrow-like thunder-bolt in his right hand, and with his eagle close at hand. Card V in those Tarot packs that replace the Pope is very similar to this *tarocchi* Jupiter.

From Court de Gebelin on, writers have identified this card as the Hierophant, the high priest of the Eleusinian mysteries. In the sense that the Christian mystery took over from the mystery of Eleusis, and the Pope is its high priest, this identification seems thoroughly justified. As Pitois put it: 'This prince of occult doctrine is seated between two columns of the sanctuary. He is leaning on a cross with three horizontals, and describes with the index finger of his right hand the sign of silence on his breast. At his feet two men have prostrated themselves....'

Oswald Wirth, on the other hand, portrayed a story-book Pope, very similar to the traditional representation. Two monks kneel before him, and he blesses them with his right hand. There are none of the extra occult symbols that Wirth put into so many of his Tarot cards.

Waite, also, restrained himself in the design of this card. His Hierophant sits on the throne, with two kneeling monks before him. His right hand is raised in benediction, and his left holds the triple cross. The crossed keys of St Peter are at his feet.
Interpretation: This card is the male counter-part of card II, the Woman Pope. Where she represents intuition, the Pope represents analytical intelligence. The keys that he holds are the keys of knowledge, the blessing he bestows is the blessing of understanding.

At Memphis, the ancient capital of Egypt, the bull Apis was worshipped as a symbol of divine procreativity. When each Apis died, he was identified with Osiris, and in due course the cult of Oserapis developed. Alexandria was established by the Greeks in

Above: the 'prince of occult doctrine' described by Pitois. *Left*: the 'Gringonneur' Pope with his two cardinals. *Far left*: card V in the 'Spanish' pack closely resembles the World in the traditional Tarot

the Nile delta in the fourth century BC, and the chief deity of the place became Serapis, adopted by the Greeks from the Egyptian Oserapis. A magnificent temple was built for the new god, where his statue represented him as a bearded and throned figure. similar to Zeus. To symbolise his connections with the underworld (of which Osiris was king), he was attended by the three-headed dog Cerberus. It seems very likely that this may be the origin of the heads of the three figures kneeling before the Pope; it is also significant that, at the time the first Tarot cards were designed, the badge of the Pope, Alexander Borgia, was a bull.

As Zeus or Jupiter, then, the Pope represents natural law and justice; as Osiris, or his priest, he represents redemption; as Serapis he represents healing. He is the adviser, the confessor, the confidant. But he may also symbolise the repressive aspects of a too rigid orthodoxy. Taking it all in all, therefore, we may identify the Pope with the firm foundation of our lives, the laws of the universe which may not easily be transgressed; but it is essential that we should understand how those laws have been framed.

L'AMOUREUX.

6 L'AMOVREVX 7

6 GLI AMANTI GLI AMANTI 9

6 Diritto: LA NOTTE

6 Vau

LOS ASTROS

Vau 6

6 Rovescio: IL GIORNO

A VENVS XXXXIII 43

THE LOVER

VI

THE LOVERS.

VI The Lover, or The Lovers

(French: *l'Amoureux*   Italian: *gli Amanti*   German: *die Liebenden*)

The first five cards of the Tarot pack appear to be well-defined images whose significance goes back into antiquity without much change, but this sixth card begins to show some of the confusion between different images that gradually crept in as the cards were copied from one cardmaker to another. At least three separate images have been incorporated into the traditional card, and account for its evident ambiguity.

These are (1) the pair or pairs of lovers strolling and talking together, while Cupid (or some cherubs) aims his darts from a cloud above; (2) the legend of the Judgment of Paris, unable to make up his mind between the charms of Hera, Athene and Aphrodite; and (3) the man unable to make his choice between virtue and vice, sometimes symbolised in the middle ages as the Choice of Hercules.

In the traditional design a single Cupid aims his arrow at a young man who has a woman at each side; one of these figures might be considered less good-looking than the other, but it is difficult to tell. The cloud from which Cupid leans has been transformed into a glorious sun.

The eighteenth century Swiss card is very similar to the traditional in its graphic grouping, but the three figures comprise a pair of lovers observed sardonically by an elderly man leaning on a staff.

There is little doubt that the original subject of this card was 'The Lovers'. The 'Gringonneur' card shows no less than three pairs promenading, while two cherubs aim their arrows; the da Tortona pack shows a single pair – presumed to be Duke Filippo Maria Visconti and his first wife, Beatrice di Tenda – in front of a magnificent pavilion over which hovers a blindfolded Cupid; the 'Bembo' card is similar, except that the Cupid is on a pedestal and there is no pavilion, and the loving pair are believed to be Francesco Sforza and Bianca Maria Visconti; and the *minchiate* cards feature a crowned prince kneeling at a girl's feet beneath a menacing arrow that Cupid is just about to loose. The *tarocchi*, on the other hand, show us Venus bathing, attended by her handmaidens; blindfolded Cupid stands to one side, with his bow, and overhead fly Venus's doves.

Oswald Wirth revealed himself strongly in favour of the image of the man unable to make up his mind: his young lover stands undecided between two beautiful girls, one a princess with 'a small but costly crown', the other ragged, barefooted, with flowers in her hair.

Pitois opts for the third concept: he calls this card 'The Two Roads'. It shows, he says, a man standing motionless at a crossroads, with his arms crossed on his breast. Two women personifying virtue (with a

Left: the 'Gringonneur' portrayal of the Lovers shows a typical courtly scene of the fifteenth century. *Below*: Pitois calls this card 'The Two Roads'

fillet of gold round her head) and vice (crowned with vineleaves) point out the two ways to him. 'Above and behind this group the genius of Justice, borne on a nimbus of blazing light, is drawing his bow and directs the arrows of punishment at vice.'

Waite's card for The Lovers makes some kind of combination of concepts 1 and 3. It shows Adam and Eve: Eve stands in front of the Tree of Knowledge of Good and Evil, round which is wound the snake; Adam stands before a tree of flames. Behind them an angel raises his arms in benediction.

Interpretation. The most important feature of this card is the element of choice: this is implied even in the earliest form of the card, because the lovers have undoubtedly chosen each other, even if they are not represented at the actual moment of choosing. The nature of the choice to be made will, of course, depend upon the context in which the card is found. In spite of the sexual nature of the imagery, you must not assume that the question is necessarily one of love or marriage. It may be connected with any aspect of your life.

The outcome of choice is decision, followed by commitment. Some commentators have interpreted the traditional card of The Lovers as a young man and woman swearing their vows before an elder. Certainly, this card demands an end to vacillation; whoever receives it when cards are read must make up his or her mind to undertake a specific course of action.

At the same time, the card emphasises the difficulty of making the correct decision. Cupid's arrow points menacingly, like a bolt from heaven ready to fall upon anybody who takes a wrong step. Poor Paris! whichever goddess he chose (and he chose Aphrodite) he made an enemy of each of the others. The choice may lie between love and all the passions of the body, or the ascetic life of the intellectual. Which is the vice and which is the virtue? this is the question that many find impossible to answer.

VII The Chariot

(French: *le Chariot*   Italian: *il Carro*   German: *der Wagen*)

Here is an image that occurs in all the different sources we have been considering: in the *tarocchi*, in the *minchiate* cards, and in the earliest Tarots. In the *tarocchi* it is the chariot of Mars: it does not seem to be drawn by anything, and Mars sits on a sort of plinth, his sword over his right shoulder and a dog (one of the dogs of war?) at his feet. In the *minchiate* a naked female figure rides on the top of a wagon, which is drawn by two horses, one of them ridden by a groom. She holds a wide ribbon behind her shoulders with the words 'Viva Viva'.

The image is essentially the same in the da Tortona and 'Bembo' packs; but the woman is richly dressed and crowned and carries an imperial orb in her hand. Two white horses draw the car, and in the 'Bembo' pack there is no outrider. In the 'Gringonneur' pack the figure is that of a soldier holding a battleaxe. The most important feature of this card, however, is that it is coming straight towards us, and the artist, unable to cope with the problem of perspective, has drawn the two horses pulling in divergent directions. This feature was copied in many later packs.

The traditional packs follow this line – indeed, perspective has been evaded further and the hindquarters of the horses are invisible, while the wheels on each side are turned even further outward. The principal difference is that the triumphal car itself appears much more like that of Mars. A crowned king stands inside it under a draped canopy, showing only the upper part of his body and carrying a sceptre in his right hand. In Swiss Tarots the upper part of this image has become entirely divorced from the rest: the upper half of the card portrays the king (with the sceptre in his left hand); the lower part contains a complete carriage drawn by two horses.

The Oswald Wirth design is similar to the traditional, but there is a very significant difference: the chariot is drawn by a white and a black sphinx. These, according to Pitois, are respectively Good and Evil – 'the one conquered, the other vanquished'.

Pitois described this card in some detail. It is 'The Chariot of Osiris', and represents a war chariot, square in shape, with a starred

Above: the 'Chariot of Osiris' as described by Pitois. *Right*: the fiery chariot of Ezekiel's vision, as illustrated in the 'Bear' Bible. *Further right*: the triumphal chariot of military power, from the 'Gringonneur' pack

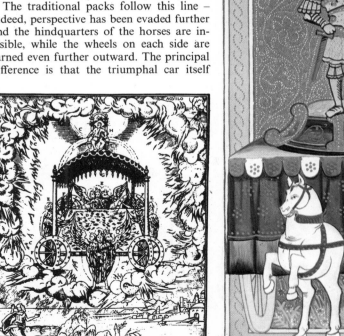

LE CHARIOT

7   LE CHARIOT   7

IL CARRO

7 Diritto: APPOGGIO

LAS AVES y LOS PECES

7 Rovescio: PROTEZIONE

A.   MARTE XXXXV   4

THE CHARIOT

THE CHARIOT.

VIII

LA JUSTICE

8 **LA JVSTICE** **7**

LA GIUSTIZIA 8

LA GIUSTIZIA 8

8 Diritto: LA VIRTU'

8 Heth

DESCANSO ó REPOSO

8 Rovescio: LA CONSULTANTE

B **·IVSTICIA· XXXVII·** **37**

VIII

JUSTICE

XI

JUSTICE .

baldaquin held up by four columns. The 'armed conqueror' carries a sceptre and a sword, and he is crowned with a fillet of gold decorated at five points by groups of three pentagrams.

Waite's design follows the same lines as Wirth and Pitois, but the canopy is smaller than on any other card, to leave room for the walls and towers of a city to be visible behind the chariot.

Interpretation. The chariot is a triumphal one, in which a military conqueror is paraded through the streets to celebrate his success. Indeed, it is this card that has given the word 'trump' to the English language, derived directly from the word 'triumph'. It is the war-chariot of Mars, the Indian *juggernaut*, clearing everyone before it or crushing them beneath its wheels.

But it is also the fiery chariot of Ezekiel's vision, the *merkabah* or Throne Chariot of God that Jewish mystics believed they could attain in trance. The way by which they ascended, through the heavenly halls of the *hekhaloth*, was very like the ascent of the sefirothic tree.

The Chariot, then, represents achievement, success, ultimate victory; and not only in a material but also in a spiritual sense. But it is very important to take care that one is not carried away by this success, running down and destroying everything that lies in the chariot's path; eventually the chariot may itself be overturned, and what began in triumph will end in defeat – perhaps, in spiritual destruction.

VIII Justice

(French: *la Justice*   Italian: *la Giustizia*   German: *die Gerechtigkeit*)

Four cardinal virtues were recognised in antiquity: Justice, Fortitude, Temperance and Prudence. To these, Christians added Faith, Hope and Charity. All seven were represented in the *minchiate* cards, but strangely the grouping was changed, so that cards numbered VI to VIII represented Temperance, Fortitude and Justice respectively, while Prudence was grouped with the Christian virtues as cards XVI to XIX. The Tarot pack retains Justice, Fortitude, and Temperance, numbered VIII, XI and XIV respectively.

This figure is once again a simple medieval image. The female Justice, wearing a head-dress which is not a crown but some sort of mobcap (or perhaps a star-shaped halo), sits upon a throne holding a sword in her right hand and a pair of scales in her left. The only variants on this are that, in the *minchiate* pack, these objects are in the opposite hands, while the Swiss Tarot has Justice in some form of armour, standing.

For various reasons, principally because he wanted to relate the Tarot cards in the right order to the signs of the zodiac, Macgregor Mathers decided to number this card XI rather than VIII, transposing it with Fortitude. This order was adopted by the Golden Dawn: Waite, therefore, and Crowley and other occultists who follow the same persuasion, all have Justice as the eleventh card.

Wirth, however, gave Justice the number VIII, and the figure he designed did not differ significantly from the traditional. Even Pitois' description, supposed to be of an ancient Egyptian mural, is almost identical. He called the card 'Themis': 'a woman seated on a throne wearing a crown armed with spear points: she holds in her right hand an upward-pointing sword and in the left a pair of scales.'

Waite, also, adhered closely to the traditional form, the only major difference being that his Justice wears a square-cut crown.

Interpretation: Themis, whom Pitois identifies with this card, was the ancient Greek goddess of justice and good advice, but she was also the interpreter of the will of the gods and had the gift of delivering oracles.

The Card of Justice, therefore, can be taken to represent the careful weighing of advice, or the equilibrium that can result

The figure of Justice changes very little from pack to pack; from the 'Gringonneur' (*left*) to Pitois' 'Themis' (*above*). Note, however, that the Waite pack (*below, left*) has this card numbered XI, and Justice in the 'Spanish' pack is numbered VIIII

VIIII

L'ERMITE

L' ERMITE

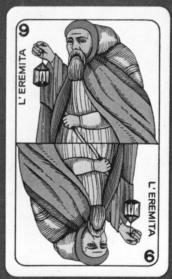

9 L'EREMITA

L'EREMITA

9 Diritto: LA GIUSTIZIA

9 Teth

LA JUSTICIA ó LA PAZ

Teth 9

9 Rovescio: DISACCORDO

A· ·SATVRNO·XXXXVII· ·47·

VIIII

THE HERMIT

IX

THE HERMIT.

when all forces are balanced one against another; but it can also advise us to weigh a situation very carefully before committing ourselves to an irrevocable course of action. By development from this it can be seen as a card that symbolises the way in which man- kind can take a hand in controlling its fate, rather than submit to blind chance. At the same time it warns us that adherence to nothing but the most rigorous logic can lead to bigotry, narrow-mindedness and excessive severity.

IX The Hermit

(French: *l'Ermite* Italian: *l'Eremita* German: *der Weise*)

Here is another medieval image that is hardly changed from pack to pack. In the 'Bembo' and 'Gringonneur' Tarots, and in the *minchiate* pack, the figure is a bearded hunchback in monkish robes carrying an hourglass. In the *minchiate*, he walks with crutches, and the hourglass is carried on his hump; the head of a sitting deer can be seen beyond him. It seems likely that this figure is connected with that of Saturn, in the character of Kronos with his hourglass and scythe, which occurs in the *tarocchi*.

In its traditional form, this card shows a man in a hooded cloak walking towards his right; he carries a lantern in his right hand and a walking stick in his left. He may be known alternatively as the Capucin.

Oswald Wirth's design was substantially the same; but where all the traditional packs show the Hermit with his hood on his back, Wirth's wears his hood up. He is accompanied by a small snake, which is reared up beside him; this was added by Wirth presumably to give colour to the proposal by Lévi that this card should be represented by the Hebrew letter *tet*, which signifies the serpent.

Although the Alliette (Etteilla) pack is not being considered here, it is worth noting that his Capucin, card number XVIII, is walking toward his left, as in the *minchiate*, and is accompanied by a dog. Alliette also gave this card the significance 'the Traitor', which, as we shall see, really belongs to card XII.

Pitois describes the traditional card, under the name of 'The Veiled Lamp': 'an old man who walks leaning on a stick and holding in front of him a lighted lantern half hidden by his cloak'.

Even Waite hardly changed the representation on this card: his hermit also has his hood up, however, and the light of the lantern is a hexagram star.

Interpretation. This card is concerned with time in all its aspects. Kronos, one of the oldest of the Greek gods, consumed each of his children as it was born; we may interpret this as a mythic representation of the way in which we all must succumb to Time:

'Time, like an ever-rolling stream
Bears all its sons away'

or of the attempts that we all make to stop the passage of time. The hourglass is a symbol of time, but it has an added significance in that it can be reversed at any moment. This is why Kronos, later known to the Romans as Saturn, is also related to Ouroboros, the serpent with the tail in his mouth. The hermit, who spends his life in solitary contemplation, is attempting to defeat time in his own way: its passing means nothing to him.

But this card is also concerned with the wisdom that time brings. The lantern that the hermit carries reminds us of the philosopher Diogenes, who had nothing but contempt for temporal power, and who carried a lantern in the dark, looking for one honest man.

In his negative aspects, the Hermit represents the tendency to escape from the responsibilities of everyday life: the holy man usually has every justification for withdrawing from the world around, but nevertheless his existence in his cell is in some ways a privileged and protected one, which he may exploit to his advantage. Knowledge and wisdom, too, may be misapplied; perhaps it was this aspect of the Hermit which caused Alliette to name this card the Traitor.

Another figure which has changed relatively little is the Hermit. In the Alliette and 'Spanish' pack (*far left*), however, card VIIII represents Justice. *Above*: 'The Veiled Lamp' of Pitois

X The Wheel of Fortune

(French: *la Roue de Fortune*   Italian: *Rota di Fortuna*   German: *das Glücksrad*)

The Wheel of Fortune has undergone extraordinary modifications, from the medieval image of the 'Bembo' pack (*right*) to the Egyptian exoticism of Pitois (*above*). Titian's 'Allegory of Prudence' (*below*) explains the identification of this card with Prudence

This card bears one of the most powerful of medieval images, and lies appropriately at the heart of the Tarot pack. It has also undergone more distortion in the course of time than almost any other Tarot image, with the addition and removal of all sorts of significant images.

The turning wheel was used by medieval artists and thinkers to symbolise many different aspects of life: from the daily motion of the sun and planets to the cycle of punishment in hell. The traditional form of the wheel of fortune showed three figures on the wheel, and a fourth below it. Seated at the top was a crowned king, with the word *Regno*; (I reign); ascending on the wheel was a young man with the word *Regnabo* (I shall reign); descending on the wheel was an older man with the word *Regnavi* (I have reigned). The figure below the wheel was an old man on hands and knees, with the words *sum sine regno* (I am without reign).

The 'Bembo' card of the Wheel of Fortune is very like this; blindfolded Fortune sits at the centre of the wheel, but the figure at the top of the wheel has become a cherub with ass's ears, The *minchiate* card is similar, but without the figure of Fortune: the man at the top of the wheel, holding an orb in his hand, has a complete ass's head, and the descending figure has a rather devil-like head. The card in the 'Gringonneur' pack, which has rather remarkably been identified by all commentators as Fortune, is in fact The World, and will be described under that heading.

The 'traditional' Tarot card design takes these medieval tendencies a little further. The top of the wheel is occupied by a crowned monkey, holding a sword in his left paw, and with some kind of wings or high-shouldered cloak behind him. Another monkey, wearing a sort of striped skirt, descends on the wheel; while what could be either a monkey or a dog ascends. There is no fourth figure on the ground and, although the wheel has a cranked handle, there is nobody turning it.

This card in the Swiss pack is interesting in that it departs further from the traditional design than any other in this pack. Fortune's wheel stands on the edge of a cliff, and she herself, almost naked, is cranking it. Seated on the top of the wheel are a young couple in late eighteenth century dress: the man appears unconcerned, but the girl is looking apprehensively over her shoulder at the abyss beneath. Below her, a young man is just falling from the wheel. Interestingly, a rosebush blooms between the supports of the wheel.

Eliphas Lévi was responsible for the next development in the design of the Wheel of Fortune. In his *Key of the Mysteries* he reproduced a drawing of 'the tenth key of the Tarot': in this the crowned monkey has become unequivocally a winged sphinx, the ascending figure is a dog carrying the winged staff of Hermes, and the descending figure is a horned devil with a trident. These three figures are labelled respectively *Archée* ('made highest'), *Azoth* (a word invented by alchemists to describe a hypothetical first principle) and *Hyle* (the raw material of man, the substance of his purely animal nature). This design was followed by Oswald Wirth, but without the three labels; in addition, Wirth's wheel is supported in some kind of crescent-shaped boat, with the serpents of Asklepios twined about the support.

Pitois' description is clearly based on Lévi's ideas. The card is called 'The Sphinx': on the right side of the wheel Hermanubis 'the spirit of God', tries to climb the wheel, while on the left Typhon, the spirit of evil, is cast down. 'The Sphinx, balanced on top of the wheel, holds a sword in its lion's paw. It personifies Destiny ever ready to strike left or right . . .'

Waite's design moves even further away from the traditional. Derived from a drawing

LA ROUE DE FORTUNE

10   LA ROVE DE FORTVNE   ▼

10
ROTA DI FORTUNA
ROTA DI FORTUNA
10

10 Diritto: LA SALUTE

10   Jod

ר

Jod   10

LA
TEMPLANZA

10 Rovescio: PRETE

B   PRVDENCIA XXXV·   35

THE WHEEL OF FORTUNE

WHEEL of FORTUNE.

The significance of the Tarot trumps

in Lévi's *Sanctum Regnum*, the wheel is now a stylised circular shape, bearing the letters R-O-T-A, which can also be read as T-A-R-O, and between these the Hebrew letters *yod-he-vau-he*, the name of God. At the top of the wheel sits a sphinx, the jackal-headed figure of Anubis rises at the right, and a serpent descends at the left. The stylised spokes of the wheel are decorated with the alchemical symbols for mercury, sulphur, salt and water, and in the four corners of the card (echoing the traditional design of the card called The World) are the four mystical animals of Revelation: man, the eagle, the bull and the lion.

Interpretation. The cycles of the lunar month and the solar year, the cycle of generation and regeneration – 'birth, copulation and death' – the wheel of the sun itself, the wheels within wheels of fate, the circular transformation from one to another of the Aristotelian elements (earth, fire, air, water): all these meanings and many more are comprised in the symbols of this card.

The king with the ass's ears of the medieval image is Midas, who could turn everything into gold: in a musical contest between

Apollo and the satyr Marsyas, Midas voted for Marsyas, and in revenge Apollo gave him the ears, which he had to hide by wearing a Phrygian cap.

The later metamorphosis of the figures on the wheel may well be the incorporation of another piece of medieval imagery: one of the figures for the cardinal virtue of Prudence, which is otherwise missing from this pack. As Cicero, the Roman orator, put it in the first century BC: 'Prudence consists of . . . Memory, Intelligence and Foresight'. These three parts of Prudence were frequently represented by a three-headed figure with the heads of an elderly man or wolf, a mature man or lion, and a young man or dog, respectively.

This card, then, signifies change, and the ability to experience change prudently: knowing (to quote Cicero again) 'what is good, what is bad, and what is neither good nor bad'. And the card reminds us that few changes are permanent and irreversible; sooner or later an upward swing of fortune is followed by a fall, the wheels of destiny turn slowly but they always turn full circle in the end.

XI Fortitude or Strength

(French: *la Force*   Italian: *la Forza*   German: *die Kraft*)

The second of the classical virtues can be represented by a number of minor variations upon a single image. The 'Gringonneur' card shows a seated woman who is breaking a column in half, apparently using some sort of 'karate chop'. There are two rather different representations of Fortitude in the da Tortona and 'Bembo' cards: the former shows a woman holding the jaws of a snarling lion, and the latter is a picture of Hercules with his club subduing the Nemean lion. In the *minchiate* pack and the *tarocchi*, these images are combined as a woman, attended by a lion, snapping a pillar in two.

The traditional packs all follow the example of da Tortona; the only remarkable feature is the broad-brimmed hat worn by the woman, which is very similar in style to that worn by the Magician. The Swiss pack, however, chooses the image of Hercules – although he has laid down his club and is wrestling with the animal.

Oswald Wirth followed the traditional design without modification. Pitois, similarly, identified this card as 'The Tamed Lion': a young girl who with bare hands is closing, without effort, the jaws of a lion.

In fact, it is impossible to tell, in the design of any card described so far, whether the woman is closing, opening or merely holding the lion's jaws. Waite's design, however, makes it quite clear that Strength is closing the lion's jaws; although a garland of flowers, which appears to link the girl with the lion, nevertheless makes this a gesture of somewhat ambiguous significance.

Above: Pitois identified this card as 'The Tamed Lion'. The broken column of the 'Gringonneur' card also appears as an attribute of Fortitude in the *tarocchi*. Note that Waite's card is numbered VIII

LA FORCE

11 LA FORCE

LA FORZA

LA FORZA

11 Diritto: LA FORZA

11 Caph

LA FUERZA

11 Rovescio: IL SOVRANO

FORTEZA · XXXVI

FORCE

VIII

STRENGTH.

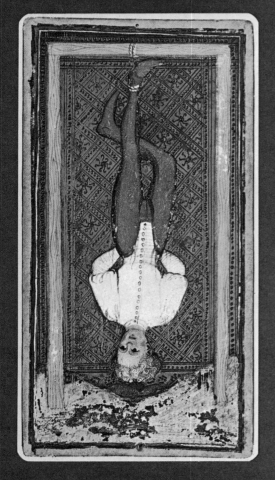

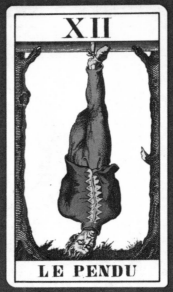

LE PENDU

12   LE PENDV

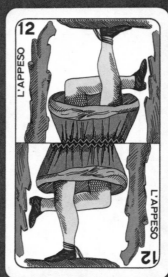

12 L'APPESO

L'APPESO 12

12 Diritto: LA PRUDENZA

12   Lamed

Lamed   12

LA PRUDENCIA

12 Rovescio: IL TRIBUNO

THE HANGED MAN

THE HANGED MAN.

Interpretation. The woman wrestling unarmed with the lion is Cyrene, nymph of the goddess Artemis (Diana). She was seen by Apollo who fell in love with her and carried her off in his chariot to Libya, where she gave birth to Aristaeus, who became the equivalent of the Thessalian god Pan.

The breaking of the pillar reminds us of another personification of strength, the Biblical hero Samson, who (although blinded) brought down the pillars of the temple. He was often represented as a Biblical equivalent of Hercules, holding a lion's jaws in exactly the way portrayed on this card. But the most evocative image for medieval man was of course that of Hercules himself, the archetypal hero of the Greeks. He spent twelve years under the orders of Eurystheus, the king of Greece, and performed twelve heroic labours, the first of which was killing the Nemean lion. While wearing the skin of this lion as a robe, Hercules was invincible.

This card, then signifies strength: strength of purpose, spiritual strength and moral courage, as well as sheer physical strength. Its message can be one of warning, meaning that bravery and resolve will be needed to meet a coming danger. And it can also suggest caution against abusing one's strength, using it to dominate others, whether physically or spiritually. The man who uses his intellectual superiority like a goad is as guilty of this as the man who bullies others by the strength of his arm.

XII The Hanged Man

(French: *le Pendu* Italian: *l'Apesso* German: *der Gehängte*)

No card in the Tarot pack has provoked more discussion than this one. Court de Gebelin, rightly realising that the pack lacked a card for Prudence, decided that this was it. 'You find it in its correct place between Fortitude and Temperance, a man hung by the heels. But why is he hung? This is the work of a presumptuous cardmaker who, misunderstanding the beauty of the allegory, has taken upon himself to correct it. . . . Prudence can only be represented in an intelligible manner as a standing man who, having put one foot forward, has lifted the other and now stands there examining the ground where he can place it safely. This card, then, is the man with his foot suspended, *pede suspenso*; but the ignorant cardmaker has made it a man suspended by his feet.'

For Court de Gebelin, in other words, the card is upside down, and it appears, as he described it, in an eighteenth century Belgian pack. The argument is very plausible, and it is fortunate that we have surviving cards from the oldest packs to show that it is wrong. For this card in the 'Gringonneur' pack is clearly of a young redheaded man who has been hung by one foot from the crossbar of a gibbet. This was the old punishment for debtors:

He by the heels him hung upon a tree
And baffl'd so, that all which passed by
The picture of his punishment might see

as Spenser put it in *The Faerie Queene*, some 400 years ago. In each hand the man holds a bag of coins that he has come by unlawfully. This is Judas, with the thirty pieces of silver he earned by betraying Christ; and, as the Bible says, he took a rope and hung himself. This is the card otherwise known as The Traitor.

In the 'Bembo' pack, the hanged man has his hands presumably tied behind his back, and his legs are crossed in a shape like the figure 4; this is the image that was adopted for all the 'traditional' cards. Even in the

From the earliest packs, the Hanged Man has been unequivocally hung by his feet; only a surviving eighteenth century Belgian pack antedates Court de Gebelin's insistence that this is a representation of a prudent man with one foot poised, printed upside down by mistake. Alliette and related packs, however, devote card XII to a representation of Prudence

Swiss pack it is substantially the same, although the crossing of the legs is not represented clearly, and the position of the arms is also rather vague.

Wirth's Hanged Man is very similar, but two bags of money can be seen, one beneath each armpit, with gold and silver coins falling from them. Pitois' description includes an attempt to explain the graphic symbolism of the figure. He calls it 'The

307

Sacrifice': 'a man hung by one foot from a gallows which rests on two trees each of which has six branches cut from the trunk. The hands of this man are tied behind his back, and the bend of his arms forms the base of an inverted triangle the summit of which is his head. It is the sign of violent death encountered by tragic accident or in expiation of some crime, and accepted in a spirit of heroic devotion to Truth and Justice. The twelve lopped branches signify the extinction of life, the destruction of the twelve houses of the horoscope. The inverted triangle symbolises catastrophe.'

Only Waite's design is significantly different. Instead of a gibbet between two trees, the man hangs from a T-shaped cross. His legs are crossed in the 4-shape, and his arms are behind his back, but there is a bright halo about his head.

It is noticeable that there is no consistency in which foot the figure hangs by. On some cards he hangs by the left foot, on others by the right, and on at least one of the 'traditional' packs – the Swiss 1JJ pack published by Müller – he hangs by both.

Interpretation. In spite of the connection with Judas, and the gruesomeness of the idea of a hanged man, it is incorrect to regard this as a card of evil meaning; it is significant that, in nearly every representation, there is no look of discomfort on the man's face, despite his position.

Several commentators have drawn attention to the parallel with the words of Odin in The Lay of the High One:

Wounded I hung on a wind-swept gallows
For nine long nights.
Pierced by a spear, pledged to Odin,
Offered, myself to myself;
The wisest know not from whence spring
The roots of that ancient rood..

The tree was Yggdrasil, the World Tree, and Odin was the Norse god of the dead, but it would be unwise to pursue the parallel too closely. One-eyed Odin, with his eight-legged horse, who moved among the heroes as an old man in a wide-brimmed hat and cloak, is not the hanged man of the Tarot. Perhaps, however, the myth of Odin, initiated into the mysteries by nine nights of pain, is one form of a tradition that goes back into the mists of antiquity. For the idea of the man who is redeemed by suffering, and who by his suffering also redeems others, is far older than the stories of Odin, of Christ, of Mithra, or of any other god-like being. We remember, in particular, Attis, often represented as a handsome young man hung upon a tree.

The meaning of the Tarot is not always as it seems, and as we look at them the shapes shift and change. Judas the traitor, the symbol of faithlessness, becomes the initiate of the mysteries, the agent who sets the fore-ordained drama in motion: as we impose one personality upon him, he shifts easily into another. Odin was known as a shape-shifter, but the greatest of all was the 'Old Man of the Sea', Proteus. He could change his form at will: the important point was not to be frightened by the changes, when he would relent and give advice drawn from his knowledge of the events that were to come.

The card of the Hanged Man, then, may mean what you will. It symbolises adaptability and the desire to learn; it brings knowledge of the future and new understanding of the past; it means change – not the slow inevitable change of the Wheel of Fortune, but sudden violent change, demanding sacrifice. Yet it counsels you not to fear that change, but to face it bravely.

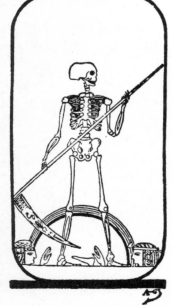

Although Death appears mounted on a horse in the 'Gringonneur' and da Tortona packs, he does not reappear in this form until the design of A. E. Waite (*bottom, far right*). The Spanish 'Great Patriarch' (*centre, far right*) is clearly derived from the traditional card VIII, the Lovers

XIII Death

(French: *la Mort*   Italian: *la Morte*   German: *der Tod*)

Here is another powerful symbol from medieval iconography, the image of Death as a skeleton mounted on a horse and carrying his scythe, trampling over the fallen bodies of kings, popes and cardinals. This is how he appears in the da Tortona and 'Gringonneur' packs, and in the *minchiate*. In the first two of these packs he has a white scarf bound round his head with the ends flying; this same feature is repeated in the 'Bembo' pack, but Death here is standing, with a strung bow in his hand. In another fifteenth century pack, by Cicognara, he stands with his scythe over his shoulder, leering in a cardinal's broad hat and cape: the words *son fine* (it is the end) emerge on a ribbon from his mouth.

Traditional packs are all very similar. Death, a naked skeleton, walks forward with his scythe in the reaping position, over a field in which heads, hands, feet and bones

are the main crop. In the Swiss pack the stance is identical, but the field is clear.

Oswald Wirth chose the same image as the traditional packs, and like them placed a crown upon one of the heads; there is no apparent additional feature in his design. Pitois also described this card without modification, giving it the name 'The Scythe' and interpreting it as the emblem of destruction and perpetual rebirth of all forms of Being in the domain of Time.

Waite's design, as might be expected, takes the elements from a number of different cards and combines them in an idiosyncratic way. Death is without a scythe, or a weapon of any kind, but he is dressed from head to foot in black armour. He rides a white horse and carries in his left hand a black banner with a white five-petalled heraldic rose. In the field through which he rides are a dead king, a child, a

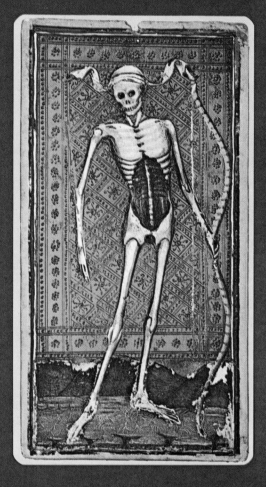

LA MORT

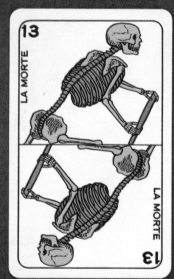

13 Diritto: MATRIMONIO - UNIONE

DEATH

DEATH.

for the wretched peasant: it was the only institution of democracy. The figure of Death was a warning of the vanity of worldly wealth and position. His scythe was the scythe of Saturn and of Time, the scythe with which Kronos castrated his father Uranus.

So, while Death takes away, he also restores: every conclusion is also a new start. The field that he reaps, with its human remains like a charnel house, is also the field where Jason sowed the dragon's teeth to grow as armed men.

Death, indeed, is the symbol of transformation. In many of the traditional Tarot packs, Death is not named for fear of bringing ill-luck by mentioning him; and it is no coincidence that this card is number thirteen; but, as with The Lovers or The Hanged Man, its true significance depends upon the context in which it is found. We have seen how the Wheel of Fortune represents change of a cyclic, recurrent kind, and how the Hanged Man means change through sacrifice and the sudden reversal of circumstances; the card of Death can also symbolise change, but of a transforming kind, the passage through ordeal to some sort of rebirth. All the mystery cults of antiquity initiated their members by some kind of ceremony in which they enacted death and rebirth; in certain cults the novices descended into Hades like Orpheus and afterward, like him, returned to the earth's surface. The myth of Orpheus tells how, when he returned from Hades, he was torn to pieces by the Thracian women; his head was thrown into the river Hebrus and carried to Lesbos, where it caught in the fissure of a rock and there remained, delivering oracles. Is the crowned head in the corner of Death's field perhaps this head of Orpheus, still uttering oracles?

woman who appears to be in despair, and a bishop praying; behind them, a river flows at the foot of a bluff, and the sun rises between two towers on the horizon.

Interpretation. For medieval man, death was the great leveller. It was the same for kings, queens and princes of the church as

XIV Temperance

(French: *Tempérance* Italian: *la Temperanza* German: *die Mässigkeit*)

Here is the fourth and last of the classical virtues, portrayed in a traditional medieval way. In every pack, from the 'Bembo' and 'Gringonneur' to those of Wirth and Waite, we find the same figure. A woman – generally standing, but in the 'Gringonneur' pack and the *minchiate* sitting – pours liquid from a jug held in one hand to another jug held in the other. In the early packs she is crowned like the other virtues, but in the traditional packs and those that follow she has wings like an angel.

To modern man, brought up to believe that 'temperance' means moderation in the use of alcohol, the figure seems to be pouring water into wine to dilute it; but to medieval man the significance was more likely that of division: halving the contents of one jug by pouring some into the other.

Pitois gave this card a very different

meaning – 'The Solar Spirit: Initiative'. He described it as the Spirit of the Sun pouring the vital sap of life from one urn into another, 'the symbol of the combinations which are ceaselessly produced in all parts of Nature'.

Even Waite's design for this card does not depart far from the traditional image. Temperance, pouring from one chalice to another, stands beside a pool with one foot in the water. Behind her a path leads to the mountains and the rising sun, and beside the pool are yellow irises.

Interpretation. The ancient Greeks represented Iris very much like the traditional figure of Temperance: she wore a long flowing tunic and flew on her errands with a pair of golden wings. When the gods returned to Olympus she waited on them, serving ambrosia and nectar. Her companion in these duties was Ganymede, the cup

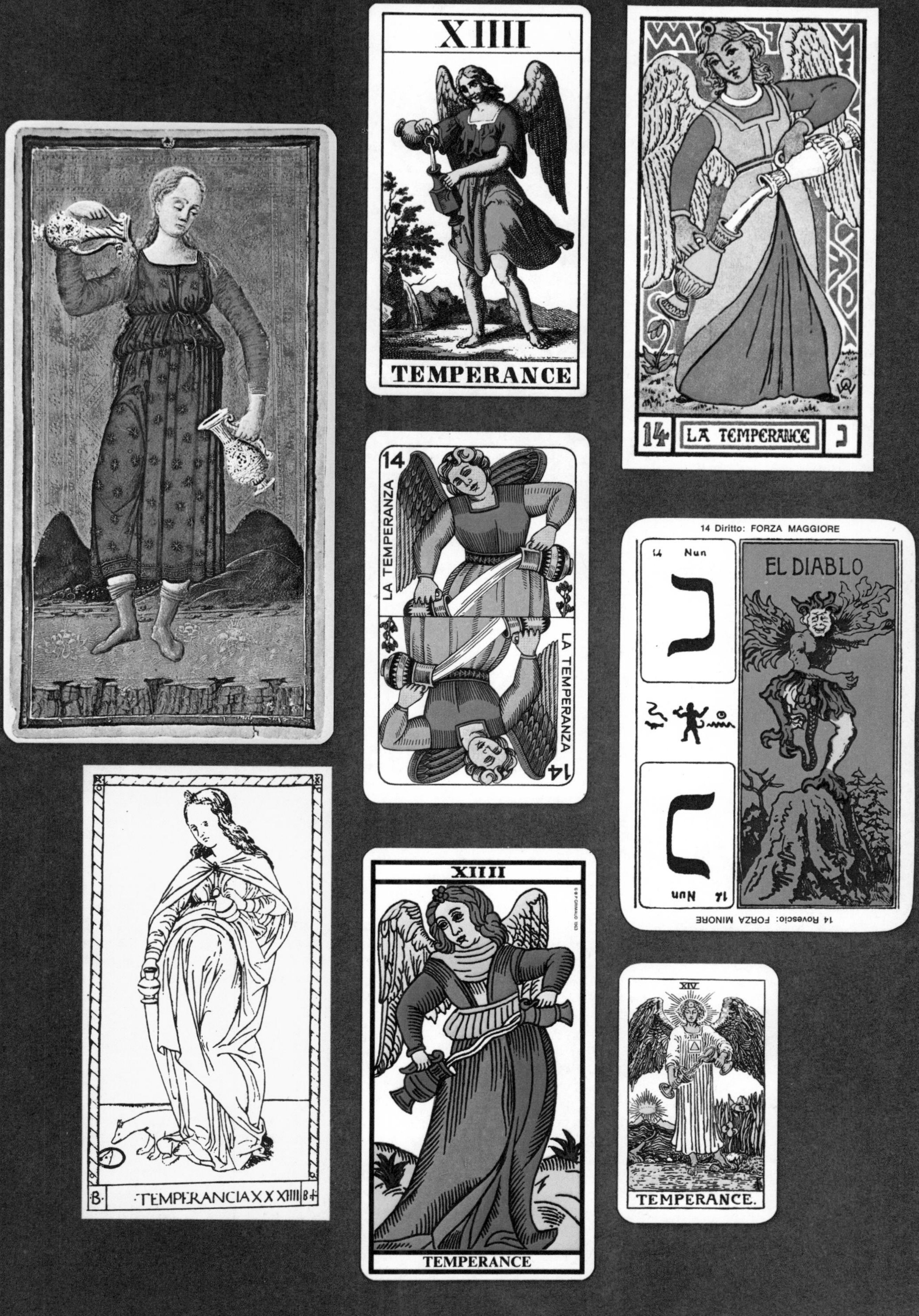

XIIII
TEMPERANCE
14 LA TEMPERANCE
14
LA TEMPERANZA
LA TEMPERANZA
14
14 Diritto: FORZA MAGGIORE
14 Nun
EL DIABLO
14 Nun
14 Rovescio: FORZA MINORE
TEMPERANCIA XXXIIII
XIIII
TEMPERANCE
XIV
TEMPERANCE.

The significance of the Tarot trumps

Above and right: medieval iconographers confused, deliberately or by accident, the figures of Ganymede (identified as the astrological Aquarius) and Iris, in their representation of Temperance

bearer; in primitive times he appears to have been thought of as the deity who sprinkled the earth with rain, and early astrologers identified him with Aquarius. It seems likely that medieval iconographers, either deliberately or by mistake, confused Iris with Ganymede.

No doubt they also infused this image with the significance of Christ's miracle of turning water into wine. The chalice of wine that changes into blood is a very powerful symbol in the celebration of the mass, and perhaps there is also a memory of the Eucharist as the second-century Gnostic Marcos celebrated it, with two chalices, one of water and one of wine, which he mixed together.

Few commentators have found very much to say about the significance of the card of Temperance: the image is a very simple one, and the concept behind it is equally simple. Temperance, of course, is not confined to alcohol; it means moderation in all things. Combined with this, too, is the concept of mercy; and the metal-worker who 'tempers' steel, bringing it exactly to the desired degree of hardness and elasticity, also knows the meaning of the word. Indeed, to keep one's temper, to be temperate in action and opinion, to keep a room, or an oven, at an even temperature – all these uses come from the same source. The card Temperance, appearing with other cards, will modify their significance, and always for the better.

XV The Devil

(French: *le Diable*   Italian: *il Diavolo*   German: *der Teufel*)

Eliphas Lévi's Goat of Mendes was supposed by him to be the idol worshipped by the Knights Templar. Its appearance contributed significantly to Oswald Wirth's design for the card of the Devil. The Spanish pack (*far right*) gives card XV to a figure that is obviously the Magician

Significantly, this card is not known in the 'Gringonneur', 'Bembo' or da Tortona packs. It appears first in the *minchiate*, a horned figure with leathery wings, animal feet and a belt of hissing snakes, purposefully marching across the card with his trident. The number of this card in the *minchiate* is XIV, part of an apocalyptic foursome which otherwise comprises the Hanged Man, Death and the Ruined Tower.

It is in the 'traditional' packs that a new element emerges. The winged figure stands on some kind of a pedestal, holding in his left hand something that might be a sceptre or a sword but which, in some designs, bears an unexpected resemblance to the object (torch, key or piece of the mystery plant *haoma*) held in the left hand of so many statues from temples of the Roman god Mithra. Two lesser devils stand each side, fastened by a cord about the neck to a ring in the front of the pedestal. In certain packs, none of the figures has the usual short, goat-like horns, but rather a helmet from which sprout antlers; and the central figure wears a kind of breastplate with exaggerated breasts and sometimes an animal-like face at his belly.

The Swiss pack, however, returns to the medieval image: the devil has short horns, a curly tail concealing his nakedness, and cloven hoofs. He carries a pitchfork, and a woman sits despairingly at his feet, her head in her hands. The eighteenth century Belgian Tarot pack also has a devil of medieval derivation.

Wirth's design once more shows the influence of Eliphas Lévi. The Devil has become Lévi's invention, the 'Goat of Mendes', which he supposed to have been the idol worshipped by the Knights Templar. This has wide curling horns and a bearded face like a mountain goat, above a naked body with a woman's breasts, legs covered in green scales, hairy calves and cloven hoofs. The two minor devils are of fairly orthodox form, and are fastened to the central ring by what is called a 'cable-tow' in freemasonry. But among the symbolic additions to this card are the glyph which covers the goat's genitals – a combination of the sign for Mercury and the *crux ansata* – and the lettering of the words 'solve' and 'coagula' on the right and left arms respectively. 'Solve et coagula' ('Liquefy and solidify' is the closest translation) was the basic principle of medieval alchemy. As always with Lévi's modifications there is

LE DIABLE.

15 LE DIABLE

ħ

ʊ

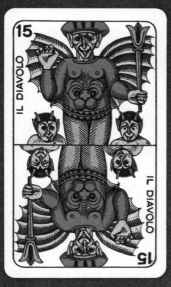

IL DIAVOLO

15 Diritto: MALINCONIA

15 Sameck

EL FALSO ADIVINO

15 Rovescio: INDISPOSIZIONE

XV

THE DEVIL

XV

THE DEVIL.

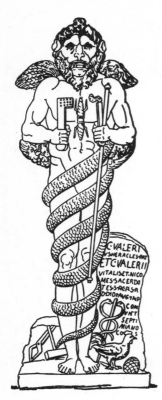

little or no justification for these changes and additions to the Tarot figure.

By comparison, Waite's design is positively conventional, but it contrives deliberately to reflect the design of his card for The Lovers. The pose of the bat-winged Devil is similar to that of the angel, and the two captive devils are a man and a woman. The Devil's right hand is raised in a strange gesture, the first and second, and third and fourth, fingers together, with the glyph of Saturn on the palm; and his left holds an inverted torch.

Interpretation. Medieval people knew very well who the Devil was: they recognised his angelic origin, but they gave him features derived from all the non-Christian gods whom they saw as threats to their religion.

First of all this is 'the frightful, the terrible Typhon', the monstrous offspring of Hera, the same creature as Set, the evil brother of Osiris. 'All that is creation and blessing comes from Osiris; all that is destruction and

perversity arises from Set.' The Egyptians represented Set with a forked tail and two stiff square-cut ears; later these ears became horns.

But the helmet with antler-like horns from the traditional Tarot is the helmet of Kernunnos, the Celtic god of pre-Roman times. And the goat horns and feet are those of the Greek god Pan, who finally came to represent the universal god, the Great All.

Above all, however, as has already been indicated above, the Devil of the Tarot incorporates many features derived from the religion of Mithraism, which flourished at the time when Christianity was first struggling to establish itself. Mithra was one of the most ancient of gods: he appears in the earliest Indian texts, the Vedas, and was well-established before 1400 BC. He appears as an important god in Zoroastrianism, where his adversary is Ahriman, the representative of Zervan, whom the Romans called Saturn.

In Mithraism, Zervan was represented in various similar ways. He usually had wings and the head of a lion, and carried a pair of keys; sometimes he had claw-like or cloven feet, and a serpent twined about his body like the tail of Set; sometimes the lion head was featured on his belly. Mithra himself was generally represented standing between two smaller figures, one carrying a torch the right way up, the other carrying it inverted.

We can see, then, that this card symbolises above all the power of the adversary: if plans are being made, it represents the way in which circumstances seem to conspire against the realisation of those plans; and it represents the darker, subconscious side of human nature, which often causes us to act against our best interests. It can mean an enemy; but it can also mean a friend whose personality is so strong that he can influence our decisions, for good as well as bad. Whenever the card of the Devil appears, it signals caution: plans should be looked at with care, decisions reconsidered.

Above: the Mithraic figure of Zervan, with attendant torch-bearers (dadophori), discovered in a mithraeum in Ostia. *Right*: the horned figure of Set (*left*) leads two attendant figures by ropes, exactly as on the Devil card

XVI The Tower

(French: *la Maison de Dieu*   Italian: *la Torre*   German: *das Haus Gottes*)

A tower, struck by lightning. In the traditional packs the tower has a crown-like castellated top which has been tilted sideways by the bolt of lightning; bricks and tongues of flame are falling on both sides, and two male figures are tumbling to the ground. In the 'Gringonneur' pack these figures are absent, and the top of the tower is undisturbed, but stones and flickers of flame are falling on the right-hand side. The card does not appear in the surviving 'Bembo' pack, nor in the da Tortona pack, where the World card has been wrongly identified as the Tower; in *minchiate* packs a naked woman, presumably Eve, is emerging from a

doorway in the tower, closely followed by a man, while fire falls from heaven.

Oswald Wirth's version is substantially the same as the traditional; one of the falling figures wears a small crown, and the lightning flash comes from a sun partially visible in the top right corner. This also is how Pitois described it.

In the Waite design, the crown-like top of the tower has become a real crown, which has been blasted off, but otherwise it remains substantially the same as the traditional Tarot cards.

Interpretation. This is yet another card of the Tarot which combines a very considerable

XVI

LA MAISON DE DIEU

16 LA MAISON-DIEV

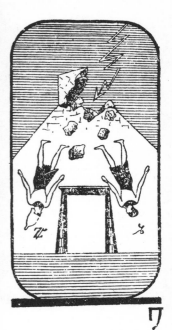

Above: In spite of its Egyptian style of design, the Pitois card is very similar to the traditional cards. The Spanish pack (*left*) devotes card XVI to the Last Judgment

16

LA TORRE

LA TORRE

16

16 Diritto: CAUSA GUADAGNATA

16 Ain

16 Rovescio: CAUSA PERDUTA

JUICIO FINAL

XVI

THE TOWER OF DESTRUCTION

XVI

THE TOWER.

The significance of the Tarot trumps

Right: a representation of the falling tower from the Golden Legend, in Reims cathedral; and the figureless Ruined Tower of the 'Gringonneur' pack.
Far right: with characteristic perverseness, the Alliette and related packs make card XVII Death

number of strong medieval images. The most obvious is a story from the Golden Legend which tells how, when the Holy Family fled from Herod, their entry into each town caused the pagan temples and altars to tumble. Representations of this story appear in carvings in several medieval cathedrals.

Next to this, we must consider a combination of the story of Pentecost, in which the descent of tongues of flames from heaven caused the disciples to speak in different languages, with the story of the Tower of Babel, whose builders were made to speak, each with a different language, as punishment for their presumption in building a tower up to heaven. The *minchiate* representation is clearly connected with the expulsion of Adam and Eve from the Garden of Eden, and there are also echoes of the story of the destruction of Sodom.

The true medieval meaning of Maison de Dieu (or, more commonly, Maison-Dieu) is 'hospital', but it seems more likely that 'House of God' is intended, and that the reference is either to the Golden Legend, or to the striking of the temple in Jerusalem by lightning at the time of the crucifixion.

The meaning of the card is punishment: for presumptuous pride, for the pursuit of forbidden knowledge, or for actual transgression of the moral code. It can also stand for pride itself, for male sexuality, or for the finger of God raised in warning. In certain contexts it may represent the gift, or the confusion, of foreign tongues; and finally it can symbolise the burning flame of divine inspiration, which must be received with humility lest it should destroy.

XVII The Stars

(French: *l'Étoile*   Italian: *le Stelle*   German: *die Gestirne*)

The usual English name of this card is 'the Star', but its Italian and German names show it for what it really represents: the whole of the celestial sphere.

Medieval philosophers imagined the planets turning about the earth in a succession of seven spheres; outside these turned the celestial sphere, and beyond this the *primum mobile*, the 'prime mover', and the *prima causa*, or First Cause. All these are represented in the 'Mantegna' *tarocchi*, but only the signs of the zodiac and the Sun, Moon and stars are included in the *minchiate*.

The *minchiate* card justifies the use of the title 'the Star', for it clearly shows one of the magi, following the star that hung over the

stable at Bethlehem, and bearing his precious gift in his right hand.

The early Tarots, in contrast, all show a crowned female figure, facing right and holding up a single eight-pointed star. In the 'Bembo' pack the star is in her left hand; in one of the surviving cards by Cicognara, the star is in her right hand, and she holds a hooded falcon on her left wrist.

The traditional packs introduce an entirely new element: a naked, or near-naked, woman, who kneels on the shore with two pitchers, emptying one or both into the water. Above her the sky is full of stars: sometimes seven and sometimes eight, generally with one much bigger than the rest.

XVII.

L'ÉTOILE

17 **LES ETOILES**

17 LE STELLE · LE STELLE 17

17 Diritto: MORTALITA'

17 Pe

LA MUERTE

17 Pe

17 Rovescio: ROVINA

B· SPERANZA ·XXXVIIII· 39

XVII

THE STAR

XVII

THE STAR.

The significance of the Tarot trumps

Below: the Star of Hope, as Pitois described it

Often there is a tree in the distance, with a bird perched on its summit.

The Wirth design is very similar, but the eight stars are of varying sizes, and the tree has been replaced by a bush with a single rose, with a butterfly on it. Pitois identifies the figure as that of Hope 'which scatters its dew upon our saddest days; she is naked in order to signify that Hope remains with us when we have been bereft of everything'.

In Waite's design, the naked woman empties one pitcher into a pool, and the other upon dry land; the bird perching on the distant tree is an ibis.

Interpretation. Who is the naked woman? Is she Hope, as Pitois and others have suggested? Certainly, in the da Tortona pack and the *minchiate*, Hope is portrayed as a crowned woman, her hands joined in prayer, but with her gaze fixed upon a ray of light, in a pose very similar to that of the figure in the 'Bembo' and Cicognara designs.

Further investigation suggests that she is of far more ancient lineage. The Persians, whose priests were the magi, worshipped Mithra together with the goddess of the waters, Anahita, who was also identified with the planet Venus. The Sumerians in their turn connected Venus with Inanna, who eventually became Aphrodite of the Greeks, born from the wave of the sea and carried naked to the shore. In the 'Mantegna' pack,

Venus bathes naked in a pool, pouring water on herself from a pitcher; and the bird which appears on so many of the Tarot cards turns out to be a dove, the most well-known of the symbols associated with Venus.

In this card Venus, or Aphrodite, is taken as the symbol of all the planets and stars beyond the sun and moon; she is the goddess of the waters of rebirth flowing from 'behind the region of the summer stars'; she is the source of the dew that falls from heaven just before the dawn.

The bird perched on the tree may be a dove or a hawk; both represent the soul. Or we may remember the dove and the raven that Noah released from the ark.

The significance of this card is, first of all, rebirth and new beginning. The morning star signals the arrival of Aphrodite to awaken Adonis; the pitchers emptied into the pool remind us of the bath of rejuvenation, and of the fountain that stood at the heart of Paradise and fed the rivers of the world; the dove, or raven, represents the re-emergence of Earth from the waters after the Deluge.

The presence of the goddess known as Anahita, Inanna, Aphrodite or Venus also promises pleasure, and we recall the rich gifts brought by the magi to Bethlehem. Above all, the distant stars symbolise hope and the promise of salvation.

XVIII The Moon

(French: *la Lune*   Italian: *la Luna*   German: *der Mond*)

Right: the development of the Tarot card of the Moon shows the combination of various concepts associated with the moon, such as the hounds of Diana and the astrological sign of Cancer. But card XVIII in the Spanish and Alliette packs is the Hermit

This is another medieval image that we can see gradually changing from one thing into another. In the 'Gringonneur' pack the image is the simplest: two astrologers are observing the crescent moon, measuring her orb with dividers, and making calculations in a book. A second element enters in the 'Bembo' pack: here the goddess Diana stands with the crescent moon in her right hand, and a broken bow in her left. The usual *minchiate* design is similar to the 'Gringonneur' except that there may be only one astrologer; but there is another *minchiate* design which represents Diana, the crescent on her head, striding along with one of her hounds.

It is from these disparate elements that the traditional Tarot card has evolved. This shows the moon shining full in the sky; the two astrologers are replaced by two of Diana's hounds, baying at the moon; and from the waters below (for the moon rules over the waters) crawls a crayfish-like animal which is in fact the zodiacal sign for Cancer, the 'house' of the moon. At each side of the landscape behind the baying hounds can be seen a squat tower.

In the Swiss pack, this design has undergone the same kind of dissociation as the Chariot in the same pack. The card is effectively divided in two: in the upper half

the crescent moon shines while a young man, his dog beside him, serenades a girl on a balcony; and in the lower half Cancer, flanked by two shapes looking like primitive shellfish, stands against a wall in which two blank-looking doors are half visible to left and right.

The Wirth design once again follows the traditional design fairly closely: the crustacean is a little more crab-like in its form, and one of the dogs is white while the other has been turned into a dark grey wolf. Pitois calls this card 'Deceptions'. The Waite card, also, is similar; it also has a dog and a wolf.

Interpretation. The moon, which changes its form so rapidly, and which can be found each night in a different part of the sky, has long been the symbol of fickleness. Its apparent connection with the menstrual cycle (indeed, the word 'menstruum' as well as 'month' may well have come from the same root as 'moon') has made the moon representative of all that is changeable in women. The huntress goddess Artemis, the Roman Diana, was renowned for the way in which she turned vindictively on those who fell in love with her, or who tried to take advantage of her femininity.

Ancient astronomers – not, of course, those of inland Asia or the Mediteranean countries – soon discovered the connection

LA LUNE

18 LA LVNE

18 LA LUNA · LA LUNA 81

18 Diritto: L'EREMITA

18 Tsade

EL ERMITAÑO

18 Tsade

18 Rovescio: TRADIMENTO - FELLONIA

A· LVNA XXXXI· 4I

XVIII

THE MOON

XVIII

THE MOON.

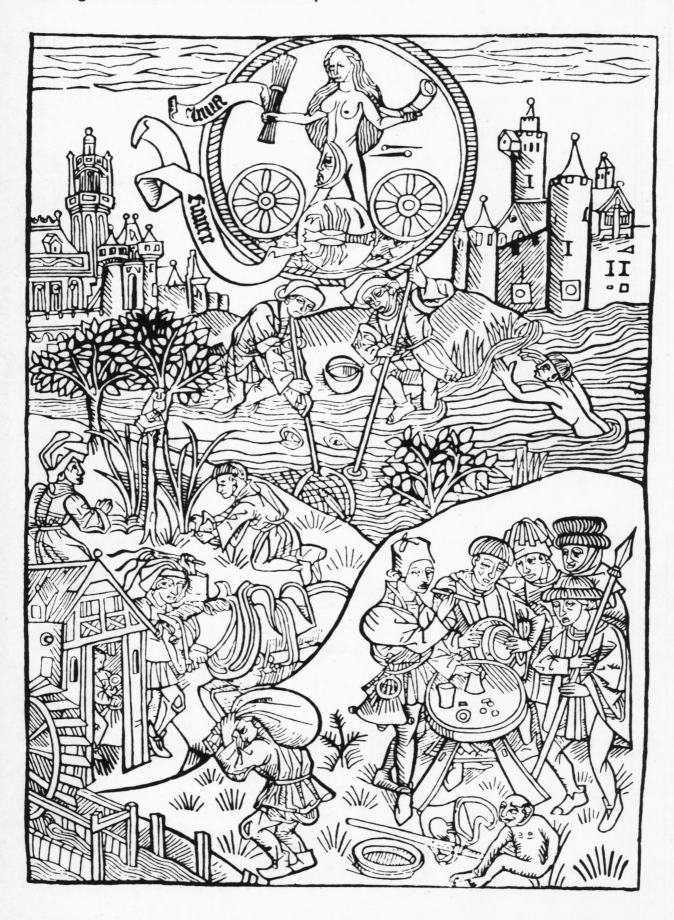

of the moon with the tides, and in medieval astrology she was believed to control all activities connected with water. Many engravings, illuminations and wood-cuts illustrate this connection, representing the moon in her chariot above scenes of boating and fishing, watermills at work and ships setting sail. And there is almost invariably one other activity which links the moon with another card of the Tarot pack: in one corner a travelling mountebank will be found, performing the cup-and-balls trick exactly like the Magician of card I.

Perhaps because, in earlier days, all women were thought to have weaker minds than men; perhaps because the moon was believed to exert its tidal influence on the liquids of the body, and particularly the brain – but it was long believed that the moon was associated with madness, making men and women 'lunatics'. Legends abound of those who were driven insane by sleeping in the light of the full moon, and nightmares and weird dreams were also associated with her influence. Witches rode abroad in the light of the moon, changing their shape, and bringing misfortune to those on whom they cast their spells.

This card is the symbol of uncertainty, of changeability. It warns us that we should not put our full trust in appearances, that even those things and people that we put most reliance upon may unaccountably let us down. The dogs who howl at the moon are pursuing an unattainable ideal.

Far left: In this woodcut from *Die Wirkungen der Planeten* (1470), the Magician is seen plying his trade under the influence of the Moon. Note the very strange position of his feet. *Left*: the design of the 'Gringonneur' card incorporates the two astrologers who were subsequently transmogrified into hounds. *Above*: the Pitois version of the Moon. *Below*: the Pitois version of the Sun

XIX The Sun

(French: *le Soleil*   Italian: *il Sole*   German: *die Sonne*)

The sun in splendour, his full face pouring down heat upon the earth, while on the ground below two children stand together in front of a low wall: this is the traditional design for this card, exemplified in a variety of different packs.

But it did not begin quite in this way. The 'Gringonneur' design is of a young fair-haired woman, walking alone with a distaff in her hand, spinning thread; above her the full sun shines down, and the origin of the wall may perhaps be seen in the incised gold background which represents the earth behind her. The 'Bembo' pack shows a cherub, carrying the sun on high as a shining face. The 'Mantegna' *tarocchi* represent the sun-god Helios driving his quadriga drawn by white horses across the sky, with the young Icarus falling to earth below; oddly, and without explanation, a scorpion (reminiscent of the crayfish on the Moon card, but not astrologically associated with the Sun) floats in the sky above.

In the *minchiate* pack, the Sun shines down upon a pair of seated lovers; and the Swiss pack, which often shows many deviations from tradition, is almost identical in its design.

The Wirth design is only a slight modification of the traditional form: the two figures are a young man and woman, standing in a flowery circle. Pitois identifies the subject as 'The Blazing Light: Earthly Happiness'. The Waite design, however, is significantly different: a single naked child, carrying a huge banner on a staff, rides the back of a white horse, while behind him the sun shines into a walled garden which is crowded with sunflowers.

Interpretation. Many commentators have identified this card with the god Apollo but, although Apollo was closely connected with the Sun, he was never represented in this form. If we take this to be Helios, then the two children may be his two sons by Perse, Aeetes and Perses; or his two daughters Circe and Pasiphae; or his children by Naera, Phaetusa and Lampetia, the guardians of his flocks. Perhaps they are the boy Aeetes and the girl Circe, who lived together on the island of Aeaea, where Circe was the goddess of love. She is best remembered for the enchantments by which she turned all the companions of Odysseus into swine when they landed on her island.

On the other hand, the appearance of these

LE SOLEIL

19 LE SOLEIL

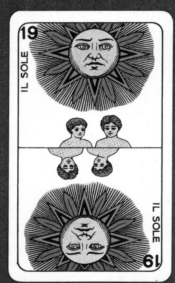

19 IL SOLE

IL SOLE 19

19 Diritto: CATASTROFE

19 Coph

LA DESTRUCCION DEL TEMPLO

19 Rovescio: PRIGIONE

·SOL·XXXXIIII·

THE SUN

THE SUN .

The design of the Sun is subject to more variations than almost any other card. From solitary woman spinner to cherub, from the Gemini to a pair of lovers and so full circle back to a naked infant on a white horse, the figures on this card have added a wide variety of meanings to its interpretation. *Above*: the astrological sign of Gemini. The 'Destruction of the Temple' (*left*) is assigned to this card in the Spanish pack

by making flames flicker above their heads.

The Sun has always been of the greatest importance to mankind: it is the source of all life, warming and nourishing animals and plants, and its disappearance at night, or during an eclipse, fills primitive man with fear. Above the tropics, the gradual strengthening of the Sun in spring, and its weakening in autumn, were occasions of great religious festivals. Apollo, who represented the Sun, became a god of many different functions. He made the crops ripen, and protected them from pests; he killed from a distance, but he also healed sickness; he was also so pre-eminent among the lesser gods that he became the god of prophecy and divination for certain communities.

It is when we go further back, to the Babylonian god who came before Apollo, that we find a possible explanation for the scorpion in the 'Mantegna' card. The sun-god of the Babylonians was Shamash, who rode in his chariot each day across the sky, and returned each night to his home in the mountains of the East. Every morning, the doors of the mountain were opened, to let out the chariot, by the scorpion men who defended them.

Primarily, this card symbolises splendour and triumph, health and wealth, everything good that the Sun brings. The two young people below, whether they are children or lovers, are joined in friendship or affection. But we must remember that solitary figure with the distaff, in the 'Gringonneur' card. Is this Clotho, who spins the thread of every human life? And is one of the two children really the enchantress Circe? Beware the deceptions that are practised in the full light of day, 'the destruction that wasteth at noonday', and remember that the scorpion, who waits motionless in the sunlight, is also a symbol not only of treachery but of the possibility of self-destruction.

two children in the traditional design may be yet another example of confusion in copying this card from one cardmaker to another. In the 'Bembo' pack the World is held aloft by two cherubs, very similar to the one who holds aloft the Sun; alternatively, these may be the Dioscuri, or Gemini, from the *minchiate* pack. During the voyage of the *Argo*, Zeus showed his favour for these two

XX The Judgment

(French: *le Jugement*   Italian: *l'Angelo*   German: *das Weltgericht*)

The concept of the Last Judgment is one that extends through many different religions, but all the Tarot representations are concerned almost entirely with its Christian significance.

The traditional card shows an angel, the Archangel Michael, armed with a trumpet and leaning down from a cloud in a blaze of light. The trumpet bears a banner with a cross on it. A number of naked figures, generally three, are rising from the grave below. The Swiss card is very similar, but there are four figures, and the angel is very much less impressive and has no banner on his trumpet.

The image is substantially the same in the very earliest Tarots: in the 'Gringonneur' and da Tortona pack two angels lean out of a cloud; in the 'Bembo' card, God himself

is seen in heaven. The subject is absent from the *tarocchi*, which are concerned solely with human knowledge, and in the *minchiate* there is some doubt as to whether the angel flying over a town and sounding two trumpets is really the herald of the resurrection. The words 'Fama Vola' (Reputation flies) which appear on the card have caused it to be known as 'the Fame'.

Oswald Wirth's design bears a close resemblance to the traditional one. The cross on the angel's flag is slightly more complex, and he bears on his head a strange red cap fronted with a gold disc, but most of the graphic elements – the cloud and the light rays coming from it, the position and sex of the three resurrected figures – are disposed in exactly the same way. Pitois described this card as 'The Awakening of the Dead:

LE JUGEMENT

20 LE JVGEMENT ל

20 L'ANGELO

L'ANGELO 20

20 Diritto: FORTUNA - DIGNITA'

20 Resch

ל

LA RUEDA DE LA FORTUNA

20 Resch

20 Rovescio: ELEVATEZZA

JUDGEMENT

JUDGEMENT.

Renewal'. 'A Spirit is blowing a trumpet over a half-open tomb. A man, a woman and a child, a collective symbol of the human trinity, are shown rising from this tomb. It is a sign of the change which is the end of all things, of Good as well as of Evil.'

Waite's design also is very little changed from the traditional. There are more resurected figures in the distance, and each of the dead is risen from his or her own tomb, which 'float on the waters of emotion'.

Interpretation. Medieval man believed without question in the Last Judgment. Many religions teach that there is judgment of the dead; the concept of the Final Assize of the Dead comes partly from Judaism and partly from Zoroastrianism, and is about 2500 years old. Christianity shares with the latter religion the idea that there is both a judgment of the individual immediately after death, and a mass judgment of all humanity at the Last Trump.

This card signifies punishment or reward; it reminds us that we must be called to account for all that we have done, all that we have left undone, all that we have thought or planned. Rewards are few, while the penalties for failure are many, but we must remember that we learn through suffering. Through pain and disappointment we rise to final achievement.

The card of the Last Judgment is linked with the card of Death; through change and transformation we shall reach the ultimate reckoning.

The design of the Last Judgment has changed very little over the centuries. The so-called 'Wheel of Fortune' in the Alliette-type packs is clearly derived from the traditional design for the World (see following pages). *Below* the Last Judgment, from the cathedral of St-Lazare at Autun. Christ sits in majesty within a mandorla, the holy shape which reappears in the design of the World

XXI The World

(French: *le Monde*   Italian: *il Mondo*   German: *die Welt*)

Below: Pitois' Crown of the Magi: 'the sign with which the Magus decorates himself when he has reached the highest degree of initiation'. *Below right*: this card from the 'Gringonneur' pack has consistently been wrongly identified as Fortune. *Far right*: the 'Spanish' card of the Tyrant may represent Scipio Africanus the younger, the 'scourge of Carthage', who was granted a Roman triumph, and it clearly has close affinities with the Chariot

This is another example of what began as a relatively simple medieval image, and gradually accrued all sorts of significant additional elements. In the 'Bembo' pack, this card shows two winged cherubs, holding up a globe which contains a vast castle, standing on a rocky island surrounded by water, while overhead the stars blaze in the sky. In one of the da Tortona cards from the Visconti family collection a half-length figure of a woman, with a trumpet in her right hand and a wreath in her left, presides above a grand arch; below, there is a complete landscape, with ships on the sea, sailors in a river boat, mounted soldiers and a fisherman, hills, towers, castles, streams, fields, houses and meadows. By comparison, the 'Gringonneur' card is almost crude: a female figure with sceptre and orb stands on a globe which portrays walled towns on a succession of little hills. This globe is surrounded by a green sphere of air, and floats among stylised blue waves. It is this card that has been wrongly identified for over a century as 'Fortune'.

The World does not figure in the *tarocchi*, but the figure of Jupiter in this pack clearly contributes something to the development of the traditional image. Jupiter sits in an almond-shaped framework, holding an arrow to represent one of his thunderbolts in his right hand. On the top of the framework perches an eagle, a girl sits in the lower part, and wounded soldiers lie about.

The next stage in development occurs in the *minchiate*. Here, as in the 'Gringonneur' card, a female – but naked now, and with wings – stands on a globe ringed about with a sphere of air. She holds an arrow in her right hand, and a crown in her left; at equal distances round the globe are four winged heads to represent the four winds.

So we come to the traditional design for this card. A naked female figure, her left leg raised in the strange figure 4 shape we have already seen in the Emperor and the Hanged Man, and holding in either hand a rod like that held by the Magician, stands inside an almond-shaped wreath. At the four corners of the card are a winged man, an eagle, a bull and a lion. The Swiss design is similar, but the naked girl stands on both feet, and holds nothing in her hands but a narrow drapery (floating freely over the figure's shoulder in the traditional design); the wreath is more open and nearly circular and, while the bull and the lion appear in the lower corners, only the eagle appears above, flanked on either side by a bird of indeterminate species.

Wirth's card shows a complete re-working of the traditional design elements. The wreath is completely circular, and the figure appears to be running to the right, carrying both rods in her left hand. The four 'Beasts' are still in the corners, but their character has somehow been lost in the re-drawing. Pitois identifies this card as the Crown of the Magi ('The Reward') and describes it as a garland of roses surrounding a star; at equal distances around the garland are the four heads. Surprisingly, allowing for the differences in style, the Waite card is almost identical with the traditional one.

Interpretation. Let us look first at the significance of the four heads in the four corners of the card. It is easiest to tabulate their significance in medieval iconography:

Bull	Luke	earth
Lion	Mark	fire
Man	Matthew	water
Eagle	John	air

These four also came to stand for the four corners of the earth, or the four directions from which the winds blew; so we have the well-known night spell 'Matthew, Mark, Luke and John, Bless the bed that I lie on'. Paul Huson, in *The Devil's Picture Book*, compares this with the cabalist's

Before me Uriel, Behind me Raphael
At my right Michael, At my left Gabriel

LE MONDE

21 LE MONDE

21 Diritto: TIRANNIA

ODIO AFRICANO — EL DÉSPOTA

21 Rovescio: TEMERITÀ.

COSMICO·XXXIII

THE WORLD

THE WORLD.

and refers this further back to the ancient Babylonian spell:

Shamash before me, Sin behind me

Nergal at my right, Ningirsu at my left

Particularly interesting is the fact that the symbols of these four ancient gods are: for Sin an old man, for Ningirsu an eagle, for Nergal a lion, and for Shamash (in his form as Adad, god of prophecy) a bull.

There is no suggestion that this indicates a more ancient ancestry for the Tarot; but it is evidence of how old imagery of this sort can be, and how it can be passed on from generation to generation, becoming modified to fit the beliefs of the time.

The four beasts also remind us once again of the vision of Ezekiel; perhaps the figure within the wreath is a distorted image of the angelic visitor in the fiery wheel. But it is also the *spiritus mundi*, and, if we think of the four beasts as representing the four elements of Aristotle, it is the fifth, *aether*, or the philosopher's stone of the alchemists.

The almond shape of the wreath is the mandorla, one of the holiest of haloes, and the figure also has a close resemblance to medieval portrayals of Christ at the resurrection. A carving in Chartres Cathedral shows Christ in a mandorla, surrounded by the four beasts.

With the twenty-first card of the Tarot we have come full circle. The number 21 is itself magic: it is the sum of the first six numbers, and it is the product of 3×7, two numbers of great magical significance, while the sum of its component figures is also 3.

This card, therefore, means fulfilment, completion, arrival at a goal; yet, in spite of the holy and magical images that it incorporates, it is essentially a material world that we see here, the material world with which the spiritual world interpenetrates. It may indicate the end of one cycle of life, but we begin again on the cycle above, knowing that we have not yet attained release from the body.

MERCVRIO XXXXII · 42

Right: the development of the Fool over the centuries clearly shows his relationship to two cards from the *tarocchi*, the Beggar (*near right*) and Mercury (*above*). As Mercury is also related to the Magician this happily completes the circle of the Major Arcana

The Fool

(French: *le Mat*   Italian: *il Matto*   German: *der Narr*)

And so we come to the central enigma of the Tarot Pack: the un-numbered Fool. But there is no doubt that he belongs here, for this card appears in the earliest Tarots. In the 'Gringonneur' pack he is a giant figure, more than 4 metres tall, clad in a yellow and red cap with ears, fool's motley and a loincloth. Between his hands he holds a string of fourteen gold discs, or beads, or perhaps brass bells; and four young men play about his feet. In the 'Bembo' pack he is ragged, with straw or feathers in his hair.

In the *minchiate* he is also a giant figure, or perhaps an adult among children; he is dressed in traditional fool's costume, with cap and bells and a toy sceptre, and he is playing with two figures who come a little above his waist. Two other designs contributed to the next stage in the development of this card. Firstly, there is the *minchiate* card of Diana (described above with the Moon); she is walking very much in the way of the Fool in the traditional pack, and one of her hounds walks behind her on a leash. Secondly, there is the Beggar card of the first series in the *tarocchi*: this shows a large and near-naked man, leaning upon a staff while dogs bark and prance at his heels.

The traditional card, then, shows us a bearded man dressed in motley with bells about his neck. With his left hand he is carrying over his right shoulder the typical tramp's stick with belongings tied in a cloth; in his right hand he holds a walking staff. The graphic quality of the design is very strong, and owes nothing to the cards that antedate it.

Behind the Fool prances a dog, and in some designs he appears to be tearing a hole in the Fool's breeches. Much has been read

into this by commentators, but we must beware. A common item of dress for several hundred years was single hose, held up by strings known as 'points'; and it was quite common for the points to break, letting the hose hang down and exposing the naked flesh beneath. Other designs show the dog, sometimes so badly drawn that it looks more like a cat, actually biting the Fool's leg. We recall the nursery rhyme lines (a description of the first appearance of wandering gypsy bands in Europe):

Hark, hark, the dogs do bark

The beggars are coming to town;

Some in rags and some in bags

And some in velvet gown.

In the Swiss pack, the Fool looks very much like a *commedia dell'arte* character, in his particoloured suit, with bells on his cap and at his knees. He has no dog or belongings, and his staff is replaced by a short baton.

In Oswald Wirth's design the animal is undeniably a cat, or some other fierce feline. The Fool is clearly wearing single hose, and both have fallen down; he is dressed in motley, but without bells. Between his feet a flower droops; this is the same flower that Wirth included on several other cards – upright between the feet of the Magician, opening at the feet of the Emperor, and in full bloom in The Stars.

At some point in the seventeenth or eighteenth century, another element entered the design of this card. It probably came from Belgium, where packs of the early eighteenth century reveal a number of significant deviations in design; and it shows the Fool walking unaware toward the open jaws of a crocodile. In the Wirth card the crocodile is scarcely visible as a pair of

LE MAT.

LE FOV

IL MATTO

IL MATTO

78 Than

LA LOCURA ó EL

ALQUI-MISTA

78 Rovescio: INETTITUDINE

MISERO 1.

THE FOOL

THE FOOL.

The significance of the Tarot trumps

Above: the Crocodile of Pitois.
Right: the giant Fool of the 'Gringonneur' pack resembles the huge figures paraded in numerous Lent carnivals

green jaws appearing over a distant beam of wood, but Pitois seized on this with enthusiasm, describing this card as 'The Crocodile: Expiation'. The Fool, he says, is 'a blind man carrying a full beggar's wallet about to collide with a broken obelisk, on which a crocodile is waiting with open jaws'.

Rather surprisingly, Waite did not incorporate this animal in his design. His Fool, a handsome young man with a rose in his left hand and his eyes on the sky, is about to step over a precipice; he is dressed in brightly decorated clothes, and carries a wallet on a stick over his right shoulder. The dog prances joyously beside him, and behind him the sun rises high in the sky.

Interpretation. The first point to be discussed is the meaning of the name *le mat* or *il matto*. Because the card is so named, and because it portrays a fool, this name has come to mean 'fool', but its derivation is very far from this. This is exactly the same word that appears in the Spanish 'matador', or in the word 'checkmate' in chess. It comes from a very old Persian word meaning 'to kill', or 'to put an end to'.

Do not suppose, however, that the Fool is death or an agent of death. He is not a messenger, nor an actor with a part in the drama. But, at every fateful moment, he is somewhere at hand, doing nothing himself but apparently there to observe that whatever should be done is done. He is the end of things, the conclusion, expected or unexpected; he is Fate.

He represents also the fickleness of Fate, and this was the function of the king's fool of the middle ages: he was there to remind his master that kings are but men, and that their deaths are as untimely and as inevitable as any other's. The fool was a privileged person, and (in theory, at least) whatever he chose to do went unpunished; a tradition that derived from the saturnalia of Roman times and, perhaps, from even older days, when a young man would be chosen for sacrifice at the year's end and would be allowed to behave exactly as he wished until the day he was to die. The Fool is the only card of the Major Arcana to survive in the modern pack of playing cards; he is the Joker, the card which can be used in place of any other in the pack.

And he is also the Fool of God, the shaman entranced with the wonders of the universe, the holy madman who lives a charmed life. He represents the best of luck – but it *is* luck, and likely to turn at any moment. When the Fool appears in a spread of Tarot cards, tread carefully: *he* may escape the snapping jaws of the dog behind and the crocodile in front, but will *you*?

Card	Gods, goddesses, mythical beings	Interpretation
Magician	Hermes/Mercury/Tehuti	Man in search of knowledge; the answer he seeks
Woman Pope	Hera/Juno Isis	Intuition, inspiration; the subconscious memory; lack of foresight
Empress	Demeter/Ceres Ishtar	Human understanding, femininity, sensuality, beauty and happiness
Emperor	Dionysos	Masculinity, independence, creativity, action
Pope	Zeus/Jupiter Serapis	Advice; justice; healing
Lovers	Cupid Venus/Aphrodite Paris	Choice, decision
Chariot	Mars	Achievement, success; danger of defeat
Justice	Themis	Caution in taking advice; control of one's fate
Hermit	Kronos/Saturn	Time; wisdom; withdrawal
Wheel of Fortune	Midas	Change; prudence; the eternal return
Fortitude	Cyrene Hercules/Samson	Strength of purpose; coming danger
Hanged Man	Attis Odin Christ Proteus	Adaptability; desire to learn; violent change and sacrifice
Death	Uranus Orpheus	Change by transformation, rebirth
Temperance	Iris (Ganymede)	Moderation, mercy; modification
Devil	Typhon/Set Kernunnos Zervan	The adversary; caution
The Tower	Babel Sodom Adam and Eve	Punishment; pride; divine inspiration
The Stars	Anahita/Inanna/Aphrodite/Venus	New beginning; pleasure; salvation
The Moon	Diana	Uncertainty; changeability
The Sun	Shamash/Apollo Circe	Splendour, health, wealth, affection; treachery
Judgment		Punishment or reward; final achievement
The World	Shamash Sin Nergal Ningirsu	Fulfilment, completion on a material level
The Fool		Fate; luck; the end

Some other Tarot packs

JUDGMENT

THE MAGICIAN

THE FOOL

LA·MOUR

LE·DIABLE

ROUE·DE·FORTUNE

L'EMPEREUR

Although a wide range of Tarot card designs have been featured on the previous pages, there is a considerable number of other packs available, either revived from traditional designs or newly-drawn.

Top left: Judgment, the Magician and the Fool, from the 'Tarot Classic' pack printed by Müller for US Games Systems. This pack is based upon original woodcuts by Burdel dating from 1751, and is fully described in *Tarot Classic* by Stuart R. Kaplan. It will be seen that in style it is very similar to the 'Marseilles' pack of Grimaud. *Centre left*: the Lovers, the Devil, the Wheel of Fortune and the Emperor, from an eighteenth century Belgian pack recently re-published in facsimile. *Bottom left*: the Lovers, the Magician, Temperance and the Moon, from the 63-card 'Bolognese' Tarot published by Viassone of Turin. *This page*: two contemporary designs. *Right*: the Moon, the Chariot, the Fool and the Queen of Swords from the 'Gypsy Tarot' designed by Walter Wegmüller, published by Sphinx Verlag, and described by Sergius Golowin in *Die Welt des Tarot*. *Below*: the Tower, the Woman Pope, Death and the Hermit from the pack designed by David Sheridan, which is described in full in *The Tarot* by Alfred Douglas

THE TOWER

THE PAPESS

DEATH

THE HERMIT

5
The significance of the minor arcana

ROI DE DENIER   REINE DE DENIER   VALET DES ÉPÉES

Above: three court or 'coat' cards from the Minor Arcana of the Müller 1JJ pack: the King of Cups, the Queen of Coins and the Jack of Swords

We have discussed in detail the significance of the Tarot trumps – the major arcana: they comprise a set of very powerful medieval symbols, as we have seen, with their roots in ancient history. You need only a short acquaintance with them to begin to discover what particular meaning they have for you; and from this point it is easy to use them for divination. But the minor arcana – substantially, almost identical with an ordinary pack of cards – are a very different matter. Of the fourteen cards of any one suit, nine (from two to ten) differ only in the number of suit symbols per card; and between the court cards and aces of the different suits, the differences are of degree rather than of kind. The novice, attempting to attribute a different significance to each card, has very little to guide him.

When you come to practise divination by cards by one of the methods described in the following chapter, it is only important that you know what each card means for you. Eventually you must make this interpretation for yourself on the basis of experience, but in the meantime it helps to know what significance is attached to each card by tradition. In many packs designed in the twentieth century, considerable attention has been paid to the minor arcana,

making each card clearly distinguishable and so more easily given an individual interpretation, but in traditional packs there is no sign of this. You will find, therefore, that many different meanings are attributed to these cards, and it is only possible here to give you the most traditional interpretation, applicable also to 52-card packs.

In the following chapter, the methods of divination first described are those making use only of the major arcana. When you have some experience you can go on to the more complex methods, and you will then need to know the interpretations below.

Cups, chalices, hearts
Ace: the home and domestic happiness. The meaning will be modified by other associated cards, so that we may find visitors to the house, change of residence, domestic quarrels, or feasts and parties.
Two: Success and good fortune; but care and attention will be necessary to secure it.
Three: Imprudence: impetuous decisions threaten favourable undertakings.
Four: A person not easily won: a bachelor or spinster, or a marriage delayed.
Five: Jealousy without foundation; or inability to make up one's mind, resulting in delay and avoidance of responsibility.

Six: A sign of credulity. You may be easily imposed upon, particularly by untrustworthy associates.

Seven: Fickleness and broken promises. Be on your guard against over-optimistic friends or thoughtless acquaintances.

Eight: Pleasurable company and good-fellowship; parties and planned celebrations.

Nine: The fulfilment of dreams and desires; good fortune and wealth.

Ten: Happiness in the family, perhaps unexpected success or good news.

Valet, Knave or 'Jack': A close friend; not always contemporary, for it may signify a long-lost childhood friend or sweetheart.

Knight: A false friend, a stranger from far away, a seducer; passing fate, to be seized before it vanishes again.

Queen: A faithful, loving woman, gentle and pleasing.

King: An honest and well-intentioned man, but hasty in his decisions and therefore not one to be relied upon for advice.

Rods, batons, clubs

Ace: Wealth and professional success; life-long friends and peace of mind.

Two: Disappointment and opposition from friends or business partners.

Three: A sign of more than one marriage; it may also be interpreted as a long engagement to one person, followed by a sudden marriage to someone else.

Four: Beware the failure of a project, which may result in financial loss, or itself be due to lack of money. False or unreliable friends play a part.

Five: Marriage with a wealthy woman.

Six: Profitable business in partnership.

Seven: Good fortune and happiness, but beware someone of the opposite sex.

Eight: Covetousness: someone is likely to make use of money that is not his own.

Nine: Disputes with friends; obstinate quarrels.

Ten: Unexpected good fortune, the cause or outcome of a long journey; but it may be accompanied by the loss of a dear friend.

Valet, Knave or 'Jack': A sincere but impatient friend; well-meaning flattery.

Knight: Providential help from a friend of the family; support from an unfamiliar source.

Queen: An affectionate and kindly woman, although inclined to be temperamental.

King: An honest and sincere man, generous and faithful.

Swords, spades

Ace: Misfortune, bad news, tidings of death; spiteful emotions.

Two: Change, removal, loss of home, separation.

Three: A journey, misfortune in love or marriage.

Four: Sickness, financial embarrassment, jealousy – all sorts of minor misfortunes which will delay any project in hand.

Five: Success in business, harmony in partnerships – but only after obstacles have been overcome. Beware ill-temper and discouragement.

Six: Only perseverance will enable you to bring your plans to fruition.

Seven: Quarrels with friends, and many troubles as a result.

Eight: Be cautious in all your undertakings: those who seem to be your friends may be revealed as rivals.

Nine: Reputedly the most ominous card of all: it may signify sickness, misfortune, all kinds of unhappiness.

Below: from an Italian double-headed pack: King of Swords, Queen of Rods and King of Cups

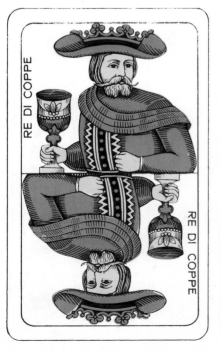

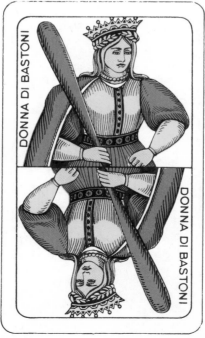

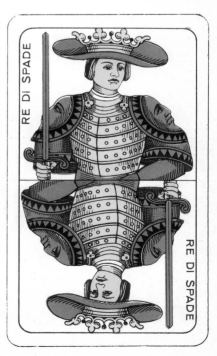

The significance of the minor arcana

KING of PENTACLES.

KING of SWORDS.

QUEEN of SWORDS.

Above: six court cards from the pack designed by A. E. Waite and executed by Pamela Coleman Smith. Every single card of the minor arcana has a distinctive design. *Below*: six court cards from the 'Ancien Tarot de Marseille' of Grimaud

Ten: Another ominous card: grief, imprisonment or, at the very least, the negation of all good indications.

Valet, Knave or 'Jack': A lazy or envious person, a hindrance in any undertaking, or perhaps an impostor, even a spy.

Knight: Romantic chivalry, inclined to extravagance, but brave and enterprising.

Queen: Treachery, betrayal, malice; a widow or a deserted person.

King: A man whose ambition over-rides everything.

Coins, pentacles, diamonds

Ace: An important message, or perhaps a valuable gift.

Two: A passionate love affair, but opposed by friends.

Three: Quarrels, lawsuits and domestic disagreements.

Four: Unhappiness arising from neglected or unfaithful friends; perhaps a secret betrayed.

Five: Unexpected news; its outcome may well be business success, realisation of an

THE KNAVE OF SWORDS

THE KNIGHT OF SWORDS

THE QUEEN OF CUPS

KNIGHT of WANDS.

QUEEN of WANDS.

KING of CUPS.

ambition, or a contented marriage.

Six: Early marriage – but also an early end to the marriage, and bad indications for a second.

Seven: Lies, rumours, unkind criticism; an unlucky gambler.

Eight: A marriage late in life; perhaps a journey; quite possibly a combination of the two.

Nine: A compulsion to travel, a taste for adventure, the desire to see changes in one's life.

Ten: Above all else, this card means money – but as the objective, not necessarily as the result, of your activities.

Valet, Knave or 'Jack': A selfish or jealous relative, or a messenger bringing unwelcome news.

Knight: A patient and persevering man; an inventor or discoverer.

Queen: A coquettish woman, given to interfering in others' affairs; scandal and rumour.

King: A hot-tempered, obstinate and vengeful man, dangerous when crossed.

THE KING OF MONEY

THE QUEEN OF MONEY

THE KNIGHT OF CLUBS

6
Divination by the Tarot

This is not the place to enter into a discussion concerning fate: whether events are pre-ordained, and what (if anything) one can do to change one's destiny. Think of yourself as an astronaut, fired from Cape Kennedy in a spaceship at the time of your birth. At Mission Control in Houston, every factor controlling your flight has been calculated before lift-off; it is possible for every adjustment to be made before your flight so that, if nothing goes wrong – and if, above all, you do nothing at all – the spaceship will automatically carry you to your destination. But sometimes things do go wrong: there is a minor interruption in the fuel feed, a solar cell does not charge properly, an electrical connection comes loose. And you, bored with your cramped surroundings, may begin to interfere with the operation of the ship. It may be no more than a movement of your body which changes the trim of the craft, or perhaps you decide to tinker with the switches. In Houston, minute changes in the flight of the spaceship will be detected a long time before you become aware of them, and instructions can be radioed to you to correct for them.

The astrologer, the crystal-gazer or the Tarot card reader can all be likened to Mission Control. By some psychic process they become aware of your original 'flight plan' and of the deviations that you are making from it. They can warn you of the changes you will have to make to avoid disaster. The horoscope, the pattern of the cards, or the crystal itself, all provide a focus of concentration which helps them to 'tune in' to you.

Even if you cannot accept the suggestion that such a flight plan exists – if you believe that your flight through space and time began as an accident – you are yourself aware of your flight, and of what you are doing to control it; the psychic adviser, like an experienced flight engineer, can warn you of the probable outcome of your actions. This is the significance and value of 'divination'.

Tarot cards present us with one of the most flexible and useful methods of seeking advice concerning what the future may hold in store. A number of cards are selected, and laid out in a particular pattern and order.

The Tarot cards must be read like the pages of a picture book. If we take only the 22 trumps, they can be arranged in 1,124,727,000,777,607,680,000 different sequences; add to this the incalculable number of groups of two, three, four or more and you will see that a selection of these trumps can portray every conceivable situation – and there are still 56 cards which have not entered into the calculation!

But how can we arrange it so that the group of cards we choose represents the situation we want it to? Some psychic researchers believe that even a completely random selection of cards, picked for instance by a sophisticated electronic machine, can be influenced by human beliefs and desires, but there is no need for us to go as far as this – and few people could afford such a machine in any case. Dealing out the cards by hand, and then selecting some of them, is a sufficiently effective method.

The important thing is to place yourself in as intimate a relationship with the cards as you can manage, without being consciously aware of what cards you are selecting. By concentrating all your mind upon the problem on which you are seeking advice, and by making a deliberate choice of a group of cards, but *without seeing their faces*, you will bring your psychic abilities into play so that, when you turn them over, you will be finely tuned to interpret their significance.

Take the 22 trumps face upward, and sort through them until you find a card which represents for you the situation on which you are seeking guidance. Then place the remaining cards face downward in a single pack and shuffle them as often as you wish. Remember to turn the cards as you cut them, so that some will be reversed. Then deal them out into three piles, putting each card on to whichever pile you think right – there is no need for each pile to contain the same number of cards, but it is probable that each will consist of between five and nine cards. Finally, concentrate very hard and choose one of the piles. Remember always to keep the cards the same way up as that in which you originally dealt them.

On a sheet of paper you should have made a little sketch to remind you of the way in which you are going to 'read' the cards. For instance, after placing the card that you first selected to represent the situation – the 'significator' – face upward on the table, you may decide to deal two cards (or one, or three) to its right to represent the events leading to this situation, two to its left to represent the future trend if you make no changes, two or three below to represent adverse influences, and the rest above to indicate the action you should take. You can deal the cards straight off the top of the pile you have chosen into their appropriate positions, or you can introduce a further element of choice by dealing them face downward, in the order you *feel* is right, before turning them over – but it is essential that you know what each card is to represent as you do this, and that is why you should keep the sketch of the layout beside you. After a little practice, you will no longer need this sketch and, like a child who has learnt to read, you will instinctively place the cards in the correct order as you lay them out one by one on the table before you.

Let us look at one or two examples and study how they may be interpreted. Experienced practitioners recommend that one should not read cards for oneself – it is considered too dangerous – but for the beginner there is no other way to obtain experience and understanding. If there is someone very near and dear to you who will give you their full sympathy, then it is best to practise with their help, but if, as is most likely, you are compelled to spend most of your study time by yourself, try not to seek advice on subjects that are of critical importance. Your problems must be serious ones, because consulting the Tarot cards is not a game, but to begin with let them be ones in which you can make mistakes without harm: deciding on a family outing, what new clothes to buy, or whether to renew an old acquaintanceship, for example. In this way you will be able to test the interpretation you have made, and so learn by your experience.

Example I

A young and unmarried woman has reached a critical point in her life: should she continue to develop her career, or should she accept the inevitable disruption of that career which will follow marriage? She is deeply in love with a man older than herself; this is not her first love affair, and she is confident that this is the man she would like to marry.

Because this is a matter of deciding between two well-defined alternatives, she chooses the Lovers as the significator. The selected pile of cards, when it is dealt out, contains eight cards, and it is remarkable that seven of these are reversed. Only the Woman Pope is unreversed, suggesting that the young woman should follow the dictates of her head rather than of her heart. To the right of the significator we find the Hermit, reversed, and the Sun, also reversed: the former obviously represents the older man, and the appearance of these two cards, both reversed, could indicate that the young woman is subconsciously not nearly so confident about her love as she would have us believe. But the reversed Hermit also signifies a lack of objectivity, and the reversed Sun suggests deceit; perhaps the man himself is not entirely faithful to the woman.

To the left of the significator, the reversed Empress together with the reversed Moon would imply strongly that, if the woman continues in her present course, letting her heart rule her head, her future will be a very uncertain one. As we have already noted, the Woman Pope is the dominant card in this spread, representing feminine intuition; the reversed Magician above can be read as suggesting that it is better for the woman to remain in her present state, even if it seems to hold out little promise of excitement in the near future, rather than take a step that she will later regret.

Below the significator, the combination of reversed Pope and reversed Justice represent bad advice of which the woman should be extremely wary.

This spread of cards and its interpretation is particularly interesting in that it has not directly answered the question that was asked. The young woman has been warned that her lover may not be all that he seems, and advised that it would be better not to change her present condition, but she has not been told that following a career will necessarily be her best course in the long run. And the Tarot, like all systems of divination, is mischievous: slyly these cards suggest that perhaps the advice they have given should be looked at more closely, and carefully weighed before any irrevocable decision is taken.

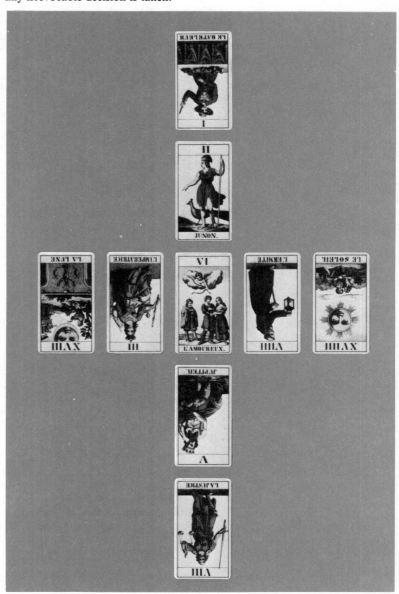

Example II

An elderly father is considering making over his estate to his son many years before his expected death: he is very concerned to discover whether he will continue to be properly looked after.

Although tempted to select the Hermit as significator, the questioner quite rightly chooses the Emperor, which properly represents him as a man still in possession of power and wealth. The selected pile dealt out is found to contain only seven cards.

To the right of the significator is the Sun reversed, which represents the events leading to the present situation. The questioner's physical powers are declining; it may transpire that there are several children between whom he has to decide – which of them will look after him best? To the left, the Lovers reversed, coupled with the Pope, suggest that the likely outcome of any request for advice is going to be of little value, since preservation of the status quo is probably the best course; this is reinforced by the cards below the significator, where the Judgment, counselling caution, is paired with the Devil reversed, suggesting that the questioner has really very little to worry about. The two cards above the significator, Death and the Fool, tell the questioner that he should continue to control his own destiny, and should not put his fate in the hands of another.

This particular spread of cards also does not directly answer the question asked, but in this case the interpretation provides rather more advice than was sought. The questioner learns that his powers of decision-making are unimpaired, and he is warned only that he should take good care before committing himself irrevocably. The cards also suggest that, if he has more than one child, it might be worthwhile consulting the Tarot on which is the most likely to handle his estate properly and look after him well in old age.

These two examples suffice to show how this very simple layout of cards may be used for practice in divination while you are learning to recognise and interpret the individual cards. Over the years, many authors have devised all sorts of complicated spreads, some of which we will now investigate. For the first few examples, we will continue to restrict ourselves to the Major Arcana, but for any spread it is, of course, possible to utilise any of the 78 cards of the pack. Later examples will show how most, or indeed all, of the pack may be used. We will assume that you have reached sufficient proficiency to be able to read the cards for someone other than yourself: it is now most important that all the shuffling and cutting of the pack should be done by the questioner. He or she should have a particular question in mind, and concentrate upon it, as this shuffling and cutting is carried out.

The 'Celtic' Cross

In consultation with the questioner, select one of the Tarot trumps to be the significator, and place it face upward on the table in front of you. Then get the questioner to shuffle the remaining 21 cards as often as he or she likes, cut them, and place them in a pile face down on the table some way to the left of the significator.

1. Turn over the first card (from left to right, so that it continues to point in the same direction, upright or reversed, as placed by the questioner). Place this card directly on top of the significator, saying 'This covers him (or her)'. This card represents the present atmosphere in which the questioner lives and works.

2. Turn over the second card and place it across the first, saying 'This crosses him'. This represents any immediate influences which may affect, or (in particular) conflict with, the interests of the questioner.

3. Turn over the third card, placing it above the first group of cards and saying 'This crowns him'. This represents the ultimate goal or destiny of the questioner; it may also represent his (or her) ideal aim in the subject under investigation.

4. Turn over the fourth card and place it below the central group, saying 'This is beneath him'. This represents the foundation of the question, the basic events and influences from the past which have brought about the identity and personality of the questioner.

5. Turn over the fifth card, placing it to the right of the central group, saying 'This is behind him'. It represents the recent past, and the effect it has had upon the present condition of the questioner.

6. Turn over the sixth card and place it to the left of the central group, saying 'This is before him'. This represents future influences that are likely to come into play in the near future.

These first six cards should now be interpreted, to show all the influences that will affect the answering of the question. Remember that your interpretation may sub-sequently be modified by the way in which you read the remaining cards, and that you are dealing only with the present condition of the questioner. Now you can proceed to deal with the specific enquiry made of the cards by the questioner. The last four cards are to be placed one above the other to the right of the cards already on the table.

7. Place the seventh card in position, saying 'This answers him'. This card represents the present position of the questioner, and may give directly the answer to the question. No final interpretation should be given, however, until all ten cards have been laid out and read.

8. The eighth card is placed above the seventh, with the words 'This strengthens him'. It represents people and factors which may have an effect upon the questioner.

9. The ninth card is placed above the eighth with the words 'This defines him'. It shows the inner feelings, emotions and intuitions of the questioner, and may also reveal secrets which the questioner is trying to keep concealed.

10. The tenth card is placed at the top of the right-hand row, with the words 'This ends it'. It reveals the end-result of everything represented by the preceding cards, and should be read as the conclusion of a continuous story which they tell.

Example III (see following page)

The questioner is a self-confident, capable mother of a family of three children. The two eldest have already left school; she finds herself with time on her hands, and is considering taking up a job. But the youngest child is still at school, and the mother is worried that this child may not yet be sufficiently mature, and may feel neglected if the mother goes out to work. What is the best thing to do?

The significator chosen here was the Empress, who was thought to represent most closely the situation of the questioner. The Woman Pope, dealt out as the first card to cover the Empress, confirms that this is indeed a question involving a woman, and the conflict that may arise between her material condition and her intuitive desires. It is particularly interesting that the second card, laid across the first, is its male counterpart, the Pope. The questioner has told us nothing about her husband, and his attitude to her problem; indeed, there is no way of telling whether he still lives with her, or is still alive – this card may even represent the youngest child about whom she is so concerned, or may suggest that the advice to be given her by you will conflict with her own desires. It is only when the full story is unrolled that the true significance of this card can be determined with confidence.

The third card, which crowns the group, is Justice, the card of decision: it tells us that the questioner hopes to receive carefully weighed advice upon which she can act immediately, but it also warns her that this is unlikely to be the case, and that she should consider the matter further before committing herself irrevocably. And the fourth card, the Magician, makes it clear that she alone must take responsibility for her decision, at the same time reinforcing your suspicion that a male influence is somewhere at work.

The fifth card, standing for the recent past, is the Hanged Man reversed. Right way up, this card symbolises a new understanding of what has gone before, and the likelihood of sudden change. Reversed, it suggests that the questioner has not learnt sufficient from past experiences, and indicates that perhaps she considered the same problem before, and rejected the step that she is now considering again. The sixth card, the Tower reversed, stands for the future, and adds to your understanding of the situation. The questioner is full of guilt because she wishes to do something that she thinks is likely to harm the structure of her family; but you can reassure her, telling her that her desire is a perfectly natural one. Nevertheless, it is one that is not likely to be fulfilled – at least, not as soon as she thinks.

So far, the first six cards have helped to throw light on the situation, giving a better understanding of the factors involved, and revealing certain aspects of the situation that the questioner kept hidden from you. The next four cards help you to answer her question, and give her the advice that she urgently desires.

The seventh card is the Fool, reversed. At the very point in the reading at which you expect the answer, there is no answer at all. Go carefully: Fate gives you a clear warning here, uncertainty piled upon uncertainty. Happily the eighth card is reassuring. Strength and resolve will come to the questioner's rescue; but she must use it with care and understanding, not seeking to impose her domination upon others weaker than herself.

The ninth card, the Devil reversed, shows that the questioner is herself aware that her strong personality can represent a danger to her family; but she can take heart, for her influence is a beneficial one. The last card is the Judgment, also reversed, and it tells you that no decision is a final one, that there is always an opportunity to redress a wrong and to admit honestly that one has made a mistake.

You can now ask the questioner about her husband; you may guess that he is still alive and with his family, but that he is a kindly, easygoing man who will support his wife in whatever course she decides upon. You can tell her that the decision she makes must be hers and hers alone, but that you think she is still not sufficiently sure about her situation and that of her child to make such a decision. She must look deeper into her motives and be sure that she is not letting selfish considerations over-rule her instincts as a mother and a wife. Then she can consult the Tarot again.

The Nine-Card Spread

Very similar to the Celtic Cross is the nine-card spread; it omits only card 2, which represents the immediate influences which may affect, or conflict with, the interests of the questioner. Interpretation of the other cards remains unchanged.

Example IV
The questioner is a middle-aged man, but still full of youth and enthusiasm. He has a good job, at which he works well, but he is dissatisfied with it. It does not give him sufficient opportunity to express his individuality and make use of the creative powers which he already feels weakening. Should he leave his present job and set up on his own account?

Here the significator agreed upon by the questioner is the Hermit, the elderly man setting out alone into the world in his search for truth.

The first card turned up indicates the present circumstances of the questioner: the Woman Pope, symbol of the desire to forsake rationality in favour of intuition, to give up the safe and mundane and embark upon a career that is more precarious but also more emotionally satisfying. And the second card, representing the questioner's ideal goal, is the Judgment, the card which itself means final achievement after difficulties.

The third card is the foundation of the question, and in this case it is the Magician, the man seeking an answer – the cards are stating the question so clearly that the questioner need not have said a word! The fourth card, to the right, represents the immediate past and the causes of the question: it is the Stars reversed. Right way up, this card represents rebirth and new beginning; reversed, it tells us that the questioner no longer finds in his present job any exciting hope for the future.

The last card in this group, the fifth card, reveals the probable future if current trends remain unchanged – what the questioner may expect if he does not make the break that he is contemplating. It is Death, reversed; it suggests that the questioner's gloomy view of his circumstances is largely justified. He can expect some gradual change, but neither for the better nor the worse, at least in a material sense; spiritually, he has little to look forward to but a gradual decline of his abilities over the coming years, until he reaches retirement.

Now we come to the four cards on the right. The reversed Pope says, in effect, 'Don't ask for advice, follow your instincts'. The Wheel of Fortune offers the desired change, but advises prudence; others are equally ambitious, and the questioner will have to compete with them. Fortitude, reversed, suggests that the questioner is subconsciously unconfident of his abilities, and warns him that he needs more resolution if he is to succeed. But the Fool, striding happily into the unknown, crowns this spread of cards with encouragement. He is the youthful companion of the Hermit, the spirit of adventure, the young in heart upon whom the gods continue to smile. The dog, symbol of faithfulness, goes joyfully with him. The change that the questioner is considering is a dangerous one, and he could fail; but if he goes forward with confidence and determination, he will be undoubtedly a happier man.

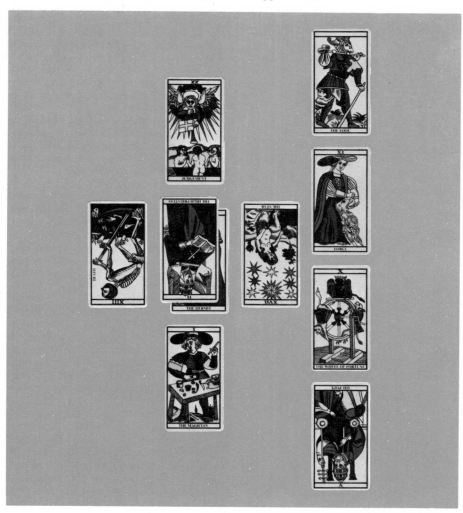

The Tree of the Qabala

The form of the sefirothic tree can be used, like the Celtic cross, as a pattern upon which to lay the cards and interpret them. The accompanying diagram shows how the ten sefiroth are related to each other. The tree is made up of three triangles, with the tenth sefiroth, Malkuth the Kingdom, below them. Each triangle contains two opposing concepts, and a third which reconciles them. Some qabalists have proposed an eleventh sefiroth, Daat, or Knowledge, and in this position we may place the significator.

The Jewish mystics imagined themselves slowly ascending the tree from sefiroth to sefiroth; while they visualised inspiration as a 'lightning flash' which descended the tree by the same path, filling each sefiroth with its flow of energy. Tarot cards on the sefirothic tree should be read in the same way: as a slowly developing story from the bottom to the top, and then in a final vision of illumination from top to bottom.

Example V

The questioner is a woman at the crossroads of her life. Her husband has left her, leaving her pregnant, and she has begun divorce proceedings against him. She is deeply in love with a man who does not want children, and has asked her to go with him to a distant foreign country. She is being wooed by another man who would happily adopt the child when it is born. And she is also tempted to return to the career that she gave up for her first marriage.

It is very clear that one card above all others

is suitable as the significator: the Lovers, because it symbolises the difficulty of choice between several alternatives. Placed at the position of Daat, it completes the 'trunk' of the tree.

At the foot of the tree is the sefiroth of Malkuth, the Kingdom. This is of the earth most earthy, the purely material basis from which we begin our slow climb. Here the first card is the Empress, reversed: the body of woman, but sunk in idleness and sensuality. Above her lies Yesod, the Foundation, the public self, representing the emergence of individuality from the generality of Malkuth. This second card is the Chariot, also reversed. Our questioner finds great difficulty in expressing her individuality; she feels herself spiritually subjugated.

The next sefiroth is Hod, or splendour, representing the visible products of human activity, those things which people do by choice to show their awareness of spirituality. Here the Sun, again a reversed card, warns us that health and wealth must be struggled for, and there are many who will try to oppose our efforts. The questioner cannot expect anything to come easily.

The fourth card lies on Netsah, representing the enduring qualities, the instinctive aspects of creativity. The card is the Hanged Man, promising progression after sacrifice. Struggle against it as she will, the questioner knows in her heart that she must make that sacrifice, and that only good can come of it.

The fifth card lies on Tifereth, or beauty, the essential self, the silent 'watcher' of the balance between outward display of emotion and inner feeling. The questioner is represented in this sefiroth by the Wheel of Fortune, reversed: all about her is change, and there is a great danger that she will not act prudently, unable to reconcile the emotions that pull her one way and the other. For on Geburah, signifying power and good judgment, the Stars are also reversed; and on Hesed – love, mercy, the inner emotions – stands Death. The emotions she directs towards others are misplaced, and there is little hope of a satisfactory outcome; and her inner feelings must undergo a complete change. Somehow or other she must give up something that she loves.

We come now to the last three cards, representing the highest qualities of the intellect. The eighth card is on Binah, which is understanding, and the ninth on Hokmah, which is wisdom. Justice is the eighth card; the questioner has a good brain, which she should use to its full; but she must beware of narrow-mindedness and bigotry. Fortitude is reversed as the ninth card: she lacks resolve, letting those emotions that we have seen to be in such a turmoil obstruct her in doing what she knows in her heart to be right. At the head of the tree is Kether, the Supreme Crown; the reversed Pope tells her that the advice she is to be given is not the advice she expects.

The slow, analytical ascent of the tree is

complete; now you must make the synthesis, the sudden downward flash of inspiration. There is only one course for the questioner to follow: she must give up all that she thinks she loves, not only the man but the child as well. Only sacrifice and purgation, physical as well as spiritual, will bring her eventual contentment. The Wheel of Fortune at the centre of the tree will turn again, and perhaps the whole tree with it.

Turn the whole arrangement of the cards up the other way and study it again. Now the significator is the Chariot, standing for success; the Pope, representing justice and redemption, rules in the Kingdom. Yesod is the Lovers reversed: the choice has been made, the alternatives rejected. In Hod, the

splendour of men's works, Fortitude stands supreme; and in Netsah the scales of blind chance have been tilted firmly for ever. Death, reversed, is now Geburah, for the change has cleared away all the old emotions; and the Stars of hope shine out, promising love and mercy in Hesed. The Hanged Man, Death's companion, is reversed in Binah; and the Sun in all his glory fills Hokmah, the sefiroth of wisdom. Crowning all is the Empress, the true feminine principle.

So much for methods of laying out cards using only the Tarot trumps; now let us take a look at various schemes that make use of the full pack of cards. One of the simplest of these is that given by Papus in *The Tarot of the Bohemians*.

The Method of Papus

Papus's 'Rapid Process'

1. Select from the minor arcana the suit that refers to the kind of advice required: Rods for business matters, Cups for affairs of the heart, Swords for legal questions or a dispute of any kind, and Discs for money matters.
2. Shuffle this suit, and ask the questioner to cut them.
3. Take the first four cards from the top of the pack and, without looking at them, arrange them in a cross as shown on the right.
4. Take the major arcana, shuffle, and have them cut for you as before.
5. Ask the questioner to take out seven cards

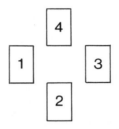

from the major arcana without looking at them, and shuffle them.

6. Ask the questioner to cut the pile of seven cards, and then take the top three and lay them face down as indicated in the diagram on the left.

Read the cards as follows: 1 represents the *commencement*, 2 the *apogee*, 3 the *obstacles*, and 4 the *fall*; I represents the influences that have affected the matter in the past, II indicates the influences of the present, and III shows what will affect and determine the future.

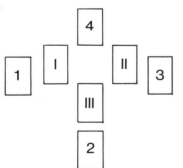

Papus's 'More Elaborate Process'

1. Shuffle all the minor arcana together, and have the questioner cut them.
2. Take the first twelve cards from the pack, laying them out in a circle.
3. Shuffle the major arcana, have them cut by the questioner, and get him to choose seven cards.
4. Place the first four in a smaller circle within the first circle, opposite numbers 1, 10, 7 and 4 respectively, in that order. Lay the remaining three cards as a triangle within this circle, so that the final arrangement is:

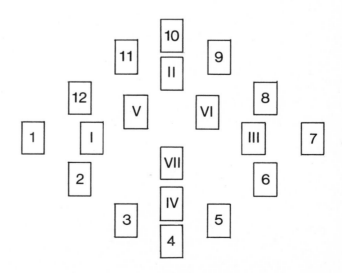

The twelve minor arcana represent progressive phases of the event during the development represented by I, the commencement, II, the apogee, III, the decline or obstacle, IV, the fall. Cards V, VI, and VII represent respectively the past, present and future.

The Horsehoe Spread

This method gives a straightforward answer to a specific question.

After having shuffled the complete pack, major and minor arcana together, ask the questioner to cut them. Then take the first seven cards from the top of the pack, and lay them face upward in the following order, taking care not to reverse the cards as you do so.

Card 1 refers to influences in the past.

Card 2 indicates the present circumstances of the questioner.

Card 3 reveals the future in general terms.

Card 4 indicates the recommended course for the questioner to take.

Card 5 reveals the attitudes of those surrounding the questioner.

Card 6 indicates obstacles that may stand in the way.

Card 7 suggests the probable final outcome of the problem.

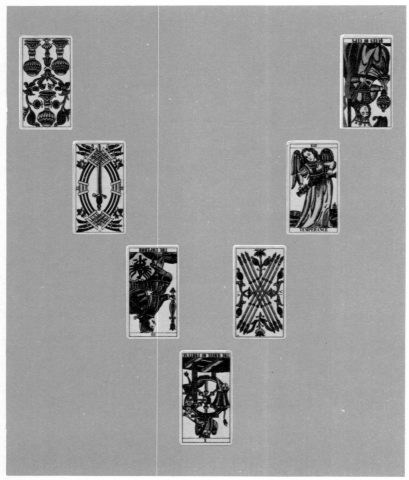

Example VI

A young man, who has taken over the flat of a friend, to whom he is paying a rent, is being threatened with eviction by his landlady because the friend is behindhand with payments on the lease. What will be the outcome?

The first card, which represents past influences, is the Three of Cups reversed, revealing that what might seem to be an imprudent undertaking (becoming the sub-tenant of a friend who is unreliable) was in reality a sensible step. But the second card, indicating present circumstances, is the Seven of Swords, symbolising a quarrel involving the friend.

The third card, which reveals the general nature of what is to come, is the Emperor reversed, suggesting that legal power will be dissipated in fruitless activity.

The fourth card, the Wheel of Fortune reversed, advises the questioner to do nothing: he should accept change if it comes and not act impetuously without wisdom.

The fifth card, standing for the attitudes of those associated with the questioner, is the Six of Rods, signifying profitable partnership; and Temperance in the sixth position suggests that few obstacles stand in his way. Finally, the seventh card, the probable final outcome, is the Queen of Cups reversed. This tells us that a quarrelsome woman will be thwarted in her attempts to provoke discord.

The meaning of this card reading is clear: the young man should remain patient, because his friend will not desert him. The rent will be paid, and the landlady will not succeed in her plan to evict him.

The 'Italian' Method

Here is another method, the Italian, which is said to correspond most nearly to the original method of divining with the Tarot.

1. Shuffle, cut, spread out the whole pack face downwards. Have 22 cards drawn and spread them before you as they are drawn, from the left to the right in three series of seven plus one.

The first seven give general information as to the immediate past.

The second seven relate to the present, and especially to the actual anxieties of the client.

The third seven deal with the immediate future, and the remaining card indicates the final resolution.

2. Connect the separate meanings of the cards in fives (counting so that there are three cards between every two consulted), starting from the first on the left.

3. Reshuffle the whole pack, have it cut and 48 cards drawn which are made up into 12 packs of 4 each, the meaning of each being:

    I. The personality of the client
    II. Money matters
    III. Family relations
    IV. Parents (father, mother and their property)
    V. Pleasures, personal satisfaction

    VI. Colleagues, collaborators, current relations
    VII. Marriage, lawsuits
    VIII. Health
    IX. Personal merits and their results
    X. Actual good or bad luck
    XI. Assistance and protection
    XII. Unpleasantnesses and misfortunes

4. If it is desired to be more precise, reshuffle, cut and have 15 cards drawn which are spread out from left to right, then 15 more, which are placed in a stack on one side.

Start the interpretation again, beginning with the first card on the left, in fives as before.

Then give the stack of 15 to the questioner, asking him to draw one which he will place on that card spread out which interests him most. This gives the supreme enlightenment.

The Methods of Macgregor Mathers

In his slim volume on the Tarot, Macgregor Mathers outlined three methods of increasing complexity, which will be described in succession.

First method

The full pack of seventy-eight cards having been shuffled and cut, deal the top card on a part of the table which we will call B, the second card on another place which we will call A. (These will form the commencement of two heaps, A and B, into which the whole pack is to be dealt.) Then deal the third and fourth cards on B, and the fifth on A; the sixth and seventh on B, and the eighth on A; the ninth and tenth on B, and the eleventh on A. Continue this operation of dealing two cards on B and one on A, till you come to the end of the pack. A will then consist of twenty-six cards, and B of fifty-two.

Now take up the B heap of fifty-two cards. Deal the top card on a fresh place which we will call D, and the second card on another place C. (This will form the beginning of two fresh heaps, C and D.) Then deal the third and fourth cards on D, and the fifth on C; the sixth and seventh on D, and the eighth on C, and so on as before through these fifty-two cards. There will now be three heaps; A = 26 cards, C = 17 cards, and D = 35 cards.

Again take up the heap D of 35 cards, and deal the top card on a fresh spot F, and the second card on another place E (so as to make two fresh heaps E and F). Now deal the third and fourth cards on F and the fifth on E, and so on as before through these 35.

There will now be four heaps altogether. A = 26 cards, C = 17 cards, E = 11, and F = 24. Put F aside altogether, as these cards are not to be used in the reading, and are supposed to have no bearing on the question.

Take A and arrange the 26 cards face upwards from right to left (being careful not to alter the order), so that they are in the form of a horseshoe, the top card being at the low-

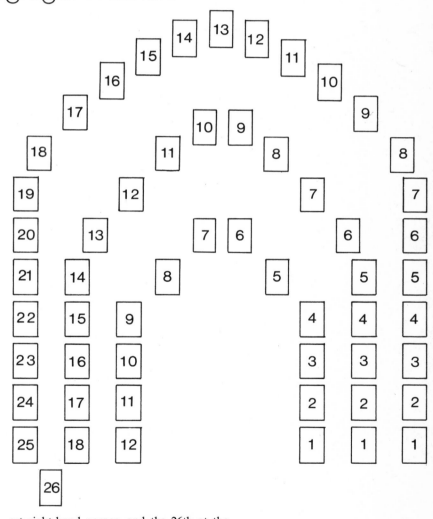

est right-hand corner, and the 26th at the lowest left-hand corner. Read their meanings from right to left as before explained. When this is done so as to make a connected answer, take the 1st and 26th and read their combined meaning, then that of the 2nd and 25th,

Divination by the Tarot

and so on till you come to the last pair which will be the 13th and 14th. Put A aside, and take C and read it in exactly the same way, then E last.

This is a very ancient mode of reading the Tarot, and will be found reliable.

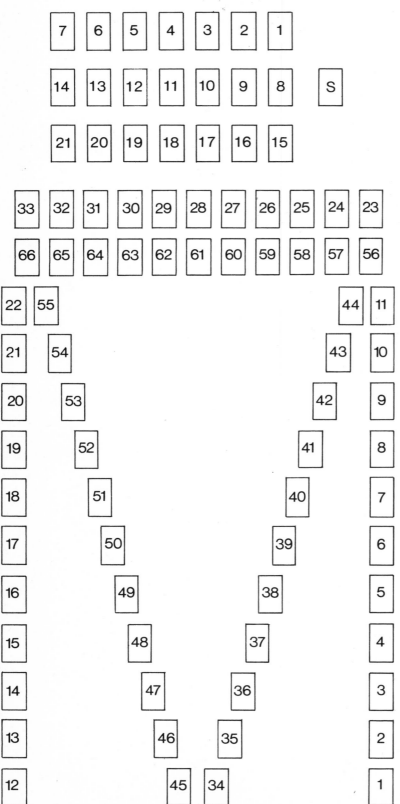